COURT AND CONSTITUTION
IN THE TWENTIETH CENTURY

The New Legality, 1932-1968

By *William F. Swindler*

MAGNA CARTA: LEGEND AND LEGACY

COURT AND CONSTITUTION IN THE 20TH CENTURY

The Old Legality, 1889-1932

The New Legality, 1932-1968

The Constitution of the United States:
A Twentieth Century Interpretation (in preparation)

COURT
AND
CONSTITUTION
IN THE
TWENTIETH
CENTURY

v. 2

The New Legality
1932-1968

by William F. Swindler

THE BOBBS-MERRILL COMPANY, INC.
Indianapolis and New York

The Bobbs-Merrill Company, Inc.
A Subsidiary of Howard W. Sams & Co., Inc., Publishers
Indianapolis · Kansas City · New York

To My Mother

Foreword

This study of the constitutional issues of the present was originally intended to be one volume. When it became necessary to divide it in two so as to preserve the essential background detail without making the whole project unwieldy, the division fell fortuitously at the point in time where the tenor of constitutional argument was to undergo a fundamental change. Thus the first volume was determined to cover the subject from the nineties to the coming of the Great Depression, and was entitled *The Old Legality, 1889-1932.* The present volume, tracing the struggles from the New Deal to the end of the Warren Court, describes the development of *The New Legality, 1932-1968.*

Three cycles are discernible in this period: the crisis in which new constitutional concepts demanded by the pressure upon the American economic system in the thirties clashed with and overcame the old constitutionalism of *laissez-faire;* the ensuing dialogue over the shape and extent of the new constitutionalism, in the course of which a new dichotomy of new conservatives and new liberals (the schools of restraint and activism) emerged in the period of the Stone and Vinson Courts; and, finally, the conception of a Federalism in which the rights of national citizenship were to place the individual American in a new relationship to his government—the epochal achievements of the Warren Court.

Strikingly enough, political events in 1968 brought the present volume to a logical stopping-point—the return of the White House to Republican control, coupled with the proffered resignation of Chief Justice Warren, effective in June, 1969. These developments signalled the end of a period of bold innovation in constitutional law for which only the history of the Court under John Marshall offers a plausible counterpart. Even had the Democratic administration and the Warren Chief Justiceship continued, it may be conjectured that this particular momentum of the Warren Court would have slowed. With the assertion of a national citizenship which guaranteed equality of vote, equality of racial opportunity and equality of all sorts and conditions of defendants under the criminal law, the jurisprudence of the Warren Court was essentially completed.

While the story of the Court and the Constitution in the twentieth century has been one of ongoing debate, the Old Legality was essentially the record of a Congress (and, periodically, an Executive) ideologically in advance of the judiciary. After the New Deal—specifically, after the showdown of 1937—the roles were reversed, and in the period of the Warren Court the ideological gap between the Court and Congress progressively widened. Whether this contributed to the social upheaval in American society of the sixties—reminiscent of the social and economic conflicts of the generation following the Civil War, but far more virulent and general in its effects—is a speculative matter which will have to await the perspective of the seventies.

The current volume is organized along lines similar to the first—a narrative in which major constitutional developments are placed in the context of political and social developments of the same date, followed by a series of, appendices covering in greater detail some of the particulars of constitutional history. There are some additional features in the present volume: First, because of the peculiar circumstances attending the appointment of Supreme Court Justices after 1937—i.e., the result of Franklin D. Roosevelt's determination to change the ideology of the Court—the politics of each of the appointments has warranted more elaborate description. Second, because of the sweeping ideological changes which in fact have come about in the judiciary in this period, detailed analytical notes have been added to Appendix A (showing the politics of judicial appointment throughout the entire Federal court system) and Appendix E (showing the juxtaposition of statutory provision, argument of counsel and composition of the bench in the "swing" cases of the New Deal era). A third development of the dimensions of the present volume was to have been an appendix containing the text of the Constitution itself, annotated with opinions from the principal cases cited in both volumes of this study. This material has also outgrown its original conception and is now being prepared for publication as a final, supplementary volume to be entitled, *The Constitution of the United States: A 20th Century Interpretation.*

More than three decades of observation and reflection have gone into the conception of this study; more than three years of writing and half a dozen years of research have been involved. Many persons have earned debts of gratitude in the process, but the passage of so much time makes it difficult and indeed impracticable to acknowledge specifically even the major instances of suggestion, assistance and encouragement. The forbearance of the writer's own family over the extended period of research and writing certainly deserves an expression of heartfelt gratitude. The cooperation of many, many librarians and correspondents is too often taken for granted—and special mention at least should be made of the continuing help of the staff members of the Manuscripts Division of the Library of Congress, the library of the Supreme Court, the Department of Justice and the National Archives.

Special thanks should go to Mrs. Elizabeth Drewry and her staff at the Franklin D. Roosevelt Library in Hyde Park, New York, whose readiness to provide all manner of services on the spot made the visits to that depository as pleasant personally as they were rewarding professionally. The cooperation of the directors of the Harry S Truman Library in Independence, Missouri and the Dwight D. Eisenhower Library in Abilene, Kansas—particularly in view of the fact that the author's requests for aid in research had to be accommodated by mail and required local search for documents by the library staffs—is a tribute to the intelligent cataloguing of Presidential papers which makes possible such esoteric means of running down needed documentary materials and supplying them by photocopy.

The two volumes of *Court and Constitution in the Twentieth Century* have appeared respectively in the years marking the one hundred and eightieth anniversary of the establishment of the Federal government under the Constitution, and of the formal opening of the Supreme Court of the United States. They have undertaken to cover the significant developments in the second century of that Constitution as affected by national and world events— political, social and economic—in an argument which, especially in the four decades of the New Legality, has been chronically and increasingly acerbic. As the writer has stated in the introductory remarks for the first volume, he has striven to describe the progress of the argument with relative objectivity, although his own persuasions are evident in the course of the exposition.

Again, as in the introduction to the first volume, the writer expresses the hope that this study may be helpful in demonstrating the continuing viability of the American constitutional proposition.

WILLIAM F. SWINDLER

Williamsburg, Virginia
January, 1970

Contents

PART I

The Decade of Crisis

We are under a Constitution, but the Constitution is what the judges say it is, and the judiciary is the safeguard of our liberty and our property under the Constitution.

Charles Evans Hughes, address at Elmira, N.Y.
May 3, 1907

Chart I THE HUGHES COURT

	1926	1927	1928	1929	1930	1931	1932	1933	1934	1935	1936	1937	1938	1939	1940	1941	1942	1943	1944	1945
President	COOLIDGE			Mar. 4	HOOVER			Mar. 4	ROOSEVELT											Apr. 12
Chief Justice	TAFT (R.-Ohio)			Feb. 3	Feb. 24 HUGHES (Chief Justice) (R.-N.Y.)											Jul. 1	STONE (R.-N.Y.)			
	HOLMES (R.-Mass.)				Jan. 12		Mar. 14 CARDOZO (D.-N.Y.)						Jul. 9	Jan. 30 FRANKFURTER (D.-Mass.)						
	VAN DEVANTER (R.-Wyo.)											Jun. 2	Oct. 4 BLACK (D.-Ala.)							
	McREYNOLDS (D.-Tenn.)															Feb. 1 BYRNES (D.-S.C.)	Oct. 6			
	BRANDEIS (D.-Mass.)													Feb. 13 DOUGLAS (D.-Conn.) Apr. 17						
	SUTHERLAND (R.-Utah)												Jan. 18 REED (D.-Ky.) Jan. 31							
	BUTLER (D.-Minn.)														Nov. 16 MURPHY (D.-Mich.) Feb. 5					
	SANFORD (R.-Tenn.)				Mar. 8 STONE (R.-N.Y.)											Oct. 6 JACKSON (D.-N.Y.)				Jul. 31
	Sargent			Mar. 5	Mitchell			Mar. 4			Cummings ROBERTS (R.-Pa.)		Mar. 2	Jan. 20 *	Jan. † Sep. 5	Biddle				
	Mitchell			Jun. 1 ‡ Apr. 17	Thacher			Mar. 5	Biggs	Mar. 15	Reed			Jan. 29 Jackson	Jan. 29 Biddle	Oct. 6 Fahy				

*Murphy †Jackson ‡C. E. Hughes, Jr., resigned when father became Chief Justice.

The shaded portion represents the period of Hughes' Chief Justiceship in relation to the periods immediately preceding and following. The long tenure of the four conservatives Van Devanter, McReynolds, Sutherland and Butler, augmented by the vacillating Roberts, offset the equal tenure of the liberal Brandeis and the moderate liberal Stone, Cardozo, Brandeis and Stone—with Hughes himself frequently in association—provided the nucleus for the Legality, but seven years of Hughes' Chief Justiceship were to elapse before this bloc of four could be converted into a majority with the addition of Black. Thereafter, however, the creating of the New Deal Court with Frankfurter, Douglas, Reed and Murphy proceeded swiftly.

1/Progressives in Power: Harvest Home

TWO MONTHS BEFORE his ninety-first birthday, early in January, 1932, Oliver Wendell Holmes sent President Hoover his resignation from the Supreme Court. Steadily declining health, Holmes wrote, compelled him to break off "the affectionate relations of many years and the absorbing interests that have filled my life." In reply, Hoover assured him: "I know of no American retiring from public service with such a sense of affection and devotion of the whole people." His eight colleagues on the bench concurred, expressing "our keen sense of loss and our warm affection." Holmes' twenty years on the Supreme Judicial Court of Massachusetts and his twenty-nine on the nation's highest court, wrote Chief Justice Hughes, had been marked by opinions which "have been classic, enriching the literature of the law as well as its substance." Holmes acknowledged the Justices' letter graciously; "for such little time as may be left for me," he replied, "I shall treasure it as adding gold to the sunset."[1]

This Presidential election year marked another sunset—not golden, but dark with menace—for an age that virtually coincided with the half-century of Holmes' judicial career. The period from the early 1880's to the early 1930's had been the heyday of American free enterprise, and many of Holmes' own opinions had been a kind of commentary on the promises and problems, the accomplishments and costs of the *laissez-faire* capitalism which had reached maturity as the last quarter of the nineteenth century began and was approaching its *dénouement* as the third decade of the twentieth century came on. "Justice Holmes," wrote Hughes in reminiscence, "was in no sense a crusader, nor did he share the views of the [reformers and] promoters of the statutes which he so readily sustained. He held them valid not because he believed in them but because he believed in the right of the legislature to experiment." He remained committed to a concept of authority in government adequate to regulate the economic process—something which the protagonists of *laissez-faire* had been steadfastly denying since the seventies. Sardonically, he had

3

even suggested that his own epitaph might perpetuate his view by reading, "Here lies the supple tool of power."[2]

In 1883 when Holmes ascended the Massachusetts bench, the Supreme Court of the United States was accepting as "settled doctrine" an interpretation of the Fourteenth Amendment which, for the next fifty years, would insulate much of the free enterprise system from both state and Federal regulation. In 1932, when he stepped down from the Supreme Court, the system itself appeared to be in its final agonies. Yet Holmes remained calmly consistent with an oft-repeated (and usually minority) conviction that constitutional freedom particularly protected the critics of the existing order: "Surely it cannot show lack of attachment to the principles of the Constitution that [one] thinks it can be improved," he once had said.[3]

Between the years 1883 and 1932 stretched a long history of litigation as the American capitalist fought off Populist and Progressive, outgrew the crudities of the early era of trusts, but never relaxed his grip upon the industrial process. The steady growth of corporate organization since the turn of the century had come to be recognized, by the end of the prosperous 1920's, as "the industrial unit with which American economic, social, and political life must deal," there being "apparently no immediate limit to its increase."[4]

For Holmes himself, the basic responsibility of the judge in these circumstances had been to avoid "read[ing] his conscious or unconscious sympathy with one side or the other prematurely into the law." His own lifelong conviction of "the limited validity of legal principles" as well as " 'the stinking sense of justice' that bedeviled the proper administration of the law" had given him patience to abide the unvarying conservative credo that protection of free enterprise from government meddling was fundamental constitutional morality. Time, he had remarked in another context, had destroyed many fighting faiths, and it might indeed deal similarly with this one.[5]

The prospect seemed real enough. The crumbling of the *laissez-faire* system was evident all about in the winter and spring of 1932. "We are living through a period of grim pessimism—worse than anything I have known," Harold J. Laski wrote to Holmes that May. He added: "Unless I gravely miss my guess the foundations are being laid of a position out of which, all over the world, there is no egress save through social conflict; and the price we may have to pay for that is hardly likely to be worth the results."[6]

*   *   *

Hughes himself had been compelled to broach to Holmes the matter of his resignation, and it had been, he recalled, "a highly disagreeable duty." Holmes had been one of three Associates from Hughes' first tenure on the Court—along with Van Devanter and McReynolds—while Brandeis, a fellow crusader from the early years of the Progressive Movement, had ascended the bench only a week after Hughes' departure to accept the Republican Presidential nomination in 1916. The associations of his second tenure, beginning in February, 1930, had promised to be particularly rewarding; in addition to the familiar faces from his prior service, there was Justice Stone whom he had known both as a fellow lawyer in New York and as a fellow Cabinet member in the Coolidge administration. Sutherland and Butler he knew by professional association, while Justice Roberts he regarded as a highly competent jurist who proved to be "most agreeable throughout the entire period of my service as Chief Justice."[7]

Yet it had become evident, with the opening of the fall term in 1931, that Holmes' magnificent physique and mental stamina were faltering, and by January a group of the Justices had formally requested the Chief to persuade the nonagenarian to step down. Hughes had done so, couching the suggestion in the kindliest terms he could think of, and Holmes had acquiesced promptly and without rancor. He asked the Chief only to locate the appropriate statute on the subject of judicial resignation, so that he might cite it in the letter which he proceeded to write.

The statute to which Holmes referred was a fateful one. At this point in time, on the brink of a constitutional upheaval unparalleled in national history, Justices of the nation's highest court, alone among the members of the Federal judiciary, relied for their continued salaries solely upon the good faith of Congress. Where the other judges could "retire" rather than resign, thus remaining technically in service subject to special assignment and thus protected by the constitutional provision against diminution of their income during tenure, Justices of the Supreme Court could only withdraw from full-time active duty by formal resignation. Congressional enactments on the subject, in 1869 and 1919, had been half-measures at best, in effect assuring the resigning jurist that the government could be relied upon to preserve the rate of pay to which he was entitled as of the date of his resignation.[8]

In August, 1932 the last Hoover Congress, obsessed with the necessity of cutting government expenditures in the face of the relentless depression, passed an economy act fixing $10,000 as the maximum pension for any government employee. It amounted to cutting Holmes' retirement pay in half—and, in Hughes' opinion, abruptly halting the plans of two other members of the Court to step down. Although Holmes himself was not in straitened circumstances—and, indeed, upon his death he would leave the bulk of his estate to the very government which had treated him so shabbily—it was a matter of shame which ultimately aggravated the constitutional crisis itself.[9]

Both Willis Van Devanter and George Sutherland, as Hughes saw the situation in retrospect, were prepared to follow Holmes into private life "had it not been for the failure of Congress to make good its promise to continue to pay in full the salaries of Justices who resigned." If his recollection was correct, a less penurious attitude on the part of Congress would have encouraged the stepping down of two of the Court's most intransigent conservatives, thus dissolving the monolith of *laissez-faire* on the bench and rendering perhaps unnecessary Franklin D. Roosevelt's confrontation with the Court and Congress in 1937. Or, had Roosevelt himself fully appreciated the simple economics of judicial retirement, an unequivocal pension law early in his administration might yet have averted the debacle.[10]

Clairvoyance was a commodity in short supply, however, in the dread winter of 1932. The free enterprise system, discredited and reeling from one disaster after another, appeared truly to be *in extremis*. Defeatism hung like a deadly fog in the air of Washington, distorting the vision and compounding despair. One foreboding correspondent wrote in his diary, "I come home from [Capitol Hill] every night filled with gloom," while another diarist, in the same vein, declared: "No one can live and work . . . this winter without a profound sense of uneasiness." It seemed to matter little whether Congress or the Court was essentially "liberal" or "conservative"—whatever those terms meant to the men who used them; the people had lost faith in all leaders.[11]

Yet men sensed that Holmes' departure created an intellectual vacancy of magnitude, that a profound responsibility lay upon the President to find a worthy successor. It was all very well to say, as Felix Frankfurter did, that Holmes was one who "serenely dwelt above the sound of passing shibboleths," or for a Washington editorialist to declare that "the best tribute that can be paid to Justice Holmes is to name as his successor . . . a jurist of the Holmes type."[12] For laymen and professionals alike, Holmes had come to represent the epitome of the noble judge. Such men were rare.

*   *   *

The name of Judge Benjamin N. Cardozo of the New York Court of Appeals was formally presented to Hoover by Senator Robert F. Wagner almost immediately after the announcement of Holmes' resignation. The law faculties of Yale and the University of Chicago promptly added their endorsements, and in swift succession a number of voluntary statements of support followed. From various parts of the country, other nominations were made, including an assortment of favorite sons, but a tally of names received by the White House within ten days of the Holmes resignation showed Cardozo's to have been advanced substantially more often than all the others combined. The flood of approval for this single jurist was, remarked a correspondent, "quite without precedent" in political history.[13]

Although Hoover hesitated briefly—the chief apparent reason being that there were already two members of the bench, Stone and Hughes, from New York—on February 15 he formally submitted Cardozo's name, and prompt and unanimous Senate approval followed. Senator James Couzens of Michigan hailed it as "an excellent thing in the interest of public confidence in the Court," while Senator William E. Borah of Idaho told Hoover that he considered Cardozo as belonging to his own state as much as to New York. Professor Zechariah Chafee, Jr. of Harvard stated approvingly that Hoover had very properly "ignored geography and made history."[14]

The man who could inspire such encomia had had an unusual career. A graduate of Columbia College at nineteen, with a master's degree at twenty, he had studied with such intensity in law school that he was able to pass the bar without completing work on his professional degree. For two decades he had specialized in appellate work, accepting the briefs of other lawyers to be argued before the state court of appeals. At thirty-three he had published his first work, a definitive treatise on the jurisdiction of that court, and at forty-three he had been elected to the state trial bench*—only to be appointed, six weeks later, to a vacancy on the court of appeals. In 1917 he had been elected to a full fourteen-year term on the nomination of both political parties. "Able and upright, conspicuously deserving a full term," the *New York Times* had said upon that occasion. Now, upon his advancement to the high bench of the United States, the same journal remarked: "The universal acclaim with which President Hoover's nomination of Judge Cardozo has been received is a wonderful tribute to the place which a wise and upright judge may come to hold in the esteem of even a turbulent democracy."[15]

The Chief Justice was delighted with the appointment. He had known Cardozo from childhood, and his own son had been a onetime law clerk under the new Associate. He was, said Hughes, "one of the outstanding jurists of his time, a rare spirit with whom it is a privilege and constant delight to be associated." At sixty-one, the successor to Holmes brought with him eighteen years of judicial experience from the New York state courts, and a wealth of lectureships and writing that was transplanted readily into the fertile soil tilled by his predecessor. "There are few precepts for the judge," Cardozo had written a few years earlier. "All the more, in this uncertainty, I am impelled to the belief that, until the political departments have acted, the courts . . . are free to make choice of the conclusion which shall seem the most in keeping with the traditions of the law, the policy of the statutes, the dictates of fair dealing, and the honor of the nation."[16]

In this vein, the chief judge of the New York Court of Appeals had found the "yellow dog" labor contract inimical to state law, the workmen's compensation statute susceptible of broad rather than narrow construction, and the single constitutional provision of universal importance to be "the principle of free thought, not . . . for those who agree with us but freedom for the thought that we hate."[17] His opinion adapting common law contract to the automobile age had become a classic: "Precedents drawn from the days of travel by stage coach do not fit the conditions of travel today," he had declared in 1916. "The principle that the danger must be imminent [in order to establish a manufacturer's duty to the user of the machine] does not change, but the things subject to the principle do change. They are whatever the needs of life in the developing civilization require them to be."[18]

*   *   *

The euphoria surrounding Cardozo's appointment did not deter the conservatives in their dogged apologetic for the old order. The *Oklahoma Ice* case, denying a state authority to limit competition in the interest of ensuring a minimum income to the existing licensees, was decided within a month of the

---

*Called the Supreme Court in New York.

new Justice's appearance, although Cardozo himself took no part in it.[19] Within the following month, however, the new Justice did write an opinion—a dissent, in which he was significantly paired with Brandeis and Stone. California's constitution had provided for suability of corporation officers in cases of alleged misappropriation of funds, and Sutherland, speaking for the Court majority, had ruled that repeal of this state constitutional provision could not affect rights of suit created prior to repeal without conflicting with the Federal Constitution's injunction against impairment of contracts. The only contract rights, said Cardozo, were between the litigants; the liability imposed upon the corporation officers was created by law, not by contract, and was subject to change as the law was changed. It was straining the meaning of words as well as the intent of the law and the accepted practice of the California courts, said Cardozo, to insist upon a literal and mechanical enforcement of the contract clause.[20]

In the penumbra of the Hoover administration, the Hughes Court usually acquiesced, however reluctantly, in a broadening application of state regulatory power in the attempt to cope with deepening economic disaster. Thus, a California law authorizing the enjoining of unreasonable waste of natural gas, and an Oklahoma statute limiting oil withdrawals from underground reserves, were both upheld.[21] But the Court's grim determination to check the growth of Federal regulatory power, and to apply the narrowest construction to constitutional rules where private interests were affected, continued unchanged. The three dissenters, joined by Roberts, protested strongly against a narrow majority holding by McReynolds, which excused a major oil corporation from Federal tax liability on income from property leased from state school lands. To permit such a tax, McReynolds declared, was tantamount to subjecting state land to a Federal tax.[22]

An employer was relieved of liability to a workman under the Federal Longshoremen's and Harbor Workers' Act by the same narrow reasoning, with Brandeis, Roberts and Stone in dissent (prior to Cardozo's appointment). It was not until the late spring of 1932 that Cardozo found himself writing a majority opinion on a constitutional issue—reversing a lower court judgment in which a Negro voter had sought unsuccessfully to recover damages from an election official who had refused him a ballot. Dismissing the argument of state officials—as well as the dissent of the four hard-core conservatives—Cardozo declared that political parties in charge of primaries "are not acting in matters of merely private concern" but as an adjunct of the political process subject "to the mandates of equality and liberty that bind officials everywhere."[23]

The balance of four conservatives, three liberals and two middle-of-the-road Justices was evaluated by Zechariah Chafee of the Harvard Law School at the end of 1932: "Justices Van Devanter, McReynolds, Sutherland and Butler almost always hold together," he conceded. "This group is large enough to be in the majority in most cases"—since the addition of only one middle-of-the-road Justice was needed—"but time is against it. The manner in which its members approach constitutional problems is almost completely discarded in the leading law schools and this will necessarily have a great influence upon the bar and the judges in the next quarter century."[24]

"The living Constitution . . . is still complicated by hang-overs of old ways at common law," Walter Nelles of Yale was to write shortly thereafter. "Judges have not given up the practice of presenting decisions as consistent both with original intent or meaning and with precedents. And since they attempt this seriously and sincerely, their constructions of right and reason are often warped, and sometimes even kept from counting, by supposed obligations of fidelity to the past."[25] David E. Lilienthal of Chicago, who would soon be a key figure in New Deal policy, was writing that "where an acute economic emergency exists the customary constitutional principles applicable to the protection of property . . . may temporarily be modified or, if the emergency is sufficiently acute, set aside entirely until the emergency period has passed."[26]

"In other words," Lilienthal concluded, "due process of law is a relative concept and its application to any particular situation depends largely upon the social and economic conditions prevailing at the time and place." To this A. H. Feller of Harvard added: "The complicated credit economy of our day is built on a foundation of public confidence, the cement of which is the system of legal rules relating to private rights. When the foundation is shaken by doubts of the economic soundness of the structure, the cement of legal rules loses its strengthening force. . . . A principle of elasticity . . . becomes a necessity in times of stress."[27]

Edward S. Corwin of Princeton, whose scholarship would particularly be relied upon in the constitutional crisis of 1936-37, wrote: "To present-day economic and social conditions the doctrines [of Marshall and Story] have little if any relevance for a community which intends to remain democratic; and if 'realities must dominate the judgment,' as the Court has said they must, the outlook for such doctrines is not bright. . . . The first requirement of the Constitution of a progressive society is that it keep pace with that society."[28]

These were representative of the jurisprudential writing with which Chafee contrasted the constitutional opinions of the Court's conservatives. They were the logical consequence of a trend of scholarship critical of mechanistic reliance upon precedential authority—if indeed that common law technique was even relevant to constitutional adjudication—against which Taft had inveighed from his days in the White House to the end of his Chief Justiceship. They would be fundamental ingredients in the constitutional debates that lay directly ahead.

*   *   *

In the fall of 1928 when Herbert Hoover had been elected President, most Americans had little reason to question the glowing rhetoric in his speech made some ninety days earlier in accepting the Republican nomination.

Following "the policies of the last eight years," Hoover had proclaimed, the country would continue its progress and would "soon with the help of God be within sight of the day when poverty will be banished from the nation." The voters had given the engineer politician a spectacular demonstration of their confidence; his popular vote margin over Al Smith of New York had been more than six million, and the electoral vote had been 444 to 87. Five states of the old "Solid South" had gone into the Republican column for the first time since Reconstruction, primarily a reflection of the Protestant agrarian prejudice against the Roman Catholic, big-city Smith.

It was all but impossible, during most of the year that followed the election, for Hoover and the American public to conceive that a decade of unprecedented well-being and material advancement was already on the verge of disintegrating. It was totally beyond possibility for them to understand that the long history of industrial growth, dating from the early seventies and surviving panics, depressions, reforms and a major war, could now with dismaying swiftness be coming to its end. At his inaugural, and in various public addresses throughout 1929, Hoover spoke confidently of the great natural wealth of the nation and the demonstrated capacity of its people to convert these resources into an endless chain of consumer goods—a system which in his view had already attained a self-perpetuating status.[29]

Blinding optimism was not a monopoly of the Republicans. In the summer of 1929 John J. Raskob, chairman of the Democratic national committee, declared that "anyone not only can be rich, but ought to be rich." The path to wealth, said Raskob, had been clearly marked since the early twenties: systematic, continuing investments in "good common stocks." The First World War campaigns to encourage rank and file Americans to invest in government savings bonds had made millions of persons aware of the opportunities to be sought in more speculative securities as the decade of normalcy wore on. Vast numbers of citizens of modest to moderately good incomes began to withdraw savings to buy stocks—and, when money was insufficient to buy them outright, to buy on margin. The mania for installment purchases of luxury goods, fomented by "super salesmen" of the twenties, still further committed the average American to an economy of credit which he scarcely understood.[30]

The movement away from the farms and into the cities had continued unabated throughout the period; in 1920 the census showed 54,000,000 persons in urban areas as compared with 51,000,000 in rural, while ten years later the figures stood at 68,000,000 and 53,000,000.[31] A major consequence of this movement was the unprecedented percentage of adults who had thus become dependent upon wages and salaries paid by industry; by 1929 it was estimated at 80 percent. Another consequence was the development of a chronic pool of unemployment, which in the last half of the twenties was reported at figures varying from 1,500,000 to 1,800,000. Concentration of control of industry, which had begun in the age of the industrial trust, accelerated in the age of finance capitalism and the holding company. Many of the latter, it would subsequently be revealed, were as precariously financed as the most irresponsible marginal purchases in the stock market.[32]

The prosperity of the past decade, under the best of circumstances, had been uneven; despite the efforts of the farm bloc in Congress over the years, nothing effective had been devised to help American agriculture recover from its catastrophic overexpansion in the single year 1917-18. The final defeat, in the spring of 1928, of the McNary-Haugen farm bill, after four years of continuous effort to get it through Congress, had unequivocally expressed the *laissez-faire* convictions of the incumbent Republican administration. In vetoing the relief measure, Calvin Coolidge had castigated it with a passion not thought possible in the taciturn New Englander. Only the naked threat to the entire American system as he knew it could provoke such emotion. The proposal, said the President, had half a dozen major flaws: foremost was the plan for price stabilization through government purchase of surpluses, "naively implying that the law of supply and demand can thus be legislatively distorted." The corollary plan for equalization taxes was the second evil: "It would be difficult indeed to conceive of a more flagrant case of the employment of all of the coercive powers of the government." Following these in the order of demonology were the vast bureaucracy necessary for implementation of the act, the encouragement of profiteering, overproduction and the stimulating of foreign competition.[33]

In returning the measure—virtually a first draft of the early New Deal relief laws—Coolidge urged Congress to consider the legitimate alternative of a legislative program encouraging farmers to organize and administer their own controls. In a peroration which itself was virtually an anticipation of the language of the judicial conservatives in reacting to the early New Deal legislation, Coolidge firmly declared: "Such a program is in accordance with the American tradition and the American ideal of reliance on and maintenance of private initiative and individual responsibility, and the responsibility of the government is discharged when it has provided conditions under which the individual can achieve success." Chief Justice Taft, beaming approval at a statement from the White House which so precisely reflected his constitutional philosophy, had told associates that the veto message was a "sockdolager."[34]

Thus the decade of the twenties had ended in a cloud of conservative antipathy for the needs of the nation's agriculture. In the year of Coolidge's final veto of the farm bill, more than thirty-eight percent of America's farmers lived on lands valued at less than $40 an acre. Mining was still a depressed and depressing area of the economy which bound hundreds of thousands of people to a life of virtual serfdom, and both from farms and mines there was a steady flow of unemployables into the urban areas. The result was that by 1928 sixteen major cities were spending $28,000,000 annually—near the practical limits of their own revenues—on charity.[35]

Thus had conditions developed into a state unprecedented in any previous crisis in economic history. The emptying of savings accounts in the orgy of installment buying of luxury goods and marginal buying of stocks, the dependence of four-fifths of the adults upon wages paid by industry, the gross overcapitalization of many enterprises and the commitment of production to goods for which payment could be systematically postponed—all of these were features unknown to classical economics, and all of them had the potential of disastrous reciprocal effects upon each other. Then, as the first anniversary of Hoover's election approached, came the horrendous stock market collapse. In the last week of October, 1929 more than $15,000,000,000 in market values of stocks had been wiped out, and by the last week of December the year's losses were estimated in excess of $40,000,000,000.[36]

*   *   *

Unbelieving, and apparently incapable of decisive action, the Hoover administration watched the glittering structure of *laissez-faire* crumble inexorably in the next three years. Industrial construction declined by 90 percent in this period; unemployment increased by 700 percent. Bank failures skyrocketed, and thousands of businesses closed overnight without even the formality of announcing bankruptcy. In nine disastrous months of 1930, the number of jobless in the nation doubled—from 3,000,000 to 6,000,000—and in the twenty-four months to follow it would double again. On April 1, 1933 United States Steel reported that it had no full-time workers left on its payrolls.[37]

Disaster had come with brutal swiftness. From the vision of a new automobile every year, and a comfortable home for a well-fed family with indefinitely increasing means, the national scene in three years had come to be dominated by long soup lines, street corner apple stands, and shacktowns which everywhere were sardonically named "Hooverville." By the fall of 1931, five cities—Chicago, Cleveland, New York, Philadelphia and St. Louis—reported that their expenditures for relief had increased at rates ranging from 125 to 400 percent over the previous year. In December, 1930 Philadelphia had registered 6,590 families for relief; by the following December the number had grown to 47,779.[38]

Twelve hundred persons lived in the "Hooverville" in St. Louis, constructed as in scores of other cities out of packing boxes with burlap covers for the window openings and grouped around communal cooking areas. The St. Louis community was built on the Mississippi levees, that in New York just under Riverside Drive facing the Hudson. A census of the denizens seldom located any professional tramps; almost to a man, they were jobless mechanics, carpenters, draftsmen, steelworkers, who had exhausted all savings, borrowed on insurance policies which had then lapsed, lost even the benefits of union membership when they had been unable to keep up their monthly dues. Chicago, which raised $10,000,000 in special relief funds for the winter of 1931-32, exhausted the money before the winter was out. In calling for another fund of similar size, Mayor Anton Cermak bluntly warned the more fortunate citizenry: "I say to the men who may object to this public relief because it will add to the tax burden on their property, that . . . it is the best way of insuring that they keep that property."[39]

Amid the debris of *laissez-faire,* the Hoover remedial measures were circumscribed by the gospel of non-interference by government with the free enterprise system. Direct Federal relief to the unemployed was thus ruled out from the beginning, and Hoover's first efforts in the fall of 1930 focussed upon setting up a national program of voluntary self-help to be undertaken by states and local communities. It was fundamental, said the President, to "preserve the principle of individual and local responsibility." Two months later he was moved to propose to Congress an appropriation of $100-150,000,000 for public works construction. A year later, Hoover submitted a plan for a Federal lending agency, which was created as the Reconstruction Finance Corporation, with authority to advance up to $2,000,000,000 to banks, life insurance companies, building and loan associations, railroads and farm mortgage groups. In July, 1932 the RFC lending authority was increased by another $1,000,000,000 and a Federal Home Loan Bank established to stave off mortgage foreclosures and encourage new home construction.[40]

Still the economy plummeted, and the President confessed himself at last incapable of devising any further efforts to cope with the disaster. As it was, he had already been driven to the absolute limits of government action within the frame of reference to which he and his economic convictions were confined. Repeatedly, and ever more plaintively, he inveighed against "haphazard experimentation" and declared his resolve not to "turn to a state-controlled or state-directed social or economic system in order to cure our troubles." To the end of his administration, Hoover protested that "ordered freedom" was the only standard by which the American system could be defined, and that the sole test of this freedom was the guarantee of "equality of opportunity for every individual." The man who had performed the miracle of feeding starving Belgium during the First World War, it was bitterly declared, had been unable to find any means of feeding his own people.[41]

*   *   *

Franklin D. Roosevelt in 1932 found himself politically in circumstances reminiscent of those confronting his distant cousin three decades earlier. Like the Rough Rider, the squire of Hyde Park took over a party dominated by conservatives. While the liberal elements were united behind him, he had to steer his way to the nomination between the whirlpool rivalries of Al Smith and John Nance Garner, with Woodrow Wilson's son-in-law, William Gibbs McAdoo of California, breaking a prospective deadlock in his favor as William Jennings Bryan had broken one in favor of Wilson in 1912. Like Theodore Roosevelt, the present nominee conceived of the Presidency as embodying all of the power necessary to meet a national emergency unless there was an explicit constitutional injunction *against* executive action, but he would be continually challenged by conservatives insisting instead upon an explicit constitutional authority *for* executive action.

The Democratic platform for 1932 was a somewhat irrational amalgam of conservative and progressive propositions. On the one hand, it had planks urging greatly reduced government spending, unemployment and retirement benefits under state laws, and a balanced national budget; on the other hand it supported "every constitutional measure that will aid the farmer to receive for basic farm commodities prices in excess of the cost of production," regulation of securities exchanges and full publicity for all offerings of stocks and bonds. Its most popular feature was its unequivocal call for repeal of the Eighteenth Amendment.[42]

Equally ambivalent, or downright contradictory, were positions taken by Roosevelt in the course of his campaign—due in part to the disparate commitments of the Democratic party itself, and in part to the composite advice the nominee received from the specialists he gathered around him, to whom reporters soon gave the name of "Brain Trust." The group did indeed reflect a unique political effort to draw upon the resources of the academic community. By coincidence, three of the early leaders of the group were recruited from Columbia University—Adolf A. Berle, Jr. of the law faculty, Rexford G. Tugwell, a specialist in agricultural economics, and Raymond Moley, a brilliant member of the Barnard College faculty of the university. Two lawyers close to Roosevelt, Samuel Rosenman and Basil O'Connor, completed the group.[43]

Through Moley as liaison officer, the nonpolitical advisers were kept in contact with party veterans such as Newton D. Baker, Owen D. Young, Bernard M. Baruch, Melvin A. Traylor, Guy A. Thompson of the American Bar Association and Colonel Edward M. House, as well as leading Senators: Cordell Hull, William H. King, Joseph T. Robinson, Key Pittman and Thomas J. Walsh. From a wide range of authorities in the political and academic communities, Roosevelt drew the elements of his speeches; the September 14 speech at Topeka outlining the New Deal farm policy was, Moley recalled, the "direct product of more than twenty-five people."[44]

Like the first Roosevelt, this one had the facility for phrases which caught the imagination. Early in the spring, prior to the nomination, the New York governor had proclaimed his intention to campaign on behalf of "the forgotten man at the bottom of the economic pyramid," while in his acceptance speech he had pledged himself "to a new deal for the American people." Yet the deliberate attempt in his campaigning to avoid alienating groups of voters led to statements that made strange reading in later years. Roosevelt decried Hoover's tendency "to center control of everything in Washington as rapidly as possible," and declared that "reduction in Federal spending" was "one of the most important issues of this campaign." It sometimes sounded, said one New Dealer, as though the Republican and Democratic candidates had taken to speaking their opponent's lines.[45]

On October 5 in a speech at Baltimore the candidate departed from his prepared text to make a revealing comment on the Federal judiciary: "After

March 4, 1929, the Republican party was in complete control of all branches of the government," Roosevelt declared, and then went on: "—the legislature, with the Senate and Congress; and the executive departments and I may add, for full measure, the United States Supreme Court as well." The Republicans thought they saw an issue. Congressman James M. Beck of Pennsylvania, a former Solicitor General, told reporters with righteous indignation that the Court "never has been controlled by any political party, and it saps the foundation of our government to impute to the highest court of the land a statement that in spirit or actions it is partisan." At Indianapolis on October 9, Hoover demanded, "Does that statement express [Roosevelt's] intention to attempt to reduce that tribunal to an instrument of party policy and political action for sustaining such doctrines as he may bring with him?"[46]

Roosevelt did not respond to the Republican jabs, although the day after the Baltimore speech he told Senator James F. Byrnes: "What I said last night about the judiciary is true"; however, he added, "I shall not make any explanations or apology for it." The teapot tempest that boiled up may have suggested to him the delicate line of distinction between criticisms of the Court's jurisprudence and criticisms of the Court as an institution, but the candidate could not have sensed the possible depth of the institution's own resentment. Four years later, in the carnival of retribution being wrought upon New Deal legislation, Mrs. Eugene Meyer expressed her dismay to Justice Harlan F. Stone; he replied to her that "some members of the Court, being only human, were much offended by Roosevelt's conduct"—apparently a reference to the Baltimore interpolation—"and were going too far during their anger."[47]

In the closing weeks of the 1932 campaign, the furore soon subsided. Almost from the outset, it had been apparent that the only question to be settled in November was the size of Roosevelt's victory. Even so, the answer was astounding: the New Deal candidate received 27,821,857 votes to Hoover's 15,761,841, and Roosevelt carried forty-two states with 472 electoral votes to the Republican's six states and 59 electoral votes. Only Taft had suffered a more complete political disaster up to that time.

*   *   *

With such a victory, including party control of both houses of Congress, political progressivism had been presented with its greatest opportunity in the twentieth century. Aside from the margin of triumph, the chief difference between the circumstances in which the Square Deal and the New Freedom had come to power on the one hand, and those attending the advent of the New Deal on the other—the desperate emergency which confronted the nation in 1932—served to give the reform program of Franklin D. Roosevelt a far greater urgency. In 1901 and 1913, the inaugurations of reform Presidents had been in the context of expectation of a broader distribution of the benefits of the good life in America. In March of 1933, the need was to undertake to save the American economic system itself—if it should prove worth saving.

The Norris "Lame-Duck" Amendment to the Constitution was formally announced as adopted the month before Roosevelt's inaugural. While it could not affect this event, the sickening slide of the country into deeper and deeper depression emphasized the urgency of a prompt change-over of administrations following a national election. Between December 1, 1932 and March 4, 1933 the index figure for national production dropped from a record low of 64 to an incredible 56. In the same period, the number of bank failures had reached such proportions, and were occurring with such frequency, that in February Louisiana officially decreed a one-day bank holiday to try to relieve the mounting panic; by the time of the inaugural, twenty-one states had taken similar action for varying periods.[48]

The prospect confronting the President-elect was unrelieved in its grimness. The previous spring, the country had been shocked to read that one-fourth of all the land in the state of Mississippi had gone under the auctioneer's hammer to satisfy delinquent taxes. State and local governments were hopelessly in debt. Georgia reported that more than 170,000 school children had had to be dismissed from classrooms for want of money to provide heat, light or teachers, while the city of Akron, Ohio ended its school year owing its instructors more than $330,000. In worst condition of all was Chicago, where teachers met their classes until they were literally too weak from lack of food to stand at the blackboards; the city paid them in tax-anticipation warrants which, when revenues failed to materialize, proved to be worthless.[49]

Dairy farmers in Wisconsin blocked shipments of milk to markets, and dumped the cans' contents into the ditches beside the roads. In Iowa and Nebraska, agents seeking to foreclose on mortgages were driven out of the counties. On the eve of the inauguration, stock and commodity exchanges in New York, Chicago and Kansas City closed down. The familiar world, Mrs. Meyer noted in her diary, was "literally rocking beneath our feet." Gerald W. Johnson could recall the observation he had written exactly twelve months before: "The average American is not the man he was three years ago. He has aged with great rapidity since that 16,000,000-share day in the Stock Exchange, and one characteristic of increasing maturity is increasing disbelief in fairy tales of any kind."[50]

*   *   *

A fairy tale of capitalism, to which Hoover and the Republicans desperately clung, was that government lacked the capacity to act in a crisis such as had arisen. No action, Hoover insisted, was permissible except in a form calculated to encourage private initiative—and if private initiative could not be stimulated to action itself, paralysis and eventual death for the system had to be accepted. Both Roosevelt and Hoover considered the authority vested in the Chief Executive by the Trading with the Enemy Act of 1917; for Hoover, it was coterminous with the First World War and thus provided no legal basis for present emergency power to be exercised by the President.

Roosevelt himself was somewhat doubtful as to the continuing force of the wartime statute, but he relied on his Attorney General-designate, Senator

Thomas J. Walsh of Montana, for an expert opinion. Walsh advised that in his view the Trading with the Enemy Act was still in effect, and Roosevelt, accepting this view with the further suggestion that the new Congress ratify the interpretation, proceeded to plan his actions accordingly. Since the statute gave the Chief Executive power to prohibit trade in gold or silver as well as the hoarding of these metals, Roosevelt later wrote, "I determined to use this power to close all the banks in order to prevent complete chaos on the Monday following Inauguration Day, which was a Saturday."[51]

The desperate emergency called for decisive steps like this, on a number of fronts. The threat of total national bankruptcy had never been so great. The steady flow of gold out of the country, the rapid drop in price levels and the equally rapid fall in economic productivity of all kinds were placing an intolerable strain upon the banking system. Roosevelt concluded that two emergency measures were imperative—one, a universal bank holiday to give the financial institutions of the country a gasp for breath, the other, a legislative formula for helping them to cope with the emergency confronting them when they reopened. On repeated occasions in February, the retiring President sought to persuade Roosevelt to join with him in a statement aimed at restoring confidence in the banking system—but on terms which, by assuring the country that no government interference with the system was contemplated, would short-circuit most of the New Deal. Roosevelt consistently rejected the bait.[52]

March 4, 1933 was a bleak day, overcast, with blustering winter winds. "We are at the end of our string," exclaimed the outgoing President, as if in final warning to his successors that all possible solutions to the crisis had been tried and had failed. But Roosevelt, as the long-delayed moment of accession approached, was in rising spirits. He had written warmly to Chief Justice Hughes: "I think it is interesting that a Governor of New York is to administer the oath to another Governor of New York," and expressed the hope of "seeing more of you than I have had the opportunity of seeing for many years." Hughes, delighted at the new President's proposal to repeat the entire inaugural oath, replied that "I especially prize the opportunity of being associated with you in our great American enterprise."[53]

The oath administered, Roosevelt swung to face the crowd, his face turning grave, his chin "thrust out defiantly as if at some invisible, insidious foe," said one correspondent. "This," the new President proclaimed, "is a day of national consecration." It was also an avowal of commitment to action. The "rulers of the exchange of mankind's goods have failed," he told the nation, because their efforts to cope with the crisis "have been cast in the pattern of an outworn tradition. Faced by failure of credit they have proposed only the lending of more money. Stripped of the lure of profit . . . they have resorted to exhortations, pleading tearfully for restored confidence. They know only the rules of a generation of self-seekers." Hoover, his brow repeatedly drawn in knots of disagreement, could only listen glumly. But millions of Americans riveted to their radios heard the words with a vague stirring of hope.[54]

It was absurd, in the President's view, to say that the American political and economic system lacked the means to deal with the crisis. "Our Constitution is so simple and practical," he continued, "that it is possible always to meet extraordinary needs by changes in emphasis and arrangement without loss of essential form." While strict constructionists stirred uneasily at the words, the speaker continued: "It is to be hoped that the normal balance of executive and legislative authority may be wholly adequate to meet the unprecedented task before us. But it may be that an unprecedented demand and need for undelayed action may call for temporary departure from that normal balance of public procedure."

He was prepared, Roosevelt went on, to "recommend the measures that a stricken nation in the midst of a stricken world may require"; Congress, alternatively, would be expected to "bring to speedy adoption" these measures or others of its own devising. Should these courses of action be unavailing, Roosevelt concluded, he would then "ask the Congress for the one remaining instrument to meet the crisis—broad executive power to wage a war against the emergency, as great as the power that would be given me if we were in fact invaded by a foreign foe."[55]

*   *   *

Reaction to the Inaugural Address was generally favorable. "He is a leader who means to lead," said the *Louisville Courier-Journal*, while the *Boston Transcript* declared that if dictatorial power were needed, "such is the desperate temper of the people that it is welcome." Another observer added: "We prefer to believe at this moment that Mr. Roosevelt has come to understand that the changed times demand a new technique and a basically new approach to the problems of society."[56]

The mingled misgivings and hopes that responded to the address were also directed to the new Cabinet which now was sworn in. Its members could not be categorically described as zealous reformers; indeed, in Secretary of State Cordell Hull the group was headed by a courtly, old-line Wilsonian who linked the New Freedom of twenty years before to the reforms in prospect for the present. There was another link with the past in Harold L. Ickes of Interior, an old Bull Mooser, crustily honest and as relentless in his search for "malefactors of great wealth" as Teddy Roosevelt had ever been. Henry Morgenthau, Jr., Under Secretary of the Treasury who would early in the New Deal succeed the elfin William Woodin as Secretary, was a Dutchess County neighbor of the Roosevelts, and both he and Woodin were fiscally orthodox, if not conservative. Big, bluff Jim Farley, Postmaster General, was one of the last of the political party managers in the mold of Mark Hanna.

These were the forces of restraint in the President's official family—with the exception of Ickes, whose old-line Progressivism steadily metamorphosed into vigorous New Dealism. Another zealous reformer, with ties in Progressivism, was to have been Attorney General Walsh, but the fiery old liberal had died on the very eve of the inauguration. His place had been taken—only as a stop-gap, in the opinion of many—by Homer Cummings of Connecticut, a competent professional lawyer but a pale likeness of the man Roosevelt was apparently seeking as the chief law officer of the administration. The principal innovation in the Cabinet appointments was Frances Perkins of Labor, the first woman to attain Cabinet rank, veteran of consumer lobbying activities and social welfare organization, godmother-to-be of Social Security. But even Henry A. Wallace of Agriculture, rumpled, mystical Iowan, did not at this point present the image of a militant; his father had been in the same Cabinet position under Harding.[57]

Outside the Cabinet, and supplementing the original Brain Trust, a number of other men would soon be making their names as Roosevelt lieutenants. They included a regiment of young lawyers for whom the depression had revealed, in Felix Frankfurter's words, that "the Holy Grail was no longer deemed to be exclusively in New York." Frankfurter himself, a Roosevelt intimate since the early twenties, directed dozens of Harvard law graduates into the ranks of the New Deal as he had formerly recruited them for Wall Street law firms. Four of his selections would play key roles in the drafting of regulatory and reform statutes for the first two New Deal Congresses: Professor James M. Landis, an expert on legislation; Benjamin V. Cohen, a Wall Street investor whose knowledge of stock market customs added realism to securities laws; and Thomas G. Corcoran and Donald R. Richberg, both of the Reconstruction Finance Corporation.[58]

Paramount among the Roosevelt advisers was Harry Hopkins, alternately hard-bitten and hypochondriac, whose sense of social justice was born of the shock of his original contact, as a small-town Iowan, with the squalor of New York's lower East Side. Hopkins, too, represented continuity with the earlier Progressivism—his credentials in social work were earned in the days of the New Freedom, while he had spent the decade of normalcy in slum eradication projects from New York to New Orleans. His first role in the New Deal was as Emergency Relief Administrator, but with the death of Roosevelt's confidante, Louis M. Howe, Hopkins logically advanced into that role.[59]

But dominating these men and filling the screen of his times was Franklin D. Roosevelt himself. William Allen White, who had watched political pretenders and practitioners of all seasons for almost half a century, would comment after the spectacular returns in the 1934 Congressional elections that the President had "been all but crowned by the people." He presented the heroic image that men sought for the apocalyptic era in which they found themselves—the massive, handsome head, the resonant voice, the Inverness cape, the jaunty cigarette holder, the personal courage which had overcome crippling affliction, the ever-present sense of destiny electrified Americans everywhere. Wilson's Under Secretary of the Navy, Cox's running mate in the Democratic disaster of 1920, victim of infantile paralysis which seemed to close his political career, then victorious Governor of New York and now the strong man demanded for the unparalleled crisis—his ultimate appeal, wrote Judge Samuel Rosenman in 1945, was to millions of persons who were convinced that "he associated himself personally with each of them in each one's aspirations for something better in life."[60]

*   *   *

In his first day in office, the new President made clear that the words in his inaugural were not mere rhetoric. He issued a call for the 73rd Congress to meet in special session March 9, and then released his proclamation of a national banking holiday until the session opened. Under the emergency order of March 5, all transactions were suspended in banks, trust companies, credit unions and building and loan associations; certificates of claims against assets were permitted to make possible elementary business transactions; an embargo was placed upon the export of gold, silver and currency, with future exports when authorized to be under license of the Treasury Department.

The first step—freezing the financial system in place until remedial measures could be taken—had thus been carried out. Roosevelt directed Moley and William Woodin, the new Secretary of the Treasury, to turn at once to the drafting of the remedial legislation, and to have it ready within ninety-six hours when Congress met. In company with leading bankers—holdovers from the Hoover administration led by Ogden L. Mills, and Walter Wyatt, general counsel of the Federal Reserve Board—Woodin set to work; in the early morning hours of March 9, the Emergency Banking Relief Act was ready. In the forenoon, a handful of Congressional leaders had seen typewritten copies of the bill—there was no time to set it up in type—and at four o'clock that afternoon it was passed by unanimous vote of the House of Representatives. By seven-thirty in the evening the Senate had also passed it, and by nine o'clock the President had signed it into law. Bold and swift action, indeed, had at last been provided for a stricken nation.[61]

The pattern of New Deal emergency legislation in general was sketched in the Emergency Banking Relief bill. After ratifying the acts of Roosevelt and Woodin under the Trading with the Enemy Act, the bill vested in the executive branch of the government a broad authority over transactions in credit and currency, provided criminal sanctions against gold hoarding and unlicensed export, directed the Comptroller of the Currency to conserve the assets of insolvent national banks, authorized the Treasury to reopen sound banks in the Federal Reserve System under special license, and permitted the Reconstruction Finance Corporation to subscribe to preferred stock in national banks and trust companies. Most importantly, the bill granted emergency power to the Federal Reserve to issue bank notes up to 100 percent of the value of government bonds in member banks, and authorized the Secretary of the Treasury to call in all gold metal and gold certificates in the country. Six weeks later, the United States would officially go off the gold standard.[62]

"In the short space of five days it is impossible for us to formulate completed measures to prevent the recurrence of the evils of the past," Roosevelt had said in his message to Congress. After passage of the banking statute, the President added, there would be two other measures "of immediate urgency." Once these were out of the way, "we can proceed to the consideration of a rounded program of national restoration." Two days after it had adopted the bank bill, Congress approved a bill cutting back Federal expenditures by an estimated half a billion dollars. Two days later it began debate on a bill to bring back light wines and beer in anticipation of early adoption of the Twenty-first Amendment; the measure went to the White House on March 22.[63]

Thus had the Hundred Days begun. By the time Congress adjourned on June 16, a dozen other major legislative measures would be adopted and the New Deal "rounded program of national restoration" would be on the way to implementation. On March 21 the White House submitted a proposal to Congress to establish a Civilian Conservation Corps, to give outdoor summer employment to a quarter of a million young men and at the same time bolster the Federal conservation program. Ten days later the proposal was on the President's desk for signature.[64]

The legislative pace inevitably slowed down in April. Three weeks of frenzied activity, unprecedented in history, had left Congress in a state of emotional exhaustion. Besides, the measures that continued to flow from the White House were bringing up more complex issues with more varied grounds for debate. The following month was spent in such debate, but thereafter, between mid-May and mid-June, a crescendo of new enactments brought the first New Deal Congress to its climax. The Federal Emergency Relief Act established a system of grants direct to the states for unemployment relief through a system of modest work relief projects; Harry L. Hopkins was named the administrator of the program. The Tennessee Valley Authority was created, with David Lilienthal as administrator, to the delighted disbelief of Senator George W. Norris, its advocate since the First World War. A landmark multiple-purpose project of flood control, power generation, and the integrated economic development of the whole area, the TVA was an example of state planning and control, said a disgruntled Congressman Joe Martin of Massachusetts, which surpassed the Soviet Union's most ambitious efforts.[65]

A Federal Securities Act, requiring full disclosure to investors of information concerning new issues of stocks and bonds and providing for the registration of the issues with the Federal Trade Commission, became law on May 27. A national employment service, to cooperate with state job-placement agencies and realize one of the earliest goals of the Progressive Movement, was established by an act of June 6. A Home Owners Refinancing Act, the Glass-Steagall Act creating the Federal Deposit Insurance Corporation, the Farm Credit Act to refinance farm mortgages, and the Emergency Railroad Transportation Act simplifying rate-making and strengthening administrative surveillance of railroad holding companies—all were adopted in a matter of ten days.[66]

*   *   *

Although the succession of New Deal measures forced their way through Congress to a steady obbligato of grumbling, three major actions of the special session were to plant the seeds of future constitutional challenge to the Roosevelt concept of the emergency power of government. One, which was the logical consequence of earlier executive actions in the money crisis, took the form of a joint resolution of both houses on April 19, cancelling the gold clause in all public and private obligations, and making all debts payable in legal tender. The formal testing of this resolution, eighteen months hence, would initiate the judicial review of most of the New Deal.[67]

Far more fateful were the Agricultural Adjustment Act of May 12, and the National Industrial Recovery Act of June 16. These two bills, in the view of Roosevelt and the Brain Trust, provided the catalyst for the general program of national reformation which would flow from the emergency enactments of the Hundred Days. The agricultural reform bill, the President conceded in forwarding it to Congress, was "the most drastic and far-reaching piece of farm legislation ever proposed in time of peace." Conservatives were quick to agree. Indeed, as their spokesmen began to regain their voices after the climax of crisis in the first week of the new administration, it was charged that in the plan for control of agricultural production the New Deal had at last revealed its intention to create a collectivist society.

Congressman James M. Beck of Pennsylvania, former Solicitor General and a respected constitutional lawyer, opened the attack upon the farm bill and the political philosophy of the administration in general. Except as to agricultural products in interstate commerce, Beck declared, the proposal lacked "any grant of power to the Congress by the Constitution, which would justify the passing of this legislation." As for the plea of national emergency, he went on, "I think of all the damnable heresies that have ever been suggested in connection with the Constitution, the doctrine of emergency is the worst. It means that when Congress declares an emergency there is no Constitution."[68]

A firm administrative regulation of agricultural production and processing was envisioned in the bill. Only by such controls, argued Rexford Tugwell and his associates, could farm purchasing power be revived. It was necessary to deal with the chronic problem of surplus crops and bring prices for marketed produce back to a parity with the period 1909-14, the pre-war levels considered normal for corn, cotton, rice, wheat, hogs and dairy produce. The bill proposed to accomplish these related objectives through a subsidy, giving benefit payments to farmers who voluntarily reduced acreage or crops and deriving the funds for the payments from a special tax levied on processors of farm products. Supplementing these basic features of the AAA was a provision for the refinancing of farm mortgages through Federal Land Banks.[69]

Beck warned that "we are making the Secretary of Agriculture a czar for the agricultural interests of the country, with . . . a power such as was never dreamed before over the products of the farm and over the processors who convert them into useful commodities." The rule against unreasonable use of the licensing authority applied against a state government in the *Oklahoma Ice* case, he prophesied, would be directed against the Federal government when the farm relief bill was tested in the courts.[70] But the farm bloc, so long denied adequate legislation, was not to be put off; ultimately, the bill passed both houses by substantial margins.

The National Industrial Recovery Act was the climax to the work of the Hundred Days. Its basic premise, and indeed the premise of the entire New Deal, wrote Moley, was that a reformation of the capitalistic system was essential, and that it would necessarily take the form of "cooperative business-government planning to combat the instability of economic operations and the insecurity of livelihood." Like Theodore Roosevelt and the other protagonists of the New Nationalism two decades earlier, the New Dealers accepted the fact of bigness in industry; it then became the duty of government "to enable the whole people to enjoy the benefits of mass production and distribution" and "to devise, with business, the means of social and individual adjustment to the facts of the industrial age." In retrospect, Moley conceded that the administration made a fundamental mistake in trying to make NIRA—a temporary, emergency program for reviving industry—a medium through which to try to lay the foundation for the long-range development of "a balanced and dynamic economic system."[71]

Conservatives like Beck disliked NIRA from the outset. The concept to him was proof positive that the American people were "going to have a new Constitution, not formally framed or ratified, but the executive usurpation." The three Columbia professors he pictured as the new Founding Fathers, as "Professor Moley takes the place of George Washington, and Professor Tugwell that of Hamilton, and Professor Berle that of James Wilson." With the proposed bill, Beck declared, added to the epochal legislation already enacted, "the President will exercise over production, transportation, banking and other instrumentalities of commerce greater power than those enjoyed by all of his predecessors, either in times of war or peace. In that sense he will be the economic dictator of America."[72]

Despite conservative eloquence, the administration bill came through both houses with substantial margins of victory, and was hailed by the President as representing "a supreme effort to stabilize for all time the many factors which make for the prosperity of the nation and the preservation of American standards."[73] Drawing upon precedents from the First World War, as he had done for his emergency banking proclamation, Roosevelt and his advisers proposed a program of self-regulation by industry through codes of fair competition drawn up by various trade associations. The codes sought to control volume of production and set price levels fair to both manufacturers and consumers, while Section 7a of the statute guaranteed to labor the right of collective bargaining. Actions under the codes were exempted from the operation of the anti-trust laws. Title II of the statute created a Public Works Administration which, by providing for consumer purchasing power among unemployed, was intended to prime the industrial pump represented in the National Recovery Administration.[74]

*   *   *

The torrent of New Deal legislation, unparalleled in its volume and most of it unique in subject-matter, literally inundated the traditional political and legal landmarks of the nation. There could be no blinking the fact, said Newton D. Baker, that the special session of the 73rd Congress had "bundled up and passed over to [the President] more power than any man ever had before him." While the more drastic statutes carried a two-year terminal date—when, it was hoped, the deepest crisis would have passed—many were now reminding themselves that in his campaign speeches Roosevelt had repeatedly advocated a "permanently safe order of society."

The legislation of the Hundred Days, it was generally understood, had been the creation of key members of the original Brain Trust—Berle, Moley and Tugwell—with a conservative counterweight provided by the Director of the Budget, Lewis L. Douglas. It remained, therefore, simply to refer to the fundamental ideas of these men, expressed in their writings over the years, to discern that they shared the feeling expressed by Progressives of the era of the New Freedom—measures that proved good in war or depression were not any less effective when the emergency had passed. The wastefulness of a competitive economy denied any regulatory direction from government, as Tugwell had argued in *The Industrial Discipline and Governmental Acts,* published that same year, was an evil of prosperity as much as of depression.[75]

The year before, Berle and his associate, Gardiner C. Means, had written an even more challenging study, *The Modern Corporation and Private Property,* which traced the evolution of control of the corporation in the twenties from the nominal control of the stockholders to the actual control of the holder of a majority of shares (or an effective minority of shares) and concluded: The developments of the postwar era had "cleared the way for the claims of a group far wider than either the owners or the control. They have placed the community in a position to demand that the modern corporation serve not alone the owners or the control but all society."[76]

The third of the original Brain Trusters would be the first to revolt. Raymond Moley, for whom the speed of change brought about by the legislation of the Hundred Days seemed disturbingly like "playing ninepins with the skulls and thighbones of economic orthodoxy," was increasingly concerned because Roosevelt was so unconcerned at what had happened in the special session of Congress. Moley scanned the basic ideas which had been written into law and saw nothing less than a revolution: banking legislation which set the stage for unification of state and national banking systems and for credit control equal in degree to monetary control; through a revision of RFC authority, coordinated with the Farm Credit Administration and the Home Owners' Loan Act, the conversion of the government of the United States into a gigantic investment and mortgage banker; a "yardstick" for public utility rates made possible by the TVA; a tightly unified transportation system envisioned in the Railroad Transportation Act; and the underwriting of economic subsistence for millions of farmers through the AAA, for millions of unemployed through the several work relief programs, and for millions of wage earners through the National Industrial Recovery Act.[77]

"The hazards and responsibilities this combination [of experimental legislation] involved might well have given the most intrepid social explorer some qualms," Moley wrote in retrospect. "But I was never conscious of a moment's doubt in Roosevelt's mind that he could wisely and safely administer discretionary powers too staggering even to be fully comprehended by the electorate at large. His courage," Moley concluded with grudging admiration, "was absolute."[78]

*   *   *

Whether or not the first New Deal legislation was conceived as temporary or as a blueprint for permanent reorientation of the economic system, the undeniable fact was that it departed drastically and dramatically from the traditional concept of lawmaking. In the Anglo-American common law tradition, as Roscoe Pound had pointed out years before, statutes enacted by state legislatures or by Congress ultimately had to find some accommodation within that tradition as administered by the judiciary. A statute which introduced a new principle of law, he wrote, might conceivably take the place of a former common-law principle, or at least be given a parity of authority. It was more likely, however, to be narrowly applied to its subject-area, leaving the main course of the common law unchanged.[79] He might have added that American courts, as the ultimate interpreters of written state and Federal constitutions, and interpreting them in the common-law tradition, could make yet another response to an esoteric statutory concept by ruling it void because in conflict with a constitutional limitation.

It was obvious that so sweeping a statutory program as that of the Hundred Days would sooner or later be subject to judicial test. The strategy of the New Dealers was to postpone the test as long as possible, so as to consolidate as much as possible the gains to be made under the legislation. It would be eighteen months before the first significant administration measure would reach the Supreme Court, and almost two years before a certain "Black Monday" in May, 1935.

For the conservatives, the prospect of relative success for the emergency statutes was the most forbidding feature of the New Deal. "The present generation of Americans are such invincible pragmatists," Congressman Beck declared, "that they are only concerned with the immediate advantages of a given policy and not with the questions of fundamental and permanent importance." In surrendering their traditions to the type of strong central administration required to deal with the disasters of the hour, he charged them with lacking the "spirit of constitutional morality." Judge John J. Parker —who had reason to know the depth of reform feeling against *laissez-faire*— added that "while we are willing to cooperate patriotically in any effort to relieve the economic distress, we have not surrendered the faith that life, liberty and the pursuit of happiness are the inalienable rights of man, and that governments exist solely for the purpose of securing these rights."[80]

*   *   *

Although there were modest indications that the first New Deal legislation had had beneficial effects upon the economy, the fall of 1933 was not a time for general optimism on the part of the administration. The defection of some of the early enthusiasts, the increasing restlessness of the business community under the regulations of the NRA codes, and the sluggishness of wages and prices generally were matters of concern. In October the Commodity Credit Corporation was organized under the AAA to extend loans to farmers on their crops. Shortly thereafter, in an effort to permit the government to take "in its own hands the control of the gold value of our dollar," the RFC was authorized to create a government market for newly mined gold and to attempt to limit the devaluation of the dollar on the world market. While the crop loan program was moderately successful, the "commodity dollar" effort was a conspicuous failure.[81]

When the 73rd Congress reconvened in January, 1934, monetary stabilization was at the top of the administration agenda. Within the month, Congress had responded by enacting the Gold Reserve Act, which among other things authorized the President to limit the devaluation of the dollar to a figure between 50 and 60 cents in relation to its gold content, and to impound gold stocks held by the Federal Reserve System. Although the effectiveness of the legislation depended upon public confidence more than upon economics, it served the political objective of forestalling the efforts of financial interests to compel a formal return to the gold standard and thus left the control of the currency and its value in government hands.[82]

A fresh stream of reform legislation poured from this second session of the New Deal Congress. The protection of agrarian interests was further bolstered by the Farm Mortgage Refinancing Act, which made possible the refinancing of farm debts by exchanging the new agency's bonds for consolidated farm loan bonds and investing these directly in farm mortgage loans. A Crop Loan Act was passed a few weeks later, while in April the commodities subject to AAA benefits were extended by the Jones-Connally Farm Relief Act and the troublesome situation in cotton dealt with by the Bankhead Cotton Control Act. The work relief program was vastly enlarged, bankrupt municipalities were offered relief through the Federal courts, government regulation of the stock market was strengthened by creation of the Securities and Exchange Commission, and a greater control over radio broadcasting was effected through establishment of the Federal Communications Commission.

The legislative output of 1934 was substantially greater than, if not so spectacular in content as, that of the special session of 1933. Its technical detail was assurance to conservatives that the emergency controls over the nation's economic life, which had been the theme of the first year's legislation, were now being converted into a permanent system. In May, before the session of Congress was ended, Representative James W. Wadsworth of New York warned that at the elections in November the President "undoubtedly would attempt to make permanent all or most of the temporary measures voted thus far." Ogden Mills initiated the criticism which was to become standard for the remainder of Roosevelt's administration; the New Deal, he declared, was an undisguised "despotism."[83]

Constitutional issues were beginning to be raised with increasing frequency, and the administration undertook to meet them on the hustings. "The fate of the Constitution framed in Philadelphia could not, of course, be predetermined on the basis of conditions then existing," Secretary of State Hull told a commencement audience at the College of William and Mary that June. A new understanding of a constitutionalism responsive to new needs was essential, he added. A month later at the National Press Club in Washington, Attorney General Cummings observed: "So long were common precepts of right and wrong unheeded in our national thinking and ignored in many phases of our national life that it was a natural shock in many quarters when an administration made bold to proclaim that certain old virtues were to be revived and their vitality reasserted."[84]

Thus the New Deal prepared for its first test at the polls, with a succession of addresses alternating between a suggestion that a new constitutional order had been born of necessity, and a suggestion that the basic objectives of the administration were to return to fundamental, homely values in American life. Indeed, the most valid criticism which liberals could level against the New Deal was that thus far it had neglected two reform measures which progressive thinkers considered keystones to all the rest—social security and the guarantee of the rights of organized labor. In a year of Congressional elections, without a Presidential contest to focus public attention on national issues, Roosevelt preferred to demonstrate the success of his emergency measures and to throw his weight behind promising Democratic candidates in local contests.

The tactics paid off. Contradicting political tradition, the party in power gained rather than lost Congressional strength in the mid-term elections—and, in fact, gained substantially. Ten seats in the Senate and ten in the House were added to the Democratic majorities. With such a mandate, the New Deal could turn its attention to the next stage in its legislative program—enacting the measures which would indeed make permanent the reforms of society which had been the ultimate, but never attained, goals of the eras of Theodore Roosevelt and Woodrow Wilson.

2/New Deal and
Old Court

W HEN HE BECAME Chief Justice, Hughes later wrote, he was "well aware of the cleavage on the Court." His personal conviction was that such labels as "liberal" and "conservative" meant little, and were "not infrequently used to foster prejudices and . . . serve[d] as a very poor substitute for intelligent criticism. A judge who does his work in an objective spirit, as a judge should," Hughes continued, "will address himself conscientiously to each case, and will not trouble himself with labels." Nevertheless, the Chief confessed that men like McReynolds and Butler were "resolute [in their] determination to maintain their conceptions of the constitutional protection of property rights, were disposed to agree with each other, and . . . had a strong influence on Justices Van Devanter and Sutherland. The disposition of these Justices to work together was strengthened by their common disagreement with certain views held by Justice Brandeis, and his elaborate and forceful expositions intensified opposition."[1]

Hughes was careful "not to identify myself with any group on the Court," but in the context of national crisis this policy, if anything, seemed more likely to aggravate matters than to solve them. The four adamant conservatives held one end of the ideological spectrum while Brandeis, Holmes and Stone had sought to create a counterbalance on the other end—leaving the Chief Justice and his junior Associate, Owen J. Roberts, in the center. The center, as events were to show, was an untenable position. Since Hughes, like his predecessor Chief Justice Taft, understood his responsibility to be to seek to "marshal the Court" on major decisions, the Justices in the center were continually being compelled to yield that position to create a majority for one extreme or the other.

The Chief was continually nonplussed, perhaps hurt, by the charges that he was a vacillator; the accusation was worse than the labels of "liberal" and "conservative" which he professed not to notice. Even the rebutting argument, made by some students of the Court, that Hughes joined the conservative bloc only when Roberts' defection made it a majority anyway, had an apologetic and defensive connotation. He pointed to his record as a crusading Progressive in the gas and insurance lobby investigations in the early years of the century, to his record as governor of New York, to his opinions as an Associate Justice from 1911 to 1916. There had been no public doubt of his liberalism then.[2] Like many another veteran in public life, however, Hughes was failing to perceive that a new generation had attained majority in the intervening years, and this generation regarded the past record as largely irrelevant.

There was also the fact that the constitutional issues which were to come on for review under the New Deal either had no historical antecedents by which the Court could be guided, or directly challenged precedential authorities and demanded rejection of past decisions. In such circumstances, even the so-called liberals on the bench were sometimes to pause —either to consider the consequences of making new law in the case of questions without clear antecedents, or the consequences of overturning long-established rules of law in the case of the direct challenge of the New Deal statutes.

In addition, there were the subtleties of raising constitutional issues, almost never understood by laymen or even by some professionals, which made all the difference in the intellectual choices open to the Court in any given case. Felix Frankfurter was to remind Roosevelt of this fundamental consideration when the first New Deal cases were coming on: "What a difference it makes in the Court's application of 'the law,'" he wrote to the President, "how statutes are drawn, how they are administered, how they are tested by the right selection of cases, how these cases are treated in lower courts by judges, district attorneys and government counsel, how they are handled and argued before the Supreme Court itself."[3]

Another future Justice, Robert H. Jackson, was to make the same point: Indeed, until the great judicial battle of the mid-thirties, the government was often precluded from engaging in a vital constitutional issue because counsel for opposing parties in a test case had prepared the issue in the form of a private suit. Or, over the years—with Richard Olney's strategy in the 1895 *Sugar Trust* case being only a typical example—statutes like the original Anti-Trust Act could be tested before the Court on issues strictly limited to the record of the specific case which might be chosen as the vehicle for the test.[4]

Every member of the Hughes Court was aware of the subtleties which surrounded and often clouded the large questions in major constitutional cases. Counsel for the conservative establishment in American economic life, who represented the most knowledgeable men in the legal profession, were also aware of and capable of employing the devices. In the judicial baptism of fire which the zealous reformers of the New Deal were to undergo, these facts of life would have to be learned by the liberals as well.

* * *

In mid-November, 1934, with a Congress unmistakably returned by the voters to continue the program Roosevelt had inaugurated, the executive and legislative branches were to operate in a degree of coordination that the Square Deal had never known and the New Freedom had enjoyed only briefly. It yet remained to determine the judicial reaction. Roosevelt's attitude toward the courts, aside from the extemporaneous comment in the 1932 Baltimore speech, was fairly to be described as inchoate. Of constitutionalism generally, he had observed—again, extemporaneously—at the opening of the 1933 Conference on Mobilization for Human Needs, that "if the state has done everything it reasonably should do" in seeking to deal with social and economic disaster, "then obviously the Federal government must step in, because, while it isn't written in the Constitution, nevertheless it is the inherent duty of the Federal government to keep its citizens from starvation."[5]

In a "Fireside Chat," in the early stages of the 1934 Congressional campaign, Roosevelt had approvingly quoted Chief Justice White's deprecation of "the constant habit which prevails when anything is opposed or objected to, of referring without rhyme or reason to the Constitution as a means of preventing its accomplishment." It was the President's indirect reply to the conservative effort to make the constitutionality of the New Deal laws a campaign issue. Two weeks earlier, in Independence Hall in Philadelphia, Woodrow Wilson's third and last Secretary of State, Bainbridge Colby, had orated against "impractical and claptrap theorists in government," and had declared: "The unemployed of the moment and the other victims of the depression are not victims of the Constitution," which he eulogized as a charter for "encouragement of industrious living by the pledge of protection to even the humblest worker, in the enjoyment of the fruits of his labor."[6]

Colby's *laissez-faire* generalities were joined with a speech on the same occasion by Col. Robert R. McCormick, publisher of the *Chicago Tribune,* who stated flatly: "The men who are violating our Constitution defend their actions on the ground that they are taking away the rights of a minority of the people to the profit of a majority." Two days after Roosevelt's "Fireside Chat," the first of a number of conservative groups received a charter of incorporation in New York, under the name of the Constitutional Protection League, "to uphold and defend the Constitution of the United States and the constitutions of the forty-eight states of the United States, and to expose and resist internal and external socialism and communism and the promotion of these doctrines."[7]

The electorate had given their answer to the rightists, but it was increasingly evident that the challenge to the New Deal was about to be carried to the courts. Already in 1934, a newspaper tally indicated, 232 prosecutions had been brought by the AAA and NRA, and of the 99 which had been adjudicated, 76 had been decided in the lower tribunals in favor of the government.[8] Unless the laws themselves could be overthrown, the prospect was clear that the New Deal would soon have a powerful record of successful litigation to give its reforms permanent force. The conservatives were hastening to carry the constitutional issue to review in the highest court; in December following the administration victory at the polls, John W. Davis, 1924 Democratic Presidential candidate, gave a radio address under the auspices of the American Bar Association in which he cited five "yardsticks" in the Constitution with which the invalidity of New Deal measures was to be measured:

First, said Davis, was the theory of limited and delegated power in the Federal government, under which any act "must be appropriate and necessary to carry out the specific duties that have been assigned to it." Second was the principle of separation of powers and non-delegability of legislative power to the executive. Third was a literal definition of interstate commerce which denied the use of the commerce power for broad regulation. Fourth was the freedom from government interference which he was confident was to be found in the guarantees of due process. Finally, there was the limitation on the use of the tax power for regulatory purposes.[9]

The speech was a recapitulation of the dominant conservative jurisprudence from Fuller to Taft; the organized bar, in sponsoring the speech, had indicated the tenor of the conservative attack. The attack itself was already under way.

*　　　*　　　*

"Mr. Roosevelt, it should be known, is determined to carry through his reformation of the social system on broad lines," reported a Washington correspondent as the new year 1934 opened. The likelihood that the President "would encounter an obstacle in the attitude of the Supreme Court has been considered," the report continued, and some White House advisers had raised the question of "reconstituting" the tribunal. "To accomplish such a move," in the writer's opinion, "the President would need nothing more than he already has: a majority in both houses of Congress, first to change the statute fixing the size of the Court, and thereafter to get his nominees confirmed by the Senate."[10]

A certain amount of progressive concern had been laid to rest by the decision of January 8 (*Home Bldg. & Loan Assn. v. Blaisdell*), upholding the Minnesota emergency statute placing a two-year moratorium on farm mortgage foreclosures. Speaking for the five-to-four majority, Chief Justice Hughes had accepted the policy statement in the statute that a public emergency existed and the reserved police power of the government was being exercised to cope with the emergency. Accepting Cardozo's earlier minority view, Hughes affirmed the argument that the statute did not violate the Federal Constitution in the matter of impairment of contracts. All contracts, said he, are made subject to the subsequent necessity of government to exercise its inherent powers, and where the exercise of the power does not extinguish but only suspends performance of the contract in the public interest, the wisdom of the legislature in calling its police power into operation is not a justiciable issue.[11]

The New Dealers were to have second thoughts, however, on reading Sutherland's eloquent dissent for himself and Justices Butler, McReynolds and Van Devanter. "He simply closes his eyes to the necessary implications of the decision who fails to see in it the potentiality of future gradual but ever-advancing encroachments upon the sanctity of private and public contracts," Sutherland declared. There could hardly have been a more pointed reference to the emergency legislation of the 73rd Congress. He then quoted the conservative oracle, Thomas M. Cooley: "The meaning of the Constitution is fixed when it is adopted, and it is not different at any subsequent time when a court has occasion to pass upon it." It is essential, Sutherland argued, to "place ourselves in the position of those who framed and adopted it"—without any thought of whether the position had relevance for the present. The ultimate question, the dissent contended, "is not whether an emergency furnishes the occasion for the exercise of . . . state power, but whether an emergency furnishes an occasion for the relaxation of the restrictions upon the power imposed by the contract impairment clause." That clause, in Sutherland's view, restricted state power irrespective of emergency, disaster or human suffering.[12]

Even more encouraging to the administration, although it came upon another five-to-four division, was the Court's holding on March 5 in *Nebbia v. New York*, where Justice Roberts, the other middle-of-the-roader, ruled valid a New York statute creating a milk control board with powers to fix minimum and maximum prices for retailers. Connecticut, New Jersey and Ohio, with comparable price-fixing statutes, filed briefs *amici curiae*. While the Roberts opinion stressed the proposition that both property rights and contract rights were relative rather than absolute, and that due process only required that the provisions of a statute not be capricious or arbitrary, its greatest significance lay in its sweeping expansion of the "public interest" doctrine into a universal rule.

"It is clear," said the Justice in reviewing the cases in which the doctrine had been alternately broadened and narrowed over the years, "that there is no closed class or category of businesses affected with a public interest, and that the function of courts in the application of the Fifth and Fourteenth Amendments is to determine in each case whether circumstances vindicate the challenged regulation as a reasonable exertion of governmental authority or condemn it as arbitrary or discriminatory."[13]

Justice Butler, writing for the four hard-core conservatives, did not challenge the majority expansion of the "public interest" doctrine so much as he sought to argue that the circumstances of the New York milk control law did not vindicate it as a reasonable exercise of governmental power. Any concept of jurisprudence, the dissent protested, "which permits facile disregard of the Constitution as long interpreted and respected will inevitably lead to its destruction. Then, all rights will be subject to the caprice of the hour; government by stable laws will pass."[14]

A narrow but important judicial line of argument had thus been established by the spring of the second year of the New Deal: The Hughes doctrine of emergency use of latent police power in the mortgage moratorium case, and the Roberts extension of the "public interest" doctrine in the *Milk Authority* case, encouraged the more optimistic to believe that these two members of the Court, joined with the three liberals, might find common cause in upholding the New Deal statutes when they came on for review. Against this hope, however, were two weighty arguments—one, the reluctance of the Court, including the liberal constructionists, to find in the Federal government the same degree of police power that it found in the states, and the other, the flaws in draftsmanship and conceptualization which were all but inevitable in the hastily enacted emergency legislation of the Hundred Days.

*   *   *

By January, 1935 the Court had handed down its first opinion on a New Deal statute and had heard oral argument on a group of cases challenging administration action in abrogating gold clauses in contracts and government obligations. The careless draftsmanship in both cases proved to be the crux of the matter, and the optimists among the Presidential advisers professed to see no serious threat to their general statutory program emerging from either series of cases. In the "hot oil" decision in January the government lost its effort to enforce provisions of the NRA Petroleum Code—but the optimists took heart from the fact that the point was a procedural one which could be remedied by statute if the NRA as a whole were found valid. Indeed, Harold Ickes noted in his diary that at a dinner the same week of the oil decision Justice Roberts "assured me that he is entirely in sympathy with what we are trying to do in the oil matter and that he hoped we would pass a statute that would enable us to carry out our policy."[15]

Hughes, speaking for a majority of eight, was particularly concerned at the slipshod methods by which the regulatory codes had been promulgated. In oral argument the previous December, Brandeis had brought out in questions directed at government counsel that there was no general publication of the executive orders by which the codes were put into effect, and that the means by which parties could determine their liabilities were involved and time-consuming.*[16] Executive lawmaking of this type, Hughes declared, was an irresponsible delegation of the power of Congress. The whole rationale of administrative procedure, he declared, was based upon the assumption that Congress would lay down broad guidelines of policy rather than leave the administration of any regulatory statute to the "unfettered discretion" of the Chief Executive.[17]

---

*As a result of this judicial criticism, the *Federal Register* was established shortly thereafter.

The same close questioning of government counsel, reflecting in this instance a general judicial doubt as to the morality of Congress' acts, attended the arguments on the gold clause cases. Attorney General Cummings —who had upset earlier predictions that he would not remain long in the Cabinet—had been the main force behind the Gold Reserve Act of 1934 by which the gold content of the dollar had been reduced. Cummings' official opinion on the government's constitutional power to enact such a provision had prompted Congress to pass the bill. But whether the opinion would be corroborated by the Court, in the light of the obvious challenge that the law impaired both public and private contracts, was another question.

Throughout the fall of 1934, the Attorney General had kept his staff busy bolstering the printed brief with additional points to be developed in oral argument. He had relied on the rationale of Hughes' opinion sustaining state government authority in the *Minnesota Mortgage Moratorium* case, but whether the Court would extend the concept to gloss over an explicit constitutional limitation in the contract clause was entirely conjectural.[18] What, indeed, would happen if there were an adverse holding on the gold clause cases was a question which suddenly began to fill the administration with dismay. Worried at the Justices' general attitude in the course of oral argument, Cummings shortly after his appearance in the Court summoned his staff to consider what action might be taken in such an eventuality. Meanwhile, although a judicial defeat promised to visit economic catastrophe on the nation, conservatives reveled in the present administration discomfiture. The *New York Herald-Tribune* saw the New Dealers receiving their come-uppance for having "brushed aside the Supreme Court as they brushed aside Congress and the Constitution," while the *Chicago Journal of Commerce* predicted that the oil case would "rock the foundations of NRA, AAA and all the other host of alphabetical upstarts."[19] What was to happen to the economy of the nation if liability for payment in gold should overnight increase the demands upon the government by more than a hundred million dollars was not discussed.

Attorney General Cummings personally appeared to argue the government's brief in four of the five *Gold Clause* cases. In three major cases involving the gold clause in private contracts, he was joined by future Justice Stanley F. Reed, then RFC general counsel, while on a case involving the gold clause in government bonds he argued with the Assistant Attorney General, Angus D. MacLean. The fifth case, involving Federal currency denominated as gold certificates, MacLean argued alone.[20] The week following the oil decision was taken up with the oral presentations, and at their end Cummings reported in detail to the Cabinet on what was involved.

Since a dollar's worth of gold was currently worth $1.69. the Attorney General pointed out, a decision against the government would mean that any holder of paper redeemable in gold could compel payment of an extra sixty-nine cents on each dollar. The result, as Ickes quoted Cummings, would be "economic chaos and heavens knows what might happen." Cummings, while guessing that "the government will probably win by a divided opinion," suggested two courses of action in the event of an adverse ruling: enactment of a statute asserting the government's sovereign immunity from suit on such claims, or a statute increasing the number of Justices "at once so as to give a favorable majority." "It wouldn't be the first time that the Supreme Court has been increased in size to meet a temporary emergency," Ickes observed; by singular coincidence, it had been a comparable question of the government's power over legal tender, three-quarters of a century before, which had been resolved by the first Court "packing."[21]

Cummings had not exaggerated the disastrous prospect for the fiscal stability of the government—as well as of thousands of corporations with gold clauses in their private obligations—if the decisions were to be adverse. Wholesale bankruptcy of both business and government was apparently unavoidable. As an immediate response to an unfavorable decision, Roosevelt advised his Cabinet, he was prepared to issue a proclamation of national emergency prohibiting for ninety days the payment of any contract at a rate exceeding $35 an ounce for gold, the figure fixed by the President under the Gold Reserve Act of 1934.[22]

Beyond this, however, the President was resolved to take yet more drastic action. He had drafted a radio address to the nation, to be given directly following the Court opinions if they went against the government. Citing the almost certain bankruptcy to which an adverse decision would doom railroads and corporations, and the homeowner whose monthly mortgage payments would instantly increase by 69 percent, Roosevelt was prepared to announce: "To stand idly by and permit the decision . . . to be carried through to its logical, inescapable conclusion would so imperil the economic and political security of this nation that the legislative and executive officers must look beyond the narrow letter" of the contract to preserve the interest of the nation.[23]

*   *   *

On February 18 the Court convened to deliver its opinions; across town at the White House, the Cabinet assembled and waited for the outcome. At the offices of the Securities and Exchange Commission, Chairman Joseph P. Kennedy conferred with the other commissioners on the possibility of ordering the stock markets closed; after a lengthy discussion, it was agreed to wait until the Court opinions were handed down, and uneasily the meeting adjourned. Open telephone lines from the President's office to the marshal's office in the Supreme Court were set up and at the Court itself long columns of spectators—reminiscent of a fateful May day in 1895 when the *Income Tax* case was adversely decided—queued up for admission. At the Treasury, Morgenthau's aides stood ready with emergency proclamations to be released as soon as their chief received a directive from Roosevelt.[24]

As the news came in over the teletype and by the open phone lines, it became evident that the government had won its cases, but by the narrowest of margins. The majority was five to four in all decisions, while in one the

fifth member of the majority—Justice Stone—dissented in part. Hughes
undertook the task of writing all of the majority opinions. With reference to
the private contract cases, but without directly extending into Federal law
the principle of the *Minnesota Mortgage Moratorium* case, the Court in essence
accepted the Cardozo argument that payment clauses in any private instrument are subject to the exercise of the government's monetary power. By
virtue of this power, Hughes declared, "there attach to the ownership of
gold and silver those limitations which public policy may require by reason
of their quality as legal tender and as a medium of exchange." Accordingly,
contracts, "however express, cannot fetter the constitutional authority of
Congress."[25]

Turning then to the question of the rights of a holder of a gold
certificate which the government required to be surrendered, Hughes answered
in the negative the proposition that the holder was entitled to more than
the equivalent face amount in legal tender. Even though gold itself had
become worth more than the face amount in legal tender, the holder had not
suffered a loss for which he was entitled to compensation.[26]

Most difficult of all was the question presented in *Perry v. United States,*
a suit brought by a New York attorney in his own person on a 1917 Liberty
Loan bond providing that "principle and interest hereof are payable in
United States gold coin of the present standard of value." There could be
no question but that the several emergency monetary enactments of the
Hundred Days, if valid, amounted to a repudiation of a promise made by
the United States. Stated another way, if the repudiation were to be validated,
such a finding "necessarily imports that the Congress can disregard the obligations of the government at its discretion and that, when the government
borrows money, the credit of the United States is an illusory pledge." Since
such a doctrine would in short order destroy the fiscal integrity of the nation,
Hughes and seven of his colleagues ruled the repudiation unconstitutional.[27]

But, having castigated the New Dealers for their fast and loose handling
of the very public credit they were seeking to preserve, Hughes then proceeded to save them from the consequences of their own actions. It was one
thing to assert that the holder of a government bond was entitled to the gold
redemption promise therein; it was another thing altogether to permit him to
be unjustly enriched by the accident of currency depreciation under emergency
conditions. Perry sought payment of his $10,000 Liberty Bond in $16,931.25
in depreciated currency; but, said Hughes, the case "is not the same as if gold
coin had remained in circulation." It was within the monetary power of the
government to withdraw gold from circulation, and as in the case of private
contracts and gold certificates, "the restraint thus imposed upon holders of
gold coin was incident to the limitations which inhered in their ownership
of that coin and gave them no right of action."[28]

McReynolds, in a bitter dissent for the hard-core conservatives, flatly
declared that, "under the guise of pursuing a monetary policy, Congress
really has inaugurated a plan primarily designed to destroy private obligations,

repudiate national debts, and drive into the Treasury all gold within the country in exchange for incontrovertible promises to pay, of much less value." Obligations, McReynolds declared, "cannot be legally avoided by prohibiting the creditor from receiving the thing promised." "Loss of reputation for honorable dealing will bring us unending humiliation," he expostulated; "the impending legal and moral chaos is appalling." Distraught by what he considered the enormity of the decisions, McReynolds added a despairing extempore: "As for the Constitution, it does not seem too much to say that it is gone. Shame and humiliation are upon us now!"[29]

*　　*　　*

The rationale of Chief Justice Hughes in the *Gold Clause* cases was a preview of the jurisprudence which he was to strive to preserve amid the constitutional chaos which lay ahead. Remaining firmly committed as he was to the ideals of the Progressive Era, with their emphasis upon the necessary adjustment of the American social and economic structure to the demands of different generations, he was at this point also committed to the preservation of the precedents in the American constitutional tradition. In 1935 neither Hughes nor the majority of his Court was prepared to yield in this matter despite the revolution which, though momentarily bloodless, was in full storm. The security and consistency apparently offered by the tradition of *stare decisis* often seemed to be the only true hope for survival as the value systems of the capitalism of the past seventy years were being swept away.

Yet, in the *Gold Clause* cases, the Court majority recognized the unacceptable alternative to denying the government the emergency power it had claimed. Like John Marshall more than a century and a quarter earlier, Hughes sought, particularly in the *Perry* decision, to define the limit to the government's power at the same time that he sustained the power itself. No opinion since *Marbury v. Madison* had so astutely pronounced a rule of law and in the same instance demonstrated why the rule could not be given its literal effect. As the *San Francisco Chronicle* commented, "The Constitution has been stretched, perhaps, but not beyond its limit of elasticity."[30]

The distinction between elasticity and inconsistency was the fundamental concern of the Chief Justice: the necessity for discerning those precedents by which to stand and those which had become irrelevant. The ultimate choice—as Hughes would come to perceive after the supreme crisis of 1937— was between a constitutional regime addressed to a socially decentralized people who had made up the United States of the nineteenth century, and the regime demanded by the economically centralized nation of the twentieth. More than that: the incapacity of individual states to cope with the chain reactions set off by the depression was inexorably leading to the proposition that only national action—a subject for which American experience offered no precedents—could effectively cope with nationwide challenges.

In the final analysis, however, it was the stability of the Court's decisions which, for Hughes, was the paramount consideration. He shared Taft's conviction that constitutional decisions should be the embodiment of "consistency in its course." He could not be charged with lack of prescience in failing to anticipate Felix Frankfurter's concept of the "erosion of time" upon all legal rules. And he was currently caught between the Court conservatives, for whom precedential authority was doubly valued because it was rooted in the *laissez-faire* principles they were fighting to preserve, and men like Brandeis and Cardozo, willing to seek new positions where the principles upon which precedent was grounded had become obsolete.

Hughes' travail in the next two years, accordingly, would be in proportion to his readiness or reluctance to abandon established prior guidelines in the Court's jurisprudence. The chimerical economics of *laissez-faire* was manifestly played out, but on what bases was a new economics, and a modern constitutional law, to be constructed? There was, as Hughes recognized in the gold issue, an ultimate sovereign right of self-preservation which could neither be defined nor circumscribed by a formal constitutional clause. What other elements of an ultimate sovereign plenary power were to be discovered in the national government created by the Constitution? Emergencies, he had written in an opinion early in his Chief Justiceship, could not create power which did not already exist but they could arouse latent power already present. Emergencies, by definition, were crises of the moment; what of the signs which pointed to the permanent end of an era?[31]

*   *   *

The narrowness of the decisions of early 1935—against the government in the *Panama Refining* case and in favor of it in the essentials of the *Gold Clause* cases—disturbed liberals everywhere. "Five-to-four Supreme Court decisions on the constitutionality of Congressional acts, it seems to me, are illogical and ought not to occur in a country such as ours," Senator Norris declared. The week following the *Gold Clause* cases, the House of Representatives judiciary committee formally reported out a plan to permit Justices eligible for retirement to do so on full pay, subject to temporary assignments to lower Federal courts. Shortly thereafter, however, the measure was voted down after floor debate.[32]

Another more challenging bill was introduced in the Senate by Hugo L. Black of Alabama, providing for direct appeals to the Supreme Court whenever acts of Congress were held unconstitutional by a lower court. The act as proposed by Black would require the high tribunal to hear the case within ten days and prepare its formal opinion within a stipulated time thereafter. Although it was one of a cluster of proposals which were advanced in one house or another at the time, Chief Justice Hughes was concerned about it sufficiently to request permission for himself and Justices Brandeis and Van Devanter to appear before the Senate judiciary subcommittee to testify against it. They viewed it as a procedural proposal which would seriously impair the regular work of the Court without accomplishing what Black expected it to accomplish. No more was heard about the proposal; the prospective appearance of the three members of the Court before a Congressional committee, however, would be remembered when another judiciary bill came up two years hence.[33]

Hughes could claim with some reason that during his Chief Justiceship the process of modernizing judicial procedure, begun under his predecessor, was now being completed. Taft's keystone concept—the drafting of uniform rules for procedure in all Federal courts—had not been realized in his own lifetime, but in the spring of 1934 the Hughes Court was able to announce the completion and promulgation of the first criminal rules, and three years later the civil rules would be announced, both with the long-solicited authorization of Congress.* The new structure for the Court itself, made possible by the pioneering work of Taft, was also completed under the Hughes administration and in the summer of 1935 the tribunal would at last move into its own home.[34]

Still, these improvements of the form and physical facilities of the Court did nothing to reassure the New Dealers of a modernization of its thinking. Major reform legislation was coming on for review, and the vacillation of the Court from one five-to-four decision in January to another in February was not calculated to fill anyone with confidence. Early in the spring, Cummings sent a memorandum to his Assistant Attorney General, MacLean, asking him to see if any study had been made of the "question of legislation which would not cut off the right of the Supreme Court to pass on constitutional questions, but would limit it somewhere with a view to avoid 5 to 4 decisions." Norris, convinced that this would require a constitutional amendment, was already at work on a draft of such a document.[35]

Meantime, Cummings was undertaking to improve the caliber of Justice Department lawyers who would have to carry the oral argument on the New Deal cases soon to be reviewed. When, in March, the courtly but inept old Solicitor General, J. Crawford Biggs, tendered his resignation, the Attorney General lost no time in bringing Stanley Reed from the RFC to reorganize the trial division of the Department. Other men of demonstrated ability—Robert H. Jackson of the Treasury, Charles E. Wyzanski, Jr. of Labor, Paul Freund of the Reconstruction Finance Corporation, and others—were quickly drafted into the ranks.[36]

On March 13 and 14, Assistant Attorney General Harold M. Stephens and Washington lawyer Harry Schulman presented oral argument for the government in a case challenging the constitutionality of the Railroad Retirement Act of 1934. On April 1 and 2, the Frazier-Lemke Federal Farm Bankruptcy Act came on for argument, with John W. Davis leading the attack of the petitioners and Congressman William A. Lemke of North Dakota and Harry H. Peterson, attorney general of Minnesota, arguing the cause for the mortgagor-respondent. On May 2 and 3 came the major case of the term—*Schechter Poultry Corporation v. United States*—with Solicitor General Reed

---

*Cf. Appendix C.

and Donald R. Richberg as special assistant to the Attorney General presenting the oral argument for the United States. Just before *Schechter,* Reed also argued for the government on a case testing the power of the President to remove a member of the Federal Trade Commission without Congressional approval.[37]

*   *   *

With the test of the National Industrial Recovery Act in *Schechter,* the New Deal was approaching the critical period in the judicial review of its emergency program to deal with the depression. The speed with which the statute had been drafted and passed by Congress, under the desperate pressures of the Hundred Days, had made inevitable a confusion of objectives and procedures for carrying out its provisions. The key provision, for the drafting of regulatory codes by industrial representatives in conjunction with government administrators, smacked distastefully of the cartelization which had plagued European economics for the past several decades. Equally serious was the ambivalence of administration leaders themselves; Attorney General Cummings was known to be unenthusiastic about, if not actively opposed to, the whole idea of regulatory codes.

The situation had tended to become demoralizing as, with the slight improvement of business conditions in 1935, public and industrial support for the act began to wane. Administrators, uncertain of their ground, urged the Justice Department to test the constitutionality of the law, and Cummings persistently demurred while searching, he said, for a suitable case. General Hugh Johnson, a bluff and blundering head of the program, seriously embarrassed Justice Brandeis by publicly announcing that he had been in regular consultation with the Justice while drafting the implementing regulations. Much more mortifying was the discovery by Justice Department attorneys, as they prepared an appeal based on the regulatory provisions in a petroleum code, that the provisions had been inadvertently omitted from the final draft of the code—thus throwing a series of pending cases out of the courts.[38]

Reed and Richberg, accordingly, had a heavy burden of argument to make before the Court when *Schechter* eventually came on for review. Richberg himself had made a number of public statements concerning the desirability of amending the statute before it had to be tested, while privately he had expressed to professional colleagues grave doubts as to the likelihood of a favorable judicial holding. Now, following Reed's effort to distinguish the Recovery Act's emphasis upon "fair competition" from the long line of anti-trust cases concerning "unfair competition," Richberg sought to establish the compatibility of the challenged law with the Sherman and Clayton Acts. The ultimate effect of the Recovery Act, he suggested, was further to limit acts of "unfair competition" without defining new standards of "fair competition."[39]

The near-sophistry with which the government's argument was threatened in this line of reasoning was typical of the whole defense. So much which had seemed elemental in the fervor of drafting the statute had by now paled to vague and contradictory objectives. Certainly, the *Schechter* case had not been the strongest one on which to try to defend the Recovery Act. The business itself was only indirectly engaged in interstate commerce, and the challenging attorneys aimed at the weakest points of the statute which Richberg had hoped would be corrected by subsequent Congressional action. The worst that could happen, as Richberg and everyone in the Roosevelt administration keenly realized, would be a sweeping finding of unconstitutionality in the entire law. The most practical ground for hope, Richberg felt, was that the Court would confine itself to a procedural detail or a single section of the statute which could then be remedied by legislation, as in the "hot oil" case.[40]

Then, in triphammer succession, came the four fateful decisions—and the New Dealers realized that the worst had happened. The first case, invalidating the railroad pension law, was a five-to-four division; the remainder were thunderous in their unanimity. The railroad case, handed down three weeks before the others, pointed to a break in the previous coalition of liberals and middle-of-the-roaders: Justice Roberts had rejoined the conservatives and wrote the majority opinion, while Hughes wrote the dissent for himself and the liberals.

Roberts' defection, unpalatable as it was in providing the narrow margin of government defeat, was somewhat less than surprising. On March 11 he had joined with the majority and had written the opinion holding unconstitutional a Kentucky gross sales tax as a denial of the equal protection of the laws guaranteed by the Fourteenth Amendment;[41] three weeks later, he again had written the Court opinion in a case denying a Negro voter a suit against the Texas Democratic party for barring him from the primary elections.[42] But the grimmest element in the present majority opinion was Roberts' adamant position on the issue of any Federal authority to establish a pension system.

In striking down the Railroad Retirement Act, Roberts was unequivocal in his condemnation: key provisions of the statute, lumping individual railroads together in an industry-wide pension plan, extending eligibility to all employees of a minimum of one year's service, and compelling a deposit of funds with the Treasury Department and making carriers insurers of employee contributions, all amounted to a taking of employers' property without due process. "The act," Roberts declared categorically, "is not in purpose or effect a regulation of interstate commerce within the meaning of the Constitution."[43]

Hughes' rebuttal was emphatic. Buttressing his criticism with an elaborate review of the jurisprudence of the commerce clause, he charged the majority with going out of its way to prevent Congress from seeking "to overcome the objections by a new statute." If the classes of persons covered, or the basis of the payments, or even the unitary system under which all railroads were covered had been singly or separately objectionable, these features "found to be inconsistent with the requirements of due process could be excised and other provisions substituted." By gratuitously pronouncing the subject itself outside the scope of the commerce power, Hughes objected, the majority had placed a totally unwarranted limitation upon that clause of the Constitution.[44]

The dissent was highly revealing of the approach which Hughes and the liberal minority had sought to take on New Deal issues—treating the specific features which might be found invalid in such a manner as to serve as guidelines for Congress in amending the legislation. It had been thus that the "hot oil" decision had been handled. The refusal of the unyielding conservatives to recognize the ultimate need for, and the possibility of, broadening Federal authority was made unmistakable; and how totally bankrupt the conservative concept was would itself become unmistakably clear in a matter of a few months when the negative doctrines of the present majority were, one after another, to be rejected by the same Court which was now pronouncing them so confidently.

*   *   *

It was no comfort to the New Dealers, however, to speculate whether the knot of willful Justices might in fact be making its last stand. The contrary prospect in May, 1935 was that, in a succession of reactionary decisions, all or most of the reform measures of the recent Congresses would be emasculated and the United States as a nation rendered impotent. One man—Owen J. Roberts—seemed to hold in his own hand the capacity to frustrate the majorities of both houses of Congress, the President of the United States, and more than 27,000,000 American voters who had underwritten the New Deal in 1932.

On May 27, in three successive opinions, the Court swept away two of the major statutory landmarks of the Roosevelt administration and, in a third case, slapped the President himself in the face.

Speaking for seven members of the Court—with Cardozo and Stone concurring in a separate opinion—Chief Justice Hughes invalidated the National Industrial Recovery Act in a categorical denial of Congressional power even more sweeping than the Roberts opinion which he himself had criticized three weeks before. As in the *Panama Refining* case, the majority found Congress guilty of having improperly delegated its legislative function to the executive branch without adequate guidelines; but Hughes then went far beyond the "hot oil" opinion and, like Roberts in the railroad pension case, gratuitously pronounced the drafting of an industrial code authority to be outside the scope of the commerce power. Substantially withdrawing from the position he had taken in the *Minnesota Mortgage Moratorium* case, Hughes declared: "Extraordinary conditions may call for extraordinary remedies. But the argument necessarily stops short of an attempt to justify action which lies outside the sphere of constitutional authority. . . . Those who act under these grants are not at liberty to transcend the imposed limits because they believe that more or different power is necessary."[45]

Cardozo and Stone, confining themselves to the issue of delegation of authority, found the concept of government-enforced privately devised regulatory codes to be a sufficient defect to strike down the statute. In their view, NIRA-type codes permitted the President to extend a general Congressional regulatory statute to any commercial activity "upon the recommendation of a trade association by calling it a code. This is delegation running riot."[46]

Brandeis, the great liberal, read the unanimous opinion in the next case invalidating the Frazier-Lemke Federal Farm Bankruptcy Act (*Louisville Joint Stock Land Bank v. Radford*). Under the provisions of the statute, a bankrupt farmer was permitted to purchase his property at the current appraised value and make deferred payments for a six-year period; or, if the mortgagee protested such a purchase, the bankrupt could obtain a stay of proceedings for five years and continue in possession of the land under control of a court. The fatal flaw in the provisions, said Brandeis, lay in the taking of substantial rights in the mortgaged property from the mortgagee and transferring them to the mortgagor; this was an undeniable taking of property without due process. "If the public interest requires, and permits, the taking of property of individual mortgagees in order to relieve the necessities of individual mortgagors, resort must be had to proceedings by eminent domain," Brandeis concluded; the government, rather than the primary party in interest in the mortgage, must retain the power of action.[47]

Sutherland, again speaking for a unanimous Court, delivered the unkindest cut of all in a case involving Roosevelt's removal of a hold-over member of the Federal Trade Commission, William E. Humphrey. Although the President had relied upon a majority opinion of the Taft Court asserting the Chief Executive's "inherent power" to remove subordinates in the executive branches of the government, an opinion in which Sutherland had concurred, the present opinion conspicuously avoided reference to this precedent. Roosevelt's action in removing an obstructionist member of an administrative board, Sutherland declared, "threatens the independence of a commission" created by Congress for the specific purpose of exercising independent administrative powers.[48]

*   *   *

"Black Monday" shook the nation. "When men like Stone, Cardozo, Brandeis and Hughes believe that the Constitution compels them to decide as they did in this case," said one writer with reference to *Schechter*, there was no flexibility to be found in any clause of the document. Sidney Hillman of the International Ladies' Garment Workers' Union was particularly incensed at Brandeis' position; having devoted his life to closing the sweatshops, said the labor leader, "he has now cleared the way for their reopening."[49]

Richberg, who had argued the government's case in favor of NIRA, observed in retrospect: "I do not believe that the briefs and arguments . . . had much to do with the opinion except in providing a basis on which the Court could rule against a government experiment which ran contrary to the political and economic predilections of the Justices."[50]

The White House was a scene of disaster. Richberg telephoned the Court's judgments in the three cases directly to the President. Roosevelt was stunned, particularly at the absence of any dissenting voices. "Well, where was Ben Cardozo? How did he stand?" he asked Richberg. "And what about old Isaiah*?" Robert H. Jackson, who was in the White House office while the telephone conversation took place, perceived that the liberals' defection left Roosevelt dazed, disbelieving.[51]

Roosevelt's inability to discern the particular reasons for the progressive bloc aligning itself with the conservatives was shared by the New Dealers generally; but for the President, it betrayed a fundamental lack of understanding of the individual convictions which made up the composite jurisprudence of the Court. Brandeis' dislike of the centralizing tendencies of big business in general was never a secret. It had been well known in the days of the New Freedom, and here, where a combination of sloppy draftsmanship and evidence of industrial abuse of the code authority was presented to him in the *Schechter* case, he was prepared to accept Hughes' lead. His opinion in *Radford* was equally explainable: he opposed government evasion of responsibility and found it improper to cast farm mortgage relief in the form of an undue weighting of the scales in favor of one party to a mortgage. As for the *Humphrey* case, he had been one of the dissenters in the original opinion on the subject in the Taft Court; untrammeled executive power, he was convinced, was an eminent threat to freedom.[52]

As for Cardozo and Stone, they had made their position clear, although not totally unequivocal, in their separate opinion in *Schechter*. By disassociating themselves from Hughes' doctrine that the "effect" upon interstate commerce of a regulatory authority might be direct or indirect as determined by the Court—a doctrine which harked back to the *Sugar Trust* case of 1895—they had sought to focus the action of the Court upon the overly vague nature of the Congressional delegation. Stone confessed, in a letter to John Basset Moore, that he was aware "that in many respects industry in the United States has become national and that the power ought to reside somewhere to treat some features of it at least nationally." But he hoped that Congress would do its job with better craftsmanship in its next attempt.[53]

The NRA, whatever its shortcomings, had been a symbol of the entire recovery program of the New Deal, and it was bitterly contended that, since it had only a short while remaining before it expired, a less doctrinaire decision could have guided Congress toward a practical reorganization of the

---

*A familiar name for Brandeis.

code concept. The uncompromisingly hostile tenor of all the opinions, however, lashed the President and his advisers and drove Roosevelt to make his first direct criticism of the Court. "The big issue is this: Does this decision mean that the United States government has no control over any national economic problem?" Roosevelt asked his press conference on May 31. A narrow concept of the authority of the Federal government under the commerce clause, he added in a phrase which instantly made headlines, had put the country back in "the horse-and-buggy age."[54]

The President then undertook to spell out what he considered to be the underlying question of the twentieth century: On "a very, very great non-partisan issue," he told the correspondents, the nation had now "to decide one way or the other. I don't mean this summer or winter or next fall, but over a period, perhaps, of five years or ten years we have got to decide: whether we are going to relegate to the forty-eight states practically all control over economic conditions, . . . or . . . whether in some way we are going to turn over or restore to . . . the Federal government the powers which exist in the national governments of every other nation in the world to enact and administer laws that have a bearing on, and general control over, national economic problems and national social problems."[55]

This was, at last, the issue which in reality had been crystallized from early in the twentieth century; it had been raised first under the Square Deal, and again under the New Freedom. "After all," said Roosevelt in a letter to a Florida jurist, "we do not want to take away states' rights but, at the same time, there are a good many problems which, under modern conditions, can be solved only by Federal action."[56]

*   *   *

The first and most urgent practical need following "Black Monday" was to salvage some administrative procedure out of the wreckage caused by the Court decisions. Cummings recommended to Roosevelt, with reference to the consequences of the *Alton Railroad* decision, that Congress be asked to create a fact-finding commission to determine upon the type of legislation which could operate within the framework of the judicial rule. The labor lobby in the House of Representatives, however, contended that the issue could be met simply by splitting in two the major objectives of the original law. Complementary but separate statutes, accordingly, were drafted with reference to the retirement system and the tax support program for the system, and were signed by Roosevelt in August. Although preliminary tests in the trial courts were initiated, the laws were superseded in 1937 by comprehensive legislation on railroad labor and retirement benefits approved by all parties in the industry, and this—within the changed climate of judicial opinion by that time—disposed of the problem.[57]

The NRA staff was reduced to a skeleton force to deal with government contracts negotiated by Federal attorneys with suppliers who agreed to be bound by the conditions formerly administered by code authorities. By executive orders in June, the labor boards under the NIRA were regrouped under a revived National Labor Relations Board, which in turn was supplanted by a board created by the Wagner Act of July 5.[58] To deal with the chaos in the coal fields which had resulted from the collapse of the price-control program under the NIRA when it was invalidated, Senator Joseph Guffey of Pennsylvania drafted a Bituminous Coal Conservation Act, which created a government commission to draft and administer a code authority.

"Manifestly, no one is in position to give assurance that the proposed act will withstand constitutional tests," Roosevelt wrote Congressman Samuel B. Hill of the House Ways and Means subcommittee. He added, however, that "the situation is so urgent and the benefits of the legislation so evident, that all doubts should be resolved in favor of the bill, leaving to the courts, in an orderly fashion, the ultimate question of constitutionality. A decision by the Supreme Court relative to this matter would be helpful as indicating, with increasing clarity, the constitutional limits within which this government must operate. . . . I hope your committee will not permit doubts as to constitutionality, however reasonable, to block the suggested legislation."[59]

The letter to Hill created a furor as news media proceeded to quote its final sentence out of context. It was, shouted conservatives, a shocking indication that the administration proposed to proceed on its legislative course in defiance of the Court. The day after the President signed the Guffey bill into law, the Carter Coal Company of Pennsylvania launched its suit to find the statute unconstitutional. The Liberty League, an extremist group of wealthy right-wingers, denounced the act as having been dictated by United Mine Workers leader John L. Lewis himself.[60]

Although the government had bowed to the *Schechter* decision by withdrawing hundreds of suits which were pending in the trial courts at the time of the adverse ruling by the Supreme Court, the extent of conservative hostility in the lower courts themselves was reflected in the torrent of restraining orders granted to defendants in actions still in progress. Judges Charles I. Dawson of the Western District of Kentucky and Merrill E. Otis of the Western District of Missouri were particularly eager to vent their spleen on the New Deal. "The scheme of regulation of the strictly local affairs of the citizens of the country, attempted to be set up and enforced under the Recovery Act, has no place in our system of government," Dawson said substantially before the Supreme Court invalidated NIRA, "and it is futile for its defenders to attempt to justify it on constitutional grounds."[61]

A year later, Dawson took the same position toward the Tobacco Control Act: it was, he declared, "the plainest kind of an attempt to accomplish an unconstitutional purpose by the pretended exercise of constitutional powers."[62] Otis, in another case substantially in advance of the *Schechter* decision, sneered at the humanitarian motives in the attempted child labor provision of NIRA: Congress, he declared, "cannot prohibit the movement in commerce of harmless things because, forsooth, they are manufactured by child labor, or by vegetarians, or by teetotalers." Following the decision, and referring to the Wagner Act by which the labor provisions of NIRA had been revived, Otis dogmatically contended: "Never can these relations be any part of commerce."[63]

As the months passed, however, no clear-cut administration policy to deal with the chaos created by the Court became evident. There was speculation, as 1936 came on, that the Court issue might become the main theme of the Presidential campaign, but the President was disposed to avoid it. On the other hand, he was beginning to despair of being presented with an opportunity to affect the composition of the judiciary through retirements, and he remarked to Harold Ickes that even Brandeis, "as he got older, was losing sight of fundamentals." Frankfurter, Roosevelt confided, was "heartbroken over it and did not like to discuss it."[64]

Throughout the remainder of 1935 the President contented himself with lofting "trial balloons" in the periodicals and reviewing the situation occasionally with his official family. In the late summer, George Creel of *Collier's* made note of a statement dictated by Roosevelt in the course of an interview, looking toward the next group of New Deal statutes coming on for review in the October term of Court. Given the attitude of the judiciary the previous May, said the statement, "it is possible the President will get another 'licking.' If so, much will depend on the language of the licking. In event that unconstitutionality is found, perhaps the decisions will point the way to statutory amendments. If, however, the Constitution is construed technically; if it is held . . . that the present generation is powerless to meet social and economic problems that were not within the knowledge of the Founding Fathers, and therefore not made the subject of their specific consideration, then the President will have no other alternative than to go to the country with a constitutional amendment that will lift the Dead Hand, giving the people of today the right to deal with today's vital issues."[65]

The interview was in line with the letter to Congressman Hill, inviting the Court to propose guidelines for legislation which it would find acceptable. It also suggested that Roosevelt was giving some consideration to a constitutional amendment on the subject of the legislation or of the Court itself. This approach was discussed in a Cabinet meeting near the end of December, 1935; of the several possible solutions to the current judicial crisis, said the President, packing the Court was "a distasteful idea," while the proposal for a series of amendments to validate each reform statute as it was nullified was impractical. He then commended to their study the latest proposal by Cummings—a single amendment affirming the power of judicial review but providing that Congress, after an intervening election, could reenact any statute declared unconstitutional by the Court. The proposal, by no means novel, conceived of a function in Congress of overriding judicial vetoes of legislation as it could override executive vetoes.[66]

The fact was that no single course of action seemed to offer substantial promise of settling all or most of the problems involved. Any constitutional amendment was subsequently subject to judicial interpretation, and as avid a reader of history as Franklin Roosevelt knew all too well that appointees to the Court, once in office, were independent of legislative or executive direction.

*   *   *

As though it were impatient for Armageddon, the Court in 1936 cast one affront after another into the teeth of the New Dealers. On January 6, by a majority of six to three, it struck down the Agricultural Adjustment Act, companion pillar with the NIRA of the original emergency recovery program. The issue had been eloquently argued; both Reed and Cummings, with eight other lawyers, were on the government's brief, opposed by George Wharton Pepper, former Republican Senator from Pennsylvania, and seven other attorneys. Groups from a dozen states filed briefs *amici* in support of the law.[67]

Pepper cast his argument in the defense of *laissez-faire,* with a fervor that was reminiscent of Joseph H. Choate's peroration on the *Income Tax* case four decades earlier. It was, in fact, a continuation of the same worn theme: "I am standing here today to plead the cause of the America I have loved," Pepper told the Court. "I pray Almighty God that not in my time may 'the land of the regimented' be accepted as a worthy substitute for 'the land of the free.' "[68]

Justice Roberts, a faithful friend of Pepper's and one whose own instincts responded with ardor to such an apostrophe, wrote the majority opinion which destroyed the AAA and saved the receiver of the Hoosac Mills Corporation from regimentation. Aware of the growing public resentment at the Court's consistent position, the Justice began defensively: "It is sometimes said that the Court assumes a power to overrule or control the action of the people's representatives. This is a misconception. The Constitution is the supreme law of the land ordained and established by the people. All legislation must conform to the principles it lays down. When an act of Congress is appropriately challenged in the courts as not conforming to the constitutional mandate, the judicial branch of the government has only one duty—to lay the article of the Constitution which is invoked beside the statute which is challenged and to decide whether the latter squares with the former. . . . This Court neither approves nor condemns any legislative policy."[69]

Applying his yardstick, Roberts determined that the taxing power of Congress was applicable only to matters of general welfare, and it was not to the benefit of the general welfare, he concluded, to coerce and regiment citizens. More objectionable than that, declared Roberts, was the fact that the subject-matter—agriculture—was something not within the jurisdiction of Congress but only of the states. Ignoring more than three-quarters of a century of Federal aid to farmers in scores of activities, the Justice declared: "The power of taxation, which is expressly granted, may, of course, be adopted as a means to carry into operation another power also expressly granted. But resort to the taxing power to effectuate an end which is not legitimate, not within the scope of the Constitution, is obviously inadmissible."[70]

ᴵ It was, said Stone in dissenting for himself, Brandeis and Cardozo, "a tortured construction of the Constitution." Judicial review, he reminded the majority, was subject to "two guiding principles of decision which ought never to be absent from judicial consciousness. One is that courts are concerned only with the power to enact statutes, not with their wisdom. The other is that while unconstitutional exercise of power by the executive and legislative branches of the government is subject to judicial restraint, the only check upon our own exercise of power is our own sense of self-restraint."[71]

The majority's contention that "a levy unquestionably within the taxing power of Congress may be treated as invalid because it is a step in a plan to regulate agricultural production and is thus a forbidden infringement of state power," Stone disposed of swiftly: "While all Federal taxes inevitably have some influence on the internal economy of the states, it is not contended that the levy of a processing tax upon manufacturers using agricultural products as raw material has any perceptible regulatory effect upon either their production or manufacture." Equally fallacious, in Stone's view, was the contention that "while the Constitution gives to Congress, in specific and unambiguous terms, the power to tax and spend, the power is subject to limitations which do not find their origin in any express provision of the Constitution and to which other expressly delegated powers are not subject." In truth, Stone pointed out, the spending power of Congress "is in addition to the legislative power and not subject to it."[72]

United States v. Butler effectively killed the most productive single statute of the first New Deal. As Robert H. Jackson pointed out, the success of the farm program which had developed under AAA stimulus had been substantial: In less than three years, the price of wheat rose from 38½¢ to 81½¢ a bushel, cotton from 6½¢ a pound to 11½¢, and hogs from $4.06 per hundred pounds to $10.22. Even greater increases in purchases of farm implements and machinery, and in mail order sales, were recorded between 1933 and 1935, and the effect on the rest of the economy was described by the conservative National City Bank of New York as the most significant factor in business recovery for the period.[73] But for the Court majority, data such as these were irrelevant; the important thing was the mechanical yardstick which Roberts had devised.

Roosevelt himself, still apparently undecided as to a remedial plan and willing to let popular pressure continue to build up, told his Cabinet on January 24, 1936 that word was "coming to him from widely separated parts of the country that people were beginning to show a great deal of interest in the constitutional questions that have been raised by recent Supreme Court decisions." In this regard, the President hinted, he would not be entirely dismayed at "the Supreme Court declaring one New Deal statute after another unconstitutional," since by this process he believed that "a real issue will be joined on which we can go to the country."[74]

He was beginning to settle on the issue. In the light of the permanent division of the Court—after *Schechter*, no decision setting aside a major New Deal mustered a unanimous opinion[75]—it was becoming evident to him that the solution, if any, was not a constitutional amendment but a modernizing of the thinking of the tribunal itself. By February, Senator Norris, formerly an advocate of the amendment route, had apparently come to the same conclusion, for in an address on the *Butler* decision he declared that it was not the Constitution which needed changing. "I think the decision is an amendment to the Constitution," he said, "but that is not a new thing. The Court has amended the Constitution before. In fact, the Supreme Court now, in effect, for all practical purposes, is a continuous constitutional convention." By its own decisions, Norris concluded, the Court had served notice that amendatory steps would not cure legislation it regarded as undesirable. "The people," he observed, "can change Congress, but only God can change the Supreme Court."[76]

The increasing determination of the conservatives to block progressive legislation was only exacerbated by their equal interest, if the occasion presented itself, to blacken the public image of New Deal agencies. This was blatantly evident in the majority's gratuitous commentary casting aspersions on the motives of the Securities and Exchange Commission in a case handed down April 6. The SEC had already withstood a constitutional challenge, and its record of performance was by now becoming popular with both public and the capitalist market. The Commission had been born out of the public outrage at the disclosures in the renowned stock market investigations conducted by a Senate Committee under a special attorney, Ferdinand Pecora.

Through the winter of 1934, under Pecora's relentless examinations, the greatest names in Wall Street had been identified before the country as self-serving opportunists who developed a fantastically profitable stock-jobbing sideline while seeking the main chance for their friends and themselves. On the strength of this investigation, Congress was able to supplant the emergency stock exchange act of 1933 with the 1934 legislation creating the SEC.[77] Its drastic powers over suspect dealings in securities offerings on the nation's markets were regarded by many financiers with dismay; its very operating principle, which was to end *laissez-faire* activity on the exchanges, stuck in the throats of conservatives.

Then, in *Jones v. Securities Commission*, the Court was asked for a rule of statutory construction. A dealer in oil royalties who had submitted a registration statement to the SEC as required by the statute undertook to withdraw the statement when the Commission questioned its validity. The defendant then contended that by withdrawing the statement he had removed himself from the Commission's jurisdiction and was not liable for refusal to answer its questions. Sutherland, speaking for a majority of six, lost no time in giving the rule of construction requested; a witness who wished to avoid embarrassing testimony compelled by an administrative agency could do so by use of this tactic.

But Sutherland did not intend to stop with that. Although the Commission had pursued its inquiry against the registrant on the assumption that it was within its statutory authority, the Justice declared: "The action of the Commission finds no support in right principle or in law. It is wholly unreasonable and arbitrary . . . because to the precise extent that the mere will of an official or an official body is permitted to take the place of allowable official discretion or to supplant the standing law as a rule of human conduct, the government ceases to be one of laws and becomes an autocracy."[78]

The majority opinion's *in terrorem* statement of "dangers that wait upon the abuse of power by officialdom unchained," Cardozo's dissent drily remarked, "is so fraught with truth that it can never be untimely." But, he reminded Sutherland and the other conservatives, there was equal danger in misrepresented securities which "pass current in the market," and in a judicial finding that a suspected perpetrator of misrepresented securities may "stifle an inquiry by precipitate retreat on the eve of his exposure." To condone such practice, the dissent perceived, was to place control over the effectiveness of the administrative process in the hands of the private parties who were supposed to be subject to its surveillance.[79]

Sutherland's provocative dictum reflected a long-rankling conservative dislike of administrative scrutiny of sharp dealing which, in Cardozo's phrase, the *laissez-faire* capitalist preferred to shrug off as "peccadillos, or even perhaps as part of the amenities of business." The "unguarded language of Mr. Justice Sutherland," wrote James M. Landis in 1938, had "the effect, if not the purpose," of breeding distrust of the whole process of government supervision of economic activity through the regulatory agency. "For months thereafter," Landis reported, "every effort to deal with fraudulent promoters was met by the accusation that Star Chamber tactics were being employed."[80]

*   *   *

The obsession of the conservatives with denying to Congress all legislative power to remedy the ills of the national economy was demonstrated again in May, when a five-to-four majority struck down the Guffey Act. Inasmuch as this was one of the measures by which the New Deal had sought to salvage some of the most substantial gains under the NIRA after it had been invalidated, there could be no mistaking the conservative intentions—or obliviousness to the public need. Where Roosevelt had ventured the hope that the judicial review of the Guffey Act would, if unfavorable, at least suggest the constitutional guidelines to be followed in subsequent legislative efforts, the majority called only for unconditional surrender.

There was little or no rational basis for arguing that mining was anything but an interstate, interrelated process. The industry, indeed, stood midway between the segments of the economy represented by agriculture and those represented by manufacturing, railroading and the interstate corporations. It was, under most circumstances, virtually the life force of the latter three segments. Yet for decades mining had been plagued with marginal profits for operators and submarginal living for workers, and until the NIRA had provided an effective brake, the entire industry had been declining into a permanent depression.

When the Guffey Act came on for review, seven states filed briefs *amici curiae* in support of the statute. Yet Sutherland, speaking for the narrow majority, chose to mingle the outworn clichés of *laissez-faire* with the equally irrelevant doctrine of states' rights. "The proposition, often advanced and as often discredited, that the power of the Federal government inherently extends to purposes affecting the nation as a whole with which the states severally cannot deal or cannot adequately deal, and the related notion that Congress, entirely apart from those powers delegated by the Constitution, may enact laws to promote the general welfare, have never been accepted but always definitely rejected by this Court," he declared.[81]

Reciting a long list of nineteenth-century precedents, Sutherland continued: "The states were before the Constitution; and, consequently, their legislative powers antedated the Constitution. Those who framed and those who adopted that instrument meant to carve from the general mass of legislative powers, then possessed by the states, only such portions as it was thought wise to confer upon the Federal government; and in order that there should be no uncertainty in respect of what was taken and what was left, the national powers of legislation were not aggregated but enumerated—with the result that what was not embraced by the enumeration remained vested in the states without change or impairment."[82]

Having reiterated this dogma of the narrow constructionists of the past hundred years, Sutherland then turned his attention to the evils in the Guffey Act. In drafting the law, Congress had sought with particular care to avoid what it understood to have been the defects in the NIRA; it had set out a detailed process of price regulation under government surveillance, and in a separate title had revived the labor relations phase of the old Soft Coal Code. Then, uncertain of the fate of the new statute before the Court, Congress had sought to make the two titles severable in the event that one was declared to be unconstitutional. Sutherland simply used the invalidity of the labor relations title to nullify the entire statute; since the two in effect were interdependent, he concluded, the one would be inoperative if the other was.[83]

Chief Justice Hughes, although he appeared to acquiesce in the majority's hostility toward the labor relations section of the act, cried out in protest at the high-handedness of the majority in ignoring the plain intention of Congress to sever the titles if only one was found void. Cardozo, speaking for the liberals, suggested that both titles in fact were legitimate subjects of Congressional action. Since the regulating of interstate commerce in reference to coal prices was tacitly accepted as within the power of Congress, it followed that stabilizing prices would "go a long way toward stabilizing labor relations by giving the producers capacity to pay a living wage." Congress, declared Cardozo, was not "condemned to inaction in the face of price wars and wage wars" which had reduced the coal industry to near chaos. "The liberty protected by the Fifth Amendment does not include the right to persist in this anarchic riot," he said. "The free competition so often figured as a social good imports order and moderation and a decent regard for the welfare of the group."[84]

It was not New Deal regulation alone, but the principle of government interference with any element of the free enterprise system at which the conservatives were ultimately aiming in their all-out effort to turn the tide of economic history. The previous December, in a case invalidating provisions in a Vermont income tax law which had exempted income from loans secured by property in the state which was already taxed, a six-to-three majority found that the state law infringed upon the privileges and immunities clause of the Fourteenth Amendment. The technical flaw lay in a companion provision exempting unsecured loans made within the state. Sutherland, again speaking for the majority, had ruled that this improperly discriminated against loans secured by property outside the state, dismissing the explanation that the exemption was actually intended to avoid double taxation.[85]

Ironically, the conservatives had created a substantially broadened concept of national citizenship—ordinarily anathema to states' rightists—in order to strike down a state legislative policy. Stone, speaking for the three dissenters, warned the majority of its sowing the seeds of its own undoing: If the restraint upon state action in the privileges and immunities clause "were extended more than is needful to protect relationships between the citizen and the national government," he wrote, "and it did more than duplicate the protection of liberty and property secured to persons and citizens by the other provisions of the Constitution, it would enlarge judicial control of state action and multiply restrictions upon it to an extent difficult to define, but sufficient to cause serious apprehension for the rightful independence of local government."[86]

Careening more rapidly down the road of "judicial control of state action" in its unheeding effort to insulate its concept of capitalism from all government, another five-to-four majority invalidated the Municipal Bankruptcy Act of 1934. McReynolds, taking over the argument for the conservatives, insisted that the statute permitted the states, through the indirect route of Congressional legislation, to evade the impairment of contracts clause in the Constitution. As the Justice phrased it, the Congressional relief proffered to municipal corporations staggering under the burdens of the depression was made to appear to be a Federal plot to "impose its will and impair state powers" by providing a way for cities to seek, as public corporations, the same type of relief in the Federal courts that bankrupts which were private corporations had enjoyed throughout the national history. "To hold that this purpose must be thwarted by the courts because of the supposed affront to the dignity of a state, though the state disclaims the affront and is doing all it can to keep the law alive, is to make dignity a doubtful blessing," wrote Cardozo for the four dissenters.[87]

On June 1, in the final vindictive judgment of an incredible term, the Court by still another five-to-four decision *(Morehead v. New York)* declared unconstitutional the New York state minimum wage law for women. With grim delight, Justice Butler turned back the calendar nearly four decades and in a sweeping opinion undertook to insure that never, under any circumstances, should the state government any more than the Federal government find a means of thus interfering with the free enterprise system. The disposition of the New York law was simple, in his view; it had been settled fifteen years before in *Adkins v. Children's Hospital.* To attempt to regulate the conditions of women's bargaining with employers was to deny their constitutional equality with men. That equality in turn assured them of the constitutional freedom of contract—"part of the liberty protected by the due process clause. Within this liberty are provisions of contracts between employer and employee fixing the wages to be paid. In making contracts of employment, generally speaking, the parties have equal right to obtain from each other the best terms they can by private bargaining."[88]

Where was the freedom, asked Stone in dissent, for "those who, because of their economic necessities, give their services for less than is needful to keep body and soul together? But if this is freedom of contract no one has ever denied that it is freedom which may be restrained, notwithstanding the Fourteenth Amendment, by a statute passed in the public interest." Even conceding that *Adkins* might have been valid when it was adjudicated, Stone continued, "we have had opportunity to learn that a wage is not always the resultant of free bargaining between employers and employees; that it may be one forced upon employees by their economic necessities and upon employers by the most ruthless of their competitors. We have had opportunity to perceive more clearly that a wage insufficient to support the worker does not visit its consequences upon him alone; that it may affect profoundly the entire economic structure of society. . . . Because of their nature and extent these are public problems. A generation ago they were for the individual to solve; today they are the burden of the nation."[89]

*   *   *

The *Morehead* decision outraged the liberals, pained those who considered themselves objective observers, and left even the conservatives with a sense of betrayal. The decision, wrote Harold Ickes, preserved "the right of an immature child or a helpless woman to drive a bargain with a great corporation. . . . Such a decision is not even as modern as the horse-and-buggy age. This is positively medieval, and I am frank to say that if this decision is constitutional, we need either an entirely new or a radically amended Constitution. If it isn't constitutional, then we need a different Supreme Court."[90]

In a matter of eighteen months, the hard-core conservatives had overturned more than a dozen Federal and state laws in their zeal to stamp out every vestige of regulatory power they could reach. As though the devotees of the last remnants of *laissez-faire* were pursuing a death wish, they repeatedly held up the talisman of limited government and a free economy as they remembered it from their imagined golden age. Moreover, the irreconcilable attitude of the judicial opponents of progressivism was forcing the political opposition to progressivism into an untenable position. It was clear, Roosevelt said in a press conference the day after *Morehead,* that the sequence of opinions handed down since January, 1935 had created a " 'no-man's-land' where no government—state or Federal—can function."[91]

3/Court Reform Revisited

I F FRANKLIN D. ROOSEVELT was in any doubt as to the nation's feelings concerning his administration, his mind was set at rest the morning of November 4, 1936. Carrying forty-six of the forty-eight states, with a popular vote margin of more than 10,000,000 over the Republican Alf Landon and a clutch of splinter parties, the President also won a Democratic majority of 77 to 19 in the Senate and 328 to 107 in the House. The Court question had been touched on in the briefest possible manner during the campaign. In his acceptance speech in June at Philadelphia's Franklin Field, Roosevelt had referred to "economic royalists" who had "created a new despotism and wrapped it in the robes of judicial sanction." The party platform had contained a plank, drafted by Richberg and endorsed by Cummings, which proposed that if reform legislation continued to run afoul of judicial review a "clarifying amendment" (unclarified in the plank) be submitted to the people.[1]

The President made few other references to the judicial problem in the course of the campaign; it remained for Henry Wallace to publicize the fundamental issue that had taken shape in the past eighteen months. On July 1 he published his book, *Whose Constitution? An Inquiry into the General Welfare,* in which he set forth the problem in contemporary terms: In 1936, Wallace wrote, "the situation seems rather more favorable to Federalism than it was in 1787. . . . Only the large corporations, the Republican party, New England, the Liberty League and most of the newspapers of the country are apparently for states' rights at any costs."[2]

"To interpret the Constitution in the light of the spirit of its framers is one thing," the Secretary of Agriculture continued. "To interpret it in the light of economic conditions as they were in 1787 when the Constitution was drawn up is another. . . . The doctrine of states' rights, now invoked by the Supreme Court, was a barrier to progress even in 1787, and was the cause of a terrible conflict in 1861. Today, the states mark no economic boundaries that make sense, and they provide only limited instruments for action to meet modern problems. Long ago the great corporations managed to break down states' rights when they interfered with corporate expansion. Today it is clear that states' rights are being invoked not for the rights which they defend, but for the privileges they protect."[3]

While Farley and other stand-pat campaign managers felt that Wallace's book might tend needlessly to churn up the waters, Roosevelt himself was enthusiastic on running through it. "I hope you sell 100,000 copies," he wrote the author. If it did not become a best-seller, nevertheless it put the public on notice that the issue of judicial review would have to be settled before the next term was very old. Wallace's approach was essentially a campaign argument; the real best-seller, appearing on the eve of the election and unleashing a vitriolic attack on the august members of the Court itself, was *Nine Old Men,* written by the authors of the recent best-selling *Washington Merry-Go-Round,* columnists Drew Pearson and Robert S. Allen.

Both liberals and conservatives in government knew, said Pearson and Allen, "and seemed to take a grim joy in that knowledge, that their opposing social and economic philosophies were speeding toward a head-on crash not merely between judiciary and executive, but between the doctrine of omnipotent intransigence and the thesis that no nation or people can stand still." With alternate breeziness and brutality, the authors then dissected each of the members of the Court: Charles Evans Hughes "has swung back and forth from liberalism to economic stultification with greater ease than the daring young man on the flying trapeze"; Stone was a conservative who had deserted the establishment; Butler, "the bruiser"; Roberts, the "Philadelphia lawyer"; Brandeis, a lonely crusader seeking "to better men's economic and social ideals"; Van Devanter, the fanatical reactionary with the "neurotic pen"; Sutherland, Harding's "lame-duck" appointee; Cardozo, "the hermit philosopher"; and McReynolds, the "Supreme Court's greatest human tragedy."[4]

The *Nine Old Men,* with its muckraking and iconoclasm, was the type of popular discussion which Roosevelt sensed was needed to arouse the country at large; the President was forced to admit the correctness of Farley's statement that there had not been "a sufficient excitement among the people" about the Court and the Constitution. With the Pearson-Allen book on so many people's tongues, the opportunity for a public move might at last be at hand.

Midway between the dignified though partisan analysis of Henry Wallace, and the calculated debunking of Pearson and Allen, the scholarly argumentation of Edward S. Corwin added another dimension to the dialogue. In December, 1936 and January, 1937, Corwin was commissioned by the *Philadelphia Record* to prepare a series of articles which would seek to bring readers up to date on the developments that had created the current impasse. Corwin reviewed for the laymen the constitutional lawyer's definition of judicial review, sketched the historical development of both the Court and the Constitution, and discussed the jurisprudential propositions in the recent cases overthrowing New Deal reform statutes.

The current problems confronting Congress and the White House, Corwin declared, could only be resolved by an about-face by the judges or an affirmative effort to counteract the prevailing ideology by law. "Congress unquestionably has powers whereby it could bring the Court [to terms]," the writer conceded, but it "is properly embarrassed in employing them by the consideration that in doing so it would seriously harm the prestige of the Court." There was also the obvious fact that "the present situation would be considerably aided by one or two resignations from the bench." But in the final analysis, the author concluded, the Court would have to save itself.[5]

*   *   *

In retrospect, those close to Roosevelt came to realize that he had all but decided upon his course of action before the November election returns; the heady margin of his victory only gave him vast added confidence that the action could be pushed through. Corwin's articles had touched the heart of the matter; any amendment to the Constitution itself would either prove ineffective while the majority on the bench persisted in its present line of interpretation, or would prove unnecessary if either the attitude or the personnel were altered. The matter ultimately and inevitably came back to the Court itself.

Roosevelt returned to Washington from Hyde Park shortly after the election and immediately sent for Attorney General Cummings. The two men evaluated the work which had been going on under Department of Justice direction throughout 1936, with a team of researchers including Corwin of Princeton and William Draper Lewis of the American Law Institute, developing the case for every conceivable approach to the problem. While the President did not indicate to Cummings that he had completely made up his mind which course to follow, he sent him away with clear instructions to wind up the work as expeditiously as possible so that a choice of methods could be made. Cummings conferred daily with Roosevelt for the remainder of November, slipping into the White House office by a private entrance so as to avoid arousing observers' curiosity.[6]

Donald Richberg, busy with the Justice Department task force, also developed a complete legislative draft of his own which proposed the retirement of members of the Supreme Court on full pay at the age of 70 with the right of assignment to special judicial functions. This, Richberg was to argue, was the most likely way of accommodating the constitutional provision that members of the Court were to be appointed for life (literally, "during good behavior") with "a compensation which shall not be diminished during their continuance in office." As the work progressed, Solicitor General Reed also was brought into the now narrowing circle of the most confidential advisers, along with Judge Rosenman and, peripherally, Thomas G. Corcoran.[7]

Roosevelt apparently took no one else into his confidence, and his main reliance was upon Cummings. As the new year began, the President went to work on his Second Inaugural Address with a view to planting a few oblique references to what would be coming. On the day it was delivered, one of the favored Washington correspondents, Raymond Clapper, was given an even broader hint: Richberg told Clapper that "Roosevelt is in an audacious mood and is . . . thinking of proposing to pack the Supreme Court by enlarging it." The President, Richberg went on, was "determined to curb the Court and put it in its place, and will go ahead even if many people think it unwise."[8]

The Inaugural Address itself suggested that something was in the offing. In the emergency, short-term remedies of the first New Deal, Roosevelt told his audience, the country had come to recognize "a deeper need—the need to find through government the instrument of our united purpose to solve for the individual the ever-rising problems of a complex civilization." The year 1937, the President noted, marked the hundred and fiftieth anniversary of the Constitutional Convention which "created a strong government with powers of united action then and now to solve problems utterly beyond individual or local solution."

"Nearly all of us recognize," the President continued, "that as intricacies of human relationships increase, so power to govern them also must increase—power to stop evil; power to do good. The essential democracy of our nation and the safety of our people depend not upon the absence of power, but upon lodging it with those whom the people can change or continue at stated intervals through an honest and free system of elections. The Constitution of 1787 did not make our democracy impotent."

Pointing to "one-third of a nation ill-housed, ill-clad, ill-nourished," Roosevelt declared: "Our pledge was not merely to do a patchwork job with secondhand materials. By using the new materials of social justice we have undertaken to erect on the old foundations a more enduring structure for the better use of future generations."[9]

Two weeks earlier, in his message at the opening of Congress, Roosevelt had indicated more clearly that the ultimate question was one of constitutional interpretation rather than amendment. "During the past year there has been a growing belief that there is little fault to be found in the Constitution of the United States as it stands today," the President said, articulating his own maturing conviction. "The vital need is not an alteration of our fundamental law, but an increasingly enlightened view with reference to it. Difficulties have grown out of its interpretation; but rightly considered, it can be used as an instrument of progress, and not as a device for prevention of action."

The concluding portion of the message was even more pointedly directed to the problem: "The judicial branch . . . is asked by the people to do its part in making democracy successful. We do not ask the courts to call non-existent powers into being, but we have a right to expect that conceded powers or those legitimately implied shall be made effective instruments for the common good."[10]

Thus Franklin Roosevelt had cast the die. The Court, and not the Constitution, must yield in the face of the demands of the 1930's.

*   *   *

The President had reason to assume that, whichever course he chose, the progressives in Congress and the majority of his own party would follow his lead. The progressives were ideologically committed to some form of action in the matter, while the unprecedented reelection in November made Roosevelt apparently undisputed master of the Democratic bloc. The mood of Congress, also, seemed to be congenial to some type of plan to curb the Court. No sooner had the session begun than more than a dozen bills on the subject had been introduced, while Senator Joseph Robinson of Arkansas had told the press on the eve of the opening that a lawful power to enact reform legislation "should be established either in the states or in the Congress."

The Supreme Court holdings of the previous term, Robinson conceded, were a serious bar to action, and in his view a remedial constitutional amendment would be required. However, he said, "I do not preclude myself from supporting any legislation which I am convinced would make possible reasonable control by public authority" over economic and social questions.[11]

The Senate majority leader reflected, in his own personality and party record, the congeries of loyalties and interests with which Roosevelt would have to deal in the Court fight. An old-line Populist and a Wilsonian Progressive, Robinson had undergone the kind of mellowing that characteristically overcame Southern Senators in the course of tenure and seniority. Seniority and party loyalty were, indeed, Robinson's primary assets. He had accepted a draft to run as Al Smith's Vice-Presidential mate in 1928. He had floor-managed virtually all of the reform legislation of the early New Deal, although much of it had stuck in his own throat. Now he would be the man to depend upon in pushing a measure which he had already condemned to cronies as "pretty raw."

Yet Robinson *would* be one to be depended upon, for several reasons. He was the gentleman of the old school, with party loyalty a part of his personal code of honor. He was a responsible politician who took seriously the job of being the majority leader. Finally—and doubtless in that order of consideration—there was a promise the President had made, to give the Senator the first vacancy which might open on the Supreme Court. At the age of sixty-five, Robinson's appointment would belie the administration claim that it sought to people the judiciary with younger men. At the stage of economic conviction to which Robinson had come, his appointment would make a mockery of the effort to liberalize the philosophy of the Court itself.[12]

In this hour, men like Joseph Taylor Robinson would have to be counted on to seek to push the bill through Congress. And yet, as the time of decision drew near, Roosevelt held no planning conferences with the majority leader or any other member of the Senate. For that matter, the President was consulting few if any persons outside the Cummings task force. As hindsight was to show, this was the first of many errors. The lofting of trial balloons in the communications media might have tested the winds of public opinion— although, to be sure, previous efforts to read the signs had been disappointing in their evidence of public apathy. Certainly the failure to take key Senators and Representatives into his confidence on so important a matter robbed Roosevelt of a vital opportunity to persuade them to undertake the job of pushing the bill through and preparing the way in advance.

As Cummings later explained it, the extreme secrecy on the part of the White House was dictated by a desire to catch the opposition unprepared. Even more persuasive was the indication that the President was hesitating over a number of details in the projected bill. Everyone involved in the plan was busy searching out stronger points to be developed; the Attorney General himself recollected that he had uncovered, in the course of a book on the Department of Justice which he and his aide, Carl McFarland, were writing, a particularly useful quotation from a report by McReynolds when he had been Wilson's first Attorney General. It stated the proposition eloquently for the retirement of jurists at a specified age. In his report for 1913, McReynolds had commented that some Federal judges "have remained upon the bench long beyond the time that they are able to adequately discharge their duties," and added:

> I suggest an act providing that when any judge of a Federal court below the Supreme Court fails to avail himself of the privilege of retiring now granted by law, that the President be required, with the advice and consent of the Senate, to appoint another judge, who would preside over the affairs of the court and have precedence over the older one. This will insure at all times the presence of a judge sufficiently active to discharge promptly and adequately the duties of the court.[13]

There was no reason, Cummings argued, why the McReynolds recommendation should not be applied to Supreme Court members as well; if an appropriate retirement age—70 years had been McReynolds' suggestion—were settled upon, six of the nine current Justices could be replaced forthwith. Meantime, the research went on. Taft and Hughes had both written influential works on the Court and the Constitution which, the New Dealers concluded, might also contain materials to be used against the conservatives of the present. Roosevelt, always a student of history, reviewed his own recollections of the basic authorities on the Constitution, and correspondents who saw him in the weeks following the election were struck by his voluminous knowledge of the arguments in Madison's *Notes* on the 1787 Convention and Elliott's *Debates* on ratification.[14]

Several members of Congress with instincts for this sort of thing made shrewd guesses as to what the White House was up to; Raymond Clapper noted in his diary that Hugo Black of Alabama had outlined to him the proposal almost precisely as it came to Capitol Hill, although Steve Early, Roosevelt's press secretary, assured Clapper that Black had talked with the President only about the Federal Maritime Commission during a recent appointment. Congressman Hatton W. Sumners of Texas, after listening to the emphases in the Inaugural Address, had hastened to reintroduce a bill he had drafted at the previous session, calling for retirement on full pay whenever members of the Court elected to avail themselves of the privilege.[15]

*   *   *

Dissimulation reached its climax on February 2, when the White House held its annual formal dinner for members of the Court and a concourse of distinguished guests. The Roosevelt advisers knew that the time to introduce the bill was at hand; within a week, government counsel would begin oral arguments on the next group of New Deal laws coming on for review, including such vital measures as the National Labor Relations Act and Social Security. The President, for a number of reasons, chose to postpone action until after the judiciary dinner; among other things, said Rosenman, it heightened Roosevelt's zest for the dramatic. Senator William Borah, watching the Chief Executive in hearty repartee with Hughes and Van Devanter, was reminded of "the Roman Emperor who looked around his dinner table and began to laugh when he thought of how many of those heads would be rolling on the morrow."[16]

The formal social function did have its ironies; among the White House guests were all of the conservatives and vacillators, but only one of the liberals, Cardozo. Stone was recuperating from a stubborn illness, and Brandeis was following a rule of long standing against attending such affairs in the evening. Cummings felt that the elaborate conviviality was not in good taste. "I feel too much like a conspirator," he whispered to Rosenman. The judge told the Attorney General that he had the same feeling.[17]

Even now, however, and despite his radiating confidence, Roosevelt was not entirely satisfied with the Court message. It lacked the warmth and persuasiveness, for which he had been striving so long, to touch a responsive chord in the public mind. After the dinner, he asked Richberg and Rosenman once more to try their hands at strengthening it. The President, Rosenman was convinced, fully appreciated the momentous nature of what he was about to attempt. "It was the only time I can recall," he wrote in retrospect, that Roosevelt "seemed worried after deciding upon a course of action."[18]

Some forty-eight hours after the Supreme Court dinner at the White House, Roosevelt called his Cabinet into special session. The time had come to let them in on the secret, along with the leaders of Congress whose advance briefing had been so cavalierly neglected. Sumners, as chairman of the House Judiciary Committee, and his counterpart, Senator Henry F. Ashurst of Arizona, appeared on invitation along with Speaker William B. Bankhead and the party leaders on the floor, Robinson of Arkansas and Congressman Sam Rayburn of Texas. The tight security against premature publicity was still in force, but Corcoran had prevailed on Roosevelt to let him break the news in confidence to "old Isaiah." Brandeis, Corcoran predicted, "sure won't like it"—and he was never more correct.[19]

Roosevelt, who so often resorted to elaborate and indirect prefaces to a course of action and, like the astute politician he usually was, called in all the key men whose responsibility would be to carry out his strategy, had decided in this critical juncture to rely on surprise and speed. Telephoned calls announcing the Cabinet meeting had gone out late the evening of February 4, with the request that the call be kept in strict confidence; the meeting itself was set for 10 o'clock, an hour before a special press conference and two hours before the message and the accompanying bill would be introduced on the Hill.[20]

Just before Roosevelt entered the room, a sheaf of mimeographed papers was brought in and distributed; they contained the texts which were ready for dispatch to Congress. Then, before the assemblage had time to digest them and begin an exchange of ideas among themselves, the President was wheeled in. Rapidly he began to speak, outlining the main points on the papers and explaining why he had decided on "a legislative rather than a constitutional amendment" approach. Among other things, Roosevelt said, "he understood that there had already been collected a large sum of money in New York by Liberty League influence to prevent the adoption of any amendment." In any event, said the President, judiciary reform was manifestly within the legislative competence of Congress although care had to be taken not to permit changes in the bill which might make it possible to hold it unconstitutional.[21]

The reactions of his listeners—for Roosevelt very pointedly avoided giving any opening for questions—were variously described. To Ickes, Robinson seemed to indicate "a mild assent," although others recalled his staring down at the conference table while the President spoke, his face deeply flushed. Ashurst did volunteer a preference for the legislative approach over an amendment, which he had previously been inclined to advocate.[22]

Congressman Sumners, in whose committee it was assumed that the bill would begin its course through Congress, never took his eyes off Roosevelt. The only point at which he might have indicated approval, said Ickes, was the President's inclusion of Sumners' own retirement plan for the Court. Bankhead appeared to Ickes "to be distinctly 'pokerish.'" But there was no conversation, even when Roosevelt hastily left the meeting with the remark that he did not want to be late for his press conference. Wordlessly, the Congressional leaders drifted to the front door of the White House, where two cabs were summoned to take them off to the Capitol. It was then that Sumners made a pronouncement to the companions riding with him.

"Boys," he said, "here's where I cash in my chips."[23]

*   *   *

What incensed both liberals like Brandeis and conservatives like Sumners was the manifest deviousness of the Presidential message. As it would be read to Congress, the plan purported to be prompted by a general need for alleviating judicial congestion and for improving the administration of the business of the lower courts, as well as for expediting the review of constitutional questions. The matter of ideology was hardly a question for discussion, but even the matter of "packing" the Supreme Court was almost casually and parenthetically introduced by reference to the accompanying draft bill— which obviously the White House expected to be passed with hardly a comma changed.

After a general summary of past Congressional enactments on the judiciary, including varying the number of Justices on the Supreme Court, the message observed that "today a new need for legislative action arises because the personnel of the Federal judiciary is insufficient to meet the business before them." The burden on the Supreme Court, the message continued, had been superficially lightened by Taft's efforts to have Congress broaden its discretionary powers of review. But Roosevelt made a vice out of this virtue by asserting that, when this amounted to denying review in 717 out of 867 cases in one term, it could not be said that "full justice is achieved when a court is forced by the sheer necessity of keeping up with its business to decline . . . to hear 87 percent of the cases presented to it" by private litigants.

The speciousness of this argument was quite apparent to anyone familiar with the administrative concept for which Taft, and subsequently Hughes, had striven. Moreover, it had virtually nothing to do with the matter of constitutional decision. Having suggested the overload on the judiciary, however, the President had the opening for his main point: "A part of the problem of obtaining a sufficient number of judges to dispose of cases," he said, "is the capacity of the judges themselves. This brings forward the question of aged or infirm judges—a subject of delicacy and yet one which requires frank discussion." Many of the judges currently at retirement age in the Federal system, he observed, felt compelled by economic necessity "to perform the duties of their offices to the very edge of the grave."

Drawing on the research of Cummings' staff for the past year, Roosevelt reminded Congress that in 1869 a retirement bill had been drafted which had provided for retirement at the age of 70 or, if the incumbent did not retire, appointment of an additional judge to assist in the work of the court. The particular provision had been dropped before final passage.[24] Then, sidling up to the underlying issue, Roosevelt continued:

> Modern complexities call also for a constant infusion of new blood in the courts, just as it is needed in executive functions of the government and in private business. A lowered mental or physical vigor leads men to avoid an examination of complicated and changed conditions. Little by little, new facts become blurred through old glasses fitted, as it were, for the needs of another generation; older men, assuming that the scene is the same as it was in the past, cease to explore or inquire into the present or the future. . . .
> Life tenure of judges, assured by the Constitution, was designed to

place the courts beyond temptations or influences which might impair their judgments; it was not intended to create a static judiciary. A constant and systematic addition of younger blood will vitalize the courts and better equip them to recognize and apply the essential concepts of justice in the light of the needs and the facts of an ever-changing world.[25]

The measure thereupon recommended the appointment of additional judges "in all Federal courts, without exception, where there are incumbent judges of retirement age who do not choose to retire or resign." If such a judge is not incapacitated, the additional member of the bench would help with the crowded state of the docket, while "if the capacity of an elder judge is in fact impaired, the appointment of an additional judge is indispensable."

The importance of the government's participating of right in litigation when an act of Congress was called into question gave Roosevelt his further point of argument. "In the uncertain state of the law, it is not difficult for the ingenious to devise novel reasons for attacking the validity of new legislation or its application. While these questions are laboriously brought to issue and debated through a series of courts, the government must stand aside."* Moreover, without an expediting act to secure prompt review of the constitutional question, the Court "is assuming an additional function and coming more and more to constitute a scattered, loosely organized, and slowly operating third house of the National Legislature."[26]

The details of the message were reviewed by the President with the press corps with considerably greater zest than with the audience in the Cabinet meeting. Roosevelt struck Clapper as being highly exhilarated, "keyed up, but in a buoyant and bright mood." His reading of passages from the message was calculated "to wring most laughs out of sideswipes at [the] Court, particularly on passages regarding retirement on age." The correspondents entered into the spirit of levity; what, asked one member, about a judge who "had lost the mental capacity to resign?"[27]

On Capitol Hill, no one laughed. A number of members of Congress who had been working on their own disparate bills aimed at coming to grips with the reactionary rulings of the past term considered that the ground had been cut from under them without warning. Dark thoughts turned to Wilson's historic blunder in ignoring the Senate in the drafting of the Treaty of Versailles. As for the Vice-President of the United States, whom Ickes had been astonished to find sitting through the Cabinet meeting entirely silent, he signified his feeling in the view of Joseph B. Keenan, one of the administration trouble-shooters on the Hill. Keenan saw John Nance Garner in the Senate corridor immediately after the reading of the message; he was "holding his nose with one hand and energetically making the Roman gesture of the arena, thumbs down, with the other."[28]

*   *   *

See p. 124 and Appendix C.

About an hour after the message had been read to Congress, a page slipped from behind the curtain which formed the backdrop to the Justice's bench in the Supreme Court chamber and passed behind the members' chairs, as unobtrusively as possible handing each man a set of papers. It was nevertheless a totally unprecedented action, so disconcerting that the lawyer presenting his case came to a momentary halt in oral argument, noting that the jurists were all intently studying the papers. Thus did the Chief Justice of the United States and the Associate Justices learn of the specific details of Roosevelt's plan to answer their nullification of New Deal legislation.[29]

The news apparently had not been a complete surprise, although it was equally apparent that on this day the Court was distinctly preoccupied. Brandeis, forgetting the normal procedure for entry, had come through the curtain before anyone else, then turned in confusion to go back just as Hughes entered followed by the rest of the Court. Brandeis had turned again and seated himself. Down in the press room afterward, a wag commented that the old liberal was probably the only one who had dared to show himself after the message; but the clerk, distributing copies of the day's opinions to reporters, shook his head. "My God," he murmured, "the Court is punch drunk."[30]

Brandeis, of course, had already been apprised of the measure; Hughes had been expecting something like it for months; Roberts was reported to have mentioned to his brethren that he intended to resign if any such measure were actually adopted. There had been a long conference among the Justices on the next afternoon, the United Press reported, in which the resignation question was again fervently discussed. Protest withdrawals from the bench were periodically to be rumored as the weeks went by. In April, when the Congressional debate was in full fury, Presidential Secretary Marvin McIntyre forwarded a note to Roosevelt quoting Senator Gerald P. Nye of North Dakota: "Justice Brandeis is going to resign and give the President hell for his bill and then, if that does not defeat the bill, and Congress goes ahead with it, the whole crowd is going to resign—the whole darn crowd."[31]

Felix Frankfurter, Roosevelt's confidante of many years, urged the President not to retreat. Some means "had to be found to save the Constitution from the Court, and the Court from itself," he wrote on reading the news of the Court bill. Within a fortnight he had submitted to the White House a concise memorandum summarizing the constitutional decisions of the twentieth century which in his view had made possible "an impasse created by a blind and stubborn majority on the Court." Chief Justice Hughes' subsequent behavior Frankfurter was to describe as fully political as Roosevelt's, while he "wrote sharply" to Brandeis about joining with Hughes and Van Devanter in aid of the fight against the bill.[32]

In the intensifying heat of the debates in and out of Congress, men like Frankfurter failed to realize that, from the Court's standpoint, the overriding issue was the independence of the judicial branch. As the ultimate guardians of that separation of powers so long held to be the touchstone of the American constitutional system, the Justices of various ideologies tended to close ranks (although, it would appear from Stone's attitude,* not entirely)—and to look to their Chief to determine on a course of action. Hughes, in turn, relied regularly upon Brandeis and Van Devanter for advice; it had been these three who had offered opposition on an earlier occasion to Senator Black's judicial procedure proposal.

Congress under the Constitution, beyond question, could change—and in the past indeed had changed—the number of Justices on the Court. As to the matter of the legislative power to define the jurisdiction of the Court aside from the specific stipulations in the Constitution, Taft himself had invoked this power to effect his administrative reforms in 1922 and 1925. The political motivations in the Judiciary Act of 1801, whereby the new administration of John Marshall was thwarted for a year before having an opportunity to pronounce its rule on judicial review, was a vivid chapter in constitutional history. And the Congressional action to eliminate two Court positions when they became vacant—to deny Andrew Johnson the opportunity to appoint Justices—followed by the law raising the number back to nine when Grant was ready to "pack" the bench, made it clear that if Roosevelt and Congress were able to work in harmony at this hour, the proposed judiciary act of 1937 would become a reality.[33]

The President, incredibly blinded by the personal victory he had won at the polls the previous November, had already handicapped himself substantially by his callous disregard of the niceties of soliciting Congress' cooperation. Should the Court exploit the situation—or could it—by departing from its own practice of non-participation in any seemly manner and thus widening the split? Or were there other means by which an effective refutation of the New Deal case could be given? Since this was a policy decision affecting the Court as an institution, it was obvious that the Chief Justice would have to take the lead.[34]

Hughes' immediate problem was to establish a case for credibility in the matter of the decisions soon to be handed down, so that it would not seem that they had been coerced or influenced by the White House message of February 5. For the fact was that the Court had already decided, in a dramatic about-face, to reverse not only the *Morehead* case but the older decision of *Adkins v. Children's Hospital* on which it had been based. The opinion, however, had not yet been delivered, and to deliver it now would seem like an accommodation under pressure. On the other hand, Hughes was politically canny enough to see that a timely release of the decision, when it would have a predictable effect on the Congressional debate on the Court bill, was not to be passed by.[35]

Already in January, in fact, a unanimous decision favorable to the government had been handed down, upholding the Silver Purchase Act of 1934. The Court could also point to the fact that, even in the torrent of invalidating

---

*Cf. note 38 below.

opinions in the spring of 1936, a majority had upheld the legislation establishing the Tennessee Valley Authority. But the problem, in terms of professional integrity as well as of politics, was formidable; coming up in the immediate future were reviews of major New Deal statutes, many of the features in them resembling features in earlier laws which had been held void.[36]

For the present, the Court merely presented its impassive facade to the public. In the rising cacophony of debate precipitated by the judiciary bill, the judiciary itself would remain in appearance the only unperturbed institution on the American scene.

* * *

The New Dealers had taken for granted that the Court bill would hand conservatives of all shades a popular issue around which to rally. The Republicans, flattened in disaster in November, could not but rejoice at the opportunity now presented to them; never able to take the offensive in the election campaign, they now eagerly seized upon the role of defenders of the Constitution by defending the Court which had been the great ally of the old order. The Democrats, dominated by a Southern oligarchy congenitally hostile to reform measures which tended to galvanize social minorities (especially Negroes) and enlarge the sphere of Federal authority, could also find in the Court bill an opportunity to rebel against their own President under the guise of principle.

What most astonished administration leaders, however, was the failure of the liberals and independents in Congress to respond in the anticipated manner. LaFollette, Norris and Burton K. Wheeler of Montana had been expected from the outset to lend their names and prestige to any measure which was calculated to bring the judicial conservatives to account. Roosevelt heard with disbelief that Norris had issued an unequivocal statement within hours of the delivery of the message to the Senate: "I am not in sympathy with the plan to enlarge the Supreme Court." Aside from his disdain for the evasiveness of the Presidential approach to the basic problem, the Nebraskan perceived the dangerous precedent in the proposal to increase the size of the Court; what, Norris asked, if Harding rather than Roosevelt had sponsored such a bill?[37]

Most Congressmen felt that the proposal was intentionally extreme, so that some horse-trading could be discussed as time wore on. Also, it was hoped that if the Court itself began to backtrack the White House might withdraw the measure altogether, claiming that its purpose had been served. Another alternative was to break up the bill, which after all was an omnibus treatment of problems of varying intensity within the judicial area. The Sumners bill for retirement at full pay not only had the appeal of fairness, but it was conceivable that it might produce the effect Roosevelt really desired in his own enlargement proposal—to encourage one or more members of the Court to step down.

In a real sense, Congress had brought this problem on itself by its miserly attitude toward Justice Holmes when he left the bench. If a law could be enacted to protect jurists against similar actions, it was highly likely that one or more would soon take advantage of the provision. Justice Stone, in a roundabout message to administration leaders, had hinted that one or two members of the Court would in fact do so. Accordingly, the bill which Sumners had revived in January, in anticipation of Roosevelt's more drastic action, was now pushed through both houses and sent to the President for signature.[38]

If Congress believed that the Sumners law would soften the President on the matter of the February 5 proposal, it was to be disappointed. Roosevelt, still supremely confident that the measure he had submitted would make its way through both houses, laughed in the faces of a Congressional committee which made the suggestion to him. The offensiveness of the behavior persuaded some wavering members to decide then and there to join the all-out opposition, but Roosevelt remained convinced that the groups in American society who had benefitted most from the reform statutes—and by the same token presumably had suffered most from judicial nullification—would back him up.[39]

These groups were, most conspicuously, the farmers and union labor. As for the farmers, the President was painfully to learn what experienced Washington observers had long known: not only were agrarians of the thirties among the most conservative elements in society, but "their persecution complex made them the least grateful and the most greedy of all lobbies. . . . Their organizations could never be trusted to repay their obligations, for they regarded whatever they received as an inadequate part payment of the national debt of an unhappy agriculture." Even when kicked in the face by the first AAA decision, it was recalled, some farm groups had given public thanks for delivery from "regimentation."[40]

As for labor, it was doing its best to throw away its gains of recent months, and to alienate public and Congressional opinion in the bargain. At the moment, nearly a quarter of a million General Motors workers were on strike or about to be laid off, as the militants among the union organizers developed the "sit-down" strike as a means of industrial insurrection. William Green's AF of L and John L. Lewis' CIO glowered at each other across a growing number of jurisdictional battlefields and—far from rushing to the President with assurances of their united backing—periodically informed the White House that they expected a pay-off for their support in the 1936 elections.[41]

But most rankling of all was the opposition expressed among the old-time liberals in Congress itself. First there had been Norris' flat condemnation of the proposed bill. Then came the announcement of Montana's Wheeler—old Progressive, scourge of the Teapot Dome malefactors, Tom Walsh's colleague, Vice-Presidential running mate with "Fighting Bob" LaFollette in the Progressive Party effort of 1924: Wheeler not only would oppose the bill, but would lead the fight against it in the Senate Judiciary Committee. Senators Bennett Champ Clark of Missouri and Hiram Johnson of California had also indicated their intention to oppose the administration on the matter. It was becoming apparent that the New Dealers were going to have to rely upon an unlikely trio of Southern conservatives to carry the brunt of the attack in the Senate— James F. Byrnes of South Carolina, Roosevelt's "personal envoy" in the upper chamber; Joe Robinson of Arkansas, who held the President's promise to deliver to him the first Court vacancy; and Pat Harrison of Mississippi, who expected to succeed Robinson as majority leader if and when he ascended the bench.[42]

*   *   *

"If Roosevelt goes to the country on this, we will know he is really worried," Clapper noted in his diary after talking to Steve Early on February 8. Within a few weeks, the President's advisers were to be preparing two speeches in which he would be doing just that. The furious public argument which had begun immediately after the publication of the Court message was evidence, at last, that a spark of interest had been lighted on the subject, but the opposing forces appeared to be splintering hopelessly. While some local bar associations endorsed the plan, the prestigious American Bar Association skated on the thin ice of barratry by offering to make its services and speakers available for any who wanted to contest the proposal. Even within the White House counsels, the strategists were beginning to divide; Cummings and his group clung to the indirect attack on the conservatives by stressing administrative requirements of the bill, while Corcoran and Jackson were urging an end to dissimulation and a direct attack on the basic issue.[43]

By early March, the direct approach had won out, and Roosevelt would make two fighting speeches—one, on March 4, would serve notice to the party membership that they were expected to fall in line; the other, a Fireside Chat, would seek to reason with the people at large. Thirteen hundred of the faithful crowded into the Mayflower Hotel ballroom, at $100 a plate, to hear their leader issue a clarion call for support (i.e., pressure) to see the bill through Congress. Five days later the nationwide radio broadcast to "My Friends" put the issue more emotionally than bluntly. The President concentrated his argument on the growing charges of "dictatorship" made jointly against his effort to dilute the judicial opposition by "packing" and his insistence that he could be trusted "to make American democracy work."[44]

Once having started down the wrong road, Roosevelt seemed incapable of finding the way back. He rejected the suggestions of some of his advisers that he hold out a hint of consideration for any alternate proposal from Congress. Having missed a chance to divide the opposition, he then disregarded the original strategy, which had called for letting the opposition talk itself out first, and approved the plan to begin committee hearings with a parade of administration witnesses.

At once the advocates of the Roosevelt bill ran into trouble; with the active cooperation of the American Bar Association, blue-ribbon lawyers from major law firms went to work on the witnesses' arguments and fed the committee members a steady supply of challenging questions. Cummings, clinging to the indirect attack which was his brainchild, and Jackson, aggressively pushing a direct attack on the judicial decisions of recent years, virtually cancelled each other out. It was quite evident—to everyone but the President and his hard core of advisers—that the scales were beginning to tip permanently toward the opposition.

*   *   *

Senator Wheeler listened to the testimony as well as the public appeals of the New Dealers—both Cummings and the President made fervent radio speeches as the hearings of friendly witnesses before the Judiciary Committee came to an end, while long-retired Justice John H. Clarke also added his public support for the bill. Wheeler also received a private plea from Tom Corcoran, relayed from the White House, not to permit his name to be linked with the conservatives in opposing the measure. It was the second time within the year, in fact, that Corcoran had served as a White House emissary on the Court question; the previous spring it had been a Roosevelt suggestion that Wheeler himself sponsor a bill to add three new members to the bench.[45]

"I told Tom," wrote Wheeler later, that "the Court was like a religion to the American people"—like religion, it was sometimes more emotional than rational. A Court-restricting plank had been put in the Progressive platform of 1924 and, Wheeler recalled, it had been "used devastatingly against us from one end of the country to the other." That experience had persuaded him that only a constitutional amendment could overturn the *laissez-faire* jurisprudence of the twenties—but the New Dealers had already concluded that an amendment, even if effective, would be too slow a remedy.[46]

Now, as administration witnesses were winding up their testimony, the Montana Senator, in company with William King of Utah and Warren Austen of Vermont, decided to call upon Chief Justice Hughes. They proposed that Hughes himself appear as the first opposition witness, confining himself to answering the charge upon which Roosevelt had laid such stress, the inability of the Court to keep up with its case load. "I was entirely willing to do this for the purpose of giving the facts on the work of the Court," the Chief later wrote. However, he suggested to his callers, he would prefer to be accompanied by Justice Brandeis, "because of his standing as a Democrat and his reputation as a liberal judge."[47] The three Senators left the Hughes office in jubilation; since Hughes and Brandeis, as well as Van Devanter, had at an earlier date offered to appear before the Judiciary Committee in opposition to Senator Black's bill, it was reasonable to assume that they would testify again.

Hardly had he got to his own office, however, than Wheeler received a telephone call from Hughes. Brandeis, said the Chief, had advised against a personal appearance, and Van Devanter had concurred. Their argument was that, unlike the appearance against the Black bill on procedural changes, to appear now would be "to testify on a matter affecting their own integrity."

The objection was difficult to refute, but it did little to lighten Wheeler's disappointment. What did lighten it was a second telephone call—this time from his married daughter; Mrs. Brandeis had just left her house, said the message, and her parting words had been: "Tell your father I think he's right about the Court bill."[48]

Was this another of those cryptic communications from behind the judicial curtain, like Stone's hint of imminent retirements or Brandeis' threat of mass resignations? Since Brandeis and Wheeler were friends of many years, the Montanan lost no time—it was Saturday afternoon, before testimony of opposition witnesses would begin on Monday. He hurried to the Brandeis apartment. Had the Justice a proposed alternative to an appearance before the committee? "Call up the Chief Justice," Brandeis told Wheeler, "and he will give you a letter." Startled, Wheeler demurred; but in due course Brandeis arranged the telephone call and the Senator made the request.[49]

It was now five-thirty in the afternoon on Saturday, but Hughes expressed himself as willing to go to work, locating his secretary and preparing a draft for Monday morning. The draft evolved in the wee hours, for by Sunday forenoon the Chief advised Wheeler that he had something to show Brandeis and Van Devanter. That afternoon, when the Senator called at the Hughes home, the Chief met him at the door with the final copy. "The baby is born," he said with a smile.[50]

What then followed, according to Wheeler's autobiography, was a remarkable conversation. Hughes motioned his caller to a chair, obviously preparing to make some further comments. The men had not known each other well, although each had begun his public career in the heyday of the Progressive Movement. Each had, in that era of fervent reform, directed his share of invective at the *laissez-faire* doctrines which overlay virtually all of the constitutional pronouncements of the time. Beyond that, the only contact between the two had been a potentially awkward one in the present context: Wheeler had been one of those who had spoken out against Hughes' nomination as Chief Justice in 1930.

Still, the Chief now spoke as one old-time Progressive to another. What, he mused, might have been the story of New Deal legislation of the past few years if "we had had an Attorney General in whom the President had confidence, and in whom the Court had confidence, and in whom the people had confidence." As it was, Hughes declared, "the laws have been poorly drafted, the briefs have been badly drawn and the arguments have been poorly presented. We've had to be not only the Court but we've had to do the work that should have been done by the Attorney General."[51]

Did the Chief Justice, as Wheeler remembered the comment,* mean that Cummings and Roosevelt between them, impatient for legislative formulae

---

*Hughes makes no mention of such a conversation in his biographical notes; see Bibliography. As for the aptness of the comment, if made in such terms, see the special note in Appendix E.

which would effect instant reforms, had pushed through statutes which might have been sustained if better written? The fundamental thrust of the comment, in any event, was that the Chief Justice had often found no means of upholding hasty legislation which had been poorly drafted. The Senator might have reflected that it had indeed been Cummings who had prepared many of the New Deal bills—and particularly that it was Cummings who had directed the preparation of the particular bill which was now the center of the storm. But more important than that was the clear indication of Hughes' commitment to the fight on the Court proposal. The Chief was in the fight to the finish.

*　　*　　*

The devastating effect of the Hughes letter when it was read at the opening of the Judiciary Committee session on March 22 was all that Wheeler could have hoped for it. Senator Ashurst guessed, when Wheeler announced that he wished to open the session with a special communication, that it was going to be something which would "blow us out of the water."[52]

The Chief Justice aimed directly at the weakest argument in the administration bill—Cummings' insistent point that the judiciary was unable to keep up with its work. Far from being behind, wrote Hughes, the Court was presently fully abreast of its docket. "When we rose on March 15 . . . we had heard argument in cases in which certiorari had been granted only four weeks before—on February 15."

In utter silence, the committee room occupants listened as Wheeler read on, each paragraph in the letter succinctly rebutting a specific argument advanced for the administration bill. While he had not been able to obtain specific endorsement of the letter from all members of the Court, wrote Hughes, he was permitted to disclose that Brandeis and Van Devanter supported it, and he felt confident in assuring the committee that the rest of the Associates (he did not qualify Stone's position) would approve in principle.[53]

As for the Court's practice of refusing to review the majority of petitions, Hughes reiterated Taft's favorite argument: any litigant who had enjoyed a fair trial in a court of original jurisdiction, and a review of the case in the Court of Appeals, had all that he was entitled to expect as a private party. "If further review is to be had in the Supreme Court," Hughes said, "it must be because of the public interest in the questions involved."

Turning then to the main point in the administration bill—the adding of members to the bench—Hughes dealt with its validity as an administrative matter. Increasing the number of men would not increase efficiency, he declared; rather, it "would impair that efficiency so long as the Court acts as a unit. There would be more judges to hear, more judges to confer, more judges to discuss, more judges to be convinced and to decide." Then, for good measure, he disposed of the alternate argument that the Court might be divided into civil and criminal divisions like a trial court; if the cases before the highest tribunal in the land were important, he said, they warranted a decision by the whole Court and not part of it. In addition, the Constitution provided for "one Supreme Court," not two or more.[54]

* * *

Having committed the Court to a definite position on the judiciary proposal, Hughes concluded that it was no longer necessary to hold back the
decision on the Washington state minimum wage law, overruling both the
Morehead and *Adkins* cases. The administration, dazed and groggy from the
body blow dealt by the letter, was about to have the wind knocked out of it
by four consecutive decisions which, upholding the reform laws, on any
other occasion would have filled the New Dealers with joy.

The Hughes letter to the Judiciary Committee had been a brilliant defense
against New Deal charges; with the four decisions of March 29 (one week
later), the Chief Justice went over to the attack. Although, throughout the
long weeks of the judiciary bill debates, no one formally invited debate on
the issue of Court ideology, neither did anyone doubt that it was the fundamental issue. Accordingly, to group together four cases which emphatically
upheld the reform view would tacitly—but no less emphatically—rebut the
charges that the Court was hopelessly in the grip of hidebound reactionaries.

The key case, *West Coast Hotel Co. v. Parrish,* had been argued the
previous December, and at that time the Justices had divided, four to four,
Stone being absent because of a severe illness which kept him from returning
to the bench until February. The even split would have sustained the judgment of the Washington state supreme court, which had already upheld the
statute, but it would not have provided a clear-cut answer to the general
constitutional question. Hughes perceived that a majority in favor of affirming
the state court judgment—assured by Stone's known attitude on the question—
would affirmatively dispose of an issue on which the progressives for forty
years had waged a forlorn struggle. After the Roosevelt Court message, it
was simply a question of effective timing of the release of the opinions.[55]

West Coast Hotel Co. v. Parrish presented a Washington state law
regulating wage minimums for women and minors in substantially similar
form to what had been held invalid in the New York case the previous term.
Hughes, speaking for the five-to-four majority, rather lamely contended that
the New York court had found itself bound by the rule in *Adkins v. Children's
Hospital* and had thus not raised a constitutional question. The Washington
court, said Hughes, "has refused to regard the decision in the *Adkins* case as
determinative and has pointed to our decisions both before and since that
case as justifying its position." The Washington case, accordingly, "demands
on our part a reexamination of the *Adkins* case."[56]

"The Constitution," the Chief Justice continued, "does not speak of
liberty of contract. It speaks of liberty and prohibits the deprivation of liberty
without due process of law. . . . But the liberty safeguarded is liberty in a
social organization which requires the protection of law against the evils
which menace the health, safety, morals and welfare of the people." By thus
focussing the tenor of the opinion upon the due process clause instead of the
contract impairment clause, Hughes found the rationale to sustain the minimum
wage law.[57]

Sutherland's dissent was eloquent and carefully reasoned, but it was a eulogy for a now dying socio-economic viewpoint. He could find no legal justification for a law which stressed a minimal need for sustenance over the value of the employee's time to the employer. The need of the individual, Sutherland insisted, was solely the concern of the individual and not of society.[58]

Having reversed itself in *Morehead*—although it protested that it was able to distinguish the New York case from the Washington case—the Court on the same day proceeded to reverse itself on the *Radford* case of the spring of 1935 which had held the Frazier-Lemke Federal Farm Bankruptcy Act unconstitutional. In *Wright v. Vinton Branch,* the question was the validity of the revised Frazier-Lemke statute—and here the Court, speaking through Brandeis, concluded that Congress in revising the law after the *Radford* decision had intended to avoid the constitutional defects of the original law. But the provisions were largely the same and the effect of the statute, to offer mortgage relief to impoverished farmers, was now held a proper exercise of legislative discretion where formerly it had been held not to be.*[59]

In another case decided this same day, Stone read the Court opinion sustaining a Federal tax on firearms against an allegation that the tax purpose was regulatory rather than revenue-producing. The Court, said Stone, "will not undertake, by collateral inquiry as to the measure of the regulatory effect of a tax, to ascribe to Congress an attempt, under the guise of taxation, to exercise another power denied by the Federal Constitution."[60] Although the opinion was unanimous, it could not but sound strange in the ears of the conservatives and erstwhile vacillators, who had said precisely the opposite on a number of occasions in the past.

Stone read another unanimous opinion, completing the quadrilateral of opinions on this "White Monday," sustaining the new railroad labor legislation of 1934 which had amended the Railway Labor Act of 1926. Again the conservatives acquiesced in the holding, although the language sounded strange and harsh to their ears. Where, only a few short months before, the majority had been saying that labor relations were not part of the elements of interstate commerce which were under Federal jurisdiction, Stone now led the Court to declare that Congress had broad authority to regulate any part of the activity of railroads which in its judgment (not the Court's) affected the interstate movement of the roads themselves.[61]

The *Virginian Railway* case was regarded by progressives as a hopeful straw in the wind, indicating the possible outcome of the test of the Wagner Act which would soon be decided. Argument of the NLRB cases had taken place the week after the Court reorganization bill had been sent to Congress, and the administration had thrown all its legal resources into the presentations. Both the Solicitor General and the Attorney General, with eight special

*See note in Appendix E.

assistants drawn either from the government or the District of Columbia bar, had participated in oral argument and the written briefs. The four favorable decisions on March 29 had suggested a shift of the Court back to a progressive position; the labor case opinion of April 12 would indicate more definitely whether the shift was reasonably likely to be permanent. If so, its effect on the Court fight in Congress would obviously be substantial.

By a five-to-four majority, with the hard-core conservatives in dissent, the Chief Justice asserted the validity of the Wagner Act. The right of employees to organize and bargain through elected representatives, said Hughes, was as lawful as the right of management to select its own officers and agents; it therefore followed that "Congress was not required to ignore this right but could safeguard it," and in the public interest "could seek to make appropriate collective action of employees an instrument of peace rather than of strife."

"Although activities may be intrastate in character when separately considered," the Chief Justice went on, "if they have such a close and substantial relation to interstate commerce that their control is essential or appropriate to protect that commerce from burdens and obstructions, Congress cannot be denied the power to exercise that control." The right of employers to hire whom they would was not denied, said Hughes; the purpose of the statute was rather to protect the right of any person hired to join with others in a collective bargaining process. Thus, after four decades of wrangling, the "yellow-dog" idea had been shot in the head.[62]

*   *   *

The forces in Congress opposing the administration Court bill rejoiced at the NLRB decision because it appeared to dispose of the remaining arguments in favor of the bill; the White House exulted at the news of the decision because it was taken as a sign that the Court had responded to the threat contained in the bill—but the bill itself was more needed than ever. This was Corcoran's argument; without the enactment of the proposal after its effect had been demonstrated, he contended, the Court would be all but invited to return to its old position.[63]

Certainly Franklin Roosevelt felt in the NLRB decision, as his distant cousin had felt in the *Northern Securities* decision,* that he had been responsible for a reversal of doctrine. In his opinion, the threat in the judiciary bill had been the key, and he told his press conference the following day that in place of a constitutional "no-man's land" the country now found itself in "Roberts' Land." The difficulty he had with the decisions, said Roosevelt, was in knowing whether the Court would limit the commerce power in its new liberal definition to collective bargaining or whether it would give the definition a general application.[64]

---

*Theodore Roosevelt and the *Northern Securities* case strategy are discussed in *The Old Legality*.

But the case for the judiciary bill in its original form was becoming more difficult to maintain. Jackson, who had favored all parts of the proposal at the outset, felt that it had been badly timed—the psychological moment for introducing it, he told Clapper, would have been the previous spring in the shock of public resentment at the reactionary rulings of that term. Since then, he pointed out, there had been no recent decision to dramatize or justify it. The fact was, Jackson concluded, that if the Court sustained the Social Security law and in time upheld the second AAA, "it will have gone as far as anybody could expect it to go," and reorganization would be irrelevant.[65]

Jackson himself argued the government's brief in the Social Security case on May 5. His whole argument, he told Clapper, "was pointed at Roberts. I was arguing to a one-man Court." The case thus stressed "the arguments that would appeal to the conservatives"—the tendency of pension laws to encourage thrift, the impact of the depression on the thrifty rather than the shiftless, the fact that the retirement and jobless benefits could be financed by borrowing as well as by taxes. "Chief Justice Hughes apparently was afraid I was not going to bring that out," Jackson recalled, "because before I got to it he asked a question" about the dependence of the plan upon the tax.[66]

The likelihood that Hughes would be favorably inclined toward the government argument, and the hope that the "one-man Court" would be reached by the line of reasoning Jackson had followed, gave ground for optimism that the Social Security law would be upheld. Anticipating that this would remove virtually the last vestige of the administration's argument for its judiciary bill, the Senate Judiciary Committee on May 18 made its adverse—and savagely critical—report on the bill. In perfect timing, it seemed, Roosevelt himself received a letter from a Supreme Court Justice; Willis Van Devanter was announcing his intention to retire at the end of the current term.

Everything, it seemed to the President's battered general staff, was conspiring to deny the New Deal any satisfaction in the shift which seemed to have been effected in the judicial position. The retirement disposed of the argument that until there was a change in Court personnel, there could be no assurance that the shift would be anything but temporary. At the same time, it opened up Roosevelt's commitment to the conservative Senator Robinson. If the President did not honor his promise to put Robinson into the first Court vacancy, the party revolution would make the Court rebellion look like a tea-party, but if he appointed Robinson he would, by his own act, continue and encourage the conservative position on the Court.[67]

To make matters worse, the news of Van Devanter's prospective retirement was all over Capitol Hill by that afternoon, and Senators were crowding around Robinson to offer him their congratulations. While they themselves had made much about choosing principle over party in fighting the Court bill, they lauded Robinson for having chosen party over personal preference, supporting a measure he did not himself believe in so as to demonstrate to the White House a loyalty which must be rewarded. Roosevelt, who had first been catastrophically overconfident, now became disastrously bull-headed; the fight, he told his weary generals, would go on—and he would have to give thought to the filling of the Court vacancy.[68]

Refusing to see the defeat which was staring him in the face, the President called for a continuing floor fight on the bill which, in the formal language of the committee, had been reported with a recommendation that "it do not pass." In less than a week, the Court itself would apply its knockout blow, with two decisions upholding the Social Security law in its several key aspects.

*   *   *

Senator King of Utah—one of the original trio who had called on Hughes to bring him into the Court fight—delivered the adverse report of the judiciary committee. In some of its more temperate language, the report castigated the administration proposal as "a needless, futile, and utterly dangerous abandonment of constitutional principle" which would "make the Constitution what the executive or legislative branches of the government choose to say it is—an interpretation to be changed with each change of administration." King asked the Senate to reject the bill "so emphatically . . . that its parallel will never again be presented to the free representatives of the free people of America."[69]

Cardozo spoke for the Court in the two cases the following week which rounded out the remarkable ninety days in which most of the major propositions of the "second round" of New Deal reform laws were upheld. The arguments against the jobless benefits and the retirement benefits sounded like voices from the grave of *laissez-faire:* the statute invaded the domain of the states, it imposed a Federal control over the states, it undermined the rugged individualism of the worker. Patiently, Cardozo disposed of them all. There was no coercion on the states in a system which left them free to participate or not in the program—they, more than any other parties in interest, the Justice observed, "would be sorely disappointed if it were now to be annulled."

A system of unemployment and retirement benefits which affected the public welfare affected it nationally, Cardozo said, and therefore required Federal administration even with state participation. Far from being a breakdown of the Federal-state relationship, it strengthened it through a cooperative plan of mutual benefit. He might have added that, with the Social Security Act, Congress had brought about a state of modern economic democracy which was almost universal in the western world.[70]

The unequivocal endorsement of Social Security, on the heels of the affirming of the Wagner Act, had disposed of all of Roosevelt's major arguments against the Court ideology. The alternating pattern of Congressional

attack; and judicial follow-up had battered the White House program merci-
lessly, and while no one confirmed it in so many words there was hardly any
doubt that each party had delivered its own blows with a full awareness of the
timing of the delivery. Roosevelt, wrote Ickes in retrospect, "was out-
maneuvered in the end, largely by Chief Justice Charles Evans Hughes."[71]

It was clear, by the end of May, that the Court fight was over—for all
but Roosevelt and his dwindling force of strategists. Frankfurter recognized the
handwriting on the wall. "I wish it were in my power to persuade you now
to drop so much of the bill as relates to the Supreme Court," he wrote the
President on May 25. There was still time to make a graceful gesture, said
Frankfurter, and in the same occasion to suggest that the bill had actually
accomplished the fundamental purpose of bringing a rule of reason to the
bench.[72]

Having reversed itself so unmistakably on all of the major reform
issues advanced by the second New Deal Congress, it was inconceivable that
the Court would deliberately reverse these latest decisions. Whether Hughes
had engineered this turn of events as a matter of basic professional conviction
or as a matter of political opportunism—and in the nature of the circumstances, there was an inevitable admixture of these—the fact was that he had
carried the thing off with brilliance and aplomb. If it was a total defeat for
the *laissez-faire* viewpoint which had dominated constitutional law for sixty
years, Hughes had given it the appearance of a spectacular victory for the
Court.

For Roosevelt to continue in his original line of reasoning was, on the
other hand, to exchange what in effect was a sweeping victory over *laissez-
faire* constitutionalism for a political disaster. For now even the staunchest
liberals were defecting; in July, Governor Herbert L. Lehman of New York
would write Senator Wagner urging him to vote against the Court bill. Now
even defeat was to be ignoble; what might have been a Waterloo was becoming
something closer to Custer's last stand.[78]

Incredibly, Roosevelt still refused to break off the engagement; the fight
would drag on into the summer, deepening the schism between the White
House and Congress until it became certain that the main legislative history
of the New Deal had come to an end. Clapper, seeking an explanation for
Roosevelt's behavior, suggested rather unconvincingly that the President felt
he could not let down those who had fought for him in Congress. A more
likely explanation, if there was any, was that Roosevelt had himself burned
all his bridges and had no means of retreat. Even more important was the
irritating question of Robinson.[74]

Then, in July, Robinson suddenly died. An intense, lumbering man in
middle life, he had driven himself physically and emotionally to the breaking
point on repeated occasions in the bitter and unrewarding struggle of the
past six months. His professional epitaph was the final judiciary act which

in the late summer the hostile Congress passed as a mark of the President's complete defeat. It related to a variety of useful procedural changes—but the propositions on additional judges in Federal courts where "aged or infirm" members were still on the bench, and the concept of "new blood" to bring new ideas into American constitutionalism, were gone without a trace.

4/The Shaping of a New Court

BEFORE HE LAUNCHED his fateful reorganization bill, Roosevelt received some advice from Henry Ashurst, chairman of the Senate Judiciary Committee. "It will fall to your lot to nominate more Justices of the Supreme Court than any other President since George Washington," Ashurst told the President. "You will nominate four, possibly five" new members to the bench. From the perspective of January, 1937, with the likelihood that the conservatives would at least hang on long enough to strike down the remaining New Deal statutes, the prediction offered little promise of substance. From the perspective of August, 1937, amid the wreckage of not only the Court bill but much of the legislative program with which Roosevelt had planned to consolidate the New Deal, there was at least room for second thoughts.[1]

Yet the question would remain forever unanswered whether the ideological shift which manifested itself really was affected by the Congressional developments in the winter of 1937. It was one thing to argue that the decisions that spring were distinguishable from the adverse rulings of 1935-36 and hence did not represent a conscious about-face on the part of the Court—and it was another to declare that, without the threat of the judiciary bill, they would in fact have been distinguished. The prospect that they would have turned out as they did, from the New Dealers' viewpoint before the fact, was conjectural in the highest degree.

It had been, as Roosevelt had written New York Attorney Charles Burlingham, a gamble that he could not afford to make; whether the price he had paid for certainty had been too great, he could not at this moment say. As it would turn out, he would indeed be able to appoint more Justices to the Supreme Court than any President since Washington—eight, rather than Ashurst's guess of a possible five, and a ninth choice fell to him when he was able to advance Stone to the Chief's chair on Hughes' retirement. Even if Roosevelt had served only two terms, his five appointees through 1940 would have ensured a reasonably permanent liberal majority.

Thus with the opening of the fall term of Court in October, 1937, whether or not the judicial fight had contributed directly to the state of affairs, a new Court would begin to take shape; and before the end of Hughes' Chief Justiceship in 1941, it would already have planted the seeds of a new constitutional jurisprudence dealing with the social and economic realities of the twentieth century. Half a century before, Melville Fuller's Court had crossed a watershed; now, in the closing years of the 1930's, Hughes' Court had crossed another.

* * *

Robinson's death had relieved Roosevelt of the harrowing need to dispose of the promise to place him on the bench, but the problem of selecting Van Devanter's successor remained. On August 4, the President told Ickes that he felt the choice "ought to come from the Wisconsin-Illinois-Indiana circuit, which had not had a man on the Supreme Court bench for many years." Within the week, Roosevelt also received from Cummings a series of *curricula vitae* on eleven prospects, including seven state judges, the dean of the University of Wisconsin law school, Solicitor General Reed, and Senators Black of Alabama and Minton of Indiana.[2]

The difficulty was going to be in obtaining Senate confirmation; both on Capitol Hill and in the White House, the bitterness of the six-month Court battle still ran very deep. Among other things, the opportunity to defy the Roosevelt leadership on the judiciary bill had emboldened the conservatives within the Democratic majority to oppose reform proposals which, during the first four years of Roosevelt's Presidency, they had not dared to question. A liberal like Wisconsin's Dean Lloyd K. Garrison, Roosevelt sensed, would be likely to be pilloried in the course of the Senate's "advice and consent."[3]

Yet a liberal was vital at this juncture, if only to keep Hughes and Roberts committed. Such a man added to the triumvirate of Brandeis, Cardozo and Stone would establish a bloc of four at the moment that the old conservative bloc was correspondingly being reduced. Hughes, who had made such a point of identifying himself with the liberal decisions of the past spring, would be virtually compelled to go along with the new bloc and thus ensure a majority. Casting through the remaining names on the list, Roosevelt eliminated the state judges either as doubtful in their liberalism or risky prospects before the Senate; Reed, who was Cummings' candidate, he dismissed as "a good man but without much force or color."[4]

This left what, for the President in the present situation, had been the rather obvious choice from the beginning: the Senate, with its traditions of collegial courtesy, would be compelled to accept a nominee from among its own members—indeed, while Robinson was living, it would not even have considered anyone else. There would also be a wry satisfaction in witnessing the resurgent right-wingers in the chamber vote approval for an all-out reformer such as either Black or Minton.

Had Roosevelt followed the reasoning he had given to Ickes, the choice would have been the Indiana Senator from the neglected Seventh Circuit.

As for Black, the President had told Ickes that the Alabaman wasn't as able a lawyer as Minton, but there were other considerations. Minton was young and well entrenched in Indiana politics, while Black was manifestly too liberal for his state and was facing such a hard fight for reelection that he had indicated his temptation to retire at the end of his current term. Here, it appeared, might be the best solution of the matter: a vigorous Southern progressive would be a much-desired addition to the present Court, and would be even more galling as a nominee to his Senate associates.

Indeed, the nominee had been galling his colleagues since he had first arrived in the Senate in 1926, promptly aligning himself with the Norris advocates of a renewed Federal development of power facilities in the Tennessee Valley. Since this included a World War I nitrate facility at Muscle Shoals, in the domain of the Alabama Power Company, the move hardened conservative opposition in his home state. Although he had been able to win reelection in 1932, the opposition continued to grow as Black volunteered for front-line service in the New Deal. His bill to introduce a thirty-hour work week in industry was considered too radical even for the most zealous administration advisers, and it was superseded by the National Industrial Recovery Act (which Black criticized as being of doubtful constitutionality). But he was again in the forefront on the Social Security Act and was joined again with Norris in a fervent campaign for the Public Utility Holding Company Act.[5]

Before the Court reform bill, which he unhesitatingly supported, the Alabama Senator had firmly established his credentials as a New Dealer. The Court would be already "one ninth packed," said Herbert Hoover when he heard the news of Black's nomination. But liberals were hardly more enthusiastic about the matter than the conservatives; Black's ruthless tactics as a Senate investigator—first of air-mail contracts, where it was charged that he rashly advised Roosevelt to cancel the agreements with a few favored airlines and let the Army planes carry the mail, which resulted in disaster—provoked extreme critics to charge him with resorting to Nazi tactics. The outcry doubled in volume when, in a probe of public utility lobbying, he threatened to seize thousands of Western Union telegrams in his search for evidence of wrong-doing.[6]

"Power," wrote a biographer, in Black's view was "something to be made the most of, and it never occurred to him that there need be an apology for so using it." His character bore the scars of the harsh struggle to rise from a modest background to political success. "Various experiences of his life," wrote Frankfurter, an early admirer, "have been calculated to make him a bit of an Ishmaelite—to expect every hand to be raised against him, and therefore, at times to be unwarrantedly suspicious when nothing but friendliness is intended."[7]

Wheeler, who had led the fight against the Court bill, felt that Black's nomination was nothing but a reward for his efforts in Roosevelt's behalf. Other critics, even less tolerant, professed to be aghast at his meager experience in legal practice, while periodic complaints about his association with the Ku Klux Klan were made. The now long-alienated Ray Moley in *Newsweek* declared that Black "looms only as a destroyer, an attacker, an inquisitor," while in his own state the *Birmingham Age-Herald* spoke faintly in praise of his "fundamental sincerity and his broad mental character," but predicted that "he may not prove the great judge."[8]

In any event, Ickes noted as the nomination went to the Senate, it had "certainly succeeded in stirring up the animals." Although the Senate appeared to be disposed to let the matter go through without objection, Vice-President Garner—another who had now alienated himself from the administration—called three different times for any objections. Finally Hiram Johnson of California and Edward Burke of Nebraska caught the cue and formally voiced the objections which automatically referred the matter to the Judiciary Committee.[9]

The conservative hope, obviously, was to gain time to rouse the legal establishment and, perhaps, give them a chance to denigrate the nomination in some manner. The oft-voiced—and sometimes suspect—criticism of "lack of judicial experience" was at least worth reading into the record for such embarrassment as it might give the President. The idea of exploiting the matter of Black's past association with the Ku Klux Klan did not seem very obvious; it was no particular secret, as Ickes put it, that "undoubtedly he came to the Senate with the support of the . . . Klan. . . . Considering his state, he probably had to make concessions to local sentiment, outrageous as it was, in order to win his Senate seat."[10]

"One issue that is being raised is a constitutional one and there is some substance to it," Ickes went on. "This Congress passed an act increasing the retirement pay of Supreme Court Justices to $20,000 a year. Is this an increase in emoluments which under the Constitution would constitute a bar to the appointment of any member of this Congress to the Supreme Court? Undoubtedly there is some validity to this argument and even if Black is confirmed, the question may arise to plague him in the future."*[11]

It was not a constitutional detail but a personal and political dislike that formed the nucleus of Senate challenge, however. Carter Glass of Virginia reacted to the suggestion that Black's nomination was a victory for the common people by sneering that "they must be God-damned common," while the anti-New Deal *New York Herald-Tribune* deplored the selection for being "as menacing as it is unfit."[12]

Black's behavior did not endear him to all his colleagues, in Congress any more than later on the Court; his prosecution of witnesses in the Post Office hearings seemed to many at the time to be excessively aggressive. His sharp tongue seldom spared any opponent, in the Senate or outside, and his periodic exposure of lobbies of various kinds trod heavily on sensitive

---

*Such a question was raised—unsuccessfully. *Ex parte Levitt,* 302 U. S. 633 (1937).

toes. Suspicion and intolerance were qualities that his critics ascribed to him throughout much of his public life.[13]

Still groping for an issue, Senator Royal S. Copeland of New York fired a random shot by stating that he felt "so outraged by this proposal to put a Klan sympathizer upon the bench that it is difficult to discuss the matter in temperate language." Senator Burke sought to develop the issue by stating that he had a witness to Black's induction into the order. But Senator Borah, while unenthusiastic about the nomination, cut off the line of argument by stating that there was "not one iota of evidence that Senator Black was a member of the Klan." By August 17, the nomination was confirmed by a vote of 63 to 16.[14] His official commission was issued the next day.

*   *   *

The conservatives were determined not to let the matter rest; anti-New Dealers in Congress and out recognized that with the nomination of a liberal to replace Van Devanter the President had managed to salvage a substantial victory out of the defeat on the Court bill, and they burned with a desire to nullify it in any way possible. The Klan issue showed the greatest promise, even though sufficient damaging evidence could not be dug up before confirmation. Ironically enough, it was the prototype of the white Protestant Anglo-Saxon hierarchy, who viewed approvingly from a haven of respectability what the bully-boys of the Ku Klux Klan practiced in the backwoods of the deep South, who would raise the most righteous outcries in the next few weeks.

While practical politicians and political observers everywhere were aware, as Ickes put it, that in the twenties and thirties there were few Southerners in public life who were not *pro forma* members of the Klan, it was easy to strike a pose as a liberal and a foe of intolerance by denouncing the organization. Genuine conservatives and liberals alike joined in a sincere condemnation of what it stood for, and there could be little serious dispute over Franklin Roosevelt's own personal and public position on the issue. But to be able now to show that the leader of the New Deal, the defender of the "forgotten man," had—if only through carelessness—put a Klansman on the Supreme Court would be a perfect, as well as vindictive, triumph.[15]

Obviously, interested parties were at work on the possibilities; by early September the *Pittsburgh Post-Gazette* had dug up enough to run an initial story which was sold to a national syndicate, the North American Newspaper Alliance. The story purported to reveal Black's initiation in 1923 into the hooded organization and his resignation in 1925 when he began his campaign for the Senate. Thereafter the information became even more tenuous, but was said to prove that he had been reinstated as a life member in 1926.[16]

The foes of the New Deal were delighted with the havoc the news promised to wreak in the groups from which Roosevelt had drawn much of his strength. The Roman Catholics and the National Association for the

Advancement of Colored Peoples beleaguered the White House with demands for the new Justice's resignation or, more vaguely, for his impeachment. The Jews, perhaps more sophisticated in their discernment of the political opportunism implicit in the exposé, were less vocal in their response. The American Bar Association, after voting down a proposal for an investigation of Black, agreed upon a constructive suggestion that the Senate henceforth conduct public hearings on judicial appointments.[17]

Meantime, Hugo Black was nearing the end of what had started out as a restful European vacation; the news stories leaped the Atlantic and followed him wherever he went. Among them, he doubtless saw a report that Roosevelt, gravely upset by the revelation, had stated that he would have no comment until Black himself had returned home and had made his own statement. The Justice had developed a dislike for the metropolitan newspapers in general from his days in Senate investigation, and the treatment he received now did not soften his attitude. When he arrived in Norfolk, Virginia at the end of September, he told the throng of reporters that he would make his answer "in such a way that I cannot be misquoted and that the nation can hear me."[18]

The national radio broadcast which Black delivered on October 1 undoubtedly reached a record audience; the speech was largely defensive, and put the best face on the matter that was possible. The Justice began with an apostrophe to the Constitution and the Bill of Rights—the latter, he observed, "is the heart of the Constitution"—but none could foresee then how accurately the statement would come to describe his own constitutionalism. He moved on to a deprecation of the "planned and concerted campaign" which, directed at himself during his absence from the country, was "calculated to create racial and religious hatred." The tendency of the campaign, he declared, was to "revive the spirit which in 1928 caused a national campaign to be waged largely upon issues unworthy of a free people."

More than half of the speech was delivered before Black came to the matter for which millions were listening. He said:

> The insinuations of racial and religious intolerance made concerning me are based on the fact that I joined the Ku Klux Klan about fifteen years ago. I did join the Klan. I later resigned. I never rejoined. What appeared then, or what appears now on the records of the organization, I do not know.
>
> I have never considered and I do not now consider the unsolicited card given me shortly after my nomination to the Senate as a membership of any kind in the Ku Klux Klan. I never used it. I did not even keep it.
>
> Before becoming a Senator I dropped the Klan. I have had nothing whatever to do with it since that time. I completely discontinued any association with the organization. I have never resumed it and never expect to do so.[19]

Whatever remained of the speech was hardly heard; the morning newspapers had launched upon a Saturnalia of vituperation, some with extras before the evening was over. The liberals were staggered and unable to offer any mitigating argument, while the conservatives ran the gamut of charges and demands. Some screamed for the Justice to resign, others mourned at the permanent stain upon the ermine of the judiciary, many relieved themselves in personal vilification of the man himself. October 4, when the new appointee was formally to be sworn in, was described in handbills distributed around Washington as "Black Day."*[20]

For the second time in 1937 Franklin Roosevelt had ended up in a seriously discredited position with reference to the Supreme Court. His attempt to discomfit the Senate by selecting Black as his nominee had precluded him from consulting the leadership and preparing the way for the handling of the appointment. Had he undertaken a conciliatory course, the men who took the Klan identification for granted, and discounted it realistically, could have softened the attack if it ever had had a chance to be mounted. But the squire of Hyde Park seemed destined now to rush from one political disaster to another; in 1938 he would attempt to purge recalcitrant Congressmen of this unruly session by invading their own bailiwicks to speak against them—a tactic which predictably ended in conspicuous failure.

Thus, as the President began to be presented with opportunities to modernize the thinking of the Court, he lost permanently the opportunity to enlarge upon the broad-gauged legislative basis for the New Deal which had begun in his first term. For the rest of his tenure in the White House, Roosevelt would have to govern primarily by the use of liberally interpreted executive powers, with such occasional statutes of a reform nature as the mood of Congress would sanction. While the logic of economic trends in the 1930's had pointed inescapably to the assumption of responsibility for society's well-being by the national government, its actual implementation proved to be a near thing. In the nick of time, the judiciary had begun to perceive the requirements of the age; henceforth, as the Court was reconstituted, it would be the medium to preserve and effectuate what Congress, before the breach with Roosevelt, had begun.[21]

*   *   *

During the judiciary reorganization fight, individual members of the Supreme Court had been deluged with letters from many parts of the country beseeching them not to resign during the struggle. Now, as the prospect became more certain that Roosevelt might effect the basic changes he sought without further Congressional action, the conservative pleading began again. It was generally understood that Justice Sutherland had been as ready as Van Devanter to leave the bench, and one correspondent wrote anxiously hoping that he would continue on the Court "for a long time, and certainly . . . during this present administration." But in January, 1938—on

---

*Black, like all justices, took two oaths of office—one on formal delivery of the commission, the other on the first day on the bench.

the eve of the White House dinner for the Court—the veteran jurist submitted his resignation. He had only waited that long, said Hughes, so that there would be a seemly interval between his and Van Devanter's retirements.[22]

Chastened by the Black fiasco sufficiently to listen to his advisers, Roosevelt heeded Cummings' renewed recommendation of Stanley A. Reed. He was certainly a nominee as circumspect and unobtrusive as Black was bellicose. While his judicious objectivity made some New Dealers suspect the extent of his commitment to progressivism, it could not be disputed that his record before the Court was unequalled—every New Deal law that he had defended on review before the tribunal had resulted in a government victory.[23]

Reed had been one of the small group of insiders who had worked on the ill-fated judiciary reform proposal, but with tempers now cooled this did not seem likely to provoke any Senate criticism. Indeed, knowledgeable lawyers in the chamber were well aware of his accomplishments as Solicitor General in building up a high-caliber staff of Federal trial counsel, thereby vastly improving the efficiency with which the government was able to handle its briefs. The work of Reed and his men was in such striking contrast to the bumbling efforts of his predecessor, J. Crawford Biggs, as to cause speculation as to how some earlier New Deal cases might have gone if Reed's group of trial lawyers had been in charge. It was possible to conjecture that, with some government victories in 1935, the debacle of 1937 might have been avoided. In any event, the criticism of Attorney General Cummings, made by Hughes to Wheeler in the heat of the Court fight, was more justly to be directed to Reed's predecessor.[24]

Within a week after Sutherland retired, Roosevelt sent Reed's name to the Senate, and the nomination was approved without incident. On January 31, he was sworn in. Thus, within six months, Roosevelt had found his opportunity to replace two of the hard-core conservatives; a confirmed liberal majority of five, augmented by the commitment of Hughes and Roberts, had been established.

In another six months a third vacancy developed, with the death of Justice Cardozo, who had long been ailing. Roosevelt felt that the time had now come to add the man he had long been wanting—Felix Frankfurter. There would be some difficulties, the President suspected, although not of the dimensions of the furor over Black. Part of the opposition, however, was to be expected from those who, with bland hypocrisy, had deplored the anti-Semitism of the Klan. More deep-rooted would be the conservative hostility toward the man who had almost singlehandedly staffed the New Deal agencies with daring and capable young lawyers now busily cementing these agencies into the government framework.

Cummings, while favorable to Frankfurter, warned Roosevelt of the cranks who would be waiting to testify against him in the Judiciary Committee. A more important political consideration was the complaint of Western

Senators that their section of the country, long neglected, was entitled to a representative on the bench. But weighty arguments lay on the other balance: just as Cardozo's nomination had been prefaced by an outpouring of public and private endorsements, most of them spontaneous, now a similar flow of supporting statements began coming into the White House. The Harvard professor, it was earnestly argued, was the logical successor to the "scholar's seat" which had been occupied by Story, Holmes and Cardozo himself.[25]

The scholarly qualifications were ample: Frankfurter had been the co-author of two authoritative works, on *The Labor Injunction* and *The Business of the Supreme Court*, as well as a long list of shorter studies and law review articles. His biographical sketch of Holmes was already considered a classic, while his trenchant articles in the *New Republic* throughout the twenties had won a wide readership. His prowess as an attorney had been equally impressive; he had followed up Brandeis' famous brief on the first Oregon minimum wage case with a powerful brief of his own in the second case (*Bunting v. Oregon*), and had been counsel in *Adkins v. Children's Hospital*—his argument in 1923 having finally been vindicated in the 1937 holding in *West Coast Hotel Co. v. Parrish*.[26]

But the most spectacular of Frankfurter's activities in the years before the New Deal had been his involvement in the case of two Italian-Americans named Nicola Sacco and Bartolomeo Vanzetti. The semi-literate radicals, charged and convicted of murder of a payroll courier and his armed escort, were tried in an atmosphere as hysterically hostile as that of the Haymarket defendants' cases half a century before. Like the anarchists in Chicago then, the anarchists in Boston in 1920 had been tried, many declared, for their political beliefs rather than for their involvement in the murder. After half a dozen years spent in vain efforts to obtain appellate review of their convictions, Sacco and Vanzetti were executed. Frankfurter, in a concise but scathing analysis of the flimsy evidence and careless procedural practices of the trial court, succeeded in outraging all the proper Bostonians—and particularly President A. Lawrence Lowell of Harvard, who had served on a three-member special commission which found no evidence warranting commutation of sentence or pardon.

A founder of the American Civil Liberties Union and one of the most active special counselors for the National Association for the Advancement of Colored Peoples, Frankfurter had assumed radical dimensions in conservative eyes long before any thought of his nomination was entertained. Roosevelt elected to wait until the volume of endorsements had built up sufficiently to overcome any serious opposition to the nomination.

From the Senate, Norris of Nebraska helped dispel the agitation of the Westerners with an unequivocal endorsement; from the bar, Robert H. Jackson urged the President to appoint a man who, like Frankfurter, would be able "to face Chief Justice Hughes in conference and hold his own in discussion." From the Cabinet, Ickes expressed the warning to Roosevelt that he could not expect to keep passing by the Harvard scholar in the expectation of giving him the following appointment: it would be a great loss, he said, if the expected opening did not materialize and thus Frankfurter could not be appointed. Finally, at the urging of Irving Brant, editor of the *St. Louis Star-Times*, Roosevelt himself sent for Justice Stone and sought his suggestions. Stone addressed himself to the problem of regional representation on the Court; the President, he said, could find a good enough man in every circuit of the Federal judiciary, but "you could not get a distinguished Court that way." The spectrum of opinion thus having been spanned, F. D. R. was satisfied; he proceeded to send Frankfurter's name to the Hill.[27]

Stone discerned another telling point with Roosevelt: the need to have a powerful intellect to counterbalance the forceful personality of the Chief Justice. There was no denying that, of all the individuals drawn into the fierce vortex of the judiciary debate of 1937, Charles Evans Hughes alone had emerged with enlarged stature. He was Chief in fact as well as title. Already he had accomplished one of the most remarkable jurisprudential shifts in the Court's history, preserving the dignity of the high bench while guiding it in an almost complete break with the past. At this particular juncture, Hughes dominated the Court as no Chief Justice had done since John Marshall.

But if the Court was to be genuinely and permanently reformed, as Roosevelt sensed it, the commitment to liberalism would have to be made by new men. The Chief, as Stone told Roosevelt, was "exceedingly clever." If he detected the slightest divergence of views among the liberals at the conference table, he would "get his big toe in and widen the cleavage." It was not a matter of suspecting that Hughes had any desire to turn the Court back to a pre-1937 position, but it was a definite question of whether the Court under Hughes would unequivocally devise a post-1937 viewpoint. The President, Stone, and others, said Harold Ickes, "recognized the importance of putting on the bench a man like Frankfurter who is capable of meeting the Chief Justice in the fields both of law and social policy."[28]

*   *   *

Of all the comments on Frankfurter from his advisers, the most prophetic Roosevelt received was from Ickes. The knowledgeable lawyer said: "If you appoint Frankfurter, his ability and learning are such that he will dominate the Supreme Court for fifteen or twenty years to come. The result will be that, probably after you are dead, it will still be your Supreme Court." Neither of the men could foresee that, in most of the *thirty* years to follow, it would be three of Roosevelt's first four appointees who would be the catalysts for the modern Constitution which would grow up after the New Deal.[29]

On January 5, 1939 Frankfurter's name was sent to the Senate; the Old Guard attitude manifested itself at once in a motion to refer the nomination to the judiciary committee for hearings on the "fitness" of the nominee. The sources of the disgruntlement were soon identified: One group pointed to Frankfurter's role in the long protest against the conviction and execution of Sacco and Vanzetti, followed by his active participation in the work of the American Civil Liberties Union, as evidence of his radical sympathies. Another grumbled over Frankfurter's foreign birth, although the real reason for this line of protest was expressed by one who identified himself as the national director (and, as it turned out, sole member) of the Constitutional Crusaders of America.

"Why not an American from Revolution times instead of a Jew from Austria just naturalized?" asked the Crusader. Senator Norris, with dry humor, speculated that "an American from Revolution times would be too old."[30]

Although he believed that there might be improprieties in his own appearance before the committee, Frankfurter overcame his reluctance and accepted its invitation to answer questions. Norris, who had been an early Frankfurter supporter for the Justiceship, kept the proceedings orderly, although Senator Pat McCarran of Nevada insisted on probing into the candidate's personal philosophy. Did Frankfurter, McCarran asked, subscribe to the doctrines of Karl Marx or of that latter-day radical, Harold J. Laski? "Senator," Frankfurter replied, "I do not believe you have ever taken an oath to support the Constitution of the United States with fewer reservations than I have or would now, nor do I believe you are more attached to the theories and practices of Americanism than I am." The audience at the committee hearing cheered the statement to the echo.[31]

Frankfurter was confirmed without a dissenting vote on January 17, and was sworn in by the end of the month. Two weeks later, Louis D. Brandeis notified Roosevelt of his wish to retire, and the President had his fourth opportunity in nineteen months to select a Justice for the Supreme Court.

A paramount consideration for this fourth appointment was the representation of the area west of the Mississippi. A perennial candidate—his name came up at each vacancy on the Court—was Senator Lewis B. Schwellenbach of Washington; now his name was placed near the top of the list, in company with Dr. Robert Maynard Hutchins of the University of Chicago, Dean Wiley B. Rutledge of the University of Iowa, and Chairman William O. Douglas of the SEC.

Rutledge was strongly endorsed by Irving Brant, but it was clear that the President did not want to follow the Frankfurter appointment with another man directly out of the academic environment. To groom Rutledge for a subsequent appointment, Roosevelt shortly thereafter would nominate him to the Court of Appeals for the District of Columbia. Hutchins, who was also an academician, did have the added appeal of being from Chicago which had not been represented on the Court since Fuller's tenure. Douglas was a *bona fide* Westerner, but his professional life was identified with New York, New Haven and Washington, D. C. Momentarily, therefore, it seemed that Schwellenbach at last might be named.

"This appointment," Ickes wrote after conferring with the President on March 12, "has never appealed to me for two reasons. In the first place, I do not think that Schwellenbach is a good enough lawyer and in the second place, I am not sure that he has an intellectual grasp on the principles of liberalism and what it means. Undoubtedly he would go along, at least to a certain extent, with the liberals already on the Supreme Court, but in the shift of public opinion over the coming years no one could be sure where he would eventually land."[32]

This commentary, although Ickes' personal one, was indicative of factors being considered as the reshaping of the Supreme Court became an accomplished fact. Black's selection had been something of an accident, and Reed's had been unobjectionable from the standpoint of his competence as an attorney and his general disposition in favor of progressivism. Frankfurter's appointment had been the first clear example of the type of man the New Deal really sought for the reconstituted judiciary. Now, in the case of the fourth selection, the type of consideration exemplified in Ickes' comment was fundamental. The Court which was being constructed now was intended to articulate and then bring to full flower a constitutional law which would perpetuate the progressive goals of the twentieth century.

With the opportunities for appointments following the defeat of the original Court bill, the President was satisfied. Statutory reorganization was no longer necessary, he told a press conference in August, 1938, "because, in effect, we obtained 98 percent of all the objectives intended by the Court plan." In a radio address delivered in New York on Constitution Day, September 17, he mused: "Perseverance of leadership combined with patience has always won." For the Constitution to have become, and continue to be, "a workable instrument of government," the President went on, "its words needed men in every succeeding generation to administer it, as great as the men who wrote it." And the greatest of these men, he declared, had been those "who have sought to make the Constitution workable in the face of the new problems and conditions that have faced the American nation from year to year."[33]

Battle-wise now after his struggles with Court and Congress during the past five years, Roosevelt had been devoting the main years of his second term to consolidating the gains which had been won in these struggles. Those who now comprised the guiding force for the New Deal were the tried and proven generals of the past engagements: Ickes, Perkins and Wallace in the Cabinet; the indefatigable Corcoran and the brooding Hopkins in the White House itself; Marriner Eccles of the Federal Reserve System, Douglas of the SEC, Robert H. Jackson of Justice, and a finely trained team of young lawyers and economists in the Departments of Agriculture, Labor and the Treasury.[34]

Black and Reed could be said to represent the outlook of the first New Deal years—the former Senator who had fought on the Hill for most of the administration reforms, the former Solicitor General who had salvaged the government's prosecuting mechanism after the first judicial disasters. With Frankfurter, the intellectual consolidation of the new constitutionalism had begun; the Harvard constitutional expert brought to the Court the resources with which to begin the transition from the jurisprudence of Chief Justice Hughes which, after the purging experiences of the constitutional cases from 1935 to 1937, had become essentially a restatement of the ideals of the early Progressive Movement. Douglas—and, subsequently, Jackson—was selected as a mind which could enforce Frankfurter's developing rationale.

To replace Brandeis, the economist who for more than half a century had been a student and critic of the *mores* of capitalism, there was manifestly demanded a liberal who understood thoroughly the mechanics and mentality of modern industrialism. Once that requirement became clear, Douglas emerged as the only logical selection. Hutchins of Chicago, who had tried to entice Douglas to his own faculty, called him "the outstanding professor of law in the nation," and the wide scholarly acceptance of his first work on corporation law and the zeal of Columbia and Yale Law Schools to bid against each other for his services bore out the tribute. Two years with a leading Wall Street law firm, and four years with the Securities and Exchange Commission, had rounded out his qualifications. Nor did the financial community have reason for misgiving at his selection; after the devastating government investigation of the New York Stock Exchange the preceding year, resulting in criminal convictions of several top-ranking Exchange personnel, the SEC could have dictated its own terms for reorganization. Douglas' approach had been firm and brusque, but reasonable and fair-minded.[35]

Thus the "Western seat" would go to a man who indeed had come from the West, who had herded sheep and ridden boxcars en route East, and whose abiding interest in conservation—although not so evident at this stage in his career—would accommodate the interests of that section. On March 21 Roosevelt settled the matter by sending a personal note to Schwellenbach, telling him that he had made his choice between "two old friends—you and Bill Douglas"—and that "I need you and the party needs you and the country needs you in the Senate. The cause of a liberal democracy," the President wrote cheerfully, "is at least equal to, and probably more important than, any individual Supreme Court Justiceship." Schwellenbach acknowledged the letter on March 25, confessing that the news was disappointing but that "I do appreciate very much the statement as to the reasons for the choice."[36]

Others, far from being disappointed, were delighted. "I threw up my hat with joy over Bill Douglas' nomination," Harold J. Laski wrote to the President. "He is second only to Felix in the list of those I want to see there. One more good resignation (by death or art is indifferent to me) and it really will be 'our' Supreme Court." Brandeis, though equally pleased, was more restrained. He simply wrote Douglas: "I wanted you here in my place."[37]

*   *   *

At forty-one, Douglas was the youngest appointee to the Court in the twentieth century and one of the youngest in history. His age focussed attention on the average age of the Court itself, now that Roosevelt was doing something about the "nine old men." Black had been fifty-one when he had been appointed, Reed fifty-four and Frankfurter the oldest at fifty-seven; the average age of the four now was fifty-one—as against an average of seventy-seven for the four men they replaced. In 1937, before the ranks of the Hughes Court began to thin, the average for the nine Justices had stood at seventy-two years of age; in 1943, after six years of Rooseveltian appointments, it would be fifty-six.[38]

What was of more fundamental importance was the ideological shift and the background of the men who had gone onto the bench in the past twenty months. Republican critics sneered at "political lawyers" and "police court judges," and it was true that the background of the four New Deal appointees was in definite contrast to that of the men they replaced.* Both Cardozo and Van Devanter had had substantial judicial experience prior to their appointments, Brandeis had enjoyed a distinguished career as a practicing attorney, and Sutherland, while a career politician, also had maintained an extensive law practice.

Their successors were men of a newer breed: What was more important in Hugo Black's fifteen years of practice as a police judge, prosecuting attorney and trial lawyer was his insight into the earthy problems of the Negro sub-culture in Birmingham, the relationships between criminality and poverty, the desperation of families harassed by tenement landlords and time payments to used-furniture dealers. The perspective of law gained in this context fitted rather better into the jurisprudence of the depression than the corporation law of Butler, Sutherland or Van Devanter.

If Reed was a "political lawyer," his ten years in government practice— following seventeen in private practice—had been under both Republican and Democratic administrations, and his thorough knowledge of the customs and procedures of various regulatory agencies uniquely equipped him to guide the New Deal cases through the judicial challenges of the mid-thirties.

The men who were truly different were Frankfurter and Douglas— essentially academicians, inclined by training and temperament to scan the law as a social phenomenon and to conceive of a jurisprudential perspective for the issues of the time. Their closest counterpart on the Court as they found it was Harlan F. Stone, whose own articles in the *Columbia Law Review* during his professorial tenure had contributed to significant changes in the law.[39]

———————

*See Appendix A.

Roosevelt's successive terms in office were to give him the opportunity not only to place new men on the high tribunal but to make significant changes in the intermediate appellate courts of the Federal system as well. In the ten circuits and the District of Columbia, he would appoint fifty-four judges—almost one-third of those who had been appointed by all the Presidents since Benjamin Harrison, and enough to fill all the positions on the appellate benches.* Although most of these did not excite public attention in the manner of Supreme Court selections, the long-term effects were perhaps even more fundamental.[40]

That they would be Democrats was to be taken for granted, for throughout the national history the Chief Executive had made his selections for appointive offices from within his own party. Only three Republicans and one Independent were among Roosevelt's forty-six lower court and eight Supreme Court nominees. That they were also predominantly New Deal Democrats was also to be assumed, although harder to demonstrate. Three—Sherman Minton of Indiana, Fred M. Vinson of Kentucky and Wiley B. Rutledge of Iowa—would be elevated to the Supreme Court in due course. Others like Thurman W. Arnold of Connecticut, Francis Biddle of Pennsylvania, Homer T. Bone of Washington, Armistead M. Dobie of Virginia, Jerome N. Frank of New York, Herbert F. Goodrich of Pennsylvania and Otto Kerner of Illinois were either party faithful or New Deal intellectuals, or both.[41]

Altogether, Roosevelt was to appoint more than 180 members of all the courts in the Federal system; with the addition of 120 appointments made by President Truman, there would be a total of some three hundred judges selected by New Deal executives for the Supreme Court, Courts of Appeal, District Courts and several special courts of the Federal bench. While many of these men (and women) were to be distinguishable as New Dealers more by their politics than by their philosophies, they inevitably added up to a judiciary which had reached professional maturity in the years when the jurisprudence of *laissez-faire* had been declared bankrupt. Steadily supplanting the jurists who had made up the Federal system in the years from William Howard Taft's Presidency to his Chief Justiceship, these appointees over the two decades of the Roosevelt-Truman administrations permanently closed the books on the judicial history of the past.[42]

*   *   *

When Justice Butler died in November, 1939 Roosevelt was in the midst of a process of regrouping the forces of his administration. Harry Hopkins was now Secretary of Commerce and Frank Murphy of Michigan was Attorney General—the replacements for "Uncle Dan" Roper and Homer Cummings giving the Cabinet a substantial realignment to the left. The President had also succeeded, in the face of a Congressional resistance which had stiffened markedly since the Court fight, in obtaining legislative sanction for a general reorganization of the executive agencies. The primary objectives

---

*See note in Appendix A.

of the New Deal had mostly been won, in the judicial tests since 1937, and the outbreak of World War II in Europe that fall had turned national attention from the lingering issues of the depression decade to the threatening prospects of the forties.

As the New Deal became more solidly entrenched in all branches of government, the need for personal solidarity gave way to increasing cases of palace intrigues and the accommodating of individual ambitions. With the third term an unsettled and controversial matter, administration Democrats and long-disgruntled old-line Democrats were maneuvering for control of the party, and Roosevelt, who had done little to keep a viable political system operative, contributed to the schism by his clumsy 1938 effort to purge recalcitrant party members in Congress. The zeal of the new Attorney General—Murphy had been given the post as a bit of political salvage after his defeat in the Michigan gubernatorial race in 1938—in seeking indictments against political bosses suspected of breaking Federal laws had seriously embarrassed Democrats in Illinois, Missouri and New Jersey. Finally, organized labor had challenged Roosevelt to choose between the union vote and the Southern wing of the party with John L. Lewis' diatribe against Vice-President Garner as a "poker-playing, whiskey-drinking old man." The attack had split the Cabinet as well as the Texas delegation, where a young Congressman named Lyndon B. Johnson had declined to join a manifesto in support of Garner.[43]

Within the Department of Justice, there was new unhappiness; Robert H. Jackson, now Solicitor General, made no secret of his disappointment at not having been named as Cummings' successor. Nor was he enthusiastic about the flurry of criminal cases which Murphy had instituted against all manner of organizations and individuals, and even less about Murphy's proposal to use tax evasion charges as a means of going after subversive groups. Murphy had galvanized the Department as soon as he took office, creating a new civil rights division and flying to various regional meetings of government lawyers to deliver "pep talks" for more vigorous law enforcement. The ex-governor liked to describe his philosophy of life as a "social priesthood"; some of his detractors suggested that it was nearer to ultimate divinity in his mind.[44]

In any event, Roosevelt and his closest advisers valued Jackson so highly that every effort would be made to satisfy him. If he wanted the Attorney Generalship, could Murphy be shifted to another Cabinet post? Murphy himself opted for Secretary of War, but the occupant, Harry H. Woodring, declined to follow Cummings and Roper out of office. The President could hardly request his resignation—not only did Roosevelt hate the thought of firing anyone, but Woodring would control the Kansas delegation to the Democratic convention of 1940, and Roosevelt needed a hedge against either a third-term fight or the right to choose the party's nominee at that time.[45]

Thus the vacancy in Butler's seat on the Supreme Court figured conspicuously in the solution of a major political problem. There were a number of better-qualified candidates; both Rutledge and Jackson were urged upon Roosevelt as intellectual superiors to the ex-governor of Michigan. But Murphy was by instinct a politician who appealed to other politicians, and New Dealers in the Senate remembered his unhesitating support of labor in the rash of sit-down strikes in Michigan two years before. There would be little trouble in getting the nomination approved on the Hill, and it would put an active liberal on the Court while opening the desired Cabinet post for Jackson. Early in January, Murphy's name went to the Senate, and after a flurry of protest from conservative witnesses at the committee hearings, the nomination was approved without dissent.

With Murphy's addition, the fundamental reshaping of the Court was completed. The remaining Roosevelt appointments—Byrnes, Jackson and Rutledge—merely rounded out the accomplishments. Except for Rutledge, whose appointment came near the end of the Roosevelt years and who never attained the intimacy with the President that the others enjoyed, there was one common characteristic of the New Deal jurists: they all maintained a contact with the White House—Frankfurter the closest, Reed the least, but Black, Byrnes, Douglas, Jackson and Murphy being fairly voluble in their communications with F. D. R. With Stone's more indirect but nonetheless effective methods of exchanging ideas with the Executive, and with Hughes responding to Roosevelt's approaches as far as he considered propriety would permit, the President had at last achieved a rapport with the Court.

Frankfurter, who had been an adviser of Roosevelt's since the earliest years of his governorship in New York, continued to counsel the President into the war years; it was at his urging that Henry L. Stimson was brought into the bi-partisan Cabinet established in the national emergency. Douglas, periodically mentioned as a running-mate for or successor to F. D. R., kept regularly in touch with the White House. Murphy—whose competence as a jurist impressed Frankfurter less and less (he referred to him as "my baby Brother")—was to pester the President continually for an assignment to action during the conflict, and meantime toured the Washington cocktail circuits assiduously. Reed communicated through Ickes and others close to the Cabinet, while Black never hesitated to express an opinion on major issues in public or in private.[46]

*   *   *

However, it was not Presidential rapport but studied judicial reorientation which ultimately demonstrated the fact that the new Court was now in being. In the popular mind, the change was calculated, strategic—it could be pinpointed on March 29, 1937 with the decision upholding the Washington state wage-hour law and thus dealing a mortal blow to the Roosevelt judicial reform bill. Because Justice Roberts, a chronic vacillator, had been the fifth man of the majority both in *West Coast Hotel Company v. Parrish*, upholding such a law, and in the *Morehead* case invalidating such a law, his "switch in time that saved nine" was to become as celebrated in the political folklore of the nation as Justice Shiras' presumed shift in the *Income Tax* case of 1895.

Hughes, Frankfurter—although at the time he was convinced that Roberts *had* made a political shift—and Roberts himself were all to deny, at various times, the reason for the change in view, or even that there *was* a change in view. In his biographical notes, the Chief Justice was to declare that Roberts had indeed voted with the liberals to affirm the Washington state court decision upholding the wage-hour law, in the conference held in December, 1936. Roberts himself, in a memorandum he gave to Frankfurter at the time of his retirement in 1945, insisted that the fault in the first decision (*Morehead v. New York*) had been in the failure of counsel for New York to ask the Court to distinguish that case from the rule in *Adkins v. Children's Hospital.* Frankfurter, making public this memorandum in a 1953 tribute to Roberts in the *University of Pennsylvania Law Review,* added a retraction of his earlier opinion and declared: "The crucial factor in the whole episode was the absence of Mr. Justice Stone from the bench, on account of illness, from October 14, 1936 to February 1, 1937."[47]

Putting *Morehead* and *West Coast Hotel Company* into the context of the series of decisions that came in 1937 and the next several years, however, several questions still remained to be answered.

On June 1, 1936 Justice Butler, speaking for his three conservative colleagues and Justice Roberts, ruled invalid a New York law governing minimum wages to be paid women and minors, relying on the *Adkins* precedent. The petitioner in the case, said Butler, was not entitled to ask that the *Adkins case* be overruled, and intoned: "Freedom of contract is the general rule and restraint the exception." He stressed the courts' responsibility to distinguish between hours of labor, which might justify legislative regulation, and compensation for labor, which did not. On March 29, 1937 Chief Justice Hughes spoke for Roberts and the three liberals in overruling *Adkins* and thus destroying the basis for the *Morehead* holding of nine months earlier.

The reasoning was tenuous in the extreme. In Hughes' words, the minority (of four Justices, lacking Roberts) in *Morehead* "thought that the New York statute was distinguishable" from *Adkins* and could have been upheld without reference to *Adkins*. The majority in that case had noted that the New York court had invalidated its own statute because it was *not* distinguishable from *Adkins* and had affirmed the New York ruling without inquiring into whether the *Adkins* rule was valid or validly applied. But in *West Coast Hotel Company* the former minority (now reinforced by Roberts) had affirmed the Washington state court in upholding its own statute—but rejected the argument, offered in the *amicus* brief of the state attorney general, that the *Adkins* rule was distinguishable; it now simply held that *Adkins* was invalid.

The whole matter turned on Roberts' attitude. In his 1945 memorandum, the then retired Justice insisted that he had felt bound, in the *Morehead* case, by the fact that New York's brief "had not asked us to re-examine or overrule *Adkins,*" while in the briefs for Washington in the *West Coast Hotel* case, "for the first time, I was confronted with the necessity of facing the soundness of the *Adkins* rule." The fact was that even some of his Associate Justices were mystified at this reasoning; Roberts reported that he "heard one of the brethren ask another" what was the matter with him.[48]

Judge Rosenman stated flatly that after the argument in the Washington case, Roberts was reported to have changed his vote. This was true, if one knew that the change was not within the one case but from the vote in *Morehead* to that in *West Coast Hotel Company*. Hughes himself denied persistent reports that he had had a talk on the facts of political life with Roberts at the time of the December, 1936 conference. There was, finally, the fact that Roberts wrote no concurring opinion in either of the cases, so that he did not have to give an intellectual accounting for his actions. On the other hand, to note the similarity of the majority reasoning in *Morehead* with Roberts' own opinions in *Carter Coal Company* and in *Schechter* was to be the more impressed with the contrast in *West Coast Hotel Company*. One could only speculate: if the Washington and New York cases had been decided together, either in June, 1936 or in February, 1937, what would have been the majority view?

*   *   *

The case that most dramatically confirmed the new judicial mentality—the opinion of April 12, 1937 upholding the Wagner Act—required a definite reversal of the propositions central to the arguments of Hughes in the *Schechter* and Roberts in the *Butler* cases, and of Hughes' concurring opinion in the *Carter Coal* case. In May, 1935, speaking for the Court in the opinion invalidating the NIRA, Hughes had elaborated upon the differentiation between "direct and indirect" effects upon interstate commerce; those in the "indirect" category, he had declared, were beyond the reach of Federal authority. "If the commerce clause were construed to reach all enterprises and transactions which could be said to have an indirect effect upon interstate commerce," Hughes contended, the Federal authority would extend far into the economic areas of the states. Labor relations, under the circumstances, he found to be a subject only "indirect" in its effect on interstate commerce and hence outside the reach of Federal regulation.[49]

Roberts was even more categorical in his opinion for the Court, invalidating the AAA in January, 1936, ringing the changes of the old theme of delegated (and hence limited) powers of the Federal government and reserved powers of the states. Hughes joined in this majority. In the *Carter Coal* decision in May, 1936 Roberts joined in Sutherland's majority view which stringently applied the "direct or indirect" test to the limitation of Federal authority. As for Hughes, his concurring opinion declared that if "the people desire to give Congress the power to regulate industries within the state, they are at liberty to declare their will in the appropriate manner, but it is not for the Court to amend the Constitution by judicial decision."[50]

To uphold the National Labor Relations Act in the face of these decisions required a substantially altered definition of the "direct or indirect" effect of labor relations on interstate commerce, and an abandonment of the proposition that only an amended Constitution could sustain the extension of Federal power into this subject-area.

While Hughes, in the *NLRB* cases, did not take notice of the fight over the judicial reorganization plan then raging in Congress, he did go so far as to state that the Court members could not "shut our eyes to the plainest facts of our national life." By this, he said, he meant that when "industries organize themselves on a national scale, making their relation to interstate commerce the dominant factor in their activities," it could not be denied that their labor relations had a "direct" effect on these activities and hence on interstate commerce. Yet no amount of sophistry could camouflage the fact that what was treated as unconstitutional in May, 1936 had become the test of constitutionality in April, 1937, eleven months later. McReynolds put it very bluntly in his dissent: "Every consideration brought forward to uphold the act before us was applicable to support the acts held unconstitutional in cases decided within two years."[51]

When another April came around, McReynolds and Butler had become the only survivors of the ravages of judicial reorganization through retirement and new appointment. To Hughes' opinion for the majority, upholding the amended Municipal Bankruptcy Act, McReynolds could only point out that the decision had to overrule the *Ashton* case of 1936, despite the Chief Justice's assurance that the two cases could be distinguished. The sweeping decision in the earlier case had indeed seemed to proscribe any action by Congress in the matter of legislating relief for local governments in financial crisis. The simple fact was that by now the four dissenters, including Hughes, had become the majority—a majority so sufficiently solidified that not even Roberts' reversal of his position in *Ashton* was significant. With the changes in the Court brought about by time, it was now a foregone conclusion that the new majority would proceed to a substantive overturning of many positions once taken on the questions of national authority.[52]

5/Seedtime of a Modern Constitution

I N THE FOUR TERMS of the Supreme Court beginning in the fall of 1937 and concluding in the spring of 1941, the full effects of the New Deal struggle to modernize the Court began to be manifest. The once monolithic core of adamant conservatism steadily eroded, and the reversal of the narrow decisions of the first part of the decade steadily continued. Indeed, after the *Bituminous Coal Act* decision in the spring of 1936, no major act of Congress was found unconstitutional in any part for the next seven years.[1] There had to be, said Thomas Reed Powell, a necessary conversion of judicial thought "if anything approaching a democratic government were to continue"; and the changes in this period, wrote another observer, "are not just a shift in attitude in the application of old principles. They constitute modification and even complete rejection of the principles themselves."[2]

What was more significant than the unequivocal broad construction of constitutional clauses formerly narrowly construed, however, was the affirmative development of a new frame of reference for Federal government in the second quarter of the twentieth century. The liberalism that now pervaded the Court, concluded an observer in 1939, was characterized not merely by "approval of New Deal laws that once might have been overthrown," but by a determination to assert Federal guarantees of a wide variety of civil rights. Henceforth, Princeton's Professor Corwin predicted, the judiciary would not spend its energies in attempting to play "economic power against political power," but would place increasing emphasis upon "the human values of free thought, free expression, and fair play."[3]

Robert H. Jackson, who by the end of this four-year period would be a member of the Court, saw the withdrawal of the judiciary from a rigid attitude toward social legislation as logically complemented by its increasingly active role in opposing legislative intermeddling with civil rights. "Ordinarily," he wrote, "legislation whose basis in economic wisdom is uncertain can be redressed by the processes of the ballot box or the pressures of opinion. But

101

when the channels of opinion and of peaceable persuasion are corrupted or clogged, these political correctives can no longer be relied on, and the democratic system is threatened at its most vital point. In that event the Court, by intervening, restores the processes of democratic government; it does not disrupt them."[4]

Neither Corwin nor Jackson—nor, it may be assumed, the members of the Court themselves—recognized at the time the full implications of the shift of ideological poles that was taking place in the closing years of the thirties. The broadening guidelines as to areas of Congressional action meant that Congress rather than the Court was to be the judge of the reasonable extension of Federal authority with reference to social and economic institutions in the United States as a whole. Conversely, the gradually increasing commitment of the judiciary to a Federal oversight of individually guaranteed rights meant that the national government, at least to a degree as great as for the states, would henceforth be responsible for these rights, and in its paramount position would be prepared to assert them even as against the states. This would be the ultimate harvest of the new constitutionalism; the period from 1937 to 1941 was its seedtime.

*   *   *

The commerce clause was the obvious starting point for the exposition of the new constitutionalism; even in the periods of maximum conservatism, the Court had generally conceded that the Federal authority was express and extensive in the interstate area. Now, in the space of four terms, the Court affirmed half a dozen New Deal statutes and overruled its own earlier restrictive doctrines in other cases. In 1938 the Public Utility Holding Company Act of 1935 was held to be well within the commerce power. The following year the Court upheld the Tobacco Act of 1935, and the Agricultural Marketing Act and AAA of 1938—both of which had been passed by Congress virtually in defiance of the Court's earlier rulings. Two other acts of Congressional defiance, the new Guffey Coal Act and a wage-hour law challenging the old rule of *Hammer v. Dagenhart,* were also upheld.[5]

The tenor of the new constitutionalism was expressed in Hughes' opinion in the *Holding Company* case. When Congress had determined "what it considers to be the factual situation and the need of Federal supervision" in the area of interstate commerce, in prescribing penalties for the violation of its rules "Congress has a wide discretion," and may withdraw from violators the access to interstate commerce itself.[6] Hughes made the definition of Congressional authority substantially broader in the *Tobacco Act* case in January, 1939: "Where goods are purchased in one state for transportation to another the commerce includes the purchase quite as much as it does the transportation." More than that: "The fact that intrastate and interstate transactions are commingled on the tobacco market does not frustrate or restrict the Congressional power to protect and control what is committed to its own care."[7]

"It is of the essence of the plenary power conferred that Congress may exercise its discretion in the use of the power," the Chief Justice concluded. "Congress may choose the commodities and places to which its regulation shall apply. Congress may consider and weigh relative situations and needs. Congress is not restricted by any technical requirement but may make limited applications and resort to tests so that it may have the benefit of experience in deciding upon the continuance or extension of a policy which under the Constitution it is free to adopt. As to such choices, the question is one of wisdom and not of power."[8]

Building upon this proposition, Roberts extended it in the second *AAA* case; any reasonable regulation which fosters and protects interstate commerce is within the competence of Congress. "The motive of Congress in exerting the power," said the onetime vacillator, "is irrelevant to the validity of the legislation."[9] *United States v. Butler* received its *coup de grace* in the decision upholding the Agricultural Marketing Agreement Act, where Justice Reed disposed of the issue of delegation of power: It is no argument against the constitutionality of a statute, he declared, "to say that it delegates broad powers to executives to determine the details of any legislative scheme. This necessary authority has never been denied" (although Butler, McReynolds, Hughes and Roberts denied it in accompanying dissents). Where Congress identified the purpose of the regulation and the standards by which the purpose was to be worked out, said Reed, within this framework "Congress need specify only so far as is reasonably practicable."[10]

From the *Rock Royal* case upholding the regulation of agricultural commerce under authority delegated to the Secretary of Agriculture, it was a short step to the upholding of price regulation in the coal industry. Where the public interest was safeguarded by placing the price-fixing machinery in the hands of public agencies, even though, as under the AAA, private interests might have a participating role, the process was within the paramount power of Congress over interstate commerce.[11]

The rediscovery and reaffirmation of latent authority in the Federal government was strikingly demonstrated in the case of *United States v. Lowden*. Where the Court, in the *Alton Railroad* case slightly more than three years earlier, had found a railroad pension plan to be outside the realm of interstate commerce and a taking of carriers' property without due process of law, it now found such pensions substantially within the jurisdiction of the Interstate Commerce Commission. Notwithstanding what was said in the *Alton* case, Justice Stone wrote, the Court could not now say "that the Congressional judgment that those conditions [of labor welfare] have a relation to the public interest . . . is without rational basis."[12]

It was in the categorical repudiation of the child labor rule in *Hammer v. Dagenhart* that the Court in February, 1941 reached the zenith of the new jurisprudence. "Congress," declared Stone, "following its own conception of public policy concerning the restrictions which may appropriately be imposed

ate commerce, is free to exclude from the commerce articles whose
e states for which they are destined it may conceive to be injurious
to the public health, morals or welfare, even though the state has not sought
to regulate their use."

"Such regulation," Stone concluded, "is not a forbidden invasion of
state power merely because either its motive or its consequence is to restrict
the use of articles of commerce within the states of destination and is not
prohibited unless by other constitutional provisions. It is no objection to the
assertion of the power to regulate interstate commerce that its exercise is
attended by the same incidents which attend the exercise of the police power
of the states."[13]

Thus, after half a century of backing and filling, the Court had come
unequivocally to acknowledge that a plenary power over interstate commerce
was vested in Congress, and that Congress was the sole judge of the appropriate use of this power. The new constitutionalism, in this, was returning to
the concept enunciated by John Marshall a century before, that the commerce
power "is complete in itself, may be exercised to its utmost extent, and
acknowledges no limitations other than are prescribed in the Constitution."[14]

* * *

The contract clause of the Constitution was the next most important
medium for an extension of the governmental authority. In a case involving
the validity of an Indiana statute providing tenure for public school teachers,
Justice Roberts for the majority held that, where the public interest warranted
it, a legislature could bind future legislatures to a contractual agreement
with its teachers. An attempt in new legislation to extinguish the contract
would properly raise a Federal question under the contract impairment
clause, he concluded. "Our decisions recognize that every contract is made
subject to the implied condition that its fulfillment may be frustrated by a
proper exercise of the police power," Roberts acknowledged; "but we have
repeatedly said that, in order to have this effect, the exercise of the power
must be for an end which is in fact public and the means adopted must be
reasonably adapted to that end."[15]

"The power is ours, when the impairment of an obligation is urged
against a law, to determine for ourselves the effect and meaning of the contract as well as its existence," Cardozo had declared in an earlier case in
the same term. The Court held that school district and road district bonds
exempt from taxes in effect when they were issued could be subjected to
new forms of tax subsequently enacted, without impairing a contract obligation of the state.[16]

Having thus delineated circumstances where the state, as in the tenure
act, was barred from extinguishing a contract made by one of its public
agencies, and where, as in the bond case, it was reasonably permitted to
limit the benefits flowing from such a contract, the Court addressed itself
to the lingering contract questions in the gold bond issue raised early in

the New Deal. "The obligation devolving upon the United States" at the time of calling any of its obligations, said Hughes in an opinion written by Cardozo, depended solely upon the law as it prevailed at the time of accelerated maturity. A call prior to the Congressional acts suspending specie payments did not commit the government to a payment in a form forbidden after the enactment.[17]

As for privately issued bonds carrying an option of payment in gold or in foreign currencies, the Court affirmed a bankruptcy case holding that under the gold suspension acts of Congress a bondholder was limited to the value of the bonds determined by domestic currency. Since the purpose of the legislation, said Black for a unanimous Court, was to "outlaw all contractual provisions which require debtors, who have bound themselves to pay United States dollars, to pay a greater number of dollars than promised," private parties cannot create vested rights which will frustrate a constitutional power of Congress.[18]

*   *   *

The resurgence of Congressional authority was also marked in a series of cases concerning the scope of the taxing and spending power. An opinion unanimously sustaining the Public Works Administration—and written by Justice Sutherland—demonstrated the completeness of the pendulum swing. A private utility, declared Sutherland in repudiation of many an earlier declaration to the contrary, has no standing to seek to enjoin the expending of public funds on a municipal power plant. Where the private utility has no exclusive franchise and the municipality exercised its own freedom of choice in seeking Federal funds for the purpose, no right is violated on which an action can be maintained.[19]

The theory of tax immunity of all government obligations, so long applied as to seem a part of the Constitution itself, also began to be qualified in the new jurisprudence. A vague area between income from state activities subjectively described as "essential governmental" and exempt from tax, and other activities classified as non-essential and liable to tax, had simply led to confusion. Worse, said Justice Black, it led to discrimination by dividing government employees into tax-paying and non-tax-paying groups when uniformity is "the objective of every just government." The case involved a Federal tax levied upon the incomes of employees of the New York Port Authority, a public agency created by compact between the states of New York and New Jersey. Although concurring in the majority opinion upholding the tax as a reasonable burden upon state employees, Black urged that the whole question be more exhaustively examined.[20]

Earlier the Court had denied tax immunity to attorneys for services involving liquidation of insolvent corporations where their fees were paid by the liquidated entity rather than by the state,[21] and in the same term had denied tax exemption on incomes of lessees of state school lands.[22] By the spring of 1939, Black's view had come to prevail, and the Court by a majority of seven held that "the theory that a tax on income is legally or economically a tax on its source is no longer tenable." The case involved a state income tax upon employees of a Federally chartered public corporation, and thus presented the other side of the coin to the *Port Authority* case. So far as the leading cases of the past, asserting such immunity in the instance of either state or Federal employees, were concerned, said Stone for the majority, they were expressly or impliedly overruled.[23]

Two months later, Justice Frankfurter in an opinion completed the cycle by finding Federal judges' salaries liable to tax, overruling a classic case to the contrary which had rested on the supposed constitutional prohibition of decreasing salaries of the judiciary during incumbency. The prior interpretation, declared Frankfurter, "was contrary to the way in which it was read by other English-speaking courts" and had met with "wide and steadily growing disfavor from legal scholarship and professional opinion."[24]

*   *   *

In the field of labor law, the Court swept away the "yellow-dog" doctrines of the *Adair* and *Coppage* cases,* sustained various phases of the Wagner Act and strengthened the Norris-LaGuardia Anti-Injunction Act. The National Labor Relations Act empowered the NLRB to compel employers to withdraw recognition of company unions when this amounted to coercing or dominating their employees in the exercise of guaranteed rights of independent collective bargaining, Stone declared in enforcing two Board rulings against the Pennsylvania Greyhound Lines.[25]

Chief Justice Hughes, in upholding the labor law against a claim that food processing was intrastate and separable from interstate commerce, moved the Court further away from its negative position in the first *Guffey Coal Act* decision and distinguished several earlier cases which had enthroned the narrow view. The test, "where Federal control is sought to be exercised over activities which separately considered are intrastate," said Hughes, is whether "there is a close and substantial relation to interstate commerce in order to justify the Federal intervention for its protection." This would not satisfy those, the Chief Justice conceded, "who seek for mathematical or rigid formulas."[26]

With the sweeping validation of the National Labor Relations Act, the Court had committed itself to a whole new body of labor law; hardly any of the orthodox common law concepts of master and servant—the very terms derived from a simpler handicraft age—had effective application within the new jurisprudence. Especially was this true after the remarkable twelve months from December, 1936 to the end of 1937, when militant labor organizing campaigns, spearheaded by the CIO and sensationalized by the sit-down strike, effected a spectacular breakthrough in union recognition. John L.

---

*These cases, as well as the Child Labor cases, are discussed in *The Old Legality, 1889-1932.*

Lewis, the craggy-browed veteran of long labor wars in the coal fields, and his lieutenant, Philip Murray, were the field marshals. The first major victory came when a lengthy sit-down strike in the General Motors plant in Flint, Michigan won the company's recognition of the auto workers' union. Within a month, Big Steel capitulated without firing a shot.[27]

After this, a succession of the citadels of the open shop came to terms with organized labor; UAW membership soared in a matter of weeks to 400,000, and that of the steel workers' union to 325,000. In quick succession other automotive manufacturers (except Ford) and other steel companies (except Tom Girdler's "Little Steel") made contracts with the unions. The major rubber manufacturers, textiles, radio manufacturers and General Electric followed one upon another into the area of collective bargaining. What had been an impossible dream for the labor leaders of the past half century—the systematic unionization of the major part of industrial America—was suddenly accomplished in little more than a year.[28]

The upholding of the NLRA in the *Jones & Laughlin Steel* case was, of course, the handwriting on the wall which the more astute of the country's business leaders were well able to read. Unionization followed as a matter of course, and the hoary fiction of freedom of contract between labor and management was quietly laid to rest. Conservatives through their spokesmen in Congress decried the sit-down strike as far-advanced socialism and took the administration's refusal to call out the troops as evidence of a definite conspiracy to destroy capitalism. The extreme aggressiveness of the CIO also roused a certain dread among the middle classes. Flushed with his spectacular successes in the winter of 1937, John L. Lewis was prepared to launch a bloody strike against the holdout steel companies and presumed to suggest greater Presidential help for labor in return for the workers' support in the 1936 elections.

But the preponderance of legal and economic advantage was on the side of the wage-earners; state as well as Federal authorities were virtually unanimous in declining to use armed forces as strike breakers, and indeed the Federal statutes now prevented the transporting of strike breakers across state lines. Senator LaFollette's Civil Liberties Committee exposed the systematic violence employed by the most virulent union-hating employers, and the Walsh-Healey Act made real the threat of withholding government contracts from corporations which conspired to violate existing labor laws. The "damned unpopular" device of the sit-down strike, Roosevelt believed, would cause the unions to renounce it of their own accord in due course.[29]

From *West Coast Hotel Co. v. Parrish* in March, 1937, restoring to the states the authority to establish minimum wages for women, to *United States v. Hutcheson* in February, 1941, extinguishing the anti-trust liability of labor unions under the Sherman Act, the Court followed a consistent line of decisions which tended, on the one hand, steadily to broaden the constitutional foundations upon which labor law would rest and, on the other, to strengthen the jurisdiction of the Labor Board itself. With the growing disposition to limit reviewable questions from all administrative agencies,* the Court thus encouraged the NLRB to fill in vast areas of the law with its own rulings on the details.[30]

The Railway Labor Act of 1926 was substantially enlarged by a decision in the spring of 1937, a Wisconsin labor code was upheld, the power of lower Federal courts to issue injunctions in cases of peaceful picketing was withdrawn, and labor disputes growing out of Negro protests against discriminatory employment practices were brought within the protection of the law.[31] As for the sit-down strike, the Court agreed that employers had the right to protect their property from strike-induced sabotage, and to replace strikers with other workers provided that any reinstatements of striking employees should not turn upon the penalizing of individuals for union activity. Local unions which were not company-dominated were accepted as bargaining units, and where strikers refused to bargain with an employer altogether the government, in Justice Stone's phrase, would not compel him "to seek out his employees and request their participation in negotiations."[32]

Governmental obstructionism in favor of the open shop was struck down in a case brought against "Boss" Hague, mayor of Jersey City, in his refusal to issue a permit for a public meeting which was to plan a union drive among the city's companies. A Labor Board finding that the CIO had been chosen as the bargaining unit in a bona fide employee election, said the Court, would not give the AF of L a cause of action. Nor would a Board order excluding a company union from the election ballot give management a cause of action. An employer tactic in the form of executing separate employment contracts with individual employees, when made the basis of an employee complaint, could be forbidden by the Board, for, as Stone said, "the public right and duty" vested in the Board extends "not only to the prevention of unfair labor practices by the employer . . . but to the prevention of his enjoyment of any advantage which he has gained by violation of the act."[33]

In February, 1941 Stone spoke for a unanimous court in *United States v. Darby,* unequivocally overruling the decisions against child labor laws of the era of normalcy. With this and a companion case affirming the constitutionality of the Wage-Hour Act of 1938, the statement of the new labor jurisprudence came full circle, and as a Washington commentator put it, "the New Deal was finally legitimatized, its last major social reform riveted into place." *Darby* did indeed symbolize the completeness of the judicial transformation; Justice Black, as a Senator, had been one of the draftsmen of the statute which had invited the Court to repudiate the past.[34]

The sophistication of the new jurisprudence was demonstrated in a landmark case in April, 1938; for states' rightists who loudly complained that

---

*See Appendix D.

the trend of contemporary decisions was sanctioning a smothering Federalism, *Erie Railroad Company v. Tompkins* confounded their argument. Reversing a rule of almost a century's standing,[35] the Court speaking through Brandeis declared unequivocally: "Except in matters governed by the Federal Constitution or by acts of Congress, the law to be applied in any case is the law of the state. . . . Congress has no power to declare substantive rules of common law applicable in a state. . . ."[36] The prior doctrine, enunciated by the venerable Joseph Story, had looked to a consistency or uniformity of rules of decisions in Federal courts throughout the land; but where the rule differed from that of the state in which a particular Federal court sat, a party could find himself subject to opposing doctrines of common law depending on whether he tried his case in a state court or the Federal court. The true uniformity of justice to be sought, Brandeis had argued for more than a decade, was consistency on the same rule of decision within the state where the litigants found themselves, whether the case was in the state or the Federal court.[37]

The Court had voluntarily withdrawn an authority which it had asserted and the legal profession had accepted for almost a century. Now it manifested a disposition to relax its long-continued surveillance of the rulings of administrative agencies as well. Since 1912[38] the Court had insisted upon reviewing not only the rulings but the evidence on which they were based. Now Frankfurter, for the Court, explicitly rejected the practice and the "obfuscating" reasoning behind it. The judgment of any expert body, he declared, should be permitted to stand if there was any warrant for it.[39] In an earlier case in the same term, he had declared that an appellate court was limited in its review of administrative decisions to the correction of questions of law, and properly should leave to the agency the carrying out of the legislative policy committed to its care.[40] Roberts, in another opinion, had added that where the Court of Appeals had found the agency to have acted according to accepted standards of due process, the finding was not reviewable in the Supreme Court.[41]

Frankfurter, like Holmes and Brandeis, took a pragmatic view of constitutional rules in the opinion relaxing judicial surveillance over legislative acts or administrative decisions implementing policy. "The equality at which the 'equal protection' clause aims is not a disembodied equality," he observed in a 1940 case. "The Fourteenth Amendment enjoins 'the equal protection of the laws,' and laws are not abstract propositions. They . . . are expressions of policy arising out of specific difficulties, addressed to the attainment of specific ends by the use of specific remedies. The Constitution does not require things which are different in fact or opinion to be treated in law as though they were the same." Older rules and precedents, Frankfurter concluded, were always subject to the likelihood of being "worn away by the erosion of time."[42]

*   *   *

Above all other decisions symbolic of the new constitutionalism, in the final years of the depression decade, were those concerning civil liberties and the subjects of restraint upon the states laid by the due process and equal protection clauses of the Fourteenth Amendment. Recurrently throughout this period, the Court showed its commitment to the Frankfurter dictum on the "erosion of time"; rules of long standing were reexamined, and the recent cases involving cardinal principles of individual rights were heard over when there was reasonable doubt as to the sufficiency of the earlier decision. Ever more prominent was the concern that a right preserved to a citizen of the United States by his Constitution should not go unprotected.

Half a century had passed since Justice Harlan's dissent in *Plessy v. Ferguson,* where a majority of the Fuller Court had found that when transportation facilities were separate but (hypothetically) equal, the Fourteenth Amendment did not proscribe segregated sections of those facilities. "Our Constitution is color blind," Harlan had protested, "and neither knows nor tolerates classes among citizens."[43] Now came a Negro seeking admission to the University of Missouri law school. In denying the application, the state cited the separate and equal facilities of the state-supported Lincoln University for Negroes, the statutory provision for the addition of professional schools therein as they might be required, and the alternative provision for payment of tuition for Negroes to obtain the professional education in neighboring state universities.

It was not enough, Chief Justice Hughes declared; the fact was that no law school was in operation at Lincoln University, and to compel a Negro student to go outside the state to obtain professional training that was available within the state for white students was discriminatory.[44] Missouri solved the difficulty by activating a law school at its state Negro institution; later it would be compelled to add other professional schools, at mounting costs, to stay within the letter of the Hughes decision. An economic wedge had been entered into the *Plessy* doctrine but it would be two decades before a social wedge would be added and, under the hammer blows of *Brown v. Board of Education,*[45] the "separate but equal" doctrine would be splintered.

*   *   *

The nagging question of the law and morality of wiretapping, a residue of the sickly jurisprudence of the prohibition era, also came up for further review. The Court found an opportunity, in the Communications Act of 1934, to rule inadmissible in Federal courts evidence obtained by Federal agents by means of intercepted messages; two years later the rule was extended to apply to wiretapping—"fruits of the [same] poisonous tree," as Frankfurter called the methods.[46] Beyond this, however, the Court could not muster a majority to support a more definitive prohibition.[47]

The requirements of due process and fair dealing led to a warning directed at administrative agencies that all parties before them were entitled to reasonable opportunity to hear the charges or complaints of an adversary party, and to have opportunity to meet them.[48] From this proposition the Court advanced into the subject of the rights of defendants in criminal trials to have the benefit of adequate legal advice. While the Court had earlier adopted the proposition that, under the Sixth Amendment, the right to counsel in criminal cases was a constitutional requirement in Federal law, and in an Alabama case in 1940 asserted that under the Fourteenth Amendment a reasonably adequate opportunity for service of counsel was required, the beginnings of a new doctrine of defendants' rights were relatively modest.[49] The road from the Missouri segregation case to the ultimate desegregation decision was to be a long one; the road from *Avery v. Alabama* to *Gideon v. Wainwright* [50] would be longer and even more tortuous.

But this was, nevertheless, a time of germinal new ideas. The labor case of *Hague v. CIO* had incorporated a judicial policy of vigorous enforcement of freedoms under the First Amendment, which was reasserted in *Thornhill v. Alabama,* outlawing an anti-picketing statute as an infringement upon freedom of speech.[51] Equally an infringement was a Georgia ordinance requiring a permit to distribute printed matter within the city limits, invalidated along with similar laws in California, Massachusetts, New Jersey and Wisconsin.[52] And where the publications or utterances were in the nature of religious views, the state was barred by the First Amendment from any regulatory acts which tended to hamper the right to disseminate these views.[53]

The Court made progress slowly in this area. In conflicts between "the liberty of conscience, and the authority . . . to safeguard the nation's fellowship," Frankfurter observed, "judicial conscience is put to its severest test." The Court majority in 1940 was not prepared to hold that a school flag-salute law infringed upon religious freedom sufficiently to invoke a constitutional prohibition.[54] But the question had been raised, and in a judicial climate where all questions were subject to reconsideration, the possibility of reversal was always open; indeed, a reversal of the flag-salute ruling came within three years.[55]

By the end of the depression decade, the Court's fundamental rules of constitutional law had moved to the opposite end of the spectrum from the position of 1930, or 1936. The commerce and tax powers of Congress, long urged by legal scholars as virtually plenary, had finally been freed of "spurious dialectic," as one journal described it. Freedom of contract and impairment of contract were no longer a rationalization of *laissez-faire,* "mischief sanctified by time." Labor as an economic unit had been put into balance with capital, and freedoms guaranteed to the individual were becoming increasingly a matter of Federal concern. "The new constitutionalists hold that each age of Americans must reinterpret the Constitution in the light of changed social and economic conditions," wrote a correspondent as the Court adjourned in June, 1941.

"Never in its history," wrote another pair of observers, "has the Court so searchingly pondered its office, asked what matters lay within its distinctive competence, insisted that unsuited tasks be left to other agencies." Not only had the modern constitutionalism come to recognize the present and look toward the future, but it had committed itself to a process of interpretation which precluded a reverting to the past. "The Court has created doctrine," the writers concluded, "which stands in the way of its own lapse into legalism."[56]

*   *   *

In the irony of history, it was the new Court brought into being by the great fight over reorganization of the judiciary which saved the New Deal from the political wreckage wrought by the fight itself. An astute Republican observer, Wendell Willkie, clearly understood that by the opportunities for his appointments, the President had accomplished "exactly what he would have accomplished if he had won the Court fight." The support won by Roosevelt in the judiciary, coming at the moment that Congress was slipping away from him, suggested to Willkie the ultimate safety in the "tripartite government of checks and balances; for even as the Executive obtained a Court with a strong bias in his favor, Congress grew increasingly independent."[57]

The fight over the judiciary bill had indeed been a disaster for the administration. Conservatives, particularly among the Southern Democrats, found encouragement and strength for their program of defiance, and Roosevelt's ill-conceived plan to seek to "purge" recalcitrant Congressmen in the mid-term elections brought on a second humiliating defeat within the next year. How bitterly Congress had turned against the White House was demonstrated in November, 1937 when a special session had been called to consider recommended legislation on agriculture, wages and hours, and reorganization of the Executive Department. After five weeks the session adjourned without having enacted a single proposal.[58]

After the administration forces regrouped themselves and launched a new campaign in the 1938 session, they were able to prevail upon Congress to enact the second Agricultural Adjustment Act and the Fair Labor Standards Act. In 1939 the Administrative Reorganization Act was passed— together with the Hatch Act, a rebuke to the New Deal aimed at prohibiting Federal office holders below the policy-making level from active participation in politics, a result of allegations of political abuses in WPA ranks during the 1938 elections. When, in August, 1939, the Social Security Act was substantially broadened, it marked the last major legislative accomplishment of the New Deal.[59]

Conservative opposition to Roosevelt was vastly strengthened in the fall of 1937 by the sudden and disastrous collapse of the recovery program. It was a staggering blow to the nation as well as to the self-assurance of the New Dealers. As a Brookings Institution economist put it, the period between September, 1937 and May, 1938 was characterized by "the most rapid . . . shrinkage in business activity which has ever been recorded in the United

States." In October, 1937 the stock market averages fell more than 75 points in a wave of selling that was sickeningly reminiscent of another October eight years before. In less than four months, steel production fell from 80 percent of capacity to less than 20, income payments declined by a billion dollars, and industry profits by 78 percent.[60]

What filled reformers with dismay was the fact that the presumed remedies in the economic system undertaken since 1933 had proved no more effective than the measures of the Hoover administration before them. Moreover, the cause or causes of the collapse were harder to discern. There was no tight money market, no excessively high interest rates, no over-abundance of durable goods on the market. Accusations flew thick and fast, the conservatives blaming the sudden new burden of social security taxes and the rise in labor costs brought on by unionization, while the New Dealers talked darkly of a deliberate conspiracy on the part of capital to discredit the recovery program.

As conditions worsened, the New Deal itself split into two camps over the "recession"—a word selected to avoid the embarrassing suggestion that the Roosevelt administration had become a victim of the same economic forces that had struck Hoover. Morgenthau, convinced that a quickly balanced budget and a disclaimer of government spending would reassure the business community, urged this course upon the President. The larger and steadily increasing opposition, advocating resumption of relief spending and a new program of public works, was led by aggressive liberals like Hopkins and Ickes, Douglas and Jackson. So long as the bottom did not fall out of the economy, Roosevelt was inclined to listen to Morgenthau; after the stock market debacle in October, he swung gradually to the other view.

The result was a final commitment of the administration to a vast increase in deficit spending (or compensatory spending, as the euphemists put it). Where, in the early summer of 1937, the administration was looking to the elimination of the deficit by 1939, the failure of the economy to respond to any other measures at length forced Roosevelt's hand. In the spring of 1938 the President sent a message to Congress recommending doubling of the WPA rolls, appropriating of $3,000,000,000 for relief and recovery programs, and an expansion of RFC loans. In June, a week after it created a joint legislative-executive committee to look into the whole economy, Congress passed the Emergency Relief Appropriation Act.[61]

*   *   *

More than the recession—which, for reasons as obscure as the never-persuasive ones offered for the collapse, ultimately came to an end—the burning question throughout most of 1939 and early 1940 was the Presidential election coming up that fall. Would Roosevelt defy tradition and seek a third term? It was a question of vital concern to all progressives. The political events of the past three years had shown clearly that broad reform measures were meeting increasingly stubborn opposition from the long-tenure con-

servatives in Congress. Without a dynamic progressive in the White House—
and certainly with a reactionary—Congress might well be expected to seek
to turn back the clock. Even the Court was not yet entirely safe—by early
1940 Roosevelt's four appointments had only replaced two conservatives,
the others filling the vacancies created by Cardozo's death and Brandeis'
retirement.

Wherever the President looked, the Democratic party presented a discouraging picture. Vice-President Garner had tacitly lined up with the opposition in the Court fight and had become the logical favorite-son candidate
of the Southern wing. Postmaster General Farley conceived of himself as
the best Cabinet prospect to carry on Roosevelt's policies—but the overwhelming prospect of a Roman Catholic candidate's defeat only added
to the more substantive argument that Farley was not, intellectually or politically, committed to progressivism. Harry Hopkins, whom Roosevelt
regarded as his real ideological heir, lacked both the physical and political
strength for the attempt. Other New Dealers were too esoteric or unknown to
the voting public to be serious prospects.[62]

Overshadowing these considerations was the steadily growing threat
of the Second World War. Throughout the domestic reform program of the
past eight years, the sneers of fascism at the capitalistic system's efforts to
heal itself had provided an ugly obbligato; but far more deadly was the
international prospect which developed when Adolf Hitler finally precipitated all-out aggression on September 1, 1939. Poland had been crushed
in less than a month, Russia had met the Nazi threat by securing its borders
at the expense of Finland and by absorbing the Baltic states; by the spring
of 1940 Denmark and Norway, the Netherlands and Belgium had been over-
run, and by summer the battle of France was over. After ten months of
Blitzkrieg, a tremendous military machine had occupied most of the western
coastline of Europe, confronting the Western Hemisphere beyond the lonely
barrier of Britain.

How, Roosevelt had to ask himself, would another man in the White
House deal with the threat from abroad? Isolationist sentiment was at its
height. In July, as France crumbled and the prospect of a Nazi juggernaut
seizing permanent control of the Continent became starkly real, a congeries of
non-interventionists met in Chicago to form the America First Committee.
Although it included responsible public men and women, it nevertheless
based a fundamental appeal to the lunatic fringe of American society, and
provided grist for the anti-New Deal forces which insisted that there was an
administration conspiracy to take the United States into the war.[63]

An isolationist Congress had already sought to trammel the Executive
Department in its conduct of foreign affairs by enacting the Neutrality Act
of 1937, and while in 1939 the arms embargo in the earlier statute was
repealed, there was still substantial and vocal hostility to official actions in
support of the belligerents. Roosevelt had to act as boldly as the letter of the

law would permit; in June, 1940, when the evacuation of Dunkirk left Britain with a virtually unarmed military force, the President dispatched more than $43,000,000 worth of ships, planes, guns and munitions as the start of a Lend-Lease program that bought time for a slowly rearming America.[64]

Finally, to return to the New Deal reforms of domestic society in the past eight years, there was the question of how they would fare in the event of American involvement in a global war. The liquidation of the New Freedom after 1917, accompanied by the direct attack of a predatory judiciary, was a vivid lesson in recent history. While the leading Presidential prospects of both parties appeared to have a realistic view of the world situation, many of them seemed likely to use war as an excuse for terminating the domestic program. Among the Republicans, there was the brash young Thomas E. Dewey of New York—he "threw his diaper" into the ring, Ickes scornfully remarked—and the conservative Senator Robert A. Taft of Ohio, as well as a politically unknown Indiana-born public utilities lawyer named Wendell Willkie. Everything considered, Frances Perkins concluded, Roosevelt was pushed into a third term decision because there simply was not "any alternative."[65]

*   *   *

For the new constitutional order which had been cultivated in the face of the coming storm, the election of 1940 offered two deeply significant object-lessons. One was that the center of gravity for American liberalism had shifted permanently to the urban areas; while Willkie cut deeply into Roosevelt's 1936 strength, his greatest gains were in the farm belt. The New Deal won in the metropolitan areas; every city of more than 400,000, except Cincinnati, went to the Democratic candidate. Illinois' electoral votes were won by a scant 94,000 plurality, thanks to a 295,000-vote lead in Chicago. The pattern was repeated in Missouri, New York and Wisconsin. The election of 1940, William Allen White concluded, had been a vote between urban and rural political faiths.[66]

More precisely, it was an election decided by the overwhelming preferences of the densely populated and economically rehabilitated ethnic and exploited groups in the cities. "Republican hopes were blocked out in factory smoke," wrote Samuel Lubell. The urban groups, he found in a post-election analysis, "had awakened to the consciousness of the power of their numbers" as well as to the "recognition through patronage, benefits and new opportunities" which had come from the New Deal. Many foreign-born or first-generation voters responded *en masse;* in some Polish-American precincts, the vote for Roosevelt was twenty-five or thirty to one.[67]

Equally important as a lesson from the November returns was the type of campaign that Willkie himself had waged. While it was widely recognized that he was a political amateur who said in straightforward fashion what a professional politician would instinctively phrase more ambivalently, he represented the philosophy of the new conservatism emerging from the depression. Like Dewey in 1944, he would excoriate the New Deal administration but would speak softly about New Deal reforms. Indeed, one of Willkie's major campaign addresses contained specific promises to continue both the National Labor Relations and Fair Labor Standards Acts, to broaden social security, to preserve the gains made in public power and conservation, and to continue rural electrification, commodity loans and crop insurance.[68]

While Willkie did not express the ultimate convictions of die-hard conservatives in the Republican leadership, he had, as one writer said, "speeded the process of making New Deal reforms part of a common heritage which would not be affected by the party in power." For this, the party's Old Guard destroyed him as a serious candidate for 1944; yet, by this very act and the manifest reason for it, the Republicans alerted the country to the prospect that the reforms of the thirties might yet be destroyed. The voter reaction to the threat compelled the conservative party control to pay lip service to the reforms; the Republican platform for 1944 carried a plank endorsing the measures that Willkie had endorsed in 1940.[69]

So at last the new constitutionalism was established, and sheltered against the threats at home and abroad during the four years of global conflict. From fifteen years of depression and war, the United States would emerge a nation in ideology as well as in fact.

PART II

The Decade
of Challenge

But in determining whether a provision of the Constitution applies to a new subject matter, it is of little significance that it is one with which the framers were not familiar.

Harlan F. Stone, C. J., in *United States v. Classic,* 313 U. S. 299, 316 (1941).

Chart II THE STONE AND VINSON COURTS

Years: 1938 · 1939 · 1940 · 1941 · 1942 · 1943 · 1944 · 1945 · 1946 · 1947 · 1948 · 1949 · 1950 · 1951 · 1952 · 1953 · 1954 · 1955 · 1956 · 1957

Presidents: ROOSEVELT · TRUMAN · EISENHOWER

Justices (by seat)

Seat	Justices and states	Notable dates
Chief Justice	HUGHES (R. - N.Y.); STONE (Chief Justice) (R. - N.Y.); VINSON (Chief Justice) (D. - Ky.); WARREN (R. - Calif.)	Jan. 30; Jul. 1; Apr. 12; Jun. 24; Sep. 8; Oct. 5; Jan. 20
2	McREYNOLDS (D. - Tenn.); BYRNES (D. - S.C.); RUTLEDGE (D. - Ky.); MINTON (D. - Ind.)	Jan. 31; Feb. 1; Oct. 3; Feb. 15; Sep. 10; Oct. 12; Oct. 15
3	FRANKFURTER (D. - Mass.)	Jan. 24
4	BLACK (D. - Ala.)	
5	DOUGLAS (D. - Conn.)	
6	BUTLER (D. - Minn.); MURPHY (D. - Mich.); CLARK (D. - Tex.)	Nov. 16; Feb. 5; Jan. 31; Jul. 31; Oct. 1; Feb. 15
7	REED (D. - Ky.)	
8	STONE (R. - N.Y.); ROBERTS (R. - Pa.); JACKSON (D. - N.Y.); HARLAN (R. - N.Y.)	Jan. 20; Oct. 6; Sep. 5; Jul. 31; Oct. 1; Jul. 19; Oct. 8; Mar. 28
9	BURTON (R. - Ohio)	Apr. 17; Oct. 8

Solicitors General

Jackson; *Murphy; Biddle; Fahy; McGrath; Perlman; ‡McGranery; Clark; Brownell; Sobeloff	Jan. 29; Sep. 5; Nov. 15; Oct. 3; Jul. 1; Jan. 31; Aug. 11; Mar. 27; Dec. 2; Jan. 21; Nov. 8; Feb. 24; Mar. 28

*Murphy †Jackson ‡McGranery || Recess appointment, not acted on by Senate; Cummings resigned March 1, 1953. Between Perlman's resignation August 15, 1952, and Cummings' appointment, and from Cummings' resignation until February 24, 1954, the duties of office were performed by First Assistant Solicitor General Robert L. Stern.

§ McGrath resigned October 7, 1946; Assistant Solicitor General G. T. Washington performed the duties of office until July 31, 1947.

The shaded portion represents the high-water mark of New Deal influence on the Court for the end of the Roosevelt and the whole of the Truman Presidencies. Frankfurter, Black, Douglas, Reed and Jackson, together with the two Chief Justices of this period, ensured so firm a majority—enlarged during the brief tenure of Rutledge and the succession of Murphy and Clark to a total of eight of the positions on the bench—that a new division, into schools of activism and restraint, was able to develop in place of the old division between conservatives and liberals on the Hughes Court.

6/Aftermath of Revolution

THE END OF THE 1940 term of Court marked the end of Hughes' Chief Justiceship. At seventy-nine, he could retire with the satisfaction of knowing that he had weathered unprecedented constitutional storms with fair success, whatever tempests might lie ahead. The bitterness of the 1937 fight was past, and between the Court and the White House a genuine cordiality prevailed. After administering the oath of office to Franklin D. Roosevelt for the third time, Hughes jocularly told the President that he had been tempted in the midst of the solemn occasion to protest: "Franklin, don't you think this is getting a trifle monotonous!" On Hughes' birthday on April 11, Roosevelt had sent "affectionate regards & best wishes," and when, two months later, the Chief Justice wrote the President his resignation, Roosevelt received it with genuine distress.[1]

Of all the men who had headed the Court, Charles Evans Hughes had experienced the most variegated challenges both to its own integrity and to the constitutional system under its surveillance. The only man to have served two separate tenures on the bench, Hughes had been regarded in 1910 as a judicial spokesman of the twentieth century reform which had first climaxed under Theodore Roosevelt and was about to reach a second climax under the New Freedom of Woodrow Wilson. Hughes as Associate Justice had supported both state and Federal power in the areas of workmen's compensation, the organizational rights of labor, and the regulation of working hours for women and minors. Had he remained on the bench in 1916—instead of being replaced for too brief a time by John H. Clarke—the progressive minority on the Court in the twenties would have been substantially stronger.

How much the temper of progressives themselves had changed by 1930, when Hoover nominated Hughes for the Chief Justiceship, was manifest in the acrimonious debate over his confirmation. Norris of Nebraska, voicing the old Populist fear of the money power, complained that after leaving the bench to run for the Presidency, Hughes had devoted most of his professional career to representing great corporations before the Court itself. It was inopportune, added Borah of Idaho, to propose such a man, however distinguished, at a time when "coal and iron, oil and gas, and power, light, transportation and transmission have all practically gone into the hands of a very few people." Although Hoover had the party votes to ensure confirmation, the 52-to-26 result encouraged the insurgents to renew their fight—successfully, this time—when the nomination of Judge John J. Parker came to the Hill.[2]

Thus Hughes had assumed the Chief Justiceship harrowed by the increasing sense of disillusionment for the long-venerated economic order of things. The onrushing depression was about to consummate the discrediting of *laissez-faire,* with a totality never conceived in the most impassioned oratory of the Progressive Era. The uncompromising resistance of the *laissez-faire* zealots on his Court was to precipitate the confrontation between the Court and the New Deal. While the clumsy White House effort at curbing the Court was to present Hughes himself with his historic opportunity to reassert, as it had not been done since Marshall's day, the independence of the judicial branch of government, the inevitable result had been to demonstrate beyond all reasonable doubt the commitment of the judicial branch to its role in the policy-shaping process of government.

In the four years since the great Court fight, Hughes had presided at the liquidation of the old *laissez-faire* Court and the old *laissez-faire* constitutionalism. For the Chief Justice himself, it had been a matter of coming back to the persuasions of his early progressivism, and a recognizing of the fact that the New Deal had achieved an economic revolution which was now permanent. Many still decried the fact, but a dwindling number of Americans denied it. "Hughes," wrote the *Nation,* "had the acumen to recognize the inevitable, and that is the larger part of statesmanship."[3]

*   *   *

How completely the past breach had been healed was demonstrated in Roosevelt's invitation to Hughes to call at the White House to discuss the matter of his successor. The President had his own candidate—Attorney General Robert H. Jackson—but he listened as Hughes offered the counterargument for his Associate Justice, Harlan F. Stone. The different preferences were understandable enough; Stone, like Hughes, represented the type of jurist annealed by the experiences of the age of normalcy and the Great Depression. Jackson was the prototype of the new man bred by the depression itself.

The selection of a Chief Justice of the United States always revolved about a number of considerations—predominantly political. If merit and ability were to be the primary criteria, George Washington had been advised in seeking the first Chief Justice, someone other than John Jay ought to be selected—but if politics were the paramount consideration, then no one *but* Jay. John Adams had hastily selected Marshall in order to complete the "Federalizing" of the bench, and Andrew Jackson had elevated Roger B.

Taney to relieve a personality conflict within his Cabinet. Melville Fuller had won confirmation over protests of "cronyism" in his close political identity with Grover Cleveland. And while William Howard Taft had been selected virtually by Republican popular demand, Hughes' own confirmation had been the target of furious progressive criticism.[4]

It was a truism of history, of course, that many Associate Justices had been the intellectual peers or superiors of most of the Chiefs—from Joseph Story to Oliver Wendell Holmes and Felix Frankfurter. Nevertheless, as administrative head of the Court (and, after Taft's lobbying from the bench for the law creating the Judicial Conference of the United States, head of the whole Federal judicial system) the Chief Justice represented a Presidential appointment of lasting influence. Most Presidents in the course of their administrations had been able to appoint one or more Associate Justices; up to now, there had been only eleven occasions to fill the post of Chief Justice.*[5]

Whether these considerations weighed very heavily with Roosevelt neither Hughes nor Frankfurter, who were summoned to counsel him on the appointment, was afterwards disposed to say. To both, the President made clear his strong desire to see Jackson on the bench, and preferably in the center chair. Neither Hughes nor Frankfurter disputed Jackson's ability— indeed, he was regarded by a vocal number of professionals as one of the most gifted lawyers in the history of the Justice Department. Frankfurter, whom Roosevelt invited to the White House on Hughes' suggestion, confessed that on personal grounds he also would prefer Jackson. But overriding considerations, Frankfurter declared, favored Stone: he had proved his abilities as a jurist during nearly fifteen years on the Court, he was a moderate and creative constitutional thinker—and, what was of increasing importance in the face of approaching conflict with the Nazi war machine, the appointment of a Republican to the Chief's chair would contribute to much-needed national unity.[6]

The President, almost apologetically, told his Attorney General that the choice would have to go to Stone. Jackson professed to concur in the decision; at least, with Stone's advancement to Hughes' chair Jackson was able to fill the vacant Associate's seat. As it turned out, Roosevelt was able to touch all political bases on Court matters by nominating, at the same time, Senator James F. Byrnes of South Carolina to fill the long-empty chair of McReynolds, who had retired the previous February. With a Republican Chief Justice, a New Dealer and a conservative Democrat to bring the Court back up to full strength, Roosevelt's reshaping of the judiciary was thus virtually completed.

---

*Of these, Washington nominated three—Jay, John Rutledge (whose appointment the Senate refused to confirm), and Oliver Ellsworth. John Adams appointed Marshall, Jackson appointed Roger B. Taney, Lincoln appointed Salmon P. Chase, Grant appointed Morrison R. Waite. The modern appointments are described in the two volumes of the present study.

The Roosevelt-era Court had, indeed, been rounded out by a series of domestic and international events of magnitude. The 1938 mid-term elections, defeating several New Dealers and conspicuously returning Congressmen whom the President had sought to purge, were an unmistakable sign of resurgent conservatism. Roosevelt had recognized it clearly enough, for his 1939 message to the opening of Congress had contained no proposals for bold new legislative attacks on social or economic ills. Correlatively, the growing menace of the militant fascists in Europe and Asia diverted public attention from local reforms and filled the nation with a sense of common peril. Finally, the fact that the Supreme Court had become firmly committed to a broadened view of governmental powers—had, indeed, saved the New Deal after Congress had declared its independence of the White House— persuaded Roosevelt and most of the liberals that the issue of the judiciary had finally been settled.

*   *   *

"Last week," observed *Time* after the announcement of Stone's appointment, "the U. S. realized how much it liked the idea of a solid man to follow Charles Evans Hughes. And solid is the word for Chief Justice Stone—200 lb. with heavy, good-natured features and a benign judicial air."[7] The comment was typical of the general approval expressed by periodicals and professional journals. As the second man to have been advanced from the bench to the presiding chair,* Roosevelt's choice was considered to be superior to Taft's advancement of Edward D. White. The fact was that there was something of the same logic in both courses of action: aside from the political effect of choosing a member of the opposite party, both Presidents had been persuaded that the choice was the best means of ensuring continuity in the current jurisprudence of the bench, by capitalizing upon an insider's familiarity with procedures and personalities.

Stone, the moderate liberal, and Roberts, the ambivalent, were now the last remnants of the pre-1937 Court. Seven new men in the short space of four years—with a change in administrative emphases as well, with Stone's elevation—had altered the bench as much as the reversals of former constitutional positions. After 1941, the Court was to deal with the fundamental problem of what its own role was to be, and what the new constitutional fabric was to be. One Washington observer discerned this fact clearly at the end of Stone's first term. The bench, he wrote, was dividing itself once more into liberals and conservatives. "The core of the new liberal minority are Black and Douglas; of the new conservative majority, Roberts and Byrnes, neither New Dealers. While the others remain more difficult to predict, Murphy tends toward the liberals, Reed, Jackson and Frankfurter toward the conservatives. . . . The most interesting tendency to be noted is the steady movement of Justice Frankfurter to the right."[8]

---

*Hughes' appointment as Chief Justice, fourteen years after his resignation as Associate Justice, is hardly analogous.

The ideological terms were relative; they had littl[e]
the liberal-conservative dichotomy of 1937, and the fa[
]stitutionalism which had crystallized at the beginning o[f
]ing to such a division in itself attested to the fact that a[
]new frame of reference was being phrased. In point of[
]Frankfurter who provided the two poles of thought w...
the legislative crusader, zealous to give the expressions of Con[g]
broadest judicial construction, and Frankfurter, the academician, demanding
that Congress rather than the Court determine how broad the effect of its
own acts should be. Both were committed to an affirmative role of government
in the regulating of modern economic processes, so that in this they were both
utterly removed from the inertial concept of government functions under the
constitutionalism of *laissez-faire*.[9]

Aside from this, the encomia for the retired Hughes, revolving about
his judicial statesmanship in steadying the helm during the stormy passage from
reaction to modern progressivism, tacitly endorsed the assumption that his
successor would follow the same course. From personal conviction as well
as from a sense of moral obligation, Stone acknowledged his intention to
adhere to the "historic shift of emphasis in constitutional interpretation."[10]
Indeed, the nature of his own matured persuasion had been clearly delineated
in his opinion in *United States v. Darby*. Addressing himself to the status of
the Tenth Amendment, which had become a sentimental refuge for states'
rightists in the progressive development of the new constitutionalism, he had
declared:

> The Amendment states but a truism that all is retained which has not
> been surrendered. There is nothing in the history of its adoption to
> suggest that it was more than declaratory of the relationship between
> the national and state governments as it had been established by the
> Constitution before the Amendment or that its purpose was other than
> to allay fears that the new national government might seek to exercise
> powers not granted, and that the states might not be able to exercise fully
> their reserved powers. . . .
>
> From the beginning and for many years the Amendment has been
> construed as not depriving the national government of authority to
> resort to all means for the exercise of a granted power which are ap-
> propriate and plainly adapted to the permitted ends.[11]

*   *   *

With seven New Deal appointees on a Court presided over by a Chief
Justice of such a turn of mind, it appeared that the equanimity which had
developed in the last four years under Hughes would continue in course.
The turbulent record which in fact the Stone Court was to compile not
only astonished the country but demonstrated beyond any doubt that the
appointees were no one's rubber stamps. As one commentator put it, the
Court "had much young blood and few hardened legal arteries."[12]

The complete disinclination of his colleagues to settle into harness may
well have surprised the new Chief Justice. While he repeatedly protested his

ect for dissent and persuasive argumentation of opposing views, he could
t have been prepared for the release of energy kept in check to the end of
Hughes' administration. While the conflicts of personal and jurisprudential
beliefs had already been implanted with the appointments of men like Black,
Frankfurter, Douglas and Jackson, the crisis of the judiciary fight of 1937 and
the arduous responsibility of making an intellectual about-face without losing
face had submerged the major differences between the Justices. As a veteran
of that transition himself, Stone had a right to assume that his Associates
would continue in their prior attitudes; immediately upon the announcement
of his appointment, the *United States News* confidently declared that he would
"find no sharp divergence of opinion among his colleagues."[13]

For a variety of reasons, Stone's Court was in fact to contrast dramatically
with the administrations which preceded and followed it. There was the manifest incompatibility of specific individuals among the new Justices which
could not be indefinitely played down. There was the extraordinary impact
of the Second World War, which fell upon the nation within six months of
Stone's advancement; not only did all-out conflict present the Court with a
torrent of urgent constitutional issues, but in three specific instances the war
disrupted the Court's work by removing members on whom the Chief Justice
had expected to rely. Thus, early in 1942, Roberts was called away to participate in the inquiry over the Pearl Harbor debacle and a few months later
Byrnes resigned to take an assignment of long-range economic planning for
the war period. At the end of the conflict, in 1945, Jackson would be borrowed from the bench to prosecute the war crimes trials in Nuremberg.

Added to these factors was the lack of rapport with the White House
on the part of the Chief Justice at the same time that several of his Associates
continued to enjoy warm relations with the President. Stone's contacts with
Roosevelt had never been particularly close. He resented a compromising
situation in which the President had placed him and Frankfurter in 1939,
when a news item obviously "leaked" from the White House implied that
Roosevelt had sought their advice on ignoring statutory prohibitions against
budgetary deficits. Murphy's surprise decision to accept a military commission
while remaining on the Court—an act as quixotic as it was patriotic—was
manifestly encouraged by and known to the President while it had remained
a secret to the Chief Justice. A few months after Murphy's arrangement to
serve with the armed forces during Court recess, Stone was irritated by
another Presidential effort to involve him in what he regarded as essentially
a political affair—heading a commission to evaluate the conflicting plans for
synthetic rubber production.

Not that the new Chief was above occasional "leaks" and news "plants"
himself. During the Court fight of 1937 he had hinted to administration
sources that some resignations were in prospect which in all likelihood would
solve Roosevelt's Court problem. He had not been impressed with Black,
the first New Deal Justice, and had passed along comments "not for attribu-

tion" suggesting that the appointee was a politician in judicial clothing. He was also the butt of malicious stories by Roosevelt-haters, particularly one that had it that the President, as a law student at Columbia, had failed a course in constitutional law taught by Stone as professor.[14]

Another, though minor, vexing matter was the recurring rumor that Stone would remain in the Chief Justiceship only briefly; in the summers of 1942 and 1943 there were flurries of unconfirmed stories that he would soon be stepping down to make room at the top for Justice Jackson. While these were annoying, the chief disturbing element in them was the manifest maneuvering of the old-line New Dealers to "get" the remaining members of the "nine old men." For the most ardent of the surviving progressives of the 1930's, Stone's liberalism was much too pedestrian, and his disposition to let discussion drag on interminably, both in conferences and on the bench, was to invite a situation where, in Jonathan Daniels' phrase, "antagonism sharpened in exasperation."[15]

As a matter of fact, since his first coming onto the bench Stone had been at work seeking to extend to constitutional law in general the "rule of reason" which White and Holmes had developed with reference to the anti-trust cases of the previous generation. In 1927 he had dissented from a majority finding that a Pennsylvania license fee on travel agencies was a "direct" burden on interstate commerce. The fairer test, he argued, was not whether the burden was direct but whether it was reasonable or unreasonable. Ten years later he had won the majority to his view, and wrote the Court opinion upholding a South Carolina highway regulation imposing weight limits on interstate truck- ing. The "unreasonable" burden on interstate commerce he identified in 1945 in an Arizona law fixing the limit on the number of cars to be hauled on interstate trains passing through the state.[16]

*   *   *

Stone's approach to constitutional change, however, was the approach of Holmes and Hughes—skeptical and moderate rather than activist and affirmative—and in the context of law and government which had evolved in the New Deal this approach seemed old-fashioned at best. For the New Deal had accelerated two trends in law and government which substantially altered the frame of reference for judicial review. One was the vast expansion of administrative regulatory activity under the agencies which implemented the proliferating statutory programs; the other was the equally vast expansion of the use of the Presidential executive order to create, revise and reorient many government activities under color of a general grant of authority from Congress.

This had been the point of major concern for the old Court in the *"Hot Oil"* case: while the constitutionality of the legislative delegation of power to a non-legislative agency had been tacitly recognized since the first judicial test of the Interstate Commerce Commission Act, the Court ultimately came, in the first New Deal reform statutes, to the question of the adequacy of safe-

guards in the legislative delegation. Committed to the proposition that delegation could not be a wholesale transfer of the legislative function to an executive
branch, the older Hughes Court had proceeded to strike down all such delegations it encountered in the first New Deal laws. When Congress subsequently
built in what were considered to be adequate checkreins or guidelines, the
Court persuaded itself that the delegation was constitutional.*

The problem of the administrative process had been agitating the legal
conservatives since the days of the New Freedom. In 1932, before the New
Deal had begun to take recognizable form, former Solicitor General Beck
had written a book, *Our Wonderland of Bureaucracy,* in which he decried
the proliferation of regulatory boards in the past decade. For the American
Bar Association's Special Committee on Administrative Law, however, the
danger point had been exceeded after March 4, 1933; in the next fifteen
months, it reported at the association's meeting in the summer of 1934, the
Chief Executive had issued six times as many executive orders as during the
period 1862-1900, and 10 percent of all that were known to have been
issued in the nation's history, while the "legislation" formulated by the National
Recovery Administration it declared would have filled ten thousand pages.[17]

At the same meeting the special assistant to the Attorney General, Carl
McFarlane, suggested that the sudden spurt in administrative agency development might well be "a belated recognition of the true functions of government,"
but it remained for James M. Landis, in the 1938 Storrs Lectures at Yale, to
document the case for the fundamental shift in law and procedure which had
resulted from this development. The administrative process, he declared,
sprang "from the inadequacy of a simple tripartite form of government to
deal with modern problems," and in the economic breakdown of the thirties
the agencies had emerged as an expression of government's concern for "the
public well-being of . . . industry." The fundamental difference under the
New Deal, Landis concluded, was that the administrative agency took as its
responsibility not merely the policing of specific industrial acts but a surveillance of the entire sector of the economy with which the acts dealt.[18]

Once having proposed a principle of validly delegated legislative power
to non-legislative branches of government, the reconstituted Court had found
few occasions to suggest that in either executive orders or administrative
regulations these branches had exceeded the limits of the Constitution. The
result—over a steady rumble of conservative protest—was the swift expansion
of affirmative powers by the Presidency and the administrative agencies and
the coming into being of what would henceforth be called "the positive state."
Its emergence had been certified by Hughes himself, in *West Coast Hotel Co. v.
Parrish,* when he declared that constitutional liberty "is liberty in a social organization which requires the protection of law against the evils which menace
the . . . welfare of the people."[19]

---

*See Ch. 5 and the note in Appendix E.

This altered concept of government—the affirmative duty to devise and administer regulations of social and economic conduct in the large interests of society—was the aftermath of the revolution of 1937-41, with which Stone's Chief Justiceship was to deal. So fundamental a change in American political theory inevitably required that most if not all of the constitutional propositions of the past be reconsidered and restated. That process in itself was an invitation to heated dialogue which became the most conspicuous feature of the Stone Court.

*   *   *

Viewed from the perspective of an ascendant nationalism established in the jurisprudence of 1937-41, the Court over which Stone had assumed administration looked distinctly different from the aspect it had presented in the introverted political economy of the depression. Black, the first of the Roosevelt appointees, had from the outset been the tradition flouter, dissenting a record number of times in his first term of Court and voicing the New Deal political credo so precisely that it was at first rumored that his opinions were actually being written by Thomas G. Corcoran. His years in Congress inclined him naturally to the concept he steadily developed: broad attribution of legislative intent in statutory construction. His ardent progressivism prompted him from the outset to challenge all long-established rules of economic jurisprudence.[20]

In his first term, Black had excoriated the judicial standard for utility rate-making—"reproduction cost, new"—which had been devised in 1898; the fiction that a corporation was a "person" within the meaning of the Fourteenth Amendment, suggested by Roscoe Conkling in 1882 and accepted by the Court from 1886; and the proposition that a Federal common law existed outside the common law of the individual states, a tenet set out by Joseph Story in 1842.[21] Brash though the protests seemed, the rate-making rule had been modified in favor of Brandeis' long-urged "prudent investment" test by the spring of 1944; the case of *Erie Railroad v. Tompkins* had overthrown Story's doctrine by the fall of 1938, while the convenient corporation loophole had become well policed if not plugged.[22] Aggressive in manner and scathing in language, Black had been "unsettling the law" since he had come onto the bench. It sometimes seemed, as one observer wrote, that he sought "to wrest domination by sheer shock of insolence toward his brethren, not excepting the Chief Justice."[23]

When Felix Frankfurter had joined the Court, the stage was set for the clash of ideas and personalities which would come into the open during Stone's administration. Reactionary commentators had labeled the Harvard professor the Machiavelli or the Iago of the New Deal; proper Bostonians were as outraged at his appointment as they had been with that of Brandeis three decades before. But by the time Stone became Chief Justice, Frankfurter was being cast in the role of a conservative by virtue of his function as a counterweight to Black's hyperactivism. In truth, observed Fred Rodell of

Yale, Frankfurter's conservatism was relative; having come onto the Court with a definite concept of what the judicial function should be, he remained consistent in his position while subsequent appointments like those of Douglas and Murphy had lined up support for Black's position to the left of him.

The activist New Dealers on the Court thus "kept pushing ahead of [Frankfurter] in their approach to new problems, whereas Frankfurter merely wanted to take the protests of Justices Holmes and Brandeis against decisions of the past, turn them into the law of the present, and then call it a day."[24] Discursive in his thinking and writing, at the same time that he was deliberate in his application of orthodox constitutional doctrine, Frankfurter invited critical reaction almost as naturally as did Black. Indeed, the first sign of friction appeared very soon after he came onto the Court, when the man who had written the definitive book on the labor injunction upheld an injunction in a Chicago strike because of evidence of past acts of violence by individual members of the union concerned. Both Black and Reed in dissents castigated the opinion as a flagrant disregard for the guarantees of free speech.[25]

Douglas took occasion to criticize another Frankfurter opinion which limited some of the procedures of the Federal Trade Commission, quoting diametrically opposite reasoning from earlier writings by the Harvard law professor. Before the end of the Hughes Court, it was said, at least six Justices—Black, Douglas, Murphy, Reed, Roberts and Stone—had been moved to record critical dissents from one or another of Frankfurter's views.[26]

Thus the seeds of discord had been planted and nurtured for several terms before Stone assumed the administration of the Court. The truth was that, from a long-term view, Roosevelt had followed no consistent policy in selecting his Justices. They had, through 1941, been chosen from a combination of short-term ideological and political expediencies. Indeed, the appointees' continued appetite for political action was blamed for the antics which brought the Stone Court into such a parlous public image. Byrnes, who chafed the most for the field of public affairs, stayed the shortest time; "Felix Frankfurter . . . made no bones about his coziness with the White House in the Roosevelt days. Jackson hoped for a bigger political plum"—as did Douglas—while "Black made speeches before the National Citizens' Political Action Committee. Justice Murphy was the most indefatigable cocktail-partier in the capital (where cocktails are invariably spiced with political dope)."[27]

*   *   *

All of the Justices, indeed, had contributed to the tensions which had built up by 1941. Stone had clearly been the source of the inside information which had provided several critical articles on Black's erratic behavior in 1938. The vehemence of the criticism and the needless harshness of the description of the Alabaman's shortcomings—"lack of legal knowledge and experience, deficiencies in background and training"—could not but leave deep scars on the memory. Stone had greeted the second Roosevelt appointment with considerable relief; Reed, an adroit advocate and a lawyer instinctively respectful of precedent, promised to be a steadying force. Then had come Stone's most profitable contact with the White House, when the President, at the instigation of a mutual friend, had sent for him to seek advice on Cardozo's replacement. Stone had heartily endorsed Frankfurter.[28]

Yet within the 1938 term, all three of the New Deal appointees had taken a series of pot-shots at each other, and Frankfurter had been an occasional source of irritation. Urbane and personable in most circumstances, the Harvard savant could betray flashes of intellectual arrogance in the heat of argument, and was given at times to lecturing his colleagues as if they were still students. As for Douglas, who in fact had been a student of Stone's at Columbia, the future Chief Justice approved of his competence demonstrated in a variety of New Deal positions, although he confided to a member of the bar, Charles C. Burlingham, that he wished Douglas had been "seasoned in active practice a little more."[29]

Douglas bolstered the wing of the new Court created by Black; his appeal, wrote Arthur Schlesinger, Jr., was to the " 'hardboiled' liberals who propose to escape the usual sense of liberal futility by concentrating on results at the expense of scruples." He was followed onto the bench by Murphy of Michigan, who had a passionate concern with the advancement of every type of civil liberty; but Murphy's chafing eagerness to be at the center of the action in the war program kept him plaguing the White House for special assignments while it diminished his usefulness and availability for the continuing business of the Court.[30]

There was, finally, Roberts. With Stone, the only survivor of the turbulence of the mid-thirties, he could still be looked to as "the chief expostulator against change." Yet he did not represent a rallying point for intellectual counter-insurgency, for he had "abandoned most of his former restricted view of the constitutional scope of the national power." Thus, on the eve of his Chief Justiceship, Stone had a fair, close-at-hand knowledge of the qualities of most of his colleagues. As for the two newcomers who were appointed at the time of his advancement, he had an enthusiastic opinion of the retiring Attorney General's abilities while Byrnes he knew chiefly as being Roosevelt's most recent trouble-shooter in the Senate.[31]

As for Stone himself, he had instincts which inclined him alternately to the Black-Douglas and then to the Frankfurter-Jackson poles of thought. Self-restraint was for him a cardinal judicial virtue, and in this he was sympathetic with Frankfurter's general rule of Court conduct. Yet he was emphatic in his conviction that the legislature should be given the widest constitutional latitude in exercising its lawmaking powers, and here he was closer to Black's persuasion. Like virtually all of the Court, Stone was intellectually committed to the necessity of a broadly defined authority for government in general and national government in particular, but he was not disposed to seek to reduce the divergences of individual views in the matter to something of an institutional commitment. Years before, Taft had sensed Stone's administrative weakness; he lacked the capacity, Taft told Hoover, for "massing the Court" so that its collective voice would be unequivocal.[32]

Thus for various reasons—the relaxed tensions after the internecine struggle and subsequent reorientation of the Hughes regime, the succession of intellectual shocks created by wartime developments, the juxtaposition of a number of able and aggressive men (specifically, Black, Douglas, Frankfurter and Jackson) each determined to endow the new constitutionalism with his own concept of the *Zeitgeist*—the Stone Court was predestined to be a jurisprudential congeries. A leading Washington observer remarked: "Once it was feared that the eight Roosevelt-appointed Justices might act as a unified bloc. Now they are castigated for making a sort of judicial hash of the law." *Time* put it more extremely; it had become "the most divided Court in U. S. history—and for that reason, one with little prestige."[33]

*   *   *

Dissents, if not dissension, were conspicuous in the first two terms under Stone. Thomas Reed Powell of Harvard and C Herman Pritchett of Chicago both noted that from the fall of 1941 to the spring of 1943, Black dissented forty-six times and Frankfurter forty. In most of the cases, Douglas and Murphy joined with Black, while Jackson, Reed, Roberts or Stone joined with Frankfurter. Yet dissents were often hardly distinguishable from the welter of concurring opinions; here the inclination of the members of the Court to come to the same general conclusion while splitting two or three ways on the rationale of the case, created an uproar in the legal world. In a profession where the literal outcome of a case is often of secondary significance while the reasoning behind the decision is the guideline to the subsequent course of the law, the continual changing of judicial minds left precedents in chaos.

On a judicial "Black Monday"—January 3, 1944—the lid blew off the bubbling cauldron. A gaggle of fourteen cases inspired more than thirty separate opinions, most of them concurring in the results but flying into a variety of reasons for concurrence. In one remarkable case in which Douglas, for the five members of the Court who joined with him, upheld a Federal Power Commission ruling on utility rates, Frankfurter wrote a dissent substantially longer than the Court opinion; thereupon, Black and Murphy, concurring in the Douglas holding, wrote what was frankly described as a criticism of the "wholly gratuitous assertion as to constitutional law in the dissent of Mr. Justice Frankfurter." Frankfurter had charged the Court with flouting the prior rule on rate making established within the due process concept of the Taft Court. Black protested that this "highly controversial due process doctrine" had not been accepted by Congress and that "we feel compelled to say that we do not understand that Congress voluntarily has acquiesced in a constitutional principle of government that courts, rather than legislative bodies, possess final authority over regulation of economic affairs."[34]

On scrutiny, Black's dissent from Frankfurter's dissent was essentially a reiteration of his own familiar insistence upon judicial accommodation of legislative prerogative. But his real concern was with Frankfurter's often abstruse approach to the issue of the case; on the heels of the *Hope Gas Company* case, Black dissented even more vigorously from a Frankfurter dissent in a patent decision. Responding to Douglas' majority holding that one who sells unpatented devices for use in a patented combination is not liable as a contributory infringer of the patent, Frankfurter observed that "the doctrine of contributory infringement is an expression both of law and morals." With a Holmesian flourish, Frankfurter conceded that the validity of the doctrine was not before the Court but added that "litigants and lower courts ought not to be embarrassed by gratuitous innuendoes against a principle of the law which, within its proper bounds, is accredited by legal history as well as ethics."[35]

Black's "disagreement with this dissenting opinion," he wrote, "runs much deeper than the mere question of whether the Court has here discussed the so-called formula of contributory infringement at an improper or inopportune time. It seems to me that the judicial error of discussing abstract questions is slight compared to the error of interpreting legislative enactments on the basis of a court's preconceived views on 'morals' and 'ethics.' " He concluded his condemnation by observing: "It has long been recognized that a socially undesirable practice may seek acceptance under the guise of conventional moral symbols. And repeated judicial assertion that a bad practice is hallowed by morals may, if unchallenged, help it to receive the acceptance which it seeks." He was impelled to write the concurring opinion, Black said, "in order that silence may not be understood as acquiescence in the views expressed in the dissenting opinion of Mr. Justice Frankfurter."[36]

The emphatic identification of the Associate with whom they disagreed was not unprecedented, but the language Black chose and Murphy supported in denouncing the Frankfurter commentaries added substantially to the concern of the profession. An experienced member of the Supreme Court bar—Stone apparently had little trouble in confirming that it was Burlingham—wrote to the *New York Herald-Tribune* that "a growing tendency to disagree" was undermining public confidence. "One of the least desirable practices that has grown up in the Supreme Court in recent years," Burlingham continued, "is the concurring opinion in which a Justice who agrees with the decision but is dissatisfied with the language of the opinion or its implications insists on expressing himself in his own words." When the concurring opinion proceeds to a direct attack upon the opinion of another member of the bench, the writer warned, it was a "breach of judicial propriety . . . in violation of the high tradition and dignity of the Court."[37]

*   *   *

Before the month was out, Roberts struck back at the activists, with Frankfurter joining in his protest. Where Black and Douglas had criticized the gratuitous introduction of philosophical ruminations, and Burlingham had decried the multiplicity of concurring opinions which diluted the effect of majority opinions, Roberts protested against the "tendency to disregard precedents" which had "become so strong in this Court of late as, in my view, to shake confidence in the consistency of decision and leave the courts below on an uncharted sea of doubt and difficulty without any confidence that what was said yesterday will hold good tomorrow, unless indeed a modern instance grows into a custom of members of this Court to make public announcement of a change of views and to indicate that they will change their votes on the same question when another case comes before the Court."[38]

The sarcasm of the last phrase in his statement was directed at those who, having upheld certain restrictive state laws in two recent cases, had reversed themselves in a subsequent case after a public expression of error. The problem was one of the most fundamental gravity, Roberts declared. "Counsel and parties will bring and prosecute actions . . . on the not improbable chance that the asserted rule will be thrown overboard. Defendants will not know whether to litigate or settle for they will have no assurance that a declared rule will be followed. But the more deplorable consequence will be that the administration of justice will fall into disrepute. Respect for tribunals must fall when the bar and the public come to understand that nothing that has been said in prior adjudication has force in a current controversy."[39]

Roberts' outburst followed by a few weeks a dissent by Frankfurter directed at a doctrine of the majority opinion by Douglas which Frankfurter criticized as "a wholly novel doctrine of constitutional law" which should not "be resorted to gratuitously."[40] The continuing crossfire between members of the Court, wrote a correspondent in the *New York Times*, represented "a carefully measured criticism, motivated by an unconcealed impatience or anger."[41] He could have pointed, on March 6, to a dissent written by Jackson in which Frankfurter, Reed and Roberts joined, in which the majority opinion by Douglas was condemned with renewed fervor: "The Court is not enforcing a policy of Congress; it is competing with Congress in creating new regulations in . . . a field peculiarly within legislative rather than judicial competence."[42]

Although conservatives throughout the profession reacted to the judicial turmoil precipitated by the New Dealers with an "I told you so" attitude, they could not stop there. At its 1944 meeting the Texas State Bar Association formally endorsed a resolution warning that "the Supreme Court of the United States is losing, if it has not already lost, the high esteem in which it has been held by the people," based on the belief that "it had always remained free of political, personal and unworthy motives." Noting that the Court had lately "repeatedly overruled decisions, precedents and landmarks of the law, of long standing, without assigning any valid reason therefor, . . . or basing its decision on casuistry and sophistry rather than logic," the Texas lawyers concluded that the Court "has subjected itself to the suspicion, widely held, that it speaks, or undertakes to speak, in the voice of the appointing power, rather than the voice of the law."[43]

In their eagerness to denigrate the New Deal itself, spokesmen of the Texas and American Bar Associations overstated their case; on questions of newly recognized authority in government to legislate on any issues of national concern, there was no division on the Court. Yet to the extent that the new constitutionalism had made room for itself by overthrowing ancient propositions which had drawn their strength from the old *laissez-faire* mentality, the conservatives of the bar were merely repeating the arguments of 1937. This did not minimize the fact, however, that the language of the bar toward the judiciary, as Kenneth C. Sears of the University of Chicago observed, was "highly uncomplimentary, not to say insulting."[44]

* * *

The view of outsiders in which the Court appeared to have become an armed camp turned against itself tended to be oversensationalized. The conflicts, wrote Max Lerner, were between men who "share many common basic premises which the members of the Court did not share ten years ago." The matter went back to the fact that in 1937 the Court and the Constitution had undergone a total reversal of attitudes and thrusts; the remaining years under Hughes had confirmed the new orientation—and the five years under Stone were the years in which a new body of interpretation was replacing the precedents upon which the old legality had rested. The period of time was highly concentrated, and thus added to the impression of erratic dialectic; it was easy to forget that the constitutional law of the old legality had been hammered out in the same manner but over a much longer period of time.[45]

On reflection, the Chief Justice could consider that most of his Associates were conducting their dispute on a reasonably high plane. Black might be sarcastic and over-aggressive, but he and Frankfurter at least spoke to each other in private. Douglas and Stone continued a personal friendship that dated from Douglas' first coming to Washington. Reed and Rutledge were both kindly in nature, and when in disagreement would never consider resorting to invective. Even Murphy, who tended to be self-righteous in his liberalism, left the main contentions to his colleagues in the activist bloc.[46]

This left—rather conspicuously—Roberts and Jackson as the chief provocateurs. Roberts, who had vacillated throughout so much of his tenure on the Court, had now settled down into a position of protest substantially to the right of everyone else. His outburst of criticism in the winter of 1944 had grown into a torrent of objections that was recorded in fifty-three dissents in the term ending in June, 1945. With the final effort, Hoover's appointee wound up his fifteen years and submitted his resignation: how bitterly his final barbs had been resented by his brethren became apparent when the Chief Justice sought to discharge the amenities of farewell. Stone drafted a letter which was hardly remarkable for its cordiality, and circulated it to his other members of the Court; Black objected to language which he considered too generous, and prepared his own draft at Stone's suggestion. After an embarrassing number of weeks passed without agreement, no letter was ever sent.[47]

Roberts, in a sense, was a whipping boy for both elements on the bench. Black declined to express a "sense of regret" at the Justice's departure because he felt nothing of the sort, while Frankfurter and Jackson contended that a mild tribute to Roberts' "fidelity to principle" was the least that could be said in recognition of his departure. It had been Roberts' misfortune to have remained on the bench too long; a retirement with Hughes in 1941 would have ended his career on a note of reasonable accommodation of the new jurisprudential climate. As it was, Roberts was driven back toward his old convictions by the vehemence of Black's judicial radicalism, while the subtleties of Frankfurter's argumentation did not equip him to deal on equal terms with others in the intellectual mélée of Stone's Court. The equivocal position of the rest of the Court on the fact of his departure was, in a sense, a reflection of the equivocal nature of Roberts' own constitutional position.[48]

In the final analysis, Roberts' handicap as a constitutional lawgiver was his inability to break with the past while entertaining a sympathy for the arguments favoring change. He spent his time on the Court seeking for a firm continuity from the old legality to the new, never understanding how the revolution of 1933-37 had destroyed the possibility of continuity. His theory of a constitutional yardstick against which to measure the validity of any constitutional issue was totally unreal; such a standard of measure was invariably subjective, and the subjectivity in the long run was not that of an individual jurist but of the collective mentality of the age. He ultimately accepted Hughes' commitment to the new order, but largely on faith; he was completely lost in the alternating hypotheses of Stone's Court.

With the resignation of Roberts, Jackson was to provide the final and most spectacular pyrotechnics of the five years of Stone's administration; mercifully for Stone himself, he had died before the explosion occurred.*

*   *   *

The Roberts vacancy introduced a new element into the Court's evolution; after eight years in which Roosevelt had made his historic number of appointments, a new President now had the responsibility of nomination. Would Harry S Truman's selection amount to a terminating of the New Deal process, by placing on the Court a more conventional, even pedestrian intellect to dampen the volatile elements that Roosevelt had set in motion?

*See Ch. 8.

Truman, only recently settled into his job, knew little about the current members of the Court, except that the restless political instincts of men like Douglas and Jackson had thrust them into the power struggle that had punctuated the fourth term maneuvers of 1944.

Truman had been used by Roosevelt to make the national Democratic ticket more acceptable to all elements in the party in 1944, as Roosevelt had used Henry Wallace four years earlier to stifle the conservative rebellion which had begun to take shape around Garner. But Wallace had been denominated Roosevelt's "personal" choice in 1944 at the same time that Truman—who was not even aware of the plan until the convention was in session—was simply the "official" choice. He had not even served as Vice-President long enough to be briefed on such vital national matters as the atomic bomb or the long-range plans for postwar policy. In addition, he was beset with the problem of finding replacements for a number of key administrative positions as Roosevelt appointees now began to drift away.[49]

The veteran New Dealers who stayed on in White House circles were anxious to encourage the new President to continue the Roosevelt pattern of selecting proved liberals—which was tantamount to naming Democrats as well. In an undated memorandum prepared for Truman's background information, it was argued that historically "Presidents have almost invariably let the swing of the election returns control judicial appointments and have made no attempt to balance the Court by crossing party lines in making appointments." Still more important, the memorandum conceded, was "a judge's liberalism or conservatism."[50]

Since Truman's personal experience was in the Senate—his national reputation, indeed, had grown out of the circumspect conduct of his committee investigating wartime contracts—it was from the Senate that he made his choice. Harold H. Burton, an Ohio Republican and close friend from committee days, thus was taken to represent the type of jurist to be sought by the new administration. A circumspect lawyer like Reed, Burton would definitely not "enlarge the 'advanced' wing of the Court," although some observers described him as "a nonpartisan, but noncrusading, progressive in action." In any event, it seemed clear that the President's intention was to try to bank the fires of controversy, and the subsequent judicial appointments of the Truman administration were to support this effort.[51]

Stone commented on Burton that he was "a very agreeable person, and I believe will be a good man." However, the Chief Justice would end his term without having been consulted by the White House on either of the appointments made after his own advancement to the presiding chair. Rutledge, who replaced Byrnes, had been even less known to Stone than Burton; indeed, Rutledge had been selected largely on the recommendation of Frankfurter and Irving Brant of the *St. Louis Star-Times*. Stone never enjoyed the confidential relations with the White House that Taft had experienced with Harding or Hughes with Roosevelt.[52]

*   *   *

On April 22, 1946 Justice Douglas for a five-to-three majority—Jackson having been absent in Nuremberg for the term—delivered an opinion overruling three earlier cases which had stood for the rule that an alien who refused to bear arms could not be naturalized. To the argument that, even though overruled, the principle in these cases had been adopted by Congress, Douglas replied: "The silence of Congress and its inaction are as consistent with a desire to leave the problem fluid as they are with an adoption by silence of the rule of those cases." Although Stone, as an Associate Justice, had dissented in the earlier cases, he now dissented from the opinion overruling them. Persuaded, as Douglas was not, that Congress had indeed adopted the rule of the earlier cases, the Chief Justice considered that the Court was bound by a legislative policy decision rather than by its own early adjudication. His closing words were characteristic of his credo: "It is not the function of this Court to disregard the will of Congress in the exercise of its constitutional power."[53]

With this statement, Stone's voice faltered. Black and Reed, the senior members of the bench on his right and left hand, who had anxiously watched the Chief's behavior, helped the bulky figure rise from his seat and leave the chamber. By that evening, the twelfth Chief Justice of the United States had died. The opinions in *Girouard v. United States* reflected the history of his five-year administration in which a kind of ideological merry-go-round seemed to have been in motion. Members of the Court had systematically overruled, or drastically construed, principles of case law and state and Federal statutes covering most of the spectrum of public and private law. Justices had frequently changed sides in succeeding cases involving the same broad issues, although they were not always so lucid in their reasons as Stone had been in his closing dissent. In five terms, Stone had never succeeded for long in "massing the Court"; his own persuasion, as reflected in the *Girouard* dissent, combined elements of Black's ideal of legislative independence and Frankfurter's ideal of judicial restraint.[54]

What, laymen and lawyers asked themselves when the news of Stone's death became public, had been the ultimate accomplishment of his Court? Stone himself, as the *Washington Post* summarized the record on the twentieth anniversary of his appointment in 1945, "has shared in, and indeed has greatly shaped, a significant expansion of the judicial view respecting the scope of Federal authority in the economic sphere." At the same time, the writer put as fair a face as he could on the administrative record: "He has never sought to govern his fellow Justices, but he has brought to their deliberations an atmosphere of tolerance and friendliness which has served to temper the vigor of their intellectual differences."[55]

Be that as it might, a member of the bench who subsequently became its Chief would in the final analysis be judged by what the Court itself had achieved under his administration. The tumultuous dialogues of the past five years often seemed to be exercises in futility, compared with the cleancut break with the past which had been effectuated by the Hughes Court. The Stone Court, in a sense, had no past; it had been launched, on the eve of the Second World War, upon a new course for which the old charts provided little practical guidance—of necessity, much of the case law of these five years had consisted of a detailed repudiation of past propositions. In this period, nineteen state laws had been held void—in only five cases by unanimous decision; twenty-five earlier decisions of the Court itself had been overruled, almost all with diverging concurrences and a number of eloquent dissents.[56]

This, standing alone, was a negative record. Yet the jurisprudence of Stone himself represented a continuum from the constitutional revolution of the thirties to the dominant nationalism forged by World War II, just as the equally lengthy tenure of Black, Douglas and Frankfurter would make possible a continuum from the reformed constitutionalism of the New Deal Court to the reformed Federalism of the Warren Court.

The New Dealers in Stone's Court had been iconoclasts, eagerly hunting down surviving idols to make sure they were overthrown. The activist bloc, for the period that it commanded the support of four members of the Court, systematically exploited the long-established policy of bringing up for review any cases thought desirable by four Justices, which might present the opportunity for challenging an old principle. Where the four could persuade one more member to their view, the principle could indeed be refuted or restated. If second thoughts then took possession of one or more of the Justices, another opportunity for discussion and reconsideration of the recently asserted proposition could be created rather promptly through certiorari requested under the "rule of four."

Principles, in this context, became relativistic, the rules of decisional law transitional, and constitutional practice essentially experimental. It was a significant coincidence that the Stone Court paralleled the years of the Second World War; the massive social and economic shifts which were being brought about by total mobilization of persons and resources were everywhere discernible, and demanded a juridical response which had to be phrased out of something more relevant than many of the familiar old propositions of law. The disposition of Stone and his colleagues not to shrink from the task was their ultimate vindication.

7/Experimental
Constitutional Law

THE ALTERNATING CURRENTS of the Stone Court flowed between the poles of activism and restraint. The approach to constitutional issues, on the parts of the frequently changing components of the respective poles, was eminently empirical, and this contributed to the public image of continuing chaos in the decisional rationale. Yet some leaders of the legal profession discerned a vital force at work: a modern Court, said the president of the Nebraska State Bar Association in 1944, had come to accept the fact that "in the law general propositions can never acquire the haughty aloofness they possess in mathematics and in a number of theologies. . . . Precedence cannot be indiscriminately accepted by the judges."[1]

As the jurisprudence of the Stone Court developed, it was increasingly evident that the old concept of *stare decisis* was of decreasing weight. For the activists, and more often than not for the whole Court, "the promulgation of doctrine, believed by them to be sound, was evidently thought to be more important than stability in the law or predictability of decision," wrote a critic in 1943.[2] In the five-year record of the Court, non-dissenting* decisions rose to 50 percent and more, with the parties to the dialogue continually changing. Yet this disparate sequence was developing a new consistency; the kaleidoscope progressively repolarized through the concurring opinions of Black, Douglas, Frankfurter, Jackson and Murphy was steadily devising a more sophisticated philosophy for the constitutional law which had been implanted in the seedtime of 1937-41.

A unanimous Court, speaking through Jackson in *Wickard v. Filburn*, aptly illustrated the emergent theme as it related to the commerce power.

---

*The term is used to indicate a decision in which all the Justices agreed on the holding but not on the *ratio decidendi*.

Pointing out that Marshall himself had defined this power "with a breadth never yet exceeded," the opinion reviewed the period of desuetude extending through most of the nineteenth century when there was "little occasion for the affirmative exercise" of power, and the circumstances instead encouraged the Court to apply the negative force of the commerce clause in limiting state action in the subject-area. As a consequence, said Jackson, when Congress asserted reentry into the area with enactment of the Interstate Commerce Act and the judiciary was called upon to interpret the scope of the Federal power, it found itself narrowly channeled within the body of negative decisions enunciated over a period of nearly a century. The crisis of the 1930's, accordingly, had compelled the Court to face up to the fact of the obsolescence of the precedents: "the relevance of the economic effects in the application of the commerce clause . . . has made the mechanical application of legal formulas no longer feasible."[3]

Jackson was, essentially, paraphrasing Stone himself, speaking a decade before against the reflex-action judicial response to precedents. "Law guided by precedent which has grown out of one type of experience," Stone had said, "can only slowly and with difficulty be adapted to new types which the changing scene may bring." For the reform-minded new members of the Court, this was a fundamental article of faith. In a famous passage in 1932, Brandeis had corroborated Stone by compiling an impressive catalog of prior decisions which had been overruled—highlighted by Fuller's asserted reversal of "a century of error" in the *Income Tax* case of 1895—and now, in the second term of the contemporary Court, Justice Reed drove home the point with a list of fourteen cases since 1937 which had been overruled.[4] The readiness to change new landmarks as well as old, while a source of concern to conservatives, became the characteristic of the experiment-minded bench of the early 1940's.

*   *   *

The ultimate extreme was illustrated in the decision in 1940, upholding a state law compelling school pupils to pledge allegiance to the flag, and a decision a year later which was punctuated by a vigorous series of dissents to the current case (a license fee imposed on distributors of religious literature) as well as the flag-salute decision. In the prior case, Frankfurter for the majority had argued that "personal freedom is best maintained . . . when it is ingrained in a people's habits and not enforced against popular policy by the coercion of adjudicated law." In the license case, Black's dissent stated the antithesis of the Frankfurter argument: "Certainly our democratic form of government, functioning under the historic Bill of Rights, has a high responsibility to accommodate itself to the religious views of minorities, however unpopular and unorthodox these views may be." Both the flag-salute and the license requirement, Black—together with Douglas and Murphy—declared to be ripe for overthrow.[5]

Jones v. Opelika was a typical divided opinion. The Court upheld convictions of members of a religious sect which refused to apply for licenses to vend religious literature, but four Justices dissented and three of the four wrote individual opinions. Reed, speaking for the majority and relying on *Gobitis* and similar cases, warned that First Amendment rights "are not absolutes to be exercised independently of other cherished privileges, protected by the same organic instrument." In his view, "the proponents of ideas cannot determine entirely for themselves the time and place and manner for the diffusion of knowledge or for their evangelism. . . . The ordinary requirements of civilized life compel this adjustment of interests."

Stone, in dissent, pointed out that if one who refused to pay a license fee was thereby prevented from practicing a tenet of his religion, the license acted as an unconstitutional control upon the belief. Murphy added that the persecution of unpopular dissenters was the specific evil which the First Amendment had sought to extirpate, and Black then followed with his declaration that the flag-salute case, having been decided against the same sect, required reversing along with *Opelika*.[6]

Encouraged by this hint from the bench, counsel for the Jehovah's Witnesses renewed their efforts, while on the Court itself the fifth man of the 1942 majority—Byrnes—gave way to Rutledge. In the spring of 1943 the flag-salute and license cases were overturned, with Jackson, won over to the libertarian view, delivering the opinion of the Court. "The very purpose of a Bill of Rights," declared Jackson, "was to withdraw certain subjects from the vicissitudes of political controversy, to place them beyond the reach of majorities and officials and to establish them as legal principles to be applied by the courts." If there were any absolutes left, the opinion concluded, they would at least include the specific guarantees set out in the Constitution and its Amendments.[7]

While the guarantees of the First Amendment came to be described as "preferred freedoms," the activists—with the momentary support of Jackson and later of Rutledge—were prepared to renew the argument that any guarantees of the citizen were guarantees against infringement by any government. Although this view had been negated in the past, the current judicial temper encouraged the continual reexamination of old assumptions. The "advanced" liberals kept alert for the opportunity to present the case; phrased in its broadest terms, as the incorporation of the first eight Amendments in the Bill of Rights into the Fourteenth Amendment's restraints upon the states, it did not come before the Court until 1947. Then, and again in 1949, it was rejected by the majority, although men like Black, Douglas and Rutledge remained persuaded that it represented the shape of the future.[8]

The alternative to total incorporation was twofold: The jurisprudence of the Fourteenth Amendment could be steadily enlarged without specific reference to incorporation; and, correlatively, the nature of national citizenship and the rights therein to be protected by the Federal authority against the states could be progressively restated. In the case of the first alternative, Rutledge was philosophical; even though it was "a piecemeal wisdom," he observed, it should not be rejected "merely because it hobbles toward the truth with backward glances."[9]

*   *   *

The second alternative was to be advocated in a case which arose early in the 1941 term, to be decided again by a non-dissenting majority. A California statute which sought to bar entry into the state by any non-resident "indigent person" was held invalid by the formal majority of five, speaking through Justice Byrnes, on the ground that the commerce power barred any state's attempt "to isolate itself from difficulties common to all of them by restraining the transportation of persons and property across its borders."[10]

In a concurring opinion three Justices—Black, Douglas and Murphy—urged that a stronger constitutional principle was to be found in the privileges and immunities clause of the Fourteenth Amendment and the proposition that the right "to move freely from state to state is an incident of *national* citizenship." In a separate opinion, Jackson went even further. The Court should not hesitate, he declared, "to hold that Federal citizenship implies rights to enter and abide in any state of the Union at least equal to those possessed by aliens," and "that a man's mere property status, without more, cannot be used by a state to test, qualify, or limit his rights as a citizen of the United States."[11]

Byrnes himself had apparently been inclined to the Jackson viewpoint but had been talked out of it by Stone. The Chief Justice argued eloquently that such a construction of the privileges and immunities clauses "has been repeatedly rejected for more than half a century"—hardly a telling argument when the constructions of the past half century were being so systematically challenged by the Court.[12]

Jackson criticized the Court for its chronic hesitation when presented with an opportunity to give the privileges and immunities proviso more effective force; and yet Stone himself took the lead in speaking for the majority and urging that the rights of national citizenship rested on something more significant than the commerce clause. Stone was prepared to add to the "preferred freedoms" the right of the Federal government to assert jurisdiction in state Congressional primaries. To the argument that the constitutional provision as to Congress' authority over "the time, place and manner" of holding such elections had been adopted long before the development of the concept of the primary, the Chief Justice replied that the statement was beside the point.

Rejecting the narrow historical argument of Black, Douglas and Murphy, Stone admonished them: "Words, especially those of a constitution, are not to be read with such stultifying narrowness." It was obvious, he pointed out, that the commerce clause was drafted with no prescience as to the invention of interstate wire and wireless communication, and if the purpose of the elections clause was to ensure fair and representative choices of members of Congress, any element which was introduced into the process of recording a choice was part of the subject which the Constitution intended to make Federal business. "If we remember that 'it is a Constitution we are expounding,' " Stone said, "we cannot rightly prefer, of the possible meanings of its words, that which will defeat rather than effectuate the constitutional purpose."[13]

Returning to the subject of the commerce clause, Stone was unreserved in his conviction of the plenary power of Congress. Holding that the Federal power to regulate the price of produce in interstate shipment extends as far into intrastate areas as is necessary to make the regulation effective, the Chief Justice declared: "It follows that no form of state activity can constitutionally thwart the regulatory power granted by the commerce clause to Congress. Hence the reach of that power extends to those intrastate activities which in a substantial way interfere with or obstruct the exercise of the granted power."[14]

But the broadening view of national power was not to mean that state power, used to effect a basic constitutional purpose, could not also be upheld. In sustaining a New Jersey statute which permitted adjustment or composition of all claims of the creditors of an insolvent municipality, Frankfurter speaking for the Court dismissed the argument that the statute violated the impairment of contracts clause. "Impairment of an obligation means refusal to pay an honest debt; it does not mean contriving ways and means for paying it," he said. "The necessity compelled by unexpected financial conditions to modify an original arrangement for discharging a city's debt is implied in every such obligation for the very reason that thereby the obligation is discharged, not impaired." To hold such state action in conflict with the Constitution would be "indeed to make of the Constitution a code of lifeless forms instead of an enduring framework of government for a dynamic society."[15]

*   *   *

In a liberal Court, remarked *Newsweek,* "its members in practice are asserting the highly individualistic traits characteristic of liberalism." In the spring of 1942, it was Jackson's turn to oppose a view of national power which other members of the bench upheld. The facts in issue involved an Ohio farmer who had accepted an Agricultural Marketing Agreement to limit his wheat acreage, and who resisted the government's effort to collect a penalty for overplanting on the claim that the wheat had been grown for his own chickens, not for market. Jackson wrote the opinion upholding the government, but not before he had protested that "whereas regulation of interstate commerce itself requires no justification beyond the will of Congress, . . . regulation of what is neither interstate nor commerce does depend on at least a reasonably probable effect of some kind." Otherwise, he said, the division of Federal and state authority was meaningless.[16]

In the same term, Stone spoke for a unanimous Court in defining the desired process of coordination between state and Federal authority in the subject: "When Congress has not asserted its power under the commerce clause, and state regulation of matters of local concern is so related to interstate commerce that it operates as a regulation of that commerce," there must be a balancing of the public interests by the Court. Other things being equal, Stone concluded, state power would be left unchallenged where it did not impede the flow of interstate commerce or "the national interest in the regulation of commerce by a single authority."[17]

Stone dissented, and Jackson dissented in part, in a case the following year which broadened the reach of the Interstate Commerce Act itself to include interstate insurance business. Insurance, it had been declared in the heyday of *laissez-faire,* was not commerce. Now, Black ruled for the majority that since the business of insurance was interstate it was subject to the regulation of Congress; Jackson protested that although a business was interstate it was not necessarily subject to the statute concerned with earlier definitions of commerce and should wait upon Congressional expression of intent to regulate such businesses.[18] Stone voiced regret that the majority opinion "overturning the precedents of seventy-five years governing a business of such volume and of such wide ramifications" should as a consequence create a new series of judicial and legislative efforts to resolve "the doubts and uncertainties inseparable from a realignment of the distribution of power in our Federal system."[19]

Yet the authority of the state within its own jurisdiction was firmly endorsed. The full faith and credit clause, said Stone, is not to be treated "as the means of compelling one state wholly to subordinate its own laws and policy concerning its peculiarly domestic affairs to the laws and policy of others. Where such conflict of interest arises, it is for this Court to resolve it by determining how far the full faith and credit clause demands the qualification or denial of rights asserted under the laws of one state . . . by the public acts and judicial proceedings of another."[20]

In the area of administrative regulatory processes, the Court strengthened the proposition that regulatory agencies were presumed to have adhered to statutory limitations upon their actions and that private parties were presumed to have acted under any administrative regulations with the intent that their actions would have the consequences they did have.[21] It also struck down a state law in conflict with a Federal agency regulation,[22] and reaffirmed the position taken by the late Hughes Court that if substantial evidence, as accepted by administrative specialists, could be found to support a ruling, the Court would not disturb it.[23]

*   *   *

Throughout the existence of the Stone Court, the Second World War and its demands brought from the government an unprecedented torrent of regulatory measures bristling with challenging constitutional questions. Many of these, stemming from the circumstances of the emergency, were not to be adjudicated until after the war itself, but the matter of individual rights

which had been ambivalently (not to say negatively) discussed in the First
World War demanded readier answers in the peculiar complexities of the
Second.

Some of the executive steps taken to meet the emergency dated from the
First World War, and others from the period of growing danger manifest in
the first two years of the Nazi assault on Europe. In the case of the latter, the
experiences of England and Canada provided some guidelines to constitutional
action. Within a week of the outbreak of hostilities in 1939, Roosevelt issued
a proclamation of limited national emergency; by the summer of 1940, the
exportation of aviation gasoline was limited to the Western Hemisphere. By
that fall, the sale of scrap iron and steel to Japan was embargoed, and by
February, 1941 potentially hostile ships and aircraft were denied approaches
to American military zones in the Pacific. By May, 1941 Roosevelt converted
the limited emergency order into one of unlimited emergency and by July
Japanese property in the United States was frozen.

The question of the extent of executive power to take such steps was
regarded as academic; even in such cases, however, it was significant to note
that the exercise of the power took no regular form, sometimes coming as
an executive order, sometimes as a "directive" and sometimes simply as a
letter of authorization.[24]

After Pearl Harbor, scores of wartime agencies were created overnight,
occasionally by statute but in most cases by a further assertion of executive
authority. A tally of wartime functions created under existing offices or
assigned to new entities especially created for the job and for the duration,
showed substantially more than a hundred. While many business executives
were recruited to handle specialized projects requiring full-time attention,
regular heads of executive departments of the government found themselves
assuming a succession of new portfolios. Harold Ickes, in addition to his
regular office as Secretary of the Interior, was Petroleum Coordinator for
War, Solid Fuels Administrator, chairman of the National Power Policy
Committee, member of the Council of National Defense and member of
the Liaison Committee for War Relocation. The Secretaries of Agriculture,
Commerce and War held equally diversified positions in wartime programs
related to their regular posts.[25]

The proliferating programs and agencies by 1943 led Congress to establish a succession of supervisory committees—of which the Special Committee
Investigating the National Defense Program, headed by Senator Harry S
Truman of Missouri, became the prototype and one of the most effective.
Particularly as, in 1943, expanding programs of price controls, priorities and
rationing came into effect, watchdog committees were established by one or
the other houses of Congress to undertake, as the Truman Committee observed in its first annual report, "a constant check . . . into the activities of
the defense agencies when it is possible for the Congress to require remedial
action to be taken before it is too late."[26]

The First World War had accelerated the trend toward centralized administration of productive activities. The Second World War increased the corporate or nationalized organization of American economic life to a degree proportionately greater. During the years of combat, and after, as Americans found themselves subjected to a vast number of Federal authorities, so they would tend increasingly to look to the Federal government for the protection of their rights within the metamorphosis of American society.

*   *   *

The general authority of the President in the conduct of foreign affairs had been sweepingly affirmed in 1936. Sutherland, speaking for the Court, had asserted that the Executive necessarily had to have in international matters "a degree of discretion and freedom from statutory restriction which would not be admissible were domestic affairs alone involved."[27] For a dynamic President, this was more than enough encouragement to act boldly in dangerous times; by the first summer of the war, Roosevelt warned Congress that if it failed to adopt his recommended program of maximum prices fixed for farm produce by statute, he would be compelled to use his war powers as Executive to fix them.[28]

The Court for the most part was prepared to back up any reasonable assertion of legislative or executive authority in the face of national emergency. The Price Control Act of 1942 was accordingly upheld two years later. With the war still in progress and in a critical shifting of advantage, the Court ruled that the degree of latitude to be allowed to an administrator to whom Congress delegated power was a question solely for Congress to determine. "The Constitution as a continuously operative charter of government does not demand the impossible or the impracticable. It does not require that Congress find for itself every fact upon which it desires to base legislative action."[29] If ultimate opportunity for judicial review of an administrative action under this delegated authority is available, the Court added in a companion case, the fact that it is deferred in the public interest of having the action take immediate effect is not a denial of due process.[30]

How far the demands of wartime security should be permitted to go in the suspension or curtailment of constitutional rights was a related question of national powers which was addressed to different circumstances in the First and Second World Wars. Relocation of enemy aliens was an unquestioned prerogative of sovereignty; but curfews and confinement of American citizens of foreign antecedents, particularly Japanese-Americans, presented a much graver problem of law and morals. Gordon Kiyoshi Hirabayashi, a citizen of the United States, charged that the military commander of the West Coast defense area in which he resided had infringed upon his rights under the Fifth Amendment in ordering the curfew.

Stone, speaking for the Court, pointed out that the Fifth Amendment contained no equal protection clause, although at the same time he confessed that distinctions between citizens because of their ancestry "are by their very nature odious to a free people whose institutions are founded upon the doctrine of equality." However, he reluctantly concluded, it was obvious that "in time of war residents having ethnic affiliations with an invading enemy may be a greater source of danger than those of a different ancestry." Douglas, troubled at the holding even though he felt compelled to concur, suggested that Hirabayashi might seek a test of his loyalty other than by defiance of a valid military order. Murphy, with even greater concern, concurred with the observation that the order went "to the very brink of constitutional power."[31]

The four different opinions in the *Hirabayashi* case accepted the government's plea of overriding national danger. After Congress enacted a more drastic security statute, specifically excluding Japanese-Americans from certain areas, the uneasy unanimity disappeared. Although a narrow majority upheld the statute, Black in speaking for the Court pointed out that had the exclusion been motivated by racial bias rather than racial identification with an enemy, it would have been unconstitutional. Acknowledging, too, that by December. 1944 when the case was decided the threat of invasion had clearly passed, he emphasized the controlling circumstances of the spring of 1942: "We cannot—by availing ourselves of the calm perspective of hindsight—now say that at that time these actions were unjustified."

Roberts, in dissent, felt that the exclusion order under the law was unconstitutional when the individual was denied any opportunity to prove his loyalty as a citizen. Murphy protested that a racial discrimination was an inescapable conclusion and thus violated guaranteed rights. Jackson, while adding his disagreement, urged the Court to face up to the fact that military orders were in their nature a threat to personal liberty, but that to look for effective review of such orders by the judiciary was "wholly delusive."[32]

Ironically enough, the naturalized citizen in these circumstances fared better than the natural-born citizen. Citizenship once conferred by naturalization could not be cancelled at a later date, the Court declared, merely because with the passage of time an individual's political views had become unpopular. "No citizen with such a threat hanging over his head could be free," warned Murphy for the majority.[33] Complementing this decision, the Court the following year rejected a government attempt to cancel a naturalization because it was unable to prove fraud in the individual as of the time of naturalization.[34]

It was, indeed, the manifest intention of the Court to avoid the excesses of curtailment of civil rights which had marred the history of the First World War. In *Hartzel v. United States* the Court unanimously reversed a conviction under the 1917 Espionage Act where a citizen had been charged with seeking to impede the war effort through critical publications.[35] In another case, the long struggle of Harry Bridges, a militant, foreign-born longshoreman, to resist deportation reached the high tribunal after an extended series of prosecutions in the lower courts. Speaking for a five-to-three majority, Douglas found that the Deportation Act's provision for expulsion of alien Communists was not intended to include all radicals whose aims, while coinciding in part with Communists', "nevertheless fell far short of overthrowing the government by force and violence." Hearsay evidence on which the deportation order was based, Douglas declared, was not admissible in situations where individual rights were put in jeopardy.[36]

The decision followed by four years another decision sustaining an appeal by Bridges from a state contempt citation based upon his vigorous criticisms of cases pending in the Los Angeles superior court. In this landmark case, strictly limiting the contempt power to disorders in the courtroom itself, Black for a five-to-four majority had asserted the paramount authority of the guarantees of free utterance under the First Amendment as a limitation upon the inherent power of the judiciary itself.[37] The second *Bridges* case, in the spring of 1945, asserted still more firmly the responsibility of the government to show the "clear and present danger" which would justify the curtailment of a "preferred freedom" even in time of national crisis.[38]

The concept of national citizenship was still far from the broad definition it was to receive in the later Court, however, and thus the long-submerged rights of the Negro and the recently qualified rights of the urban voter were to be frustrated for another decade and more. In the case of *Screws v. United States* in May, 1945 the Court at once revealed the extent of its own ambivalence and the lingering reluctance to find in the Federal authority the only effective safeguard for such rights.

In this case Robert Hall, a young Negro, had been arrested by Georgia county officers on a theft charge, handcuffed and beaten to death in the courthouse square. Upon the state prosecutor's bland disclaimer of any investigative responsibility in the absence of a complaint, a prosecution was initiated in the United States District Court under the Federal Criminal Code's extension of the Civil Rights Act of 1866. The trial resulted in a conviction which was then affirmed by the appellate court, and thereafter carried for review to the Supreme Court. In an example of non-concurrence remarkable even for Stone's Chief Justiceship, Douglas wrote an opinion for four members of the bench, Rutledge concurred separately in an opinion which sharply criticized the Douglas view and the Roberts dissent, and Murphy dissented separately for reasons similar to those in Rutledge's concurrence. The dissent by Roberts, Frankfurter and Jackson devoted itself primarily to upbraiding Douglas and his three associates for reversing the lower courts rather than dismissing the action altogether.[39]

The reversal of the lower Courts, because of what Douglas considered too broad a construction of the Federal criminal statute, was an involved piece of apologetic. It upheld the government in invoking the Civil Rights Act in such a case as this, but insisted that a new trial was nevertheless required to keep the prosecution within the limits of definable standards of liability. The alternative, in this view, would be to hold the statute void for vagueness; any right of national citizenship had to be found specifically within the Constitution or law enacted thereunder. Stone's bold extension of the protection of a national right in other cases, said Douglas, rested upon a definite guarantee of voting rights in Section 2 of the Fourteenth Amendment; it was necessary to find an equally definite standard of criminal liability in the present case. This could be done, said the Douglas opinion, by narrowly construing the act so as to make the criminality definite and certain and also to preserve "the traditional balance between the state and the national government in law enforcement."[40]

Rutledge, who made it clear that he would have preferred to sustain the convictions, chose to support the Douglas opinion in order to ensure a majority for the constitutionality of the law. However, he decried the narrowness of the reasoning. It was justified, he said, neither by the nature of the offense nor by the threat of a Federal-state conflict. "The right not to be deprived of life or liberty by a state officer who takes it by abuse of his office and his power" is a definite Federal right, Rutledge declared. As for the threatened intrusion of the national government into the area of state criminal jurisdiction, he noted that such fear had been expressed in the Congressional debates on the original Act but "not realized in later experience. Eighty years," he concluded, "should be enough to remove any lingering vestige."[41]

Murphy dissented. Like Rutledge, he preferred to affirm the convictions rather than to send the case back to the trial court in order to preserve a narrow construction of Federal law. "The significant question, rather, is whether law enforcement officers and those entrusted with authority shall be allowed to violate with impunity the clear constitutional rights of the inarticulate and the friendless. . . . But where, as here, the states are unwilling for some reason to prosecute such crimes the Federal government must step in unless constitutional guarantees are to become atrophied."[42]

The principal dissent, written by Roberts, protested against finding any constitutional basis for a Federal prosecution. The statute, it was contended, was confined to "state action"—violations by the state or the state's agents of a limitation laid by the Amendment upon the states. Through more than twenty pages of argumentation which ranged from eloquence to sophistry, the dissenters insisted that the Federal prosecution for an unjustifiable homicide—which even with conviction as a denial of civil rights carried a relatively minor penalty—improperly invaded the state sphere of criminal jurisdiction. For Jackson, joined in this opinion, it was a total withdrawal from the argument he had once made in favor of more effective definition of the privileges and immunities of national citizenship. For Frankfurter, it was a basic element in his developing doctrine of judicial restraint.[43]

* * *

The Court in the *Screws* case made an initial, though narrow, opening in the prior doctrines which had denied access to Federal courts for the exploited minorities in American life. In commenting on the decision, at least one observer mused at the habitual judicial refusal to recognize "that the threat to civil liberty from state and local governments and from private individuals and groups of individuals has always been *at least as serious as the threat from the Federal government*" sought to be contained by the Bill of Rights.[44] Yet the alternative—incorporation of the Bill of Rights into the rationale of the Fourteenth Amendment—was to be thwarted repeatedly by various circumstances; twenty years after the *Screws* decision, although the doctrine therein was slowly extended, the incorporation question was still denied by the Court.[45]

Still, the decision in this case prepared the way for a steadily developing jurisprudence of Federally protected civil liberties. The following month a four-to-three majority* refused to assert a constitutional rule which evolved more than fifteen years later in the reapportionment cases.

In *Colgrove v. Green* the Court was presented squarely with the question of whether a failure of a state to apportion its Congressional representation on an equitable population basis was a justiciable issue. As in the *Screws* case, the result was a wide split in opinions: Frankfurter, taking advantage of his opportunity to advance his argument for Federal restraint, wrote the opinion in which Reed and Burton joined. Rutledge, even more ambivalent than he was in *Screws,* felt that the issue was justiciable but was not one in which the Court ought to exercise its jurisdiction; for, said Rutledge, quoting a concurring opinion of Frankfurter in an earlier case, "it is the very essence of our duty to avoid decision upon grave constitutional questions, especially when this may bring our function into clash with the political departments of the government."[46]

In his growing concern over the tentative theses being periodically advanced in constitutional law by the New Deal and post-New Deal Court, Frankfurter had been steadily retreating into a doctrine of self-limitation which would become his main contribution to mid-century constitutional theory.† The dogma which he had evolved had been pronounced just a week earlier in a case in which the majority held invalid a Congressional act which sought to bar alleged subversive parties permanently from government employment. To Black's opinion for a five-to-two majority holding such an act to be a bill of attainder specifically outlawed by the Constitution, Frankfurter had replied in a concurring opinion that "the judicial function exacts considerations very different from those which may determine a vote in Congress." Avoiding a collision with Congress was something more important than administrative strategy, Frankfurter contended, for while "Congress can readily mend its ways, or the people may express disapproval by choosing different representatives, . . . a decree of unconstitutionality by this Court

---

*Chief Justice Stone had died in March, and Justice Jackson was in Nuremberg.

†Cf. Ch. 9.

is fraught with consequences so enduring and far-reaching as to be avoided unless no choice is left in reason."[47]

The *Colgrove* case, involving a refusal of the Illinois legislature to undertake a redistricting to accommodate population changes, appeared to Frankfurter to be an apt example of the sort of issue calling for judicial abnegation. The constitutional history of the nation, he declared, was full of illustrations of just such a position on the part of the Court. Its refusal to consider the validity of legislative actions, he concluded, stemmed from the fact that "due regard for the effective working of our government revealed this issue to be of a peculiarly political nature and therefore not meet for judicial determination."

Frankfurter did not deny that there was a proper Federal interest in the fair apportionment of electoral districts, but he insisted that it was the exclusive concern of Congress. "If Congress failed in exercising its powers" to compel Illinois to establish an equitable electoral process for its representatives in Congress, "the remedy ultimately lies with the people," the Justice declared. "Whether Congress faithfully discharges its duty or not, the subject has been committed to the exclusive control of Congress."[48]

Rutledge agreed; to inject the judiciary into the reform of the electoral process, he feared, was to upset a political balance of nature. "The right here is not absolute," he wrote. "And the cure sought may be worse than the disease."[49] Black, protesting for himself, Douglas and Murphy, replied that when the clear result of malapportionment is "to deprive some citizens of an effective vote, the admitted result is that the constitutional policy of equality of representation has been defeated. Under these circumstances it is the Court's duty to invalidate the state law."[50]

Thus, for the first time, the Court skirted the edges of the political thicket of reapportionment. It preferred in this period not to explore into the problems which might lie hidden in the depths.

The underlying moral issue of the apportionment cases, now and in the future,* was the responsibility for judicial action where an independent branch of the government had proved negligent in its own responsibility. For men like Frankfurter, the answer to such a question was inescapably and emphatically negative. The separation of powers was an unalterable principle of representative government, and the accountability of the elected branches of the government to the electorate was of the essence of democracy. For men like Black and Douglas, the justiciability of the issue derived from the fact that a paramount constitutional right in a democracy was the individual's right to an equal vote in the electoral process; the judicial responsibility for protecting that right was augmented by a legislative default in the matter of its own accountability.

Like the issue of effective enforcement of constitutionally guaranteed minority rights, the issue of effective reapportionment in the effectuation of

---

*Cf. Ch. 15.

constitutional democracy was to remain for settlement in the trilogy of epochal decisions which would climax the jurisprudence of the Warren Court.

*   *   *

The third of the issues to comprise the jurisprudence of the 1960's had been implanted early in the history of the Stone Court. In June, 1942, in the case of *Betts v. Brady,* the question had been raised whether the right to counsel in the case of indigent defendants in any felony case was guaranteed under the Sixth Amendment by extension to the states through the Fourteenth. A decade earlier, the Court had held that such a right was constitutionally required in capital cases,[51] but it was not now prepared to enlarge this into a universal rule. To do so would require a further advance into the area traditionally reserved to the states. "To deduce from the due process clause a rule binding upon the states in this matter would be to impose upon them . . . a requirement without distinction between criminal charges of different magnitude or in respect of courts of varying jurisdiction," said Roberts for a six-man majority.[52]

While it was true, said the opinion, that "the Fourteenth Amendment prohibits the conviction and incarceration of one whose trial is offensive to the common and fundamental ideas of fairness and right, and while want of counsel in a particular case may result in a conviction lacking in such fundamental fairness, we cannot say that the Amendment embodies an inexorable command that no trial for any offense, or in any court, can be fairly conducted and justice accorded a defendant who is not represented by counsel."[53]

That, said Black for himself and Douglas and Murphy, was not the question in the current case; rather, the question was a narrower one as to whether this specific defendant had been denied due process. There was no doubt, Black urged, that if the case had arisen in a Federal Court the Sixth Amendment would have made the right to counsel a fundamental requirement. The stumbling block, therefore, was the refusal of the Court majority to incorporate the Sixth Amendment into the Fourteenth, and the result, said Black, was "to defeat the promise of our democratic society to provide equal justice under the law."[54]

The majority in *Betts* did not categorically deny the argument that under certain circumstances the guarantees of the Sixth Amendment were susceptible of application to state criminal proceedings through the Fourteenth. As a succession of critics were to observe, however, its equivocal application of the Sixth to the question of right to counsel, through Roberts' concept of a "fair trial" doctrine, was to make *Betts* an obstacle to the guarantee of the right more than a means of effectuating it.[55] For the next twenty-one years, a succession of decisions would vacillate between the upholding and the denying of the right to counsel in less than capital cases, each relying upon the Court's application of the *Betts* doctrine to the circumstances of each argument.[56]

Eventually and inevitably, the courts would have to accept the proposition that if due process required the guarantee of legally trained counsel in any type of felony it required the guarantee in all. Criminal liability, and the requirement of a free society that the defendant's rights were to be ensured, did not admit of a discrepancy between state administration and Federal, or between some states and others. To arrive at that conviction, however, the judiciary had to proceed from the present experimentalism, through the intellectual counterpoint of the Vinson Court, to the ultimate acceptance in the sixties of a progressively broadening concept of absolute rights vested in the people of the union.*

*   *   *

The accelerating trend of reversal of older constitutional rules, begun in the last four years of the Hughes Court, continued at the same pace during the Stone Chief Justiceship. In the century and a quarter prior to 1936, there had been forty-four instances in which the Court had acknowledged that it was specifically overruling one or more of its earlier decisions. Sixteen more cases were added in the years between 1937 and 1941, and another fifteen in the years between 1941 and 1946. Even in the slower-paced Court under Vinson, another thirteen instances of overruling previous cases were recorded, while in the Warren Court between 1953 and 1967 there were at least thirty more.† In the three decades following the great judiciary battle of 1937, the number of decisional laws supplanted by newer rules of constitutionalism was half again as many as in the hundred and twenty-five years before that date.[57]

The Stone Court also continued the trend of the later Hughes Court in upholding state laws which accommodated the concept of a broadened regulatory authority and overturning those which were found to infringe upon a Federally guaranteed right. Stone himself had led the way in finding invalid a California law regulating non-resident entry into the state—in contravention of the commerce clause, according to five Justices, and in contravention of the privileges and immunities clause, according to the other four.[58] A Georgia law which imposed criminal liability upon an employee quitting his job while owing money to his employer was held to be a peonage statute in violation of the Thirteenth Amendment.[59] The supremacy clause of Article VI was declared to supersede a Florida law imposing an inspection fee on fertilizer brought into the state under Federal soil conservation statutes.[60] A Texas statute requiring union organizers to secure a license from the Texas secretary of state was held to violate the freedom of assembly guarantee of the First Amendment,[61] and in the closing days of the Stone Court a Virginia "Jim Crow" law was set aside as an unreasonable state burden upon interstate commerce.[62]

The function of the Supreme Court in the post-New Deal era, as Stone himself phrased it in memorial services for Justice Sutherland in 1944, was to "determine the boundaries and distribution of power under a Federal

---

*Cf. Ch. 16.
†Cf. Appendix E.

constitutional system."[63] It was Stone's destiny to have assumed the administration of the high tribunal at the time when, in Learned Hand's phrase, "the latent equivocation" in the reformed constitutionalism under Hughes "reappeared as the field of combat changed."[64] Of necessity, in these circumstances a dialogue had to develop in which the range and ultimate boundaries of the new constitutional authority could be threshed out. The basic proposition, paraphrasing Jefferson, was that the power of government belonged to the living. For Stone as well as for Black, Douglas, Frankfurter and Jackson, the application of the proposition rested upon Holmes' familiar aphorism: the growth of the law was experience.[65]

In the steadily accelerating pace of the World War II era—the pressures of all-out war, the revolution in technology, the uprooting of a whole population and moving it *en masse* to centers of production—the testing of experience was condensed into a short time span of high intensity. Juristic answers to pressing new issues were demanded, even if they were manifestly tentative. Non-concurrence in judicial opinion under these circumstances was both predictable and desirable; in the ferment of crisis, all constitutional propositions tended to become relativistic.

A nostalgic view of the past crept into Stone's memorial to Justice Sutherland on December 18, 1944. The confident reliance on familiar rules of *laissez-faire* economics and constitutionalism in Sutherland's prime contrasted poignantly with the turbulent atmosphere of his own Court. Recalling Sutherland's description of his own mind as one which "put a great deal of faith in experience and very little in mere experiment," the Chief Justice underlined the reversal of the intellectual poles which had taken place in his own time. As much as for Sutherland's past, Stone spoke for his own in adding: "He was profoundly convinced that ill-considered experimentation in government in pursuit of passing fashions in legislation, and the loose governmental control of administrative officers, would in the end prove to be the real enemies of true democracy, and a grave danger to constitutional government. Among those who did not share fully his views of constitutional functions, few would be so bold as to deny those dangers."[66]

The essential difference between Stone and Sutherland, said Chief Justice Vinson in pronouncing the eulogy for his predecessor three years later, was Stone's disposition to follow Holmes in reserving judgment on his own first principles. The tolerance for dissent and concurring opinions under Stone's Chief Justiceship, said Vinson, was a natural consequence of his having witnessed, throughout his own tenure, the ultimate triumph of many views expressed as dissents in earlier years. "To Harlan Stone," Vinson concluded, "the great hazard to the perpetuation of constitutional government was narrow and illiberal construction of constitutional provisions."[67]

*   *   *

In a sense, the enactment of the Twenty-Second Amendment was another manifestation of the unstable political compounds created in the process of war and postwar change. Stone himself, never having been close to Roosevelt and having had distasteful experiences in several of his contacts with the President, had viewed the centralization of Federal power in the Executive, and the breaking of the anti-third-term tradition, as ultimate threats to the future of two-party government. Nor had he been persuaded by the argument that, having run for a third term in 1940 under the threat of approaching war, Roosevelt would be compelled by the same logic to run a fourth time when the war was in progress. But both Stone and Roosevelt had been removed from the scene by the time Congress undertook to write a political tradition into the letter of the Constitution itself.

The proposed Amendment, Alexander Wiley of Wisconsin told the Senate in March, 1947, "should be considered apart from discussion of the personality of the late President Roosevelt. It is not intended as a criticism of him, and prejudices for or against him should not be considered."[68] Whether Wiley himself believed this, few others in public life did; proposals to limit the Presidential and Vice-Presidential terms to one or two, or to vary the length of the term, were commonplace in the assorted amendments introduced in successive Congresses of the twentieth century,* but none had been given serious consideration until now.

For many, it was a spiteful gesture directed at the memory of the New Deal leader. "My God, can't they let the man rest in peace?" Congressman Adolph Sabath of Illinois had exclaimed when the Amendment was first debated in the House. "Had President Roosevelt been a Republican the stand of both parties would be the reverse," declared the *Philadelphia Bulletin,* no uncritical devotee of the late occupant of the White House. The truth was, however, that it was not entirely a Republican, or even a conservative Democratic, cabal that provided the groundswell in favor of the proposal. Rather, it was a deep-rooted concern of Congress collectively for its independence from a dominating Executive, although, to be sure, the concern was most acute among the most conservative.[69]

Virtually every strong-willed President had touched off an irrational resistance in Congress at one time or another. The first Roosevelt and Wilson (and Hoover for other reasons) had been virtually *non grata* on Capitol Hill in the closing months of their administrations, and the second Roosevelt's troubles had grown steadily since the fiasco of the judiciary bill of 1937. Although Pearl Harbor had driven Congress again into following his leadership, the abrasive elements in the relations soon worked themselves back to the surface. In 1943, Congress overrode an Executive order fixing a wartime ceiling on salaries, and passed the controversial War Labor Disputes Act over his veto.[70]

The crisis in New Deal-Capitol Hill relations (for the Progressive Movement by now was little more than a trusteeship of the Executive branch) came

---

*Cf. Appendix B.

in February, 1944, when Roosevelt sent back a tax bill which, he declared, provided relief "not for the needy but for the greedy." It was, moreover, a masterpiece of obscurantism, said the President, and was "squarely the fault of the Congress of the United States in using language in drafting the law which not even a dictionary or a thesaurus can make clear." Congress reacted with the same vehemence with which it had heard the earlier Roosevelt's charge of sloppy draftsmanship. In a seizure of emotion which caused tears to stream down his cheeks, Alben Barkley of Kentucky told the Senate that he did "not propose to take this unjustifiable assault lying down." Thereupon he resigned his position as administration floor leader—and was instantly re-elected by acclamation.[71]

"It is natural that Franklin Roosevelt, hungry for the Presidency's power as his birthright, should exemplify the man who helps himself," wrote Richard E. Neustadt. And, he added, "the natural conservatism of established institutions" made a Congressional resistance to Roosevelt's power a predictable action, an attempt to check "reforms that would give him a clear advantage over them." More than the New Deal enactments of the depression years, the Administrative Reorganization Act of 1939 had tended to consolidate the legislative opposition; the regrouping of some fifty governmental units under the Executive, streamlining controls in the interest of greater efficiency, created an obvious stereotype to be decried as "dictatorship."[72]

Even more foreboding, so far as the political balance of power between Congress and the White House was concerned, was the continuing support of Roosevelt by various blocs of voters. When, in the 1940 elections, many of the farmers deserted his banner, the labor and foreign-born vote became even more solidly united behind him, while the pressures of war in 1944 held numerous other electoral groups in line. "One of the principal arguments for representative government," wrote Edward S. Corwin, "has been that it assures the responsibility of the governors of society by imposing on them the constant necessity of obtaining a fresh consensus. But when a powerful pressure group or combination of groups furnishes the core of a legislative majority, their easy maneuverability in respect of issues that do not touch their own central interest renders easy the descent into 'government by bloc and blackmail.'" In Roosevelt's case, the President, rather than Congress, had obtained control of this core.[73]

*   *   *

Thus Wiley, for all his assurances, revealed the Senate majority's true feelings toward Roosevelt when he continued, in his argument for the Twenty-Second Amendment: With the Amendment, he said, the people "can settle one of the fundamental issues which was left unsettled by the founders of the Republic. That issue is whether or not the principle of long continuance in office by so-called indispensable leaders—called by some the *Fuehrer-Prinzip* —is compatible with our republican form of government." If there was "any lesson to be learned from the past twenty years," Wiley declared, "it is that power in the hands of any man or group, if it remains there long enough, has a tendency to become dangerous to the general welfare."[74]

In rebuttal, Lister Hill of Alabama warned that the proposed Amendment "would place the wisdom of the people in a strait-jacket. It would be a limitation on their right of free election. . . . There is a vast difference between a rigid prohibition in the Constitution, absolutely denying such a right to the people, and a custom under which the people ordinarily do not exercise the right." The whole thing, Hill concluded, "is a political issue, and that is all there is to it."[75]

In the end, it proved to be a political issue, the post-mortem on the New Deal itself. Supported by Southern conservatives, the Republican majority beat down all efforts to make the Amendment more flexible, and particularly to submit the question to ratifying conventions rather than to the Republican majorities in many of the state legislatures. On March 12, 1947 the Senate approved the proposal, 59 to 23 with 13 not voting. The House approved overwhelmingly on March 21, and ten days later the legislatures of Maine and Michigan had recorded their ratifications. Eighteen states had ratified it by the end of the year, but the momentum dropped thereafter. It was not until another wave of conservatism swept the state and Congressional elections in 1950 that the momentum picked up again; the needed thirty-sixth state, Minnesota, completed the ratification process in February, 1951.

To the extent that the Amendment was a petulant conservative action after the fact, it was of little effect; Roosevelt himself had by now been dead six years, while the issues out of which the New Deal had been born were largely settled. The primary progressive question of the twentieth century— when the American people would in fact recognize that they were *in* the twentieth century—was already past. Not even a conservative majority in Congress, or an oncoming Republican administration in the White House, would suggest any serious program of dismantling the legislative structure that had been erected in the twelve years under Roosevelt. As for the Court and the Constitution. the new judicial concepts which had been vociferously evolved in the experimentalism of the Stone Court had already begun to stabilize within the prosaisms of Vinson's Chief Justiceship.

8/The Vinson Interlude

THE 1947 DECISION of a conservative Congress to prepare a questionable limitation on Presidential terms to be written into the Constitution was a logical part of a sequence of events which, in the end, made it clear that the New Deal era was over. First had been Roosevelt's death itself. Harry Truman, thus suddenly propelled into the White House, found himself inundated by issues which moved the depression-born crusade a distant age away. In the world of 1945, with the collapse of the Axis war machine in Europe and shortly thereafter, to the ominous roar of an atomic explosion, in Asia as well, totally strange new problems materialized in profusion. Demobilization, the pressure to remove price controls, the ravenous appetites demanding long-denied consumer goods, the restless labor forces planning long-restrained tests of strength with management, the vacuum in employment resulting from the cessation of war production and the inevitable delays of conversion to peacetime manufactures—the problems seemed to grow in geometric ratio.

Next, in 1946, had come the death of Chief Justice Stone, revealing the parlous administrative state of the Court itself. From an eight-man balance (caused by Jackson's long absence) which often manifested itself in unsatisfactory four-to-four decisions, the membership now fell to a seven-man skeleton force which had to try to cope with the accelerating volume of opinions which normally mark the final weeks of a term. Overseas, Justice Jackson continued his role as American prosecutor at the war crimes trials in Nuremberg against a background of grumbling at the hardship worked on the undermanned Court by his absence and outspoken criticism of the idea of the trials themselves and the participation of a jurist in a prosecutor's role.

Jackson, indeed, was now being mentioned repeatedly as the most likely prospect to succeed Stone; it was recalled that Roosevelt had wanted to place him in the Chief Justiceship five years before, and newspaper speculation had it that the choice now lay between him and Douglas. But as the weeks went by without a selection, it became less obvious that either man would be chosen. There were further rumors that at least two and perhaps three members of the Court had threatened to resign if Jackson was elevated. Truman invited both Charles Evans Hughes and Owen J. Roberts to call at the White House and discuss prospective appointments with him, but still no inkling of who the choice would be or when it would be made issued from the Executive.[1]

Of all the men on the twentieth century Court, perhaps only William Howard Taft had exceeded Robert H. Jackson in his yearning for the Chief Justiceship. Yet combinations of circumstances and personalities seemed always to frustrate Jackson's ambition. In 1941, it had been Hughes' persuasive argument for Stone's superior qualifications for the needs of the moment which had led Roosevelt to elevate Stone. Whether or not Roosevelt intended to elevate Jackson when Stone left the chair, the fact was that now in 1946 Roosevelt was gone. There was also the fact that Jackson had quickly developed a bitter antipathy for Hugo Black, while his conflicts with Frank Murphy had carried over from their days in the Justice Department. Now, added to this, was Jackson's distant removal from the Court activities while the war crimes trials were in progress. Sidetracked once more when the Chief Justiceship opened up, Jackson could only watch this opportunity passing him by with an agony which finally would reach a point of explosion.[2]

Truman recognized the importance of finding the right man for the job. On the one hand was the desirability of keeping the Court in the same general constitutional channel into which it had been guided by Hughes and Stone, while on the other was the need for bringing under control the undisciplined behavior of the Justices which had all but become an open scandal. In the final analysis, however, the President in this as in his other selections turned to men—his critics called them cronies—whom he had come to know intimately in political life. He found his own prescription for a Chief Justice in a man whose career in some respects resembled Truman's own.

Fred M. Vinson was the son of a county jailer in Kentucky, who had worked his way through Centre College in Kentucky, and its law school, then proceeded through the familiar pattern of private practice and appointments as local prosecutor to two terms in Congress. For services rendered to the New Deal, he had been appointed to the Court of Appeals for the District of Columbia and had put in six years of competent service. The war years had marked his swift rise to the top ranks of the administration: Roosevelt had made him Director of Economic Stabilization in 1943, and 1945 had witnessed his rapid progression from head of the Reconstruction Finance Corporation to Director of War Mobilization and Reconversion to Secretary of the Treasury. He was, said a Washington correspondent, one of the most experienced men in government, and "a borderline New Dealer, as strongly anti-Socialist as he is anti-reaction."[3]

To the question of his ability to bring an unruly bench under control. there were various answers. His "good nature and tact" were cited as factors in his favor, although professional lawyers expressed the belief that he would follow an administrative policy somewhere between Hughes' firmness and Stone's looseness of rein. Others regarded the prospect with a certain sardonic amusement; the leading recalcitrants on the Court—Black, Douglas, Frankfurter and Jackson—it was observed, were all the intellectual superiors of the new Chief. He was, as another observer put it, a "sound" man, recognized as expert in fiscal questions and competent in matters of legal orthodoxy, however underdeveloped might be his judicial philosophy.[4]

* * *

Whatever might be Vinson's qualifications and shortcomings, they were almost immediately forgotten in the shockwave of an unprecedented outburst, directed by Justice Jackson against Justice Black, in a letter sent from Nuremberg to the Judiciary Committees of the House and Senate. Opening with an endorsement of Vinson as "an upright, fearless and well-qualified man," Jackson said that he had been moved to write his open letter in order that the "situation" on the Court should be "made clear."

"Many have assumed," the absentee jurist wrote, "and the impression has been cultivated, that [the new Chief] faces a mere personal vendetta among Justices which can be soothed by a tactful presiding officer. This is utterly false. The controversy goes to the reputation of the Court for non-partisan and unbiased decision. Further suppression of facts will not help Mr. Vinson and will afford continuing basis for irresponsible rumor and innuendo. This 'feud' has been so much and so long publicized that Congress has a right to know the facts and issues involved."

The development which touched off the current controversy, said Jackson, revolved about Justice Black's participation in a split decision sustaining contract rights of the United Mine Workers, who had retained Black's onetime law partner, Crampton Harris of Alabama, as their appellate counsel. This followed an earlier labor dispute in which a narrow vote favorable to Harris involved Black in the majority opinion.[5] What aroused Jackson's ire, he wrote, was his colleague's behavior when the defeated parties in the *UMW* case asked for a rehearing with Black excluded from participation.

"I did not say that it was wrong of Mr. Justice Black to sit," Jackson told the committees, "but I did say that it was for him to decide and that responsibility for approving his decision should not be by inference put on the Court." The rehearing petition was denied on the ground that the Court had no power to exclude one of its members—non-participation or disqualification was left to the discretion of the individual—but Black, according to Jackson, wanted the record to show a simple *per curiam** denial rather than commenting on the exclusion request.[6]

---

*I.e., an opinion "by the Court" as a formal institution would give no reasons for the ruling.

"Mr. Justice Black became very angry and said that any opinion which discussed the subject at all would mean a 'Declaration of War,'" Jackson stated. "I told Justice Black in language that was sharp, but no different than I would use again, that I would not stand for any more of his bullying." Yet he repeated that he did not want to be understood as saying that "Black's sitting in the *Jewell Ridge* case involved lack of honor. It is rather a question of judgment as to sound judicial policy. . . . However innocent the coincidence of these two victories at successive terms by Justice Black's former partner, I wanted that practice stopped. If it is ever repeated while I am on the bench, I will make my *Jewell Ridge* opinion look like a letter of recommendation by comparison."[7]

"Seldom in this city of recurring sensations," wrote a correspondent, "has there been such surprise" as in the Jackson cable. "For months there has been gossip that the two men disliked each other cordially, personally and professionally. By Mr. Jackson's friends, Mr. Black has been accused of a 'domineering and sneering' attitude; by the adherents of Mr. Black, the New York Justice is castigated as one who came to Washington as a New Deal liberal, but has turned too far toward the conservative side."[8]

Not only Washington, but the country and the international legal community, rocked with the sensation of Jackson's communication. Truman himself declined direct comment, other than to reveal in due time that Jackson had communicated to him the sense of his open letter prior to the announcement of Vinson's appointment and that the President had asked him to reconsider releasing it. "After Jackson's public quarrel with Justice Black," Truman wrote in retrospect in 1951, "of course I couldn't make him Chief Justice."[9] The President apparently meant that, upon hearing privately from Jackson of the proposed letter, he came to the conclusion that an outsider would have to be chosen.

The decision to make the letter public, Arthur Schlesinger, Jr. speculated, was "the act of a weary and sorely beset man, . . . tormented by the certainty that the Chief Justiceship had now passed forever out of his reach." The questionable taste in lifting the veil of secrecy which normally covered the internal activities of the Court occasioned much journalistic tongue-clucking. A Gallup public opinion poll released later in the month showed that a substantial number of Americans had come to have a lower regard for the Court as an institution, and a firmer conviction that its decisions were politically motivated.[10]

The fact was that the New Deal Court had been made up, *ad hoc* as it were, of a group of strong-minded men who had little in common except their zeal for overhauling and modernizing American constitutional law. Black, caustic and aggressive, invited both personal and ideological counter-attack. Frankfurter, who clearly regarded himself as the trustee of the Roosevelt reforms, often badgered appellate counsel as he would a law student in a classroom. Murphy's mild-mannered contrast to these men often seemed to verge on sanctimoniousness. But the most volatile of all was Robert Houghwout Jackson: as political an animal as Black, as keen an intellect as Frankfurter, he even exceeded Murphy in his ultimate conviction of his own righteousness, at the same time that he was honestly aware of his acuity as an attorney.

Upon examination, Jackson's quarrel with Black—like his earlier quarrels with Murphy—stemmed from a combination of factors which exaggerated the importance of the immediate issue. As the former chief trial officer for the government, Jackson had found himself regularly compelled to abstain from participating in a judicial review of cases in which he had earlier appeared. He had apparently been outraged to find that Black felt no similar compulsion to abstain from participating in the review of cases which had come to his former law firm long after he had left it. In Murphy's case, Jackson had been outraged to hear that Murphy had planned to continue as Attorney General for an indefinite period after his confirmation as Asso-ciate Justice—thus not only delaying Jackson's own advancement to Attorney General but (in Jackson's view) needlessly multiplying the potential cases in which Murphy himself would have to abstain from review. To these conflicts of principle, and conflicts of constitutional ideology, conflicts of ambition only added to the explosive potential.

The Court, in the latter years of the Stone Chief Justiceship, had become a battleground between Black and Douglas on the one hand and Frankfurter and Jackson on the other. Each faction wooed the remaining Justices, with Murphy tending toward the activists and Reed and Rutledge toward the advocates of judicial restraint. Since Roberts and his successor, Harold Burton, also inclined to the Frankfurter camp, those outside the Court who saw Black and Douglas as the only remaining stalwarts for the old New Deal tradition regarded any possible promotion of Jackson to the Chief's chair as a serious advantage for the new (and relative) conservatism. There was strong suspicion that Black's supporters outside the Court—with or without the Justice's clandestine support—launched a powerful undercover campaign to frustrate Truman's reported inclination to elevate Jackson.[11]

*   *   *

It was among the political partisans, galvanized by the resurgence of conservatism produced by postwar reaction against reform movements in general, that the Jackson-Black disagreement stirred the most vociferous response. In the Senate, Scott Lucas of Illinois called for the resignations of both men "to preserve the integrity of the Supreme Court," and Styles Bridges of New Hampshire proposed that Congress draft a law defining the conduct of various members of the Court as outside the pale of the constitutional provision that members of the bench "shall hold office during good behavior." Harrison E. Spangler, Republican spokesman, laid all of the blame on Roosevelt's doctrinaire attitude toward the Court and his inade-quacies in the selecting of judges.[12]

The more rabid New Deal haters in the House shouted for an investigation by Congressional committee, and, more vaguely, for some kind of censure of the responsible parties. The Senate Judiciary Committee, to whom the unsolicited Jackson letter had come, saw no practical course of action to be taken, and issued a statement to that effect: "If any question is presented by this communication we lack authorization or jurisdiction to determine it at this time." Any complaint, the committee observed, would have to come in the form of formal charges from the House of Representatives, on which impeachment proceedings could be based. No one except a scattering of extremists in either House seemed disposed to want to go so far.[13]

An attempt to go even further was the joint proposal of a constitutional amendment by Senators Bridges and James Eastland of Mississippi, to limit the number of appointments to the Supreme Court to be made by a single President. Only four such appointments could be made, according to the plan, while any other vacancies during the same Presidential term would be made as interim appointments by the House of Representatives. To ensure that the New Deal Court would be "unpacked" forthwith, the amendment called for the removal of the four last Justices to be appointed by Roosevelt —Douglas, Murphy, Jackson and Rutledge. The real objective of the proposal was revealed in a ranting speech in which Eastland berated the Court as being "bent on legislating social reforms which have failed of passage in Congress."[14]

This, in the final analysis, appeared to be the crux of the matter. Eager to broaden the judicial definition of labor rights, particularly under the Fair Labor Standards Act of 1938, the Black-led activists on the Court had written a succession of opinions, of which the *Jewell Ridge* case and its companion were significant elements, substantially strengthening the unions' bargaining position under the statutes. The current interest of the CIO unions, in particular, was in shortening the working day by compelling employers to recognize that the day began from the moment the laborer came onto the premises until the moment he left. "Portal to portal" was the rallying slogan of the union leaders in the year following the end of the war.

The case which brought the activist bloc to its extreme point of challenge to Congress was *Anderson v. Mount Clemens Pottery Co.*, in which Black, as senior Justice after Stone's death and before Vinson's appointment, again assigned the writing of the opinions. In this case as in *Jewell Ridge*, the zealously pro-labor Murphy wrote the majority opinion citing the earlier cases which had ,incensed Jackson as authority for the proposition that compensable employee time was any time "controlled or required by the employer and pursued necessarily and primarily for the benefit of the employer and his business." Thus a statutory work period, Murphy concluded, "includes all time during which an employee is necessarily required to be on the employer's premises" and must be held within the wage period covered by the Wage-Hour Act.[15]

Burton, speaking for himself and Frankfurter, hinted at the course of action open to Congress by protesting that the intent of the statute was not "to set aside long established contracts or customs which had absorbed into the rate of pay of the respective jobs recognition of whatever preliminary activities might be required of the worker by that particular job."[16] But the primary force which was generated against the majority opinion came from industry, which was aghast at the prospect that suits for back overtime now made possible by the *Mount Clemens* rule could run into billions of dollars.

The Fair Labor Standards Act had made mandatory a minimum wage for a forty-hour work week with time and a half for overtime, thus writing into law a standard bargaining feature of the great breakthrough in unionization in 1937.* In the course of the next eight years, the labor contract in compliance with this law had become all but universal—although the Wage-Hour Administrator regularly admonished both labor and industry that his interpretation of what constituted a work week within the definition of the law was subject to judicial modification.[17] The drive of the United Mine Workers, whose time involved in "portal-to-portal" employment underground was the most substantial in nature, led to the series of Court tests which culminated in the sweeping doctrine set out in *Mount Clemens.*

The postwar reaction of the American people—a retreat from the reform-mindedness which had been maintained not only by the war but by the tumultuous disputations of the depression before it—was reflected in the Congressional elections that fall. For the first time since 1932, the Republicans gained control of both houses of Congress; "the majority of Americans," observed *Time,* "had cast a protest vote" against the various frustrations of the time, including "price muddles, shortages, strikes, black markets, government bungling and confusion." Republican leaders began avidly discussing the candidates for the Presidential campaign two years hence, only superficially aware of three new faces which had appeared in Congress as a result of the polls—Joseph McCarthy, Republican of Wisconsin in the Senate, and the Congressmen Richard M. Nixon, Republican of California, and John F. Kennedy, Democrat of Massachusetts. GOP leaders in Congress were even more concerned about their legislative program; after fourteen years, they had a catalog of old scores to settle, the largest of all being with organized labor.[18]

*   *   *

For the conservatives, two glaring shortcomings existed in the nation's labor legislation—the lack of any restraining policies in the National Labor Relations Act and the tendency of the courts to expand the minimum-wage concepts of the Fair Labor Standards Act. For the former, Senator Robert A. Taft of Ohio was already formulating a remedy; for the latter, the conservative majority in Congress, goaded by the *Mount Clemens* decision on

---

*Cf. pp. 106-107 *supra.*

"portal-to-portal," was preparing an unprecedented legislative rebuke to the Court itself.

The debates on the "portal-to-portal" law quickly developed into a party issue, with the substantial Republican majority alternating between a protestation that it wanted justice for both capital and labor and a declaration that the New Deal labor statutes had been vehicles for a perpetuation of Democratic power. Southern Democrats joined in referring to the Wage-Hour Act as a "cancer" they would like to see excised entirely from the body of law; and conservatives of all colors eagerly stressed the fact that since the wage rights set out in the statute were solely by grace of Congressional act, they could be curtailed by amendatory legislation.[19]

The debate soon involved the Court. Congressman Clare Hoffman of Michigan declared that the lawsuits now reportedly accumulating on back "portal-to-portal" pay "are the result of a decision of Justice Murphy and four of his associates" which had made a gift of "$6,000,000,000 worth" of back overtime to the CIO. "Way back in 1937," Hoffman recalled, "Justice Murphy gave us the sit-down strike in Michigan, and you gentlemen from the other states have had the benefit of that over the years. The action of the then governor of Michigan was a gift to the CIO—which enabled it to exist."[20]

In the Senate, Wiley of Wisconsin opened the debate by stating that the country had moved from "the era of unsettled labor conditions . . . to an era of uncertainty for management," and that the "portal-to-portal" bill was intended to help reestablish a balance of interests in wages and hours. Forrest Donnell of Missouri, floor manager for the bill, added that aside from relieving capital of the threat of billions of dollars in liability incurred by virtue of an unanticipated judicial interpretation, the proposed legislation sought to ensure that "the opportunity for the recurrence of such a condition of surprise and disaster to American industry" would be eliminated. With this oblique way of stating that the bill was limiting the jurisdiction of the courts in future "portal-to-portal" suits, the conservative majority overrode all protests and passed the bill.

The direct rebuke to the activist bloc on the Court was made clear in the unprecedented language of the law's policy statement: "The Congress hereby finds that the Fair Labor Standards Act of 1938, as amended, has been interpreted judicially in disregard of long-established customs, practices and contracts between employers and employees, thereby creating wholly unexpected liabilities, immense in amount and retroactive in operation.*[21]

*   *   *

Although the Supreme Court, in the same month as the enactment of the "portal-to-portal" law, sustained a contempt citation against John L.

---

*See note on Congressional response to Supreme Court interpretation of statutes in Appendix D.

Lewis and the United Mine Workers for defying a strike injunction, the wide divisions of opinion in the case, reminiscent of the Stone Court in its most disjunctive temper, did not mollify a Congress bent on revising the National Labor Relations Act as drastically as it had modified the Wage-Hour Act.

Throughout the forties, in the face of no-strike pledges in the interest of the nation's war effort, Lewis had successfully employed the threat or the fact of walkouts to force concessions for his miners. To forestall any work stoppages in the wave of strikes sweeping the postwar economy, the government had taken over the operation of all important mines and in the spring of 1946 had executed an agreement between Lewis and Department of the Interior Secretary Julius Krug. Ever ready to tear up any agreement if he found the conditions worsening for his men, Lewis served notice of termination of the agreement in the fall. The administration forces held firm, and the District of Columbia court issued a temporary restraining order until it could determine whether a union could unilaterally terminate the agreement. Upon the union's ignoring of the order, the court imposed a fine of $3,500,000 on the UMW and $10,000 on its president.[22]

The workers promptly raised the question of the injunction under the Norris-LaGuardia Act on appeal, whereupon the Vinson Court divided into five groups. The Chief Justice, joined with Burton and Reed, determined that the statute did not apply to injunctions sought by the United States, and that in any event a temporary order for the purpose of determining the right to strike was within the power of the trial court.[23] Jackson concurred separately, arguing that the Norris-LaGuardia Act on its face relieved the Court of taking jurisdiction in the matter of injunctions; Frankfurter, one of the godfathers of the statute, concurred for a diametrically opposite reason. Black and Douglas concurred in part but declined to support the condition imposed by the majority under which the $3,500,000 fine was to be reduced to $700,000 on compliance with the order to terminate the union's defiance.* Murphy and Rutledge categorically dissented.[24]

"In our complex society, there is a great variety of limited loyalties," Vinson observed, "but the overriding loyalty of all is to our country and to the institutions under which a particular interest may be pursued." For a man who was criticized, upon being appointed Chief Justice, for a lack of a manifest judicial philosophy, the statement was to become a main point of reference in the philosophical conflicts which the seven years of his administration were to witness. His position with respect to Lewis and the UMW was unequivocal; the restraints of the anti-injunction act did not run against the government, and a private party to an agreement with the government could not take unilateral action to dissolve the agreement.[25]

Frankfurter, concurring, differentiated between an injunction forbidding a strike and what he saw in the District Court's action as an injunction against

---

*The fine was ultimately set at $1,400,000.

starting a strike until the question of the parties' rights under the agreement could be analyzed. "If one man can be allowed to determine for himself what is law, every man can. That means first chaos, then tyranny." To that extent, he was compelled to support the majority opinion; beyond that, however, Frankfurter insisted that the legislative history of both the Norris-LaGuardia and the War Labor Disputes Acts denied the argument that the government was exempt from the restraints upon injunctions.[26]

Murphy's objection was cast in terms of the ultimate morals of the government action: "If seizure alone justifies an injunction" where a government sympathetic to labor feels compelled to prevent a strike in the national interest, he pointed out, "some future government could easily utilize seizure as a subterfuge for breaking any or all strikes in private industries." Rutledge added, in a separate dissent, that "under 'a government of laws and not of men' such as we possess, power must be exercised according to law; and government, including the courts, as well as the governed, must move within its limitations."[27]

*   *   *

It was Senator Robert A. Taft's conviction, also, that the governed as well as the government should be subject to a rule of law, and he discerned in the state of postwar labor a tendency toward an irresponsible use of economic power for which existing statutes provided no counterweight. Given his particular conservative heritage, it was not surprising that he should see in the Wagner Act as it had existed for more than a decade a serious imbalance in industrial relations. He appeared in the position of negotiator of a sweeping legislative revision of the labor laws at a moment when all of the conservative complaints about labor's growing power were given focus and impetus by the Republican landslide in the 1946 Congressional elections.[28]

Just as the progressives throughout the 1920's had held out doggedly against the predominant conservatism of their era, so the conservatives had dug themselves in, after the Wagner Act in the heyday of the New Deal, to await a change of political climate. Now that it had come, liberals cried out that the calendar was about to be turned back; like most such cries of calamity, this one was to prove exaggerated—even though it was evident that a substantial modification of the labor law was going to be undertaken and that the conservatives had the votes to sustain it. The ultimate fact was that, however much the conservatives would have wished to eradicate what had been done in the labor field by the New Deal, they only succeeded in a legislative definition of what labor relations were to be in the post-New Deal world. The Wagner Act had been devised to deal with an industrial economy in which organized labor had no vested rights; the 1947 legislation to which Taft's name was to be attached had to deal with an economy in which labor's vested rights had come to be on a parity with those of capital.[29]

Still, the other lawmaker whose name would be identified with the new labor code obviously thought in terms of the old days of *laissez-faire* and freedom of contract. Congressman Fred A. Hartley of New Jersey spent twenty years in the House of Representatives, and his tenure from 1929 to 1949 coincided with the apocalypse of normalcy, the struggle for New Deal reform, the strictures of the war period and the disillusionments and intellectual fatigue of the postwar years. In the flush of conservative revival in 1947, he declared that "as a result of labor laws ill conceived and disastrously executed, the American workingman has been deprived of his dignity as an individual."[30] Hartley was to claim, after the extreme proposals of the House version of the bill had been trimmed out in conference committee, that his effort to wipe out the Wagner Act altogether was part of a strategy to ensure some sort of bill being adopted. "We put everything we could into the House bill so we would have something to concede and still get an adequate bill in the end," he told a reporter. Until the more balanced Senate version was evolved, however, Hartley plainly hoped to push through an omnibus bill which would have something for every hue of conservatism among Republicans and Southern Democrats.[31]

Hartley's own attitude seemed to characterize the House temper on the bill. A caterwauling debate erupted in the course of hearings before the Committee on Education and Labor with a parade of witnesses dominated, according to one labor sympathizer on the committee, by employers who had been cited by the NLRB for unfair practices. Five volumes of testimony from more than 130 witnesses were compiled, but not necessarily referred to in the course of the debate on the House floor. The minority report of the committee charged that the bill reported out had not even been subjected to a full committee discussion, and indeed had been written by the majority before testimony had been taken.[32]

Riding roughshod through the House, the Hartley bill reached the Senate as Taft's own bill was coming on for debate; in the ultimate decision to shelve the latter in favor of the House bill, the Senate was able to moderate the tone of the measure and sustain most of its changes in conference committee. On June 6, by a vote of 54 to 17, the Senate passed the bill and sent it to the White House. Overwhelmed by the conservative uprising in Congress, the liberals called upon the country to besiege the Executive with veto requests; already, in his struggle with a hostile Congress, Truman had sent nearly two dozen vetoes back to Capitol Hill, and most of them had been sustained.[33]

West Coast labor announced plans for a "veto caravan," reminiscent of Coxey's "army," to march on Washington, while Mayor William O'Dwyer of New York announced an official municipal "veto day." There was little doubt, however, that the President had already made up his mind. In the two weeks* that the measure lay upon his desk, a correspondent reported, it was subjected to intensive analysis by Truman's closest advisers, but their studies

---

*Ten legislative days.

were essentially intended to provide points to be stressed in the veto message.[34]

A Democratic President, the trustee of the New Deal tradition, had no choice but to have the record show that he had disavowed the effort to revise one of the cardinal provisions of the reforms of the thirties. His breaking of both the railroad and coal strikes of 1946 had soured labor's political leaders, and their inaction in the fall elections had contributed to the debacle which overtook the Democrats and made possible the 80th Congress. The attitude of this Congress in attacking both the Wagner and Wage-Hour laws made clear that labor had leaped from the frying pan into the fire, and a Truman veto made logical the return of labor's political support in 1948. The veto also cut the ground from under the bruited third-party movement under Henry Wallace, and while it made a lot of people angry, "his advisers," said *Time,* "hoped that they would be mostly people who would not vote for him anyhow."[35]

The House of Representatives overrode the veto within minutes after the message was received. In the Senate, Wayne Morse of Oregon, Glen Taylor of Idaho, Harley Kilgore of West Virginia and Claude Pepper of Florida organized for a filibuster, intended not to kill the measure but to delay action until, they hoped, Truman's radio broadcast of his veto message might have some effect on constituent reaction. It was in vain; Taylor spoke for eight hours and 25 minutes, Morse one minute less than ten hours. Thereafter the Senate overrode by a substantial margin.[36]

*   *   *

The Taft-Hartley Labor-Management Relations Act of 1947, said Senator Walter George of Georgia, was a legislative step in the direction of breaking "the stranglehold of the labor bosses." For David Dubinsky, president of the International Ladies' Garment Workers' Union, it was "a snake-bite into the heart of American liberties." As experience was to prove, the statute was less a rejection of the elemental rights of labor organization than it was a shift in philosophy; where the Wagner Act had charged management with the sole responsibility for precipitating industrial strife, the new law asserted that labor had grown to a state of equal responsibility.

In the same vein, the 80th Congress concluded that the National Labor Relations Board, which had carried to a logical extreme the dual administrative functions of prosecutor and judge, required a division of functions into regional directorates responsible for investigation and a fact-trying board independent of its general counsel. The law sought to meet the widely held public conviction that Communists had infiltrated many unions by requiring an abjuror's oath of union officers. It outlawed the closed shop—under the euphemism of the "right to work," a slogan developed by conservative state legislatures in drafting local laws on the subject—as well as secondary boycotts and jurisdictional strikes, two matters of substantial public irritation.[37]

Ironically for the conservative majority in the 80th Congress, the enactment of the Taft-Hartley law had two major consequences: it drove organized labor back into political activism in the interests of the Democrats, and it dealt with a major area of Federal administration by substantially enlarging, rather than reducing, Federal power. For labor, which would seek unsuccessfully to repeal the law in future Congresses, and only in piecemeal fashion to be able to modify some of the 1947 provisions, Taft-Hartley became a fetish of diminishing appeal to the rank and file as the succeeding decades of prosperity refuted the dire predictions of the time.[38]

For the American people, the legislative session of 1947 prepared the way for a clearcut choice in the oncoming Presidential elections: The Twenty-Second Amendment, the "portal-to-portal" act and the Taft-Hartley law represented the alternatives the Republicans had to offer to the New Deal and post-New Deal era. Truman himself, in a masterful political stroke, summoned the Congress into special session on the eve of the election to demonstrate his charge that its negative attitudes made it "the worst Congress in history."[39]

Nonetheless, the confident Republican party smelled victory in the 1948 campaign. Thomas E. Dewey, deft and politically powerful, alternated between apostrophes to the good old days and ambivalent positions on modern economic and social legislation already rooted in American life. Truman, plodding over thousands of miles of campaign trails, seemed incapable of firing the old enthusiasms first touched off by Franklin Roosevelt. He provided pyrotechnics, to be sure, and knowledgeable political observers concluded that his audiences came to enjoy the show. "Give 'em hell, Harry," hardly seemed like a battle cry of liberal resurgence; one professional pollster declared the election settled by early September, and Dewey's homestretch speeches were concerned largely with what harm a defeated administration could do in the remaining weeks between November and January.[40]

Added to Truman's travail were the substantial splinter parties—Wallace's frenetic Progressives and Strom Thurmond's South Carolina-based "Dixiecrats," both aimed at seeing that the incumbent in the White House was defeated. Thurmond's "States' Rights" Democrats, indeed, presented the real issue confronting the nation—whether it was possible at this stage in the twentieth century to reverse a trend away from localisms, both economic and political, which had been steadily accelerating for fifty years. More than a million persons swung thirty-nine electoral votes to the party in affirmation of the idea as well as in protest against the powerful civil rights plank written into the Democratic platform that year.[41]

The stunning defeat of Dewey in the face of a conspiracy of hostile factors was less important in itself than the remarkable consequence of the election as a whole: Two years after they had elected a smothering conservative majority to Congress, the American people turned them out and installed an equally substantial progressive majority. The Democrats who regained control of both Houses of Congress were men pledged to the introduction of a broad range of new social and economic legislation which would replace the New Deal with the Fair Deal—widened Social Security, an attempt at repeal of Taft-Hartley, a new statutory role in public housing, and an affirmative program to enforce the civil rights of all disfranchised Americans. Men like Paul Douglas of Illinois, Estes Kefauver of Tennessee, and Hubert Humphrey of Minnesota entered the Senate to make good the pledges.[42]

*   *   *

The legislative proposals of the Fair Deal reflected the changing interests and requirements of a new society: broader Social Security coverage, higher minimum wage scales, the National Housing Act and similar enactments were structures erected on statutory foundations laid down in New Deal days which the people had now come to assume were permanent features of national life. In the existing aura of prosperity, they were advanced with less of the crusading tenor of the Roosevelt years. A more sophisticated public had come to take progressivism for granted, and their principal manifestation of their convictions was in overturning the 80th Congress and installing the 81st.

As events were already demonstrating, the real burning issues of the late forties were revolving around loyalties to or subversion of existing institutions. The problem had presented itself after the First World War, but its appearance as an aftermath of the Second was complicated by the beginning of the so-called "cold war," the emergent Communist imperialism in Europe and the outbreak of the Korean conflict in 1950. For men like Howard W. Smith of Virginia, the threat of foreign-born subversives had led to the Alien Registration Act of 1940, the judicial review of which was soon to come in the Vinson Court. For doctrinaire witch-hunters like McCarthy of Wisconsin, non-conformity of all types was by definition prospectively disloyal. For Pat McCarran of Nevada, the cycle was completed in 1950 with the passage of his Subversive Activities Control Act over Truman's veto, substantially enlarging the proscribed areas first defined in the President's own loyalty program.[43]

This shifting of political focus in the later 1940's in turn determined the nature of the constitutional business with which the Vinson Court would be primarily concerned. While the validity of reform legislation and the question of a steadily broadening Federalism would still require a certain amount of judicial attention, the fundamental matter of civil rights, as defined, circumscribed or protected by the Federal Constitution, ultimately came to dominate the dialogue.[44] "The New Deal spirit of jurisprudence," wrote one observer, had reached its zenith in the disparate majorities of the Stone Court; with Vinson, so far as the new jurisprudence was concerned, "the march is now largely in place." At the end of the Truman administration, the same writer would comment: "The transition from the New Deal Court to the Fair Deal Court has been a great change. In matters of economic policy, the machine runs in the same general direction as did the Roosevelt Court, but such vigor, militancy and spirit of innovation as the earlier Court had is gone."[45]

A major reason for this gradual quiescence was the sudden deaths, in 1949, of the fifty-six-year-old Frank Murphy and the fifty-five-year-old Wiley B. Rutledge, thus removing two of the prototypes of the New Deal Court. To fill these two vacancies, Truman followed the same practice he had initiated with the first two appointments, relying on men with whom he had intimate personal acquaintance or whose careers had progressed along the same general course as his own. In terms of personnel, accordingly, the Roosevelt Court became the Truman Court; for the four Truman appointees, men of moderate views as well as moderate abilities, tended to align with the three apostles of restraint—Frankfurter, Jackson and Reed—to reduce the Black-Douglas bloc both in numbers and in volume of argumentation.

The reduction of the activist bloc to two meant, among other things, that they could not compel the Court to review all facets of civil liberties on certiorari as they had formerly done under the "rule of four." Conversely, as the easy-going Vinson encouraged the tribunal to limit the number of cases for which full oral argument and full opinions would be required each term, the intellectual leaders like Black, Douglas, Frankfurter and Jackson were able to devote more time to the elaboration of their own jurisprudential expositions.*

Tom Clark, a genial Texan who had spent seven years in the Department of Justice without compiling a particularly notable record, was a protégé of Senator Tom Connally and through his influence was advanced by Truman to Attorney General. Although he was approved by the Senate without any serious question, the Judiciary Committee in 1953, probing into embarrassing questions of vote frauds in the ex-President's Kansas City bailiwick, invited the Justice to testify as to his role in the Justice Department's perfunctory investigation. Clark declined to appear before the committee, and a movement to subpoena him was defeated.[46]

Sherman Minton of Indiana was recommended to Truman by J. Howard McGrath, Clark's successor as Attorney General. The President needed little urging; he remembered Minton as the New Deal whip in the heyday of the Roosevelt reforms in the Senate, and after his defeat for reelection he had been selected by Roosevelt as one of the administrative assistants in the White House and shortly thereafter had been named a judge of the Court of Appeals. Pugnacious and pedantic—his critics sometimes said that the bellicosity with which he asserted the law was in inverse ratio to his knowledge of it—Minton was considered by most contemporary students of the Court as the poorest of Truman's unremarkable selections for the high tribunal.[47]

Added to its varied shortcomings, the Truman administration never succeeded in extricating itself from the shadow of the Roosevelt image, and its own accomplishments and the quality of its own personnel always had to submit to comparison with the heroic proportions of the New Deal in its heyday. The Cabinet which replaced the Roosevelt men could hardly be

---

*Chs. 9 and 10.

called distinguished. Ex-Justice James F. Byrnes and former Chief of Staff George C. Marshall were somewhat anomalous choices as Secretaries of State. Dean G. Acheson was a substantial advance as their successor, although he soon became a target of the McCarthyite hysteria. Another target—of the professional liberals and Zionists—was James V. Forrestal, last secretary of the independent Navy Department and first secretary of the new Defense Department; his proposal to rehabilitate Germany as a Western partner and to give the Arabs a day in court on the proposed state of Israel threatened serious embarrassment to the Truman campaign in 1948. Julius Krug in Interior and Louis Johnson in Defense created even more explosive troubles for Truman. Indeed, in the five years following Roosevelt's death there were no less than twenty-one changes in Cabinet positions.[48]

Justice was in the worst administrative situation of all. Clark, reportedly disappointed at having lost the Chief Justiceship to Vinson, was promised the next Court seat and spent most of his time as Attorney General for the next two years waiting for the opening. Rhode Island Senator J. Howard McGrath, Democratic National Chairman, succeeded him in 1949 and was fired in 1952 amid a welter of charges of general administration corruption which the Justice Department would not or could not run down. For the remainder of Truman's term he was followed by James P. McGranery, a political henchman whom the President had earlier rewarded with a Federal judgeship. Not since Hoover's administration had the Attorney General's office compiled such an indifferent record of accomplishments.[49]

*   *   *

For all its diminished capacity for further experimental essays in constitutional law, the Vinson Court with fair consistency upheld the Federal power in all instances in which it was called into question. In June, 1947 a seven-to-one majority, with Jackson disqualifying himself, affirmed the paramount authority of the United States over tideland oil reserves lying off the shore of California. Despite the zealous advocacy of private oil interests in favor of a state title to the lands, Truman had instituted an original suit through the Department of Justice to confirm the Federal government's title. Black's opinion, while conceding that Congress could limit the Attorney General's authority to bring such an action, found that until such time as Congress acted the Executive branch could proceed to test the title.[50]

The interest of the Federal government in tidelands oil resources, said Black, was a trust for all the people of the nation and overrode the interests of a particular state within whose coastal area the resources happened to be situated. Three years later, Douglas spoke in similar vein for a six-to-one majority, with Clark and Jackson abstaining, in a suit brought by the United States against Louisiana; the same day, in a suit against Texas, the majority dropped to five to three, but the Federal interest was still upheld. Three years later, Congress responded to the oil companies' pressures and adopted a statute waiving the Federal rights in the tidelands oil areas.[51]

The Court upheld the Hatch Act curtailing political activities of certain classes of government employees, by a four-to-three majority, with two Justices abstaining. By a similar accidental majority of four to three, it upheld the so-called "anti-Petrillo" statute under which Congress sought to curb the leader of the musicians' union in his insistence upon the employment of minimum numbers of union members by broadcasting stations. The wartime statute defining the terms on which the government would renegotiate contracts as its requirements for services and supplies changed was affirmed by a non-dissenting majority (with Douglas dissenting in part); and the military authority of the United States to conduct the Japanese war crimes prosecutions was affirmed in an unusual *per curiam* opinion from which Murphy dissented and in which Douglas concurred in a lengthy opinion.[52]

In most of these cases, an undercurrent of uncertainty manifested itself. Black dissented from the Hatch Act decision with the observation that there was "nothing about Federal and state employees as a class which justifies depriving them or society of the benefits of their participating in public affairs," or which warranted Congress' acting "so drastically to stifle . . . spoken and written political utterances and lawful political activities." Murphy and Rutledge joined in Reed's protest against the "anti-Petrillo" law because it was vague definition of criminal liability.[53]

In the Japanese war crimes case, Jackson filed an unusual memorandum appended to the Court's order of oral argument, explaining in a lengthy but not very clear statement why he considered himself not disqualified by virtue of his role as prosecutor in the Nuremberg cases. The Court without him would be evenly divided over the question of whether the Japanese petition for habeas corpus should be heard; to have a hearing on the constitutional issue denied by default, Jackson declared, would be harmful to the nation's position in the law of nations. When the Court proceeded therafter to deny the petition after argument, Jackson abstained from participating.[54]

This type of consistency effected through ambivalence became increasingly a characteristic of the Vinson Court in the face of inexorably growing varieties of cases involving complex moral issues. The cases themselves reflected the temper of the "cold war" with its own ambivalent objectives of building up a deterrent military force abroad while seeking to promote the good life at home as well as abroad. NATO and the United Nations, the Truman Doctrine and the Marshall Plan, the unprecedented security policy embodied in the Atomic Energy Act, the prospect of an indefinitely partitioned Germany, an increasingly socialized Great Britain and a massive disintegration of Nationalist China as a mainland force—these, coupled with the economic pressures on all fronts, combined to produce an almost manic state of the public mind.

Pervading all issues of the day was the increasingly obsessive quest for a standard of loyalty which was constantly on the verge of being translated into a requirement of conformity, periodically exacerbated by the hysteria of Joseph McCarthy, the other-wordly quality of the trial of Alger Hiss, the

conviction and execution of atomic spies Julius and Ethel Rosenberg. The
atmosphere of suspicion had been clouding since 1938, when the House Un-
American Activities Committee had first begun its investigations under the
chairmanship of Martin Dies of Texas. It had been rebuked, but hardly
deterred, by the 1946 report of the President's Committee on Civil Rights
which deplored the resort to outlawry and repression which characterized
the Dies group's approach to the issue of internal security. The Court, by
an equivocal five-to-two majority, had struck down a disability statute in
United States v. Lovett the same year; it was only the beginning, however, of
a long series of cases which were to test the capacity of the judiciary to
identify and protect the basic values of American democracy.[55]

*   *   *

Vinson undertook to articulate his own position on civil rights in a
1950 case challenging the anti-Communist oath required by the Taft-Hartley
Act of union officers. "Congress could rationally find that the Communist
party is not like other political parties in its utilization of positions of union
leadership as means by which to bring about strikes and other obstructions
of commerce for purposes of political advantage," he declared; and although
matters of personal belief are not ordinarily relevant "to permissible subjects
of government action, this does not lead to the conclusion that such circumstances are never relevant."

The problem of 1950, said Vinson, "is not the same one that Justices
Holmes and Brandeis found it convenient to consider in terms of clear and
present danger. Government's interest here is not in preventing the dissemination of Communist doctrine or the holding of particular beliefs because it is
feared that unlawful action will result therefrom if free speech is practiced.
Its interest is in protecting the free flow of commerce from what Congress
considers to be substantive evils of conduct that are not the products of speech
at all."[56]

American Communications Association v. Douds was another badly
divided opinion. Clark, Douglas and Minton did not participate in the case,
Frankfurter and Jackson dissented in part and Black *in toto*, so that Vinson's
elaborate rationale represented the view of only three Justices. Frankfurter
conceded that it "would make undue inroads upon the policy-making power
of Congress" to hamper its power to ensure industrial peace by insulating
from its power those whose purpose was to disrupt that peace. To be consistent with the Court's painstaking development of a doctrine of broad
legislative discretion, he said, it was necessary to presume in favor of the
validity of legislation aimed at dealing with a particular mischief. "I cannot
believe," said Frankfurter, "that Congress has less power to protect a labor
union from Communist party domination than it has from employer domination."

"The task of this Court to maintain a balance between liberty and
authority is never done, because new conditions today upset the equilibriums

of yesterday," Frankfurter observed. "The Court's day-to-day task is to reject as false, claims in the name of civil liberty which, if granted, would paralyze or impair authority to defend existence of our society, and to reject as false claims in the name of security which would undermine our freedoms and open the way to oppression."[57]

Black, for whom the civil liberties issues of the Vinson Court would provide the ultimate focus for his jurisprudence, warned against the easy assumption that a curtailment of constitutional liberty could be limited to minimal requirements of national security: Such an assumption blinks the fact "that individual mental freedom can be constitutionally abridged whenever any majority of this Court finds a satisfactory legislative reason."[58]

*   *   *

The Vinson and Black doctrines alternated in the balance during the term of Court which began in October, 1950. In December Black spoke for a unanimous bench in holding that a witness before a grand jury was protected under the Fifth Amendment from being required to answer questions about the Communist party or her employment by it. When the grand jury sought the witness for further questioning and was unable to find her, it summoned her husband and asked him to disclose her whereabouts. Black, for a six-to-two majority, held that all marital communications were privileged and immune from infringement in court.[59]

Two months later, however, Vinson spoke for a five-to-three majority in finding a witness not justified in refusing to identify the recipient of party papers when she had already testified as to her prior custody of the papers. Having already testified as to the fact which might incriminate her, said the Court, the subsequent testimony did not present "reasonable danger of further crimination." For Black, Douglas and Frankfurter, the "waiver doctrine" put witnesses in a chronic state of jeopardy which the current cases had tried to avoid. On the one hand, wrote Black, witnesses "risk imprisonment for contempt by asserting the privilege prematurely; on the other, they might lose the privilege if they answer a single question. The Court's view makes the protection depend on timing so refined that lawyers, let alone laymen, will have difficulty in knowing when to claim it."[60]

Three cases in succession on January 15, 1951 demonstrated the tenuous support for the Vinson viewpoint. In a non-dissenting majority involving the right of a religious sect to hold meetings in a public park, Vinson held that the requirement of a permit for such a meeting violated the First Amendment and the refusal of a permit violated the equal protection clause In a second opinion in which Black and Frankfurter concurred and Jackson dissented, Vinson invalidated a similar municipal permit requirement on the ground that the ordinance did not require the local officials to find a danger of breach of the peace before refusing to issue the permit. Finally, in *Feiner v. New York,* Vinson spoke for a majority of five, supplemented by Frankfurter's concurrence in the result, upholding a conviction for disorderly conduct where a student harangued a group to help Negroes secure their rights by force. Black protested that the conviction grew solely out of the unpopularity of his views, while Douglas and Minton found no evidence of a present danger of riot.[61]

A relentless torrent of civil rights questions growing out of the loyalty issue continued to pour down upon the Court, and the continued ambivalence of the answers emphasized the tormented state of mind of the Justices. Did the non-Communist oath requirement in labor cases, as affirmed in *Douds,* apply to government employees? Clark, for a five-to-four majority, answered affirmatively with reference to a Los Angeles charter provision to that effect. Frankfurter, among the four dissenters, conceded that in "the context of our time, such membership is sufficiently relevant to effective and dependable government," but found that the lack of *scienter* provisions* in the loyalty oath violated due process.[62]

In the next term of Court, the Frankfurter objection prevailed and the tribunal unanimously invalidated an Oklahoma loyalty oath on the ground that it arbitrarily disqualified individuals who in good faith believed the organizations to which they belonged to be innocuous. Such a standard of disbarment, said Clark, amounted to guilt by association which was odious to the First Amendment.[63] But the problem of guilt by association was only beginning to reveal its true dimensions; in 1951 the four-year-old loyalty board program of the Executive Department was substantially revised to include all cases where, "on all the evidence, there is reasonable doubt" as to an employee's loyalty. To guide both boards and oath-takers in identifying subversive organizations, the Attorney General was authorized by executive order to prepare a list of "totalitarian, fascist, Communist, or subversive" agencies which sought to deny constitutional rights to others by violence or to alter the form of government by unconstitutional means.[64]

In April, 1951 three organizations which found themselves listed on the Attorney General's catalog sued to remove their names. The trial court sustained the government's motion to dismiss the complaints, and the Court of Appeals affirmed the judgment by a two-to-one vote. But by a vote of five to three—with five different opinions written by the majority—the Supreme Court reversed the lower courts. An arbitrary listing contrary to available facts, said Burton, takes a government agency beyond the scope of its authority and gratuitously jeopardizes the parties affected by the arbitrary act. A proceeding such as a list of subversive organizations, added Black, possesses "almost every quality of bills of attainder" explicitly forbidden by the Constitution. In an effort to synthesize both arguments, Frankfurter observed that "democracy implies respect for the elementary rights of men, however suspect or unworthy; a democratic government must therefore

---

*I.e., lack of safeguard requiring that prosecution prove the guilty knowledge of the accused.

practice fairness; and fairness can rarely be obtained by secret, one-sided determination of facts decisive of rights." The adoption of anti-democratic methods to detect subversion, said Frankfurter, sets in motion a subversive process far more dangerous to free institutions.[65]

*   *   *

Still, the Vinson wing of the Court tended to deal gently with government procedures which often built subversive cases on unsworn testimony by unidentified witnesses, watering down the propositions of the preceding cases to a point where, in Jackson's critical phrase, the majority tended to grant "relief to the group while refusing it to the individual."[66] A seven-to-two majority upheld a New York law which disqualified teachers who, after full notice and hearing, were found to belong to the state's own list of subversive groups.[67] In an unhappy time, the Court was unable to settle upon a definitive standard for the preservation of individual rights.

The climax in the Communist and Communist-association cases was *Dennis v. United States,* a testing of the Smith Alien Registration Act with the now familiar splintering of opinions by the Court. The original trial, involving a large number of admitted revolutionists as defendants, had taken nine months of unruly testimony and produced more than 16,000 pages of evidence. On review by the Supreme Court the constitutional questions centered around the First, Fifth and Fourteenth Amendments and required an answer which would restate the rationale of freedom of expression and action in a subversion-sensitive nation.

The constitutionality of the Smith Act was sustained in a cluster of opinions representing a six-to-two majority, with Clark not participating. Vinson, writing the Court's opinion for himself, Burton, Minton and Reed, found an organized conspiracy to overthrow the government, in the context of the postwar world, a sufficiently clear and present danger to meet the World War I test in *Schenck v. United States.* As for the First Amendment guarantees, Vinson observed that "neither Justice Holmes nor Justice Brandeis ever envisioned that a shorthand phrase should be crystallized into a rigid rule to be applied inflexibly without regard to the circumstances of each case. Speech," he continued, "is not an absolute, above and beyond control by the legislature when its judgment, subject to review here, is that certain kinds of speech are so undesirable as to warrant criminal sanction. Nothing is more certain in modern society than the principle that there are no absolutes. . . . To those who would paralyze our government in the face of an impending threat by encasing it in a semantic straitjacket we must reply that all concepts are relative."[68]

While he was willing to concur in the upholding of the convictions, on his principle of judicial abstinence from restricting the legislative freedom of judgment, Frankfurter was constrained to expostulate: "No matter how clear we may be that the defendants now before us are preparing to overthrow our government at the propitious moment, it is self-delusion to think that we can punish them for their advocacy without adding to the risks run by loyal citizens who honestly believe in some of the reforms these defendants advance. It is a sobering fact that in sustaining the conviction before us we can hardly escape restriction on the interchange of ideas."[69]

Black dissented by pointing out that the original indictment had nothing to do with overt acts but only with a meeting of minds to engage in writing and speech thereafter. Such a degree of pre-censorship, he said, "waters down the First Amendment so that it amounts to little more than an admonition to Congress."[70] Douglas, in a more detailed protest, suggested that the majority had affirmed a valid standard for curtailment of First Amendment freedoms but only by affirming a judgment which was initially wrong: "There comes a time when even speech loses its constitutional immunity. Speech innocuous one year may at another time fan such destructive flames that it must be halted in the interests of the safety of the republic. That is the meaning of the clear and present danger test. . . . Yet free speech is the rule, not the exception. The restraint to be constitutional must be based on more than fear, on more than passionate opposition against the speech, on more than a revolted dislike for its contents. There must be some immediate injury to society that is likely if speech is allowed." This, said Douglas, was a question which should have been submitted to the jury and made the basis of its verdict.[71]

The *Dennis* case marked the ultimate extreme to which *Schenck* had pointed in 1919; it depreciated the significance of the Holmes dissent in *Abrams v. United States* and the struggle throughout the twenties to win majority approval for the view which culminated in *Near v. Minnesota*. *Dennis* marked the contemporary ascendancy of the Vinson policy of suffering curtailment of constitutional rights on a reasonable legislative determination of clear and present danger. Where political radicalism was concerned, the majority on the Vinson Court found itself applying the doctrines of the Taft Court of the early twenties.[72]

* * *

The freedom of religion clause of the First Amendment was another stumbling block for the Court at the end of the forties and beginning of the fifties. The flurry of cases prior to the war, involving the handbill ordinances aimed at the Jehovah's Witnesses, gradually were supplanted by even knottier issues involving the use of public educational facilities for religious purposes or the releasing of student time for attendance at religious instruction. The cases alternated between the "free exercise" guarantee and the "establishment" prohibition of the First Amendment.

In a five-to-four decision, the Court in 1947 upheld a New Jersey law permitting taxpayers whose children attended parochial schools to be reimbursed from public funds for the costs of transportation to these schools. Black, speaking for the majority, held that public-supported school bus service was "public welfare legislation" to which all taxpayers were entitled.

Rutledge, for the dissenters, felt that reimbursement for transportation to church schools was a direct aid to religious activity forbidden by the Constitution.[73]

Yet Black and his majority members were opposed to an Illinois plan for releasing students from classes for periods of religious instruction of their preference in segregated parts of the school buildings; the unconstitutional element, said an eight-Justice majority, lay in the use of the school facilities for this instructional purpose.[74] When, in a later case coming up from New York, the pupils' time was released for instruction off the public premises, a majority of six upheld the law.[75]

The Illinois decision outraged church groups throughout the country; the New York decision outraged the anti-establishmentarian elements to an equal degree. The Court ducked the issue entirely in another New Jersey case, which provided for Bible-reading as part of the school ceremonies, by ruling that the plaintiffs lacked standing to be heard.[76] Thus, by the spring of 1952, the Court was approaching religious freedom issues, like the Fifth Amendment issues, with an increasingly manifest air of self-doubt.

*   *   *

The tendency of complicated contemporary issues of law to muddy waters of doctrine which had formerly seemed relatively clear, aside from the problems of the First Amendment presented in the loyalty oaths, the Communist advocacy cases, and the school and religion juxtapositions, manifested itself even more strikingly in the area of criminal law. The Vinson Court stirred up matters in 1946 by holding constitutional a search and seizure which involved a five-hour ransacking of private premises on a warrant for arrest on mail fraud which turned up instead evidence of unlawful possession of Selective Service cards. The Chief Justice, for a five-to-four majority which included the liberals Black and Douglas, held that since "the objects sought for and those actually discovered were properly subject to seizure," no constitutional immunity had been violated.[77]

Frankfurter, in an eloquent review of constitutional history, protested that this was precisely the sort of thing which had brought about the rejection of the general warrant. The fact that entry into the suspect's home was lawful, he added, merely went to the issue of trespass; the "protection of the Fourth Amendment extends to improper searches and seizures, quite apart from the legality of an entry."[78]

Douglas crossed over to the Frankfurter group in *Johnson v. United States,* where the Court held invalid an entry into a hotel room without warrant, followed by a discovery of opium and an arrest of the persons in the room. Such a proceeding, Jackson observed, put the government in the position of making an arrest to justify a search while at the same time making a search to justify the arrest.[79] But the niceties of the question became more debatable as further cases came on. Another five-to-four majority invalidated arrests by revenue officers who were led to an illicit still by the two-way radio directions of one of their own agents who had infiltrated the liquor ring. Murphy spoke for the majority in insisting that a warrant could easily have been obtained and the deliberate neglect of seeking it made the search and seizure unreasonable.[80]

Vinson led the dissenters in ridiculing a rigid hypothesis which nullified "a valid seizure of contraband materials located in plain sight in the structure in which the arrest took place." Where the issuance of the warrant would contribute nothing to the preservation of individuals' rights, Vinson said, the majority view "serves only to open an avenue of escape for those guilty of crime."[81]

Murphy's holding in *Trupiano v. United States* was overruled within a few months of his death. Minton, one of the new members of the Court, held in *United States v. Rabinowitz* that the "relevant test is not whether it is reasonable to procure a search warrant, but whether the search was reasonable."[82] With this 1950 decision, the Vinson Court settled upon a majority position which thereafter tended to remain consistent in favor of broader scope for Federal officers in search and seizure cases.

The Court moved into deeper and murkier waters as it undertook to review questions of fair trial of criminal cases in state courts, coerced confessions and denial of counsel to defendants. As evidence obtained through unreasonable search and seizure had been excluded from Federal courts, the possibility of extending the same exclusionary rule to the state courts through the Fourteenth Amendment logically suggested itself; but in both 1947 and 1949 the majority declined to go so far. To do so, argued Frankfurter, would require an incorporation of the Fourth Amendment into the Fourteenth, a prospect not anticipated by the framers of either.[83] Although the majority was willing, in *Wolf v. Colorado,* to assert as an abstract principle that individual privacy was to be kept secure from arbitrary intrusion, the Court declined to implement the principle by permitting a Federal court to enjoin the admission of evidence so obtained in a state trial.[84]

The right to counsel proved an equally difficult issue to face up to. While the majority, in *Townsend v. Burke,* set aside a conviction where the defendant was without legal assistance, its opinion was based on the sentencing judge's gratuitous comment on past records of conviction.[85] Black and Douglas, joined by Murphy and Rutledge while they lived, sought to overturn the increasingly criticized rule in *Betts v. Brady.* But to do so brought the Court back again to the question of extension of the several provisions of the Bill of Rights to the Fourteenth Amendment and hence to the states, and the majority continued to resist the logic of the proposition.[86]

The matter of confessions was complicated by another criticized case— *McNabb v. United States,* which in 1943 had held that delay in taking an accused person before the nearest judicial officer was presumptive evidence of coercion. In 1948 the Vinson Court reaffirmed the rule in *Upshaw v. United States*—but again declined to apply it to states under the Fourteenth

Amendment.[87] Even more emphatic in its acquiescence in a double standard of criminal justice in this respect was *Stein v. New York,* in which the majority concluded that since the defendants were mature men and since there was sufficient other evidence to support the charges, the fact that constitutional rights might have been infringed would not have affected the results of the case.[88]

*   *   *

The most sensitive area of all with which the Vinson Court was brought in contact was the issue of racial segregation. For half a century, the dissent of Justice Harlan in *Plessy v. Ferguson* had sat like Banquo's ghost at the elbows of succeeding generations of Justices, but the obvious social explosiveness of the subject prompted all factions on the Court to avoid the confrontation for as long as possible. The Constitution, it seemed, was not color blind. but only blind to the matter of racial equality.

The Vinson Court avoided the issue primarily by turning any constitutional question away from the "separate but equal" *versus* equal protection doctrines to a question of Federal authority under the commerce clause. Where the issue involved segregated transportation facilities, the rule against "Jim Crowism" could be enforced in interstate commerce while being left out of consideration in intrastate cases.[89] But in the matter of segregated educational facilities, the "separate but equal" doctrine had already been questioned in *Missouri ex rel. Gaines v. Canada,* and similar attacks were sustained in cases involving Oklahoma and Texas in 1948 and 1950.[90] But a direct overruling of *Plessy v. Ferguson* and a sweeping extension of the equal protection clause to the matter of racial equality was a challenge which was accepted only at the close of Vinson's Chief Justiceship; it would be part of the unfinished business to be handed on to the Warren Court.

*   *   *

The term beginning in October, 1952 would be the final one for the Vinson Court. In June of that year, in a case which required a record of seven separate opinions, the Court found a Presidential seizure of steel companies' properties to be unconstitutional. Truman's loathing of the procedure contained in the Taft-Hartley Act obviously underlay his determination to use other means to deal with a threatened strike in a time of national emergency. With the Korean War in progress, a work stoppage in steel was considered a serious blow to the government's capability for prosecuting the military action. When the issue had been referred without success to the Wage Stabilization Board, one of the several agencies created in an effort to keep brakes on inflationary tendencies, Truman ordered Secretary of Commerce Charles Sawyer to take possession of the steel mills throughout the country and operate them.

Here at length was presented the question first suggested by Theodore Roosevelt in his "stewardship" theory of Executive power: Did the President possess inherent power to act in what he conceived to be the national interest, absent any specific constitutional injunction? Justice Black, consistent with his activist philosophy, proposed to meet the issue directly—and to answer the question negatively. The man who had not heretofore hesitated to find a broad power of government in all parts of the Constitution now hesitated to find that a national emergency justified a seizure of private property because he could find no specific language to that effect.[91]

The language sounded like that of Frankfurter in his most restrained philosophy, but in this instance not even Frankfurter, though concurring, was prepared to go so far. The question of Presidential power as defined by the Constitution did not have to be reached, said Frankfurter for himself, Burton and Jackson, because the barrier to Truman's seizure already existed in specific legislation. "It is an inadmissibly narrow conception of American constitutional law to confine it to the words of the Constitution and to disregard the gloss which life has written upon them," Frankfurter admonished. Yet, having said so much, he himself was prepared only to say that in this case the Executive could proceed with seizure if Congress directed him to do so.[92]

Although Vinson, with Minton and Reed, filed an elaborate dissent, the steel case reflected the general disinclination of the Vinson Court to carry any of its constitutional arguments through to their logical extremes. Truman, by his four appointments, had reduced the former rapid pace of the new constitutionalism to a walk, often interrupted by hesitation before alternate courses encountered along the way. The continuing disparity of opinion, however, continued unabated; the observer of the institution, wrote Thomas Reed Powell, "gets the impression of a company of independent essay writers rather than of members of an official body wielding governmental power." For a decade and more, under the administration of both Stone and Vinson, the Court had been a culture bed of competing ideas of implementation of the constitutionalism conceived in the latter days of the Hughes Court.[93]

The age of the Great Depression and the decade of war and postwar were both now to give way to the new political and economic perspectives of the fifties and sixties. In the fall of 1952, resurgent Republicanism would win both the Presidential and Congressional elections, and in the spring of 1953 Vinson's death would terminate the interlude between the constitutional reforms of the late thirties and the renewed effort to articulate the constitutional requirements of the mid-century. The net result of the jurisprudential developments of the 1940's was a maturing of fundamental philosophies of three members of the Roosevelt Court as, in their continuing tenure from Hughes through Stone and Vinson to Warren, they shaped the intellectual environment in which the constitutionalism of the remainder of the twentieth century was to develop.

9/ The Transition of Liberalism

WHEN FELIX FRANKFURTER exchanged his chair as professor of law for the chair of Associate Justice of the Supreme Court, an astute observer of his lifelong studies of the personnel and procedure of the Federal bench stated: "Frankfurter does not deny authority to the world's most powerful court; instead, he pleads for self-restraint in its exercise." In the context of the judicial reaction of the mid-thirties, the restraint Frankfurter sought was the ideal of Holmes, to leave the legislature free to seek the best solutions for the people's problems. In the early sixties when he retired, the restraint Frankfurter urged had reached the opposite pole—in the context of judicial activism, to check the Court's disposition to broaden the law beyond the expressed letter of the legislative enactment or in lieu of any legislative expression. The doctrine of self-restraint had remained consistent, but the frame of reference had almost totally changed.[1]

Thus the judicial career of Justice Frankfurter, from 1939 to 1962, illustrated the gradual but almost predestined transition of that school of constitutional interpretation which, epitomized by Holmes, Brandeis and Cardozo in the heyday of *laissez-faire*, was described as liberalism—and which, after the triumph of the Roosevelt reforms and in the Kennedy-Johnson decade of the sixties, took on the appearance of conservatism. Holmes, in his philosophy a constitutional conservative, sat on the bench in an age when his skepticism and tolerance provided an enlightened contrast to the hardened conceptions of the majority. Frankfurter, all his life a liberal in philosophy, sat on the bench in a time when much of the old constitutionalism had been supplanted, and his argument for judicial abstinence seemed out of harmony on a Court which was affirmatively seeking to make a new world. Liberalism (and perhaps conservatism) in these circumstances was a relative term.

At the time of his appointment, it was suggested that Frankfurter's concise studies of Marshall, Taney and Waite and the latent supremacy of

the Federal power in the commerce clause revealed his own basic conviction: The great Chief Justice, Marshall, had established the fundamental
principle that Congressional control in the area of interstate commerce was
paramount; Taney strove with the explosive growth of national power while
intensely wishing it did not exist, and permitted "the temptation to express
right views" to break through "an attitude of judicial reserve." Waite
emerged the hero of the trilogy because he "fulfilled one of the greatest
duties of the judge, the duty not to enlarge his authority."[2]

To Augustus N. Hand ten years later, Frankfurter's record on the
bench confirmed the idea that he "has proceeded with a restraint reflecting
the conviction of a mature thinker that the solution of legal problems is by
no means simple, . . . and that the work of a judge calls for delicate and
sensitive discrimination." He had in his first decade, wrote Louis L. Jaffe, lived
up to the prediction that he would follow Marshall's view of Federal power
and Waite's disposition to avoid applying it if he could persuade himself
that one of the other branches of "the great secular trinity" of legislature,
executive and judiciary could more appropriately do so.[3]

After twenty years of Frankfurter's work on the bench, Sidney Hook
wrote: "Justice Frankfurter pleads guilty to the charge of entertaining an
'old-fashioned liberal's' view of government and law.' It is the liberalism
with which we all grew up—even those opposed to it." He had, in Hook's
opinion, confounded rather than confirmed the critics who widely alleged
that he had settled into a conservatism reminiscent of the pre-1937 Court;
Frankfurter, like most other thoughtful men, recognized that it was impossible
to return to that era. In 1959, the Eisenhower administration had made a
number of tentative efforts in that direction, but it had met with no success
and its time would soon be running out.

Frankfurter, Hook continued, "like Holmes, recognizes the difference
between . . . 'the strategic freedoms,' those upon which the functioning of a
free market of ideas depends, . . . and those freedoms which are required,
say, for the functioning of the free market in commodities. But since the
strategic freedoms are themselves not absolute, and on occasion conflict, it
is sometimes necessary to abridge a particular freedom in order to safeguard
the entire complex of freedoms on which the democratic way of life rests."
Frankfurter, said the writer, "believes that the best appeal from majority rule,
drunk and unenlightened, is to majority rule, sober and enlightened."[4]

Upon his retirement in 1962, Paul Freund wrote that Frankfurter's
consistent position had been to leave lawmaking to the legislative branch—
construing foolish laws narrowly, rather than reforming them by judicial fiat
or overruling them by judicial presumption, so as to give lawmakers a
second chance to do better.[5] In twenty-three years, as the most discerning
students of his work were able to recognize, the Justice had remained true
to the proposition that Federal power was sufficient for any Federal issue,
provided that Congress elected to implement it. The judiciary, in his view,

had acted unwisely in negating Congressional efforts in the days of Fuller, White and Taft; it was no less unwise to attempt to do so in the changed climate of the days of Hughes, Stone and Warren.

*   *   *

Even the "preferred freedoms" of Holmes and Brandeis were relative rather than absolute—this was the basis of the distinction between the liberalism of Frankfurter and the activism of Black and Douglas. What of the time, Frankfurter seemed to ask, when a choice had to be made between so-called absolutes? Whatever the choice might be, the constitutional values involved could only be regarded as relative. The identification of the "preferred freedom" always had to depend upon the circumstances. Holmes had demonstrated the distinction in his majority opinion in *Schenck v. United States*—a "clear and present danger" might warrant a limitation upon free expression—and his minority opinion in *Abrams v. United States*—freedom of expression should override any limitation when there was no "clear and present danger."[6]

This would have been, for Frankfurter, a sufficient answer, if he had been disposed to make any answer, to the criticisms which arose over his positions in the "flag salute" cases, where the New Deal enthusiasts had received their first shock of awakening to the Frankfurter jurisprudence. *Minersville School District v. Gobitis* had required a choice between the authority of government to enforce a policy uniformly applicable to all sorts and conditions of school children, and the guarantee that government would not interfere with religious belief. To compel the flag salute *did* interfere with the religious beliefs of a particular sect, but in Frankfurter's view, "to affirm that the freedom to follow conscience has itself no limits in the life of a society would deny that very plurality of principles which, as a matter of history, underlie protection of religious toleration."[7]

The overriding of *Gobitis* by *West Virginia Board of Education v. Barnette* three years later was simply an alternative choice between absolutes, in which the obligation of observing the symbolic gesture of respect to the national government was made relative by the majority in favor of the "preferred freedom" of religious belief. For Frankfurter, himself a member of a minority group, the reversal of the judicial position was intellectually appealing but jurisprudentially wrong; to reach the decision in *Barnette* required a judicial veto over a legislative policy decision. The majority position in *Gobitis,* he was persuaded, while jurisprudentially correct and intellectually repelling, was correct because it placed back upon the legislature the responsibility for modifying the policy.[8]

First Amendment freedoms, Frankfurter kept reiterating, could not be absolute in a society where volatile elements close-packed in large centers of population could abuse the freedom to the injury of public order. It was one thing, he contended, to exercise a right of provocative speech on a New England village green and another to try to exercise it in Greenwich Village.

In this he was mindful of Holmes' aphorism that the freedom did not excuse one from falsely crying "fire" in a crowded theater.[9] As for Holmes' rule of "clear and present danger," Frankfurter was persuaded that in the context of the postwar world it had come to be misapplied. In *Dennis v. United States* he observed that its tendency was "to hide from the believers in an absolute right of free speech the plain fact that the interest in speech, profoundly important as it is, is no more conclusive in judicial review than other attributes of democracy."[10]

A viable democracy, Frankfurter contended, "need not rely on the courts to save it from its own unwisdom." It was never a sound argument, in his view, that the Court "professes to act in the service of humane ends. As history amply proves, the judiciary is prone to misconceive the public good by confounding private notions with constitutional requirements." Judicial review, he admonished his colleagues, "does not give us greater veto power when dealing with one phase of 'liberty' than with another."[11]

Uncompromising in his own intellectual honesty, the Justice reminded himself that even in attempting to accommodate the legislative purpose the Court might tend to read its own predilections into the legislation. Where the statute itself was not explicit, Frankfurter urged that the Court seek guidelines for interpretation in analogous enactments of the same lawmaking body. If Congress had failed to stipulate a waiver of immunity from suit in the creating of one administrative agency, he argued early in his tenure, analogies were to be found from other laws creating other agencies of the same general type.[12]

The Black-Douglas-Frankfurter dialogue reached its most earnest proportions in the effort to incorporate the Bill of Rights into the Fourteenth Amendment. Frankfurter contended that "it would seem too late in the day" to suggest that "a phrase so laden with historic meaning" as the words of the Fourteenth "can be given an improvised content." Rather less convincingly, Frankfurter subsequently argued that incorporation would mean fixing upon the states "the limited experience of the eighteenth century."[13]

In the flux of constitutional debate in the Stone Court, Frankfurter sought to qualify the disposition of the activists to relegate the principle of *stare decisis* to an inactive status. Where it was a case of overturning decisional law which manifestly had become absolute, Frankfurter was at one with the Black-Douglas group; where the reversal of precedent amounted to nullifying a substantial body of legislative theory and enactment, he considered an overruling by the judiciary to place an unwarranted burden on the legislature.[14] The instances of obsolescence of prior judicial decisions, however, he found to be fewer than the activists discerned, and in 1944 he supported Roberts' notable protest by warning that "the tendency to disregard precedents . . . has become so strong in this Court of late as, in my view, to shake confidence in the consistency of decision."[15]

Where Congress had been silent, the Court should be also, he often declared, nor did it do to seek to divine too much from the lack of expression of a Congressional position. "The search for significance in the silence of Congress is too often the pursuit of a mirage," he stated in a 1942 case.[16] However, when the record showed that the legislature had in fact consciously considered the subject of the existing law and had failed to alter it, Frankfurter was willing to declare that the Court was bound to avoid extending the law by interpretation since this would manifestly fly in the face of Congress' own decision.[17]

On the other hand, Frankfurter concurred without reservation in a Court opinion in 1940 which declared: "The long-time failure of Congress to alter [an] act after it had been judicially construed, and the enactment by Congress of legislation which implicitly recognizes the judicial construction as effective, is persuasive of legislative recognition that the judicial construction is the correct one."[18]

*   *   *

Another point at which Frankfurter's opinions rudely jolted the liberal establishment was in the labor cases which came on for review in the forties and fifties. The temporary injunction, whose abuse he had so elaborately documented as an academician, he sustained in the John L. Lewis-UMW case because it was a legitimate exercise of a judicial power to stay private actions until the facts of the dispute could be ascertained. In the same year he warned his brethren that the Norris-LaGuardia Act was not intended to give labor unions *carte blanche* in cases which were in fact a violation of the anti-trust laws. Ten years later he told organized labor that the injunctive power was for the effective administration of judicial business and would not be permitted to "make an ally of an old enemy" in union strategy to bring management to a conference table.[19]

Frankfurter was sympathetically inclined to the old Brandeisian concept of "industrial self-government," and thus was not disposed to try to limit the effect of the so-called "right to work" laws which were eventually tested in the Court, unpopular with the unions though they were. The meaning of collective bargaining, he declared in a leading case in 1949, "does not remotely derive from the sanction of litigation in the courts." Judicially imposed solutions to issues between labor and management, he philosophized, are "more likely to discombobulate than to compose."[20]

In 1951 the Justice joined in a dissent against a majority ruling that a Wisconsin statute barring strikes and compelling arbitration was in violation of the Wagner Act. In 1957 he supported an injunction against a union seeking to strike to force a settlement rather than to follow the slower processes of the National Railroad Adjustment Board.[21] He supported the idea of judicial surveillance of union tactics to see that they did not disregard "a judicially enforceable duty of fairness to all components of the working force."[22]

Frankfurter indicated on various occasions that in his view the Railway Labor Act of 1926 represented the zenith of labor legislation, because it was a statute worked out cooperatively by labor and management and then enacted by Congress. In his view, it had adequately provided for all of the essential steps in the bargaining process, so that courts need not intervene; where experience revealed the need for amendment, a preliminary agreement between the parties most concerned could then be referred to Congress—again without judicial interference.[23]

The continuity from Holmes to Frankfurter was quite discernible in this context: In the days of *laissez-faire,* Holmes and Brandeis faulted the Court for using its final authority of interpretation to declare subject areas to be beyond the realm of legislatures; in the days of the new legality, Frankfurter and Jackson faulted the Court for using this same authority to declare the law beyond the statement of it made by the legislature itself.

"Great constitutional provisions must be administered with caution," Holmes once wrote. "Some play must be allowed for the joints of the machine, and it must be remembered that legislatures are ultimate guardians of the liberties and welfare of the people in quite as great a degree as the courts." A decade later he was again impelled "to urge that in dealing with state legislation upon matters of substantive law we should avoid with great caution attempts to substitute our judgment for that of the body whose business it is in the first place, with regard to questions of domestic policy that fairly are open to debate."[24]

Frankfurter echoed the sentiment in a communication to Franklin D. Roosevelt in the heat of the judiciary fight of 1937: "People have been taught to believe that when the Supreme Court speaks it is not [the Justices] who speak but the Constitution, whereas, of course, in so many vital cases, it is *they* who speak and *not* the Constitution." The problem remained, as he observed after two decades on the Court, "to avoid infusing into the vagueness of a constitutional command one's merely private notions."[25]

For the Justice, this would be the ideal of judicial review, avoiding decision on constitutional construction in the majority of cases in labor law and other fields of public conflict. Abstinence in the matter, Frankfurter continually argued, meant that the legislative body had another chance to recognize its own errors and correct them.

*   *   *

Frankfurter shared with Chief Justice Taft the belief that issues important only to the individual litigants should not occupy the time of the high court. The supreme tribunal, he wrote in a 1956 case, "is not a court to determine the local law of the forty-eight states." It should be limited in its jurisdiction "to important questions of general significance in the construction of Federal law and in the adjustment of the serious controversies that arise inevitably and in increasing measure in a Federal system such as ours. These questions are more than sufficient in volume and difficulty to engage all the energy and thought possessed by the Court; it should not be diverted by the correction of errors in local controversies turning on particular circumstances."[26]

Consistent with this view, Frankfurter protested periodically against the issuance of certiorari under the rule of four, when "The Four" comprised the activist bloc zealous to bring up every problem arising under the civil liberties crises of the postwar forties. Another group of cases which more often than not seemed to involve petty technicalities were those arising under the Federal Employers' Liability Act. The Justice had inveighed against the review of the majority of these cases since his days as a law teacher,[27] and his irritation with them mounted as the terms passed, and on one memorable occasion in 1957 he became so exorcised that he shouted his dissent and, according to a reporter, "grew red-faced when he discussed the facts of what he felt were ridiculous cases. He appeared to be lecturing not only his colleagues on the bench but the crowded chamber, largely consisting of lawyers, as well."[28]

Frankfurter's disposition to lecture, sometimes in a manner that appeared to be patronizing of lesser minds, tended to temper the professionals' admiration of him as a leading intellect. Lawyers presenting their oral arguments before the bench were often disconcerted to find questions shot at them apparently out of nowhere as the little Justice, rocking his chair in his course of interrogation, alternately appeared in view over the bench and disappeared. In his earlier years he was insistent upon counsel identifying the process by which they had brought their case this far. An apocryphal story, circulated for years, had it that when he asked a dignified member of the New York bar, "How did you get here?" the startled lawyer stammered, "On the night train."[29]

Like Holmes, Frankfurter relied substantially on the implications of legal history, and having come onto the Court in a period of sharp breaks with the past, he began at once to cast about for a balance. As the free-wheeling experimentalism continued under the Stone Chief Justiceship, he sought to enunciate a rule of constitutional history which first appeared in its full dimensions in his opinion in *United States v. Lovett*. The Bill of Rights, he suggested, was divided between two classes of liberties: one—deriving from "broad standards of fairness" exemplified by the concepts of due process and by the practical matter of apportioning powers between the nation and the states—he considered allowed "a relatively wide play for individual legal judgment"; the other class he found explicit—as in the guarantee of jury trial—and thus strictly limited as to the opportunities for a later Court to depart from the precedents which had been established with reference to them. These propositions, he concluded, had been "defined by history."[30]

With this dualism, Frankfurter was prepared to acquiesce in the incorporation of the first category of rights—the "preferred" or "strategic" freedoms —into the orbit of the Fourteenth Amendment. The second category, which he deprecated with the suggestion that they were absolutes of the eighteenth century, he sought to withhold in the hope that the states would develop their own equivalents.[31] Like most theses, this one had its antithesis, which Black and Douglas were quick to develop: either the principles of the Bill of Rights represented restraints upon government which were equally appropriate to apply to the states as to the nation, or their crystallization in an eighteenth-century conceptual format was as inappropriate for the one government as for the other. To this argument, Frankfurter never developed a totally persuasive answer.[32]

*   *   *

"We are not final because we are infallible, but we are infallible because we are final," Justice Robert H. Jackson commented in 1952. It was an echo of Frankfurter's own viewpoint, matured by a decade on the Court. For Jackson, as for Frankfurter, the demands of final constitutional interpretation had required a reexamination of the critiques of the process of judicial review which he had written before coming onto the bench. Yet, like Frankfurter, Jackson was persuaded that there was no basic inconsistency in his viewpoints then and now: the crux of the old liberal criticism had been the condemnation of the old Court's insistence upon applying constitutional rules to preserve the status quo. Equally to be condemned, he concluded, was the new Court's tendency to apply the same rules to overturn the status quo. The judicial function was neither to preserve nor to overturn, until a study of each issue could make possible a decision on the merits.[33]

"Liberty," wrote Jackson, "requires that coercion be applied to the individual not by other individuals but by the government after full inquiry into the justification." The activist viewpoint he decried as "wholly incompatible with faith in democracy," tending to encourage the judiciary "to correct the result of public indifference to issues of liberty." On another occasion he declared: "It is not the function of our government to keep the citizen from falling into error; it is the function of the citizen to keep the government from falling into error." To give *carte blanche* to all disorderly conduct under the guise of an absolute freedom of expression, he said in a minority opinion, was to "convert the constitutional Bill of Rights into a suicide pact." Due process of law, Jackson warned his colleagues, "is not for the sole benefit of the accused."[34]

Yet Jackson, perhaps more than Frankfurter and fully as much as Holmes, was persuaded that where the Constitution had affirmatively created a Federal power, as in the commerce clause, it was unnecessary to wait for Congress to act before striking down a state encroachment. "The practical result is that in default of action by us [the state encroachments] will go on," he warned. While he concurred in the specific case then before the Court, sustaining an Arkansas license required for transportation of liquor across its borders from one state to another, he denied the majority opinion that the state law could stand because Congress had not acted to exclude a state authority. The true understanding in this particular instance, Jackson argued, was that the Arkansas license was valid because the Twenty-First Amendment had made a particular qualification of the commerce clause.[35]

It was not Congressional preemption with which Jackson was concerned, but judicial preemption. This had been the ultimate vindication of the New Deal attack upon the old legality, in his view—and it remained as a *caveat* for the new legality as well. *Stare decisis,* or the "doctrine of precedents," as some had called it, might well need to be discounted where the precedents had been built up on the judicial preemptions of the old legality. But the erroneous precedents were those which denied an authority to the legislative branch to attempt to keep the law up to date, and to improve upon their own attempts on the basis of judicial critiques rather than judicial denial.

The ideal judicial interpretation of a statute, in Jackson's view, would provide guidelines for Congress in improving the statute by subsequent amendment. In a highly technical case, *Dobson v. Commissioner,* in 1943— an opinion which, ironically enough, was criticized as activist, "an all-embracing essay on the steadily expanding evils of tax litigation and the pressing need for judicial reorientation"—Jackson virtually cried out to Congress for reform. Although the Revenue Code of 1926 had sought to limit Supreme Court review of Tax Court findings except where the findings were "not in accordance with law," Jackson noted that more than five thousand cases had been reviewed on the basis of this exception. In specific response to this criticism from the bench, Congress in 1948 amended the section of the Tax Code which *Dobson* had pinpointed.[36]

In a dissent in *Farmers Reservoir and Irrigation Co. v. McComb,* the question before the Court was whether employees of an agricultural cooperative were exempt agricultural employees under the Fair Labor Standards Act. The majority opinion held that they were not, since they were employees of the agency rather than of the farmers. Jackson protested that the distinction was an "esoteric duplicity" for which the Court was to blame—although the Court's error as he saw it derived from a paradox in the statute itself, which sought to distinguish between agricultural production "in a normal sense" and agricultural production "in a special sense." Congress acted the same year, amending the statute to exempt a list of marginal employees whom courts or administrators had held outside the original exemptions.[37]

These were, as Jackson was proud to be told, lawyers' critiques of the law—too technical for the general public to appreciate, but of the very essence of the function of judicial review as the old liberals would have had it. It was not that the Court should not concern itself with social needs, as Jackson and Frankfurter saw it; but the remedy for social needs was primarily legislative, and if constitutional interpretation usurped a remedial legislative function it upset the political balance of nature. The good or evil of judicial reform of the law depended on the facts of the given situation, Jackson contended, and its success did not change its character.[38]

In this posture, Frankfurter and Jackson were consistent with the Holmes-Brandeis tradition—and the second John Marshall Harlan, in the Court of the fifties and sixties, would continue the tradition. In the very heyday of normalcy, Holmes had urged the Court to recognize that "a power which must belong to and somewhere reside in every civilized government" could ultimately be found within the powers enumerated by the

Constitution of the United States. The touchstone, for Holmes, was the legislative initiative in using the power, whether the legislature was state or national; and it remained for the Court "to avoid with great caution attempts to substitute our judgment for that of the body whose business it is in the first place, with regard to questions of domestic policy that fairly are open to debate."[39]

In the 1920's, a conservative majority had insisted upon substituting its judgment for that of the legislature. Twenty and thirty years later, the activists on the modern Court were still, in the view of Frankfurter and Jackson, tending to substitute their judgment for that of the legislature— and, worse, pronouncing their view of the law on subjects on which the legislature had not acted at all. For Holmes, this had been the original judicial sin; so it was for Frankfurter and Jackson, and so it would be for the second Harlan.

*   *   *

Frankfurter sought to persuade the Court always to construe the Constitution as a whole, to avoid selecting portions which best suited majority purposes. In his view, this led logically to a relativistic construction: absolutes were possible only if a favored proposition in the text of the Constitution was made the sole controlling rule in cases in that subject area; if any single proposition in the Constitution were balanced with the whole, each of necessity would become relative in value.

His desire to encourage legislatures—either Congress or the state assemblies, acting singly or in concert—to do the lawmaking and to give expression to the intent of their own laws, wherever feasible, was illustrated in *West Virginia v. Sims,* where the Court was reviewing the validity of an eight-state compact to control Ohio River pollution. The Court itself, said Frankfurter, could provide no formula for the procedure; "the delicacy of interstate relationships and the inherent limitations upon this Court's ability to deal with multifarious local problems" precluded such an approach. Since the constitutional provision for interstate compacts encouraged the idea of state legislatures delegating some of their administrative prerogatives to a joint agency, and the procedure had been arrived at "by conference and mutual concession on the part of representatives of the states so vitally interested," the reviewing function should be limited to a corroborating of the procedure by which an orderly solution of the mutual problem had been reached.[40]

"To press a juristic principle designed for the practical affairs of government to abstract extremes is neither sound logic nor good sense," Frankfurter observed in a 1946 case.[41] It was sufficient if the Court derived a consistent interpretation of specific clauses in the Constitution, and specific statues enacted thereunder, to apply to the facts of each case as it was presented. He resisted the idea of enlarging upon these principles of adjudication and thus converting them into absolutes. "Words being symbols do not speak without a gloss," he conceded, and where "the gloss may be the deposit of history, . . . a term gains technical content" which may impel a Court to apply a rule only as precedent has established it. But where the gloss "is a function of the process of judgment, the judgment is bound to fall differently at different times and differently at the same time through different judges."[42]

Black and Douglas could concur in the latter statement, and Frankfurter could concur in the Black-Douglas thesis that "basic rights do not become petrified as of any one time" and some might come close to being "eternal verities." Thereupon, however, Frankfurter and the activists parted company. The manner of enforcing basic rights was variable, in his view, and could not be reduced to a dogmatic rule which would "preclude the varying solutions which spring from an allowable range of judgment on issues not susceptible of quantitative solution."[43]

*   *   *

"The preservation of a proper balance between state and Federal responsibility in the administration of criminal justice demands patience on the part of those who might like to see things move faster among the states in this respect," Frankfurter chided his colleagues in a dissent in 1961. The dissent was written by Justice Harlan, who would assume, in the course of events, the burden of the doctrine of abstinence that Frankfurter and Jackson had maintained.[44]

Harlan, with whom Frankfurter joined in the dissent in *Mapp v. Ohio,* was protesting against the continuing effort to extend elements of the Bill of Rights to the states through the Fourteenth Amendment. Frankfurter himself had delivered the opinion of the Court, twelve years earlier, in *Wolf v. Colorado* in which the point had been first reviewed in detail. While the majority had rejected the incorporation idea, and Black had concurred in the result, the dissent in that case had included Douglas, Murphy and Rutledge. Now, despite the loss of two of "The Four," the case for the incorporation of the Fourth Amendment guarantees in the Fourteenth had prevailed.

"The security of one's privacy against arbitrary intrusion by the police—which is at the core of the Fourth Amendment—is basic to a free society," Frankfurter had conceded in *Wolf.* "Accordingly," he added, "we have no hesitation in saying that were a state affirmatively to sanction such police intrusion into privacy it would run counter to the guaranty of the Fourteenth Amendment." Even more, Frankfurter conceded: since 1914 in *Weeks v. United States,* Federal courts had applied an exclusionary rule to evidence obtained by unlawful search and seizure, and this rule "was not derived from the explicit requirements of the Fourth Amendment."[45] The exclusionary rule, then, came within the class of guarantees in the Bill of Rights which Frankfurter held to be affirmations of general and elementary principles of fairness.

After conceding this much, however, Frankfurter in *Wolf* felt that the Court could not proceed to the incorporation of the exclusionary rule into state criminal process because most of the states did "not regard it as vital." This basis for his rejection of incorporation had vanished by 1961. Justice Clark, speaking for a new Court majority, observed that "time has set its face against" the state practice obtaining in 1949 and—quite possibly on the impetus of the Frankfurter decision in *Wolf*—had accepted the exclusionary rule. Upon reexamination of the judicial position taken in *Wolf*, declared Clark, it was now time to "close the only courtroom door remaining open to evidence secured by official lawlessness," and declare affirmatively that henceforth all evidence obtained by unlawful search and seizure is barred by the Constitution from admission in state courts.[46]

Harlan, with whom Frankfurter joined, criticized the Clark opinion at length, centering its argument around Frankfurter's firm commitment to restraint: "For us the question remains, as it has always been, one of state power, not one of passing judgment on the wisdom of one state course or another. . . . An approach which regards the issue as one of achieving procedural symmetry or of serving administrative convenience surely disfigures the boundaries of this Court's functions. . . . " [47]

Three years later, Frankfurter was retired from the bench by a rapid decline in health. His legacy was an eloquent and exhaustively documented case for a self-limitation upon the judicial function. If he seemed to have ended his career as a conservative, it was as a conservative of the new constitutional order he had helped to bring about—and thus, as he himself would have put it, the term was a relative one rather than an absolute.

10/The Jurisprudence of Activism

THE HOLMES-BRANDEIS-FRANKFURTER-JACKSON concept of liberalism was a familiar theme in American constitutional history. On the other hand, the Black-Douglas concept of an aggressive and affirmative judicial process was a totally new theme. For the apostles of judicial restraint, legislative inaction did not provide a reason for judicial initiative; *per contra*, for the activists the question of legislative inaction required a judicial inquiry into the existence of a governmental obligation implicit in the Constitution. The essence of the new legality as distinguished from the old was the positive concept of constitutional duty as contrasted with the prior concept of constitutional limitation.[1]

The Frankfurter-Jackson and Black-Douglas schools gave different emphases to this concept. The latter pair, with their passionate commitment to the obligation of government-led reform, had conducted a vociferous dialogue within the Court during the Stone Chief Justiceship and had been reduced to a minority role under Vinson. Their jurisprudence would come to full flower in the Warren Court.

*   *   *

Bill Douglas, Hugo Black once said, "must have come into this world with a rush and . . . his first cry must have been a protest against something he saw at a glance was wrong or unjust." As a leading Washington figure, observed a correspondent, Douglas "is plainly of the 'angry man' mold, a type which historically has furnished the motive power for most American political changes." Like Brandeis, whom he succeeded, he instinctively distrusted bigness, in business and in bureaucracy. Bigness, Douglas once admonished a Chicago financiers' meeting, "concentrates tremendous economic and financial power in the hands of a few," and for that very reason is suspect.[2]

In the more than a quarter of a century since he had come onto the bench, Douglas had borne out most of the predictions which had been made of him at the outset. He had consistently followed the activist line, had

195

developed in the judicial sphere the beginnings of a new body of corporation law he had initiated on the Securities & Exchange Commission, and had helped push the Court boldly into the broadening of First Amendment freedoms. A gifted writer in both professional and popular media, he published nearly a score of books in which he reached far beyond courtroom audiences with his credo of the priceless beauty and value of nature, the ultimate decency of all peoples, and the enduring absolute of personal freedom.

In many views, Douglas was the best exponent as well as the best product of the New Deal era. Quadrennially throughout the 1940's, political liberals urged him for the first or second place on the Democratic ticket. Roosevelt, it was said, would have welcomed him as an ideal choice between Wallace and Truman; and Truman, it was said, might have accepted him as a running mate four years later had not the ardent pleas of conservative Democrats and his personal friendship in the Senate for Alben Barkley overridden other considerations. Like Theodore Roosevelt, Douglas was an enthusiast for the strenuous life, and his code of honor was much like Teddy's oft-repeated "don't flinch, and hit the line hard." He could convey moral indignation without appearing to be either irascible or ascetic, and his competence as an administrator had become almost legendary even before he left the SEC.[3]

As the Republican tenure of the fifties came on, Douglas was to settle down to the task of perfecting a jurisprudential system for the constitutionalism which had been forged in the intellectual excitement of the late thirties and the forties. "To him," Abe Fortas commented in 1964, "our Constitution is a mandate for strong individuals functioning in the framework of strong government. To him, government may not impinge upon the freedom of the individual. Government and the individual are equals, equal in right and dignity. . . . Beyond this right of individual freedom, government has and must have full power . . . to make the rules and enforce them."[4]

The shift of Hughes and Roberts had already changed the constitutional position of the Court when Douglas had come onto it in 1939, and thus his opinions upholding broad governmental authority both in the second Bituminous Coal Act and in the second Agricultural Adjustment Act were not remarkable innovations in themselves. Nor was it extraordinary to hear him affirm the broad power of the government to control prices under the exigencies of the Second World War. It was in his dissent in a case exempting a California public warehouse from the Price Control Act that he first elaborated upon his conviction that the primary valid purpose of such a law was to ensure equitable restraints on inflationary tendencies everywhere. To exempt a so-called public agency, he argued, "creates another point of leakage, multiplies the task of enforcement and creates a favored class of business."[5]

This was Douglas' theme as he turned his expertise upon cases brought under the Bankruptcy Act. Its significance as a rule of constitutional construction was reflected in his declaration in *Anderson v. Abbott:* "Judicial power hardly oversteps the bounds when it refuses to lend its aid to a . . . project which would circumvent or undermine a legislative policy. . . . If the judicial power is helpless to protect a legislative program from schemes of easy avoidance, then indeed it becomes a handy implement for high finance."[6]

While creditors' rights are entitled to be protected to the extent of the availability of assets of value, Douglas contended, the intent of Congress that debtors should also be afforded reasonable relief inhibited the Court from going further, "lest its benefits be frittered away by narrow formalistic interpretations which disregard the spirit and letter of the [Bankruptcy] Act," Douglas had declared in *Wright v. Union Central Life Insurance Co.* in 1940.

The man who had risen to Presidential attention by his exhaustive study of the uses and abuses of stockholder protective committees in the heyday of corporate reorganization in the 1930's became the Court authority on the equities of bankruptcy procedure and securities policies in the 1940's. Economic law was an arcane subject for most members of the bench except for corporation specialists like Butler and Van Devanter, and thus until Douglas brought to these cases a liberal's conviction that the intricacies of finance and refinancing of business should be subject to equitable concepts, Court decisions on the subject tended to be written by Justices most sympathetic with the most powerful elements in the corporation field.*[8]

From long study of the intricacies of corporate reorganization which enabled greedy men to profit unconscionably while stockholders and creditors got a fraction of their claims if they got anything, Douglas urged that a bankruptcy court had overriding public obligations. Its primary responsibility, said Douglas, was to conduct its own investigation of the facts of each case, and where this "discloses the existence of unfair dealing, a breach of fiduciary obligations, profiting from a trust, special benefits for the reorganizers, or the need for protection of investors against an inside few, . . . the court has ample power to adjust the remedy to meet the need."[9]

Douglas' thorough knowledge of the business economics implemented a succession of decisions under which the Court was able to liberalize the concept of judicial oversight of corporate activities. The hard-nosed jurist could detect the source of the evil in each area of high finance and prescribe a procedure for practicable remedy. At the same time, he was impeccably orthodox in his "attitude of uncompromising insistence on the payment of obligations."[10]

It was Douglas who provided the legal-economic argument for Black's cases against the 1898 rule of "fair value" in public utility rate making, culminating in the rule in the *Hope Natural Gas* case that regulatory agencies were free to fix rates as warranted by the factual situation in each case.[11]

---

*Brandeis, the economic expert of the liberals, of course was in the minority for most of his career.

Concerned that concentrated economic power should not result in unfair advantages to one side in the business process, he wrote a 1945 opinion affirming the right of the state of Georgia to sue a combination of railroads whose rates allegedly discriminated against Southern shippers.[12] Where rules of law purported to relieve parties of double taxation, Douglas sought to modify the rules where the relief actually amounted to a convenient means of avoiding tax claims which a government was entitled to make; Utah, he declared, could place a transfer tax on securities owned by a decedent in the case of a Utah-chartered corporation, even though the transfer was actually made in New York.[13]

*   *   *

In three decades on the Court, Hugo Lafayette Black had witnessed the reversal of more than a hundred prior judicial decisions on constitutional questions, the nullifying in whole or in part of more than a dozen acts of Congress, 165 state statutes and thirty municipal ordinances. He had been the central figure in three soul-shaking controversies, two of which had had national and international repercussions—the first over his early Ku Klux Klan affiliation, the second over his ideological debate with Frankfurter, and the third over his dispute with Jackson. In the course of thirty years, he had helped bring on the constitutional revolution in the Hughes and Stone Courts, had settled into a minority with the gradual loss of momentum under Vinson and with the first years in which the Warren Court sought to develop its own emphases, and finally had seen his fundamental tenets assume a permanent dominance in the new Federalism of the late fifties and the sixties.[14]

His name had become a synonym for activism—or perhaps positivism would have been an equally accurate term. As the years had passed, Black's central concern had become more and more the enlargement of the concepts of individual liberties embraced by the Bill of Rights, the incorporation of this extended list into a constitutional rationale applicable to state and national government alike, and the use of government power to protect the rights of exploited minorities and defenseless individuals. Black, wrote Daniel Berman, "is not convinced that in a society of abundance, a man would not still desire for himself a little more of the abundance than he is willing to concede to others. He is not certain that racial animosities will fade when the economic motives for their perpetuation disappear."[15]

To offset this perverse tendency, Black conceived of the Bill of Rights as an affirmative directive to the judiciary to scan the spectrum of social behavior for aberrations from the constitutional order. With Frankfurter, he could agree that not all injunctions of the first Ten Amendments were self-executing or independent of judicial definitions. But for the others, where Frankfurter insisted that historical experience had fixed their meaning, Black contended that they were absolutes which could not be balanced against other rights expressed or implied.[16]

The phenomenon of the power to govern, Black concluded, expanded with the needs of an increasingly interrelated society; all the more, in such case, the restraint upon government with reference to the rights and dignity of the individual—or, more positively, the responsibility of government to insure that no institutions or persons should infringe upon the rights and dignity of any individual—was a logical corollary. If Frankfurter was right in contending that the definite and certain limitations in the Bill of Rights were to be read in their eighteenth-century meaning, they would inevitably be relative rather than absolute in the twentieth century. For Black, the proliferating means by which individual rights could be jeopardized in the corporate society of the twentieth century could only mean that the concept of the enjoyment of individual liberties had to expand with the times.[17]

*   *   *

It was in the atmosphere of conformity and self-doubt, in the last years of the Truman and first years of the Eisenhower administrations, that Black's conviction of an imperative constitutional guarantee against majority oppression crystallized. The threat of Communism, underlined by Soviet power politics in the international sphere and whipped into an unreasoning hysteria by McCarthy and his abettors on the domestic front, provided abundant opportunity for protest. Under Vinson in his declining years, and under Warren in his uncertain starting period, the Court majority inclined to the support of conformity and the penalizing of noncomformity.

In the spring of 1954, Black spoke for himself and Douglas in dissenting from an opinion sustaining a deportation order for a former Communist who had belonged to the party in a period before it had become legally suspect, and who left it in disillusionment before the public in general discerned its ultimate cynicism.[18] Three years later, in the backwash of McCarthyism, Black mustered a temporary majority striking down a California court ruling which denied admission to law practice to an otherwise qualified applicant because he declined to reveal his political associations.[19] When the same case made its way back to the Court in 1961, the increased conservative weight of subsequent Eisenhower appointees overturned the former majority and sustained the denial of admission.

The second John Marshall Harlan,* speaking for the currently ascendant conservative majority, undertook at length to refute the Black thesis of First Amendment absolutes. In dissent Black answered: "The majority's 'balancing test,' " whereby a guarantee of freedom of belief may be offset by a plea of overriding public interest, "tells us that no right to think, speak or publish exists in the people that cannot be taken away if the government finds it sufficiently imperative or expedient to do so. Thus the balancing test turns our 'government of the people, by the people, and for the people' into a government over the people.

"I cannot believe that this Court would adhere to the 'balancing test' to the limit of its logic. Since that 'test' denies that any speech, publication or petition has an 'absolute' right to protection under the First Amendment,

---

*Appointed by President Eisenhower in 1954. See Ch. 11.

strict adherence to it would necessarily mean that there would be only a conditional right, for any American to express his views to his neighbors— or for his neighbors to hear those views."[20]

Three years earlier, Black had found "this whole business of penalizing people because of their views and expressions concerning government . . . hopelessly repugnant to the principles of freedom upon which this nation was founded," and added that the proscriptive trend of the fifties "is not the course of a strong, free, secure people, but that of the frightened, the insecure, the intolerant."[21] Yet the balances of the scales of justice teetered erratically in this period of challenged loyalties. Where the Court, in a six-to-one opinion in *Watkins v. United States,* admonished the House Un-American Activities Committee to adhere to elementary standards of fairness in examination of witnesses, it all but contradicted itself two years later in a five-to-four majority in *Barenblatt v. United States.*[22]

Replying to Harlan's majority holding that the asking of questions as to political beliefs, in the face of the First Amendment, was justified by the security needs of the nation, Black declared: "It is difficult at best to make a man guess—at the penalty of imprisonment—whether a court will consider the state's need for certain information superior to society's interest in un-fettered freedom. It is unconscionable to make him choose between the right to keep silent and the need to speak when the statute supposedly establishing the 'state's interest' is too vague to give him guidance." Attacking Harlan's reiteration of the "balancing test," Black observed that it was "closely akin to the notion that neither the First Amendment nor any other provision of the Bill of Rights should be enforced unless the Court believes it is *reasonable* to do so."[23]

Ideas, Black insisted, "cannot be proscribed under our Constitution," and he quoted FBI Director J. Edgar Hoover and the corroborating view of the majority in *Barnette:* "If there is any fixed star in our constitutional con-stellation, it is that no official, high or petty, can prescribe what shall be orthodox in politics, nationalism, religion, or other matters of opinion or force citizens to confess by word or act their faith therein."[24]

It cannot be too often repeated, said Black in another dissent, "that the freedoms . . . guaranteed by the First Amendment must be accorded to the ideas we hate or sooner or later they will be denied to the ideas we cherish." The statutory outlawing of the Communist party in the United States, he protested, flew in the face of the fact that the American people themselves contained it effectively at the polls. "No one need console himself," the Justice warned, ". . . that the policy of using governmental force to crush dissident groups . . . can or will be stopped at that point. The weakening of constitutional safeguards in order to suppress one obnoxious group is a technique too easily available for the suppression of other obnoxious groups to expect its abandonment when the next generally hated group appears."[25]

*   *   *

Before the domestic Communist hysteria, it had been a case of obstreperous religious minorities which had presented the same test of the absolutism of the First Amendment guarantees. The temptation to find an overriding governmental interest had trapped Black and Douglas and Murphy in acquiescing in the first "flag salute" case in 1940; two years later, in *Opelika,* they had publicly confessed their error, and the following year in *Barnette* they had rectified it.[26]

The antecedent to the California disbarment cases under the proscription of political beliefs had been encountered in a 1945 Illinois case where the applicant for admission to the bar declined to take an oath which ran counter to his religious scruples. To bar an applicant "solely because he entertains a religious belief which might prompt him at some time in the future to violate a law which has not yet been and may never be enacted," Black protested, was not only unconstitutional but irrational.[27]

The issue was substantially magnified in 1957 when the bar admission question turned upon an allegation of subversive sympathy rather than religious scruples. The clash of the Black and Frankfurter viewpoints was starkly illustrated in the majority and dissenting opinions in the first of these cases, which sustained the argument that an applicant for admission to the bar, otherwise qualified, could challenge a denial of license because of alleged radical sympathies—and in the second case, which held just the opposite—under the due process and equal protection clauses of the Fourteenth Amendment.

In the first review of *Konigsberg v. State Bar of California,* Black for the Court declared: "Because of the very nature of our democracy such [radical] expression of political views must be permitted. . . . Government censorship can no more be reconciled with our national constitutional standard of freedom of speech and press when done in the guise of determining 'moral character,' than if it should be attempted directly." Vehement criticism of public issues and public officials, refusal to answer licensing authorities' questions when based on a belief that the questions were constitutionally impermissible, and informers' charges of Communist associations, said Black, were unworthy and improper standards for denying one otherwise qualified the right to practice his profession.[28]

When the second *Konigsberg* case came on in 1961, Justices Reed and Burton of the original six-to-three majority had been replaced by Justices Whittaker and Stewart. The new five-to-four majority now adopted Harlan's former minority view, with the rationale of Black's 1957 opinion now becoming the essence of the dissent. Harlan, with Frankfurter in vigorous agreement, declared that proscription of unpopular political views was not the issue, but rather the state's immemorial right to police the practice of law. So stated, the issue "involves an area of Federal-state relations . . . into which this Court should be especially reluctant and slow to enter." But even if the inquiry into the applicant's beliefs and affiliations were judicially considered, Harlan (and Frankfurter) concluded, the state was justified in declaring that "petitioner's refusal to answer questions made it impossible to proceed to an affirmative certification that he was qualified."[29]

The diametric shift of majority views outraged the liberals and scholars, who attacked the second *Konigsberg* holding, and the conservatives in Congress, who added the first *Konigsberg* holding to a catalog of sins they would ascribe to the activists in the massive Congressional attack upon the Court early in the second Eisenhower term.*

In the postwar years, Black wrote vigorous opinions in three major cases turning upon the issue of religious freedom; he spoke for the majority in sustaining the New Jersey school bus law, and again for the majority in overturning the Illinois "released time" in public schools law. In the New York "released time" law he dissented. For him, the accommodation of any opportunity for religious instruction during hours provided for public school education, whether on or off the school premises, was a weakening of the anti-establishment clause.[30]

The culmination of the several principles of religious freedom under the Constitution came in *Torcaso v. Watkins,* a 1961 case in which Black, for the Court, invalidated a Maryland oath requiring holders of public office to affirm a belief in God. The state law, said Black, ran contrary to the specific constitutional provision that "no religious test shall ever be required as a qualification to any office or public trust under the United States"—a provision of the original document which the Justice subtly extended to the states by implication. "The test oath," he said, citing an earlier landmark opinion, "is abhorrent to our tradition."[31]

A year later Black read the most controversial of all the opinions on the anti-establishment clause, in *Engel v. Vitale.* A six-to-one majority invalidated the New York regents' non-denominational prayer prescribed for the opening of public school class sessions, and a storm of public protest instantly broke. Roman Catholic, Episcopal and Protestant leaders loudly accused the Court of having succumbed to atheism; members of Congress discerned an easy chance to go on record in favor of God and indirectly to castigate the judiciary for its signs of resurgent progressivism, and introduced proposed amendments which would reverse the decision. The so-called "Bible belt" of rural fundamentalism reacted predictably; amid the storm of recrimination, only the Roman Catholic President Kennedy and the New York regents themselves publicly suggested that the decision was to be obeyed.

In this country, Black said for the majority, "it is no part of the business of government to compose official prayers for any group of the American people to recite as part of a religious program carried on by government." The anti-establishment clause, the Baptist Justice went on, "does not depend upon any showing of direct government compulsion and is violated by the

*See Ch. 12.

enactment of laws which establish an official religion whether those laws operate directly to coerce non-observing individuals or not." The historical reasoning behind the freedom of religion provision in the First Amendment, he concluded, was an awareness that "governmentally established religions and religious persecutions go hand in hand."[32]

*   *   *

On December 8, 1941—the day after Pearl Harbor—Black delivered the Court opinion reversing a contempt conviction of Harry Bridges. "The likelihood, however great, that a substantive evil will result cannot alone justify a restriction upon freedom of speech or the press," said the Justice in the after-shock of the blow which had plunged the nation into the Second World War. "No suggestion can be found in the Constitution that the freedom there guaranteed for speech and the press bears an inverse ratio to the timeliness and importance of ideas seeking expression."[33]

Whether it was the atmosphere of war which tended to exaggerate the hostility toward minorities, or the atmosphere of reaction after the war which was hostile to nonconformists, Black felt that the guarantee of freedom of expression was constant. In the same vein he dissented, in 1947, from the majority opinion affirming the prosecutions under the Hatch Act. To impose a restraint upon government workers in the political process, he declared, "reduces the constitutionally protected liberty of several million citizens to less than a shadow of its substance."[34]

"Individual freedom and governmental thought-probing cannot live together," he warned in 1951 in *Douds*. When red-baiting and character attacks without judicial safeguards dominate government policy, he added, "the fog of public excitement obscures the ancient landmarks set up in our Bill of Rights. Yet then, of all times, should this Court adhere most closely to the course they mark." As the impulses of intolerance mounted, he pointed out, the inevitable political reaction was to let "the policeman's club . . . . take heavy toll of a current administration's public critics."[35]

"Undoubtedly, a governmental policy of unfettered communication of ideas does entail dangers," Black observed in his dissent in *Dennis*. "So long as this Court exercises the power of judicial review of legislation, I cannot agree that the First Amendment permits us to sustain laws suppressing freedom of speech and press on the basis of Congress' or our own notions of mere 'reasonableness.' . . . The Amendment as so construed is not likely to protect any but those 'safe' or orthodox views which rarely need its protection."[36]

"It seems self-evident that all speech criticizing government rulers and challenging current beliefs may be dangerous to the status quo," said Black in concurring in a Court opinion overturning an Oklahoma test oath. "With full knowledge of this danger the Framers rested our First Amendment on the premise that the slightest suppression of thought . . . is still more dangerous. This means that individuals are guaranteed an undiluted and unequivocal right to express themselves on questions of current public interest. It means that Americans discuss such questions as of right and not on sufferance of legislatures, courts, or any other governmental agencies."[37]

The proscriptive features of the Smith Act brought again before the Court the question of absolutes-v.-relatives which had first arisen in *Dennis*. An eight-member majority, characteristically divergent in its concurring opinions, substantially reduced the *Dennis* doctrine—but not sweepingly enough for Black and Douglas. Until the thrust of the law was so contained as to eliminate all danger that unpopular defendants would be tried for their beliefs instead of their actions, Black said, the American people would continue to compromise their constitutional guarantees by the ultimate appeal to coercion.[38]

The allegedly obscene as well as the allegedly subversive was also a concern of the First Amendment, in Black's view. Concurring in a unanimous voiding of a Los Angeles bookstore-control ordinance, he reiterated his fundamental theme: while today the law might be upheld because an act might be both offensive and unconventional, tomorrow the way would be open for the easy step to prosecution of what was merely unconventional. Relatively little extra burden is put on the state, said Black, to require it to prove a bookseller's awareness of obscenity at the time he offered the book for sale. The alternative, he warned, was a state censorship.[39]

*   *   *

A right to a fair trial before an impartial court was another basic guarantee of the Bill of Rights, which came on for review in the aftermath of World War II. The circumstances under which military courts, even in a state of martial law, could try and sentence civilians for offenses only remotely associated with the military establishment demanded a judicial answer. The fear of arbitrary control of civilians by military authority, said Black for the Court, "has become part of our cultural and political institutions." The established principle of constitutional law, he observed, "is that the law shall alone govern," and the law was not the military law where civilians were concerned.[40]

It was self-evident to the Justice that servicemen charged with a civilian crime were also protected by the elementary safeguards of the Bill of Rights. In his first term of Court, Black wrote the majority opinion reversing a conviction of two soldiers on leave who had been tried on charges of counterfeiting without benefit of legal counsel. "If the accused . . . is not represented by counsel and has not competently and intelligently waived his constitutional rights," Black declared, "the Sixth Amendment stands as a jurisdictional bar to a valid conviction and sentence depriving him of his life or his liberty."[41]

Nearly a quarter of a century later, Black reaffirmed his argument that the defendant's right to counsel was a fundamental guarantee of the Sixth Amendment. In between had come *Betts v. Brady,* in which Black, joined by Murphy and Douglas, had expressed doubt that any trial anywhere could be had without the right of counsel being assured the defendant. "A practice cannot be reconciled with 'common and fundamental ideas of fairness and right,' " he protested, "which subjects innocent men to increased dangers of conviction merely because of their poverty."[42] Then, in 1962, Black renewed his attack on the doctrine set out by the majority in *Betts;* the experience of two decades, he declared, had "demonstrated its basic failure as a constitutional guide."[43] The following year, in *Gideon v. Wainwright,* the majority returned to, and enlarged upon, the older principle that the right to counsel was a guarantee of the Bill of Rights which now applied to the states.[44]

Gideon was representative of Black's long career. Activism meant a patient waiting for the opportunity to persuade the majority, on the facts of the proper case, that the view consistently developed should at length be accepted. It was less a matter of eloquence in the argument than of letting the course of history make its own point.

Vigilance was a fundamental requisite in an age when complex and impersonal forces continually threatened to nullify the capacity of the individual to assert his rights in contemporary society. The insistence of the apostles of restraint that the Fifth Amendment did not apply in full force to the states through the Fourteenth came home to roost in 1959 in *Bartkus v. Illinois;* an acquittal in Federal court did not bar another prosecution—and conviction—in a state court, said Frankfurter, since it did not run counter to anything in the state constitution. For Black, the factual situation pointed up the ultimate bankruptcy of the case against incorporation.

> The Court apparently takes the position [Black wrote] that a second trial for the same act is somehow less offensive if one of the trials is conducted by the Federal government and the other by a state. Looked at from the standpoint of the individual who is being prosecuted, this notion is too subtle for me to grasp. If double punishment is what is feared, it hurts no less for two "sovereigns" to inflict it than for one. If danger to the innocent is emphasized, that danger is surely no less when the power of state and Federal governments is brought to bear on one man in two trials, than when one of these "sovereigns" proceeds alone. In each case, inescapably a man is forced to face danger twice for the same conduct. . . .
>
> Implicit in the Court's reliance on "federalism" is the premise that failure to allow double prosecutions would seriously impair law enforcement in both state and nation. For one jurisdiction might provide minor penalties for acts severely punished by the other and, by accepting pleas of guilty, shield wrongdoers from justice. I believe this argument fails on several grounds. In the first place, it relies on the unwarranted assumption that state and nation will seek to subvert each other's laws. . . .
>
> The Court's argument also ignores the fact that our constitution also allocates power between local and Federal governments in such a way that the basic rights of each can be protected without double trials. . . .[45]

*   *   *

With the examples of the great dissenters of the past to encourage him, Hugo Black continued over the years to preserve the argument for his incorporation principle; the logic of events, he was confident, in time would compel its acceptance. He had made the case for the idea in his dissent in *Adamson v. California* in June, 1947, and it provided a standard of reference over the next two decades.

The defendant in a California murder trial was convicted, after a summation by the state prosecution which, under a practice permitted in California, called attention to the defendant's failure to take the stand in his own defense. The affirming of the conviction by the majority of the Supreme Court, protested Black, reasserted the principle of *Twining v. New Jersey* "that this Court is endowed by the Constitution with boundless power under 'natural law' periodically to expand and contract constitutional standards." The majority opinion in *Twining,* in Black's opinion, "carries its own refutation," and could only be accepted as precedent if the modern Court was prepared to accept its assumption that the Bill of Rights was an eighteenth-century straitjacket.[46]

"It is an illusory apprehension," said Black, "that literal application of some or all of the provisions of the Bill of Rights to the states would unwisely increase the sum total of the powers of this Court to invalidate state legislation." If the Amendments represented the proposition that a curtailment of guaranteed personal liberties was an evil inherent in government, the proposition applied with as much force to the one sovereignty as to the other.[47]

The Stone and Vinson Courts had provided a proving ground for some of the most eloquently argued constitutional propositions in American history, by some of the most remarkable intellects to sit upon the Court in any period of its history. The first Harlan,* Holmes, Brandeis and even Cardozo had performed their functions as intellectual leaven without the benefit of the galvanic force of the constitutional revolution which was the starting point for the dialogue of the forties and early fifties.

*   *   *

"The judiciary," wrote Douglas in 1956, "is in a high sense the guardian of the conscience of the people as well as of the law of the land." While he decried the past practice of the Court in assuming the right to reform any legislative enactment or administrative decision it chose, he remained suspicious of agencies which, though nominally parts of the executive branch of government, remained "welded closely to Congressional groups through a wide variety of lobbying agencies." Agencies, he found from his own administrative experience, often had a rough-shod approach which "often imperils the rights of the citizen and produces injustice."[48]

The judiciary after 1937 tended less and less to sit as a super-legislature, but, in Douglas' view, it was necessary for it to remain alert to legislative and executive abuses of power. The Supreme Court of the United States, Douglas said in the University of Calcutta lectures in 1955, "was the product of a

---

*Grandfather of the present Justice, serving from 1877 to 1911.

political maturity that saves a people from disasters. Our government is, indeed, the result of political forces and political processes that allow for change and at the same time give some guaranty of stability. Our Court is an important part of that government—an institution that has created in our people the confidence that the humblest and the most powerful will receive the same treatment."[49]

With this increasing persuasion, Douglas was to join with Black in the mid-forties in an earnest effort to broaden the definition of the individual rights guaranteed by the Constitution. While Murphy and Rutledge remained on the bench, "the Four," as they often were called, succeeded in containing the tendency to proscribe minority activity which was the by-product of the Second World War as it had been of the First. It was Douglas who gave currency to the term "welfare state," which came to describe a society in which the well-being of its citizens was the primary responsibility of government. The term shook the conservatives who still clung to atavistic memories of a morality of "every man for himself," and it pointed to logical consequences from which even the majority on the Warren Court would occasionally shrink.

An opportunity to develop his thesis, even in minority, was presented in the 1960 case of *Flemming v. Nestor,* in which a deported radical was cut off from further payments of his Social Security benefits. Aside from the fact that the deportation turned upon a conviction for Communist affiliations prior to the Internal Security Act of 1951, the five-to-four majority sustained both the expulsion and the termination of the retirement benefits. The operation of the statute, Douglas protested, was a perfect example of the modern-day bill of attainder, and the expropriation of the Social Security benefits was a vindictive act of the government. Old-age security was a matter of right and not of charity; to deny to anyone "accrued social benefits—part of his property interests"—was an application of the medieval concept of attaint which flouted all of the principles of a free society.

"Could Congress, on deporting an alien for having been a Communist, confiscate his home, appropriate his savings accounts, and thus send him out of the country penniless?" Douglas demanded. In view of the fact that the operation of the criminal penalty was itself an *ex post facto* law in further violation of the Constitution, Douglas vainly urged the majority to face up to the task of compelling Congress itself to honor the letter and spirit of the Constitution.[50]

In 1963 the Court came to accept the portion of Douglas' *Flemming* dissent which went to the proposition that Social Security benefits were a matter of right and not a matter of grace. When South Carolina undertook to cut off unemployment compensation from an eligible person who declined to work on Saturdays because of the doctrine of her religion, the Court held the action an improper abridgment of religious freedom. While the majority thus avoided the direct answer to the question of the vested right of beneficiaries in Social Security, the logic of events had moved it substantially in the direction of affirmation.[51]

*   *   *

The thin line between abridgment of individual religious freedom and "establishment" of religious activity through any semblance of public support was a phase of civil liberty which provoked increasingly irrational criticism as the Court strove for a firm rule of construction. First dividing the issues between the anti-establishment clause and the freedom of worship clause in the First Amendment, the Court had then placed itself in a position of future embarrassment by seeking to be overly specific in a 1947 New Jersey school bus decision.

Seeking to clarify the "establishment of religion" clause, the Court had suggested that it specifically forbade government to set up a church or to enact laws "which aid one religion, aid all religions, or prefer one religion over another." Nor, added the Court, could any tax money be spent in aid of any type of religious activity, nor any government facility be used for any religious purpose. Having said so much while supporting the refunding of school bus moneys to parochial school parents, the Court was compelled to deny the released time inside public schools in the Illinois case.[52]

In two New York cases, Douglas was able to provide the Court with a narrow path of consistency between the two rules set out in *Everson* and *McCollum*. To permit students to leave public schools to receive religious instruction off the public premises, he suggested in *Zorach V. Clauson,* accommodated both the anti-establishment and freedom of religion clauses. The purpose of the First Amendment, he pointed out, was to separate church and state by insisting that "there shall be no concert or union or dependency one on the other." But, Douglas added, this was not to say that government had "to be hostile to religion and throw its weight against efforts to widen the effective scope of religious influence."[53]

A decade later, in *Engel v. Vitale*, Douglas had narrowed his perspective from his acquiescence in *Everson* and his affirmance in *Zorach,* but still was able to preserve the very minute distinctions between these earlier cases and *McCollum.* The prayer authorized by the New York Board of Regents for recital in public schools he found to conflict with the establishment provision for the same reason that released time in the Illinois case—time spent in religious activity on the public premises—had done so. The provision in the New York law that objecting students could leave the room while the brief prayer was in progress, said Douglas, was not only unrealistic but a further corroboration of the fact that the public facilities were being used.[54]

For a man whose own stern religious persuasions and broad religious tolerance made the language of the *Zorach* case seem closest to his personal convictions, the distinctions which he was required to make in the succeeding cases placed a maximum strain upon his libertarian philosophy. But co-equal with the religious heritage of the nation, Douglas found, was the tradition of protecting minority views. Both principles had to find accommodation in the constitutional context. They were not, in Douglas' view, mutually exclusive: "The smallest minority of all," he once wrote, "is in one man's conscience."[55]

*   *   *

The concern for the individual in an increasingly impersonal corporate society was the dominant element in the jurisprudence of both Black and Douglas. It led both men to a degree of cooperation not even equalled in the Holmes-Brandeis association, where the essential restraint in the Holmesian philosophy was often in contrast to the restrained activism of Brandeis. Rather, the progress of liberal thought on the Court of the fifties and sixties was a process of counterbalances between Black and Douglas on the one side and Holmes' intellectual heir, Frankfurter, on the other.

The aggressive activism of Douglas was shared with Black, as Black's ideal of individual liberty was shared with Douglas. Frankfurter's sympathy with the ultimate objectives of both was tempered by the persuasion that the essence of American democratic tradition was to leave the attainment of the objectives to the more deliberate process of electoral initiative. Both Douglas and Frankfurter were products of law school environments which had nurtured a thoroughgoing critique of the old constitutionalism, but Douglas represented the "realism" of the latter-day Yale curriculum which would have been anathema to one of his predecessors on the Yale faculty, William Howard Taft. Frankfurter, said yet another Yale professor, Fred Rodell, was an apostle of "academic adjudication," while Douglas had attacked at every opportunity 'the leave-liberty-to-the-legislature' slant of the . . . Thayer-Hand-Frankfurter school of jurisprudence."[56]

The choice of progressivism, in Douglas' view, lay between a judicial policy of scrutinizing each governmental action to determine if it satisfied a due process standard, and a policy of affirmatively enforcing the guarantees of the Constitution broadly defined. Under the reliance on due process, he declared, jurists were permitted "to roam at will in the limitless sea of their own beliefs as to reasonableness," whereas an incorporation of the principle of enforcing individual rights into the Fourteenth Amendment would compel the judges to apply the letter of the Constitution itself.[57]

Although this proposition was subjected to a stormy passage in the religious freedom cases, it formed a solid base for Black and Douglas in their insistence upon a steady extension of judicial authority in the field of civil liberties. "Men have short memories and at times forget that the Bill of Rights deliberately made it difficult for government to bring its awesome powers to bear against the citizen."[58] The Fifth Amendment clause against self-incrimination, in the view of Douglas and the majority of the Court, represented a historic step away from the Dark Ages. It was logical that, with the grudging acceptance by the Court of the incorporation of the First

Amendment into the Fourteenth, the incorporation of the Fifth should be the next small step forward.

For Black, freedom of expression was an absolute. For Douglas, while it was subject to reasonable qualification under the "clear and present danger" test, the Court had always to be alert to the likelihood that the emotions of the moment would be translated irrationally into such a danger. In his dissent in the *Dennis* case, Douglas conceded that the nature of Communism "as a force on the world scene" was relevant to the question of the "clear and present" threat to security posed by the defendants' activities. "But the primary consideration is the strength and tactical position" of the American Communists, he warned. Unless it could be established beyond reasonable doubt that their activities were on the verge of endangering the government, they remained within the constitutional protection to be afforded unpopular utterances.[59]

The violence of expression itself, Douglas said on another occasion, might be the very thing the First Amendment was intended to protect: "a function of free speech under our system of government is to invite dispute." The observation was made in a minority protest which went on to suggest that the freedom was most meaningful when "it induces a condition of unrest, creates dissatisfaction with conditions as they are, or even stirs people to anger."[60]

Yet—in a dissent from an opinion upholding the statutory requirement of registration and disclosure of affiliations—Douglas conceded that alien agitators as a group could be made subject to the law if domestic agencies were also subject to it. To require registry in order to identify propaganda groups was one thing; to publicize the membership in the group was another, for it could expose individuals to harassment in "their exercise of First Amendment rights. The more unpopular the group, the greater the likelihood of harassment."[61]

Douglas' test of balancing the national interest in security against the national obligation to preserve individual freedoms reached a climax in his opinion for a five-to-four majority in 1966, invalidating an Arizona loyalty oath for public school teachers. A law which proscribed membership in any organization without requiring proof of "a specific intent to further the unlawful aims of the organization" was unconstitutional, he declared. "A law which applies to membership without the 'specific intent' . . . infringes unnecessarily on protected freedoms. It rests on the doctrine of 'guilt by association' which has no place here."[62]

Douglas joined in a Court majority in striking down an act of Congress broadly curtailing the right to travel abroad in peacetime; "freedom of movement is the very essence of our free society, setting us apart," he wrote in a concurring opinion. "Like the right of assembly and the right of association, it often makes all other rights meaningful—knowing, studying, arguing, exploring, conversing, observing and even thinking."[63] He protested with the minority the following year when the Court sustained a specific ban on travel to Communist Cuba. Failure of Congress to fix standards whereby the Secretary of State would be required to show why the ban was justified, he declared, encouraged the invasion of private and personal rights.[64]

Douglas wrote the Court opinion in 1965 invalidating Connecticut's law against disseminating birth control information and prescribing contraceptives for married couples. The opinion presented him with the opportunity to develop the proposition, shared with Black, that "specific guarantees in the Bill of Rights have penumbras, formed by emanations from those guarantees that help give them life and substance. The right of privacy, a concept which had been knocking at the unanswered door of common-law tort for more than a generation,[65] Douglas suggested, was a vital element in the penumbra: The Third Amendment prohibition against quartering soldiers in any house in peacetime, the Fourth Amendment security against unreasonable searches and seizures, and the Fifth Amendment clause against self-incrimination, all had roots in the right of the individual to be let alone.[66]

The right to counsel in felony cases in state courts, severely limited in *Betts v. Brady,* was broadly extended in *Gideon v. Wainwright* in 1964. Black read the opinion of the Court, and Douglas concurred with the observation that "rights protected against state invasion by the due process clause of the Fourteenth Amendment are not watered-down versions of what the Bill of Rights guarantees."[67] Although, by the summer of 1967, Black and Douglas had still not mustered a Court majority in favor of the incorporation of all of the Bill of Rights into the Fourteenth Amendment, the recurring majority holdings in favor of adding to the catalogue of freedoms under the First and Fifth amounted to half a loaf for the activists rather than none at all.[68]

The disjunctive jurisprudence which characterized the Court throughout virtually all of his tenure struck Douglas as a sign of the effectiveness of the change which had occurred three decades earlier. "When an old Court is suddenly reconstituted," he told a Calcutta audience, "there will be unsettlement until the new judges have taken their positions on constitutional doctrine. During that time—which may extend a decade or more—constitutional law will be in flux. That is the necessary consequence of our system. The alternative is to let the Constitution freeze into the pattern which one generation gave it."[69]

As one of the men who led the unprecedented attack on precedents in the Stone Court, Douglas continued to be persuaded that "*stare decisis* must give way before the dynamic component of history" and that each new generation in a chronically moving society may "catch the broader vision which may require the undoing of the work of their predecessors."[70] If Douglas' credo sounded revolutionary, it also sounded familiarly Jeffersonian; both men, in their own time, had preserved the ideal of action.

PART III

Court and Constitution at Mid-Century

. . . I believe that our Constitution, with its absolute guarantees of individual rights, is the best hope for the aspirations of freedom which men share everywhere.

Hugo L. Black, J., in the James Madison Lecture at New York University, February 17, 1960.

Chart III   THE WARREN COURT

1950 1951 1952 1953 1954 1955 1956 1957 1958 1959 1960 1961 1962 1963 1964 1965 1966 1967 1968 1969

TRUMAN   EISENHOWER   KENNEDY   JOHNSON   NIXON

VINSON (D. - Ky.)

WARREN (Chief Justice) (R. - Calif.)

FRANKFURTER (D. - Mass.)

GOLDBERG (D. - Ill.)

FORTAS (D. - Tenn.)

BLACK (D. - Ala.)

MINTON (D. - Ind.)

DOUGLAS (D. - Conn.)

BRENNAN (R. - N.J.)

REED (D. - Ky.)

WHITTAKER (R. - Mo.)

WHITE (D. - Colo.)

CLARK (D. - Tex.)

MARSHALL (D. - Md.)

BURTON (R. - Ohio)

STEWART (R. - Mich.)

HARLAN (R. - N.Y.)

JACKSON (R. - N.Y.)

McGrath | McGranery | Brownell | Rogers | Kennedy | Katzenbach | Clark | Mitchell

Perlman | Sobeloff | Rankin | Cox | Marshall | Griswold

* McGranery

‡ See note on Chart II, p. 118.

† Kennedy resigned September 3, 1964; Katzenbach was Acting Attorney General until February 13, 1965.

The sixteen-year tenure of the Warren Court, covering virtually all of the Presidential administrations of Eisenhower, Kennedy and Johnson, was the longest Chief Justiceship since Fuller's at the turn of the century. Frankfurter, Black, Douglas and Clark continued for most of this period to consolidate the basic principles of the New Legality begun in the late New Deal when they were appointed. Warren himself, and Brennan, as well as the second Harlan in his own way, augmented the majority for the New Legality. Frankfurter and Harlan, together with Stewart and White, represented the pole of judicial restraint counterbalancing the Black-Douglas group of activists.

11/Congressional
Confrontation

L ESS THAN A WEEK after he had terminated his military career, in 1952, Dwight D. Eisenhower mounted a platform in a ball park in his hometown of Abilene, Kansas. It was pouring rain, and the guest of honor had to borrow a raincoat while he made an address to 20,000 persons huddled under the grandstand roof. For the first time in thirty-six years, the erstwhile General of the Armies felt free from the restraints of military protocol to voice his thoughts on the domestic scene.

The America he observed, Eisenhower told the Kansas audience and millions of television viewers, seemed to be torn by "unreasonable antagonism between economic elements" which constituted "a danger that is far easier to intensify than to reduce by depending exclusively upon legislation." He identified other elements of danger in the growing threat of inflation and the continuing burden of taxation, and above all in the "gradual absorption by the central government of functions that belong to local communities and to individuals."[1]

It was a speech calculated to warm the hearts of the old-line agrarian conservatives, but in the urban centers, where the votes were, Republican leaders were not sure of the impact of the Eisenhower words. Since the general had been the favorite of the party moderates, it would be one thing to make an appeal to the uncomplicated life of another generation, but another thing to win the votes of the millions of independents—or, as it might be better to describe them, non-Republicans—who had come to voting age in the twenty years of Democratic rule.

Ever since the close of World War II, the name of the spectacularly successful commander-in-chief of the allied forces in Europe kept cropping up in political discussions. But the first problem had been to persuade the man himself that the effort to try for political office, and in fact the highest political office, was both a duty and a practical, attainable goal. The second

215

problem was to determine whether he was a Republican or a Democrat. To the best of his knowledge, Dickinson County Clerk C. F. Moore wrote to Sherman Adams in 1951, "Mr. Eisenhower has never voted in this county," at least since the enactment of the primary voting registration law in 1927. "I don't think he has any politics," Moore concluded.[2]

That, indeed, was the general impression of both parties, and both parties had ardently wooed him as a possible candidate in the past. President Truman, as Eisenhower later described their conversation en route to the postwar Potsdam Conference, had made clear his own support of Eisenhower for a Democratic nomination in 1948. Other influential Democrats approached him with corroborating offers of support—Jacob Arvey of Chicago, Frank Hague of Jersey City, James Roosevelt and Senator Claude Pepper of Florida. The thickening plot to maneuver him into the nomination prompted Eisenhower at length to make an unequivocal refusal to consider any political office.[3]

In 1950, when he had settled into a civilian job as President of Columbia University, Eisenhower seemed to be a much more likely subject ·for a draft, and Governor Dewey of New York publicly announced that the General would be his choice for the Republican nomination two years hence. Eisenhower's return to military command of the North Atlantic Treaty powers in the winter of 1951 did not diminish the volume of importunity; both Republican and Democratic leaders shuttled regularly to Paris in an effort to win him to a commitment for the next election.

In June, 1951, more than a year before the conventions, a poll indicated that 40 percent of the Democratic voters of the country favored Eisenhower as a candidate on either ticket. Among Republican voters, the poll showed an Eisenhower lead of 50 percent over 20 for Ohio Senator Robert A. Taft and a scattering of support for Dewey and for California Governor Earl Warren. It was, in fact, the early groundswell of party commitment for Taft, who formally announced his candidacy in September of that year, that brought a redoubling of efforts by moderate Republicans to win their man. In March, although the General had made no sign of changing his position of four years before, the first Presidential primary of 1952 in New Hampshire gave Eisenhower a stunning victory over Taft, who had campaigned hard to get a head start on convention delegates.[4]

From then on, the drama had built up. Eisenhower almost overtook the favorite son, Governor Harold E. Stassen, in the write-ins in the Minnesota primary, but thereafter the cold realities of primary politics began to build Taft's delegate lead. A spectacular "steal" of Texas delegates excited the nation on the eve of the Republican convention in Chicago, and focussed attention on a fight in the credentials committee which was then carried to the convention floor. After an hours-long debate in which Taft and Dewey partisans engaged in furious name-calling, a vote of the full convention seated the disputed pro-Eisenhower delegates from both Texas and Georgia.

Then had come the actual balloting. Having dealt the Taft forces a solid body blow in the delegate fight, the Eisenhower floor managers watched the first roll call of states with mounting hopes. At the end of the first ballot, the General had 595 votes to 500 for Taft; with only nine more votes needed for the nomination, Minnesota signalled the speaker's chair. Senator Edward J. Thye roared into the microphone that his state delegation was changing its vote—and Eisenhower was assured of the convention victory.[5]

*   *   *

Many reasons were given by and for the man in the street for his support of the General for the Presidency. There was the mounting evidence of widespread corruption in the long-entrenched Democratic bureaucracy in Washington; there was the sagging fervor for reform and sustained public effort which customarily followed a major war; there was a conviction among a substantial body of the electorate that twenty years of almost unbroken control of both the Presidency and Congress by a single party was unhealthy for the two-party system. But outweighing all of these was the average American's response to the candor and warmth of the Eisenhower personality.

In the elections in November, 1952 the choice lay between a glamorous military leader who represented security in a cold war and a nostalgic sympathy for the comfortable order of things as they once had been, and an urbane and capable intellectual—Adlai Stevenson of Illinois. The issue was never really in doubt, although many thousands listened with admiration for and agreement with Stevenson's polished prose and calls to high duty. The majority of Americans, however, had simply become weary of such calls; the New Deal years of combatting depression and then foreign military danger had drained them of any zest for fresh crusades, and Harry Truman's earnest but earthy administration had further dampened a fervor for programs of national betterment. The Korean war, dragging along indecisively, contributed to a general disillusionment with foreign affairs.

This disillusionment, in two respects, handicapped Stevenson and benefitted Eisenhower. On the one hand, the Republican candidate's vapid campaign speeches on foreign policy—manifestly demonstrating that, for the moment at least, he had nothing to contribute on the subject—were entirely acceptable to an electorate wishing to forget the complexities of international life. On the other hand, Eisenhower's electrifying Detroit promise to go to Korea himself, after the election, to look into matters there, was precisely the type of assurance the majority of Americans wanted, and would find credible coming from the conquering hero of the Second World War.

Eisenhower embodied the people's yearning for a semblance of stability in the postwar world; Stevenson's contribution, essentially, was to keep the Republican victory from becoming a general avalanche. In this he was more than partially successful; it was true that Eisenhower's 33,927 549 popular votes to 27,311,316 for Stevenson was a mammoth landslide, but it was a significant and totally personal victory. The Republicans won only 48 seats in the Senate as against 47 for the Democrats and one Independent, while in the House the Republican margin was only 221 to 212.

Eisenhower, as it were, had been the successful candidate of a national good-government coalition, but the practical test of his ability would come first with his choice of the personnel of his administration. Immediately following his election, he had announced that he would seek out the best brains in the country to take over the executive departments, and while his choices presented impressive credentials, it remained to be seen how or whether they could improve upon the work of the men they were succeeding. John Foster Dulles, as Secretary of State and ranking member of the Cabinet, was a generally applauded selection; a partner in the leading New York law firm of Sullivan and Cromwell with its wide-ranging international contacts, Dulles was one of the most knowledgeable men to fill the Secretaryship of State in many administrations. His chief handicap was the public image, slightly Puritanical, more than slightly superior, which he conveyed.[6]

Indeed, the tendency of the new administration's personnel to stress their own righteousness did not endear them to the public, although throughout his two terms "Ike" would remain apart in popular esteem. The incessant prating of Vice-President Richard Nixon on the integrity of the incoming administration had almost come a cropper in the campaign when a New York newspaper broke a story about a special "Nixon fund" established by California backers to meet some of the substantial financial demands upon a man of moderate means in high government office. The "fund" was hardly more of a secret than Hugo Black's early Klan affiliation had been in 1937, but the opposition in both cases had tried to fan an issue into flame. Nixon's national radio and television defense was essentially one of confession and avoidance. The "fund," after all, was unusual but hardly censurable, and the reaction to the broadcast was a mixture of personal sympathy for a man and embarrassment at the "corny" quality of his self-vindication which discussed the mortgage on his home, his little dog, "Checkers," and the limited amount he could afford to spend on his wife's cloth coat.[7]

There was a certain disenchantment with the new administration— always excepting the President himself—bred in part by its aforementioned self-conscious declarations of moral superiority and in part by the warm welcome it extended to the conservative hierarchy in the Republican party. If Dulles represented a twentieth-century view of American obligations in world events, most of the Cabinet consisted of parochial minds obsessed with a balanced budget as the solution to all national ills. George Humphrey administered the Treasury with a fervor for cutting back Federal activities that could only warm the heart of Robert A. Taft. Sinclair Weeks took over Commerce with an air of surprised relief that twenty years of Democratic control had not destroyed all opportunity for the department to be of service to private enterprise, and began cancelling administrative controls in every direction he could reach. Charles E. Wilson, whose inept remark that what was good for General Motors was good for the country, demonstrated in his administration of Defense that the Republican premise that a successful business executive could, by definition, be a successful government officer was subject to substantial qualification.[8]

*   *   *

The new President, acutely conscious of his status as a political novitiate, tended to defer to the counsels of old-line party leaders, and these leaders, seeking to weld a powerful coalition between the Taft conservatives and the Dewey moderates, consistently urged accommodation of all factions. Against his personal instincts, the candidate had consented to appear on the same platform with Senator William E. Jenner in Indiana and Senator Joseph McCarthy in Wisconsin, even excising a tribute to General Marshall which would have rebutted McCarthy's unconscionable vilification of Eisenhower's old comrade-in-arms. Having compromised with reference to the party's most rabid character vandal, Eisenhower had little difficulty in accepting the proposal that he balance his Cabinet with rightists as well as moderates.

Thus, in addition to Humphrey, Weeks and Wilson, there was Douglas McKay of Oregon in Interior and Taft's ardent admirer, Arthur E. Summerfield, in the Postmaster General's chair. The relatively liberal wing was represented in Labor first by a union official, Martin P. Durkin, whose stay was so short-lived that he had little influence, and his successor, personnel expert James P. Mitchell. There was also the first secretary of the new Department of Health, Education and Welfare—Oveta Culp Hobby of Texas, who was occasionally suspected of "harboring egalitarian inclinations not wholly appropriate to a Republican Cabinet."[9]

But the dominant figure in the Cabinet was a thoroughly committed Dewey man—Herbert Brownell, Jr., the Attorney General, campaign manager for Dewey's New York gubernatorial campaign in 1942 and both his Presidential bids. Having deftly guided Eisenhower's own preconvention and electoral campaigns, and having served ten years in the House of Representatives, Brownell had impeccable credentials as a political adviser, while his reputation as a Wall Street lawyer made him the logical consultant to the President on matters of judicial selection. In both functions, he would prove to be one of Eisenhower's most effective lieutenants. His careful preparation of the ground on Capitol Hill in 1956 made possible the passage of the Civil Rights Act of 1957, the first such statute in modern times.[10]

The first of his opportunities for guiding the selection on a major judicial appointment materialized in September, 1953, when Chief Justice Vinson suddenly died. Eisenhower promptly requested Brownell to prepare a list of prospects from the legal profession who might have the highest qualifications for the opening.

Although he did not elaborate upon it in his interoffice communications, Eisenhower could not be unaware that the passage of time had made it likely that a significant number of appointments to the Supreme Court was apt to develop during his administration. He was also aware that these appointments would presumably affect the character of the Court as an institution. Of the eight remaining Justices, three were Truman appointees and five still represented the Roosevelt Court. As it was to turn out, Eisenhower's five appointments would replace three of Truman's and two of Roosevelt's.

Eisenhower's ideal candidate for the Chief Justiceship would have been another Charles Evans Hughes, and there was a singular coincidence in the fact that President Taft, in his original appointment of Hughes, had found it necessary to qualify a hint of elevation to the Chief's chair when it became vacant. Eisenhower, early in his administration, had discussed an appointment to the Court with Governor Warren, but he did not now consider that this was a commitment applying necessarily to the Chief Justiceship. Warren's general views, however, Eisenhower wrote after their interview, "seemed to reflect high ideals and a great deal of common sense."[11]

Among leading candidates for the vacancy were two men with primary claims upon the administration—Dewey himself, and Dulles; Eisenhower intimates insisted that if either of these men wanted the position it should go to him. When it developed that neither did want it, other names were also studied—Judge Arthur T. Vanderbilt of New Jersey, a leader in constitutional and procedural reform and a vigorous pioneer in postwar legal education; and Federal Judge Orie L. Phillips of Colorado. Both of these were struck from the list as being too old; the President, among other criteria, was seeking a man of youth and physical vigor who would be able to remain in office over a period of years and put the stamp of his personality upon the Court.[12]

The choice, rather quickly, narrowed to the name of the California governor. While there were the usual objections to his lack of judicial experience, the undemonstrated depth of his legal knowledge, and to his reputation for liberalism, there were two factors that appeared to carry substantial weight in his favor. One was his manifest ability as an administrator—the practical importance of which had been demonstrated in the Chief Justiceships of Taft and Hughes and, negatively, in those of White, Stone and Vinson. The other was the manifest political capital to be realized from a moderate, a Westerner, and an associate of California Senator William F. Knowland, who had succeeded to Senate leadership upon the death of Robert Taft.[13]

To Warren himself, the President owed no significant political debt. Although the governor had helped swing the convention in favor of seating the Eisenhower delegates in the disputed cases of Georgia and Texas, his ultimate strategy at the time had been to balance off Taft and Eisenhower forces in the hope of a deadlock from which he might emerge as the dark horse candidate. Even in the final shifting of convention balloting, the California delegation remained with Warren to the end. Any political debt that might have been owing, said *Time,* could have been satisfied with a third-class postmaster's appointment. The chief political consideration with reference to Warren and the center chair on the Court was simply the necessity that the chair be filled by a Republican.[14]

It was also known at the time that cases of historic significance were before the Court—had been argued, indeed, under Vinson and would almost certainly be reargued under the new Chief. The cases challenged the "separate but equal" doctrine of racial segregation in public schools, and they had been grouped for review as they came up to the Court from the District of Columbia, Delaware, South Carolinia, Virginia, and, by a singular irony, from the old Free Soil state of Kansas. *Brown v. Board of Education* was an action against the board of education of Topeka—and thus the leading case in this review illustrated the pervasiveness of the issue, both North and South, and the elemental character of the issue within the social fabric of the United States, which was being tested. Whichever way the Court would proceed in its decision, it would indelibly fix the public image of the new Chief Justiceship.

*   *   *

It was not hard to discern Earl Warren's assets in the eyes of a professional politician like the Attorney General. Twenty years before, as district attorney for Alameda County, Warren had led a campaign to upgrade the state attorney general's office, making it a full-time position and second in influence and prestige only to the governorship. In 1938 Warren had won the primary nominations of both parties to go into the office himself, and two years later had upset incumbent Democratic Governor Cuthbert L. Olson. By 1944, with this spectacular record of political successes, Warren's long shadow from the West was reaching to the Republican National Convention in Chicago.

Two years later the shadow grew even longer when Warren became the second governor in California history to be elected to a second term. His selection by the Dewey group for the Vice-Presidential candidacy was all but a foregone conclusion, and Dewey's defeat did not dim the Warren luster. In 1950 he won his third successive term as governor.[15]

Brownell had come to know Warren well in the course of the 1948 campaign, and the 1950 California victory added to his impressiveness as a party hope. On the other hand, it was only realistic to consider that Warren's prospects for the Presidency were now in decline: after Eisenhower's prospective eight years, there would be the ambitions of a rival Californian, Vice-President Richard Nixon, to be taken into account. What national office of magnitude remained to offer a liberal Republican of Warren's stature, except the Chief Justiceship?

Brownell, on Eisenhower's instructions, flew to California to consult Warren. Astute observers speculated that the subject was whether the governor would be willing to wait for an Associate Justiceship to open up or would insist upon the Chief's position. Within hours, Brownell was back in Washington with the answer, which was first "leaked" to a few favored members of the press corps and then, on October 1, officially announced by the President. Four days later Warren himself flew to the capital, took the oaths of office and began his duties as the fourteenth Chief Justice of the United States.[16]

The appointment met with varying reactions. Eisenhower himself observed that Warren met his requirements for "integrity, honesty, middle-of-the-road philosophy, experience in government, experience in the law." David Lawrence, the right-wing commentator, objected that a "middle-of-the-road philosophy" was a poor qualification, since there was "no middle of the road as between right and wrong in determining a judicial question." The far right-wing commentator Fulton Lewis shouted that the California governor had favored socialized medicine and was soft on radicalism. Liberals applauded Warren's refusal to support the regents of the University of California in their effort to compel faculty members to take a loyalty oath—although they faulted him for endorsing a statewide non-discriminatory loyalty oath. In the comfortable perspective of 1953, they also upbraided him for the Japanese relocations of wartime 1942.[17]

On balance, the new appointee was characterized as a modern-minded moderate; "Warrenism" had become a California synonym for policies favorable to fair employment practices, state-supported health insurance, and non-discrimination in housing. "In his unprecedented three terms as governor of America's third largest state," wrote a correspondent of the *New York Times*, "Warren signed some 10,000 bills. None were overthrown by judicial review." Almost all of the major bills, the writer continued, infringed upon some sensitive vested interest and alienated a broad spectrum of interest groups. In the politics of the state, the report concluded: "Nobody likes Warren but the voters."[18]

Whether or not the voters liked Warren as governor, the number of persons reacting to the appointment was substantial. On October 13, a White House memorandum tabulated "85 unfavorable, 31 favorable" letters which "came from all over the United States, although California writers had a plurality." Presumably the Senate Judiciary Committee had a similar volume of mail, for its chairman, Senator William Langer of North Dakota, announced that the committee would proceed to investigate "more than a hundred" protests which it had received. Although, on his own subsequent report, nine out of ten of these proved to be a waste of time, Langer continued to delay committee action; when a newspaper suggested that it was because of his pique at Eisenhower's failure to consult him on four post-office appointments in North Dakota, he made a lengthy self-defense on the Senate floor—which failed to advance the matter. Eventually, however, after hearing an unimpressive assortment of racists and rightists, the committee reported favorably and on March 1, 1954—more than five months after he had taken office—Warren was confirmed by a unanimous but untabulated vote.[19]

*   *   *

On October 9, 1954 sixty-two-year-old Robert H. Jackson suddenly died, in his automobile en route to the Court from his home in McLean, Virginia. It was an unexpected loss, bringing to a close a career of juris-prudential brilliance too often clouded over by disappointed ambitions and self-inflicted wounds of irascibility. Three times Jackson had been passed over for the highest seat on the Court. Roosevelt had been persuaded to prefer Stone's experience, Truman had ruled him out after his diatribe against Black, and Eisenhower had momentarily considered him before turning to Warren. Jackson's tenure had been marked by two major features—his non-judicial role as prosecutor at Nuremberg, a subject of vigorous intellectual disagreement, and his association with Justice Frankfurter in development of a new conservatism within the context of the new constitutionalism of the forties and fifties. The latter course, as it turned out, would be one to be followed by his successor.[20]

Eisenhower had by now developed a standard procedure for filling judicial vacancies; through the Attorney General he sought a list of qualified candidates endorsed by the organized bar, while through Sherman Adams, his special assistant, he cleared the selections with the Republican national committee.[21] On November 5 Brownell made his recommendation to the President—a second John Marshall Harlan, grandson of the great dissenter in *Plessy v. Ferguson*. How consistently the third generation would adhere to the turn-of-the-century liberalism of the first Harlan was a matter of speculation; although this Harlan was identified with the Dewey wing of the Republican party, he was also conspicuous as a partner in one of the most conservative New York law firms.

If the President had hoped to avoid the petty obstructionism in the Senate Judiciary Committee which had attended the Warren case, by the manifestly circumspect character of the present appointee, he was to be disappointed. Several factors militated against an objective and expeditious disposition of the matter. One was purely political. Within the week that the Harlan nomination was sent to the Senate, the mid-term elections wiped out the tenuous Republican majority in the upper chamber. Senator James O. Eastland of Mississippi had little trouble persuading Langer to postpone committee hearings until January when the Democrats would be back in control. Although they were from opposite political camps, each had his particular reasons for wishing to harass the nominee, the Court and the administration. Langer was responsive to the substantial Republican element disgruntled with the nominee's identification with the Dewey wing of the party, while Eastland was groping for a policy of judicial selection which would blunt if not destroy the effect of the desegregation ruling in *Brown,* a supplementary opinion on which was momentarily awaited.[22]

Another factor was the resurgent isolationism, augmented by a resurgent states' rightist reaction to *Brown,* which argued first that there was a conspiracy to elevate national power at the expense of the states and then that there was a conspiracy to impose an international authority through the United Nations upon the sovereignty of the nation itself. The fact that Harlan had been a Rhodes Scholar was, for the neo-xenophobes, prima facie evidence of his commitment to an "internationalist" jurisprudence. Taft's fellow Ohioan, Senator John W. Bricker, had sought to meet the "one world" threat even before Eisenhower took office, with a proposed constitutional amendment which would virtually nullify executive power in the conduct of foreign affairs by vesting in Congress the ultimate control of all international agreements. The Bricker amendment was a symptom of the same distortions in national politics that had allowed the festering of the McCarthyite program of character aspersion. Both were substantially the venom of rightist Republican hatred for the accomplished fact of the New Deal, and took the form of wholesale charges of Communist infiltration into government and of secret concessions in the wartime conferences at Yalta and later at Potsdam.[23]

The Southern attack on the judicial position in *Brown* took the form of a bill, sponsored by Eastland's companion from Mississippi, Senator John C. Stennis, requiring that at least half of the Supreme Court appointees in future should have had a minimum of ten years of prior judicial experience apiece. "Justices of the Supreme Court are not on that tribunal to carry out the policies of any administration," Stennis observed; "they are not there to enforce the laws or policies of any group." Experience in advocacy was of minor importance, the Senator eloquently argued, when compared with "the feel of the precedents" which should control the process of judicial review. While the argument was plausible, the ultimate motive behind it was apparent to many observers. The desegregation decision, the Southern critics contended, had been emotional rather than legal, and a jurist firmly committed to *stare decisis,* the "doctrine of precedents," would presumably have felt compelled to deny the desegregation case.*[24]

Eastland himself was more candid. After the favorable report of the judiciary committee, he told the Senate that he would still oppose the Harlan appointment for three reasons. First, he said, Harlan would not "protect the sovereignty of the United States in the fight which now is being waged by powerful, organized pressure groups on the Atlantic seaboard" to declare "the United Nations Charter, with its taint of Communism, . . . paramount to the United States Constitution." Second was the allegation that "this is a

---

*See the general discussion of desegregation in Ch. 13.

political appointment, dictated by Thomas E. Dewey and his henchmen," and third was the conviction that as a New Yorker Harlan held "views and philosophies which are different from those entertained by the rest of the country."

While insisting that he was not voting against the dissent of the first Harlan in *Plessy v. Ferguson,* Eastland went on to declare that there were "certain things that even the Supreme Court cannot do. . . . No court can compel school integration in areas where it is violently opposed by both races. . . . When the final decree is entered the net result will be simply an intensification of the contempt held by many people of this country for the Court."[25] The opposition continued its protests against the trend toward a new Federalism and "a tendency in the United States today to be international-minded instead of thinking first of our own nation," whereupon the Senate proceeded to vote on the nomination and approve it by a majority of 71 to 11, with 14 not voting. The second Eisenhower appointment to the Court had taken four months to reach confirmation.[26]

The President felt compelled to write a personal apology to the new Justice for the Senate tactics. "I regret, of course, that you were subject to the harassment and delay that was involved in the confirmation of your appointment," he told Harlan. "I assure you, however, that as I have grown wiser, I hope, in the ways of political life, such things tend to bother me less."[27]

*   *   *

Another five-month delay in confirmation awaited Eisenhower's third nomination to the Court. In the fall of 1956 Sherman Minton completed seven undistinguished years on the bench and announced his retirement; it was an ironic commentary on the recurrent Senatorial demand for prior judicial experience that Minton, whose record on that score was substantially longer than any other member's, should have contributed so little to constitutional law. William J. Brennan, Jr. of New Jersey seemed to satisfy the major requirements for speedy Senate approval—a Roman Catholic and a Democrat, an associate justice of the state supreme court since 1952, endorsed by the state and national bars, his qualifications seemed impeccable. "When I met him," Eisenhower wrote a friend, "I was immediately taken with his warm personality and his generous understanding of people and problems."[28]

Brennan went onto the Court in October, 1956; his confirmation, delayed until March 19, 1957, was caught in the backwash of McCarthyism. The Wisconsin Senator was especially incensed because the New Jersey jurist had dared to characterize McCarthy's own investigations as "Salem witch hunts" and to decry "epithets hurled at helpless and hapless victims" of "the barbarism of Congressional hearings." The Senator concluded his diatribe with a sneer: "I assume—because of Mr. Brennan's attacks on anyone who dares fight subversives in this country—that perhaps he qualifies in the minds of some Senators for a position on the Supreme Court." The increasing weariness of the Senate with McCarthy himself was demonstrated in the lack of support for his arguments; by an unrecorded vote, the Senate immediately thereafter confirmed the appointment.[29]

If Eisenhower was pained at the delay in his third appointment, he could not but have been gratified at the expedition of Senate action on the fourth; Charles E. Whittaker of Missouri was confirmed the same day. While the Brennan hearings had been dragging on with McCarthy's continued baiting, Stanley Reed, Roosevelt's second appointee, had submitted his resignation. Whittaker seemed like the type of selection which at last would appease the conservatives in the Senate. A Federal judge on both the district and appellate courts, he applied the pedestrian formula to judicial review which struck a responsive chord in the judiciary committee. "I read the law only for an understanding of its meaning, and enforce it in accordance of my understanding of that meaning," he had told his interrogators. Whittaker, who was confirmed more promptly than any of the other Eisenhower appointees to the Court, was also to rank with the least distinguished selections of the Truman era.[30]

The Truman era itself was all but expunged with the retirement of Justice Burton in 1958, and the nomination of Potter Stewart of Michigan completed the Eisenhower appointments to the Court. It was to be characterized, like three of the other four, by lengthy Senate delay in confirmation, although it was the most politically accommodating of any of the five. Senator Bricker of Ohio—Stewart was a Circuit Court Judge in his state—had personally endorsed the nomination, and, as the President was advised, since the other Ohio Senator was a Democrat and Stewart himself was a Republican, the nomination rested primarily on Bricker's recommendation. Like Whittaker, Stewart had earlier been appointed to the Federal bench by Eisenhower, so that, having won a previous Senate confirmation, it was reasonable to anticipate that there would be no delay in his confirmation for the Supreme Court.[31]

As it was to turn out, the delay on Stewart was the longest of all; six and a half months were to elapse between his appointment and final Senate approval in May, 1959, by a vote of seventy to seventeen. Of Eisenhower's five appointees, only Whittaker had enjoyed prompt confirmation. Ironically, Stewart, whose confirmation was delayed the longest, was the subject of the least personal opposition. In part the delays in several cases were protracted because the appointments had been made during a Congressional recess, but in greater part they reflected a Congressional desire to strike indirectly at the Court by an exhaustive questioning of the new members of the bench. The demands to know whether Stewart considered himself a "creative judge," whether in his opinion the Constitution meant the same thing in 1959 that it had meant in 1787, and whether he accepted the "reasoning" in the segre gation decisions—all were symptomatic of a smouldering discontent with the developing trends of constitutional decision.[32]

*   *   *

The line of cases proceeding from *Brown* was one source of complaint; the sweeping assertion of Fifth Amendment safeguards for witnesses before McCarthy and other Congressional investigators was an even greater affront to many on the Hill, and for conservatives in general there was a growing suspicion that the general tenor of decisions was in favor of a broadening Federal authority in derogation of state power. "During the past generation," wrote Bernard Schwartz of New York University, "there has been a profound change in the manner in which Americans have tended to regard the Supreme Court. . . . Veneration has, all too often, given way to vituperation," he added, and a dangerous tendency had set in, whereby the critical discussion of specific decisions was being supplanted by a systematic plan "to denounce the Justices on purely personal grounds and to seek to destroy the effectiveness of the Court itself as an institution."[33]

Vice-President Nixon had not helped matters when in February, 1956 he had commended the desegregation ruling to the Republican Club of New York, saying: "Speaking for a unanimous Supreme Court, a great Republican Chief Justice, Earl Warren, has ordered an end to racial segregation in the nation's public schools." Senator Stennis gloated: "Although the Vice-President's statement . . . has put the Chief Justice and the decision right in the middle of the forthcoming political campaign, ordinarily injurious to the Court, he has nevertheless rendered a service to the nation by openly characterizing and branding this decision for what it is, purely a political one."[34]

In March, 1957, exercised at the uncompromising position of the Court on segregation orders, ninety-six Southern Congressmen had issued a Declaration of Constitutional Principles. "The unwarranted decision of the Supreme Court in the public school cases is now bearing the fruit always produced when men substitute naked power for established law," the document began. Neither the original Constitution nor the Fourteenth Amendment had mentioned education, it continued, and the *Brown* opinion was clearly a case of nine men substituting "their personal political and social ideas for the established law of the land." The Declaration called upon the rest of the country "to consider the constitutional principles involved against the time when they, too, on issues vital to them, may be the victims of judicial encroachment."[35]

Two months later, Senator Harry F. Byrd of Virginia expressed his concern at the growing use of the "preemption doctrine," which he defined as a gratuitous declaration that any Congressional legislation on a given subject *ipso facto* supplanted and nullified state laws, whether contrary to or corroborative of the national statute. In June, a bill before the Senate

Judiciary Committee was reported out favorably, proposing to deny to the Court a power to assert a Federal preemption unless Congress had stated such an intention in express terms in any statute. Rounding out the Southern arguments against current judicial trends was an article by former Justice Byrnes, whose brief tenure on the Court had been followed by terms as wartime mobilization director, Secretary of State, and then four years as governor of South Carolina. It was imperative, Byrnes declared, that a halt be brought to the decisions which aimed at seeing "all power centered in the Federal government."[36]

A climax in paranoia was reached in the winter of 1957 when the state legislature of Georgia received a resolution, introduced by the speaker of its lower house, formally requesting Congress to undertake the impeachment of the Chief Justice and five Roosevelt and Truman appointees. (Burton had not as yet resigned.) Their "high crimes and misdemeanors" consisted of accepting awards and advancing the objectives of "Communist front organizations" including the National Association for the Advancement of Colored Peoples. The lower house approved the resolution by a vote of 107 to 33, and the state senate followed suit a week later. Congressman Carl Vinson, however, publicly refused to introduce the resolution into Congress, and declared that if any other member introduced it he would vote against it.[37]

The dénouement of the Georgia legislative resolution was not the last of the official Southern protests. From the fall of 1956 until the winter of 1958, ten memorials from the legislatures of eight states were formally presented to Congress, calling for impeachment, announcing an "interposition" of sovereign state power,* and otherwise seeking to enlist Congressional effort in the attack upon the desegregation holdings. State memorials from Illinois and Nebraska, expressing support of the judicial decisions on the school issue, reflected the attitude of the political majority, however.[38]

*   *   *

It was not integration, but subversion, which excited the more universal concern of Congress. In February, 1958 Senator William Jenner of Indiana introduced a bill which sought to deny judicial review to cases concerning contempt of Congress, loyalty and security programs involving Federal employees, and state and local laws on subversives. An uproar promptly broke out from coast to coast; the American Bar Association, which was soon to launch its own attack upon the Court, deplored the proposal as a threatened upsetting of the balance of separate powers in government, while Attorney General William Rogers, who had replaced

---

*See Ch. 13.

Brownell, warned that it was an open-ended program for reducing the Court's jurisdiction with every unpopular decision.[39]

Senator John M. Butler of Maryland proposed an amendment to the Jenner bill which would empower Congress to define the limits to the effect of any specific judicial decision, which was condemned as a more mischievous proposal than the original bill. Then, in April, came a transcript of the hearings before a subcommittee of the Senate Committee on Internal Security, accompanied by an appendix purporting to be a report of the subcommittee's "research department" and attacking the Court as an instrument of international Communism. Suspicious Senators began inquiring into the origin of the report, which was ultimately located in a non-governmental agency known as "SPX Research Associates." Upon further prodding by Senate members, an individual in Stanwood, Washington, identifying himself as one of a group of World War II intelligence officers, acknowledged authorship of the report.

"SPX," it was solemnly reported, stood for "Soviet Principle Ten," and purported to be a study of instances of implementation of Russia's "tenth principle" of class warfare, the breaking of an enemy's capacity to resist without direct military aggression. The firm conviction of the group of private individuals that the current trend of judicial rulings accommodated this principle had been written up and forwarded to the subcommittee holding hearings on the Jenner bill, and accepted by the subcommittee as its own view. With this revelation, the Butler-Jenner proposals began a steady decline back to oblivion.[40]

The fiasco in Congress in the spring of 1958 was only the introductory act in a drama of increasing tension in the summer and early fall. On July 1 the Federal district court in Arkansas granted a Little Rock school board petition to suspend integration plans for two and a half years, but the appellate court reversed the order. In late August the Supreme Court was called into special session to review the question and on September 13 the Court unanimously upheld the appellate court. In the opinion terminating its special session it replied to the mounting cadence of hostility.

In this opinion the Court took the unusual step of naming all nine Justices in support of its holding. The case, said Chief Justice Warren, "raises questions of the highest importance to the maintenance of our Federal system of government." Baldly put, the issue was whether a state, through its governor and legislature, could advise state officials that they were under no duty to obey Federal court orders "resting on this Court's considered interpretation of the United States Constitution." The answer was readily found in basic decisions in the national history: John Marshall had observed that if "the legislatures of the several states may, at will, annul the judgments of the courts of the United States, and destroy the rights acquired under those judgments, the Constitution itself becomes a solemn mockery."

Roger B. Taney had added that the constitutional requirement that every state officer should swear to uphold the Constitution reflected the framers' "anxiety to preserve it in full force, in all its powers, and to guard against resistance to or evasion of its authority, on the part of a state."

The opinion also quoted Chief Justice Hughes in a 1932 case, averring that if a governor or other state officer were able to defy a Federal court order, "it is manifest that the fiat of a state governor, and not the Constitution of the United States, would be the supreme law of the land." It was readily conceded, said the opinion, that public education was primarily a responsibility of the states; the only constitutional basis for Federal involvement derived from the requirement that equal justice under law was to be assured to all persons within the United States. The holding in *Brown,* that segregated public education was a denial of equal justice and due process, Warren pointed out, had been the unanimous holding of the Court in 1954 and again in 1955. He added that since the original holding, three new Justices had come onto the Court and were "at one with the Justices still on the Court who participated in that basic decision."[41]

*   *   *

It was in this atmosphere of bad feeling that Justice Stewart's nomination was submitted to the Senate judiciary committee in January, 1959. Earlier in that same month, Chief Justice Warren had formally resigned from the American Bar Association—a body which Justice Black had once described as the single organization in his professional career which he regretted ever having joined. At its midwinter meeting in February, the ABA made a rejoinder in the form of a report by a committee headed by Peter C. Brown, a former member of the Federal Subversive Activities Control Board, which flatly stated: "Many cases have been decided" in the contemporary Court "in such a manner as to encourage an increase in Communist activities in the United States," and internal security had been "weakened by technicalities raised in judicial decisions."[42]

The criticism of the Court thus continued to alternate between the poles of Southern hostility to integration and a general conservative worry over threatened subversion. The legal profession still rocked with the sensation of a censure of Court action contained in another committee report in August, 1958—this one at the Conference of State Chief Justices, where the committee chairman, Chief Judge Frederick W. Brune of Maryland, recommended adoption of the majority report admonishing the Supreme Court to exercise "careful moderation in . . . its policy-making role."[43]

The question "whether Federalism shall continue to exist, and if so in what form, is primarily a political question rather than a judicial question," said the Conference through its Committee on Federal-State Relations as Affected by Judicial Decisions. "On the other hand, it can hardly be denied that judicial decisions, specifically decisions of the Supreme Court, can give tremendous impetus to changes in the allocation of powers and responsibilities, as between the Federal and the state governments." Thereupon the report unleashed an avalanche of condemnation:

> We are now concerned specifically with the effect of judicial decisions upon the relations between the Federal government and the state governments. Here we think that the overall tendency of decisions of the Supreme Court over the last twenty-five years or more has been to press the extension of Federal power and to press it rapidly. There have been, of course, and still are, very considerable differences within the Court on these matters. . . .
> We believe that in the fields with which we are concerned, and as to which we feel entitled to speak, the Supreme Court too often has tended to adopt the role of policy-maker without proper judicial restraint. We feel this is particularly the case in . . . the extent and extension of the Federal power, and the supervision of state action by the Supreme Court by virtue of the Fourteenth Amendment. In the light of the immense power of the Supreme Court and its practical non-reviewability in most instances no more important obligation rests upon it, in our view, than that of careful moderation in the exercise of its policy-making role.[44]

The report went on to decry the multiple opinions and frequent five-to-four majorities on key cases. It seemed strange, the Conference declared, "that under a constitutional doctrine which requires all others to recognize the Supreme Court's rulings on constitutional questions as binding adjudications of the meaning and application of the Constitution, the Court itself has so frequently overturned its own decisions thereon, after the lapse of periods varying from one year to seventy-five, or even ninety-five years."

> These frequent differences and occasional overrulings of prior decisions in constitutional cases cause us grave concern as to whether individual views of the members of the Court as from time to time constituted, or a majority thereof, as to what is wise or desirable do not unconsciously override a more dispassionate consideration of what is or is not constitutionally warranted. We believe that the latter is the correct approach, and we have no doubt that every member of the Supreme Court intends to adhere to that approach, and believes that he does so. It is our earnest hope which we respectfully express, that that great Court exercise to the full its power of judicial self-restraint by adhering firmly to its tremendous, strictly judicial powers and by eschewing, so far as possible, the exercise of essentially legislative powers when it is called upon to decide questions involving the validity of state action, whether it deems such action wise or unwise. The value of our system of Federalism, and of local self-government in local matters which it embodies, should be kept firmly in mind, as we believe it was by those who framed our Constitution.[45]

The minority report charged that the majority statement was simply a disguised condemnation of the segregation decisions, while Solicitor General Lee Rankin described the ABA committee report as a fundamental threat to the independence of the judiciary.[46]

*   *   *

After the prolonged hearings of the judiciary committee, the Senate debate on the Stewart appointment became a litany of despair for a social order disintegrating under the impact of the emerging jurisprudence of a new Federalism. The intellectual agony of high-principled men in their hour of travail was manifest in the successive remarks of Senators Richard B. Russell of Georgia and Olin D. Johnston of South Carolina. Readily conceding the character and professional competence of Justice Stewart, Southerners one after another announced themselves constrained to oppose his nomination; their fundamental conviction was that the doctrines of the current Court were axes laid at the very roots of their way of life. There was no passionate bigotry in any of their speeches; the Senate atmosphere this May 5, 1959 had the sadness and dignity of a scene in Valhalla.

It was not Stewart the man or the jurist—indeed, in the final analysis it was not really the Supreme Court—against which the speakers were inveighing; it was the *Zeitgeist,* and the vague *corpus* of Federalism in general, which they saw as the ultimate adversary. Because, for them, the old social order had been fundamentally beneficent, they could only conclude that judicial attitudes critical of that state of being must be alien to the *ethos* of the Founding Fathers. "Feeling as I do," said Russell, "that the nomination of Mr. Justice Stewart is a part of a deliberate policy by the Department of Justice to perpetuate some recent decisions of the Court, which decisions were partly based on *amicus curiae* briefs submitted by the Department of Justice, I have no alternative. I shall vote against this nomination."[47]

The Georgia Senator saw a calculated design in the selection of the Eisenhower appointees. Convinced as he was that *Brown* flew in the face of constitutional principles, and that its corroborating cases only corroborated that fact, he added: "I am convinced that these decisions were sponsored by the Department of Justice and that, through a process of screening and making recommendations to the President, that Department has made sure that no man will be nominated to the Senate who does not wholeheartedly embrace the 1954 decision of the Court on school segregation, which was admittedly based on psychology rather than law."[48]

Senator Johnston warned that "the interpretation of the Constitution . . . to give the Federal government more power and the states less power . . . is interpreting the Constitution in reverse, because the Constitution provides that all power not delegated to the Federal government is reserved to the states." Because he was convinced that Stewart would support this trend of decision, he was confirmed in his own opposition. His colleague, Senator Strom Thurmond, after reciting a "Red Bill of Rights" which he felt had been enunciated in recent decisions, joined in Johnston's objection:

"I understand that Mr. Stewart was asked whether or not he approved of the decision in *Brown* against *Board of Education.* He stated that he did.

If Mr. Stewart believes in that decision, then he believes that the Constitution of the United States can be amended by the Supreme Court. If he believes in that decision, he does not believe in the division of power which is clearly set out in the Constitution."[49]

The ultimate confirmation of Stewart was never in doubt. The lengthy delay on the final vote was simply one more expression of Congressional unhappiness at the apparently undeviating progress of the Warren Court toward a permanent positive concept of Federalism. Already, under a Republican President and a Republican administration, the confrontation between Court and Congress had exceeded in seriousness anything since the ideological struggle in the early Marshall Court leading to *Marbury v. Madison*. In the six Eisenhower years, a culmination of frustrations had developed: the crisis point in the postwar hysteria over loyalty and subversion, aggravated by demagogues like McCarthy; the disappointment of many conservatives who had assumed (or wishfully hoped) that dislodging the Democratic administration would be synonymous with dismantling all or most of the jurisprudence of the New Deal; the death-blow to racial integration which had been dealt by *Brown,* but had only resulted in an agonizing and lingering death.

Five Eisenhower appointments represented a numerical majority on the Supreme Court, but this only made the conservative bitterness more acute at finding three of the five committed firmly to the new legality which had prevailed since 1937. If Brennan did not outdo Black or Douglas, he manifestly sympathized with their concept of a positive constitutional duty vested in modern government. If Harlan had replaced Jackson with the understanding that he would be Frankfurter's intellectual legatee, one had to remember that all of these men were conservatives only by contrast with the activists. And as for Warren, if he was not the lawyer that Hughes had been, he was an administrator far more inspiring than either Stone or Vinson—and his leadership was picking up momentum as the years passed.

On the tenth anniversary of the Warren Court, constitutional observers generally corroborated the conclusions of Philip Kurland of the University of Chicago: three fundamental propositions, each growing out of the other and all of them in a sense the inevitable consequence of the twenty preceding years of depression and war, clearly epitomized the jurisprudence of the mid-century bench. First was the insistence upon the "primacy of equality"—starkly stated in *Brown* and sounding the call to the egalitarian revolution of the sixties. Second was the undermining and eventual destruction of the classical Federal system in favor of a new Federalism which, as a consequence of equality, required uniformity of the guarantee of equality throughout the land. From that proposition grew, inevitably, the third— "enhancement of judicial domination at the expense of the powers of the other branches of government."[50]

There was little disagreement as to the accuracy of the observation; indeed, in the same instance of their acquiescence in the statement of the condition of the Court and Constitution, conservatives called upon all their resources to change the condition. The second Eisenhower term was to witness an all-out Congressional effort to do precisely that.

12/Storm on Capitol Hill

T HE SIX YEARS BETWEEN the first segregation decision in the spring of
1954 and the adjournment of the Court in June, 1960 was a period of
tension between the high tribunal and Congress unparalleled even by the
early years of the 1930's. The roles were now reversed. In the prior era the
Court had been the bulwark of the old order and Congress represented the
rising tide of insistent reform; during the Eisenhower years a coalition of
Southern Democrats and Old Guard Republicans seeking to undermine
their own President's moderate modernism kept up a continuing cacophony
against the renewed activism of the Court.

There was indeed an irony in the fact that with Eisenhower in the
White House—representing, as Emmet John Hughes was to write, "an
administration committed to conserving rather than creating, of guarding
rather than building"—the Presidency should have found itself caught
between a judiciary once more advancing upon new social and economic
issues and a vocal segment of Congress charging the Court with creating
the issues.[1] The first three appointments of a Republican President had provided a galvanic spark for an engine which had dropped to a slow idle under
the Truman judicial appointments. With Warren replacing the easygoing
Vinson, and the fresh keen minds of Harlan and Brennan replacing the
frenetic mind of Jackson and the mediocre mind of Minton, the intellectual
pace of the bench was bound to pick up.

The new Chief Justice suggested the fundamental constitutional position he intended the Court to take soon after the *Brown* decision in a speech
at the dedication of the new American Bar Center in Chicago. Amid the
fragmented loyalties and values of the postwar world, he declared, "the
extent to which we maintain the spirit of our Constitution with its Bill of
Rights will in the long run do more to make it both secure and the object
of adulation than the number of hydrogen bombs we stockpile."[2] It was a

235

phrase which could be passed over as a familiar homily: only hindsight would demonstrate how literally Warren and his new associates took the words. And yet, as hindsight would also show, the Court would have had to respond to the cold war issues with their related domestic and international involvements, whether or not the personnel had changed in the meantime.

The revitalized Court, conservatives correctly asserted, hastened the day when the American people were compelled to come to terms with the questions of segregation and civil liberties generally. The Court did not, as the conservatives complained, create the problems. The question of Negro rights in its twentieth-century context could be traced at least as far back as the First World War and its attendant technological revolution which began fundamentally to alter the whole American social structure, while the same period had marked the beginning of a long and confused debate over the logical extremes to which the guarantees in the Bill of Rights could be carried. For as long as possible, upper- and middle-class Americans had simply ignored the questions. The Second World War—completing the process of disintegration of older frames of reference—released the pent-up demands of exploited classes both at home and abroad, and drove the upper and middle classes to cover seeking to resist the torrent as it poured upon them.

In this state of affairs, the Court found itself compelled to break its new ground often unaided by either of the other branches of government; indeed, the detached or frequently wavering position of the White House tended to encourage the noisier critics of the judiciary and the desperate plans of conservatives to neutralize the constitutional propositions being enunciated. Eisenhower, after the first *Brown* decision, said no more than that it would take time for the old pattern of racial relations to be adjusted; while this was self-evident, it was not calculated to arouse many to turn promptly to the task of adjustment. Men who, however distasteful they found the decision, would have been prepared to accept it were intellectually immobilized by the equivocal expression from the President.[3]

This lack of zeal for the prospect of a social revolution, where the ultimate exclusive question was whether the revolution would be violent or non-violent, was to characterize all of Eisenhower's administration. When the Little Rock test of desegregation presented itself, the President firmly enforced the Federal authority, but there were many signs that his half-hearted attitude toward Brownell's drive to put the Civil Rights Act of 1957 through Congress had led Arkansas Governor Orville Faubus to believe that the administration would really not try to enforce *Brown*.[4]

A cooling of personal relationships between the Chief Executive and the Chief Justice had begun with the accelerating liberalism of the Court after the spring of 1955, and had intensified when, following Eisenhower's heart attack that fall, there was wide speculation that the President would

not be able to seek a second term and that Warren would be drafted by the
Republican Deweyites to run in his stead. While, for Warren, the idea of
reentering the political arena was abhorrent, for Eisenhower the speculation
was highly irritating. Rather brusquely, when he was able to return to office,
the President told a press conference that he felt the country "shouldn't
get too great a confusion between politics and the Supreme Court."⁵ While
this cloudy commentary was characteristic of many Eisenhower statements,
and while the President later disavowed any opposition to Warren's candidacy, the issue tended to make more stiffly formal the relations between
the White House and the Court.

It would be a similar story with reference to the civil liberties cases
as the outcry against them rose in Congress. If Eisenhower had been
unenthusiastic about the segregation decisions, he felt anger and frustration
at the "Communist cases." These decisions, wrote Robert J. Donovan, rapidly
deepened the chill between Eisenhower and Warren, and in the great Congressional uprising against the Court in the spring and summer of 1958,
the White House would maintain an almost unbroken silence while the
storm raged.⁶

*   *   *

The renaissance of activism did not come swiftly; in the first two and
a half years of the Warren Court, there were few straws in the wind. Except
for *Brown,* the 1953 term had only a few cases which discussed the status
of illegally obtained evidence in state and Federal criminal process, and one
case on the matter of coerced confessions. In *Irvine v. California,* indeed,
the Court majority even evinced a strong disposition to accept the precedent
of the restrictive decisions of the Vinson era. While roundly criticizing
police eavesdropping to obtain evidence upon which to base a conviction,
the five-to-three majority felt bound by the decision in *Wolf v. Colorado*
which refused to find that the Fourteenth Amendment protected defendants
in state prosecutions from unreasonable searches and seizures. "Perhaps
strict adherence to the tenor of that decision," said Clark in a concurring
opinion, "may produce needed converts for its extinction."⁷

Similarly, the 1954 term produced little challenging constitutional
doctrine. Aside from the second *Brown* decision, the Court avoided a direct
attack upon the character-aspersion aspects of the Federal loyalty program
by finding lack of jurisdiction in a loyalty review board to dismiss a government employee twice cleared by subordinate review boards.⁸ But in all
these decisions there was a fundamental proposition—the responsibility of
the Court to enforce any protection the Constitution provided against encroachments upon individual freedom by government, state or Federal. It
was readily predictable, therefore, that as the majority became more positive
in its assertion of these constitutional guarantees, the Court would find
itself upon a collision course with any other governmental agency attempting
to restrict these rights. In the security-loyalty hypersensitivity of the fifties,

the most conspicuous agency in the path of the new libertarianism was Congress itself.[9]

The stage was thus set for five momentous acts in the drama of the 1955 term—acts which provided exacting roles for the judicial members of the cast, and told the story of the renaissance of activism. Although the first—*Griffin v. Illinois*—was a time bomb set to destroy the 1942 rule in *Betts v. Brady,* it would not go off until 1963 when *Gideon v. Wainwright* would affirm a sweeping right to counsel in indigent defendants in state as in Federal prosecutions. The next three bluntly asserted the paramountcy of constitutional guarantees in the face of the Congressional investigatory process. The fifth shocked the conservative forces who had up to then been confident of their air-tight defense against the closed shop effected by the Taft-Hartley Act.

Griffin was a testimonial to the tenacity of Justice Black; he wrote the dissent in *Betts,* the opinion for the Court of a four-member coalition in the current case, and would write the opinion of the Court in the conglomerate majority in *Gideon.* Although, when *Betts* was eventually overruled in *Gideon,* the tenuous majority in *Griffin* would not be relied on, it served a fundamental purpose in weakening the force of *Betts* as precedent and preparing the way for its overthrow.[10] *Griffin* was also a building-block for Black to use in his continuing project of constructing a principle of constitutional absolutes. "The ability to pay costs in advance," in the case of the Illinois requirement for convicted defendants seeking to appeal, "bears no rational relationship to a defendant's guilt or innocence and could not be used as an excuse to deprive a defendant of a fair trial." Such a requirement, Black contended, "is a misfit in a country dedicated to affording equal justice to all and special privileges to none in the administration of its criminal law. There can be no equal justice where the kind of trial a man gets depends on the amount of money he has."[11]

The five-to-four majority in *Griffin*—Frankfurter, the fifth Justice, still resisting the Black thesis of absolute rights, had concurred separately—became a six-to-three majority in the second of the notable decisions of the term, which boldly asserted the doctrine of Federal preemption. Ironically, *Pennsylvania v. Nelson* upheld a decision of the Pennsylvania supreme court, which found that Federal legislation had superseded the state sedition law; in affirming, Warren invalidated in whole or in part the sedition statutes of forty-two states and Alaska and Hawaii. Pointing to the progression of Congressional enactments on the subject—the Smith Act of 1940, the Internal Security Act of 1951 and the Communist Control Act of 1954—the Court reached the "inescapable" conclusion that "Congress has intended to occupy the field of sedition." More significantly, Warren went on to observe that "the Federal statutes 'touch a field in which the Federal interest is so dominant that the Federal system [must] be assumed to preclude enforcement of state laws on the same subject.'" The operation of two sets of laws relating to the same criminal act, finally, suggested the danger of double punishment for the same act.[12]

In *Slochower v. Board of Education,* the majority was again five to four, with Clark being pursuaded to join the now crystallizing new bloc of Black, Douglas and Warren—and, in this instance, Frankfurter—to strike down a section of the New York City charter permitting dismissal of a public employee merely for invoking the privilege of the Fifth Amendment before a Congressional committee. "At the outset," wrote Clark, "we must condemn the practice of imputing a sinister meaning to the exercise of a person's constitutional right under the Fifth Amendment. . . . In practical effect, the questions asked [by the committee] are taken as confessed and are made the basis of the discharge." New York City was left free to make its own inquiry into its employee's fitness for his job, Clark emphasized, but any process which penalized the use of a right guaranteed by the Constitution was itself a violation of the Constitution.[13]

With this case the Court thrust itself into the maelstrom of dispute over the relative rights of individuals and their government in the context of the cold war of the mid-fifties. With McCarthy whipping public hysteria to a lather, the majority in *Slochower* found its opinion serving as a public rebuke to all investigators who cast aspersions on the invocation of the Fifth Amendment. Under the calmest of conditions, the Court would have been embarking upon a hazardous passage between ideological dangers both real and imagined, and now that it had committed itself to the adjudication it had moved a substantial distance further into the area in which the Federal guarantee of individual liberties would be the fundamental constitutional standard. Ten years later in 1966, in *Elfbrandt v. Russell,* the Court would still be grappling with the loyalty issue.[14]

Fourth in the 1955 term came *Cole v. Young,* which, like *Peters* the preceding term, avoided a confrontation with Congress on the validity of security-loyalty statutes by interpreting the statute narrowly. The Summary Suspension Act of 1950 had empowered Federal agencies to dismiss employees upon a finding that they had failed to clear loyalty board hurdles. Harlan, speaking for another six-to-three majority, declared that when the workers concerned were civil service personnel in "non-sensitive" positions, they were liable to dismissal only through established civil service procedures rather than by summary order.[15] The majority opinion confined itself to this narrow question, but in the charged atmosphere of the time, and in association with the other decisions of this term challenging the powers of Congress to deal with individuals, *Cole* only added fuel to flame.

Finally, as the term was ending, came *Railway Employees v. Hanson,* in which the Court unequivocally held that state "right to work" laws, to the extent that they sought to apply to interstate carriers, were barred by the Railway Labor Act of 1926 from a field preempted by the Federal authority. *Amici* briefs for the attorneys general of nine states, the National

Right to Work Committee, the United States Chamber of Commerce and the National Association of Manufacturers, all were filed in an effort to dissuade the Court from this position. Open shop advocates, who had been lulled into complacency by a decade under Taft-Hartley, read the opinion unbelievingly; if, on the heels of *Nelson, Hanson* reasserted the preemption doctrine, what legislation could be devised which would meet the needs of states rightists?[16]

*   *   *

In the winter of 1955 Congressman Howard W. Smith of Virginia— who had previously made his name in political history with authorship of the Smith Act of 1940—introduced a bill stipulating that "no act of Congress shall be construed as indicating an intent on the part of Congress to occupy the field in which such act operates, to the exclusion of all state laws on the same subject matter, unless such act contains an express provision to that effect."[17] This attempt to nullify the preemption doctrine of the Court was kept buried in the House Judiciary Committee for more than a year by the maneuvering of the committee chairman, Congressman Emanuel Celler of New York. This did not prevent members of the House from using it as a basis for recurrent anti-Court speeches on the floor, however.

In the spring of 1956, as Smith's bill was being pried out of committee, Congressman Noah Mason of Illinois spoke at length against "recent Supreme Court decisions and their effect upon states' rights." His objection to the preemption doctrine, he declared, derived from the fact that for the past two decades "a New Deal Congress has legislated 'all over the waterfront,' . . . and a New Deal-appointed Supreme Court has upheld such legislation." If all major statutes enacted by Congress were thus to be held preemptive, said Mason, "it is only a question of time before all power and all sovereignty residing in the states to enact and enforce laws will be taken over by the Federal government."[18]

Southern Congressmen hastened to take the floor to congratulate him. Since Mason had included the segregation cases among those which he decried as invasions of states' rights, he had presented the Southern case more effectively than any Southern member could do. Congressman James C. Davis of Georgia, joining with Mason in urging action on the Smith bill, reiterated the condemnation of the twenty-year trend in which "the Court has overruled many more outstanding cases, and in so doing has undertaken to change the meaning of the Constitution as effectively as if it had been duly amended according to the method provided in the instrument itself."[19] The fact that the cases which had been overruled might well have been judicial amendments as much as their successor cases did not seem to concern the speaker.

Congressman Smith joined the parade of spokesmen. Perhaps anticipating that the Judiciary Committee would report out a bill of more limited objectives than he had originally proposed, Smith urged that Congress prepare to enact a general prohibition of the preemption doctrine. "If your bill is going to correct one Supreme Court decision at a time," he warned, "we are . . . placing just a shin plaster on a broken leg."[20]

As Smith correctly divined, the majority report for the judiciary committee recommended favorable action on a bill "limited to the specific area of subversion and sedition" rather than dealing with "the whole span of relationship between state and Federal laws." In an eloquent minority report, Chairman Celler pointed out the fundamental problem in a bill even limited to these objectives: "Our objective at all times must be to strike a balance between the evil of seditious conspiracy and subversion, and the constitutionally guaranteed civil liberties of our citizenry. Only a national program consistent and centralized can do that," he declared.[21]

The depth of conservative hostility toward recent judicial decisions was attested both by the number of proposals introduced into the Eighty-fourth Congress—more than seventy bills sought in one way or another to curb the Court—and in the powerful organizations which appeared at the hearings on the Smith bill. The United States Chamber of Commerce, the American Farm Bureau Federation and the National Association of Manufacturers all earnestly urged the committee to endorse a broad-based law, or at least one which would definitely reject the *Nelson* and *Hanson* rulings.[22]

The version of the Smith bill reported out by the committee was acceptable neither to Congressman Smith, who considered it too narrow, nor to House liberals, who considered it too broad. Majority Leader John McCormack proposed to call up the bill under a suspension of the rules, which would have prevented an attempt to amend it back to its former broad form; Smith objected, and the bill thereupon was tabled for the rest of the session.[23]

*   *   *

Having fallen short in this effort to reverse the current trend of constitutionalism, the conservative forces were goaded to fresh efforts by decisions in the 1956 term. Again, as in the previous term, the Court dealt a succession of thunderous blows in defense of individual rights against government action. The first—*Mallory v. United States*—like *Griffin* the year before, excited professional lawyers more than laymen. It substantially enforced the rule of fourteen years earlier, in *McNabb v. United States,* excluding from evidence in a criminal proceeding any confession obtained before an accused had come before a committing magistrate in any Federal prosecution.[24] *Mallory,* with Frankfurter speaking for a unanimous Court, substantially strengthened *McNabb* by holding invalid a confession obtained from a slow-witted adolescent, in the course of several hours' interrogation before arraignment, as a violation both of the Sixth Amendment and of the Federal Rules of Criminal Procedure requiring arraignment "without unnecessary delay."[25] While the new *McNabb-Mallory* rule thus prepared the way for a series of decisions in the 1960's substantially circumscribing arresting officers' powers of interrogation, the decision in the winter of 1957 had the primary effect of exacerbating other decisions which hit closer to conservative interests.

The *Girard College* case,[26] in which the exclusion of Negroes from a Philadelphia institution under the will of its founder was held to be a denial of rights guaranteed by the Fourteenth Amendment,* rubbed salt into the wounds of the segregationists, but they were only too aware that they had no chance of rallying Northern conservatives in support of retaliatory legislation on a segregationist issue. The Smith bill still represented the most affirmative plan of action against the libertarians, but it required a new galvanic shock from the Court itself to rouse Congress to violent reaction which would either push the Smith bill through both houses, or generate an alternative. The Court accommodated; in the closing weeks of the term, four cases on the security-loyalty issue tossed a firebrand into the powder keg.

On June 3, 1957 the Court offered a prelude to the four cold war cases to come in *Jencks v. United States,* a case which itself was to provide the ultimate basis for the attempted counterrevolution in Congress. A New Mexico union leader charged with violating the non-Communist oath requirement of Taft-Hartley was confronted with testimony of two undercover FBI agents who admitted, on cross-examination, that they had regularly made reports to their Bureau on the subjects on which they were then testifying. When defense counsel moved to require the government to produce the reports for inspection by the trial judge, the government sought to protect its confidential sources of information by contending that the defense had failed to establish a preliminary showing of inconsistency between the testimony and the reports. On sustaining the government's argument, the trial proceeded to a conviction and a review before the Supreme Court. Brennan, speaking for himself and five Associates, pointed out that "the accused is helpless to know or discover conflict without inspecting the reports," and reversed the judgment. Burton and Harlan concurred, with the reservation that the trial judge rather than defense counsel should alone be permitted to examine the government's documents.[27]

Clark, alone in dissent, gave the conservatives their cue by stating the fundamental danger in the majority decision: "Unless the Congress changes the rule announced by the Court today, those intelligence agencies of our government engaged in law enforcement may as well close up shop, for the Court has opened their files to the criminal and thus afforded him a Roman

---

*The city of Philadelphia being one of the trustees made Girard College a quasi-public institution and thus subject to the *Brown* rule.

The Philadelphia Board of Trusts proceeded to substitute private parties for the city trustees, and the Pennsylvania supreme court ruled that this satisfied the Supreme Court order on the remand of the original case. *In re Girard College Trustees,* 138 Atl. 2nd, 844 (1958), app. dism. 357 U. S. 570 (1958). But see *Evans v. Newton* in Appendix E.

holiday for rummaging through confidential information as well as vital national secrets."[28] Congress was already gathering its forces in response, but as if to spur it on, the Court two weeks later staggered the nation with its four epochal civil liberties decisions. June 17 would become, in the phraseology of conservatism, "Red Monday," to rival the liberals' "Black Monday" of 1935 and the "White" one of 1937.

*   *   *

In *Watkins v. United States,* Chief Justice Warren undertook at length to curb some of the more blatant inquisitorial practices of the House Un-American Activities Committee, an agency which had first been created in the ideological conflicts of the later New Deal and had zealously exploited the atmosphere of suspicion in the postwar era. Watkins, a labor union officer, had candidly admitted his own aid and comfort to Communist causes in the past, but had declined to give the committee names of ex-Communists known to him on the ground that this information was outside the scope of their investigating powers. In reversing the resulting conviction for contempt of Congress, the Chief Justice observed that in "the decade following World War II, there [had] appeared a new kind of Congressional inquiry unknown in prior periods of American history" which "involved a broad-scale intrusion into the lives and affairs of private citizens."

"We cannot simply assume, however," said Warren, "that every Congressional investigation is justified by a public need that over-balances any private rights affected," and the most elemental constitutional safeguard would be a requirement that Congress explicitly instruct its committees as to the scope of their inquiries and the limits to their powers. In the case of the House action establishing and continuing the Un-American Activities Committee, Warren observed: "It would be difficult to imagine a less explicit authorizing resolution," which neglected to define the very term, "Un-American," or the "principle of the form of government as guaranteed by our Constitution."[29]

Having dealt the high-handed inquisitors of the Congressional committee a stinging slap in the face, the Court meted out the same kind of condemnation to state agencies. New Hampshire's attorney general, upon the direction of the state legislature that he constitute himself a one-man investigating committee to seek out violations of the state's 1951 Subversive Activities Act, focussed his attention on a faculty member of the state university. Paul Sweezy, a self-described "classical Marxist," declined to answer certain questions about his prior activities as being unrelated to the object of the investigation and was found in contempt. Warren, speaking for the Court majority in reversing the conviction, could well have been recalling his own position as governor of California in condemning the regents' loyalty oath in opening his opinion. "The essentiality of freedom in the community of American universities is almost self-evident," he observed, and the danger of distrust generated on campuses of state-supported institutions by state-instigated investigations was to require the most exacting tests of public necessity.

The burden was entirely upon the state, said the opinion, to show that its own self-protection or its need for factual information upon which to base legislative action outweighed the individual's right to privacy and security in his personal beliefs.[30] Frankfurter and Harlan, in a concurring opinion, added that the public need must be beyond all doubt to justify such an inquiry: "Inviolability of privacy belonging to a citizen's political loyalties has so overwhelming an importance to the well-being of our kind of society that it cannot be constitutionally encroached upon on the basis of so meagre a countervailing interest of the state" in this instance.[31]

Harlan spoke for the Court—although its voice was more broken than at any time since the experimentalism of the Stone Chief Justiceship—in a third case which left the conservatives aghast. In *Yates v. United States,* the Court struck the first devastating blow at the tenuous, relativistic doctrine of Vinson in *Dennis v. United States,* upon which the general validity of the Smith Act of 1940 rested. In the six years since *Dennis,* many elements of the decision had lain unhappily on the public conscience. The sweeping validation of that section of the act proscribing freedom of expression had been a *de facto* gloss upon the First Amendment, while the vague standards of liability set out in other portions of the statute did violence to the spirit of the Fourth, Fifth and Sixth Amendments.

Yates purported to "explain" the rationale of *Dennis* which had condoned these tortured variations of the plain guarantees of the Constitution; for many alarmists who read Harlan's words, however, it was not a case of returning to the standards of freedom erected by Holmes and Brandeis, but an invitation to Communism to undermine the structure of American life. Yet Harlan strove to keep the basic principles both in *Dennis* and in *Yates* in focus:

> In failing to distinguish between advocacy of forcible overthrow as an abstract doctrine and advocacy of action to that end, the District Court appears to have been led astray by the holding in *Dennis* that advocacy of violent action to be taken at some future time was enough. It seems to have considered that, since the "inciting" speech is usually thought of as something calculated to induce immediate action, and since *Dennis* held advocacy of action for future overthrow sufficient, this meant that advocacy, irrespective of its tendency to generate action, is punishable, provided only that it is uttered with a specific intent to accomplish overthrow. In other words, the District Court apparently thought that *Dennis* obliterated the traditional dividing line between advocacy of abstract doctrine and advocacy of action.[32]

Harlan's distinctions were too fine for the impatient conservatives who saw only that the net result of his opinion was to free five of the fourteen accused Communists, and to order a new trial for the others, and thus to set at naught the long prosecution which had ultimately led to the affirmed convictions in *Dennis*. A torrent of abuse poured down upon the decision. Clark's dissent, which accused the majority of usurping the functions of the jury, was widely and approvingly quoted, and David Lawrence—shades of 1895—suggested that Federal judges should be popularly elected in order to be more responsive to popular will.[33]

But the torment of conservatism was not yet ended. Rounding out this day's quadrilateral of reversals was *Service v. Dulles,* a unanimous holding of eight Justices with Clark not participating, which ordered the reinstatement of a State Department employee who had been cleared five times by departmental loyalty boards and twice by the loyalty review board. Persistent demands for further reviews had finally won from the board a finding of reasonable doubt, whereupon Secretary Dulles had ordered the employee's dismissal. The Secretary had relied on the so-called "McCarran Rider" to the security statute which gave the chief administrators "absolute discretion" to discharge employees when they found it to be in the public interest. In so doing, said Harlan for the Court, Dulles had acted in violation of his department's own rules of procedure. Having elected to follow the more exacting standards of review provided by his own agency, the opinion held, he could not thereafter disregard them and take the easier course of summary dismissal.[34]

*   *   *

The impact of *Jencks, Watkins* and *Yates* was soul-shaking for a nation which, deeply involved in an unprecedented cold war, was inclined recurrently to take seriously the alarmist contention that non-conformity in these times was a dangerous luxury. Although the heritage of both Jefferson and Marshall stressed the function of the Supreme Court as the guardian of individual Americans' freedoms—its "leading constitutional province," in the phrase of Donald G. Morgan[35]—the tribunal was now to suffer its most vehement attacks for the performance of this function. More than a generation before, in the period of reaction after the First World War, Holmes and Brandeis had fought a lonely minority struggle to keep the Court committed to that ideal; now, with the tribunal almost at one on the matter, it was rewarded by a sense of public outrage at its defense of recalcitrant radicals. The national mood of the moment was epitomized by the remark of California Congressman Donald Jackson; in *Jencks* and *Watkins,* he declared, Communism had won "a victory greater than any achieved by the Soviet on any battlefield since World War II."[36]

Specific bills to limit if not rescind the rule in *Jencks* and other libertarian decisions were poured into the Congressional hopper almost before the echoes of the opinions had died away. The Attorney General's office informed the White House that it was being inundated with calls from its regional offices requesting advice on procedure in seeking to continue prosecutions under the security-loyalty laws, and relief from the intricacies anticipated in the *Jencks* holding. The Justice Department soon laid on the President's desk a bill, drafted in large measure by Assistant Attorneys General Warren Olney III and Wilson White, intended to nullify the Court decision. It was promptly introduced in both houses of Congress by a clutch of sponsors including Congressman Kenneth Keating of New York, and Senators Eastland of Mississippi, Everett Dirksen of Illinois, Estes Kefauver of Tennessee, Butler of Maryland, Matthew M. Neeley of West Virginia, Alexander Wiley of Wisconsin and Charles E. Potter of Michigan. After a conference between Brownell and Eisenhower, a White House spokesman announced that the administration would "urge" passage of remedial legislation.[37]

A more direct assault on the Court was the Jenner bill introduced a few weeks later, which proposed to withdraw from the Court jurisdiction over questions of loyalty or subversion—as well as of state bar admissions, where the tribunal had supported applicants who refused to answer questions concerning their past political affiliations. The bill, as later amended and co-sponsored by Butler, aimed at reversing the *Watkins* and *Yates* rules, and was complemented by a bill under the prestigious sponsorship of the Judicial Conference of the United States, the Justice Department, the American Bar Association Section on Judicial Administration and the Conference of State Chief Justices. This bill sought to limit the *habeas corpus* power of the Court in state criminal proceedings to Federal questions which for certain reasons had not been raised and adjudicated at the trial level.[38]

All the measures reflected, to a degree unparalleled in Congressional history—at least back to the long debate on the Judiciary Act of 1801—a militant hostility toward the Court as an institution. The Southern antipathy for the Court growing out of the successive segregation decisions could not in itself hope to muster a Congressional majority; indeed, the anti-Court bills were introduced in the climactic weeks in which the first civil rights statute of the twentieth century was en route to final passage. Thus the Southern Democrats threw their support behind the measures which were introduced by conservative Republicans as a means of indirectly striking at the bench which had dealt the deathblow to the old social order.

But the anti-*Jencks* bill had the widest measure of support; for many moderates and liberals, the prospect of opening up the most confidential files of the executive departments to defendants' attorneys seemed to threaten the whole system of national security. The Justice Department's draft of the law, which would have circumscribed the documentary record which could be made available, was unacceptable as denying to defendants the elemental justice which *Jencks* had sought to preserve, and a succession of revised bills were drafted and substituted in the course of committee study and floor debate. Recognizing that an unwise choice of alternatives might do serious damage to the Court, Senator Joseph O'Mahoney of Wyoming—like Senator Wheeler of Montana in 1937—sought to get an expression of preference from members of the bench. Although the Warren Court produced nothing as momentous as Hughes' famous letter, a vague and roundabout message to O'Mahoney encouraged him to give affirmative support to the bill which finally was passed by Congress at the end of August.[39]

Both sides claimed victory in the final *Jencks* bill. In its key provision— "After a witness called by the United States has testified on direct examination, the court shall, on motion of the defendant, order the United States to produce any statement of the witness in the possession of the United States which relates to the subject matter as to which the witness has testified"—the law actually amounted to a codification of the rule in *Jencks* as qualified in the concurring opinion of Burton and Harlan. The following year, in *Palermo v. United States,* Frankfurter for the Court and Brennan in concurrence interpreted the new law as susceptible of empowering trial judges to compel production of any documents in the government's possession which were considered necessary "to eliminate the danger of distortion and misrepresentation" as between the complete record and the selections from it contained in the witnesses' testimony.[40]

If there was any rebuke to the Court in the *Jencks* law as finally enacted, it was the most that the anti-Court forces were able to win. Nevertheless, the effort to adopt the more drastic bills continued through the spring and summer of 1958, when the conservative impetus reached its maximum. In that period, five critical measures actually passed the House of Representatives, and by substantial margins: The limited *habeas corpus* bill, a second specifically rejecting the *Mallory* rule, another similarly negating the rule in *Cole v. Young,* a fourth revising the Smith Act of 1940 to offset the decision in *Yates,* and finally Congressman Smith's bill to disavow the preemption doctrine were all approved between mid-March and mid-August. For the first time since the Reconstruction era, a politically motivated legislative movement to invade the judicial function seemed on the verge of success.[41]

There was another reminiscence of the Reconstruction era in the Congressional sessions of 1956 and 1957: for the first time since 1875, a Federal civil rights bill was pushed through both Houses. By a supreme irony, an administration which had been faint indeed in its support of judicial decisions on civil rights—and particularly Negro rights—was forced by political circumstances to take a stand of sorts on a legislative approach to the issue. The Truman administration had struggled in vain with Congress on the matter, and the Eisenhower forces had shown no stomach for repeating the attempt during the President's first term. With "Ike" so widely adulated by the voters, the professionals told each other, there was no need to risk a split with Capitol Hill on the subject.[42]

An unhappy legislative and judicial history clouded the post-Civil War civil rights laws—a number of which had been enacted between 1866 and 1875, primarily in implementation of provisions in the Fourteenth and Fifteenth Amendments. The virtual emasculation of these statutes in the Civil Rights Cases in 1883,* and the overriding interest of the *laissez-faire* generation in interpretations of the Fourteenth Amendment to protect free enterprise rather than freed slaves, effectively muffled further demands for Federal action for the next three-quarters of a century. It was true that the New Deal had reopened the question with its scattered statutory provisions and executive orders on racial discrimination, as in the National Labor Relations Act, the program of the Civil Rights Section of the Department of Justice established in 1939, and the fair employment practices stipulated under the war contract program of the early 1940's. But a general attack on the problem had never been launched.[43]

In 1946 the President's Committee on Civil Rights, headed by Charles E. Wilson, issued a comprehensive study which declared: "The separate but equal doctrine stands convicted on three grounds. It contravenes the egalitarian spirit of the American heritage. It has failed to operate, for history shows that inequality of service has been the omnipresent consequence of separation. It has institutionalized segregation and kept groups apart despite indisputable evidence that normal contacts among these groups tend to promote social harmony." Urging a straightforward Congressional approach to the subject, the report concluded: "The achievement of full civil rights in the law may do as much to end prejudice as the end of prejudice may do to achieve full civil rights."[44] The administration's attempted response to the challenge, however, died by filibuster in the Congress of 1950.

The Supreme Court in the 1940's had made some efforts at resuscitating the civil rights objectives of the Civil War constitutional amendments and statutes. The all-white primary had been struck down in 1944, and restrictive racial covenants in real estate in 1948, while *Brown* in 1954 and *Girard College* in 1957 indicated a quickening of the judicial pace. But the fundamental problem lay in the fact that, aside from piecemeal equity actions similar to these, the Court could find no effective statutory machinery by which the government could take the initiative in these matters. The unhappy conclusion, in *Screws v. United States* in 1945 and in *United States v. Williams* in 1951, that the surviving sections of the post-Civil War acts were insufficient to permit full-scale Federal prosecutions thereunder, left the Department of Justice without adequate tools for the job.[45]

Thus had matters dragged along until the galvanic shock of Eisenhower's major heart attack in September, 1955. With the sudden prospect that the President might not be able to seek or serve a second term, the heretofore confident Republicans were confronted with a pressing need, if not for a candidate at least for a legislative achievement to attract and hold a mass of voters not normally drawn to the party. Attorney General Brownell, both from political instinct and from an affirmative sympathy

---

*See further discussion of this subject in Ch. 13.

for the concept itself, settled upon a civil rights bill as the hedge against the uncertainties of the 1956 election year.

Until the President himself was able to return to his office, the chance of having the bill go to Congress as an administration measure depended upon the Cabinet. Only Secretary Wilson, former chairman of the Truman Committee on Civil Rights, could be counted on for vigorous support; certainly the President's lukewarm position did not help. Since the bill was to be a Republican project, leading figures on Capitol Hill (being Democrats) could not be prematurely consulted. In the end, therefore, the draft of the bill to be introduced in the winter of 1956 was almost entirely the product of attorneys within the Justice Department.[46]

The measure which eventually got through Congress disappointed the most hopeful, but it did not justify the dark comments of the pessimists— after all, to have established a legislative precedent for civil rights in national law after more than eighty years was an achievement of some importance. The Civil Rights Commission established by the new law to gather information on the problems of racial discrimination was to provide the research for the herculean drafting efforts of the sixties. The 1957 statute itself concentrated its main force on protecting the voting franchise —again providing a starting point for the rights legislation of the next decade.[47]

Brownell's role in the struggles in 1956 and 1957 did not endear the Justice Department to the caterwauling conservatives, engaged in a two-front war against the Court and administration campaigns for racial equality and already incensed at the influential role of the Department in the selection of candidates for openings throughout the Federal judiciary. As the Eisenhower forces (even without Eisenhower's active backing) built up the strength to carry the bill through the two Houses, their triumph goaded the conservatives to even greater attempts to strike at their other adversary, the Court.

*　　*　　*

In July, 1957, as part of a conservative opposition to the Civil Rights Act being pushed through Congress, Senator Jenner made an impassioned and well-documented speech, addressed nominally to the sections of the act providing for judicial enforcement but actually preparing the ground for his own bill on limiting the Court's general jurisdiction. In detail, he reviewed and castigated the decisions in *Jencks, Nelson, Slochower, Girard, Mallory, Yates, Watkins* and the California bar association cases. All of these, aside from making "new law," as he described them, were symptomatic of what he felt was a fundamental issue:

> There was a time when a Justice of the Supreme Court might dissent in a case of first impression, but could be relied upon to decide the next case involving similar points in accordance with the prior decision of the Court, notwithstanding his own prior dissent. This was because

Justices of the Supreme Court respected the Court and respected the principle of *stare decisis*. Nowadays individual members of the Supreme Court are constantly busy defending their own positions, and a Justice who files a dissenting opinion on a particular point can usually be expected to stick to that opinion whenever the point is raised, thus keeping the Court constantly split.

By a process of attrition and accession, the extreme liberal wing of the Court has become a majority; and today we witness the spectacle of a Court constantly changing the law, and even changing the meaning of the Constitution, in an apparent determination to make the law of the land what the Court thinks it should be.[48]

Jenner's criticism echoed what conservatives had said of the experimentalism of the Stone Court fifteen years before, but his words were amplified in the climactic denunciation of radicalism which was approaching in the midpoint of the second Eisenhower term—and without a comment of moderation from the White House. After a final tirade against "this parade of decisions that came down from our highest bench on Red Monday after Red Monday," in which the Court held everyone wrong "except the attorneys for the Communist conspiracy and the majority of the United States Supreme Court," Jenner introduced his own bill.[49]

It was a long, hot summer. The National Association of Attorneys General of the states called upon Congress to "reaffirm and reactivate Federal and state internal security controls" weakened by *Nelson, Yates* and related decisions. The American Bar Association, meeting in London to commemorate Anglo-American traditions of freedom under law, accepted a report of its committee on Communist strategy and tactics which recommended a Congressional repudiation of the Court security cases. The Conference of State Chief Justices continued its cries of concern for the future of "the constitutional power of state governments," and the national Governors' Conference devoted much of its meeting to discussing the danger to national security and the importance of not hampering the government agencies in their pursuit of subversives.[50]

The tenor of the complaints against the Court continued unchanged into the fall of 1957 and the winter of 1958. In February Senator Stennis urged consideration by the southern regional meeting of the ABA of two changes in the matter of judicial selection and tenure: removal of the Department of Justice from the role of screening and recommending candidates for Federal judgeships, and periodic reconfirmation of appointees to the bench. In the same month, hearings opened on the Jenner bill and permitted a motley assortment of cranks as well as competent witnesses to speak their minds for and against the current judicial position. While motives were varied, the solidity of conservative determination at least in the lower house of Congress was everywhere manifest.[51]

*   *   *

In the winter of 1937, when the prospect of judicial adamance had threatened to coalesce anti-Court sentiment in Congress, Chief Justice Hughes had masterminded a strategic retreat which left the Roosevelt reform bill defeated. In the 1957 and 1958 terms of the Warren Court there was no retreat, but there was a strategic abandonment of the most exposed positions in order to consolidate the gains which had been won. Frankfurter, rather than Warren, led the way to the more defensible positions in the face of the Congressional attack by reviving his doctrine of judicial restraint.

In *Trop v. Dulles,* where the majority held that loss of citizenship as a penalty for wartime desertion amounted to "cruel and unusual punishment" forbidden by the Eighth Amendment, Frankfurter admonished his brethren: "Rigorous observance of the differences between limits of power and wise exercise of power—between questions of authority and questions of prudence—require the most alert appreciation of this decisive but subtle relationship of two concepts that too readily coalesce." The Court, Frankfurter repeated, had not been authorized by the Constitution "to sit in judgment on the wisdom of what Congress and the Executive Branch do."[52] In rebuttal, Chief Justice Warren used the same argument that the onetime *laissez-faire* majority had so often voiced: "We are oath-bound to defend the Constitution. This obligation requires that Congressional enactments be judged by the standards of the Constitution." And, he added, the Court could not "push back the limits of the Constitution merely to accommodate challenged legislation."[53]

Nevertheless, a line of decisions midway between the Frankfurter and Warren views seemed to be developing in the winter and spring of 1958. In the tangled jurisprudence of the security decisions of the fifties, it was possible to find whatever precedent was most timely, and in two decisions the Court was able to avoid carrying its *Slochower* doctrine to a logical extreme. In *Beilan v. Board of Education,* a Pennsylvania teacher loyalty oath was upheld, and in *Lerner v. Casey* the New York charter provision permitting dismissal of employees who invoked the Fifth Amendment was also sustained. Harlan made the distinctions between these and *Slochower* without seeming to indulge in excessive sophistry, by arguing that in the later cases the defendants had been refusing to respond to state rather than Federal interrogation. This may have been nonsense, but it struck the security-conscious extremists as a salutary concession. It was followed by *Barenblatt v. United States,* upholding a contempt conviction against one who had refused to testify before the Un-American Activities Committee concerning his own Communist affiliations, and by *Uphaus v. United States,* upholding another contempt citation for refusal to produce a guest list for a camp suspected of being a Communist indoctrination center.[54]

On the other hand, in *Greene v. McElroy,* the Court served notice that it was not giving up ground on the matter of fundamental individual rights to be protected against government encroachment. The *Greene* case grew out of an incident half a dozen years earlier wherein the government had revoked a security clearance for an officer of a corporation under contract with the Defense Department. Rather than lose the contract, the company fired its officer, and he then sued to compel the government to reinstate his clearance. Having been denied access to the documents on which informers had based their case against him, he sought review in the Supreme Court, where a majority of eight ruled the government action invalid. The case, said Warren for the Court, involved "substantial restraints on employment opportunities of numerous persons imposed in a manner which is in conflict with our long-accepted notions of fair procedures."

Greene, an aeronautical engineer, had found himself denied opportunity for professional employment by government action which he could not effectively combat in the courts; had this been the intent of the security statutes, said Warren, it would have been in violation of the guarantees of the Fifth and Sixth Amendments. It was not necessary to reach this question, however, the Chief Justice concluded, for the evidence suggested that the government officers had acted without explicit authorization either from the President or Congress. If the procedure had not been explicitly authorized, the case against Greene fell of its own weight; it was not for the Court to ascribe to another branch of the government a conscious intent to violate the Constitution.[55]

By this tactic of indirect constitutional testing of a sensitive statute, and a construction of the statute which accomplished the purpose of protecting individual rights without necessitating a constitutional decision, Warren developed a technique which was to serve him well in a number of funda-mental issues. It was not possible to determine whether the strategy would defeat the anti-Court measures already on their way from the House to the Senate; the Senate itself would have to answer that question.

*   *   *

The prospects for a sweeping triumph of the anti-Court forces in Congress were disturbingly strong in the late summer of 1958. With East-land in charge of the Senate Judiciary Committee, it was only a matter of time, and relatively short time, before the measures passed by the House would be favorably reported out in the Senate. Yet the progressive forces, after being divided by the confused security-loyalty issues of the early fifties, perceived certain opportunities for recouping their strength in the self-confidence and intransigence of the conservatives. The determination of die-hard Court haters to enact all of the pending bills as a succession of specific rebukes to the Court was to prove their ultimate undoing. Moreover, the possibility of increasing the Democratic majorities in Congress in the November elections meant the relative weakening of conservative strength—provided the action on the proposals could be delayed.

Already the new leadership in national affairs was beginning to show its face. With Eisenhower in the last years of his administration—thanks to prior Republican machinations which had put the anti-third term amend-ment into the Constitution—and Vice-President Nixon his heir apparent, a struggle was on for the Democratic nomination in 1960. Democratic support for the administration's civil rights program, as well as Democratic power .in striking down the anti-Court measures without appearing to be soft on Communism, offered the party's leaders substantial promise of political gain. In position to take maximum advantage of these opportunities were the Senate majority leader, Lyndon B. Johnson of Texas, and the ardent Minnesota liberal, Hubert H. Humphrey. In a minor supporting role was John F. Kennedy of Massachusetts.

The liberals' strategy was to delay action on the Court bills, to soften them with a series of proposed amendments, and to use their own support of administration measures as a *quid pro quo* to gain White House help in curbing the conservatives. Although Johnson regarded the bills with distaste, it was primarily because they threatened to dissipate the Senate majority over which he had attained a remarkably effective control. He had been long in planning the Democratic program for this session of the Eighty-fifth Congress, opening it with a Democratic "state of the Union" address which made the official Presidential message sound like an afterthought. For five years—since the beginning of the Eisenhower administration—the Texas Senator had shaped the course for the Democrats in the Senate and in the nation at large, anticipating the great events to which the laconic Republican administration made its slow reactions—the problem of military adequacy, the challenge of the Russians' initial achievements in space, the growing threat of a serious economic slowdown on the home front. Johnson, as one correspondent put it, had the "unique ability to sense the paramount— or sometimes merely the hourly—issue."[56]

As one of the front runners for the 1960 Presidential nomination, Johnson intended to make the record of the Eighty-fifth Congress his showpiece, demonstrating to the voters the Democrats' reasonableness in providing the key support for Eisenhower measures which the President's own party could not provide. Everything depended on Johnson's consummate strategy in controlling his committee chairmen and steering particular bills onto the floor or keeping them off. In his agenda, the anti-Court measures were relatively minor, although the volatile character of the social and economic forces behind them made them a threat to his grand campaign plan for the session as a whole. He was caught between the Republican-Southern Democratic coalition, which smelled blood after almost a generation of frustration, and the liberals who knew that they could not let the present conservative challenge go unanswered. Johnson had come to his moment of truth; could he, in fact, engineer the defeat of the measures without destroying his own control over the party and the party's control over the Senate?

The majority leader was faced with a formidable task. The anti-Court bills had all passed the House of Representatives by such wide margins that any substantial modification of the measures, throwing them into the hands of conference committees, would enable the House representatives to restore the most obnoxious features. If the bills were to be defeated at all, they would have to be defeated in the Senate, and their very numbers made it seem likely that at least one or two might get through in the give-and-take of debate. Whether the ambivalent President would bring himself to veto any such bills, in an election year for Congress, was conjectural.

Having delayed action for as long as possible, Johnson called up the anti-*Mallory* bill on August 19. The Senate Judiciary Committee, at least, had softened its impact by revising the opening statement to provide that evidence in criminal cases should "not be inadmissible solely because of reasonable delay" in arraignment. The word "reasonable," the conservatives vigorously protested, confirmed rather than reversed the Court holding; even with the word inserted, the liberals found the bill barely acceptable. After nine hours of debate, the Senate approved the revised measure and sent it to conference. For better or for worse, Johnson had momentarily managed to dispose of *Mallory*.[57]

Second was the Jenner-Butler limitation on Court jurisdiction in security-loyalty questions. A canvass of the votes convinced Johnson that he had the strength to table the measure, and after lengthy speeches by the bill's co-sponsors, corroborated by a spate of Southern addresses endorsing the general principle of limiting judicial authority, Senator Thomas Hennings of Missouri moved to table. By a narrow margin of 49 to 41, the measure was carried and Jenner-Butler disposed of.[58]

*   *   *

Although his sternest tests were yet to come, the majority leader seemed to have control of the situation, and both sides were hewing to the line of Senatorial etiquette. At this point, however, Senator Paul Douglas of Illinois all but broke up the meeting. Appearing in course on the agenda was a relatively innocuous proposal to provide notice of interlocutory relief against administrative agency orders; Douglas obtained the floor and proposed an amendment sponsored by himself, Wayne Morse of Oregon and Humphrey of Minnesota, which read:

> The Congress hereby expresses its full support and approval of the recent, historic decisions of the Supreme Court of the United States holding racial segregation unlawful in public education and transportation as a denial of the constitutional right to the equal protection of the laws.[59]

Pandemonium exploded the instant the Senate clerk read the Douglas proposal; the presiding officer, Senator Alan Bible of Nevada, pounded his gavel futilely while Senators milled in the aisles or shouted for recognition from the chair. By his blunt spade-calling, Douglas had jerked the genteel camouflage from the elaborate debate and revealed the naked fact of racial segregation as the real issue behind the nicely worded arguments. In the uproar that raged for many long minutes, Douglas lost the floor to Johnson, who apparently could not hear above the din, and only after a point of order had been raised was the Illinois Senator able to resume his remarks.

Behind "the smokescreen of the legal complexities in the half-dozen court measures with which the Senate has been or is about to be confronted in the closing days of the session," said Douglas, "the real issue is the Supreme Court. The amendment which my colleagues and I are proposing puts that issue out in the open, right here on the floor of the Senate." Congress had to face the issue, Douglas went on, because "prospects of leadership from the Chief Executive of our country or from any of the executive departments to encourage compliance and to discourage lawlessness are dim," and the public interest required "some such minimum declaration of our deep conviction on this basic principle."

For four years since *Brown,* Douglas reminded his colleagues, men who recognized its fundamental justice "have kept relatively silent in the Senate under a barrage of attack upon that decision and the other decisions of the Supreme Court." Meantime, there had been a carnival of abuse: "We have listened to threats of massive resistance. We have listened to denunciations of the personnel of the Court. We have heard high officials in state government openly declare that they intended to disobey the decisions of the courts of the United States. In the interest of harmony, we have kept silent, believing that the storm would pass—or at least hoping that the storm would pass."

To the argument that the current bills were not concerned with segregation, Douglas answered that "if any member thinks that by getting the bill previously under discussion out of the way, he will avert and avoid facing the issue of whether the Senate approves or disapproves the decisions of the Supreme Court in the desegregation cases, that member is mistaken." To the argument that the pending bills were not intended to be a rebuke to the judiciary, Douglas answered: "This is all part of a 'reverse the Court' campaign which stems largely, although not entirely, from the earlier decision of the Supreme Court in the *Brown* case, and the cases which have grown out of the *Brown* case."[60]

Within the rigid framework of parliamentary procedure, Douglas' proposed amendment had no remote chance of being adopted. Manifestly, adoption was not his objective, but an opportunity to remove the smiling mask which both sides had agreed to hold up to the "thinly transparent effort to overrule . . . Supreme Court decisions." Not only did Johnson dislike the exposure of the dissimulation of which all parties were guilty, but he regarded the Douglas diversion as a dangerous, perhaps fatal, interruption of the momentum which the majority leader had developed in steamrollering over the very anti-Court measures which Douglas opposed.[61]

How correct Johnson was became clear when the Smith anti-preemption bill now came up, through parliamentary maneuver, for initial vote. Again, after lengthy conservative debate in support of the measure, Hennings put his motion to table; it was soundly defeated, 39 to 46. Once more pandemonium broke out. With victory suddenly within grasp, the conservatives were on their feet shouting for a vote on the bill, while Johnson saw a catastrophic repudiation of his leadership yawning before him. The Senate chamber was a bedlam, with progressives in panic. Taking things into their own hands, Douglas and his cohorts were improvising an all-out filibuster, while Jenner and Butler, furious at the thought of being denied the kill, were trying to shout down any delaying tactics. Nixon, back in the presiding officer's chair, and aware of the crisis before the Senate, recognized Johnson for the purpose of moving for adjournment until the next day and put the question. On a record vote, adjournment carried, 70-18.[62]

*   *   *

In the ensuing twenty-four hours, a frenzied, sleepless campaign of recapturing or consolidating support for each side went on. Johnson and Humphrey for the liberals, and Thurmond of South Carolina and John McClellan of Arkansas—mightily aided by the Washington office of the National Association of Manufacturers—hunted down every available Senator and plied promises, threats and any other available arguments to hold their respective lines intact. Senator John Carroll of Colorado, who had a motion ready to recommit the bill to the Judiciary Committee, held up action during the first hours of the next legislative day, waiting for word from Johnson.

The word did not come until five o'clock in the afternoon; even then, the majority leader was unable to hope for anything more than a tie vote, with Nixon then in position to tip the scales either way. By continuing to work feverishly in the cloakrooms and on the telephone while the roll call on the motion proceeded, Johnson sought to convert the hesitant and to persuade some of the opposition simply to absent themselves when the vote came. His last hope was pinned on Senator Wallace Bennett, a Utah Republican. With the vote at 40-40, Bennett came onto the floor, answered the roll call in favor of the motion to recommit, and the Smith bill passed out of history.[63]

The victory was doubly sweet for the progressives, and doubly bitter for the conservatives as a defeat, for it was indeed double. In raising the anti-preemption bill as a proposed amendment to a bill amending the Smith Act—and in form making the latter an addendum to the anti-preemption proposal—the conservatives had tied one to the fortunes of the other. Thus, in recommitting the amended measure, the Senate had recommitted both proposals, and Johnson—having sent the anti-*Mallory* measure to conference and tabled Jenner-Butler—in bringing home the winning vote on the recommittal motion now had four of the five anti-Court bills disposed of in whole or in part.

It remained to handle the conference measures—first, the bill proposing to reverse *Cole v. Young,* which came out of conference committee and passed the House on August 22. The majority leader conferred with Senator Olin Johnson of South Carolina, and prevailed upon him not to call for the conference committee report on the floor of the Senate. Since the majority leader himself had no intention of calling for it, and with adjournment now only hours away, the fifth anti-Court bill was thus disposed of.[64]

Now, as time was running out on the Eighty-fifth Congress, the anti-*Mallory* bill came out of conference to be passed by the House as part of its final business. Under threat of another liberal filibuster, Johnson called a hurried meeting of his party policy committee, and agreed to a point of order on a rule under which new matter added to a bill by a conference committee nullified the committee report. After O'Mahoney of Wyoming was trapped into stating in the record that there was new matter in the reported bill, Carroll invoked the prohibitory rule; Nixon sustained Carroll, and at 4 o'clock in the morning of August 24, the Eighty-fifth Congress and the current legislative drive against the Supreme Court both came to an end.[65]

*   *   *

Less than six weeks after adjournment, the anti-Court coalition in the Senate was smashed at the polls; two conservatives retired and five others were defeated for reelection. While political observers doubted that the technical issues in the anti-Court measures, even as dramatized by the eleventh-hour debate in the Senate, were specific factors in the election results, the changing character of the Eighty-sixth Congress indicated a general renaissance of liberalism. In turn, this clearing of the air tended to diminish the public hysteria which had developed in the early years of the cold war. Not without misgivings, the American people were now preparing themselves to accept a future of continually shifting social and economic balances in domestic affairs, a chronic state of alert on the international scene, and a need for increasing reliance on the Federal protection of individual rights in a corporate organization of modern life.[66]

The Supreme Court, Robert H. Jackson had written in 1941, "is almost never a really contemporary institution." Life tenure meant that the judiciary in time tended to be substantially older than the elective branches of government and, with reference to Congress, to keep "the average viewpoint of the two institutions a generation apart." Thus the judiciary in most of its history, Jackson concluded, had represented "the check of a preceding generation upon the present one."[67] If events since 1941 had not borne him out, the explanation was to be found in the variety of the events themselves.

First was the fact that World War II had completed both the centralizing tendency of American economic society, and the destruction of the nineteenth-century balances of world power, begun by World War I. In its frenetic effort to recapture a sense of security in a world completely altered by two global wars and a decade of depression which had almost seen the death of capitalism, the United States had only postponed facing the question of its constitutional values in a totally new world.

Early in the nineteenth century, as the experiment in Federalism was being fairly launched, the Court under John Marshall had undertaken to point the way in which a congeries of states might find nationhood. The Seventh to Eleventh Congresses had excoriated the Court with as much vehemence as the Eighty-fifth; Marshall, in the years from 1803 to 1810, had borne the brunt of invective not excelled until Earl Warren occupied the same position a century and a half later. To accept the consequences of change had been the mark of greatness in the members of the Court in all of the period in between; in the great tradition of Story, Miller, Holmes, Brandeis, Hughes and Cardozo had come Black, Douglas, Frankfurter—and now Warren.

The long-drawn-out fight over confirmation of new, modern-minded appointees to the bench, and the epochal struggle for legislative nullification of specific judicial holdings, represented the opening campaigns in an economic Armageddon. Like most signal victories in the struggle for constitutional guarantees of freedom, the battle in the Eighty-fifth Congress had been a near thing. The average American, queried as to his personal preferences on the matter of racial equality and constitutional rights for all, would have heartily wished that he had never heard of the issues. Public opinion polls during these years listed a sizable percentage of persons in the "no opinion" category on the question of how broad the privileges of democracy ought to be.[68]

For the Warren Court, whether activist or restrained, the ultimate question could only be answered in one way, and it had become the responsibility of the judiciary in the context of the mid-century to enforce the constitutional propositions as against all restrictive force. including government itself. In his first six years as Chief Justice, Warren had defined the basic outlines of the jurisprudence of a new Federalism for the modern age.

13/The Jurisprudence of Desegregation

A MONG THE FIVE THOUSAND or more cases in the history of the United States which have touched upon constitutional subjects in the courts, perhaps a hundred have been pivotal decisions; there have been less than a dozen which have been of such magnitude as to change the course of American political and legal development. *Marbury v. Madison,* in 1803, established the principle of judicial review of Federal legislative and executive action. *Dartmouth College v. Woodward,* asserting for the next century the rigid prohibition of the clause against impairment of contracts, and *McCulloch v. Maryland,* unequivocally declaring the supremacy of Federal authority in all powers conferred upon it by the people of the United States, both were decided in 1819. *Gibbons v. Ogden* in 1824 extended the jurisdiction of the United States under the commerce clause. These were the landmarks of the Marshall Court in the formative period of American nationhood. Students of constitutional history might add other cases representing Marshall's constitutionalism, but these beyond question would be the irreducible core of Federalism as it would be recognized in the constitutional law of the next century.

In the hundred and twenty years after Marshall, only the *Slaughterhouse* cases of 1873, sounding the opening note for the long threnody on the Fourteenth Amendment, attained a comparable magnitude. Many epochal decisions, from *Dred Scott v. Sandford* in 1857 through the *Granger* cases twenty years later and the *Sugar Trust* and *Income Tax* decisions of 1895, were to be overthrown by later events or to succumb, in Frankfurter's phrase, to the "erosion of time." The same was true of many mighty judicial works wrought by the first Harlan and Holmes, by Brandeis and Taft, by Hughes and Cardozo. In the massive intellectual shift in constitutional jurisprudence between 1937 and 1945, more than a century of judicial landmarks were washed away or fundamentally altered.

Most of the judicial dialogue of the twentieth century, until the Warren Court, was perceived in retrospect to be either an accommodation of the *status quo* or an attempt—particularly in the Black-Douglas-Frankfurter disputations of the forties and early fifties—to restate American constitutionalism in terms of the new social and economic frames of reference. The primary accomplishment of the late Hughes Court and the Stone Court was to confirm the constitutional basis for the permanent changes in American life effected by the New Deal. The Black-Douglas-Frankfurter synthesis spelled out the consequences of the decisions of the Hughes-Stone period—the inevitability of a Federal enforcement of the constitutional rights of American citizens in the centralized economy emerging from the depression and the Second World War.

The Warren Court thus found itself placed in the vortex of a new Federalism which, in the generation following the depression and the war, demanded historic judicial decisions of the magnitude of those made by the Marshall Court in the original period of nascent Federalism. Critics might excoriate the one Chief Justice as they had the other; the underlying truism was that in both periods the Court was dealing with accomplished facts of national life. The Constitutional Convention of 1787 had made inevitable— if the Federal proposition in that convention was to become a reality—the type of decisions represented in *Marbury*, the *Dartmouth College* case, *McCulloch* and *Ogden*. The crisis which had brought about the New Deal and had been followed by Pearl Harbor and the ultimate confrontation with world military and economic totalitarianism, had led with equal logic to *Brown v. Board of Education*, to *Baker v. Carr*, and—as representative of the whole complex of guarantees in the Bill of Rights—to *Gideon v. Wainwright*.

*   *   *

In the year following the *Income Tax* and *Sugar Trust* cases, Justice Brown for a seven-to-one majority handed down the opinion in *Plessy v. Ferguson*, upholding as "reasonable" a Louisiana statute requiring segregated railroad cars. The opinion was broad enough to apply the "separate but equal" standard to all types of public services and accommodations. Brown rejected the assumption "that social prejudices may be overcome by legislation, and that equal rights cannot be secured to the Negro except by an enforced commingling of the two races." Social equality, said the majority, "must be the result of natural affinities, . . . and a voluntary consent of individuals," not the artificial creation of legislation.[1]

The first Harlan, speaking in dissent, stoutly denied "that any legislative body or judicial tribunal may have regard to the race of citizens when the civil rights of those citizens are involved." Social distinctions, both within and between races, Harlan recognized as a fact of life; but "in the eye of the law, there is in this country no superior, dominant, ruling class of citizens. . . . Our Constitution is color-blind, and neither knows nor tolerates classes among citizens." Social equality, he pointed out, "no more exists between two races when traveling in a passenger, coach or a public highway than when members of the same races sit by each other in a street car or in the jury box, or stand or sit with each other in a political assembly."

"The present decision, it may well be apprehended, will not only stimulate aggressions, more or less brutal and irritating, upon the admitted rights of colored citizens," warned Harlan, "but will encourage the belief that it is possible by means of state enactments to defeat the beneficent purposes which the people of the United States had in view when they adopted the recent amendments to the Constitution."[2]

The majority opinion in *Plessy v. Ferguson* was eagerly seized upon by white Americans at the turn of the century as an accurate description of the existing (and desired) state of affairs; had they been as insistent upon the "equal" as they were upon the "separate" term in the "separate but equal" doctrine, latter-day progressives would have had a harder case to make out. As it was, the majority opinion in *Plessy* was accepted as controlling, almost without reference to Harlan's lone dissent, for nearly forty years. A single case, in 1917, held invalid a municipal ordinance which zoned separate residential districts for different races, but the Court here stressed that geographic segregation was a subversion of the "separate but equal" doctrine.[3]

It was not without significance that Negroes generally in America between 1890 and 1910 were at the lowest economic and social level in the history of their race in the New World. By the end of the first half a century of emancipation, the overwhelming majority were disfranchised, all but illiterate and generally unskilled, universally scorned and crowded into the filthiest slums in cities or pushed onto the most scrabbled farm plots in the country. The twentieth century was opened, in 1900 and 1901, with two hundred and fourteen lynchings, and though a striking proportion of these mob killings took place outside the Deep South—Ray Stannard Baker described in disheartening detail such a murder in Springfield, Ohio in 1905—they were almost all perpetrated against black Americans. In the Deep South, the slave labor of the *ante-bellum* plantation was replaced by a system of tenancy and credit which, supplemented by a custom of requiring fines for minor crimes to be worked out, amounted to an effective system of modern serfdom.[4]

In 1909 the first steps were taken to organize what was to become the National Association for the Advancement of Colored Peoples, but it would require the economic holocaust of the depression a quarter of a century later before it would attain the capacity for militance—and another quarter of a century would elapse before it would spearhead a social revolution.

It was particularly ironic that in a period when the jurisprudence of the Fourteenth Amendment as it was applied to state regulatory powers in the matter of industrial activity should be proliferating, the "original understanding" of the Amendment with reference to Negro equality should have been treated with general judicial silence. Twenty-one years were to elapse between the segregated zoning case in 1917 and the 1938 case compelling the state of Missouri to provide equal though separate facilities in higher education for Negro taxpayers.[5]

Still, a judicial challenge to long-continued inequities had been launched in 1927 with a case involving all-white primary laws (although the courts were to answer ambivalently over the next fifteen years) and in 1931 with a case challenging the procedure for selecting a jury to try Negro defendants in felony cases. *Powell v. Alabama* in 1932 established the principle that defendants were guaranteed the right to counsel in capital cases under the Fourteenth Amendment, and three years later the Court reversed the capital convictions in the Scottsboro cases on the ground that there was no evidence that Negroes had ever been permitted to serve on juries in such cases.[6]

The massive awakening of the colored peoples around the world which came about with the collapse of the colonial empires in World War II provided the galvanic force for the Negro's struggle to win full judicial recognition of his rights in the late 1940's and early 1950's. Segregation on interstate passenger trains was prohibited in 1946. Within the next four years, two cases in Oklahoma and one in Texas elicited rulings from the Court that separate educational facilities in state universities did not justify a denial of Negro admissions to any state institutions, and a more fundamental decision in this same period declared unconstitutional the time-honored custom of writing racial convenants into leases and conveyances of real estate.[7]

*   *   *

It was almost universally recognized that a definitive governmental effort to remove the remaining racial barriers would have a cataclysmic reaction in social, economic and legal spheres. It would mean the overturning of a system of values and relationships which had been developing over more than three centuries—from the landing of the first boatload of Negro slaves at Jamestown in 1619 until the general loosening of the linchpins of American society in the depression thirties. For the Civil War and the Reconstruction Amendments to the Constitution had made little permanent change in white-Negro relationships in their time. The chief effect of emancipation had been to change the Negro problem from one which had been exclusively Southern to one which was ultimately nationwide, as Negroes themselves began gradually to drift to the Northern cities. School segregation was a fact not only of Southern life, but of a preponderance of the states of the union, and where it was not enforced by law it was established by economics, with schools in Negro living areas being almost universally Negro in enrollment.[8]

The Fourteenth and Fifteenth Amendments, "by making the Negro a citizen and surrounding his citizenship with constitutional safeguards, made his legal rights an important Federal question," a legal periodical mused in 1939;[9] the simple fact was, however, that the Federal government had largely ignored the question over the years. The problem was too deep-rooted to turn upon an abstract legal proposition. A rigid system of social taboos almost completely divided the races in the South and in most sections of the North as well; miscegenation was a moral and legal offense in a majority of the states of the union; racial mixing at social and recreational functions, eating together, sharing the same public sanitary facilities—or even conversing together on terms of equality—were awkward occasions in the North and almost totally ostracised in the former slave states. The very *tone* of speech between the two races, observed Swedish social scientist Gunnar Myrdal, was determined by their relative status: "the Negro was to use deferential tones and words; the white man was to use condescending tones and words."[10]

It was one thing for social theorists and reformers to emphasize the unconscionable handicap which segregation represented for the Negro; it was another to come to terms with the psychological, economic and cultural trauma which *de*segregation represented for the majority of white Americans in the South, as well as for substantial numbers of whites elsewhere in the nation. The theorists and reformers responded to the white problem in one of two ways: Either they refused to recognize its existence, or certainly its validity, as something too shameful for civilized men to discuss, or they damned it as pernicious, and prepared, whenever they had the opportunity, to ride roughshod over it. Northerners, insulated in comfortably segregated suburbs, might endorse integration in the abstract. If they lived in the path of overflowing colored zones they organized property owners' protective associations or sought frantically to move elsewhere. Southerners, who had lived for generations, in James J. Kilpatrick's phrase, with this "subconsciousness of race," had no alternative but to go on record in opposition to the principle.[11]

To say that a way of life was in jeopardy was a cliché, but it did not overstate the case; after many generations, white and black in the South had developed a *modus vivendi* which pervaded every element of social organization. The white man accepted it because it was for him the only tolerable definition of racial relationships; the black man accepted it because he lacked the leadership and power to change it. The white man said that both races preferred things this way; the black man usually said nothing. Emotionally, both races adjusted their whole lives to the fact of separation, recognizing the taboos and the compensations alike, "white and Negro coexisting in an oddly intimate remoteness," as Kilpatrick wrote.[12]

Northern liberals dismissed all of this. The case for the Negro was invariably stated by urbane, Ivy-League educated, professional men or women of black skin, while the case for the South was almost always put into the mouths of ranting bigots from the backwoods. Sincere Southern conservatives like Kilpatrick were occasionally invited to appear on nationally televised discussion programs—only to be upstaged by liberal co-panelists who seldom permitted them to make their points uninterrupted. The Southern moderate or liberal was more aware of the emotional and cultural crisis that was involved. After "a lifetime of adventures in that gap between law and custom," wrote Congressman Brooks Hays of Arkansas, the tragedy of desegregation from the Southern viewpoint was accentuated by the Southerner's fundamental hostility to Federal authority which made him regard Congressional action and Supreme Court decision as two different forms of force bills.[13]

The conflicts bred by the determination of the new Negro to push swiftly forward on all fronts to attain equality, and the whites' insistence upon gradualism at the most, bred circumstances where "the educated Negro in the South dislikes the Southern white man *en masse* as never before in our history," wrote Mississippi editor Hodding Carter. This mounting antipathy, he continued, had become mutual.[14]

All this aside, however, the ultimate reality was that a revolution had been in the making for the past two decades—and revolutions by definition aim at the destruction of the *status quo*. The New Deal had committed the United States to the proposition of equality of economic opportunity; World War II had made the proposition an attainable reality, and thereafter there could be no turning back. The successive judicial challenges to the idea of segregation throughout the decade following the war were clear evidence of the social commitment, and yet, conservatives told themselves, in the context of American constitutional law (or constitutional tradition) segregation in its fundamentals was clearly a matter of state concern. Unless the Supreme Court was prepared to federalize such subjects which had always been treated as non-federal, there seemed to be no legal opening for a constitutional attack on the fundamentals.

This line of reasoning overlooked the revolution.

* * *

The case for desegregation in public schools had first been argued before the Court in the late fall of 1952. In June, 1953 the Vinson Court ordered it to be reargued the following October and requested counsel in all the cases to discuss a remarkable range of subjects:

> 1. What evidence is there that the Congress which submitted and the state legislatures and conventions which ratified the Fourteenth Amendment contemplated or did not contemplate, understood or did not understand, that it would abolish segregation in public schools?
> 2. If neither the Congress in submitting nor the states in ratifying the Fourteenth Amendment understood that compliance with it would require the immediate abolition of segregation in public schools, was it nevertheless the understanding of the framers of the Amendment
>> (a) that future Congresses might, in the exercise of their power, under Section 5 of the Amendment, abolish such segregation, or

(b) that it would be within the judicial power, in light of future conditions, to construe the Amendment as abolishing such segregation of its own force?

3. On the assumption that the answers to questions 2 (a) and (b) do not dispose of the issue, is it within the judicial power, in construing the Amendment, to abolish segregation in public schools?

4. Assuming it is decided that segregation in public schools violates the Fourteenth Amendment

(a) would a decree necessarily follow providing that, within the limits set by normal geographic school districting, Negro children should forthwith be admitted to schools of their choice, or

(b) may this Court, in the exercise of its equity powers, permit an effective gradual adjustment to be brought about from existing segregated systems to a system not based on color distinctions?

5. On the assumption on which questions 4 (a) and (b) are based, and assuming further that this Court will exercise its equity powers to the end described in question 4 (b),

(a) should this Court formulate detailed decrees in these cases;

(b) if so, what specific issues should the decrees reach;

(c) should this Court appoint a special master to hear evidence with a view to recommending specific terms for such decrees;

(d) should this Court remand to the courts of first instance with directions to frame decrees in these cases, and if so, what general directions should the decrees of this Court include and what procedures should the courts of first instance follow in arriving at specific terms of more detailed decrees?[15]

The Court in its order for reargument specifically invited the Attorney General to participate in oral argument and to submit an additional brief. For subsequent students of the Court's progress, several facts emerged conspicuously from this order. First was the determination of the bench to have an exhaustive study of the constitutional propositions for and against the application of the Fourteenth Amendment to this subject-area, with the record showing that all sides had been given opportunity to be heard at length. Second was the decision of the Court to deal in such magnitude with the question during Vinson's Chief Justiceship—before Earl Warren's name had arisen with reference to any specific opening on the bench. Third was the fact that the Court anticipated, and was putting the Department of Justice on notice, that a sweeping and affirmative desegregation opinion would immediately vest in the Attorney General the responsibility for enforcement. Finally, in its detailed sub-sections to its questions to counsel, the Court made clear its awareness of the monumental social effects involved in such an affirmative decision.

The judicial problem was a peculiar one, created by the oblique development of the jurisprudence of the Fourteenth Amendment over the past eighty years. Not only had the judiciary, since Conkling's famous (and possibly gratuitous) aphorism of 1882, developed the Fourteenth Amendment as a standard of measurement of state police power in economic areas, but conversely it had permitted the original objectives of the Amendment to languish in tacit concession to the racial separatism which the articulate majority of the nation had so long preferred. The "privileges and immunities" of national citizenship had been defined over the decades largely in institutional terms, and even when national citizenship was held to be something distinct from state citizenship—and moreover was held to be "paramount and dominant"—until now the Federal government had not been disposed to enforce the rights of its citizens as individuals as against the states.[16]

As on so many historic occasions in the past, the Court was crowded to every doorway as argument on the cases, postponed from October to December, was finally begun. Among nearly thirty lawyers who had figured in the briefs and the supporting arguments, two men—the field commanders for the opposing views—strikingly represented the changes in American life which were finally demanding accommodation. As special counsel representing South Carolina and Virginia there was John W. Davis, now 80 years of age, Solicitor General under Woodrow Wilson, 1924 Democratic candidate for the Presidency, virulent critic of the New Deal. The Wall Street lawyer, appearing in this penumbra of his career as the advocate for the jurisprudence of separatism which had prevailed throughout virtually the whole span of the capitalistic age he represented, epitomized the old order as perfectly as the new order was epitomized in his chief opponent, 45-year-old Thurgood Marshall, chief counsel for the NAACP, grandson of a slave, destined to become the first Negro to be appointed to this Court.

Complementing the vested interests thus balanced in these lawyers was the Assistant Attorney General of the United States, J. Lee Rankin, who would reiterate to the Court the position which had been taken by the Department of Justice under Truman, now under Eisenhower, and with increasing firmness under Kennedy and Johnson: Racial segregation in the America of the mid-century had become a cancer in the body of democracy.

*   *   *

For all the elaborate briefs which had been prepared in response to the Court's order of the preceding June, including a supporting brief prepared on the authority of thirty-two leading sociologists, anthropologists, psychologists and psychiatrists reminiscent of the famous "Brandeis brief" of 1908, the principal arguments followed predictable lines. Davis earnestly contended that it "was not within the judicial power" to overturn a social system which "has stood legally for three-quarters of a century," and that the Fourteenth Amendment had never been intended to extend to the control of local public school systems. Marshall countered with the argument that the Amendment, complementing the abolitionist Thirteenth by declaring all persons born within the jurisdiction of the United States to be citizens of the same, had conferred the full rights of citizenship upon the Negro as part of the plan to abolish "the last vestige of slavery."[17]

As for the matter of ingrained social attitudes, Marshall and his associates stated flatly: "The question is whether the public policies, the prejudices, the mores of South Carolina and Virginia, or the provisions of the Constitution, shall prevail." Corroborating this general argument, Rankin declared that in the view of the Department of Justice "the Fourteenth Amendment does not permit any discrimination based upon race or color." Frankfurter shot a question as to the consistency of the Congressional policy in asserting an absolute anti-discrimination policy in the Amendment and in legislating for segregated schools in the District of Columbia, and when Rankin failed to answer to the Justice's satisfaction, Frankfurter made his own observation that in this context "legislation by Congress is like the British Empire, something that is acquired in a fit of absent-mindedness."[18]

Rather ironically, the case which had given its name to the great issue— the action against the Topeka board of education—was insisted by Frankfurter to have become moot with the action of the board that fall integrating the Topeka schools. In his characteristic fashion of engaging in a lengthy procedural colloquy with counsel, Frankfurter ultimately compelled Brown's attorney, Robert L. Carter, to concede that the issue was indeed moot. Warren intervened with the observation that since the Kansas litigants were before the Court by invitation, he for one wanted to hear the argument of Carter and the state's assistant attorney general, Paul E. Wilson. But after the Frankfurter interlude, the oral arguments in *Brown v. Board of Education* seemed anticlimactic, and they ended with both sides using only a small part of the two hours allotted to them.[19]

On the final question on which the Court had requested argument, counsel for all sides were in agreement; if integration was to be the shape of the future—and few now doubted what the judicial outcome was to be— a reasonable time would be required to adjust the public educational systems of the nation as well as the mental attitudes of the American people. For, as every realist could perceive, such an epochal holding in this subject-area would put in operation a chain reaction which would ultimately affect every other social contact in the national life.

*   *   *

Following the oral arguments in December, the Court postponed its decision for a tantalizing length of time. In part this was dictated by the obvious desire to avoid needling the Senate while Warren's confirmation was pending before it, although only extremists among the racists offered testimony against the appointment. Substantially the greater consideration, in Warren's own view, was the need to ensure unanimity in the opinion. While it was evident from the outset that there would be no dissent, the Chief was concerned, in such a momentous issue, that the Court should seek to achieve the unequivocal unity that it had demonstrated in *Marbury v. Madison.*

Equally important, Warren perceived, was the format of the opinion itself. It should be succinct, leaving a minimal target for the political attack which was certain to come and expressing only the fundamentals upon which the members of the Court would be emphatically united.[20] Thus the Court proceeded deliberately toward May 17, 1954 when the opinion was announced without advance warning; newspaper correspondents covering the Court and even the Associate Justices, as one observer concluded, were taken by surprise. Yet this was unlikely; the Attorney General and his Assistant were in the room that day, and Justice Jackson, hospitalized for some weeks by a heart attack, chose this occasion to return to the bench, in James Reston's opinion, either "to emphasize the unanimity of the Court" in this historic moment or to "be present when the history-making verdict was announced."[21]

In the Marshall tradition, Chief Justice Warren personally assumed the responsibility for speaking for the Court on this issue. He opened with a brief comment on the exhaustive analyses of the intent of Congress and the ratifying states in framing and adopting the Fourteenth Amendment, but observed that "although these sources cast some light, it is not enough to resolve the problem with which we are faced. At best, they are inconclusive." It therefore became a matter of determining the constitutional rule in the light of the present: "In approaching this problem," Warren declared, "we cannot turn the clock back to 1868 when the Amendment was adopted, or even to 1896 when *Plessy v. Ferguson* was written. We must consider public education in the light of its full development and its present place in American life throughout the nation. Only in this way can it be determined if segregation in public schools deprives these plaintiffs of the equal protection of the laws."[22]

Inasmuch as public education at the time of the Amendment was non-existent in the South and rudimentary in the North, literalists were correct in arguing that the framers could not have had in mind any matter of segregated public education. But it was obvious that the Court in the present opinion was not to be frustrated by literalism; if a subsequent development in national experience presented justiciable questions which fell within the orbit of the Amendment, specifically, as privileges and immunities of citizens of the United States, there could be no doubt that the Amendment conferred jurisdiction. "We come then," said the Chief Justice, "to the question presented: Does segregation of children in public schools solely on the basis of race, even though the physical facilities and other 'tangible' factors may be equal, deprive the children of the minority group of equal educational opportunities? We believe that it does."[23]

Relying upon the findings in two of the trial courts—in Delaware, where segregation had been rejected, and in Kansas, where it had been reluctantly upheld—the Court reiterated: "Segregation of white and colored children in public schools has a detrimental effect upon the colored children. The impact is greater when it has the sanction of law; for the policy of separating the races is usually interpreted as denoting the inferiority of the Negro group. A sense of inferiority affects the motivation of a child to learn."

It followed that "in the field of public education the doctrine of 'separate but equal' has no place. Separate educational facilities are inherently unequal."[24]

*   *   *

The first *Brown* decision, wrote James Reston, applied Cardozo's "test of contemporary social justice" and thus read "more like an expert paper on sociology" than a legal opinion. In the packed courtroom, he noted, "each of the Associate Justices listened intently. They obviously were aware that no Court since the *Dred Scott* decision of March 6, 1857 had ruled on so vital an issue in the field of race relations."[25]

Accepting the pleas of counsel for all parties that a reasonable period of adjustment be provided, the conclusion of the opinion restored the cases to the docket for yet another reargument, on the fourth and fifth questions of the earlier order, before the end of the term. Eleven months later—with six other Southern states joining the original parties—the Court speaking again through the Chief Justice remanded the school cases to the Federal trial courts for implementation. The opinion admonished the courts to be guided by "a practical flexibility" in the process of "adjusting and reconciling public and private needs." The burden would be on the school authorities, the opinion warned, to establish the fact that they were proceeding with reasonable expedition. No one doubted that whatever action would ultimately be taken by the lower courts, the high tribunal would be compelled to review the action on repeated occasions.[26]

The unanimity of the Court in both *Brown* decisions, as well as the detailed attention given by the opinions to the constitutional issues, cast the question of desegregation unequivocally in terms of the limiting effect of the Fourteenth Amendment on state sovereignty. Conversely, the Court in *Brown* committed itself irrevocably to the proposition that rights of individuals as citizens of the United States were to be affirmatively asserted by Federal authority as against restraints by the states of which these individuals were also citizens.

Thus, at last, a judicial and ideological Rubicon had been crossed. Racial integration happened to be the compelling reason for the crossing at this time, but throughout the twentieth century there had been glimpses of the ultimate course ahead. Until *Brown,* however, constitutional law had dealt with individual rights almost exclusively in terms of the specific (but limited) guarantees of the Bill of Rights, and the concern of the new constitutionalism of the late thirties and forties had been primarily with the incorporation of the Bill of Rights into the Fourteenth Amendment. *Brown* was opening a door upon a broad new proposition, the absolutism of individual rights to be protected by the Constitution.

It was this underlying proposition, even more than the fact of desegregation itself, which shocked the conservative—and particularly the Southern conservative—mind. Ingrained in the fiber of conservative political thought was the undying conviction that the Constitution defined a carefully circumscribed national government, created by the states without prejudice to their own preexisting sovereign authority. With John Calhoun of South Carolina, adherents to this view insisted that "the general government emanated from the people of the several states, forming distinct political communities, and acting in their separate and sovereign capacity, and not from all of the people forming one aggregate political community." Although this view had led to the attempt at nullification in the 1830's and to secession in 1861, the failure in both instances had never persuaded the states' rightists that history as well as political and legal logic was against them.[27]

Now, presented with a fresh challenge to the Calhoun concept, the conservative forces would make one more effort to assert a paramount state sovereignty. On January 11, 1956 the General Assembly of Virginia received a bill which solemnly declared:

> A. The several states existed prior to the formation of the United States. As states they were sovereign and without limits on their power.
> B. The several states, seeing the advantages in a central government for the conduct of certain affairs, joined together to form the United States as a separate government with certain powers.
> C. The several states joining together to form the United States were aware of the dangers inherent in a central government. To guard against these dangers, they ordained and established the Constitution of the United States which (A) gave certain powers to the central government and (B) reserved all other powers for the states.
> D. Subsequent to the formation of the United States, and the establishment of a Constitution therefor, occasions arose for extending or limiting the powers of the states. These were accomplished by amendments. . . .
> E. The action of the Supreme Court of the United States in holding that the states cannot provide separate but equal facilities for children of different races constitutes an unlawful and unconstitutional assumption of power which does not exist. An agency created by a document to which sovereign states were parties cannot lawfully amend the creating document when that document clearly specifies in Article V thereof the manner of amendment. . . .

The Founding Fathers (extended to include Calhoun) were declared by the resolution to have agreed that "in case of a deliberate, palpable and dangerous exercise of powers not granted by the Constitution of the United States, the states who are parties thereto have the right and are in duty bound to interpose. . . ." Thus was Calhoun's doctrine of nullification resurrected as the new doctrine of interposition.[28]

Under one name or the other, the proposition was endorsed or implied in related actions by a number of states. South Carolina's legislature adopted a resolution in February, 1956 declaring that the Supreme Court had "ignored the principle that the meaning of the Constitution and its Amendments does not change." The Southern "Declaration of Constitutional Principles" was introduced into Congress the next spring, condemning the *Brown* decisions as "a clear abuse of judicial power." On the heels of this instrument the Georgia legislature adopted its Resolution of Nullification

which proclaimed the Federal courts "powerless to interfere with the operation of the public schools of the states, because the Constitution of the
United States does not confer upon the general government [jurisdiction]
over such schools, or over the subject of education, jurisdiction over these
matters being reserved to the states."[29]

The grand illusion of interposition was summarily disposed of when the
Little Rock School case came before the Court in the summer of 1958. An
interpretation of the Federal Constitution by the Federal judiciary, said the
unanimously signed opinion, "can neither be nullified openly and directly
by state legislators or state executive or judicial officers, nor nullified indirectly by them through evasive schemes." The supreme law of the land, as
stated in Article VI of the Constitution, is the Constitution itself, which
every Federal and state official is sworn to uphold.[30]

The ultimate humiliation of the states' rightists came in 1960 when a
three-judge Federal court, striking down the Louisiana legislature's attempt·
to prevent integration of public schools, gave a substantial answer to the
interposition thesis:

> Apprehensive of the validity of the proposition that the Constitu-
> tion is a compact of states, interposition asserts that at least a ruling
> challenged by a state should be suspended until the people can ratify
> it by constitutional amendment. But this invocation of 'constitutional
> processes' is a patent subterfuge. Unlike open nullification, it is defiance
> hiding under the cloak of apparent legitimacy. The obvious flaw in the
> argument lies in the unfounded insistence that *pending a vote on the
> proposed amendment* the questioned decision must be voided. Even
> assuming their good faith in proposing an amendment against themselves,
> the interpositionists want too much. Without any semblance of legality,
> they claim the right at least temporarily to annul the judgment of the
> highest court, and, should they succeed in defeating the amendment
> proposed, they presume to interpret that victory as voiding forever the
> challenged decision. It requires no elaborate demonstration to show
> that this is a preposterous perversion of Article V of the Constitution.
> Certainly the Constitution can be amended to "overrule" the Supreme
> Court. But there is nothing in Article V that justifies the presumption
> that what has authoritatively been declared to be the law ceases to be
> the law while the amendment is pending, or that the non-ratification of
> an amendment alters the Constitution or any decisions rendered under it.
>
> The conclusion is clear that interposition is not a *constitutional* doc-
> trine. If taken seriously, it is illegal defiance of constitutional authori-
> ty. . . .[31]

On review of the Louisiana school case, the Supreme Court *per curiam*
affirmed the finding and the reasoning of the lower court. Interposition—
if it ever could have been considered alive—was dead, John Calhoun and his
doctrine were reinterred, and the sovereignty of the United States with reference to the rights of its own citizens had been firmly asserted.[32]

The decade after the *Brown* decisions was a litigious one, testing the
struggle of two counterforces at work in a society which had been irrevocably changed by the school cases. There was, on the one hand, a succes-

sion of extemporizing or evasive measures attempted by various state and local groups in the face of the established principle: pupil placement plans, state tuition grants to private schools where public schools had been discontinued, "grade-a-year" schedules, the option of transfer for students from integrated classrooms, and numerous variations on these. On the other hand, as conservatives and progressives alike had foreseen, school integration provided the galvanic spark for fresh efforts at eliminating racial discrimination in public housing, transportation, public accommodations and recreational facilities. The courts systematically were petitioned to adjudicate challenges to all of these efforts over the years.

* * *

By 1963—ten years after the reargument in the first school cases—the Court concluded that a reasonable time had elapsed in which its directive for integration with "all deliberate speed" should have been implemented. It had already rejected local plans which purported to group students on the basis of academic achievement, or the capacity of the individual school child to benefit outside of his "established social and psychological relationships," or documentary proof of "moral fitness" for admission.[33] Where it is "readily apparent that the . . . system proposed lends itself to the perpetuation of segregation," the Court said bluntly in 1963, no amount of academic language would serve to camouflage the fact.[34]

The "passage of a substantial amount of time since the original declaration of the manifest unconstitutionality of racial practices," declared Justice Goldberg in another 1963 case concerning desegregation of recreational facilities, made suspect any leisurely program of conversions which might have come within the "deliberate speed" test eight years earlier.[35] In 1965 the Court *per curiam* summarily ordered integration where plaintiffs showed that they were specifically being denied services to which they were entitled, solely because of the slow pace of integration.[36]

A "freedom of choice" plan in Prince Edward County, Virginia, left the matter of compulsory attendance at public schools to local option and provided for tuition grants out of the public funds for students attending non-sectarian private schools or public schools outside the local districts. The Court upheld an injunction against the county commissioners and school board, forbidding them to pay tuition grants or other public funds in aid of the evasion of the integration order and directing the trial court to require the county to levy new taxes to reopen the public schools.[37]

The capacity of local groups to devise means of evading the rule in *Brown,* demonstrated by the steady succession of cases coming before the Court in the decade following the decision, was also demonstrated in the obstructions which were thrown up against the enforcement of the Civil Rights Act of 1957. William P. Rogers, who had been one of Brownell's chief aides in the Congressional campaign for passage of the bill, had succeeded Brownell as Attorney General. His earnest efforts to enforce the law, as well as those of Robert F. Kennedy who followed him, were often frustrated by the tactics of defense counsel who continually raised constitutional issues, or by trial courts which held that the statute did not contemplate actions against state governments but only against individuals—the reverse of the classic "state action" doctrine. Local election registrars claimed authority under state law to destroy old registration records. If the registrars were named in suits brought by the Justice Department they would resign their state offices, leaving no officeholder against whom the case could be brought. As the Civil Rights Commission, created by the 1957 statute, was to observe, "against the prejudice of registrars and jurors, the United States Government appears under present laws to be helpless to make good the guarantees of the Constitution."[38]

An attempt to strengthen the 1957 statute was made in 1960, with requirements that past registration records be preserved and produced on proper court order, that states be made parties to any actions brought to enforce the voting rights under the statute, and that court-appointed referees could examine claims of individuals that they had been denied opportunities to register or vote. The changes in the law, however, did not result in any significant lessening of the dilatory strategies of the defendants. What was needed, declared the Civil Rights Commission in 1963, was far bolder Congressional action—dealing not only with the electoral franchise but with all of the other major areas of discrimination, in an integrated program of Federal action.[39]

The administration of John F. Kennedy, whose hallmark was total war on all types of racial prejudices, responded to the Commission's appeal wholeheartedly. The 1960 Democratic platform had contained an uncompromising civil rights plank, and one of the dramatic highlights of the Presidential campaign had been the swift action of the candidate and his brother to secure the release from jail of a brilliant young Negro crusader, the Reverend Martin Luther King, Jr. There was manifestly no lack of zeal for the task in the new administration of the Justice Department, yet after two years of John Kennedy's Presidency no spectacular accomplishments had been accounted for in the matter of the existing statutes and their effectiveness.

What had been spectacular was the spontaneous uprising of protest from individuals, white and black, which came about in the winter and spring of 1963. It had been preceded by months of freedom marches and sit-ins at restaurant counters, theaters and other public places, and by the gathering of many forces of conscience from across the land—clergymen, students, young lawyers and others—converging on the South, the geographic focal point of the issue of racial equality. These were the idealists; the followers of men like Martin Luther King were the activists. Beyond them, now in rising chords of fury, was a small but menacing group of revolutionists. What hesistant local trial courts had failed to accomplish, what the half-measures of 1957 and 1960 in Congress had left undone, what even the Supreme Court and the White House had declared in vain, the mass demonstrations of this year were asserting with a single voice: "We shall overcome!"[40]

*   *   *

On June 19, 1963 President Kennedy sent his new civil rights bill to Congress. It came in the wake of a furious confrontation in Birmingham, Alabama between the Reverend Dr. King's marchers and an adamant old-line city administration in which the march's leaders were summarily arrested and vicious police dogs turned loose on the rest of the demonstrators. In the shock of televised reports of the Birmingham incidents before a nation of eyewitnesses, the White House message grimly warned that such ingrained denial of equal rights "is a daily insult which has no place in a country proud of its heritage—the heritage of the melting pot, of equal rights, of one nation and one people."[41]

Kennedy accepted the conclusion of the Civil Rights Commission, that only a broad-gauged legislative attack on all aspects of racial discrimination—not alone in matters of voting but in education, housing, transportation, recreation, and accommodations for eating and sleeping—could cut off the piecemeal harassments of the segregationists. After a century of evasion of the issue, the issue itself had now reached proportions of national emergency requiring national action on behalf of national citizens.

Once more, the restless multitudes spoke their grievance as Congress permitted the Kennedy bill to drag through long debates in the summer of 1963. On August 28, a quarter of a million persons converged on Washington, from almost every state in the Union and from most of the races of man who had come to make the American. Before the Lincoln Memorial in the fading light of the afternoon they heard Dr. King exclaim: "I have a dream that on the red hills of Georgia the sons of former slaves and the sons of former slave owners will be able to sit together at the table of brotherhood."

King's vision, and Kennedy's calls to greatness, still did not push the civil rights bill faster through Congress. It was, after all, a monumental step into the future, and the death-grip of the past was proving all but impossible to break. Finally, death itself by an assassin's bullet in Dallas would provide the final galvanic shock—and a new President, born and bred in Texas, would lead the final drive to commit the government finally to the defense of all their rights for all its citizens.

*   *   *

The Civil Rights Act of 1964 presented grave questions of constitutionality, first for Congress and subsequently for the judiciary, but its enactment was a matter of political even more than legal urgency. The years of judicial pronouncements on the subject of equality of all citizens had created a new frame of reference for Congressional action. Whereas for three past generations the only truly effective pressure group with reference to civil rights legislation had been the constituency of Southern Senators and Representatives, adamantly opposed, there now appeared powerful new organizations in support: Negro agencies, vastly strengthened in political effectiveness, were complemented by national boards of religious bodies (irrespective of the degree of support they received from their local and regional church leaders), labor unions (despite locals' resistance to Negro job competition), and others.

In Attorney General Kennedy the civil rights forces in Congress had an even more resourceful leader than they had had in Brownell or Rogers. Strategic command posts were set up in the Department of Justice as well as in the White House, to coordinate efforts to advance the bill through Congress. Kennedy himself testified volubly and effectively at committee hearings, and the memory of his uncompromising drive to compel integration of the University of Mississippi had made him the lion of the hour with liberals everywhere. The organized rights lobbies mounted a strict surveillance of members of Congress, with watchers in the galleries daily checking on the voting of individual Representatives when the bill came on for floor debate.[42]

While Southern conservatives also organized—and while they had, at this stage of development, a substantial case questioning the validity of the "public accommodations" concept of the bill—they were to fight their battle almost entirely alone. Outside the South, support of civil rights had become a key to political survival, and conservatives as well as liberals sought to endorse the bill in the abstract if not in final practice. Senators Mansfield and Dirksen set up a bi-partisan planning committee which met regularly with the President, while the management of the bill on the floor was jointly handled by Hubert Humphrey for the Democrats and Senator Thomas Kuchel of California for the Republicans. Similar teamwork was developed in the House, where Congressman Celler of New York and his Republican associate in the judiciary committee, William McCulloch of Ohio, directed strategy in close cooperation with Speaker John McCormack of Massachusetts and Republican Charles Halleck of Indiana.[43]

"Stronger than all the armies is an idea whose time has come," said Dirksen, quoting Victor Hugo. It was now the centennial of the Emancipation Proclamation—a full century in which the Negro had waited for the full definition of his rights as an equal participant in American life. In the crucible of the mid-century, a new nation was being born as surely as one had been born in the 1860's. With single-minded determination, the leader in the White House and the leaders on Capitol Hill directed the campaign to see through to final triumph the bill which would assert the principle of universal equality in specific legislation as well as in the general principle of the Constitution.[44]

To make this assertion required Congress to move in its area as boldly as the Court had moved in its adjudication of the Fourteenth Amendment.

A statutory prohibition of discrimination was an affirmative declaration by the legislative and executive branches of the Federal government—and, if upheld in judicial review, by the courts as well—of the paramountcy of the rights of national citizenship. The bill as Johnson advocated it—with the unequivocal assurance that he intended to enforce it to the letter—in effect codified the law on the subject from the original statute of 1871 through the voting rights enactments of 1957 and the supplemental measure adopted in 1960.

As the bill would eventually be drafted, it carried specific and detailed provisions for the protection of voting rights, plugging gaps in the previous legislation, proscribed discrimination in any privately owned facility which held out services to the general public, provided means of policing the facts of discrimination in employment, laid down specific guidelines for the integration of public schools and other public facilities—and provided belatedly for Federal intervention in any lawsuits which alleged denial of equal protection of the laws.[45] The power asserted in the statute was drastic, as the subcommittee of the House Judiciary Committee confessed; it was the only alternative to the situation which had frustrated the acts of 1957 and 1960— "discriminatory application and administration of apparently nondiscriminatory laws."[46]

In Title II of the statute—the so-called "public accommodations" section—it was fervently declared that no peacetime law had ever gone so far in affecting private individuals' property. The Senate Judiciary Committee agreed; but to lay restraints upon the social use of private property, it urged, was not to deny the use and enjoyment of the property itself. "The institution of private property exists for the purpose of enhancing the individual freedom and liberty of human beings," the Committee declared. "This institution assures that the individual need not be at the mercy of others, including government, in order to earn a livelihood and prosper from his individual efforts." But these valuable attributes of private property, it was averred, were not diminished by denying a right to use the property to discriminate or segregate by race.

To the calamity cries that Title II established a precedent for future Congressional laws extending the guarantee of equal accommodations, the Committee quoted one of its witnesses, Dean Erwin N. Griswold of Harvard Law School: "I don't think that we have to defend against every conceivable bill that Congress might some time have to consider. . . . There is a major national problem with respect to race. There is a problem which is on the doorstep of this Congress and which must be faced and resolved by this Congress with respect to race."[47]

In asserting a permanent governmental position on the question of racial equality, Congress at last had to come to terms with the ruling case law pronounced by the Court itself in the Civil Rights Cases of 1883. Justice Bradley for the majority in that decision had categorically declared: "It is state action of a particular character" that was prohibited by the Fourteenth Amendment. "Individual invasion of individual rights is not the subject-matter of the Amendment." Where state action could not be clearly established, wrongful acts of an individual were simply to be described as private wrongs actionable in private suit.[48]

For eight decades the "state action" theory had proved a bulwark against effective Federal prosecution in cases of private denial of individual rights; cast in terms of the constitutional law of the nineteenth and early twentieth centuries, it had been all but impregnable. To convert it from an obstacle to an implementation of the new civil rights law—and particularly Title II—Congress would rely upon the continued increase in sophistication of the new constitutionalism of the mid-century. Sixteen years earlier, the Vinson Court had begun the process in *Shelley v. Kraemer,* outlawing racial covenants in real estate transfers by declaring that the private agreements could only stand if state courts enforced them. "We have no doubt," said Vinson for a six-judge Court, "that there has been state action in these cases in the full and complete sense of the phrase."[49]

Only three years before, in 1961, Douglas for the Court majority had found invalid a franchise between a state agency and a private entrepreneur which failed to enjoin the private party to "discharge the responsibilities under the Fourteenth Amendment imposed upon the private enterprise as a consequence of state participation." For, said Douglas, "no state may effectively abdicate its responsibilities by either ignoring them or by merely failing to discharge them whatever the motive may be."[50] Finally, in 1963, the Court, speaking through Chief Justice Warren, had held a government agency chargeable with liability where it effected a policy of discrimination by private storekeepers by executive action.[51]

*   *   *

Thus the Civil Rights Act of 1964, in the course of its progress through Congress, had every judicial encouragement to prescribe bold action, yet, as the opposition fully understood, a definitive enactment by Congress—thereafter affirmatively supported by the Court—would all but close the ring of Federal power to protect individual liberties. The liberal-conservative dichotomy on this proposition, outside the special pleading of the Southern Congressmen, thus approached the relativism of the activist-restrained concepts of the Supreme Court. Northerners, Midwesterners and Far West representatives were thus divided between those who felt that the broad interpretation of the Fourteenth Amendment's "state action" principle justified an all-inclusive legislative statement based on that principle, and those (including the Attorney General) who preferred to rely on the commerce clause which, though more limited in its reach, was less conjectural in terms of established constitutional decision.[52]

Kennedy was prepared to accept the more limited conceptual approach for two reasons. In the first place he felt that the breadth of interpretation of the commerce clause since 1937 made reasonably certain the upholding of the statute on review in the courts. In the second place he believed that the more restrained application of Federal power through the commerce clause would reduce the opposition to the act as a whole in Congress. Lyndon Johnson, with his profound grasp of the politics of enacting legislation in general, concurred in this view, and thus the Congressional activists were neutralized by vigorous administration support of the plan to implement Title II through the commerce clause.[53]

After prolonged hearings, floor discussion and Southern filibuster, the Civil Rights Act of 1964 ultimately was passed by the Senate in June, by a vote of 73 to 27, and by the House in early July, by a vote of 289 to 126. The judicial test came swiftly; when the Court opened in October, two major cases were already before it—one involving an Atlanta motel and the other a Birmingham restaurant, each challenging the constitutionality of the government's enforcement of civil rights under the commerce clause. Justice Clark read the opinion of the Court in both cases.

In the *Heart of Atlanta Motel* case, the proprietors cited the holding in the Civil Rights Cases invalidating a section of the 1875 civil rights statute prohibiting discrimination in inns and other public accommodations. Clark dismissed this argument quickly. The Bradley opinion, he pointed out, specifically noted that the 1875 act was not "conceived" in terms of the commerce clause. This left the Court free to apply the concept of the commerce clause set out in *Gibbons v. Ogden,* at the same time taking into consideration the fact that the "sheer increase in volume of interstate traffic alone would give discriminatory practices which inhibit travel a far greater impact upon the nation's commerce than such practices had in the economy of another day."[54]

Since the essence of the motel business was the accommodation of interstate travelers, and since it was established law that "the power of Congress to promote interstate commerce also includes the power to regulate the local incidents thereof . . . which might have a substantial and harmful effect upon that commerce," the reach of Title II was readily established under the commerce clause.[55]

In *Katzenbach v. McClung* the proprietors of Ollie's Barbecue in Birmingham contended that, aside from the purchase of foods transported in interstate commerce, they had no direct or regular relationship to such commerce within the definition of the act. Clark pointed to the exhaustive debates on this proposition in the course of enactment of the statute, and concluded that Congress acted reasonably and within its constitutional powers in determining that the act should apply to racially discriminatory policies in selling food, however indirect the relationship of any single seller to the flow of interstate commerce might be. He stated categorically: "The Civil Rights Act of 1964, as here applied, we find to be plainly appropriate in the resolution of what the Congress found to be a national commercial problem of the first magnitude."[56]

Although the Court justified the expectations of the Congressional advocates of "restraint" in thus giving a broad effect to the commerce clause as applied to Title II, it indicated in a 1966 case that the Congressional activists would also have been supported in their approach. In *Evans v. Newton,* Douglas for the Court sustained a contention that a city in withdrawing from the trusteeship of a park in order to permit its private operators to segregate it could not divest the operation of a public character. "What is 'private' action and what is 'state' action is not always easy to determine," Douglas conceded. A privately operated recreational facility denominated as a club of limited membership, he further conceded, might presumably come within the "freedom of association" principle and thus be immune from constitutional challenge.

But a private park open to every white person was essentially public in nature, Douglas concluded, and thus was "so entwined with governmental policies or so impregnated with a governmental character as to become subject to the constitutional limitations placed upon state action."[57] The ultimate test of state action, Douglas stressed, could thus be stated: "When private individuals or groups are endowed by the state with powers or functions governmental in nature, they become agencies or instrumentalities of the state."[58]

*   *   *

The Civil Rights Act of 1964 was a step toward ultimate racial equality as momentous in the political arena as *Brown v. Board of Education* had been in the judicial. It remained for group action—always denominated nonviolent whether it was or not—to hasten the day of general public acceptance of the established principle. The summer of 1963 had marked a new technique in the Negro revolution, with the widespread practice of peaceful picketing, "marches," and "sit-ins" and their counterparts. They were said by many to have accelerated—and by others to have exacerbated—the circumstances in which Congress debated and eventually framed the 1964 statute.

Was organized protest of this type protected by the "freedom of assembly" provision in the First Amendment, or was it even to be considered another form of free expression? Conversely, did it contain within itself the germinating seeds of anarchy? With such questions, a new dimension of constitutional dialogue opened in 1965 with a succession of cases on the right of demonstration.

A quarter of a century earlier, a major group of First Amendment decisions had been handed down by the Court with reference to both Jehovah's Witnesses and extremist political groups, seeking to draw a line between freedom of expression and assembly on the one hand and incitement to disorder on the other. Despite Douglas' proposition that one of the elemental functions of free speech was to invite disagreement, the Court majority had groped for a jurisprudential principle which would accommodate both the literal guarantees of the First Amendment and the police power in the preservation of public peace. The result had been a somewhat academic provision that where no substantial obstruction to public use of public ways and facilities was involved, religious or political advocates were to be undisturbed in the exercise of their rights.[59]

These constitutional pronouncements of the 1940's did not seem to fit the practical situation of the 1960's. Were organized mass protests and demonstrations different from passive distribution of religious literature or vehement exhortation from the political soap box? What was the point at which, in the legal view, an assembly changed into a mob, and civil disobedience crossed the wavering line dividing it from insurrection? As early as 1951 the Court had encountered questions like these in *Feiner v. New York*, where a six-to-three majority opinion by Chief Justice Vinson upheld the arrest of an inflammatory speaker whose words provoked a threat of riot. "It is one thing to say that the police cannot be used as an instrument for the suppression of unpopular views," Vinson declared, "and another to say that, when as here the speaker passes the bounds of argument or persuasion and undertakes incitement to riot, they are powerless to prevent a breach of the peace."[60]

Black's dissent in *Feiner* had contended that the police function should be to prevent the opposing factions from coming to blows while continuing to defend the speaker's right to be heard. The next year the Court by a five-to-four majority upheld an Illinois "group libel" statute fixing criminal liability for published defamation of minority groups. Despite his sympathy for maligned minorities, Black protested against state action which tended to narrow the right of expression which historically had been the measure of the degree of democracy in effect, and Douglas had added a separate protest: "Free speech, free press, free exercise of religion are placed separate and apart" in the constitutional framework; "they are above and beyond the police power; they are not subject to regulation in the manner of factories, slums, apartment houses, production of oil and the like."[61]

In 1963, the Court was confronted with a test of constitutional absolutes of the Black-Douglas view in reference to mass Negro demonstrations. Rejecting (except for Clark's dissent) the contention that the demonstration in a South Carolina case amounted to obstruction of public ways, Justice Stewart for the Court declared: "The circumstances in this case reflect an exercise of rights in their most pristine and classic form." Aggrieved by state segregation laws in general, the Court held, a Negro group was taking a fundamentally democratic means of making its desires known to state authorities who were in position to remedy the laws. Where the evidence showed no violence, and where the demonstration took the form of a "religious harangue" and the loud singing of the national anthem, the majority declined to sustain convictions which the South Carolina supreme court had itself confessed were "not susceptible of exact definition."[62]

As demonstrations continued, with varying circumstances and varying strategies of local law enforcement officials, the cases for review continued to come before the Court. Two Louisiana cases in 1965 offered the next medium for a judicial attempt to pronounce a workable rule on the subject. The first case involved a breach of the peace statute and a related law on obstructing public passages, while the companion case involved the same defendant in an alleged violation of a law forbidding demonstrations within a minimum distance of public buildings. The incidents arose out of a demonstration organized by the Congress of Racial Equality in Baton Rouge. Mere noise at such public demonstrations, the Court declared, could not be made the basis of a criminal prosecution which would have the effect of cutting off constitutionally permissible expression. Laws creating liability for obstructing public ways, the opinion continued, are unenforceable where the determination of what constituted obstruction was left to the discretion of local officers. In the case of the third Louisiana statute, the Court majority held that local officers had assented to the demonstration at a stated distance from the Courthouse and could not thereafter use the refusal to disperse as a violation of the law.[63]

Black, Clark, Harlan and White concurred in part and dissented in part; Black, for all his absolutist views on the First Amendment, conceded that the state law on demonstrations near a public building was based on valid considerations of public order and applied to all persons indiscriminately. All four argued further that the statute against public obstruction was reasonably susceptible of construction which would make it non-discriminatory. Thus, in the two cases of *Cox v. Louisiana,* a distinct ambivalence with reference to the law of public demonstrations had manifested itself.[64]

The divisions of opinion on the issue were manifested in another Louisiana case in 1966, in which a plurality of the Court—Fortas, speaking for himself and Douglas and Warren—held that the authorities could not prosecute Negro demonstrators for refusing to leave the premises of a segregated public library even when, in conformity with library etiquette, their demonstration was silent. Brennan concurred separately, protesting that the "overbreadth" of the local statutes should have led the Court to declare them unconstitutional, while White in a separate concurrence felt that the demand to the demonstrators to leave the library was itself evidence of discrimination.[65]

Black, speaking for himself and the other dissenters in *Cox,* contended that the Louisiana law could properly distinguish between the absolute freedom to use public ways for demonstrations and the limited freedom, applicable to all, to use public facilities of limited purpose. First Amendment freedoms, Black declared, did not "guarantee to any person the right to use someone else's property, even that owned by government and dedicated to other purposes, as a stage to express dissident ideas."[66]

Black's view prevailed in a Florida case the same year, in which a five-to-four majority affirmed convictions of demonstrators who refused to leave the premises of a jail where they had come to protest the prior arrest of a number of their fellows. To insist, as the demonstrators did, that a jail was public property on which they could exercise their right of protest, said Black, was to assume "that people who want to propagandize protests or views have a constitutional right to do so whenever and however and wherever they please." There was a limit: "The United States Constitution does not forbid a state to control the use of its own property for its own lawful nondiscriminatory purpose."[67]

*　*　*

In the series of cases flowing from the Civil Rights Act of 1964, the Court had sought to identify the reasonable limits to both private and public action within the public policy enunciated by the statute in general. While the later cases tended to warn against unreasonable assertion of their new-found powers by minority groups, when there were reasonable alternatives for the expression of their views and the advocacy of their rights, the problem of ensuring the franchise to all citizens remained to plague the law enforcement process. The "ingenuity and dedication of those determined to circumvent the guarantees of the Fifteenth Amendment," as the House Judiciary Committee put it in 1965, not only thwarted each Congressional effort at implementation but destroyed any remaining argument against Federal surveillance of the entire voting process.[68]

The statutory steps in 1957, 1960 and in parts of the 1964 law had simply failed to root out the evil of voter discrimination. On the other hand, the great bold step taken by the legislation of 1964, projecting the Federal government permanently into the arena of civil rights of all individuals, now made logical the final action on the specific matter of the franchise. Ironically enough, the constitutional authority had existed since 1870; the Fifteenth Amendment declared unequivocally: "The right of citizens of the United States to vote shall not be denied or abridged by the United States or by any State on account of race, color or previous condition of servitude." The accompanying section had also expressly stated: "The Congress shall have power to enforce this article by appropriate legislation." Yet, said the House Committee, the "historic struggle for the realization of this constitutional guarantee . . . reveals both the variety of means used to bar Negro voting and the durability of such discriminatory policies."[69]

Throughout the decades from 1870 to 1960, the tradition of state sovereignty had operated powerfully to deter Congressional action for which the Fifteenth Amendment provided plenary authority. The time had come to assert that authority, the House Committee declared: "The prevailing conditions in those areas where the bill will operate offer ample justification for Congressional action because there is little basis for supposing that the States and subdivisions affected will themselves remedy the situation." To permit the states and their political subdivisions to continue to flout the constitutional guarantee was simply to abdicate the responsibilities of national government.[70]

"The inadequacy of existing laws is attributable to both the intransigence of local officials and dilatory tactics, two factors which have largely neutralized years of litigating effort by the Department of Justice," the Committee report concluded. Thus spurred, Congress at length enacted a statute which asserted the authority originally created by the Fifteenth Amendment: the Voting Rights Act of 1965 authorized the Attorney General to institute proceedings to secure appointment of examiners under the Civil Rights Commission to inquire into discrimination in voter registration, tests and other devices for qualification to vote, and to suspend any electoral procedures which denied or abridged any voting rights under the Fifteenth Amendment. In effect, the law placed all state electoral machinery under the surveillance of the Justice Department and the Federal judiciary for a five-year period, after which the state could petition the District Court for the District of Columbia for a determination that the discriminatory procedures had been permanently eliminated.[71]

To the contention of the state of South Carolina that the 1965 statute represented a revolutionary use of the lawmaking power of Congress, Chief Justice Warren spoke for an eight-to-one majority. "This may have been an uncommon exercise of Congressional power, as South Carolina contends," Warren observed, "but the Court has recognized that exceptional conditions can justify legislative measures not otherwise appropriate." The fact that the law specifically struck down certain registration practices in three states— Louisiana, Mississippi and South Carolina—as well as partially invalidating local election laws in certain other states was justified, said Warren, by the finding of Federal courts that "substantial voting discrimination" was effected by means of these laws in circumvention of the Fifteenth Amendment.[72]

In another case involving the Voting Rights Act of 1965, a seven-to-two majority of the Court upheld the statute against a New York law requiring a reading knowledge of English as a condition of voting. The effect of the state law being to disfranchise large numbers of Puerto Ricans who read only Spanish and the purpose of the Federal statute being to ensure voting rights to all citizens of the United States, said Brennan for the Court, the Federal statute had to take precedence.[73]

To protect the civil rights of its citizens, the Federal government may prosecute private persons as well as state officers where, in concert with the officers, the private persons are acting under color of law. Thus Fortas pronounced the opinion of the Court in setting aside a trial court's action in dismissing indictments against private citizens joined with local officers as defendants against charges of murdering three civil rights workers in Mississippi. Whether the Constitution created a cause of action by one group of private citizens against another group of private citizens—and whether unspecified rights of individuals could be brought within the scope of constitutional protection because universally recognized as rights—were questions which were dealt with ambivalently by the Court as the principle of Federal protection came before it in continually varying forms.[74]

Certainly the net effect of the decade of adjudication after the historic decisions in *Brown* was to establish that anything in state law or local custom which tended to discriminate between racial groups or individual members of different races was suspect. The "mere 'equal application' of a statute containing racial classifications" was not enough to exempt it from the prohibitions of the Fourteenth Amendment, said the Court in invalidating Virginia's miscegenation statute. The basic principle of modern constitutionalism, said the Chief Justice, is the invalidity of "measures which restrict the rights of citizens on account of race."[75]

Since the citizens whose rights were being asserted were the citizens of the United States as defined in the Fourteenth Amendment, and since the rights in the course of the numerous decisions arising under this proposition tended continually to broaden, the constitutional concepts established in the segregation cases reached far beyond the racial question. *Brown v. Board of Education* had sounded the keynote of a totally new Federalism; cases epitomized in *Baker v. Carr* and *Gideon v. Wainwright* would fill in essential details.

14/Restatement of the Bill of Rights

W ITH THE ELECTION OF John F. Kennedy in 1960, both the nation and the Supreme Court entered a new phase of history. The Kennedy campaign theme, and the tenor of his soon-renowned inaugural address—to "get the country moving again"—was a call for a return to the activism of past Democratic administrations. Coming as it did after six years of crucial struggle between Congress and the Court while the White House remained conspicuously uninvolved, the Kennedy program invited a fresh campaign for broadly defined social objectives in both the legislature and the judiciary. The unprecedented appointment of the President's brother, Robert, as Attorney General signalled the determination of the incoming administration to continue—and, indeed, to accelerate—the vigorous enforcement of Federal law which had been the most creditable feature of the Eisenhower years.

Under Robert Kennedy the Department of Justice underwent a swift and sweeping liberalization; Brownell and Rogers, for all their zeal for civil rights, had done little to defuse the program of radical surveillance which had been built up in the cold war hysteria of the fifties. Now the Attorney General took steps to bring the subversive-control procedures into balance by taking in the "Welcome" sign for informers and malicious cranks who had become accustomed to "making false or irresponsible charges, not only against their neighbors, but against courageous teachers and public officials." The era of militant conformity began to pass.[1]

For the judiciary, the seeds of change for most of the sixties were planted and nurtured in the brief three years of Kennedy's Presidency. Under the new Attorney General, whose persistent diminutive of "Bobby" belied his forcefulness (his enemies called it his ruthlessness) and maturity, it was evident that the civil rights program would take on added vigor, but his reputation as attorney for the Senate committee investigating racketeering suggested that this area of law enforcement would also be expanded. The Attorney General was, in addition, deeply concerned with another subject—the rights of indigent defendants to competent legal counsel—which would speed the day when the much-criticized rule in *Betts v. Brady* would be superseded.[2]

Several other members of the new administration would play their own roles in the judicial history of the decade. Arthur Goldberg of Illinois, labor lawyer and leader in the AFL-CIO, had been named Secretary of Labor; Byron White, former Rhodes scholar and brilliant attorney, was appointed Deputy Attorney General; Thurgood Marshall, general counsel for the NAACP and one of the architects of *Brown v. Board of Education,* would soon be named to the Court of Appeals. Not the least important member of the executive family was Vice-President Johnson, whose remarkable handling of the anti-Court bills in the summer of 1958 had turned back the century's most concerted drive against judicial independence. When *Gideon v. Wainwright* at last overturned *Betts,* the case would be argued by Johnson's close personal friend, Washington attorney Abe Fortas.[3]

Justice Whittaker resigned in the spring of 1962; his five years on the bench had been characterized by technically acceptable workmanship but no inspired pronouncements on the law, as he had clung to the pedestrian formula of "reading the law for an understanding of its meaning," and applying this meaning to the facts of the case. A much more substantial loss came in the summer of the same year when rapidly deteriorating health compelled Justice Frankfurter to resign. In his twenty-three years of tenure, he had contributed an enduring counterpoint to the great theme of modern constitutionalism which had been composed by himself and his fellow Titans. Where Holmes and Brandeis, and even Cardozo, had been fated to develop a jurisprudence which for most of their tenures had represented a minority view, Frankfurter had had the good fortune to be on the Court in an epochal seminal era, an era in great measure created by his own opinions.*

Thus President Kennedy found himself presented, within a few months, with two opportunities to place men of his choice on the high tribunal. He had several definite candidates in mind: White, who had Bobby's strong recommendation; Paul Freund of Harvard, acknowledged as one of the country's leading authorities on the Constitution; Goldberg; and Judge William H. Hastie of the Third Circuit. The young Chief Executive, only just launched upon the second year of what could reasonably be expected to be an eight-year administration, indicated to his close advisers that he anticipated being able to appoint all of these men to the bench in due course.

At the moment, to replace Whittaker, he decided on White; having brought so many Harvard men into his administration, he felt it impolitic

---

*Cf. Ch. 9.

to tap Freund so soon. Goldberg he wanted badly to keep in the Cabinet, and as for Hastie, it "was just too early" to nominate a Negro, however competent. When Frankfurter retired, the same considerations still militated against the selection of either Freund or Hastie—and thus Kennedy was logically compelled to choose Goldberg.[4]

Although these were to be Kennedy's only appointments to the Court, they had the immediate effect of strengthening the activist bloc. In both the reapportionment and right-to-counsel cases which were soon to come on for decision, Whittaker and Frankfurter by their past records could have been expected to support a conservative position. In the reapportionment cases, in particular, both White and Goldberg were consistently aligned with Warren, Black and Douglas—and, concurrently in most instances, with Brennan and Clark.* As for the two appointments made by President Johnson through 1968—Fortas for Goldberg, who had been drafted for the Ambassadorship to the United Nations, and Marshall for Clark, who retired —these also were considered prospects for continuing the activist program which had enjoyed a full renaissance in the sixties.[5]

*   *   *

Kennedy had come to the Presidency with definite agenda, although his critics complained that he had none too clear a plan for implementing them. The conservatives in Congress were less vociferous than they had been in the critical years from 1953 to 1958, but they would have to be taken into account in any legislative program. Having accepted the fact of recurrent international crises as a fundamental of contemporary history, the American people had begun to cultivate a passivity toward both domestic and world affairs in general. Yet the new President sensed that a stable economy in the context of mid-century technology could not be a static economy, while the first two years of his administration were to teach him and the nation a great deal about foreign affairs in the mid-century context. The debacle of the Bay of Pigs and the Berlin wall were substantial reverses for American adventurism in diplomacy, but it was the Russo-Cuban missile crisis which warned the United States that the thermonuclear age required a permanent capability for instant response to challenge.

Thus Kennedy defined the New Frontier of the sixties: a society which had to be kinetic to survive must continually seek affirmatively to accommodate needs of various segments of that society as they developed. His successive messages to Congress in the winter of 1961 reflected this conviction. In a population now dominated by young adults, such matters as Federal aid to education, housing subsidies, job training and community development were of high priority. In a population with a lengthening life span for increasing numbers of individuals, improved Social Security and government-sponsored medical assistance claimed a priority virtually of the same level.

---

*Cf. Ch. 15.

Urban renewal or resuscitation was vital to a people who now had moved to cities and towns by a substantial majority. Stronger civil rights legislation was an inescapable consequence of the Negro revolution and the settled fact of Federal enforcement of the individual's constitutional guarantees.

Through careful timing and a willingness to accept half a loaf rather than receive none, the Kennedy administration in its first two years was able to win Congressional approval for a striking list of new legislative programs. "Ask what you can do for your country," had been the new President's clarion appeal to American idealism, and the Peace Corps bill provided a dramatic medium for response. The Western Hemisphere—despite the nihilism of Cuba—represented a neglected rampart of world security; the legislative implementation of the Alliance for Progress was a hopeful attempt to shore up this rampart. A housing act, increased minimum wage benefits, broadened community health services and a number of statutes on various aspects of child welfare were also approved.[6]

Two more Amendments to the Constitution in the early sixties reflected the Federal commitment to a broadening of the electoral franchise. The Twenty-third Amendment, after years of agitation by residents of the District of Columbia, had eventually been approved by the Eighty-sixth Congress and submitted to the people in June, 1960. Two and a half months after Kennedy's inauguration it was certified as having been ratified by vote in the necessary thirty-eight states. While not giving the District the status of a state, the Amendment afforded residents a vote in Presidential elections and yet preserved "the unique status of the District as the seat of Federal government under the exclusive legislative control of Congress."[7]

The Twenty-fourth Amendment was an essential part of the broad civil rights objectives of the Kennedy administration—and as such aroused a flurry of conservative oratory on Capitol Hill in the spring and summer of 1962. Efforts to abolish poll taxes in national elections had been made sporadically since 1939; the taxes themselves had existed in many states for more than ninety years as a means of limiting the Negro franchise which the Fifteenth Amendment had purported to affirm. Although only five states now maintained a poll tax, proposals to legislate it out of existence in national elections had been fought by Southerners over the years as an invasion of state powers over elections in general. Alternatively, the argument had been advanced that Congress lacked the power to legislate on the subject of Presidential elections, which was set out in Article II of the Constitution; a statutory provision qualifying the electoral right defined therein, it was contended, would violate the Constitution itself.[8]

Specious, or at least tenuous, as the argument was, the liberals undertook to settle the matter through a proposed amendment, and evaded the threat of having it buried in the Senate judiciary committee by introducing it as an amendment to an innocuous proposal to establish a National Monument in the original New York home of Alexander Hamilton. Senator Russell of Georgia promptly challenged the deviousness of this maneuver.

Not only did it join two unrelated matters in a single joint resolution, he pointed out, but it cast the amendment in the form of a legislative bill which would entail Presidential signature to give it effect. Thus the anti-poll tax forces were circumventing the explicit constitutional procedure for proposing amendments.[9]

However valid Russell's point was, the Senate liberals managed to override it. As matters turned out, they simply amended the preamble (the Hamilton National Monument) to eliminate it, changed the title after the measure was approved by the Senate, and thus left it as an orthodox proposal for amending the Constitution to be submitted to the states.[10] Five months later it passed the House of Representatives—and eighteen months after that, in February, 1964—it had become a part of the Constitution.

*   *   *

The judicial containment of the loyalty-security obsession of the fifties progressed steadily in the sixties, even though the margin of the majority was usually a narrow one. In 1960, by a seven-to-two majority, the Court invalidated an Arkansas statute requiring that each public school teacher file an annual affidavit listing all organizations to which he had belonged or contributed in the preceding five years. The law made no provision for keeping the information confidential or for procedural safeguards in the case of a question of qualification raised by the affidavit. Such arbitrary interference with freedom of association, said Justice Stewart for the majority, was all the more notorious when an employee serves subject to the slightest whim of his superiors which may occasion dismissal "without bringing charges, without notice, without a hearing, without affording an opportunity to explain."[11]

The bar association cases, which had excited so much criticism in Congress in 1956-58, continued to sustain the restrictive position in a five-to-four decision in 1961, with Harlan arguing that since the practice of law was a privilege subject to public license, an inquiry into subversive associations was proper. Black, for himself, Brennan, Douglas and Warren, dissented from such an attempted "balancing" of the security interest of the state against the absolute of the First Amendment.[12] Then, in 1964, the Court in *Malloy v. Hogan*—speaking through Brennan—completed the process of writing the Fifth Amendment into the Fourteenth. What *Mapp v. Ohio* had done to the rule on unreasonable search and seizure, *Malloy* now did for "the right of a person to remain silent unless he chooses to speak in the unfettered exercise of his own will, and to suffer no penalty . . . for such silence."[13]

Three years later the Court applied the rule in *Malloy* to the disbarment cases and thus substantially disposed of the issues which had first been raised in the several bar association cases.[14]

A Florida anti-subversive statute requiring state employees to swear that they had never "knowingly lent their aid, support, advice, counsel or influence to the Communist Party," when the Communist Party had in the recent past been a legal political entity in the state, was so vague as to threaten employees with unintentional perjury and was thus held invalid by the Court.[15] In another Florida case a five-to-four majority speaking through Justice Goldberg reversed a contempt citation for the NAACP for refusal to disclose its membership lists on the state's claim that it intended to check them for Communists. Qualifying its *Barenblatt* holding, the Court now held that a defendant could not be found in contempt unless the prosecution established a direct relationship between him and the Communist Party.[16] Applying substantially the same rationale as in the first Florida case, the Court the following year held invalid two loyalty oaths of the state of Washington.[17]

Moving into the field of labor law, in 1965 another five-to-four majority read by Chief Justice Warren held invalid a section of the Labor-Management Reporting and Disclosure Act of 1959 which made it a crime for a Communist to serve as an officer or an agent of a labor union. This, said the Chief Justice, violated the clause against bills of attainder in the Constitution, although he then proceeded to spell out for Congress an acceptable method of achieving the same objective in the labor statutes:

"In a number of decisions," Warren declared, "this Court has pointed out the fallacy of the suggestion that membership in the Communist party, or any other political organization, can be regarded as an alternative, but equivalent, expression for a list of undesirable characteristics." By categorically identifying all members of a group as being under a civil disability —with criminal sanctions—by virtue of their membership in the group, Congress had indulged in legislative trial and conviction. The preferred procedure, and the only constitutional one, said the Court, was to stipulate the activities which disqualified an individual in these situations and leave to the courts the determination of the facts of liability.[18]

Although in a case the following year the majority denied that this decision in *United States v. Brown* invalidated the 1950 case of *American Communications Association v. Douds* which upheld a similar section of the Taft-Hartley Act, Black and Douglas in a concurring opinion declared that it did just that. Where the current decision invalidated a section of a statute similar in language and purpose to a related antecedent statute, they argued, the only logical conclusion was that the later decision had overruled the earlier.[19]

In the spring of 1966, the Court sought to bring to a final restatement the loyalty oath problem into which it had injected itself with the *Slochower* case ten years earlier. In *Elfbrandt v. Russell* a five-to-four majority speaking through Douglas sought finally to dispose of the guilt-by-association fixation of the McCarthy era. Holding unconstitutional an Arizona law which qualified a teachers' oath by a legislative declaration of presumption of perjury for any who took the oath while maintaining any Communist association, Douglas asserted the state's responsibility to distinguish between guilty knowledge (*scienter*) and "guiltless knowing behavior." Legislation which "applies to membership without the 'specific intent to further the illegal aims of the organization' infringes unnecessarily upon protected freedoms. It rests on the doctrine of 'guilt by association' which had no place here."[20]

In a unanimous decision the Court upheld the right of a Negro pacifist to a seat in the Georgia legislature despite his opposition to the Federal government's military policy in Viet Nam. To require members of a legislature to swear allegiance to the state and national constitutions, said Warren, is not to be interpreted in such a manner as to penalize the individual member's right to express critical views on public policy.[21] In a five-to-four decision in 1967 Brennan for the Court found inapplicable to defendants a New York statute on subversive associations; "even though the governmental purpose be legitimate and substantial, that purpose cannot be pursued by means that broadly stifle fundamental personal liberties when the end can be more narrowly achieved."[22]

*   *   *

First Amendment freedoms—whether or not the Court had committed itself to Black's concept of absolutes—were affirmed with increasing breadth in the sixties. With reference to the associational disabilities of the Communists, the start was slower; in two 1961 cases, a narrow majority sustained the Smith Act against charges of unconstitutionality by reverting to the practice of the fifties, of construing the statute narrowly. Harlan, for the majority in *Scales v. United States,* construed the clause in the act proscribing membership in the Communist party as being limited to "active" members with a "specific intent" to implement the party's revolutionary aims. *Scales* sustained the courts below in finding such "active" membership and "specific intent," while the companion case of *Noto v. United States* reversed a conviction where the record failed to sustain these facts.[23]

Black, Brennan, Douglas and Warren dissented in *Scales* and concurred in *Noto,* but in each case they urged that the unconstitutionality of the membership proscription should have been declared.[24] The same division of the Court appeared in a third 1961 case, arising under the complementary Subversive Activities Control Act of 1950 requiring the Communist party to register as a Communist-action organization under section 7 of the statute.[25] Black's opinion stressed that "banning of an association because it advocates hated ideas . . . marks a fateful moment in the history of a free country." The statute as a whole, Black insisted, was unconstitutional on three grounds— the requirement for self-incrimination, the elements of a bill of attainder, and the deprivation of due process.[26]

In a companion case in 1961, the general purposes of the statute were upheld against charges of unconstitutionality, but in a series of cases in 1964, 1965 and 1966 the Court substantially reduced the scope of the law. As it turned out, it was the self-incrimination element, rather than First Amendment absolutes, which proved to be the Achilles heel in the government's cases. The Court of Appeals for the District of Columbia set the ball in motion by reversing the conviction of the party for failure to register under the 1950 act. Since an individual representing the party would have to register for it, and the government "had the burden of showing that a volunteer was available" to discharge this duty at the risk of self-incrimination, failure of the government to carry this burden made the conviction invalid.[27]

Although the Supreme Court declined to review the decision on the question of self-incrimination, holding that it was premature, the stage was manifestly set for testing the act on this question. The opportunity arose in the 1965 term when the Court unanimously (with White not participating) declared that an order of the Subversive Activities Control Board requiring individuals to register as members of the Communist party violated their privilege against self-incrimination. The absence of a stipulation in the act that this registration would not constitute a basis for prosecution of the individuals was a fatal flaw, said Brennan, but even with such a stipulation the requirement could not be validated because the information could obviously be used as a "lead" for other evidence on which to prosecute.[28]

Having thus all but nullified the 1950 statute's registration clause, the Court proceeded to nullify the act's attempted ban on travel by Communist party members. Citing the *Noto* case as finally prevailing over *Scales*, Justice Goldberg spoke for a six-to-three majority in affirming the Fifth Amendment protection for individual rights. To deny the freedom of innocent travel as punishment for association with a radical group whose unlawful aims the individual might not support, Goldberg declared, was a substantial abridgment of constitutional liberty.[29]

*   *   *

The rapid advance of the libertarian view, after the ambivalence of decisions in this subject-area in the late fifties, aroused fresh alarm among Congressional conservatives. In the spring of 1962 Senator Eastland delivered an elaborate speech in which he cited "the enormous total of seventy cases or more involving Communist or subversive activities in one form or another" heard by the Warren Court in its first seven and a half years. "Forty-six of these decisions," Eastland declared, "have sustained the position advocated by the Communists, and twenty-four have been to the contrary."

Eastland then proceeded to analyze the behavior of individual Justices. As to Black, in his record since his appointment in 1937, said the Senator, it was "impossible for a man to demonstrate greater consistency than he has evidenced": in 102 cases which had been tabulated—and the speech was massively buttressed with tables—Black had "supported the position urged upon the Court by the Communist party or its sympathizers exactly 102 times." Douglas' score was reckoned at 97 to 3, Warren's at 62 to 3, Brennan's at 49 to 2 and Frankfurter's at 69 to 34. Against the libertarians, Eastland cited Clark's relative conservatism as 21 "pro-Communist" to 61 against, Harlan's at 30 to 35, Whittaker's at 12 to 30 and Stewart's at 6 to 14.[30]

To Senator Jacob Javits' query as to "who sets the criterion that these are pro- and anti-Communist decisions?" Eastland replied: "Any lawyer with any sense at all could do it. Intelligent lawyers have done it." Upon Javits' further inquiry, Eastland said his own staff lawyers had made the compilation. Nevertheless, the speech by the chairman of the Senate Judiciary Committee—and particularly its name-by-name attribution of ideological decisions to individual Justices—was intended to make headlines. While the Mississippian's address was in the nature of an incipient filibuster against the Kennedy administration's voting rights bill, it provided an official record which could be reprinted and widely circulated by Court haters throughout the land. The following day, in an effort to refute the charges, Javits himself took the floor.[31]

"Unless one is a careful lawyer and knows the cases," Javits pointed out, "this kind of statement has a tendency to confirm in certain minds and to have them accept this kind of tommyrot." His ,listeners knew the target of the reference; for several years a growing volume of doctrinaire condemnation of the Supreme Court had been spreading through the land, largely through the efforts of the John Birch Society. At its Indianapolis meeting in December, 1958 the supporters of Boston candymaker Robert Welch's obsessive idea of a monolithic anti-Communist movement heard him propose the formal impeachment of the Chief Justice of the United States. Two years later the radical right avidly circulated a small book entitled, *Nine Men Against America*, reviving the reactionaries' standard complaints against Warren as governor for supporting the United Nations, Social Security, government housing and the Fair Employment Practices Commission.[32]

The Birchers' movement might have died the death of many previous crank movements but for two factors—the zeal of the segregationists to make their Court opposition respectable by casting it in terms of anti-Communism, and the abundant financial support coming, in one observer's words, from "Texas oil wealth, Bible Belt collection plates, and the checkbooks of California's proverbial old ladies in tennis shoes."[33]

As the libertarian decisions of the Court continued—climaxed, after the desegregation cases, by reapportionment and an uncompromising assertion of defendants' rights—the raging against the Court steadily (and systematically) increased. Its geographic orientation was striking: in California, Texas and the Deep South, road signs blatantly shouted a demand to "Impeach Earl Warren," and bumper stickers urged citizens to "Put God Back in the Schools" and to "Support Your Local Police Force." Now, in 1962, the Senate moderates felt it essential to refute the Eastland allegations lest the ranting extremists of the land seem to have an uncontested Congressional charge to support their own irrationality.[34]

Senator Thomas Kuchel of California, referring scornfully to "the pitiful, puny and highly regrettable attempt . . . made by one of our colleagues to slur and to slander the Chief Justice . . . and his colleagues," described it as "a shocking and an evil charge," only exceeded by the Birchers' previous charges against Eisenhower, Dulles and others in the past and current administrations. "It is a dreadful disservice to the cause of America and to the cause of security of our country," Kuchel declared, "for anyone to attempt to undermine our people's faith in any of our national governmental institutions."[35]

Humphrey of Minnesota joined with his colleague in calling the Eastland canards "a disservice to the cause of constitutional government" which "cannot be justified." Javits then brought the focus of the defense back to the real elements in the attack: "The so-called radical right of this country is a serious problem. . . The [Eastland] statement is not merely an isolated one. Most unfortunately, it falls upon ground which is being furrowed by many in this country." Bush of Connecticut added that if the Court were actually concerned with whether its objective judgments followed or opposed the Communist line, each Justice "would have to go to the Communist party headquarters to find out what the Communist line is before he started to reach a decision," a process he described as "the most ridiculous proposition I have ever heard." The proper approach to unacceptable judicial decisions, added Keating of New York, was by legislative redefinition of interpreted statutes rather than by a ridiculous attempt "to set up a category of pro-Communist and anti-Communist decisions."[36]

The Congressional atmosphere had changed since the cold war hysteria of the fifties. After Eastland's demagoguery and the refutation of the moderates, the Senate moved on to other business. Among small minds and in small towns of the land, however, the poison of unreasoning hatred of the Court persisted.

*   *   *

Meantime, the Court continued its affirmation of First Amendment guarantees. With reference to freedom of expression, its major decisions fell into two groups—those concerning commentary on matters of public interest and those concerning the proper limits to freedom to be effected by obscenity statutes.

New York Times v. Sullivan was actually a by-product of the developments in the Negro revolution, but like much of the jurisprudence of desegregation it had far-reaching effects in other areas. The cause of the action for libel was a full-page advertisement in the *Times* over the signature of a "Committee to Defend Martin Luther King and the Struggle for Freedom in the South," in which a city commissioner of Montgomery, Alabama alleged that he had been defamed. Although the plaintiff had not been identified by name in the advertisement, and the errors of fact in the statements in the text were minor errors of detail, the trial court accepted a verdict for the plaintiff and awarded damages of $500,000 against the committee and the newspaper.

In a divided decision the Supreme Court reversed the judgment on appeal from the Alabama supreme court. Justice Brennan at the outset rejected the contention that the state decision was not reviewable because it was a private suit without state action; the fact that the case was brought under a statute* complementary to common law libel would have been sufficient to support an appeal under the Fourteenth Amendment, Brennan declared. Nor was the Court barred from applying the First Amendment merely because the defamation concerned paid advertising rather than editorial matter. To uphold this contention "would discourage newspapers from carrying 'editorial advertisements' of this type and so might shut off an important outlet for the promulgation of information and ideas by persons who do not themselves have access to publishing facilities—who wish to exercise their freedom of speech even though they are not members of the press."

Libel, Brennan went on, could "claim no talismanic immunity from constitutional limitations," but an allegation of libel had to be considered "against the background of a profound national commitment to the principle that debate on public issues should be uninhibited, robust, and wide open, and that it may well include vehement, caustic, and sometimes unpleasantly sharp attacks on government and public officials." The constitutional rule, said the Court majority, "prohibits a public official from recovering damages for a defamatory falsehood relating to his official conduct unless he proves that the statement was made with 'actual malice'—that is, with knowledge that it was false or with reckless disregard of whether it was false or not."[37]

Two years after *Sullivan*, Brennan again spoke for the Court in extending the "public official rule" to licensees of public agencies. Douglas, concurring in part, suggested that the test should be "public issues" rather than "public officials," since it was the valid public interest in the issues which should be balanced against the injury to the individual.[38] In 1967 Brennan undertook to accommodate the Douglas proposition while extending the *Sullivan* principle to an invasion of privacy action. "Exposure of the self to others in varying degrees is a concomitant of life in a civilized community. The risk of this exposure is an essential incident of life in a society which places a primary value on freedom of speech and of press. . . . We create a grave risk of serious impairment of the indispensable service of a free press in a free society if we saddle the press with the impossible burden of verifying to a certainty the facts associated in news articles with a person's name, picture or portrait, particularly as related to non-defamatory matter."[39]

How far the *Sullivan* rule could be extended into the area of private suits for defamation or other injury to reputation was disputed between the Justices in a later 1967 case. The decision in this instance, in fact, included two cases—one by an athletic director of the University of Georgia against the *Saturday Evening Post*, the other by a retired military officer against the Associated Press. In sustaining a modified award of damages against the magazine and reversing the judgment against the news service, Harlan gave

---

*The statute provided for evidence of retraction of an allegedly defamatory publication as a condition of mitigation of damages.

the officially denominated opinion of the Court, for himself and three Associates; the remaining Justices joined in Warren's "concurring" opinion.

Harlan contended that the *New York Times* rule was not appropriate for libel actions in which public officials were not involved, and that the ordinary tort standards of reasonable or due care were sufficient for determining the issues without reference to constitutional issues. A "public figure" who is not a public official, in his view should be able to recover damages for a defamatory falsehood on a showing of highly unreasonable conduct. In the case of a well-known sports figure accused of conspiring to "fix" an intercollegiate football game, the manifestly dangerous implications in the article and the relatively lessened pressure of publication deadlines added to the evidence supporting "a finding of highly unreasonable conduct." In the case of General Walker and his alleged participation in the organized resistance of Federal marshals' efforts to ensure enrollment of a Negro at the University of Mississippi, the instantaneous demands for news by the public, the reports of eyewitnesses and the prior publicity given to Walker's statements concerning the controversy showed the wire service to have acted reasonably in accepting the correspondent's report.[40]

Warren, for whom the *Sullivan* rule offered the most practical standard for limiting liability in the interest of public information, argued that "although they are not subject to the restraints of the political process, 'public figures,' like 'public officials,' often play an influential role in ordering society." Since, in the modern world, distinctions between public and private actions had become blurred and a "blending of positions and power" made it possible for many persons out of office to influence public affairs through the continuing public interest in their activities and views, the Chief Justice held that the *Sullivan* rule should apply. Under this rule, the holding of the Court in the two current cases would be the same, but the rule itself would continue as "an important safeguard for the rights of the press and public to inform and be informed on matters of legitimate interest."[41]

The net effect of the libel cases of the sixties, from *Sullivan* to the cases of *Curtis Publishing Co. v. Butts* and *Associated Press v. Walker*, was to encourage a substantially broader freedom of public discussion where legitimate public interest in the subject-matter and reasonable objectivity in its publication could be shown.[42]

*   *   *

Did the same standards of freedom to read apply to matter which, in the view of some members of the public, actually constituted obscene or pornographic publication? In this sector of the First Amendment, the Court found an even stormier passage to be traversed.

In 1957 the Court, with Harlan dissenting in part and Black and Douglas dissenting in vigorous entirety, had sustained the convictions of a New York publisher and a California mail-order bookseller for violation respectively of a Federal and a state obscenity statute. Brennan, speaking for the Court, noted that the case presented in the context of the First and Fourteenth

Amendments the first test of an obscenity prosecution under the free press guarantee. Defining obscene material as "material which deals with sex in a manner appealing to prurient interest," he concluded that the trial court in the Federal case had correctly instructed the jury to "ask yourselves, does [the publication] offend the common conscience of the community by present-day standards?"[43]

Harlan's partial dissent turned upon the variable nature of the "conscience of the community" under present-day standards, pointing to the fact that when Edmund Wilson's *Memoirs of Hecate County* had run afoul of New York law it had been cleared in California, while judicial tests of *God's Little Acre* had brought a conviction in Massachusetts but acquittals in New York and Pennsylvania. Nor, said Harlan, should a finding of obscenity necessarily lead to the conclusion that the publication was "utterly without redeeming social importance."[44] Black and Douglas proceeded from that line of argument to cite sociological studies showing a low correlation between reading interest and delinquency and declared that "the standard of what offends 'the common conscience of the community'" clearly conflicts with the First Amendment.

"Any test that turns on what is offensive to the community's standards" is dangerously loose, Black wrote; how dangerously loose would be self-evident if "religion, economics, politics or philosophy" were the subjects rather than so-called obscenity. Community censorship, he concluded, "creates a regime where in the battle between the literati and the Philistines, the Philistines are certain to win."[45]

Although the rule in *Roth v. United States* provoked a torrent of critical comment, no one in the Court or outside it seemed able to improve upon the matter in succeeding cases. A magazine devoted to nude male portraits was barred from the mails until the Supreme Court reversed the sustaining opinions of the lower courts on appeals. Harlan, in the opinion of the Court, reiterated the *Roth* rules of patent offensiveness and "prurient interest" appeal, and suggested that for nationally circulated publications "a national standard of decency" ought to be devised. He suggested, but did not apply, a New York court's holding that "hard-core pornography" alone would violate the First Amendment protection.[46] This 1962 holding was followed by a 1964 case in which Brennan for the majority added to the *Roth* tests the necessity of finding a total absence of "redeeming social importance"; Warren in dissent questioned whether this was an acceptance of the "hard-core pornography" test and at the same time asked for a definition of such a test.[47]

Two years later the Court undertook, in three obscenity cases, to clarify the distinction between permissible and impermissible portrayals within the free press concept. The success of the effort was not notable; in a six-to-three division, with three separate opinions for the majority, Massachusetts' finding of obscenity in the book, *Fanny Hill*,* written two centuries earlier, was re-

---

*Formally entitled, *John Clelland's Memoirs of a Woman of Pleasure.*

versed. Each of the three criteria enunciated in *Roth* and in *Jacobellis v. Ohio,* said Brennan for the Court, "is to be applied independently," and in the social importance test the book could not be condemned "unless it is found to be *utterly* without redeeming social value." Douglas, in his concurring opinion, suggested that where experts disagreed on a particular book's merit, the presumption of constitutional protection should prevail.[48]

In the other two cases, the Court sustained convictions in two New York cases, one involving a publisher, Mishkin, who specifically commissioned the writing of books in which "sex had to be very strong, it had to be rough, it had to be spelled out." The other involved a publisher, Ralph Ginzburg, and his three corporations charged with mailing lascivious matter in the form of a hard-cover magazine named *Eros,* a bi-weekly newsletter entitled *Liaison,* and a small volume called *The Housewife's Handbook of Selective Promiscuity.* In the first case, Brennan for the Court held that where the publications are intended for a clearly defined deviant sexual readership, "the prurient-appeal requirement of the *Roth* test is satisfied" if the dominant theme of the publications is to the prurient interest of that group.[49] In the second case, while conceding the possible social value of the publications to medical specialists, the Court again speaking through Brennan declared: "Where the purveyor's sole emphasis is on the sexually provocative aspects of his publication, that fact may be decisive in the determination of obscenity."[50]

Still, as Harlan observed in dissent in the *Fanny Hill* case, "no stable approach to the obscenity problem has yet been devised by this Court." Retreating from his previous speculation as to a national standard of obscenity, Harlan proposed to limit First Amendment cases to material "whose indecency is self-demonstrating," while applying the Fourteenth Amendment only to a requirement that state courts "apply criteria rationally related to the accepted notion of obscenity."[51] Yet, as Douglas replied in his own dissent in the *Mishkin* and *Ginzburg* cases, to expect the Court to apply any such tests would require an omniscience "which few in our whole society possess."

This led ultimately to the conclusion, in Douglas' view, "that the First Amendment allows all ideas to be expressed—whether orthodox, popular, offbeat, or repulsive." The ultimate solution, he urged, was to leave all persons free "to pick and choose, to recognize trash when they see it, to be attracted to the literature that satisfies their deepest need, and, hopefully, to move from plateau to plateau and finally reach the world of enduring ideas." This, at the last, he considered "the ideal of the Free Society written into our Constitution."[52]

The indefinite cycle of reasoning in the obscenity cases thus encompassed the ultimately subjective tests in *Roth* and the absolutism of free publication in the Black-Douglas view. The hesitation and second thoughts which characterized successive decisions in the field seemed to reflect the sense of indecision in American society generally, as old standards of sexuality were undergoing substantial changes in full view of everyone. A suggestion of the final course of constitutionalism in this subject came in the spring of 1967, when the Court in *per curiam* decisions summarily reversed twenty obscenity convictions on review.[53]

*   *   *

In the final analysis, the tenor of most of the First Amendment decisions of the sixties—whether revolving about the insulation of "public issues" from any restraints but malicious defamation, or probing for a general theory of obscenity in the context of mid-century morality—was a persuasion that maximum personal freedom was the touchstone of a mature society. This was consistent with the basic concern of the Warren Court for the ensured equality of all persons in the enjoyment of rights guaranteed to them by the Constitution, whether they were members of minorities, individual voters entitled to equal weight in the electoral process, or accused criminals unable to assert the defenses preserved to them without the aid of professional counsel.

The obscenity question was an incident in a six-to-three decision in 1961 overruling the 1949 case of *Wolf v. Colorado* and extending the rule against admissibility of evidence obtained through unlawful search and seizure to state courts. In *Mapp v. Ohio,* allegedly obscene matter was obtained from the defendant's private premises after unlawful entry by state officers. Observing that "time has set its face against" *Wolf,* Justice Clark for the Court held that the restraints of the Fourth Amendment should now be applied to the states through the Fourteenth. To continue to tolerate a state practice of admissibility of such evidence when the Fourth Amendment forbade it in Federal courts was "to encourage disobedience to the Federal Constitution." Such an "ignoble shortcut to conviction left open to the state tends to destroy the entire system of constitutional restraints on which the liberties of the people rest."[54]

But two years later, Clark spoke for a five-to-four majority declining to apply *Mapp* to all searches and seizures resulting from forcible entry. Where the entry was based on "probable cause," resulted in lawful arrest and produced the evidence as an incident to the arrest, Clark found it distinguishable from *Mapp,* where unlawful entry was prerequisite for the search for evidence which thereafter created the "probable cause" for the arrest. In *Ker v. California,* Clark insisted that the difference in Federal and state rules of exclusion of evidence was statutory rather than constitutional.[55]

The orderly progression from original ascertainment of "probable cause" to lawful entry, lawful arrest and lawful search and seizure incidental to arrest was the standard the Court sought consistently to apply. In 1964 a six-to-three majority in *Aguilar v. Texas* set aside a conviction based on evidence obtained with an improperly issued search warrant; if the circumstances required a warrant, said Justice Goldberg, the standard for obtaining a properly issued one was the same under the Fourth and Fourteenth Amendments.[56] In *Preston v. United States* in the same year, the Court unanimously overturned a conviction based on a search (which turned up narcotics) "remote in time and place from the arrest" (for vagrancy).[57] Permission to search without

warrant, the Court continued in *Stoner v. California,* could be given only by
the defendant and not by a third party.[58] But seizure of evidence without permission after arrest for "probable cause" could be justified by the circumstances, as in a case where a blood test of a drunken driving suspect was
necessitated as quickly as possible before the evidence of alcohol in the
blood could be lost by its natural diminution.[59]

Close cases divided even the activists on the Court. In two five-to-four
decisions in 1967, the majority spoke through Justice Stewart in affirming an
arrest of a suspected narcotics peddler on the tip of an anonymous informant;
the tip created the "probable cause" upon which a lawful arrest and search
proceeded, said the majority, while Warren in dissent declared that the
decision left the Fourth Amendment guarantee to the discretion of arresting
officers.[60] Black spoke for the majority in the other case, upholding a conviction based on a search of the accused's car after his arrest on suspicion of
narcotics traffic, where the search uncovered narcotics. *Preston* was distinguishable, said Black, because in *Preston* police possession of the car was
unrelated to the arrest and the search turned up evidence unrelated to the
cause of the arrest.[61]

The development of exclusionary rules as a protection of defendants'
constitutional rights sounded the apparent (but perhaps premature) knell of
wiretapping. Relying on the prohibition in the Federal Communications Act
of 1934 against intercepted communications, the Court in 1957 had excluded
wiretap evidence obtained by state officers and turned over to Federal prosecu-
tors for use in Federal courts.[62] In the same year, however, another case
distinguished between interception and recording of conversations where one
of the parties consented to the recording.[63] Qualification of the rule began
in 1961 with the prohibiting of eavesdropping by means of an electronic
device inserted in a party wall. Although when a recording merely documented
an arresting agent's own testimony, said a six-to-three majority in 1963, or
when the testimony itself consisted of remarks made by the defendant to an
informer, said a six-to-one majority in 1966, the defense against unreasonable
search and seizure could not be asserted.[64]

In *Berger v. New York* in 1967, a six-to-three majority found a New
York state wiretap law unconstitutional and in the process dealt a *coup de
grace* to *Olmstead v. United States.* Pointing to the decision of the Department
of Justice to forbid the use of electronic surveillance for "prosecutorial purposes," Clark for the majority declared a kind of peroration for the question:
"Under our regime a man stands mute if he chooses or talks if he chooses.
The test is whether he acts voluntarily. . . . In short, I do not see how any
electronic surveillance that collects evidence or provides leads to evidence is
or can be constitutional under the Fourth and Fifth Amendments."[65]

*   *   *

All of this line of thought led to the climactic series of decisions dramatized in *Gideon v. Wainwright* and cleared the ground for a more humanitarian

basis for criminal procedure within the circumscribed area of constitutional rights. The concern of the Court with the degree of coercion in the matter of confessions was essentially interrelated to its determination that no defendant should be jeopardized in his defense for lack of professional legal aid. Accordingly, the sixties witnessed a steady progression of opinions broadening the standards of safeguards for the accused, in the face of growing outcries that the trend of decisions was demolishing the whole machinery of law enforcement.

The admissibility of confessions in criminal procedure had been a harshly debated issue for decades. As late as 1953 the Court had ruled that the only concern of the Fourteenth Amendment with the subject was to admonish courts not to admit confessions obtained under circumstances which were "inherently untrustworthy."[66] Six years later, however, the Court began applying the "trustworthiness" test on its own initiative, specifically invalidating admissions based on marathon interrogation or the threat of embarrassment or harassment to the defendant's family or friends. The test henceforth, said Warren in a 1961 opinion, was to be whether any circumstances surrounding a confession were "such as to overbear petitioner's will to resist and bring about confessions not freely self-determined."[67]

Yet even the new test of "voluntariness" had obvious weaknesses; it was, said Clark, "an elusive, measureless standard of psychological coercion" which only encouraged interrogators to use greater ingenuity in their methods. Frankfurter sought, in a companion case, to devise a test alternately for the propriety of techniques of interrogation and for the impact of the techniques upon the defendant's "mind and will."[68] Clark's opinion was a lengthy but not conspicuously enlightening rationale.

The root of the matter, Douglas suggested in a 1962 opinion, was the absence of counsel in most of the preliminary stages of a criminal proceeding, when the "potential prejudice" to the defense was at a maximum. In setting aside a conviction under Virginia's habitual criminal statute, Douglas observed that "an imaginative lawyer" might readily find issues in the defendant's past convictions which properly would raise reasonable doubt as to the validity of some of the evidence against him.[69]

With Douglas' opinion in *Chewning v. Cunningham*, the stage once more was set for the refutation of the much-maligned rule in *Betts v. Brady*, and Clarence Gideon's hand-written petition for a review of his felony conviction in Florida provided the opportunity the following year. The Court left no doubt about the constitutional issue it proposed to discuss; in appointing one of the ablest attorneys in Washington—Abe Fortas—as Gideon's counsel in the high tribunal, the order for argument invited a focus on the question: "Should this Court's holding in *Betts v. Brady* . . . be reconsidered?"[70]

In January, 1962, on a letterhead of the Florida Division of Corrections, a penitentiary inmate in a handwritten scrawl addressed the Supreme Court of the United States: "I, Clarence Earl Gideon, inform this Court that I am a

pauper without funds or any possibility of obtaining financial aid, and I beg
of this Court to listen and act upon my plea." The Florida trial court, Gideon
charged, had refused to appoint counsel for his defense; contrary to the law
of the Constitution. In that day of the lingering *Betts* rule, Gideon was wrong,
but his handwritten petition was accepted from the mass of expensively
printed writs of error and requests for certiorari, so that the Court might now
finally consider whether the law of the Constitution should be changed.[71]

How completely the climate of legal opinion had changed since 1942 was
demonstrated in the *amici curiae* briefs which accompanied the transcript of
the case. Richard W. Ervin, Florida's attorney general, had invited his counterparts in all other states to prepare such briefs; Alabama responded with an
amicus brief in support of the Florida position—and twenty-three other
states submitted briefs in support of the petitioner's position, with a supplementary brief from Oregon describing that state's post-conviction procedure.[72]

Fortas built his own case for Gideon meticulously. "It is not the issue of
whether counsel is or is not needed for a trial which is fair and decent," his
brief began. "The necessity for counsel in a criminal case is too plain for
argument. No individual who is not a trained or experienced lawyer can
possibly know or pursue the technical, elaborate and sophisticated measures
which are necessary to assemble and appraise the facts, analyze the law, determine contentions, negotiate the plea, or marshal and present all of the factual
and legal considerations which have a bearing upon his defense. Even a
trained, experienced criminal lawyer cannot—and will not, if he is sensible—
undertake his own defense."

"The law of involuntary confessions and searches and seizures as applied to the states," Fortas continued, "postdates almost in its entirety the
decision in *Betts v. Brady.*" Inexperienced laymen, unaware of the fine points
of "probable cause," waiver of privilege, or even the fact of privilege against
self-incrimination, walked headlong into traps. In this circumstance, the
distinction between capital and non-capital felonies, the one being entitled
to counsel and the other not, was invalid; if denial of counsel to any indigent
defendant amounted to a denial of due process and equal protection, the
constitutional injunction applied to all irrespective of the magnitude of the
felony charge.

Thus, Fortas concluded, if the decision in *Mapp v. Ohio* had been required to eliminate an unconstitutional disparity between courts in the matter
of admissibility of evidence obtained by unlawful search, a similar decision
overturning *Betts* on the question of right to counsel was equally necessary.
Nor, if justice was the objective, should the Court be deterred by a concern
over the retroactive effect of such a decision. In a free world, Fortas declared,
the right of counsel for the poor as well as the rich "is an indispensable safeguard . . . of justice under law."[73]

Accepting Fortas' basic argument, Black for a nondissenting Court
agreed that *Betts v. Brady* had been "an anachronism when handed down"

and should now be overruled. In a society where the government would not prosecute crimes without aid of counsel, it was unthinkable that government should deny counsel to the accused. Where state and national constitutions uniformly sought to protect the rights of defendants so that they might stand equal before the courts, a poor man charged with crime who was compelled to offer his defense without trained assistance was denied this "noble ideal."[74]

Douglas, concurring, observed that "rights protected against state invasion by the due process clause of the Fourteenth Amendment are not watered-down versions of what the Bill of Rights guarantees"—an implication that, better than incorporation, was the concept of the Fourteenth as a guarantor of many rights presently inchoate. This prompted Harlan in his separate concurrence to deny the proposition; in holding "a right or immunity, valid against the Federal government, to be 'implicit in the concept of ordered liberty' and thus valid against the states, I do not read our past decisions to hold that by so holding, we automatically carry over an entire body of Federal law and apply it in full sweep to the states."[75] Thus, with the epochal holding in *Gideon v. Wainwright,* the stage was set for another activist-restrained dichotomy in the most far-reaching case of all, in the reapportionment jurisprudence.*

*   *   *

The dichotomy was manifested almost immediately in the case following *Gideon* where a six-to-three majority, speaking through Douglas, set aside a California practice which permitted appeals through counsel where parties were able to retain lawyers but limited appeals by indigents to a review of the court record before determining whether to permit appointment of counsel. For an indigent to be "forced to run this gantlet of a preliminary showing of merit," said Douglas, "does not comport with fair procedure. . . . The indigent, when the record is unclear or the errors are hidden, has only the right of a meaningless ritual, while the rich man has a meaningful appeal."[76]

Harlan, in a separate dissent, protested the unqualified extension of the right to counsel to appellate cases. The requirement of equal protection, he said, did not prevent the state "from adopting a law of general applicability that may affect the poor more harshly than it does the rich." Uniform procedural requirements were one thing, but to "impose on the states 'an affirmative duty to lift the handicaps flowing from differences in economic circumstances' . . . would be to read into the Constitution a philosophy of leveling that would be foreign to many of our basic concepts of the proper relations between government and society." As for due process, he added, the Fourteenth Amendment did not require review of tried cases, and in any event review procedure did not involve the same type of knowledgeable forensic skill as trial procedure.[77]

Harlan, usually joined by Clark and White and frequently by Stewart, thus assumed the position of relative conservatism in the new Federalism

---

*Cf. Ch. 15.

which had once been occupied by Jackson, Reed and Frankfurter. Black and Douglas continued as the original activists, usually firmly supported by Warren and Brennan and, after Frankfurter's retirement, by Goldberg and Fortas, his successor; and after Clark's retirement by Thurgood Marshall. The established majority of liberals, accordingly, pushed the concept of individual defendants' rights as steadily as possible toward its logical extremes.

Now that a right to counsel in a trial and presumably in an appeal had been established, the next question to be determined was how far back in the accusatorial process should the right be extended. Even if due process did not require a lawyer at the pre-trial or pre-arraignment stages, was due process denied if a defendant asked for a lawyer without success, or if his lawyer sought to reach him without success? Two 1958 cases had answered in the negative, but a changed Court in 1965 held otherwise in a case where a defendant's remarks in the presence of his counsel were recorded as part of a conversation with a co-defendant secretly turned state's witness.[78] The stage was set for Gideon's fateful companion, *Escobedo v. Illinois*.

On the night of January 19, 1960 a man was shot to death in Chicago, one of the commonplaces of big-city violence which seldom occupied public attention beyond the next morning's headlines. A brother-in-law of the victim, a 22-year-old Spanish-American named Danny Escobedo, was arrested without a warrant at 2:30 in the morning, brought to police headquarters and interrogated until 5 o'clock the following afternoon, when he was released on a habeas corpus obtained by his lawyer. On January 30 another suspect charged Escobedo with having fired the fatal shots, and that evening he and his sister, the widow of the murdered man, were picked up and brought back to the station.

Escobedo's lawyer arrived shortly thereafter, but despite repeated requests of both the lawyer and the client, neither was permitted to communicate with the other. At 1 o'clock in the morning the lawyer gave up and departed, after filing a complaint with the Chicago police commissioner. Meantime, continued interrogation in both Spanish and English at length elicited statements from Escobedo indicating knowledge of the crime, and further statements which implicated him substantially. Thereafter an assistant state's attorney took down his statement, wording it carefully so as to conform with Illinois rules of admissible evidence. The undisputed record throughout this period showed that Escobedo was at no time told of his constitutional right to remain silent.[79]

Escobedo's conviction was reversed by a five-to-four opinion of the Supreme Court. Goldberg for the majority declared that the circumstances of the station house activities prior to formal charging amounted to a denial of assistance of counsel guaranteed by the Sixth Amendment and extended to the states through the Fourteenth. Although the interrogation had the superficial cast of "a general investigation of 'an unsolved crime,' " said Goldberg, in reality Escobedo "had become the accused, and the purpose of the interrogation was to 'get him' to confess his guilt despite his constitutional right not to do so."

Whatever Escobedo's awareness of his constitutional rights from prior advice of his lawyer, Goldberg emphasized, as a layman he was "undoubtedly unaware that under Illinois law an admission of 'mere' complicity in the murder plot was legally as damaging as an admission of firing of the fatal shots. . . . This was the stage when legal aid and advice were most critical." The practice of state courts in applying the *Gideon* rule, or in this instance the earlier rule of *Powell v. Alabama,* after formal charging of the accused, "would make the trial no more than an appeal from the interrogation," since "for all practical purposes, the conviction is already assured by pre-trial examination."

Goldberg answered the state's contention, and anticipated the immediate flood of protest to the *Escobedo* rule, "that if the right to counsel is afforded prior to indictment, the number of confessions obtained by police will diminish significantly, because most confessions are obtained during the period between arrest and indictment. . . . The fact that many confessions are obtained during this period points up its critical nature as a 'stage when legal aid and advice' are surely needed." The majority opinion rejected the idea that the system of criminal justice could not survive if it could not depend on "the citizens' abdication through unawareness of their constitutional rights. No system worth preserving should have to *fear* that if an accused is permitted to consult with a lawyer, he will become aware of, and exercise, these rights."[80]

Harlan's dissent found Goldberg's argument "ill-conceived," and warned that it would "seriously and unjustifiably" hamper "perfectly legitimate" methods of criminal investigation. Stewart added that for a citizen to have a right of silence when the police were investigating an unsolved murder was to strain the meaning of the constitutional guarantee; he did not consider the rule against self-incrimination in his denigration of the right of silence.[81] But it was Justice White who was bitterest in his protest.

The logical extreme, and the "goal which the Court seemingly has in mind," would be "to bar from evidence all admissions obtained from an individual suspected of crime, whether involuntarily made or not." "The right to counsel now not only entitles the accused to counsel's advice and aid in preparing for trial but stands as an impenetrable barrier to any interrogation once the accused has become a suspect. From that very moment apparently his right to counsel attaches, a rule wholly unworkable and impossible to administer unless police cars are equipped with public defenders and undercover agents and police informants have defense counsel at their side."[*] Sarcastically, White suggested that the ultimate extent of the majority doctrine would be to provide the prospective criminal with legal counsel even before he committed the crime.[82]

---

[*] A practice which was in effect in certain cities by the spring of 1967. Cf. 89 *Time*, 79 (April 14, 1967).

*   *   *

The *Escobedo* decision, handed down in the spring of 1965, provoked a substantially more vehement outburst of commentary than had the more fundamental decision in *Gideon*. Indeed, Congress had reacted favorably to *Gideon*—although, more specifically, to the previous year's report of the Attorney General's Committee on Poverty and the Administration of Federal Justice—by enacting the Criminal Justice Act of August 20, 1964. Its purpose, stated in its preamble, was "to promote criminal justice by providing for the representation of defendants who are financially unable to obtain an adequate defense in criminal cases" in the Federal courts. The scope of the act, from preliminary hearing through appeal, was broad, although after *Escobedo* it was a nice question whether it was broad enough.[83]

Amid the continuing complaints that *Escobedo* had made a shambles of law enforcement, the Court in the spring of 1966 took the unusual step of spelling out in detail what was and was not permissible in pre-trial procedure under the *Escobedo* doctrine. A "second round" of cases provided the occasion for an elaborate discussion by Chief Justice Warren for the five-to-four majority, as well as for even more elaborate dissents by Justices Harlan and White.

Consolidating a number of cases—one from Arizona, another from California, a third from New York and a fourth from the Federal court in Kansas City—under the title of the first, *Miranda v. Arizona*, Warren devoted the greater part of the five-to-four majority opinion to a discussion of details of pre-trial procedure before disposing briefly of each of the four. The fundamental issue in each, said the Chief, was the nature of "the restraints society must observe consistent with the Federal Constitution in prosecuting individuals for crime." Explicitly he described the constitutional requirements: Before any interrogation, the authorities were to make clear to the accused' his constitutional right to remain silent, and correlatively his liability in saying anything which could thereafter be used against him. In addition, he was to be advised at the outset that he had a right "to the presence of an attorney, either retained or appointed." The interrogated party could invoke any of his rights at any stage of the proceedings, and though the rights might be waived the waiver could be withdrawn at any stage.[84]

Turning to the standard police manuals on interrogation procedure which had been cited by the defendants' briefs, Warren observed that their objectives were clear: "To be alone with the subject . . . and to deprive him of any outside support. The aura of confidence in his guilt undermines his will to resist. . . . It is important to keep the subject off balance, for example, by trading on his insecurity about himself or his surroundings. The police then persuade, trick, or cajole him out of exercising his constitutional rights."

No admissions by a defendant under these circumstances, the opinion declared, could be considered voluntary. "An individual swept from familiar surroundings into police custody, surrounded by antagonistic forces, and subjected to the techniques of persuasion described above cannot be otherwise than under compulsion to speak." It followed, from this reasoning, that "the right to have counsel present at the interrogation is indispensable to the protection of the Fifth Amendment privilege," for with a lawyer present "the likelihood that the police will practice coercion is reduced, and if coercion is nevertheless exercised the lawyer can testify to it in court."

"Whatever the testimony of the authorities as to waiver of rights by an accused, the fact of lengthy interrogation or incommunicado incarceration before a statement is made is strong evidence that the accused did not validly waive his rights," Warren concluded. The irreducible fact was that the Fifth Amendment guaranteed that an individual cannot be compelled to be a witness against himself. "That right," said the majority, "cannot be abridged."[85]

Clark, in dissent, urged that the Court return to a practice of considering "the totality of circumstances" in determining the involuntariness of the confession rather than, as he put it, "in one full sweep changing the traditional rules of custodial interrogation which this Court has for so long recognized as a justifiable and proper tool in balancing individual rights against the rights of society."[86] But the principal dissents were those of Harlan and White, in both of which Stewart joined.

"I believe the decision of the Court represents poor constitutional law and entails harmful consequences for the country at large," Harlan began. The "new constitutional code of rules for confessions," he declared, tends "to negate all pressures, to reinforce the nervous or ignorant suspect, and ultimately to discourage any confession at all." Harlan emphatically denied that the thrust of the Fifth Amendment was to rule out any kind of interrogation which would persuade a suspect to abandon his resistance to the evidence. "Until today," said the Justice, "the role of the Constitution has been only to sift out undue pressure, not to assure spontaneous confessions." Where it was common knowledge "that some crimes cannot be solved without confessions, . . . the Court is taking a real risk with society's welfare in imposing its new regime on the country."[87]

It was necessary to recognize at the outset, said White in his turn, that what the majority had done in *Miranda* had been "to make new law and new public policy." This in itself was what the Court historically did at great periods of constitutional change; but while this was its proper role, it invited critical discussion of the new policy which it had evolved. White then attacked the logical consequences of the majority holding. If it was to require the presence of a lawyer, and if the lawyer was presumed to admonish the client to be silent, "the result adds up to a judicial judgment that evidence from the accused should not be used against him in any way, whether compelled or not." The fundamental flaw in the new rule, said White, was not in its philosophy but in its indiscriminate operation upon all criminal law.[88]

*   *   *

Although the Court, by a seven-to-two majority, held that *Escobedo* and *Miranda* were to be limited in their retroactivity to the date of the earlier decision[89]—June 22, 1964—state courts were almost instantly inundated with *habeas corpus* proceedings from the penitentiaries relying either on these or the *Gideon* decision. It was widely predicted that an orgy of defiance of police interrogators would follow in the wake of the sweeping decisions, with extremists predicting a general breakdown of criminal prosecutions. The fact that, by the spring of 1967, three of the four defendants in the cases affected by *Miranda*—including Ernesto Miranda himself—had been convicted on new trials (or, in one case, had pleaded guilty to a lesser crime) without use of their confessions did not particularly mollify the critics.

The fact was that in *Gideon, Escobedo* and *Miranda* the liberal, activist majority on the Court had asserted an absolutism in the Fourth, Fifth and Sixth Amendment guarantees at least equal to that which had been accorded the First Amendment in the free press and obscenity cases, or in the freedom-of-association cases before that. The dominant theme of constitutional law emerging from all of these decisions in the 1960's was the paramount importance of the individual's rights as against the rights of organized society. There might be, as the Court repeatedly protested, a "balancing" of these rights in the ultimate rationale of such cases, but the fact was that a privilege or immunity of a national citizen which the Court recognized at all was apt to be accorded more weight than all but the greatest preponderance of institutional rights which could be mustered on the other side of the scale.[90]

The sixties provided, in the Kennedy-Johnson administrations, an atmosphere congenial to a general acceptance of swiftly advancing Federalism, particularly in the vigorous program of social legislation enacted in the period from the winter of 1964 through the summer of 1965. Lyndon Johnson's fervent backing of the martyred John Kennedy's civil rights program, leading to the historic Civil Rights Act of 1964, was followed by his own election in an unparalleled avalanche of popular and electoral votes—43,126,506 and 486 to Barry Goldwater's 27,176,799 and 52, with Alabama's eleven electoral votes being cast symbolically for Senator Harry F. Byrd of Virginia. A mandate of such proportions prepared the way for the first session of the Eighty-ninth Congress. Vastly expanded Federal aid to education, Medicare, the war on poverty, the Voting Rights Act of 1965, and job retraining in the Appalachia rehabilitation program, were followed in 1966 by the automobile safety bill, the program for demonstration cities, and a stronger law on air and water pollution.

Goldwater had sought, in as straightforward a manner as he could, to call the nation back to conservative values; the magnitude of his defeat, only exceeded on the electoral vote by Roosevelt's triumph over Alf Landon twenty-eight years before, attested to the country's attitude. Americans sensed what Kennedy had so often declared, that in an age of continuing and rapid change the United States had to be continuously and rapidly responsive. This was not to say that the American people accepted the fact gladly; accepting it as inevitable, they nevertheless gave vent to their regrets that it was so, aiming their frustrations alternately at the President and the Chief Justice. A confused war of attrition in distant Viet Nam and civil insurrection in the cities on the domestic scene tended to blend with the judicial doctrines insisting upon the equal rights of minorities—Negro, Communist, criminal defendants—as a tangle of traces against which the public sporadically kicked.

15/The Ultimate Democracy

THE DESEGREGATION CASES permanently altered the social frame of reference of the United States, and the cases on constitutional rights of the individual—culminating in *Gideon, Escobedo* and *Miranda*—were equally cataclysmic in their impact on criminal law and procedure and the restraints upon the state in dealing with the individual in these circumstances. But in the final analysis of the jurisprudence of the Warren Court, nine decisions handed down in the space of twenty-six months—between March 26, 1962 and June 15, 1964—were to be the most far-reaching of all. For in the span from *Baker v. Carr* to *Reynolds v. Sims,* the rationale of representative government itself was fundamentally changed.

There was a fundamental consistency of judicial policy running through all of these landmark decisions, the net effect of which was to restate the constitutional ideals of the eighteenth century in meaningful terms for the last half of the twentieth. This was the insistence upon the equality of all citizens in the enjoyment of constitutional guarantees. The initial premise was relatively modest: if the Constitution in terms, in a specific Amendment, stipulated a specific guaranty such as freedom of expression or of assembly (association), it was universally applicable to all persons subject to the authority of the Constitution. From this premise, the rationale of the Warren Court proceeded in two parallel courses: if experience or intellectual persuasion identified other privileges than those specified, it was the duty of the Court to ratify and apply them; and if the requirements of equality demanded it, the constitutional guarantees were to be asserted against the states of the Union through the Fourteenth Amendment as well.[1]

Thus, if racial segregation was a denial of constitutional privileges and immunities, it was a denial everywhere and everywhere to be enjoined; having first determined the principle the Court was logically impelled to apply it to the states. If all men were endowed by the Bill of Rights with immunity from self-incrimination, and the right of counsel was essential in the preservation of this immunity, this proposition likewise demanded universal applicability to the states. Ultimately, the principle of equality led to the heart of democratic, representative government—to find expression at length in the new rule of constitutional law, "One person, one vote."

With a consistently substantial majority—in the nine cases on reapportionment, there were no more than three dissents in two cases, one dissent in two, and two in the other five[2]—the Court moved swiftly to its ultimate conclusion: The initial Tennessee case of *Baker v. Carr* held that an irrational basis for apportionment of representation in the lower house of the state legislature conflicted with the equal protection clause of the Fourteenth Amendment.[3] Two Georgia cases then overturned state election laws which gave unequal weight to voting in statewide elections, whether for state officers, United States Representatives or United States Senators.[4] The wheel then came full circle in a series of cases concerning representation in the upper house of state legislatures in Alabama, Colorado, Delaware, Maryland, New York and Virginia.[5] In a society "ostensibly grounded on representative government," concluded the Court in the Alabama case, "it would seem reasonable that a majority of the people of a state could elect a majority of that state's legislators," and electoral districts should not be drawn with primary reference to trees and land over flesh and blood.[6]

*   *   *

The proposition in the reapportionment cases appeared to strike at the deepest roots of American historical tradition: the Jeffersonian ideal of the independent husbandman whose virtue came from the soil he tilled and whose integrity and influence in national life should be kept forever inviolate. The great Convention of 1787, where the large and small states worked out their *modus operandi* in the form of the bicameral Congress alternating between a one-for-one representation and a popular representation, inspired the statecraft of the pioneers who created governments in the pattern of the Founding Fathers, with political and geographic divisions of representation within the borders of their states.

The proposition also struck at a "rotten borough" power base in both state and national politics—the surviving franchise in rural areas of steadily dwindling population, which so long as they were preserved gave dynasties (or machines) in these areas a disproportionate weight in the legislatures. The truism that no political interest ever voluntarily surrenders its advantage was amply documented in the apportionment cases themselves as they were briefed to the Court: whatever the requirements on representation written into particular state constitutions, the fact was that in many states, if not most, redistricting in response to changing population distribution had not occurred in many decades.[7]

Meantime, the urban and suburban dominance of the population had been accelerating. In 1920, under the impetus of World War I, the total urban census showed 54 million to 51 in the rural areas, and in 1930 the ratio had increased to 68 to 53. By 1940 the Census Bureau recognized an established social phenomenon—the absorption of former villages into the suburban areas, or the wholesale development of towns which in former times would have been classified as rural but which in reality were the residential zones for families who looked to the adjacent cities for their work and recreation. Under this redefinition of greater urban areas, the gap between the cities and the country widened at a substantially greater rate; the 1940 figures showed more than 88 million persons in the metropolitan centers as against 51 million still denominated as rural. The figures jumped to 96 to 54 in 1950, and to 125 to 54 in 1960.[8]

For more than a generation, cities had chafed under the lingering dominance of state legislatures with their "rotten" rural boroughs and legislative majorities unresponsive to accelerating urban needs. As city dwellers moved to the suburbs to escape the rising taxes which the cities in turn had to levy at the local level, a triangle of conflicting political and economic interests developed, with the new suburbanites resisting the efforts of the cities to annex them or in other ways to pursue the taxable assets acquired through the cities' economy. On the other hand the suburbanites found themselves confronted with county politics still dominated by the surviving rural courthouse rings.

Early efforts to break the rural control on electoral districting were consistently rebuffed, in White's Chief Justiceship, with the Court dismissing the suits on the ground that the question was "political" and hence to be settled only by legislative means. But as urbanization continued at an accelerating pace, the notorious indisposition of the state legislatures to carry out any effective reapportionment reflecting the changing population character called more insistently for attention. The 1930 census presented something of a crisis in Congressional apportionments as several states showed a sufficient loss of population to reduce their representation—or a shift of population within their borders which required more electoral power for their cities.

The Hughes Court, in cases coming up from Minnesota, Missouri and New York in 1932, finding that each state had lost a Congressman by the 1930 census but had failed to redistrict accordingly, ruled that the states would have to elect their Representatives at large.[9] The following year, however, Hughes ruled that the Court could not compel Mississippi to redistrict equitably because Congress had not stipulated such a requirement in its 1929 redistricting act.[10] The difference, in Hughes' cautious reasoning, lay in the fact that the 1929 act repealed certain sections of a prior 1911 statute, and made it necessary for the Court to determine the effect of the surviving 1911 sections on the 1929 law with reference to the situation in each state.[11] The fact that neither statute anticipated a loss of representation indicated the lag in political awareness of the population trends.

Except for one or two abortive efforts in the later thirties,[12] the next serious judicial challenge did not arise until 1946, in two suits attacking the Georgia county unit voting system in the case of Congressional and gubernatorial elections. In both cases the Court dismissed the appeal from the lower courts which had upheld the system, suggesting doubt as to its jurisdiction in the matters.[13] In the same year, in *Colgrove v. Green,* an Illinois apportionment case was dismissed for want of a substantial Federal question.[14] A bloc on the Court, however, was beginning to coalesce in favor of adjudication. In 1948 in another Illinois case a six-to-three majority held *per curiam:* "It is allowable state policy to require that candidates for state-wide office should have support not limited to a concentrated locality. . . . To assume that political power is a function exclusively of numbers is to disregard the practicalities of government."[15] Douglas, in dissent, rejoined: "The fact that the Constitution itself sanctions inequities in some phases of our political system does not justify us in allowing a state to create additional ones."[16]

There were two obstacles in the path of the activists seeking to apply a judicial formula to the problem of equitable apportionment. One was a holding of Chief Justice Roger B. Taney in 1849, to the effect that section 4 of Article IV of the Constitution was a "political" matter which concerned only the legislative or the executive branch of the government. Thus the Court considered itself blocked from attacking the apportionment question under the clause guaranteeing a republican form of government to the individual states. The other was the then dominant Frankfurter doctrine of restraint, which Frankfurter himself had most eloquently expressed, with reference to this question in *Colgrove:*

"Because the Illinois legislature has failed to revise its Congressional Representative districts in order to reflect great changes, during more than a generation, in the distribution of its population, we are asked to do this, as it were, for Illinois." In Frankfurter's view, relying on the Hughes formula of the early thirties, the only Federal action that was possible was Congressional action, and this could only be limited to requiring elections at large, without districts. But even this was too much for the Justice, for, he declared, it created the threat that "the aggregate minority of the people in a state, though approaching perhaps to a majority, [would] be wholly overpowered by the combined action of the numerical majority, without any voice whatever in the national councils." Coining a long-repeated phrase, he concluded that courts "ought not to enter this political thicket."[17]

Frankfurter spoke for himself, Burton and Reed, with Rutledge separately concurring; Black, Douglas and Murphy dissented. Stone having just died and Jackson being overseas, *Colgrove* was thus a four-to-three decision. However, with Vinson succeeding to the Chief Justiceship and Jackson returning to strengthen the Frankfurter bloc, it was clear that the majority of the Court would continue to adhere to this general view for some time to come.

*   *   *

The Black-Douglas minority spoke the language of the future in the dissent in *Colgrove;* under the equal protection clause of the Fourteenth Amendment, they pointed out, the judiciary had a demonstrable responsibility for "protecting and vindicating the right of a voter to cast an effective ballot."[18] Moreover, the activists contended, the judicial responsibility was not limited to Congressional districting. In 1950, where a seven-to-two majority declined to consider malapportionment in a Pennsylvania primary election, Douglas declared that "the only tenable premise under the Fourteenth, Fifteenth and Seventeenth Amendments is that where nominations are made in primary elections, there shall be no inequality in voting power by reason of race, creed, color, or other invidious discrimination."[19]

Two years later, however, the majority again rejected a challenge to the Georgia county unit system in a primary election with the declaration that a primary was not an election within the meaning of the constitutional references.[20] Still more tenuous was the reasoning of the majority in a 1956 case, where the Court accepted the tortuous argument of the Tennessee state supreme court that it could not set aside, as inoperative, a 1901 redistricting law because to do so would leave the state without a prior law to fall back on and hence without a legal government or the means of electing one.[21]

The Court was by now all but impaled on both horns of a dilemma: the exaggerated regard for "political" questions on the one hand and the manifest determination of inaction on the part of state agencies on the other. Since the early thirties, more than fifty suits on malapportionment had been unsuccessfully brought in various states, and more than a dozen had been tried in Federal courts.[22] The need to face up to the fact that, while this dilemma became more acute, growing numbers of American citizens were being denied the full effective force of their ballots, was finally thrust before the Supreme Court in the frank words of a dissent in a 1957 case coming up from the western district of Oklahoma. To the majority holding that redistricting under the Oklahoma constitution was a political question over which a Federal court could not assume jurisdiction, Judge W. R. Wallace replied:

> With no threatened conflict between the Congress and the Federal judiciary, the question simply is, "Will the Federal judiciary stand idly by and permit the mastication of a Federally guaranteed constitutional right?" At such point the question of "political issue" or "delicacy of Federal-state relationship" becomes secondary.[23]

Still probing for a chink in the seemingly impregnable wall of malapportionment erected by the entrenched interests in the "rotten boroughs" and by judicial hesitancy, Charles W. Baker and other voters in Nashville, Knoxville and Chattanooga undertook a class action in the Federal district court in Tennessee, seeking to enjoin Joe C. Carr, Tennessee secretary of state, from conducting further elections under the antiquated 1901 statute. In the summer of 1959 Judge William E. Miller ruled that the fundamental issue was one of proper jurisdiction, and referred the issue to a three-judge court. The following December the three-judge court ruled that it did not have jurisdiction over the case and that the complainants had failed to state a complaint on which relief could be granted.[24]

Thus, in the 1960 term of the Supreme Court, the question came on appeal to the Warren Court where the activist bloc, if not yet a majority, was at least en route to ascendancy. Noting "probable jurisdiction," and with the activists able to exploit the "rule of four," the case at last was set down for argument.[25]

*   *   *

An army of attorneys prepared briefs for the Supreme Court argument, attesting to the importance of the issue which at last was going to be given the attention of the Court. After an initial argument on April 19 and 20, 1961 the case was set down for reargument in an order issued two weeks later, with additional *amicus* briefs invited. The case was reargued on October 9, 1961. Charles S. Rhyne, former president of the American Bar Association, and Z. T. Osborn, Jr. argued for Baker; Jack Wilson, assistant attorney general of Tennessee, argued for the state; and Solicitor General Archibald Cox obtained special leave of the Court to argue the *amicus* brief of the United States. Altogether, eight briefs *amici* were filed, including one in the name of the governor of Oklahoma and another on behalf of the National Institute of Municipal Law Officers—all in support of Baker. A total of sixty-one attorneys worked on the various briefs and supporting statements—all but four on the side of the appellant.[26]

Rhyne developed the proposition that malapportionment amounted to "unauthorized, purposeful and systematic discrimination" against Baker and the other complainants which "distorts and reduces their rightful representation" in the state legislature. Thus they were denied "a full vote in equality with other voters" and therefore were denied the equal protection of the laws under the Fourteenth Amendment. Nor could the state rely on the Eleventh Amendment immunizing it from suits by individuals when the state action at which the suit was directed was a denial of constitutionally protected rights.[27]

Wilson's argument was to the jurisdiction. Since the state constitution made reapportionment the exclusive concern of the state legislature, he contended, and since the right to vote for members of the state legislature was derived from the state, the "result of shifts in population and the passage of time do not amount to a dilution of voting rights sufficient to show intentional and purposeful discrimination." He added the *in terrorem* claim that an adverse ruling by the Supreme Court would "seriously interrupt, if not destroy" the government of Tennessee, and closed with a citation from an old case stating that jurisdiction by a Federal court could not be established by the mere assertion of a Federal question.[28]

For the government Cox argued that the right "to be free from gross discrimination in the selection of a state legislature is a Federal right protected by the Fourteenth Amendment," and that in view of the realities of the situation the complainants had no remedy outside the Federal courts. He joined Rhyne in urging a remanding to the District Court with an unequivocal statement of constitutional finding: "In effectuating a Federal right," Cox concluded, "a Federal court is not restricted to the remedies provided by state law."[29]

A six-to-two majority accepted substantially all of the arguments offered by Rhyne and Cox, noting that with the absence of the initiative in Tennessee, a constitutional amendment on the subject of reapportionment depended on the same legislature which had neglected, over six decades, to adjust voting rights even to conform with the 1901 law. Brennan for the Court quickly disposed of the jurisdictional question; the majority of the earlier cases, from Hughes through Vinson, he pointed out, had accepted jurisdiction even where finding no substantial Federal question. Even in the four-to-three opinion in *Colgrove,* Brennan observed, at least four Justices expressed a certainty that the Court had jurisdiction—the three dissenters and the concurring Justice Rutledge. In any event, Brennan held, since the complaint "plainly sets forth a case arising under the Constitution, the subject is within the Federal judicial power," and had in terms been assigned to the jurisdiction of the Federal courts under the civil rights statutes.

A "citizen's right to vote free of arbitrary impairment by state action" had been underlined by many earlier cases involving erroneous tallies, failure to count votes, ballot-box stuffing and gerrymandering.[30] Quoting from the gerrymandering case of 1961, Brennan declared: "When a state exercises power wholly within the domain of state interest. it is insulated from Federal judicial review. But such insulation is not carried over when state power is used as an instrument for circumventing a Federally protected right."[31]

The standing of the complaining parties to sue on a constitutional right was also affirmed by the majority. Their specific claim as residents of metropolitan areas in Tennessee that their votes were not effectively weighted in proportion to metropolitan population was a specific injury as distinguished from the general right of every citizen to a government administered according to law. As to justiciability, Brennan hastened to disavow any intention to consider the *Baker* case under the guaranty clause, but declared that "the mere fact that a suit seeks protection of a political right does not mean it presents a political question."

In a lengthy discourse, Brennan described political questions—presumably non-justiciable—as questions turning upon foreign relations, the war powers of the Chief Executive, the effective dates for Congressional enactments, the status of Indian tribes and Taney's gratutious holding in *Luther v. Borden.* Since he found none of the characteristics of political questions present in *Baker,* he ruled that the District Court could take jurisdiction and should proceed in a manner "consistent with this opinion."[32]

In their concurring opinions, both Black and Clark upbraided the majority represented by Brennan for failing to deal more directly with the apportionment problem itself—prompting Stewart in his own concurrence to affirm his support of the narrower holding of the majority. For Douglas, the time had come to deal directly with the problem described in the brief of the National Institute of Municipal Law Officers: although the United States had become a predominantly urban nation, state legislative representation based on a rural preponderance of the population half a century earlier was now "determining and undermining our elections."[33]

A statistical analysis of the wide discrepancies in voting power and population distribution in Tennessee, said Clark, persuaded him that if legislative apportionment followed any policy at all, "it is to maintain the status quo of invidious discrimination at any cost"—a conclusion confirmed by unsuccessful efforts of urban voters to reform legislative apportionment at the polls or through constitutional amendment. It was well enough for the Court to practice self-restraint in matters of Federal-state relationships, Clark continued, but this was not the same as refusing to act where "the national rights of so many have been so clearly infringed for so long a time."[34]

Even more eloquent in dissent were Justices Frankfurter and Harlan. "The Court today reverses a uniform course of decision established by a dozen cases, including one by which the very claim now sustained was unanimously rejected only five years ago," Frankfurter scolded. "The impressive body of rulings thus cast aside reflected the equally uniform course of our political history regarding the relationship between population and legislative representation—a wholly different matter from denial of the franchise to individuals because of race, color, religion or sex."

The majority holding, he declared, was nothing but a "hypothetical claim resting on abstract assumptions," with no practical means for the lower court to enforce a judgment against the state. It would be better for judicial dignity to avoid making an empty gesture in such cases, said Frankfurter, and to make "a frank acknowledgment that there is not under our Constitution a judicial remedy for every political mischief." And a political question this certainly was, in his view; it involved "all the elements that have made the guaranty clause cases non-justiciable," and was in reality a guaranty clause case masquerading under the Fourteenth Amendment.

Discrepancies in representation, Frankfurter declared, were simply a fact of political life, and the history of representative government in Great Britain, the American colonies and the modern states tended to establish this fact. The extraordinary complexity of the apportionment question, turning on "considerations of geography, demography, electoral convenience, economic and social cohesions or divergencies among particular local groups . . . ancient traditions and ties of settled usage," made it all but impossible in his view to vest in the judiciary an effective rule of apportionment.[35]

"In the last analysis, what lies at the core of this controversy is a difference of opinion as to the function of representative government," said Harlan. "It is surely beyond argument that those who have the responsibility for devising a system of representation may permissibly consider that factors other than bare numbers should be taken into account. The existence of the United States Senate is proof enough of that."

Any plan of apportionment, he continued, was essentially "the embodiment of the state's choice, or, more realistically, its compromise, between competing political philosophies." In his view, "the charge of arbitrariness and capriciousness rests entirely on the consistent refusal of the Tennessee legislature over the past sixty years to alter a pattern of apportionment that was reasonable when conceived." And, he asked, was it not the responsibility of any state to determine that, by weighting electoral representation in favor of agricultural interests in order to protect them from a disproportionate burden of taxes, it was balancing the interests of its internal economy in a reasonable manner?

Where a rational basis for state action could be shown in such a situation, Harlan contended, the function of the judiciary ended. In the final analysis, he charged, "what the Court is doing reflects more an adventure in judicial experimentation than a solid piece of constitutional adjudication."[36]

*   *   *

Baker v. Carr precipitated a torrent of comment adding to the already swollen stream of oratory and publication on racial equality and the rights of defendants. In Congress, and particularly in the House of Representatives where many members suddenly found themselves confronted with the probability of sweeping changes in the composition of the familiar districts on which their own seats depended, the preponderant tone was critical, if not abusive. Frankfurter's careful historical analogies, and Harlan's own dissection of the majority opinion, were quoted repeatedly. A cascade of bills poured into the hoppers proposing a variety of statutory definitions of apportionment, constitutional amendments to ensure adequate geographic representation in state legislatures, and stays of the effect of *Baker* until the states were given time to act.[37]

Law review commentary, while critical of the judicial rationale in many instances—one influential writer described the majority holding as "politics in search of law"—generally applauded the constitutional principle involved. "With the decisions in *Brown* and *Baker*," said one, "the libertarian side of the equal protection clause has fully matured" and as a defense of individual rights "must be ranked second in importance only to the due process clause." It "is best treated as an episode in the urbanization of the American community," and "moves broadly in the direction of developing and supporting procedures necessary for the effective operation of a modern democratic system," wrote two authorities in a symposium in the *Yale Law Journal*. The consistent tenor of dozens of other professional articles was in this same vein.[38]

Frankfurter's doubts as to the practical problem of compelling state response to the judicial decision proved to be groundless. The Federal (three-judge) District Court scanned an emergency redistricting bill passed by a special session of the Tennessee legislature in 1962 and found no rational basis for its projected reapportionment. It thereupon announced that it would await a new redistricting measure from the regular 1963 session before issuing a final decree, and in the fall of 1963, while not expressing complete approval of the second measure, announced that the bill would be approved if no objections were filed within the next three months. Two years later, when a third reapportionment act was passed by the state assembly, the District Court gave its formal approval.[39]

The handwriting on the wall had been discerned everywhere; in the period between *Baker* and *Reynolds v. Sims,* nearly sixty suits were instituted in thirty-eight states to compel reapportionment by state courts or legislatures. The Council of State Governments reported in early 1965 that subsequent to *Baker,* twenty-seven states had reapportioned at least one house of their legislature. How long-needed the changes had been was reflected in the range of dates since the last apportionment; Vermont's most recent previous law on the subject dated from 1793, while many showed a lag of half a century or more.[40]

The complaint of the dissenters in *Baker,* that the question of Congressional apportionment would have been a clearer Federal question, all but invited a review (and reversal) of the prior Georgia cases in which that question had been presented and evaded. It was noteworthy that in both of the cases which now came up from Georgia, the Solicitor General filed new *amici* briefs for the United States urging reapportionment as the necessary means of protecting a Federal right. By an eight-to-one majority (the Kennedy appointees, White and Goldberg, were now on the bench) the Court in March, 1963 overturned the Georgia county unit system for elections for statewide offices, and in December, 1964—by a vote of six to three with Clark concurring in part and dissenting in part—it invalidated the system with reference to Congressional elections.[41]

Douglas and Black—the lone dissenters in *Colgrove*—respectively wrote the opinions of the Court in the Georgia cases. In *Gray v. Sanders,* Douglas observed:

> If a state in a statewide election weighted the male vote more heavily than the female vote or the white vote more heavily than the Negro vote, none could successfully contend that that discrimination was allowable. . . . How then can one person be given twice or ten times the voting power of another person in a statewide election merely because he lives in a rural area or because he lives in the smallest rural county? Once a geographical unit for which a representative is to be chosen is designated, all who participate in the election are to have an equal vote— whatever their race, whatever their sex, whatever their occupation, whatever their income, and wherever their home may be in that geographical

unit. This is required by the equal protection clause of the Fourteenth Amendment. The concept of "we the people" under the Constitution visualizes no preferred class of voters but equality among those who meet the basic qualifications.[42]

The opinion went on to comment: "The conception of political equality from the Declaration of Independence, to Lincoln's Gettysburg Address, to the Fifteenth, Seventeenth, and Nineteenth Amendments, can mean only one thing—one person, one vote."[43]

Eleven months later, in February, 1964, the case of *Wesberry v. Sanders* disposed of the remnants of the county unit system. Black, for the Court, held that nothing in the Constitution "gives support to a construction that would immunize state Congressional apportionment laws which debase a citizen's right to vote from the power of the courts to protect the constitutional rights of individuals from legislative destruction." He then declared:

> To say that a vote is worth more in one district than in another would not only run counter to our fundamental ideas of democratic government, it would cast aside the principle of a House of Representatives elected "by the people," a principle tenaciously fought for and established at the Constitutional Convention.[44]

*   *   *

It remained, however, for the Court to make clear the ultimate dimensions of the Federal rule of reapportionment. In the six cases which the Court decided in June, 1964 Chief Justice Warren assumed the responsibility of writing the majority opinions as a means of spelling out in remaining detail the proposition which had first been expressed in *Baker*. The basic principle was the same in all the cases, he declared. If the rule of "one person, one vote" was constitutionally applicable, as in *Baker,* to representation in the lower house of the state legislature, to state officers and United States Senators and governors in statewide elections, as in *Gray,* and to Congressmen, as in *Wesberry,* it remained to extend it to the upper chamber of the state legislature since it depended on a rule of equality derived from the Federal Constitution rather than on any theory of representation set out in state constitutions.[45]

Equality of voting weight would mean little, said Warren, if one house of the state legislature were apportioned and the other were not. While some issues might be compromised between the houses, "in all too many cases the more probable result would be frustration of the majority will through minority veto in the house not apportioned on a population basis, stemming directly from the failure to accord adequate overall legislative representation to all of the state's citizens on a nondiscriminatory basis."

The opinion in *Reynolds v. Sims* thereupon rejected the contention that reapportionment for both houses of a legislature rendered the concept of bicameralism meaningless, reasserted the holding in *Gray* that the "Federal analogy" in the case of state legislatures was "inapposite," and dismissed the argument, "grounded on Congressional approval, incident to admitting states to the Union, of state apportionment plans containing deviations from the equal-population principle." Companion opinions held invalid a redistricting plan which was so complex and sophisticated as to ensure "a built-in bias against voters living in the state's most populous counties," or provided an improbable remedy in the form of a so-called "floterial district."* Nor, declared the Court at the last, could the fact that malapportionment plans had been submitted to and ratified by the people of a state overcome the constitutional objection to any scheme distorting the weight of individual votes.[46]

Conservatives—and many moderates—were stunned by the June, 1964 decisions. While *Baker,* in retrospect, was beginning to seem like a reasonable statement of essential democracy—it was difficult to deny that per capita representation ought to mean just that—and even the equality of voting for statewide offices in the Georgia cases had a firm basis in logic, it now became evident that the Court was carrying voting equality to the same extreme that it had reached in the racial cases and in the rights of defendants.

Thus, by an eight-to-one majority, in *Reynolds v. Sims* the Court had invalidated an Alabama districting plan which permitted variances in its lower house so great that one vote in some counties had the weight of forty votes in others, while in the state senate the variances might be one to sixteen.[47] By seven-to-two majorities, the Court set aside a Maryland plan which gave 75 percent of the population only 30 percent of the representation (*Committee for Fair Representation v. Tawes*),[48] and procedures in Virginia (*Davis v. Mann*)[49] and Delaware (*Roman v. Sincock*)[50] which gave more than 50 percent of the representation to substantially less than half of the voters. Six-to-three majorities in *WMCA, Inc. v. Lomenzo*[51] set aside a New York constitutional formula so complicated and rigid that the state legislature could do little to ameliorate it, and in *Lucas v. Colorado General Assembly* rejected a Colorado constitutional amendment on apportionment approved by the people. The people of a state could not, even by majority vote, escape the overriding rule of equal protection in the Federal Constitution, the Court held in the Colorado case.[52]

*   *   *

Harlan, the consistent dissenter in all cases, joined by Stewart in five and by Clark in two, continued the systematic refutation of the Warren thesis which he had begun in *Baker* and continued through *Gray* and *Wesberry.* In both *Baker* and *Gray* he had demonstrated mathematically that the formula of one-person-one-vote could be irrational in itself. In *Wesberry* he warned that the holding of the Court "casts grave doubt on the con-

---

*The term "floterial" was defined by the Court as a legislative district including several separate districts which independently were not entitled to an additional representative but whose conglomerate population entitled the area as a whole to another seat in the state legislature. *Davis v. Mann,* 377 U. S. 678, 686, n. 2.

stitutionality of the composition of the House of Representatives," and insisted that the only constitutionally guaranteed right is the right to vote itself, not to have an equal weight given to the vote.[53] He shrewdly reminded the majority of the language in Article I, section 2, that the electors for members of the House of Representatives "shall have the qualifications requisite for electors of the most numerous branch of the state legislature"—an implication that the Founding Fathers had assumed that only one house would be chosen on a population basis.[54]

Following Frankfurter's example of using legal history, Harlan cited the records of the Convention of 1787 as indicating "as clearly as may be that the Convention understood the state legislatures to have plenary power over the conduct of elections for Representatives," with only one Federal agency—Congress—permitted by the Constitution to propose any guidelines. He also reviewed congressional enactments from 1842 to 1940 to support his argument.[55]

In relying on population as the sole basis for representation in any elective assembly, Harlan complained, the majority refused to consider any alternative bases of equal legitimacy—"economic or other sorts of group interests," a desire "to insure effective representation for sparsely settled areas," or "availability of access of citizens to their representatives." He then reached his climax:

> The Constitution is an instrument of government, fundamental to which is the premise that in a diffusion of governmental authority lies the greatest promise that this nation will realize liberty for all its citizens. This Court, limited in function in accordance with that premise, does not serve its high purpose when it exceeds its authority, even to satisfy justified impatience with the slow workings of the political process. For when, in the name of constitutional interpretation, the Court *adds* something to the Constitution that was deliberately excluded from it, the Court in reality substitutes its view of what should be so for the amending process.[56]

The Warren opinion answered the Frankfurter-Harlan doctrine of restraint with an unequivocal call for the total enjoyment of the right of equality in a free society. "State legislatures are, historically, the fountainhead of representative government in this country," said the onetime governor of California. But, he insisted, "representative government is in essence self-government through the medium of elected representatives of the people, and each and every citizen has an inalienable right to full and effective participation in the political processes of his state's legislative bodies."

"To the extent that a citizen's right to vote is debased, he is that much less a citizen. . . . The complexions of societies and civilizations change, often with amazing rapidity. A nation once primarily rural in character becomes predominantly urban. Representation schemes once fair and equitable become archaic and outdated. But the basic principle of representative government remains, and must remain, unchanged—the weight of a citizen's vote cannot be made to depend on where he lives."[57]

The reapportionment cases, and particularly the six epitomized in *Reynolds,* left conservatives in a state of profound shock. The decisions which followed failed to mollify those who were convinced that state sovereignty had received a mortal blow in June, 1964. Yet *Fortson v. Dorsey* in 1965 upheld a Georgia plan for a multi-member senatorial district against the lower court's finding that it failed to ensure one senator for each part of the district; as long as the district as a whole had the number of senators to which its population entitled it, said Brennan, the Federal requirement was satisfied.[58]

The next year the Court unanimously upheld a Hawaii temporary apportionment plan which used a population base of registered voters; Brennan, again speaking for the Court, found this a reasonable means of offsetting the abnormal and continually changing numbers of military personnel in temporary residence.[59] But in 1967 the Court, speaking through White, denied a Florida plan which failed to demonstrate a rational base for a 30 to 40 percent variation in the population apportioned in various voting districts.[60]

If anything, these successive decisions attested to the continuing watchfulness of the Court in the matter of reorienting the base for representative government in the United States. Two other 1967 cases, while indicating a willingness to accept geographic variances in local electoral districts at face value, nevertheless suggested that the basic proposition initiated in *Baker* could reach into city and county government processes as well.

The local issue was settled in *Avery v. Midland County,* decided in the spring of 1968. A six-to-three majority speaking through Justice White found malapportionment forbidden under the equal protection clause where a local county board included four members representing districts which varied in population from 67,906 to 414. The Court declared:

> That the state legislature may itself be properly apportioned does not exempt municipalities from the Fourteenth Amendment. While state legislatures exercise extensive power over their constituents and over the various units of local government, the states universally leave much policy and decision making to their governmental subdivisions. . . . In a word, institutions of local government have always been a major aspect of our system, and their responsible and responsive operation is today of increasing importance to the quality of life of more and more of our citizens. We therefore see little difference, in terms of the application of the equal protection clause and of the principles of *Reynolds v. Sims,* between the exercise of state power through legislatures and its exercise by elected officials in the cities, towns and counties.[61]

*   *   *

What rankled most among conservatives was the ultimate basis of the one-man-one-vote rationale: the conclusion of the Warren Court majority that the citizen whose universal voting equality was being asserted was a citizen of the United States as much as (or perhaps more than) he was a citizen of a particular state. If a "people of the United States" was becoming the paramount source of authority in the Union, what was the future role of the states as component parts of that Union? What were the "reserved powers" of the states, to which conservatives so wistfully alluded in the Tenth Amendment—or were these, in the changing context of the mid-twentieth century, powers reserved to the people rather than to the states? And if so, what people, if not the people who were citizens of the United States?

A crystallizing concept of a people distinguishable from either the states or the Union was beginning to appear in professional literature. One writer in the *New York University Law Review* in the fall of 1962 suggested that the Ninth and Tenth Amendments, which had been the ineffectual refuge of those resisting the growth of Federal power, might alternatively be the culture-bed of inchoate rights of the people, "adjacent to, or analogous to, the pattern of rights which we find in the Constitution," to be asserted against governmental restraints when and as they matured.[62]

Modern Federalism was the ultimate issue on which the climactic apportionment opinions were being challenged. As Henry Steele Commager observed, the most rabid critics "are not genuinely concerned with the powers of the states. They are concerned with the non-powers of the nation. They do not want to see state governments invigorated, carrying through broad legislative programs; they want to see the national government frustrated, incompetent to carry through legislative programs."[63] And yet, this did not describe the anomaly in its totality—for it was a protest against the general judicial doctrine of universal equality that unified the conservatism of the mid-sixties, and it was in Congress that some of the most insistent debate on the issue took place.

From the spring of 1962 to the end of 1967, a steadily intensifying attack on the jurisprudence of the new Federalism went on. Under the goading of the Tennessee and Georgia malapportionment cases, and with the zealous backing of the Court's old nemesis, the Conference of State Chief Justices, three so-called "states' rights amendments" had been introduced in the winter of 1963; they had died for lack of Congressional support and from a flurry of condemnation from legal scholars and bar associations.* The real effort to overcome the apportionment doctrines was galvanized by *Reynolds* and its associated cases in June, 1964. Over the next three years the attack developed into a campaign—shrewdly planned, quietly administered—and uncompromising.

There was a growing irrationality about the matter. While state politicians continued loudly to denounce the judicial holdings, state governments generally proceeded with reapportionment in keeping with the decisions. Thus a race against time was under way; if constitutional amendments were

---

*The text of these amendments, and the current effort to invoke a new Constitutional Convention, are discussed in Ch. 16.

sought to overturn the Court's opinions against malapportionment, how would they be received in states which had completed their apportionment reforms? In the alternative, how would a Congressional program for relief affect the situation in the reapportioned states?

The first Congressional attempt at reversal or neutralization of the Court doctrine took the familiar form of an attempted limitation on the Court's jurisdiction in a bill introduced by Congressman William M. Tuck of Virginia. While it was promptly condemned by moderates as "a smoke screen . . . to postpone the effect of . . . giving all Americans an equal opportunity to participate in legislation," others contended that the bill went to the basic issue of letting the people of a state decide, without interference, how they wished to be represented. However, Congressman L. C. Arends of Illinois revealed the premise on which many conservatives would base their action when he declared that failure to arrest the judicial decrees would destroy "the principle of a Republic of Federated States."[64]

The Tuck bill passed the House by a vote of 218 to 175, but died in the Senate—not from majority opposition but from the belief that it proposed a remedy that would come too late. Instead, Senator Everett M. Dirksen of Illinois and Senator Mike Mansfield of Montana advanced a bipartisan proposal in the form of a rider to the 1964 foreign aid appropriation act, relieving the states of all compliance with the reapportionment ruling until January, 1966—within which time, it was obviously hoped, a constitutional amendment negating the judicial decisions could be submitted and adopted.[65] Liberals countered with an alternative rider, proposed by Senators Javits of New York and Humphrey and Eugene McCarthy of Minnesota, declaring it the sense of Congress that the states should have a reasonable time to comply.[66] The maneuvers of the opposing groups eventually cancelled each other out.

*   *   *

A widely admired, though sometimes vacillating, moderate himself, Dirksen had not generally been identified with the doctrinaire states' rightists in or out of Congress. His wildly waving hair and his old-fashioned, mellifluous oratory endeared him to all factions, and his steadfast refusal to play partisan politics whenever he was convinced the national interest was at stake gave him on frequent occasions the aura of genuine statesmanship. "Shrewd, experienced, worldly, where lesser men are merely cynical," wrote one contemporary observer, Dirksen nevertheless ultimately became the image of "a Republicanism of old men, outdated ideas, and perpetual negatives."[67]

In this hour, Dirksen was being driven by a combination of motives and a deep-seated moral conviction that universal equality in the local electoral process, which automatically subordinated the rural interests, was a denial of certain basic values in American life. His own Illinois experiences —born and raised in a small city in the middle of a state politically dominated by the massed millions in Chicago—made him thoroughly aware that he had to hold fast to the downstate constituency to offset his opponents' metropolitan advantage. He was also aware that, in the mid-twentieth century, the Republican party generally was confronted with the same problem.

Thus he attracted to himself a formidable following. As Senate minority leader, pursuing a course which substantially accommodated his own party's interests, he could count on two major blocs of Democrats as well: Southern conservatives saw the practical advantage of letting the anti-Federalist case be stated by a Northern Republican; and anti-urban Democrats like Mansfield of Montana, sharing Dirksen's moral convictions and personal political necessities, likewise were disposed to vote with him.

Thus, Dirksen's 1964 defeat only encouraged him to plan a more elaborate strategy for 1965; rather than a bill proposing a statutory moratorium until a constitutional amendment could be proposed, he would offer the amendment itself. Knowing that the bill would remain blocked in the Judiciary Committee indefinitely, on July 22 he brought to the Senate floor an inconsequential bill to proclaim the dates for "National American Legion Baseball Week." Thereupon he offered as a substitute for this bill his own amendment—reminding the liberals that they had used the same tactics to get the anti-poll tax amendment out of committee.[68]

The Dirksen amendment, in the form in which it came onto the floor, proposed to permit any state by popular vote to district one branch of its legislature on the basis of factors other than population. "Because of my fidelity to the state-Federal system that our forefathers gave to us," Dirksen told the Senate, "and because I believe that there is such a thing as sovereign power in the states and there are some rights in the states," he intended to go all-out for the amendment. Moreover, he warned, if he lost this battle he would continue the war. On two points, said Dirksen, he wanted his colleagues to be clear: "The first is that I play for keeps. The second is that I use whatever weapons are in the rule book."[69]

The battle would continue for two weeks, introduced each time by the clerk's straight-faced announcement that the pending business to be discussed was the American Legion baseball week. In the course of the debates, few remarks on either side added anything new to the previous pros and cons; liberals applauded the ultimate democracy in the principle of equal voting weight for all, and decried the long resistance of rural legislatures to changing needs, while conservatives insisted upon the right of individual states to organize self-government and decried the potential neglect of rural areas by the dominant urban representation.[70]

Senator Owen Brewster of Maryland reiterated the argument that the "Federal analogy" was "inapposite." Representation by states in the United States Senate, he declared, was in itself evidence of the degree of sovereignty in the states recognized by the Constitution, but no such sovereignty attached to counties or other political subdivisions within a state.[71] Senator Birch

Bayh of Indiana stated that he shared substantially the same feelings about the primacy of local self-government as Dirksen, but proposed certain amendments to the Dirksen text to ensure that before the states assumed this prerogative the democratic guarantee of the Court decisions be accommodated. "A legislative body which frames a proposal to be submitted to the people for approval can ofttimes, by the wording in the referendum document itself, determine what the outcome of that referendum will be," he observed.

Prerequisite to any such constitutional amendment, therefore, Bayh insisted that both houses of the legislature should be reapportioned on a population basis. Such a requirement, in his view, was valid on four points: it recognized the principle that "people . . . are the most important and overriding factor to be considered in the apportionment of any legislative body"; it took into account the differing circumstances created by physical or economic geography in different states; it would establish a redistricting process which would not require continuing judicial review; and it would not require a suspended obedience to the law of the land while the amendment was being ratified.[72]

In a detailed critique of the proposal on July 29, Douglas of Illinois pointed out that the primary intent and effect of the Dirksen amendment was to revive the "rotten" boroughs of the pre-*Baker* era, that the failure of the proposal to muster a majority of the Judiciary Committee after extended hearings was an indication of its ambivalent character, and that there was no evidence that the reapportionment now being conducted under court surveillance had been attended by chaos. In a colloquy with Clark of Pennsylvania, Douglas described the danger of leaving reapportionment surveillance of state legislatures to politically minded state courts, and concluded by stressing the practical difficulty of ensuring a proportionate voter turnout on any referenda on the question which might be drafted.[73]

The ultimate issue, said Senator Joseph D. Tydings of Maryland, is "where we wish to put the high water mark of representative democracy." For him, it was unthinkable and an untenable contradiction to freeze in the language of the Constitution a variable voting franchise ensuring permanent minority domination of state legislatures. The "barons of barnyard government," in H. L. Mencken's phrase, had demonstrated their own intransigence with reference to chronically denied legislative aid to areas of their states where concentrated population cried for increased public services. The plan to remove the question from judicial review he charged removed any limits upon legislators in restoring the old inequities.[74]

On August 4 the constitutional amendment, alias a national baseball week proclamation, came to a vote. Dirksen's estimate of strength had been substantially correct; a solid phalanx of Southern Democrats, and both Democrats and Republicans from states where the political power base lay in the rural centers, lined up in favor. The final vote was 57 yeas to 39 nays, with four Senators not voting. Only the fact that two-thirds of the Senate was required in the affirmative for a proposed constitutional amendment prevented the measure from carrying; the Illinois strategist had fallen just seven votes short.[75]

Dirksen immediately served notice that he intended to do just what he had announced he would do at the beginning of the debate on his substituted bill. On August 11 he introduced a new joint resolution on the same subject. When the judiciary committee voted not to report the bill, Dirksen proceeded to block Senate action on an administration immigration measure. Not until September 8 did Senator Thomas J. Dodd of Connecticut switch his vote to Dirksen in order to break the tie; he served notice on the Illinoisan that he would not support the resolution after voting for it, however. The immigration bill then moved forward, but the judiciary committee managed to delay its own action on the Dirksen measure until March 4, 1966.[76]

*   *   *

The third defeat for Dirksen came a month later; having threshed out the issues so thoroughly the year before, the Senate was not disposed to prolong the debate. Once again, on April 20, the majority of fifty-five to thirty-eight in favor of the bill fell short of the two-thirds majority required for an amendment. Senator James B. Pearson of Kansas observed that the consistency of the ratio indicated a hardening of positions rather than a striving for some common ground.[77]

Each side charged the other with extensive lobby influence; the conservatives pointed to the civil liberties and labor interests who besieged the uncommitted, while Senator Douglas declared that public utilities and anti-labor associations were equally active on the other side. There was definite evidence of a carefully organized campaign to whip up backing for the Dirksen proposal: an organization calling itself the "Committee for Government of the People" was identified as the *alter ego* of the San Francisco public relations firm of Whittaker and Baxter which was reported to have spent very large sums of money in support of both the 1965 and 1966 Dirksen proposals.[78]

Since this was the same firm which had been retained to propagandize against Medicare when that had been the burning issue before Congress, it was hardly to be disputed that the undying conservatives of the past had a major stake in the issue. A similar public relations job had attended the movement for the "states' rights amendments" of 1963, and indeed, the next maneuver which Dirksen himself resorted to was an open invitation for the revival of those proposals. "The issue will not die and, unlike old soldiers, it will not fade away," the Illinois Senator adamantly stated after his third defeat.[79] Once more, as had happened so often in the rapid changes of the twentieth century, the American people were moving toward another constitutional crisis.

16/Views at the Threshold

I N THE SUMMER OF 1968 Chief Justice Warren offered his resignation to
Lyndon Johnson to take effect at the President's "pleasure." After a
Senate revolt over Johnson's attempt to name Abe Fortas as Warren's successor, an agreement with President-Elect Richard M. Nixon set the retirement
date as the end of the Court term in June, 1969. With this development the
constitutional history of the sixties began to draw to its conclusion. The
fifteen years from the spring of 1954, when the Warren Court had handed
down its fateful opinion in the first desegregation case, had been the capstone
for a jurisprudence which had progressed logically and inexorably from the
historic shift of the Hughes Court in the spring of 1937. In these thirty-two
years, Americans as a nation had reached full maturity, although not without
passing through a number of traumatic stages in the process.

The Court, in the closing months of Warren's Chief Justiceship, strikingly
symbolized the events of these years. Two members, Black and Douglas, were
the remaining appointees of Franklin D. Roosevelt; four others—Warren
himself, Brennan, Harlan and Stewart—represented the Eisenhower terms.
The remaining three—Fortas, Marshall and White—were the men of the
sixties appointed by the Kennedy and Johnson administrations. Harlan and
Stewart, and occasionally White, tended to be the trustees of the Frankfurter
tradition. The remainder of the Court, particularly in the days of the New
Frontier and the Great Society, had made possible the ascendancy of the
Black-Douglas school.

This majority in favor of activism, indeed, had been clinched by the
Kennedy-Johnson appointments. White had replaced Whittaker, the least
forceful of the Eisenhower appointees, and Arthur Goldberg had replaced
Frankfurter himself. Johnson's first appointment—Fortas, replacing Goldberg
who was drafted as Ambassador to the United Nations—made no further
change in the Court's orientation, but with his second appointment of Thurgood Marshall to succeed old New Dealer Tom Clark, the liberal wing attained its greatest strength.

Kennedy's appointments were relatively circumspect. No one, the Senate Judiciary Committee reported, appeared in opposition to Byron White. A zealous campaigner for Kennedy, the onetime "Whizzer" of the gridiron had rounded up a precious number of pre-convention votes for the Democratic hopeful in the Western states, and during the electoral campaign had staged a massive "Citizens for Kennedy" parade in New York City. His tenure as Deputy Attorney General had been deft and productive. The only pertinent protest, observed Senator Richard Russell of Georgia, could not be against the man but against the fact that now for many years no "genuine conservative constitutionalist" had been nominated by any President.[1]

The Goldberg nomination to succeed Frankfurter, in what some were coming to call the "Jewish seat" on the Court, won equal praise from the Senate. The conservatives were mollified by the objectivity with which this onetime labor lawyer had discharged his duties as Secretary of Labor. Goldberg had voluntarily renounced the $25,000 yearly pension for which he had qualified by his years of service as counsel for the United Steelworkers and the CIO upon accepting public office. His complete honesty in administering the program of the Labor Department had won him the admiration of employers generally. Senator Yarborough of Texas had expressed the hope that Goldberg would account for "increasing confidence in the Court" in his years of service.[2]

*   *   *

This general euphoria abruptly dissipated when Johnson offered his nominations for the bench. In the summer of 1965, following the death of Adlai Stevenson, the President surprised the nation by choosing Goldberg as Stevenson's successor to the U. N. position. Goldberg himself was dismayed; the Court, as he told close friends, had represented the peak of his personal ambition and he had looked forward to spending the remainder of his professional career there. A Presidential call being what it was, however, he had virtually no choice but to accede.

The nomination of Abe Fortas reminded Raymond Moley of *Newsweek* of the early Roosevelt appointments to the Court—"an especially pronounced return to the reformist tradition, as well as a recognition of personal and political ties." The consensus of criticism, in Congress as well as out, concerned the nominee's long and close association with the President. Fortas and Johnson had first come to know each other in the New Deal era, and Fortas had served the Roosevelt administration in a number of assignments, chiefly as a lieutenant of Harold L. Ickes. Subsequently he had joined with two other old New Dealers—Thurman Arnold of the anti-trust corps of the Justice Department, and Paul Porter, wartime price administrator—to form a Washington law firm which over the years grew to one of the most successful in a frenetically competitive domain.[3]

Fortas' intimate personal and professional relationship with Johnson also grew with the years. He helped plan the organization and duties of the

Warren Commission, appointed by Johnson to review the evidence relating
to John Kennedy's assassination. He drew up the trust in which the Johnson
family radio and television interests were placed during Johnson's public
life. When an unsavory incident involving one of Johnson's closest administrative aides became public in the course of the 1964 election campaign,
Fortas arranged for a relatively quiet disposition of the matter.

There could be little dispute over the closeness of Fortas' ties with the
President—but how relevant this was depended on the viewpoint of the
observer. The relationship was hardly any closer than Frankfurter's with
Franklin Roosevelt, different only in circumstance from the relationship
between Brandeis and Wilson, and quite analogous to the contacts between
Melville W. Fuller and Grover Cleveland. It was difficult to argue that the
brilliant professional accomplishments of a judicial nominee should be in
any way nullified by a legitimate personal and professional relationship with
the Executive who placed his name before the Senate.

What was to prove Fortas' future undoing, however, was not cronyism
but the alleged continuation of the advisory functions of an attorney after
his going onto the bench, or at least the acceptance of a retainer which
threatened to compromise his judicial position. The furore which broke out
over this incident was compounded by the Byzantine nature of Washington
law practice in firms which, like Arnold, Fortas and Porter (later Arnold
and Porter), specialized in handling the interests of wealthy clients before
administrative regulatory bodies. The expertise of senior partners in such
firms derived from things much subtler than the printed rules and regulations
promulgated by these agencies—it was a thorough knowledge of unwritten
law, an instinctive feel for the manner in which specific agencies and commissioners approached specific factual situations, the demonstrated ability
to guide clients to positions conformable with the established preferences of
decision-makers in these agencies and commissions. This knowledge, usually
gained from prior employment within the government body itself, was a
commodity of extraordinary salability in the mid-century, when scarcely any
major corporation or individual entrepreneur could operate without reference
to policies administered by one or more such agencies.

Under the circumstances, it might well have been asked whether the
nature of the clients in his administrative law practice in Fortas' case differed
significantly from the corporation and railroad law practice of many an
earlier member of the Court, insofar as his judicial objectivity was concerned. But the fundamental issue, in the *Blitzkrieg* of publicity which would
force the Justice off the bench in the late spring of 1969, was the alleged
continuation of some sort of counseling relationship with some former
clients after the appointee had exchanged the role of attorney for that of
jurist. The issue and the allegations were never formally substantiated, but the
normally news-tight Justice Department suddenly appeared to be leaking
news in torrents, all to the effect that there was "much more serious"

evidence in its possession. However that might be, the furious psychological pressure had its effect; in the middle of May, Fortas submitted his resignation to the White House and it was instantly accepted.

In the summer of 1965, of course, nothing of this could be anticipated. Fortas was known as a brilliant attorney, and the factor which rankled most with conservatives was his successful argument as appointed counsel in *Gideon v. Wainwright,* the cornerstone of the constitutional rule of a right to counsel for all criminal defendants. The opposition to Johnson's nomination manifestly drew its greatest strength from that line of decisions which had proceeded from *Gideon* through *Escobedo* to *Miranda*—and from criminal courts to juvenile courts (*In re Gault*) as well.* Such an appointee, it was reasonable to expect, would strengthen the Court majority in this position.

Although it had no part in the process of "advise and consent," the House of Representatives indulged in a certain amount of commentary on the Fortas nomination. One speaker suggested, among other things, that Justice Goldberg had simply been drafted off the bench to make a spot for Fortas, and quoted a current article in *Esquire* magazine implying that a Supreme Court appointment was the only position in public life which would entice the nominee from his lucrative law practice.[4]

For its part, the Senate Judiciary Committee divided its interrogation of the nominee between a variety of his services for the Kennedy and Johnson administrations and a fishing expedition for his views on the constitutional issues of reapportionment and defendants' rights. Fortas answered the first series of questions forthrightly and parried the others where, he explained, he either had no considered opinion or might be taking a position which would affect a case subsequently to come before the Court. After a brief flurry of further grumbling over the politics of the nomination, the Senate itself confirmed without a recorded vote.[5]

*   *   *

It was widely anticipated that Johnson's next nomination would be a Negro—specifically, Thurgood Marshall, chief counsel for the appellants in the original desegregation case, whose subsequent appointments to the Court of Appeals and then to the office of Solicitor General were felt to be preparatory steps. The opportunity came in the spring of 1967 when Ramsey Clark was appointed to his father's onetime position as Attorney General. Whether this was another Johnsonian tactic to force an opening on the Court was conjectural, but in any event the senior Clark thereupon announced his intention to retire at the end of the term to avoid any potential conflict of interest.† In June the President formally submitted Marshall's name to the Senate.

---

*Cf. Ch. 14 and Appendix E.

†As Charles Evans Hughes, Jr. had resigned as Solicitor General in 1930 when his father became Chief Justice.

The conservatives raised the hue and cry immediately. Thurmond of South Carolina candidly stated that he would oppose Marshall on the fundamental premise that the nomination would tend to solidify the liberal influence on the Court. Byrd of Virginia agreed, reminding his colleagues that he had voted in favor of Marshall on his two previous nominations to the Court of Appeals and as Solicitor General. Ellender of Louisiana concurred in these general objections, while other Southerners complained specifically of some of Marshall's liberal opinions from the appellate bench and his long professional association with reform groups which would regularly be represented in issues before the Court.[6]

The politics of the appointment, like the politics of the Fortas appointment, was self-evident; but in both cases the real question was whether a manifest but legitimate political fact should prejudice the acknowledged professional accomplishments of the nominee. It was hardly arguable that Johnson was aware in nominating Marshall that it was politically opportune to advance a Negro to the high court. Not only was the climate encouraging, but the summer of 1967, torn with wide-ranging riots in Negro slums throughout the nation's cities, represented a crisis for Democratic liberalism.

Senator Hart of Michigan called upon his colleagues to face the fact of the nominee's race honestly. While it was incidental to his personal qualifications, said Hart, "I think it is a symbol of progress, of hope, and of opportunity . . . and the nation will be the stronger." Senator Kuchel of California agreed: "I believe his selection is part of a larger process in which not only Negro Americans, but also Americans from all racial and religious backgrounds, have begun to participate in the affairs of this nation." While he supported Marshall because of his personal competence, the speaker continued, by his confirmation the Senate would in his view "express confidence in the American dream, a dream which says that every man, regardless of race, color or creed, may achieve the goals he seeks in a free society."[7]

The conservatives speaking in opposition were Southerners, but they disclaimed—and their colleagues expressed their acceptance of the disclaimers —any racial antagonism. Erwin of North Carolina, one of the Senate's acknowledged specialists on constitutional law, delivered a lengthy and scholarly discourse which could have served as a concise treatise on the conservative interpretation of the Constitution. Thurmond, in an address of almost equal length, focussed upon a series of judicial decisions with which he was in disagreement. The dialogue ran for six hours, before the confirmation at length was put to a vote. Thurgood Marshall was confirmed, 69 to 11, with 20 members not voting.[8]

*   *   *

Lyndon Johnson, whose hallmark in a quarter of a century on Capitol Hill had been political deftness, was condemned to an image as President which was often crude and blatant. He was, as many observers commented, sensitive about the contrast between the urbanity of the late Kennedy administration and the alleged earthiness of his own; a man of dignity and great moral courage on many occasions, Johnson seldom had the good fortune to be on center stage in his best moments. His espousal of the Great Society was all too readily denigrated by his critics as an attempt to rework the New Frontier into a homely version of the New Deal. In point of fact, however, Johnson displayed in many of his messages to Congress a keen perception of the total transformation of American life which had come about in the two decades since World War II.

In his leadership of the Eighty-ninth Congress, in particular, Johnson had hewn out some epochal landmarks. Building on the Civil Rights Act of 1964 with the Voting Rights Act of 1965, he had forged a statutory instrumentality for the enforcement of guarantees in the Fourteenth and Fifteenth Amendments which had been frustrated for a century. He had thrown the full weight of his administration behind two other proposals which had been thwarted for years—Medicare for the aged, and Federal aid to education. He had accurately discerned the dangerous national problems reflected in urban deterioration, air and water pollution, and transportation congestion. And the most fundamental (if also the most controversial) of all his objectives had been the attempt to carry to conclusion a war on poverty in the land.

"Throughout his long climb upward," wrote Political Columnists Evans and Novak, "Johnson's posture had always been deliberately and necessarily flexible." As a New Deal Congressman in the depression, he spoke for the impoverished back country of Texas; as a Senator, he achieved an accommodation with statewide oil interests which dominated the conservative party majority. Finally, at the Vice-Presidential level he found himself "free now at last to be as liberal as necessary for his national constituency." The frustrating war in Viet Nam had been the major pitfall of his career, even though the pit had been dug before his administration.[9]

Many spoke of the President as a complex individual, as if in apology for or expiation of some of his policies and actions. It was, to be sure, a complex age in which he was charged with the awesome duties of Chief Executive, and he was not the first American leader to lack a touch for international affairs. Johnson was accused, rather gratuitously, of over-reacting in a Dominican crisis which might well have become a debacle like Cuba. That adventure came off; his election to accelerate the American military role in Viet Nam was foredoomed on several counts. He asserted the color of authority based upon a tenuous Congressional resolution; neither military nor diplomatic intelligence cleared up the uncertainty as to the integrity of various interests in Viet Nam itself; and (more than the vociferous opposition of vested anti-war interests of various hues) the ultimate collapse of public support was bred by the inability of the American military commitment to bring off a conventional victory.

On the home front, Johnson's troubles were said by his critics to be compounded by his compulsive tendency to promise too much. Negroes, in particular, whose hopes were so often to be dashed (and often by their own too-ready assumption of what had been promised), nurtured a bitter resentment at the continuance of social and economic barriers to the better life. In four unhappy summers, from 1964 to 1967, a growing number of American cities experienced riots approaching the proportions of insurrection in the Negro ghettoes.

One of the problems of the Great Society as Lyndon Johnson offered it, wrote an observer from the London School of Economics, was the inability of Americans to distinguish between poverty and inequality. The one merely implied an appeal to the general conscience to offer some degree of economic relief; the other implied "the need for structural change, for sacrifices by the majority." Yet the poverty on which Johnson was seeking to wage war, the writer concluded, was rather a problem of inequality. The growth of inequality between 1949 and 1956, he declared, "was more striking than at any time during at least the past forty years," so that by the time of Johnson's project for equal opportunity more than a quarter of the population of employment age were found to be below the minimum subsistence level of income. It was somewhat less than Franklin Roosevelt's "one-third of a nation," but it was a problem not likely to respond quickly to a campaign such as the administration had attempted.[10]

*   *   *

In the matters of the Supreme Court and the Department of Justice, Johnson's actions were sometimes contradictory (or at least inconsistent)— and largely political in motivation. There was reasonable ground for arguing that both of his Court appointments had been the result of maneuvering to create artificial vacancies. In both cases, the men he nominated were men he was specifically interested in putting onto the bench, yet what he intended to accomplish in the process was not so readily apparent. Certainly with Thurgood Marshall's appointment the President not only broke the color barrier but definitely increased the tempo of activism. Clark, Marshall's predecessor, was an expert in judicial administration* and as an old-line state's attorney did not share the majority's readiness to short-cut all details of criminal procedure in favor of the absolutism of the defendant's rights. On the other hand, his son as Attorney General evinced throughout his tenure a pronounced sympathy for such absolutism which substantially aided the activist argument.[11]

Johnson's selection of Goldberg for the United Nations ambassadorship was also enigmatic. It was argued that he sought a skilled Jewish advocate to beard the vociferous Arab spokesmen in the U. N. in the aftermath of the "Six Days' War" in which Israel had humiliated Arab military adventurism.

---

*Clark subsequently became director of the Federal Judicial Center, a clearing house for research and programs for improvement of judicial administration in the Federal court system.

But this was tenuous at best; there were other Jewish liberals in American public life who would have been available for the purpose. Certainly, so far as the Court was concerned, Johnson's shift of Goldberg for Fortas did not change the balance for activism; and if his purpose had been to use the U. N. opening to disguise his creating of a Court opening for Fortas, it would have been more plausible to have drafted either Harlan or White, non-activists whose identity as former Rhodes Scholars would have given some color of interest or expertise in international affairs.

In the Attorney General's office, Johnson from the outset had been confronted with the problem of continuing Robert Kennedy for a decent interval after John Kennedy's death, while at the same time finding a terminal point for the Kennedy influence within his administration. Indeed, the Kennedy program of all-out prosecution of civil rights continued without diminution under his successor, Assistant Attorney General Nicholas Katzenbach. The chief difference, it was reported, was in the personalities of the men; Katzenbach, after all, had been personally on the scene when a Negro student was enrolled over state governors' defiance at both the University of Mississippi and the University of Alabama. Kennedy's intensity, it was said, often aggravated tensions in such confrontations, while Katzenbach's more phlegmatic approach tended to reduce them.[12]

In the Solicitor General's office, Johnson also inherited a strong Kennedy lieutenant in Harvard labor law expert Archibald Cox, who had been the late President's consultant on a wide variety of matters other than purely legal. As soon as Cox left to return to teaching, Johnson hurried Marshall into the position from his appellate judgeship—perhaps to broaden his dossier of experience, as well as to strengthen his record of Senate confirmations preparatory to nominating him for the Supreme Court.

To succeed Marshall in the trial post, Johnson made the somewhat anomalous choice of Harvard Law Dean Erwin N. Griswold, whose criticism of certain Supreme Court cases had occasionally ranged from virulent to vitriolic. The absolutism of the First Amendment freedoms, Griswold had written in 1963, was essentially a narrowing of the Constitution; any simple phrase taken by itself might stand as an absolute, whereas it would not necessarily be susceptible of such an interpretation when read in the context of the whole Constitution. On the other hand, he urged all parties to "take the long view" on the cases strengthening the clear constitutional guarantees of criminal defendants' rights.[13]

A man as totally political as Johnson would inevitably be assumed, sometimes wrongly, to be politically motivated in his appointments, whether for the judiciary or other arms of the government. It was true that in due course a number of deserving Texas Democrats found their rewards in some branch of the administration. This was hardly at variance with American political tradition, but where vacancies in the Federal judiciary were concerned, the President would have been well advised to take note of the potential for

Senate reaction when the politics of the appointment became too obvious. John Kennedy had learned this the hard way, when a Massachusetts hench-man without other notable qualifications had been greeted with such an outburst of protest on Capitol Hill that the nomination had ultimately to be withdrawn.[14]

In his final effort to maneuver a vacancy on the Supreme Court, Johnson might have reminded himself of Kennedy's experience. He started under sub-stantial handicaps: not only was he himself a "lame duck" President, having renounced the intention to seek reelection, but the manifest timing of Chief Justice Warren's resignation suggested an intention to reserve for Johnson the filling of this position in the face of an increasing prospect that Republican Richard Nixon would be elected in the fall. When the President compounded the matter by proposing Justice Fortas—already charged with cronyism in his original nomination to the Court—to succeed Warren and an unmistakable Texas crony, former Congressman Homer Thornberry, to succeed Fortas as Associate Justice, he invited opposition of all hues to unite against him in a spectacular challenge.

*   *   *

On June 13, 1968 Warren sent two letters to the President. The first was a formal letter citing (as Holmes, nearly four decades earlier, had cited) the pertinent statutes on the matter and advising "of my intention to retire as Chief Justice of the United States effective at your pleasure." The second was a letter of explanation, in which the Chief assured Johnson that "it is not because of reasons of health or on account of any personal or associational problems, but solely because of age" that he had decided upon his retirement. The President, in acknowledging the letters and paying tribute to Warren, announced that he would "accept your decision to retire effective at such time as a successor is qualified."[15]

This language gave the conservatives as well as narrow constructionists (if there was any difference between them) an opening for their campaign. Did a retirement offer, effective at the President's "pleasure," actually create a vacancy? And, what was of equally vital importance to the gathering opposi-tion, was the Chief Justice's offer irrevocable? The Republicans quickly added an obviously political argument that no outgoing President had a right to make so important an appointment in the closing months of his administration. Only when and as the White House joined the issue and announced that it would make an all-out fight for the nominations did the true nature of the opposition make itself clear in an equally all-out attack on Fortas' judicial behavior and constitutional beliefs.[16]

The argument over Johnson's right to appoint a Chief Justice in the last half-year of his tenure was patently political. It had been made when Grover Cleveland had nominated Fuller in 1888, and—as a telegram to the Judiciary Committee from more than four hundred law teachers pointed out—such a mentality would have denied John Adams the privilege of appointing John

Marshall in 1800. The law teachers added: "To lay it down as a general rule
that in his last year in office a President should leave judicial posts vacant
so that they may be filled by the next administration would frequently disrupt
the orderly conduct of judicial business. In addition, such a general rule would
have even more serious repercussions. It would imply acceptance of the
premise that judges are accountable to the President who nominates and the
Senators who advise and consent. Our entire constitutional structure is reared
upon exactly the opposite premise."[17]

Senator Ervin of North Carolina had his own conception of the need
of the Court and the Constitution at this juncture. It was, he told his colleagues on the Judiciary Committee, a need for Justices "both able and willing
to interpret the Constitution according to its true intent." After a lengthy
opening day's testimony by the Attorney General as to whether a vacancy
currently existed on the Court—with elaborate hairsplitting over the distinctions between retirements and resignations—the hearings turned to the political and ideological questions which were manifestly the true issue.[18]

Senator Robert P. Griffin of Michigan launched the Republican attack,
on the issue of "cronyism," while Senator Thurmond of South Carolina prepared to follow him on the most recent issues which rankled the conservative
establishment—the absolutism of defendants' rights. A third issue, calculated
to rouse the fundamentalist fervor of the hinterland, would be the question
of First Amendment freedom as it extended to allegedly obscene publications.
The Republican-Southern conservative coalition proceeded to dominate the
news of the committee hearings; whether the moderates on the committee,
certain of a favorable report on the nomination, felt it unnecessary to counter
the hostile publicity at that time, it was seen in retrospect to be a blunder.
The public was aware only of a parade of witnesses from organizations
identified as the Conservative Society of America, the Council Against
Communist Aggression, the Liberty Lobby and Citizens for Decent Literature,
whose exhibits were not always on point.[19]

In four days in July, the Roman carnival swirled about Fortas himself
as he accepted the committee's invitation to testify. Griffin and others first
questioned the Justice's continuing advisory function with the White House.
Whether the practice was to be condoned or condemned, it was hardly
unique in Fortas' case: Frankfurter's continuing aid to Franklin Roosevelt
after he had ascended the bench was well enough known; Theodore Roosevelt
had maintained a comparable contact with Justice Moody; the examples
stretched back through national history.[20]

In any event, the greater issue was one of constitutional philosophy, and
this quickly came to dominate the interrogation. Ervin quoted fervently from
the gospel of the long-deceased evangel of conservatism, Thomas M. Cooley;
indeed, the real witness had little opportunity to testify as the interminable
oratory of *laissez-faire* was read into the record by the committee member.
But if Ervin was prolix, Thurmond was vitriolic, shouting the outrage he felt

at decisions (many of them before Fortas came onto the bench) which h
police interrogation and criminal prosecution of defendants.

"Does not that decision, *Mallory*—I want that name to ring in your
ears—*Mallory*—shackle law enforcement?" the South Carolina Senator
roared. Fortas, of course, was given no chance to reply to the question, as the
speaker poured a long diatribe of his own into the hearing. When at length
the witness stated that he was constitutionally barred from commenting on an
area of law which might come before the Court on which he sat, Thurmond
called for the record to show that the witness refused to answer.[21]

*   *   *

The caterwauling in the Judiciary Committee had its desired effect; although the nomination was reported favorably to the floor of the Senate by
an eleven-to-six vote, it was instantly announced that a filibuster was being
organized to block confirmation. The dispute had now attained a high degree
of irrationality. Much was made of a report that Fortas had given a summer
seminar at the American University law school for a lecturer's fee of $15,000,
the funds having been provided by past or potential clients of Fortas' former
firm or by individuals who might have cases before the Court. Much was
also made of the issue of law and order, by Senators whose words belied
their claim to have read Fortas' small tract, *Concerning Dissent and Civil
Disobedience*, a thoughtful restatement of libertarian ideals and responsibilities.

The defeat of the Johnson nomination was inevitable when an attempt
to invoke cloture in the Senate debates failed of the necessary majority.
Minority Leader Everett Dirksen, who had at first been mildly favorable to
the nomination, saw the handwriting on the wall and switched his allegiance.
The moderates and liberals were disorganized; an awkward attempt to portray
the opposition to Fortas as anti-Semitic backfired, and efforts to compel
Nixon to take a stand on the issue were manifestly unrealistic. After a recess
for the political conventions, in which Senators tested the winds of change,
the question was finally settled in the early fall when Fortas formally requested the White House to withdraw his nomination.

It was the second time in the twentieth century that a Presidential
nomination for the Supreme Court had been rejected—although, unlike
Hoover's proposal of Judge Parker, the Fortas nomination did not suffer the
ignominy of a recorded Senate negative vote. It was also the second time in
history that a Chief Justice's nomination had been rejected.* A combination
of events had brought about Johnson's final humiliation—the cumbersome
politics of the maneuver to time Fortas' succession with Warren's retirement;

---

*John Rutledge of South Carolina was appointed Chief Justice by
Washington in the summer of 1795 and actually presided at one short
term of the Court. The Senate, incensed at his criticism of Jay's Treaty,
refused to confirm him in December of that year.

pedestrian Thornberry being added to the Court at the
ap hatreds of activism nurtured by the conservatives over
epublican hopes for victory a few weeks hence and the
the appointment for themselves. Indeed, Vice-Presiden-
Agnew, in a characteristic gaucherie, accused Warren
tivity as a Republican nominee" to have submitted his
ocratic administration.[22]

The fact was that, as the Nixon years began, the administration did indeed face the prospect that a number of changes in the Court would materialize in the near future. Two Roosevelt appointees, and possibly one or two other Justices besides Warren, were considered likely to complete their tenure in the coming four to eight years. It was not an unfamiliar chapter in the history of the Court—Taft and Harding had concentrated a key number of appointments within a single term, and Truman and Eisenhower had also been able to make a number of nominations during their Presidencies. Franklin Roosevelt's record, of course, was unlikely to be equalled, thanks to the anti-third-term Amendment to the Constitution.

The departure of Justice Fortas in May, 1969 presented the new administration with two early opportunities to alter the composition of the Court; and in the case of the new President it was evident that two fundamental factors would be likely to affect his selections. One was his own professional orientation; Nixon was the first occupant of the White House since William Howard Taft to have a broad experience in the practice of law, and presumably his scrutiny of judicial prospects would be colored by a lawyer's knowledge of the qualifications valued by a trial or appellate practitioner. Such criteria tended to be professionally conservative; added to this factor in the selection process was a politically conservative one, which observers of the White House ascribed to the accommodation of interests reached between Nixon and the Thurmond-led Southern Republicans in the course of the 1968 election campaign.

Eager to curry public support for his choice for the fifteenth Chief Justice, the President arranged to make the announcement by means of a nationally televised ceremony, followed the next day by a full-scale press conference. Judge Warren E. Burger of the Court of Appeals for the District of Columbia, Nixon told the correspondents, had satisfied three requirements he had considered as fundamental. First was Burger's apparent middle-of-the-road position (the phrase Eisenhower had once applied to Earl Warren) on the Constitution in general and criminal law in particular. Second was his prior judicial experience, a factor dear to most constitutional conservatives but of indeterminate significance in the shaping of the insights of Supreme Court members. Finally, said the President, was the fact that the nominee was not close to the White House personally—a policy position which had been followed by Republican presidents from Harding to Eisenhower, and disregarded by Democratic Presidents from Roosevelt to Johnson.[23]

Burger's contribution to the history of the Court and Constitution would be the record of the coming decade. His solid Midwestern background and his moderate to conservative opinions in the appellate court strongly suggested a return to the Frankfurter-Jackson tradition and the ascendancy of the Harlan-Stewart viewpoint of the contemporary Court. Few doubted that this was Nixon's basic objective—like Truman seeking to calm the intellectual turbulence of the Stone Court, Nixon's judicial appointments were to be expected to aim at a similar levelling off of the activism of the past decade.

The activism of the sixties, in fact, appeared to have been reaching a levelling-off of its own accord even before the summer of 1968. In its epochal decisions on segregation, reapportionment and uniformity of defendants' rights, the Warren Court had accomplished the shaping of the third and final dimension to the New Legality which had begun in 1937. The fundamental contribution of the late Hughes Court—providing the cornerstone for the New Legality—had been the constitutional assertion of a sweeping breadth of legislative (particularly Congressional) power. Since the primary tenet of the conservative jurisprudence of the Old Legality had been a restrictive doctrine of legislative power, progressive objectives from the Square Deal to the early New Deal had been consistently frustrated until the doctrine was renounced. And in the sequence of cases in which statutory proposals of the second New Deal had been consistently affirmed, in sharp contrast to the same general proposals which had formerly been negated, the Hughes Court after 1937 had conclusively defined broad legislative authority to be a fundamental principle of the modern Constitution.

The second fundamental had been supplied by the Stone Court, in the course of its disparate jurisprudence from 1941 through 1946: Once the legislative doctrine of the Old Legality had been rejected, a major body of interpretative cases in support of that doctrine had also to be overturned, and alternative judicial findings—threshed out in what at the time seemed to be a trial-and-error approach—had to be enunciated in accommodation of the broad legislative power asserted in the New Legality.

How broad, at last, this power was to be—the answer to this was the third and final dimension of the progressive jurisprudence of the post-New Deal age. The answer turned upon a fresh assertion of the restraining principles of the Constitution itself—restraining, not in the old conservative sense of limited government power to accommodate the people's needs, but in the new sense of limitations upon government action to insure the people's individual rights. This was the burden of the major decisions of the Vinson and early Warren Courts, in the context of the conformist hysteria of the fifties. Thereafter, in the context of legislative inaction on the new issues of racial equality, voter equality and criminal defendants' equality, the activist majority of the Warren Court as it attained dominance was to assert the guarantees of the Bill of Rights and the Fourteenth Amendments as self-executing. With this proposition, the New Legality attained its ultimate dimensions.

*   *   *

Amending the Constitution was the subject of a variety of discussions in the sixties. The Twenty-fifth Amendment, under the impelling circumstances of an assassination of one President and the history of a heart attack in his successor, provided emergency procedures in the event of executive disability in an age which demanded constant readiness on the part of the White House. A possible twenty-sixth amendment, endorsed by the American Bar Association and introduced in Congress after the 1968 election amid a murmur of generally favorable comment, would abolish the anachronistic Electoral College and make the Presidency, like state and national legislatures, responsive to an equal-vote electoral process. Although the proposal had been made sporadically in the past, the more favorable climate generated by the jurisprudence of equality held promise of more serious consideration at this time.[24]

But if some constitutional proposals reflected the continuing trend toward a modern Federalism, others sought to reverse the process. For, as conservatives and reactionaries alike perceived, the thrust of the jurisprudence of the Warren Court was to read the Constitution consistently as a charter of a national government, and in their alarmed view, the old idea of a Federalism existing by sufferance of the states had receded almost to the vanishing point. That it had ever had even theoretical validity had been denied by many Americans since the days of John Marshall, but it had remained a fundamental article of faith with *laissez-faire* devotees and latter-day advocates of restricted governmental powers like the dissenters from *Munn v. Illinois* to *Reynolds, Escobedo* and *Miranda*.

In an article poignantly entitled, "Heartbreaks for the Constitution," a respected Virginia lawyer in the American Bar Association *Journal* in August, 1964 reflected sadly over three decades of libertarian interpretation and concluded: "The evil is that the Court changes the meaning of the Constitution by what its apologists call interpretation. The real amendatory processes are thus circumvented in violation of the Constitution itself. Thus the changes are made by persons who have no constitutional power to amend and who by later decisions may amend it again."[25]

The same month that this article appeared, Justice Brennan was the featured invited speaker at the New York meeting of the Conference of State Chief Justices. He described himself, half-jokingly, as a Daniel walking into a lions' den. Whether he shared Daniel's good fortune was conjectural, but Brennan spoke frankly to his audience: "Of course, the Federal system's diffusion of governmental power has the purpose of securing individual freedom. But this is not all the Constitution provides to secure that end. There are also explicit provisions to prevent government, state or Federal, from frustrating the great design."[26]

It was a truism of American political history that constitutional interpretation at all times had been condemned by the adversely affected interests as reading into the Constitution what was not there. "While all declare for liberty," observed Harvard Law Professor Arthur Sutherland, "few losers will cheer a specific decision granting liberty to the other man, and him undeserving, at the cost of the man who thinks himself more worthy. But the nature of a constitution is, case by case, to extend its immunities to individuals; and in these selective judgments the society at large is not consulted."[27]

Assessing the putative correlation between landmark judicial decisions and their predicted adverse effects upon the politico-economic process, Yale Law Professor Alexander M. Bickel concluded that in the structure of Federalism the Supreme Court was the "least dangerous branch." But these detached observations did not persuade those who found both their personal interests and their social sympathies flouted by great abstract propositions handed down from the high tribunal. This had always been so; early in his tenure on the Court, Holmes had written that the quiet atmosphere was actually the quiet at the center of a storm. The storm was ever recurrent; no major decision in the Court's history failed to stir violent condemnation from some quarters.[28]

There were two eras in the history of the Court, however, which differed conspicuously from the others—and they were the ones that provoked the most virulent and concerted attacks. One was the Chief Justiceship of Marshall, the other the Chief Justiceship of Earl Warren. If men were truly measured by the enemies they made, Marshall and Warren had much in common, yet the fundamental similarity in the periods was the fact that in both the judiciary had been activist, and hence tending to lead the public to the acceptance of new potentials discerned in the Constitution. Marshall had his own answer for the limited-power, sufferance-of-the-states schools. The Preamble's reference to the "people of the United States," he wrote in 1819, was an incidental description of what had been the logical (albeit largely unconscious) act of the Constitutional Convention. It recognized the fundamental fact that the Constitution emanated from the people and was not the creation of sovereign and independent states.[29]

In Warren's Chief Justiceship, this concept of a sovereign people of the nation had become a basic premise of American constitutionalism—and had provoked the greatest cries of outrage. To accept the premise was to subordinate the concept, so dear to traditionalists, of the sovereign people of a *state,* and to concede that the welfare and interests of all people in the aggregate overrode the particular preferences of *some* people in *some* states. The concern of the activist majority on the Warren Court for the complete equality of enjoyment of constitutional rights, for the Negro, the defendant, the nonconformist, the individual voter, had a cumulative and infuriating effect upon the Court's critics.

*   *   *

One of the milder, but persistent, arguments of the conservatives was that the Supreme Court would be less disposed to flout precedent and move into strange new paths if its appointees were required to have a set period of prior judicial experience. The sobering effect of having to seek guidance from precedent in the workaday issues of the lower Federal tribunals, or from state courts, so the theory ran, would make Justices less inclined to cast their decisions in terms of broad or abstract principles and to venture into matters of policy.

An earnest recapitulation of the argument was made in February, 1965 by Senator Eastland, relying on a detailed compilation made up at his request by the Library of Congress which in his view concluded the case "against forcing the American public to be judged, in the highest judicial tribunal in the land, by men who lack the basic ingredient of 'experience' in the task to which many have been so prematurely assigned." For, he repeated, "learning to think judicially is a skill which should have been mastered before a man becomes a Supreme Court Justice. It is a skill which equips a man with the discipline necessary to discard personal notions and to decide the issues upon the basis of the Constitution, the statutes, and legal precedent."[30]

Yet, by Eastland's own documentation, none of the Chief Justices from Marshall to Fuller—a period of 110 years—had any prior judicial experience, while among the renowned Associate Justices, both progressive and conservative, in the same denigrated category were James Wilson and Joseph Story, Samuel F. Miller, Louis D. Brandeis, George Sutherland, Felix Frankfurter and Robert H. Jackson. Indeed, of the four arch-conservatives of the early Hughes Court, only Willis Van Devanter had had prior judicial experience. Both Chief Justices Hughes and Harlan F. Stone could claim previous seasoning only on the Supreme Court itself (except for Hughes' specialized work on the International Court of Justice). On the contemporary bench, the same description applied to Earl Warren, Hugo L. Black, William O. Douglas, Byron White and Arthur Goldberg (and his successor, Abe Fortas), as well as Tom Clark.[31]

The Eastland argument, and similar arguments before and after, started out to prove much and ended by proving nothing. Of those on his list with the talisman of previous experience, many had had only brief and insignificant experience with minor courts, while those with substantial judicial background were often the very movers and shakers against whom the argument was directed. Stephen J. Field's six years on the California supreme court, and Horace Gray's seventeen on the high court of Massachusetts, tended to substantiate the argument—only to be offset by Oliver Wendell Holmes' thirteen years on the same Massachusetts bench, and Benjamin N. Cardozo's eighteen as a judge in the New York courts. As for the two Harlans, the first had served a year on a Kentucky county court and the second a comparable period on the Federal Court of Appeals.*

---

*Cf. Appendix A.

The truth was that the members of the Supreme Court, both conservative and liberal, who had left their impact on the constitutional doctrine were men whose sense of history discerned the occasions when a possible change of course presented itself—and whose intellectual conditioning and social persuasion prompted them either to try the new course or continue in the old. Chief Justice Taft, who respected judicial experience for sound professional reasons, nevertheless was fully conscious of the peculiar function of adjudication in the high court; the disciplines appropriate to the trial and review of facts were readily distinguishable from the adjudication of broad jurisprudential principles in public and private law which he would have made the sole business of the Supreme Court.[32]

Justice Brennan, himself a former member of the New Jersey high court, said substantially the same thing to the Conference of State Chief Justices. "The fact is that the state high court and the Supreme Court of the United States play necessarily different roles in our judicial system," he said. His own reaction, he confessed, "upon moving from Trenton to Washington was one of considerable astonishment at learning how different the work of the two courts really is. The work of each has a character, a difficulty and a complexity of its own, and none of these has its exact counterpart in the other."[33]

Brennan concluded by urging the state justices to keep in mind the common responsibility of all American courts—"to protect fundamental constitutional rights threatened today in ways not possibly envisaged by the Framers." It remained to be seen whether he convinced anyone. For if the conservatives and states' rightists were prepared to concede the difference in judicial functions between the Supreme Court and the rest of the judicial system, it was not in terms of Brennan's "ideal of libertarian dignity protected through law." In their view, if the literal text of the Constitution was susceptible of this sort of construction, the time had come to change the text itself.

*   *   *

The Conference of State Chief Justices provided a willing instrument for the mounting conservative attack on the new Federalism in the 1960's. Its hostility to the Warren Court's doctrine of equality of enjoyment of constitutional guarantees had first been manifested in its intemperate 1958 outburst which had accelerated the anti-Court movement in the Eighty-fifth Congress. That pronouncement had been provoked by the Fifth Amendment decisions and the early defendants' rights cases. In 1962 with *Baker v. Carr,* the crusade was launched again with even greater fervor. Under the guise of expertise, the Conference statements were treated as objective documentation by conservatives everywhere who were preparing to attack the jurisprudence of national citizenship and the equality it required.

Building on the 1958 statement, the National Legislative Conference, another adjunct of the Council of State Governments, met in Phoenix, Arizona in September, 1962 to study the problem of strengthening the states in the Federal system. The need, as its committee on Federal-State relations pointed out, was for a constitutional amendment—but nothing as limited as the sub-

sequent Dirksen amendments of 1965 and 1966. Even Congress, the committee concluded, could not be trusted to turn Federal power back to the states,
and therefore a never-used proviso of Article V of the Constitution itself
was to be invoked. This was the statement that Congress, "on the application
of the legislature of two-thirds of the several states, shall call a convention
for proposing amendments."[34]

In December at the meeting of the Council of State Governments' general assembly, the committee submitted its report with a general recapitulation of the states' rights viewpoint:

> Some Federal judicial decisions involving powers of the Federal
> and state governments carry a strong bias on the Federal side, and
> consequently are bringing about a strong shift toward the extension of
> Federal powers and the restraint of state powers. This shift tends to
> accelerate as each decision forms the basis and starting point for another
> extension of Federal domination.
>
> A greater degree of restraint on the part of the United States
> Supreme Court can do much, but experience shows that it is not likely
> to be sufficient. The basic difficulty is that the Supreme Court's decisions
> concerning the balance between Federal and state power are final and
> can be changed in practice only if the states can muster sufficient interest
> in Congress, backed by a three-fourths majority of the states themselves
> to amend the Constitution. While the Founding Fathers fully expected
> and wished the words of the Constitution to have this degree of finality,
> it is impossible to believe that they envisaged such potency for the pro-
> nouncements of nine judges appointed by the President and confirmed
> by the Senate. . . .
>
> To amend the Federal Constitution to correct specific decisions of
> the Federal courts on specific points is desirable, but it will not necessarily
> stop the continuing drift toward more complete Federal domination. The
> present situation has taken a long time to develop and may take a long
> time to remedy. Accordingly, some more fundamental and far-reaching
> change in the Federal Constitution is necessary to preserve and protect
> the states.[35]

The committee thereupon submitted to the Assembly three resolutions
demanding that Congress call a Constitutional Convention for the purpose
of proposing one or all of the amendments embodied in the respective resolutions. In the paranoia of the circumstances, the committee saw betrayers
everywhere, and solemnly advised the Assembly to draft the resolutions in
their legislatures "in whatever technical form the state employs for a single
resolution of both houses of the legislature which does not require the
governor to approve or veto."[36] The *amicus* brief in *Baker* filed by the
governor of Oklahoma had warned the states' rightists that not all state
executives could be trusted to be traditionalists.

The first concern of the committee was that the Federal Constitution
should be brought irrevocably under the control of the state legislatures, thus
making the nation forever subordinate to its constituent state governments.
The fantasy of such a proposal was all too quickly inflated by the fact that

thirty-seven out of forty-five states voting in the assembly cast their votes in favor. The text of the proposed amendment confirmed the most extreme construction that could be put on it:

> Article V of the Constitution of the United States is hereby amended to read as follows:
> The Congress, whenever two-thirds of both Houses shall deem it necessary, *or, on the application of the legislatures* of two-thirds of the several states, shall propose amendments to this Constitution, which shall be valid to all intents and purposes, as part of this Constitution, when ratified by the legislatures of three-fourths of the several states. *Whenever applications from the legislatures of two-thirds of the total number of states of the United States shall contain identical texts of an amendment to be proposed, the President of the Senate and the Speaker of the House of Representatives shall so certify, and the amendment as contained in the application shall be deemed to have been proposed, without further action by Congress.* No state, without its consent, shall be deprived of its equal suffrage in the Senate.*[37]

The second of the three proposed amendments anticipated Senator Dirksen by aiming at the reversal of the apportionment decisions. It was, however, a complete reversal. Whereas the Dirksen proposal was for a limited power in the states to apportion a single house of a two-house legislature on a basis other than population, the states' rights drafters demanded complete surrender, stipulating that no provision in the Constitution should be construed "to restrict or limit any state in the apportionment of representation in its legislature," and denying jurisdiction to the Federal courts on apportionment questions. Of the state delegations answering the roll call on this proposal, twenty-six voted in favor, ten against and ten abstained.[38]

Finally, to ensure a veto over Court decisions which might survive the crippled Constitution, the committee proposed a resolution (approved by a vote of twenty-one states to twenty) creating a fifty-member "Court of the Union," to be composed of the state chief justices, to review "any judgment of the Supreme Court relating to the rights reserved to the states or to the people." The single issue before the *ad hoc* sessions of such a "court" would be "whether the power or jurisdiction sought to be exercised on the part of the United States is a power granted to it under this Constitution."[39]

In February, 1963 Senator Thurmond of South Carolina introduced the first and third resolutions in Congress, and the following month the apportionment proposal was introduced in the House by Congressman Sydney A. Herlong of Florida. Nothing came of them. In May the board of governors of the American Bar Association went on record as opposing the two measures introduced by Thurmond and, reversing the recommendation of its committee on jurisprudence and law reform, recommended to the ABA convention the rejection of the reapportionment proposal as well. At the August convention,

---

*Italics represent the new matter proposed.

the Association's house of delegates formally went on record as opposed to the reapportionment amendment and accepted the action of its board of governors on the others.[40]

*   *   *

The rejection of the "states' rights amendments" in Congress in 1963, and the narrow defeats of Dirksen's proposals in the following three years, called for a stealthier strategy on the part of conservatives, desperate agrarians represented by the far-right American Farm Bureau Federation, and a motley aggregation of anti-Federalists whose hatreds dated back to the New Deal. Quietly the groups in each state were contacted by Dirksen—agents in Colorado and Indiana credited his visits with legislative representatives in their states with organizing the movements there, and they suggested a consistent plan elsewhere. The strategic plan to invoke Article V and call for a new Constitutional Convention was under way once more.

With a minimum of attention in the state legislatures, and with a piecemeal reporting of the petitions to Congress, the plan slowly took shape. On March 18, 1967 a Washington correspondent of the *New York Times* suddenly reported that thirty-two states out of the thirty-four presumably necessary to invoke this clause in Article V had filed their petitions. Macchiavellian though the process had been, it was all but an accomplished fact; whatever the mischief it might stir up, the possibility of a convention of states had become very real, after 180 years.[41]

"The idea seems to be," said Senator Tydings of Maryland on March 22, "to get so many state legislatures to ask for a convention that Congress will be terrified into proposing the kind of pro-malapportionment amendment it has twice rejected in two years. For a Constitutional Convention, were one convened, could not be limited to the reapportionment issue, but could make wholesale revisions in our . . . Charter of Government."

However, Tydings declared, the legitimacy of a number of the petitions was subject to a serious doubt, since they had come from malapportioned legislatures, and since the subject of their petition was not uniform. He expressed the hope that "Congress will not be moved to lay open our sacred Constitution to amendment on the defective and self-serving petitions of . . . rotten borough legislatures which are no longer even in existence."[42]

As the prospect of an actual convention call became real enough to evoke other Congressional comment, conservatives as well as liberals began to have second thoughts. Senator Ervin of North Carolina, a lifelong strict constructionist, blanched at the thought of what damage might be done to the Constitution in a runaway convention. While he had frequently condemned the reapportionment decisions as "officious meddling" on the part of the judiciary, he was not prepared to give *carte blanche* to a heterogeneous gathering to make piecemeal changes in a document which William Gladstone had once described as "the most wonderful work ever struck off at a given time by the brain and purpose of man."[43]

Senator William Proxmire of Wisconsin joined with Tydings in a condemnation of the surreptitious methods by which the attempt to invoke the Article V clause had been perpetrated. Citing the attitude of legislative leaders in his own state, even though favorable to a limitation on the reapportionment doctrine, expressing doubt as to the binding force of the state petitions, Proxmire declared: "It would appear to me that many of the states acting on these memorials are doing so in the belief that they merely serve to let Congress know of state concern."[44]

Dirksen, confident that he could muster the simple majority which he had won twice before, if the two-thirds of the state petitions became a reality, let the opposition do most of the talking. Briefly, on April 19, he took the floor to ask whether, if the malapportioned legislatures were considered incompetent to petition for the convention, they were also to be held incompetent to have legislated on anything else—including their own past ratifications of twenty-five Amendments to the Constitution.[45] The point was wittily made, although the progressives were not amused.

*   *   *

Did Everett McKinley Dirksen's obsession with the concept of local self-government, freed at least in part from Federal surveillance, really mean that he intended to precipitate a crisis which might well destroy the national character of the United States? Or did he mean to reveal the full dimensions of such a crisis so dramatically that he could indeed prevail upon Congress to accept his own amendment as so much milder in the afterview? Even though colored with certain concerns for his own political self-preservation, no one questioned the basic sincerity of his conviction, but, like many high-principled persuasions, Dirksen's was tailor-made for the purposes of a vast number of selfish interests.

Those holding long pent-up hatreds of Federally enforced reform legislation of the past three decades were prepared to slip their leashes at the first opportunity. Many who had never accepted the principle of equality established in the race cases of the past decade, but who could not attack the moral rightness of the principle directly, eagerly supported the proposal to humiliate the Court in another area. Those who feared the defendants' rights decisions as coddling hardened criminals and encouraging the spread of lawlessness were impatient to limit the Federal power and toughen the criminal process once more. But beyond that, there were the reactionaries who had never accepted the principles of social welfare legislation by Congress dating back to Franklin Roosevelt's day, and who also looked upon a constitutional convention as the chance to reduce Federalism to impotence.

The news of Warren's retirement had been only one of a number of major events of 1968 which fed the frustrations of conservative and liberal alike. A public increasingly disillusioned with the indecisive and ill-defined military objectives in Southeast Asia was under harassment from a militant and somewhat self-conscious minority of self-proclaimed intellectuals and

alienated adolescents on the home front. The developments of the year, sometimes approaching the fantastic, cast varied shadows of doubt over the
electoral contests of the fall. Only one thing seemed certain: as hindsight had
shown, the enormous electoral victory won by Lyndon Johnson in 1964 had in
reality been a massive rejection of the proposal to return to *laissez-faire* as
offered by Republican Barry Goldwater. Now, in 1968, the frustrations and
discontents of the time were coalescing into an equally negative vote.

In a society where, as many declared, the majority had "never had it so
good," public dissatisfaction with the state of affairs had reached an almost
unparalleled intensity. The war—always the war—as well as inflation, racial
conflict, and the vague complaint about big government, were explanations
given by the man in the street to the poll takers. There was also the fact that,
as Hans J. Morgenthau wrote, the Johnson administration had committed
itself to "two mutually exclusive goals: the Great Society and the avoidance
of political conflict." Dissent, by such a definition, could only yield to consensus or convert itself into alienation.[46]

"There is a continuing tension in American democracy between 'the will
of the people' and the judgment of their chosen representatives," wrote former
Presidential Press Secretary Bill Moyers. He recalled a meeting of Johnson's
Cabinet, in the early months of the implementation of the Civil Rights Act of
1964. Reflecting on the disorders in Selma, Alabama which had first brought
the new machinery of the Justice Department into operation, one Cabinet
member had exclaimed, "If one only knew what the people of this country
really wanted us to do about civil rights . . ." As his voice trailed off, Johnson
had looked at the speaker gravely. "If we knew what they wanted us to do,"
the President asked, "how could you be sure that we should do it?"[47]

The year was a churning series of shocks. In April the Rev. Martin
Luther King, Jr. was shot and killed on the eve of a projected protest march
of Memphis Negroes. With the senseless slaying of the most hopeful leader
among Negro moderates, black outrage exploded violently in scores of cities
across the face of the country. In Washington, D.C., which had remained
relatively quiet during the four previous summers of urban riots, mobs stormed
and looted, then set fire to whole blocks of retail establishments on the very
edge of the main shopping district. Army troops cordoned off the White
House itself, and a light machine gun was placed in a command post on the
steps of the Capitol. The District's badly undermanned police department
could do little but watch the sacking of stores and the methodical arson which
spread over much of the southeastern sector of the city. More than ten
thousand troops were ultimately ordered into the city to regain control.[48]

Poverty, on which President Johnson had so resolutely declared war, was
the root of much of the evil. Fetid slums, a synonym for urban deterioration,
were a culture bed for virulent hatred of the police, the proprietors of shoddy
discount houses exploiting the slum dwellers, and the infested tenements
which they called home. Amid all the projected reform programs of the

American people since the crusades of the early New Deal, it was declared, there had always been overlooked a hard core of chronically unemployable—in actual numbers, more white than Negro. Fair labor standards, housing developments, civil liberties programs passed them by, while incessant advertising of consumer luxuries by newspaper, television and storefront displays continually goaded the underprivileged.

Hunger, a total anomaly in a land where surpluses and potential productive processes accounted for an undistributed food supply, was appallingly widespread. Yet it was largely unknown to the travelers of the interstate highways and the dwellers in suburbia who never saw the pockets of starvation. One had to go looking for it—in the worked-out mining areas of Appalachia, the exhausted dirt farms of the deep South, the hard-baked dust streets of Southwestern villages.

To dramatize the issue before a nation still only half convinced, the Rev. Dr. King and his co-workers had already proclaimed a spring "Poor People's March" on Washington. Like Coxey's "army" of the seventies, and the veterans' march of the early thirties, it was planned to invite the desperate and despairing from all parts of the nation to the glamorous capitol on the Potomac, there to settle down and haunt the public conscience. King's murder intensified rather than dampened the zeal to carry the project through.

*   *   *

While "Resurrection City" was opening for business in the District of Columbia, the twisting trail of campaign politics was leading toward California. The Democratic party itself seemed to be in the process of disintegrating—an unprecedented breakdown of a government which only three years before had appeared to be so firmly entrenched that Republicans considered a run in 1968 hardly to be worth the effort. The cancer of the Viet Nam war was the fatal cause; it had split the Democratic ranks in Congress, then led to a historic revolt by Minnesota's Eugene McCarthy whose primary election triumph in New Hampshire had revealed the depth of the anti-Johnson feeling in the country. Thereupon Robert F. Kennedy had entered the race himself, quickly pulled abreast of McCarthy, while trailing them both was Vice-President Hubert Humphrey, heir by default to the Johnson administration when the President himself, reading the political auguries, announced his retirement from office.

The second of the Kennedy brothers to die by an assassin's bullet fell in Los Angeles in June. Whereas the slaying of John Kennedy five years before had struck a nation with total disbelief, the slaying of Robert seemed to many like the inexorable ordering of fate. John and Bobby represented a continuity of national purpose; more than most others in contemporary politics, these young men had understood both the imperative necessity and the perils of grappling with the demands of an uprooted social organism. Robert Kennedy, wrote a correspondent, was always regarded as "John Kennedy's surrogate, driven to seek his brother's fulfillment, or his tragedy."

With both men, the same observer continued, there was the mass appeal that had characterized the Bonapartes: "They identify with the deprived, being the radical foes of all authority when they are out of power."[49]

The funeral of Robert Kennedy had its own somber poignancy. An entire nation—and, by satellite television, much of the world—watched its own passion being acted out in the slow train procession from New York to Washington. The repeated, often spontaneous mass singing of the "Battle Hymn of the Republic" at stops along the route throbbed upon the American consciousness. Hours behind schedule, the cortege left the Union Station in the capitol in rain-spattered darkness, the headlights of cars like a column of candles escorting the martyr to the grave beside his brother. John Kennedy's funeral down these same streets in the cold winter afternoon of 1963 had somehow been sublimated into a national rededication; Robert Kennedy's funeral had equal dignity, but the atmosphere was more apocalyptic, charged with a sense of wrath and final judgment.

*   *   *

Not in generations—not, indeed, since the anguished decades of the eighties and early nineties—had the American people been so beset by self-doubt as in 1968. Even in the depression thirties, as the structure of *laissez-faire* had collapsed in ruins about them, there had emerged under Franklin Roosevelt's inspiration a sudden hope for a far better future. A now greying generation which had lived through the New Deal years could recall the times with nostalgia—the quickening of energies, the kindling of ideals for a great intellectual adventure which in retrospect made the thirties seem heroic. Roosevelt had offered a fresh outlet for the pioneer spirit which, until the closing of the frontier, had made the American a legendary figure throughout the world.

The ultimate handicap of the Johnsonian age—the stumbling block in the path of the first step toward the Great Society—was the cataclysmic annihilation of all familiar references in time and space. Gradualism of all kinds was being shouted down by long-denied segments of mankind, in the United States and around the world. Instant and universal accommodation of their demands was the expectation of recently liberated peoples, aroused minorities in the cities, a disaffected generation of young adults around the globe. Intercontinental television and interplanetary scientific exploration had overnight destroyed the last vestiges of localism; now at last, in Thomas Paine's phrase, all problems of mankind were everyman's problems.

Thus the election of 1968 was a total anomaly. The American voter, having witnessed a Democratic convention in Chicago which appeared virtually to be an exercise in anarchy, was offered a choice between three candidates, none of whom did more than obliquely refer to the perilous decisions awaiting action in the seventies. George Wallace of Alabama held out a nativistic kind of nihilism; a desperate Hubert Humphrey sought to salvage Roosevelt-Truman era values; Richard Nixon tacitly suggested a return to something like the slowdown of the Eisenhower years. In the end, and by the narrowest of margins, the electorate chose the last of these.

Still, the events which had made inevitable the new legality of the past four decades were the product of long-term, historic developments which were not substantially within the control of any party or administration. Technology and social change, wrote Arthur Selwyn Miller of George Washington University, had created the national, unitary Federalism which had permanently replaced the dual Federalism to which the conservatives so fervently looked back: The necessarily centralized administration of New Deal and post-New Deal reforms, the coming of "central government by contract" which was accelerated by World War II, and the massive growth of uniform programs organized by national foundations had all made inevitable the concept of a single economic and social entity which was the United States of the mid-century.[50]

The function of the Court throughout American history, Robert H. Jackson had observed, had been to give meaning to the "great silences of the Constitution." The function had been performed by the Court from the time of John Marshall, and had varied as the national frames of reference had varied from Marshall's era of a coalescing nation to the economic centralization of the United States of Waite and Fuller. The twentieth century had experienced the reform arguments of the Progressive Era, the decade of normalcy under Taft, the revolutionary transition over which Hughes had presided, the cold war of the Truman and early Eisenhower years, until the emergence of the concept of a national citizenship with its rights protected by a Federal rule of law, in the jurisprudence of the sixties.

The restlessness of minorities, ethnic and economic, domestic and foreign; the outward expansion of human ambitions toward the universe which space technology was opening; the impact on world society of now near-instantaneous communication and incredibly rapid transportation—and withal, the chronic state of crisis arising from the challenges which these changes presented to all orthodoxy—these were prospects of the seventies which would be little affected by a change of Presidents or Chief Justices. From Fuller to Taft, the Court majority had sought to perpetuate a particular philosophy in a system of constitutional interpretation. From Hughes to Warren—and now beyond—the Court had come to accept the fact that constitutional interpretation was simply a continuing search for rules which were both appropriate and relevant in the face of successive and continuing challenges.

APPENDICES

Appendix A

Court Personnel from Hughes to Warren

From February, 1930 when Chief Justice Taft resigned until the spring of 1969 when Chief Justice Warren's tenure was ending, twenty-four Justices were appointed to the Court, one nominee was formally rejected and the nomination of another (Fortas, already on the bench, to be Chief Justice) was denied a vote on confirmation by Senate filibuster. Fortas' subsequent resignation from the Court, under a combination of publicity and pressure, was a unique episode in constitutional history. The long Democratic tenure in the White House—for all but eleven and a half of these thirty-nine years—and the shifting ideology of the age accounted for a substantial metamorphosis in the whole Federal judiciary. A statistical demonstration of this tranformation appears at the end of this Appendix.

Even if the New Deal had not come about, it seems likely that the metamorphosis still would have taken place, although the fact might not have been so striking. The coming of a generation of jurists educated under the newer and more critical faculties of twentieth-century law schools was a factor of paramount importance. Moreover, the wide geographic distribution of the law schools represented in the *curricula vitae* of the members of the Federal bench belied the claim that any single law school was the catalyst. It was true that in the early New Deal Felix Frankfurter almost singlehandedly staffed the Roosevelt administration with Harvard law graduates; John F. Kennedy, too, favored Harvard-trained men to a point of political embarrassment. But the essential fact was that legal education generally approached constitutional law with a sophistication and critical appraisal which was reflected in the mature philosophies of the great majority of the judicial appointees.

Thus the development of the New Legality was nurtured in a soil intellectually prepared during the generation in which Chief Justice Taft had complained that the law schools were seeking to undo so much of the work which his Court had sought to preserve. And it was in Chief Justice Hughes' administration that the need for a changed viewpoint reached a critical state. Those of the "nine old men" who retired from the scene after 1937 were,

357

whether liberal or conservative, products of the nineteenth-century viewpoint in legal education, while their successors were graduates of twentieth-century professional training. Being men by temperament sensitive to the unprecedented events which made up the public affairs of this period—the depression, total war, cold war, nuclear power, space pioneering and racial awakening—the products of this new legal education developed a jurisprudence that was consistently distinguishable from that which made up the Old Legality.

This is readily discernible when one compares the biographical data for the members of the Court which follow, with their respective constitutional arguments set out in the main text.

As in the corresponding material in the companion volume, the appointees to the Court are grouped by Chief Justiceships, and each group is introduced by a table summarizing the process of individual appointment, followed by a paragraph of biographical data on each individual. The name of each appointee is preceded by a number indicating his order of succession on the Court since its establishment, with the number in parentheses for his predecessor. Each group of Justices' biographical summaries is followed by a statistical recapitulation.

1.   The Hughes Court, 1930-1941

In the course of his administration, Chief Justice Hughes was to have seven new Associate Justices under him. The last five of these were appointed in a period of less than four years, and coming as they did with the traumatic ideological and political struggles of the mid-thirties, these changes in personnel put to a supreme test Hughes' own administrative abilities. The consistent deftness with which he led the Court through the maelstrom of public debate

Name of Justice	President Nominating	Date of Nomination	Date of Confirmation	Vote on Confirmation	Date of Commission	Date of Swearing-in
Hughes	Hoover	2- 3-30	2-13-30	52-26	2-13-30	2-14-30
[Parker	Hoover	3-21-30	5- 7-30	39-41*]		
Roberts	Hoover	5- 9-30	5-20-30		5-20-30	6- 2-30
Cardozo	Hoover	2-15-32	2-24-32		3- 2-32	3-14-32
Black	Roosevelt	8-12-37	8-17-37	63-16	8-18-37	10- 4-37
Reed	Roosevelt	1-15-38	1-25-38		1-27-38	1-31-38
Frankfurter	Roosevelt	1- 5-39	1-17-39	†	1-20-39	1-30-39
Douglas	Roosevelt	3-20-39	4- 4-39	62- 4	4-15-39	4-17-39
Murphy	Roosevelt	1- 4-40	1-16-40	†	1-18-40	2- 5-40

* Sixteen Senators not voting.

† Executive session, no recorded vote.

over the Constitution assured him of one of the highest niches in the American judicial pantheon.

74 (69). CHARLES EVANS HUGHES (April 11, 1862-August 27, 1948). *Eleventh Chief Justice.* Born Glens Falls, New York; studied at Colgate University and received A.B., Brown University, 1881; A.M., Brown, 1884, LL.B., Columbia, 1884; admitted to practice New York, 1884; general practice, New York City, 1884-1907; professor of law, Cornell University, 1891-93; special counsel for state investigating commissions, 1905-06; governor of New York, 1907-10; appointed Associate Justice of Supreme Court, April 25, 1910; resigned, June 10, 1916, to become Republican candidate for President. Practiced law in New York City, 1917-21, 1925-30; Secretary of State, 1921-25; U.S. delegate to disarmament conference, 1921; U.S. member, Permanent Court of Arbitration, 1926-30, Permanent Court of International Justice, 1928-30. Retired from Supreme Court July 1, 1941.

[JOHN J. PARKER (November 20, 1885-March 17, 1958). Born Monroe, North Carolina; A.B., University of North Carolina, 1907; LL.B., 1908; admitted to bar in North Carolina, 1908, and did general practice, 1908-22; special assistant to Attorney General, 1923-24; judge, U.S. Circuit Court of Appeals, 1925-1958. Author, *Democracy in Government* (1940). Senate rejected nomination by narrow vote, with large number of abstentions, as protest against continuing conservatism of Court and allegedly anti-Negro and anti-labor attitude of nominee.]

75 (72). OWEN JOSEPHUS ROBERTS (May 2, 1875-May 17, 1955). Born Philadelphia; A.B., University of Pennsylvania, 1895; LL.B., 1898; admitted to practice in Pennsylvania, 1898; private practice in Philadelphia, 1898-1901, 1905-30; assistant district attorney, Philadelphia County, 1901-04; professor of law, University of Pennsylvania, 1898-1918; special U.S. attorney prosecuting Teapot Dome oil scandals, 1924; chairman of committee investigating attack on Pearl Harbor, 1941. Resigned from Supreme Court July 31, 1945. Dean of law school, University of Pennsylvania, 1945-52.

76 (58). BENJAMIN NATHAN CARDOZO (May 24, 1870-July 9, 1938). Born New York City; A.B., Columbia University, 1889; M.A., 1890; studied law at Columbia, admitted to New York bar, 1891; appellate practice, New York, 1891-1914; elected to supreme court of New York, 1914, and appointed to vacancy on court of appeals, serving 1914-32, chief judge, 1926-32. Author, *The Nature of the Judicial Process* (1921), *The Growth of the Law* (1924), *Law and Literature* (1925), *Paradoxes of Legal Science* (1928).

77 (63). HUGO LAFAYETTE BLACK (February 27, 1886-   ). Born Harlan, Alabama; LL.B., University of Alabama, 1906; admitted to bar in Alabama, 1906; private practice, 1907-10, 1911-15, 1919-27; U.S. Army, 1917-19; police court judge, Birmingham, 1910-11; prosecuting attorney, Jefferson County, Alabama, 1915-17; U.S. Senator, 1927-37.

78 (70). STANLEY FORMAN REED (December 31, 1884-   ). Born Mason County, Kentucky; A.B., Kentucky Wesleyan University, 1902; A.B., Yale University, 1906; studied law at University of Virginia and Columbia

University; general study, University of Paris, 1909-10; admitted to bar in Kentucky, 1910, and engaged in general practice, 1910-17, 1919-29; U.S. Army, 1918-19; general counsel, Federal Farm Board, 1929-32; general counsel, Reconstruction Finance Corporation, 1932-35; Solicitor General, 1935-38. Resigned from Supreme Court February 25, 1957.

79 (76). FELIX FRANKFURTER (November 15, 1882-February 22, 1965). Born Vienna, Austria; A.B., College of City of New York, 1902; LL.B., Harvard University, 1906; admitted to Federal bar and became assistant U.S. attorney, 1906-10; law officer, Bureau of Insular Affairs, 1911-14; professor of law, Harvard, 1914-39; visiting professor, Oxford University, 1933-34; special counsel in various government cases, 1914-30. Author, *The Case of Sacco and Vanzetti* (1927); *The Business of the Supreme Court* (with James M. Landis) (1928); *The Public and Its Government* (1930); *The Labor Injunction* (with Nathan Greene) (1930); *The Commerce Clause Under Marshall, Taney and Waite* (1937); *Mr. Justice Holmes and the Supreme Court* (1939); and various law casebooks. Resigned from Supreme Court August 28, 1962.

80 (67). WILLIAM ORVILLE DOUGLAS (October 16, 1898-   ). Born Maine, Minnesota; B.A., Whitman College, 1920; LL.B., Columbia University, 1925; high school teacher, Walla Walla, Washington, 1920-22; admitted to bar and practiced in New York, 1925-27; law professor, Columbia, 1925-27; Yale University, 1927-34; secretary of a committee of the National (Wickersham) Commission on Law Observance and Enforcement, 1930-32; director of protective committee study, Securities and Exchange Commission, 1934-36; chairman, SEC, 1934-39. Author, among numerous other titles, of *Of Men and Mountains* (1959); *An Almanac of Liberty* (1954); *We, the Judges* (1956), *et al.*

81 (71). FRANK MURPHY (April 13, 1890-July 19, 1949). Born Harbor Beach, Michigan; A.B., University of Michigan, 1912; LL.B., 1914; graduate study, Lincoln's Inn, London, and Trinity College, Dublin, 1914; admitted to Michigan bar, 1914; law clerk in Detroit firm and night law teacher, 1914-17; in U.S. Army, 1917-19; chief Assistant U.S. Attorney, 1919-20; private practice, 1920-23; law professor, University of Detroit, 1923-27, and judge of the recorder's court, 1923-1930; mayor of Detroit, 1930-33; Governor-General of Philippines, 1933-36; governor of Michigan, 1936-38; Attorney General, 1939-40.

Recapitulation

Several striking features emerge from a statistical profile of the Hughes Court—even before the Roosevelt appointments. One was the sudden prominence of law school teaching among the Justices' records: Hughes himself had taught, years before, at Cornell, and his lectures on the Supreme Court at Columbia University had become a classic reference; but four of his seven new Associates had taught, full-time or part-time, for a grand total of sixty years. Columbia, Detroit, Harvard, Pennsylvania and Yale were the law school faculties with which they had been associated.

Another feature was the experience on Federal regulatory agencies included in the group's record—fifteen years, divided among three appointees. On the other hand, in the light of the recurring issue of prior judicial experience of appointees, the new men on the Court had a disparate record: Hughes, of course, was in a special category with his six earlier years on the Supreme Court and his half dozen years on one or both of the international tribunals at The Hague. Black represented, with Murphy, the other extreme of experience on local police courts. Only Cardozo, with eighteen years on the New York bench, offered the type of judicial preparation which many advocates would wish to see as a prerequisite for Supreme Court appointment.

The level of education and literacy was high: eight A.B. degrees were distributed among seven Justices, two had M.A. degrees and two had some overseas postgraduate study. All but two had LL.B. degrees; Cardozo had qualified to take the New York bar examinations without completing his degree requirements, and Reed had studied, without degree, at law schools at the University of Virginia and at Columbia. Undergraduate institutions included Brown, the College of the City of New York, Columbia, Kentucky Wesleyan, Michigan, Pennsylvania, Whitman and Yale, with graduate degrees from Brown and Columbia. Law schools attended included Alabama, Columbia (with three alumni among the appointees), Harvard, Michigan, Pennsylvania and Virginia. Overseas studies were pursued at Lincoln's Inn in London, Trinity College in Dublin and the University of Paris.

The average number of years in private practice was seventeen—about the same as for the Fuller and Taft Courts. Among public offices held by individual appointees were one term as mayor, one term as governor, two terms as United States Senator, two as United States attorney, two as local prosecuting attorney. Reed's three years as Solicitor General had been particularly effective in strengthening the government's trial and appellate work. Among the unusual records were Hughes' service as Secretary of State in the early 1920's, and Murphy's three years as Governor-General of the Philippines.

2.   *The Stone and Vinson Courts, 1941-1946, 1946-1953*

Although in many respects they contrasted with each other, these two Chief Justiceships are treated together as representing the decade following the Roosevelt revolution. Neither Stone nor Vinson really had the opportunity to develop a distinctive administration; each man served as Chief Justice for a relatively brief time, and each found his role rather pre-determined. Stone, the last appointee to the Taft Court, inherited the fundamental problem of the great constitutional reorientation of 1937-41—how to fashion a new body of decisional law in place of some three-quarters of a century of precedents whose overturning was the logical consequence of the reorientation. Vinson, whose chief function was to seek to quiet the turbulence within the Court generated by the debates under Stone, provided a time for a catching of breath and a renewal of energies preparatory to the dash for the intellectual heights in the Court to follow.

Name of Justice	President Nominating	Date of Nomination	Date of Confirmation	Vote on Confirmation	Date of Commission	Date of Swearing-in
Stone	Roosevelt	6-12-41	6-27-41		10- 6-41	10- 6-41
Byrnes	Roosevelt	6-12-41	6-12-41		6-25-41	10- 6-41
Jackson	Roosevelt	6-12-41	7- 7-41		7-11-41	10- 6-41
Rutledge	Roosevelt	1-11-43	2- 8-43		2-11-43	2-15-43
Burton	Truman	9-18-45	9-19-45		9-22-45	10- 1-45
Vinson	Truman	6- 6-46	6-20-46		6-21-46	10- 7-46
Clark	Truman	8- 2-49	8-18-49		8-19-49	10- 3-49
Minton	Truman	9-15-49	10- 4-49		10- 5-49	10-12-49

HARLAN FISK STONE (October 11, 1872-April 22, 1946). *Twelfth Chief Justice.* Born Chesterfield, New Hampshire; A.B., Amherst College, 1894; LL.B., Columbia University, 1898; admitted to bar in New York, 1899; general practice in New York, 1899-1903, 1905-10, 1923-25; professor of law, Columbia University, 1903-05, 1910-23, and dean, 1915-23; Attorney General, 1924-25. Appointed to Court by President Coolidge, January 5, 1925.

82 (66). JAMES FRANCIS BYRNES (May 2, 1878-   ). Born Charleston, South Carolina; read law and admitted to bar, South Carolina, 1903; editor, *Aiken Journal & Review,* 1903-07; court reporter, South Carolina second circuit, 1900-08; solicitor, same, 1908-10; House of Representatives, 1911-25; private law practice, 1925-31; U.S. Senate, 1931-41. Resigned from Supreme Court October 2, 1943 to become director, Office of Economic Stabilization, 1943-45; Secretary of State, 1945-47; private law practice in District of Columbia, 1947-51; governor of South Carolina, 1951-55.

83 (74). ROBERT HOUGHWOUT JACKSON (February 13, 1892-October 8, 1954). Born Spring Creek, Pennsylvania; studied law at Albany Law School and admitted to New York bar, 1913; private practice, 1913-34; general counsel, Bureau of Internal Revenue, 1934-36; Assistant Attorney General, 1936-38; Solicitor General, 1938-39; Attorney General, 1940-41. Chief counsel for international war crimes commission in Germany, 1945-46. Author, *The Struggle for Judicial Supremacy* (1941); *The Case Against the Nazi War Criminals* (1946); *The Nuremberg Case* (1947).

84 (82). WILEY BLOUNT RUTLEDGE (July 20, 1894-September 18, 1949). Born Cloverport, Kentucky; A.B., University of Wisconsin, 1914; LL.B., University of Colorado, 1922; high school teacher, 1914-22; admitted to bar in Colorado, 1922; in Missouri, 1926; in Iowa, 1935; professor of law, University of Colorado, 1924-26; Washington University, 1926-35, and dean, 1931-35; dean, State University of Iowa, 1935-39; judge, Court of Appeals for District of Columbia, 1939-43.

85 (75). HAROLD HITZ BURTON (June 22, 1888-October 28, 1964). Born Jamaica Plain, Massachusetts; A.B., Bowdoin College, 1909; LL.B., Harvard University, 1912; admitted to practice in Ohio, 1912, and Utah, 1914; private practice in Ohio, 1912-14; counsel for public utilities in Utah and Idaho, 1914-17; U.S. Army, 1917-19; practice in Cleveland, 1919-31; law director, Cleveland, 1929-32; acting mayor and mayor of Cleveland, 1931-40; U.S. Senate, 1941-45. Resigned from Supreme Court October 13, 1958.

86 (73). FREDERICK MOORE VINSON (January 22, 1890-September 8, 1953). *Thirteenth Chief Justice.* Born Louisa, Kentucky; A.B., Centre College, 1909; LL.B., 1911; admitted to Kentucky bar and practiced, 1911-24, 1929-31; commonwealth's attorney, 1921-24; House of Representatives, 1923-29. 1931-38; judge, Court of Appeals for District of Columbia, 1938-43; Office of Economic Stabilization, 1943-45; Federal Loan Administrator, 1945; Office of War Mobilization and Reconversion, 1945; Secretary of Treasury, 1945-46.

87 (81). THOMAS CAMPBELL CLARK (September 23, 1899-   ). Born Dallas, Texas; studied at Virginia Military Institute and received A.B., University of Texas, 1921; LL.B., 1922; admitted to bar and practiced in Texas, 1922-27; civil district attorney, Dallas County, 1927-34; Assistant Attorney General, 1934-45; Attorney General, 1945-49. Resigned from Supreme Court June 12, 1967; director, Federal Judicial Center, 1967-present.

88 (84). SHERMAN MINTON (October 20, 1890-April 9, 1965). Born Georgetown, Indiana; LL.B., Indiana University, 1915; LL.M., Yale University, 1917; admitted to Indiana bar and practiced, 1916-25; U.S. Army, 1917-19; practiced in Florida, 1925-28, and resumed practice in Indiana, 1928-31; Indiana public counsellor, 1933-34; U.S. Senate, 1935-41; administrative assistant to President, 1941; judge, Court of Appeals, 1941-49. Retired from Supreme Court October 15, 1956.

Recapitulation

Although there were only two law professors on the Court in the decade of the forties—Stone and Rutledge (in company, of course, with Frankfurter, an earlier appointee)—they represented thirty additional years of academic background. The new Justices of the Stone-Vinson period totalled eighty-eight years of private practice, or an average of twelve years apiece. Byrnes' twenty-six years in both Houses of Congress, and Vinson's twelve in the lower House, as well as Burton's and Minton's single terms in the Senate, added significantly to the legislative background of the Court. Jackson and Clark between them represented twenty-two years as counsel for Federal departments, and prior judicial experience included two years for Rutledge, five for Vinson and eight for Minton, on the Federal intermediate courts. Executive department positions included Justice, Treasury, wartime regulatory agencies, and Minton's brief term as administrative assistant to President Roosevelt.

Among undergraduate institutions at which five of the eight Justices studied were Amherst, Bowdoin, Centre, Texas, Virginia Military Institute and Wisconsin. Byrnes and Jackson took bar examinations without law degrees, although Jackson had studied law at Albany; LL.B. degrees were earned at Centre, Colorado, Columbia, Harvard, Indiana, Texas, with the advanced degree of LL.M. from Yale.

3. The Warren Court, 1953-1969

The sixteen-year tenure of the Chief Justiceship of Earl Warren is the longest in the present century, comparable to the twenty-two years of Fuller's Chief Justiceship which ushered in the period of the present two volumes. In this length of time, seven positions on the bench have been filled by nine different Justices, and only two Roosevelt appointees—Black and Douglas—remain from the Court prior to Warren's ascendancy. The reciprocal influences of major social and economic changes in this period, and the fresh new viewpoints brought to the judiciary by these appointees, largely explain the challenging jurisprudence which has resulted in the Warren years.

Name of Justice	President Nominating	Date of Nomination	Date of Confirmation	Vote on Confirmation	Date of Commission	Date of Swearing-in
Warren	Eisenhower	10- 5-53*				10- 5-53
		1-11-54	3- 1-54		3- 2-54	
Harlan	Eisenhower	11- 9-54*				
		1-10-55	3-16-55	71-11	3-17-55	3-28-55
Brennan	Eisenhower	10-15-56*				10-16-56
		1- 4-57	3-19-57	†	3-21-57	3-22-57
Whittaker	Eisenhower	3- 2-57	3-19-57		3-25-57	3-27-57
Stewart	Eisenhower	10-14-58*				10-14-58
		1-17-59	5- 5-59	70-17	5-18-59	
White	Kennedy	4- 3-62	4-11-62		4-12-62	4-16-62
Goldberg	Kennedy	8-31-62	9-25-62		9-28-62	10- 1-62
Fortas	Johnson	7-28-65	8-11-65		8-11-65	10- 4-65
Marshall	Johnson	6-13-67	8-30-67	†	8-30-67	10- 2-67
[Fortas	Johnson	6-27-68‡]				

*Recess appointment.

†No recorded vote.

‡Johnson submitted Fortas' name to succeed Warren as Chief Justice on June 27, 1968; after certainty of filibuster in Senate, the nomination was withdrawn on October 2. Thus the nomination of Homer Thornberry, while submitted at the time of Fortas' nomination, and contingent upon a vacancy being created by Fortas' advancement, did not become a matter for formal Senate disposition. Fortas resigned from the Court on May 14, 1969.

In the tabular summary of the appointments in this period, it is worth noting that four of President Eisenhower's appointments were recess appointments, thus contributing in some degree to the delay in their confirmation. Warren, Brennan and Stewart were sworn in and sat on the bench prior to confirmation and the issuing of their commissions, but only Brennan felt it appropriate to be sworn in a second time.

89 (86). EARL WARREN (March 19, 1891-   ). *Fourteenth Chief Justice.* Born Los Angeles, California; A.B., University of California, 1912; J.D., 1914; admitted to bar and privately practiced in California, 1914-17; U.S. Army, 1917-1919; deputy city attorney, Oakland, 1919-20; deputy district attorney, Alameda County, 1920-23; chief deputy and district attorney, 1923-1939; California attorney general, 1939-43; governor of California, 1943-53; Republican candidate for Vice President, 1948; special representative to coronation of Elizabeth II, 1953; chairman of commission to investigate assassination of President Kennedy, 1963-64. Retired from Supreme Court June 23, 1969.

90 (73). JOHN MARSHALL HARLAN (May 20, 1899-   ). Born Chicago, Illinois, grandson of Associate Justice of same name; A.B., Princeton University, 1920; B.A., M.A. (Rhodes Scholar), Oxford University, 1923; LL.B., New York Law School, 1924; admitted to New York bar, 1925; assistant U.S. Attorney, 1925-27; special assistant attorney general for New York, 1928-30; general practice with Wall Street law firm, 1931-43, 1945-53; U.S. Army, 1943-45; judge, U.S. Court of Appeals, 1954-55.

91 (88). WILLIAM JOSEPH BRENNAN (April 25, 1906-   ). Born Newark, New Jersey; B.S., University of Pennsylvania, 1928; LL.B., Harvard, 1931; admitted to New Jersey bar and practiced, 1931-49; superior court judge, 1949-50; appellate division judge, 1950-52; justice, New Jersey supreme court, 1952-56.

92 (78). CHARLES EVANS WHITTAKER (February 22, 1901-   ). Born Troy, Kansas; LL.B., University of Kansas City, 1924; admitted to Missouri bar, 1923; private practice in Kansas City, 1924-54; judge, U.S. District Court, 1954-56; U.S. Court of Appeals, 1956-57. Resigned from Supreme Court April 1, 1962; dealer relations umpire for General Motors Corporation, 1962-present.

93 (85). POTTER STEWART (January 23, 1915-   ). Born Jackson, Michigan; B.A. cum laude, Yale University, 1937; fellow, Cambridge University, 1937-38; LL.B. cum laude, Yale, 1941; admitted to practice in Ohio, 1941; in New York, 1942; practiced in New York City, 1941-42, 1945-47; U.S. Navy, 1942-45; admitted to Ohio bar and practiced in Cincinnati, 1947-54; judge, U.S. Court of Appeals, 1954-58; vice-mayor of Cincinnati, 1952-53.

94 (92). BYRON R. WHITE (June 8, 1917-   ). Born Colorado; A. B., University of Colorado, 1938; Rhodes Scholar, Oxford University, 1938-40; U.S. Navy, 1940-43; LL.B., Yale University, 1946; law clerk to Chief Justice

Vinson, 1946-47; admitted to bar and practiced in Colorado, 1947-60; Deputy Attorney General, 1961-63.

95 (79). ARTHUR JOSEPH GOLDBERG (August 8, 1908-   ). Born Chicago, Illinois; B.S.L., Northwestern University, 1929; J.D., 1930; admitted to Illinois bar and practiced in Chicago, 1929-42, 1944-52; U.S. Army, 1942-44; practiced in District of Columbia, 1952-61; general counsel, CIO, 1948-55; same, United Steelworkers, 1948-61; general counsel, industrial department, AFL-CIO, 1955-61; Secretary of Labor, 1961-62. Resigned from Supreme Court July 26, 1965 to become U.S. Representative to United Nations, 1965-69.

96 (95). ABE FORTAS (June 19, 1910-   ). Born Memphis, Tennessee; A.B., Southwestern University, 1930; LL.B., Yale University, 1933; assistant professor of law, Yale, 1933-37; assistant chief, legal division, AAA, 1933-34; assistant director, corporate reorganization study, SEC, 1934-37; counsel, same, 1937-38; assistant director, public utility division, same, 1938-39; general counsel, PWA, 1939-40; same, bituminous coal division, 1940-41; director, division of power, Department of Interior, 1941-42; undersecretary, same, 1942-46; member of D.C. law firm, 1947-65; delegate to United Nations San Francisco Conference, 1945, and London Conference, 1946. Resigned from Supreme Court May 14, 1969.

97 (87). THURGOOD MARSHALL (July 2, 1908-   ). Born Baltimore, Maryland; A.B., Lincoln University, 1930; LL.B., Howard University, 1933; admitted to Maryland bar and practiced in Baltimore, 1933-37; special counsel and general counsel, various divisions, National Association for the Advancement of Colored Peoples, 1948-61; judge, U.S. Court of Appeals, 1961-65; Solicitor General, 1965-67.

Recapitulation

Undergraduate institutions represented among members of the Warren Court included California, Colorado, Lincoln, Northwestern, Pennsylvania, Princeton, Southwestern and Yale. Law degrees came from California, Harvard, Howard, Kansas City, Northwestern and Yale (four). Two appointees had been Rhodes Scholars at Oxford and another a graduate fellow at Cambridge. A total of one hundred and twenty-seven years of private practice was represented, with an average of fourteen years per member.

Specialized law practice included Justice Goldberg's thirteen years with national labor organizations, Justice Marshall's thirteen years with the NAACP, and an equal number of years by Justice Fortas with various Federal administrative agencies. Chief Justice Warren had more than twenty years of experience as a local government attorney and four as California attorney general, in addition to his unprecedented three terms as governor. Justice Brennan's state court experience covered seven years, virtually equal to the combined Federal intermediate court records of three other appointees. Two Associates had served two years each in the Department of Justice. Fortas had taught five years as a Yale Law School faculty member. No House or Senate experience was recorded by any of the appointees.

Attorneys General from 1932 to 1968

The Department of Justice, as much as the Supreme Court, was both a progenitor and an instrument of the New Legality. At no previous period in national history, it is safe to say, had the legal officers of the government been charged with such massive responsibilities, and they were handled with varying degrees of effectiveness in proportion to the competence of the men who held the offices. History has put a pitiless spotlight on such persons as Solicitor General Biggs and Attorneys General McGrath and McGranery.

The Department in the early New Deal encountered monumental challenges—to draft, under the desperate pressure of an unparalleled depression deepening into panic, emergency legislation for which no precedents existed; then to defend, before a judiciary largely fixed in its focus upon orthodox *laissez-faire* principles, the enactments with which Congress had attempted to deal with the crisis. In the insistent haste of the times, the draftsmanship of statutes suffered, thereby magnifying the task of legal defense against attacks upon the statutes. This conspiracy of events inevitably pointed to disaster for the first New Deal legislation—compounded, of course, by the adamance of the Court majority up to 1937.

Eisenhower's reliance on Attorney General Brownell to screen candidates for the judiciary considerably enlarged upon this function of the Justice Department, at the same time that it provided critics of the courts with a whipping boy. The reliance of Kennedy and Johnson upon their Attorneys General for the vigorous enforcement of the civil rights laws and policies of the sixties again enhanced the activism of the Department in the socio-political issues of the day. Finally, since 1937 when the law explicitly permitted the government to appear as of right in cases involving constitutional issues, the Department had had a continuing role where in the past it had often been incidental or accidental.

HOMER STILLE CUMMINGS (April 30, 1870-September 10, 1956). Ph.B., Yale University, 1891; LL.B., 1893; admitted to bar and practiced in Connecticut and Washington, 1893-1933, 1939 to retirement; mayor of Stamford, Connecticut 1900-02, 1904-06, corporation counsel, same, 1908-12. Attorney General, 1933-39. Author, *Liberty Under Law and Administration* (1934); with Carl McFarland, *Federal Justice* (1937); *The Tired Sea* (1939).

FRANK MURPHY (see preceding section).

ROBERT H. JACKSON (see preceding section).

FRANCIS BIDDLE (May 9, 1886-   ). A.B. cum laude, Harvard University, 1909; LL.B. cum laude, same, 1911; law clerk to Justice Holmes, 1911-12; admitted to Pennsylvania bar and practiced in Philadelphia, 1912-15, 1917-22, 1926-38, 1945 to retirement. U.S. Army, 1915-17; special assistant United States Attorney, 1922-26; special counsel of committee to investigate TVA,

1938-39; judge, U.S. Court of Appeals, 1939-40; Solicitor General, 1940-41; Attorney General, 1941-45; member war crimes commission, 1945-46. Author, *Mr. Justice Holmes* (1942), *Democratic Thinking and the War* (1944), *World's Best Hope* (1949), *Faces of Freedom* (1951), *In Brief Authority* (1962).

J. HOWARD MCGRATH (November 28, 1903-September 2, 1966). Ph.B., Providence University, 1926; LL.B., Boston University, 1929. Admitted to Rhode Island bar, 1929; U.S. District Attorney, 1935-40; governor, Rhode Island, 1940-45; Solicitor General, 1945-46; U.S. Senator, 1946-49; Attorney General, 1949-51; private practice until retirement.

JAMES P. MCGRANERY (July 8, 1895-December 23, 1962). LL.B., Temple University, 1928; admitted to bar and practiced in Philadelphia, 1928-36; U.S. House of Representatives, 1936-43; Assistant to Attorney General, 1943-46; judge, U.S. District Court, 1946-52; Attorney General, 1952-53; practiced to retirement.

HERBERT BROWNELL, JR. (February 20, 1904-   ). A.B., University of Nebraska, 1924; LL.B., Yale University, 1927; admitted to New York bar and practiced privately, 1927-53, 1957-date; Attorney General, 1953-57.

WILLIAM P. ROGERS (June 23, 1913-   ). A.B., Colgate University, 1934; LL.B., Cornell University, 1937; admitted to New York bar, 1937 and District of Columbia bar, 1950; assistant district attorney for New York County, 1938-42, 1946-47; U.S. Navy, 1942-46; counsel, Senate committee investigating war progress, 1947-48; same, Senate committee on executive expenditures, 1948-50; resumed private practice, 1950-53; Deputy Attorney General, 1953-57; Attorney General, 1957-61; private practice, 1961-69; U.S. Representative to United Nations, 1967; member, President's Commission on Law Enforcement and Administration, 1965-67; Secretary of State, 1969-present.

ROBERT FRANCIS KENNEDY (November 20, 1925-June 6, 1968). U.S. Navy, 1944-46; A.B., Harvard University, 1948; LL.B., University of Virginia, 1951; admitted to Massachusetts bar, 1951; attorney, criminal division, Department of Justice, 1951-52; special counsel to various Senate investigating committees, 1953-55, 1957-60; Attorney General, 1961-64; U.S. Senator from New York, 1965-68; assassinated in Los Angeles. Author, *The Enemy Within* (1960); *Just Friends and Brave Enemies* (1962); *Pursuit of Justice* (1964).

NICHOLAS DEBELLEVILLE KATZENBACH (January 27, 1922-   ). U.S. Air Force, 1941-45; B.A., Princeton University, 1945; LL.B., Yale University, 1947; Rhodes Scholar, Oxford University, 1947-49; admitted to New Jersey bar, 1950, Connecticut bar, 1955; Attorney Counsel's Office, Air Force, 1950-52; law faculty, Yale, 1952-56, and University of Chicago, 1956-60; Fellow of Ford Foundation, 1960-61; Assistant Attorney General, 1961-62; Deputy Attorney General, 1962-64; Acting Attorney General and Attorney General, 1964-66; Undersecretary of State, 1966-69. Author, with M. G. Kaplan, *The Political Foundations of International Law* (1961).

RAMSEY CLARK (December 18, 1927-   ). Son of Justice Tom C. Clark; U.S. Marine Corps, 1945-46; A.B., University of Texas, 1949; A.M. and J.D., University of Chicago, 1950; admitted to Texas bar, 1951, and practiced in Dallas, 1951-61; Assistant Attorney General, 1961-65; Deputy Attorney General, 1965-66; Acting Attorney General and Attorney General, 1966-69.

Solicitors General from 1932 to 1968

J. CRAWFORD BIGGS (August 29, 1872-January 30, 1960). Ph.B., North Carolina, 1893; studied law, North Carolina, and admitted to practice, 1894; practiced in North Carolina over number of years until his retirement; professor of law, North Carolina, 1898-1900, Trinity College (now Duke), 1911-12; mayor and state legislator, 1897-98; judge, North Carolina supreme court, 1907-11; Solicitor General, 1933-35.

STANLEY F. REED (see preceding section).

ROBERT H. JACKSON (see preceding section).

FRANCIS BIDDLE (see preceding section).

CHARLES FAHY (August 27, 1892-   ). Studied at Notre Dame University, 1910-11; LL.B., Georgetown University, 1914; admitted to District of Columbia bar and practiced privately, 1914-17, 1919-24; U.S. Navy, 1917-19; admitted to New Mexico bar and practiced there, 1924-33; assistant solicitor, Department of Interior, 1934-35; general counsel, National Labor Relations Board, 1935-40, 1947-49; Assistant Solicitor General and Solicitor General, 1940-45; judge, Court of Appeals for District of Columbia since 1949.

PHILIP B. PERLMAN (May 5, 1890-August 30, 1960). LL.B., Maryland 1912. Practiced in Maryland, 1912-17, 1926-47, 1952-60. Maryland assistant attorney general, 1917-20, Maryland secretary of state, 1920-23, Baltimore city solicitor, 1923-26; Solicitor General, 1947-52; Acting Attorney General, 1952.

J. HOWARD McGRATH (see preceding section).

WALTER J. CUMMINGS, JR. (September 29, 1916-   ). A.B., Yale University, 1937; LL.B., Harvard University, 1940; admitted to practice in Illinois, 1940; staff of Solicitor General, 1940-46; private practice in Chicago, 1946-52, 1953-66; Solicitor General, 1952-53; judge, U.S. Court of Appeals, 1966-present.

SIMON E. SOBELOFF (December 3, 1894-   ). LL.B., University of Maryland, 1915; admitted to Maryland bar, 1919; city solicitor, 1919-23, 1927-31, 1943-47; U.S. Attorney, 1931-34; chief judge, Maryland court of appeals, 1947-52; Solicitor General, 1954-56; judge, U.S. Court of Appeals, 1956-present.

JAMES LEE RANKIN (July 8, 1907-   ). A.B., University of Nebraska, 1928; LL.B., 1930; admitted to bar and practiced in Nebraska, 1930-53; Assistant Attorney General, 1953-56; Solicitor General, 1956-61; private practice in New York, 1961-66; corporation counsel, New York City, 1966-present. General counsel to Warren Commission, 1963-64.

ARCHIBALD COX (May 17, 1912-   ). A.B., Harvard University, 1934;
LL.B., 1937; admitted to bar and practiced in Massachusetts, 1937-41; attorney in office of Solicitor General, 1941-43; associate solicitor, Department
of Labor, 1943-45; on law faculty, Harvard Law School, 1945-61, 1965-
present; Solicitor General, 1961-65. Author, *Cases in Labor Law* (6th ed.,
1965).

THURGOOD MARSHALL (see preceding section).

ERWIN NATHANIEL GRISWOLD (July 14, 1904-   ). A.B., Oberlin, 1925;
A.M., 1925; LL.B., Harvard University, 1928; S.J.D., 1929; admitted to Ohio
bar in 1929, and Massachusetts bar in 1935; attorney in Department of Jus-
tice, 1929-34; on law faculty, Harvard Law School, 1934-67, dean, 1950-67;
Solicitor General, 1967-present. Author, *Spendthrift Trusts* (1936, 1947);
Cases on Federal Taxation (1940); *The Fifth Amendment Today* (1955).

Note: The Federal Judiciary and the New Deal

Next in importance to the Supreme Court of the United States in the
process of interpreting and (perhaps most important) devising the means of
applying the law on Federal questions and the Federal Constitution are the
United States Courts of Appeal for the ten circuits and the District of
Columbia. Franklin Roosevelt's long tenure in the White House, which enabled him to appoint eight Associate Justices and a Chief Justice in the case
of the Supreme Court, also enabled him to make a greater number of appellate court appointments than any other President. Roosevelt's more than
fifty appointments to the circuit benches was more than the combined totals
of his distant cousin and Woodrow Wilson, who appointed twenty-one and
twenty respectively.[1] New Deal appointments amounted to approximately
one-third of all that had been made in the Courts of Appeal since their
establishment in 1891.

More important than numbers were the background and ideology of the
appointees under the New Deal. While a substantial number of the appointments, in keeping with American political practice, were made to deserving
followers—and only three to Republicans—the majority of them were twentieth-century men (and one woman), products of the same law schools that
had contributed to the critical appraisal of the *laissez-faire* jurisprudence of the
Taft and early Hughes Courts. It was not without significance that among the
appointments to the busy Eastern circuits were eight men who had received
their law degrees at Harvard during Roscoe Pound's early and imaginative
deanship—Arnold, Biddle, Clark, Edgerton, Goodrich, Magruder, Patterson
and Stephens.

Judges Justin Miller, a Stanford law graduate, Wiley B. Rutledge of
Colorado and Armistead M. Dobie of Virginia were other products of the
academic culture beds which bred the New Legality or, like Jerome Frank of
Chicago, helped to nurture it in practice. Among these dozen men were legal
educators, indoctrinating the oncoming generation of leaders of the bar in
universities from coast to coast. Trained in the critical academic environment

of the first quarter of the twentieth century, and teaching in the second quarter, they helped to shape both the study of law and its judicial interpretation.

The statistical summary which follows is limited to a few salient data on the New Deal appointees to the intermediate appellate courts. The judges are listed by circuits, and in order of appointments, with the length of their tenure on the bench, the law school and year in which they earned their professional degree, and the more prominent features of their careers prior to appointment. Admittedly, there is always a temptation to read too much into such data; but this is not to say that the emerging picture does not tell something about the pervasiveness of a more modern legal mentality which developed throughout the higher Federal courts in the course of the Roosevelt appointments.[2]

Circuit and Judges	Dates of Service	Date of Law Degree	Principal Professional Activities
District of Columbia			
Harold M. Stephens	7-27-35 3- 8-48	Harvard 1913	Utah state judge, 1917-21; Asst. Atty. Gen., 1933-35; author, *Administrative Tribunals and the Rules of Evidence* (1933)
Duncan L. Groner, C.J.	12- 7-37 3- 8-48	....	U.S. District Court, 1921-31
Justin Miller	8-23-37 9-30-45	Stanford 1914	Law faculties California, Duke, Minnesota, Montana, Oregon, Southern California, 1910-35; later President, National Assn. of Broadcasters
Fred M. Vinson	12-15-37 5-28-43	Centre 1911	See section on Supreme Court
Henry Edgerton	2- 1-38 5-28-55	Harvard 1914	Law faculties Cornell, George Washington, 1916-18, 1921-38
Wiley B. Rutledge	5- 2-39 2-14-43	Colorado 1922	See section on Supreme Court
Thurman W. Arnold	5-11-43 7- 9-45	Harvard 1914	Law faculties Wyoming, West Virginia, Yale, 1921-38; author, *The Folklore of Capitalism* (1937), *The Symbols of Government* (1935), etc.
First Circuit			
Calvert Magruder	6- 3-39 6-12-59	Harvard 1916	Law clerk to Justice Brandeis, 1916-17; law faculty, Harvard, 1920-34, 1936-38; general counsel, NLRB, Wage-Hour Div., 1934-35, 1938-39

Circuit and Judges	Dates of Service	Date of Law Degree	Principal Professional Activities
John Mahoney	2-12-40 12-18-50	Harvard 1908	U.S. District Court, 1935-40
Peter Woodbury	2-25-41	Harvard 1927	State judgeships, New Hampshire, 1928-41
Second Circuit			
Robert P. Patterson	3-21-39 7-30-40	Harvard 1915	U.S. District Court, 1930-39
Jerome N. Frank	3-27-41 1- 3-57	Chicago 1912	Legal officer, AAA and SEC, 1933-41; author, *Law and the Modern Mind* (1930) and numerous other books.
Third Circuit			
John Biggs, Jr.	2-16-37 10-30-65	Harvard 1922	General law practice
William Clark	2-25-38 3-24-42	Harvard 1915	New Jersey Court of Errors, 1923-25; U.S. District Court, 1925-38
Albert B. Maris	6-24-38 12-31-58	Temple 1918	U.S. District Court, 1936-38
Francis Biddle	3- 4-39 7-22-40	Harvard 1911	See previous section
Charles A. Jones	7-25-39 12-31-44	Dickinson	General law practice
Herbert F. Goodrich	5-10-40 6-25-62	Harvard 1914	Law faculties Iowa, Michigan and Pennsylvania, 1914-40
Gerald McLaughlin	6-14-43	Fordham 1917	General law practice
Fourth Circuit			
Armistead M. Dobie	12-19-39 2- 1-56	Virginia 1904	Professor and dean, Virginia, 1909-39
Fifth Circuit			
Edwin R. Holmes	3-20-36 11-30-54	....	General law practice
Leon McCord	6-24-38 2-26-51	....	Alabama state courts, 1916-35
Curtis L. Waller	3-10-43 7-11-50	Millsaps 1910	U.S. District Court, 1940-43
Elmo P. Lee, Sr.	12-17-43 7-26-49	La. State 1911	General practice
Sixth Circuit			
Florence E. Allen	3-21-34 9-14-66	N.Y.U. 1913	Ohio state courts, 1920-34

Circuit and Judges	Dates of Service	Date of Law Degree	Principal Professional Activities
Elwood Hamilton	3- 4-38 9-19-43	Louisville 1904	U.S. District Court, 1935-38
Herschel W. Arant	3- 4-39 1-14-41	Yale 1915	Law faculties, Emory, Yale, Kansas, Ohio State, 1916-39
John D. Martin, Jr.	9- 4-40 4- 2-62	Virginia 1905	General law practice
Thomas T. McAllister	5-22-41	Michigan 1921	Michigan supreme court, 1937-41
Seventh Circuit			
Louis Fitzhenry	6-16-33 11-18-35	Ill. Wesleyan 1890	House of Representatives, 1913-15; U.S. District Court, 1918-33
J. Earl Major	3-23-37 3-23-56	....	Illinois state attorney, 1912-20; House of Representatives, 1923-25, 1927-35; U.S. District Court, 1935-37
Walter E. Treanor	12-27-37 4-26-41	Indiana 1922	Law faculty, Indiana, 1922-30; Indiana supreme court, 1930-36
Otto Kerner	11-21-38 12-13-52	Lake Forest 1905	Illinois state courts, 1927-33; Illinois attorney general, 1933-38
Sherman Minton	5-22-41 10- 5-49	Indiana 1915	See section on Supreme Court
Eighth Circuit			
Joseph W. Woodrough	4-12-33	....	U.S. District Court, 1916-33
Charles B. Faris	6-16-35 11-30-35	Missouri 1889	State prosecuting attorney, 1892-99; state judge, 1910-19; U.S. District Court, 1919-35
Seth Thomas	12- 2-35 5- 1-54	Iowa 1910	Asst. U.S. Attorney, 1914-20; Solicitor, Dept. Agr., 1933-35
Harvey M. Johnsen	10-14-40	Nebraska 1911	Law faculty, Creighton, 1922-31; Nebraska supreme court, 1939-40.
Walter G. Riddick	12-19-41 8- 1-53	Arkansas 1908	General law practice

Circuit and Judges	Dates of Service	Date of Law Degree	Principal Professional Activities
Ninth Circuit			
Francis A. Garecht	5-19-33 8-11-48	....	Law lecturer, Gonzaga, 1911-21; U.S. Attorney, 1914-21
William Denman	2- 1-35 7- 3-57	Harvard 1897	Law faculty, Hastings, 1902-06; reform leader in California, 1908-17
Albert Stephens	6-18-37 3- 5-65	U.S.C. 1903	State and local judge, 1910-35; U.S. District Court, 1935-37
Homer T. Bone	8-12-44 1- 1-56	....	U.S. Senate, 1933-44
Tenth Circuit			
Sam G. Bratton	6- 1-33 3- 1-61	....	New Mexico state courts, 1919-24; U.S. Senate, 1925-33
Walter A. Huxman	5-23-39 4- 1-57	Kansas 1914	City attorney, 1919-21; state tax commission, 1931-32; governor, 1937-39
Alfred P. Murrah	9- 4-40	Oklahoma 1927	U.S. District Court, 1937-40

Appendix B

Proposed Constitutional Amendments, 1932-1968

This Appendix continues the statistical analysis of the subjects which agitated Congressmen or their constituents sufficiently to take the form of proposed Amendments to the Constitution, which appears in the companion volume to this study. Like that analysis, this is divided roughly into decades, Table I being the period (1932-40) of the New Deal, Table II the decade of World War II and the postwar Truman years, Table III in the main covering the Eisenhower administration and Table IV the Kennedy-Johnson decade (1961-68). The statistics through the year 1962 are derived from *Proposed Amendments to the Constitution of the United States of America* (Senate Document No. 163, 87th Congress, 2d Session), which covers the period from 1927 to January, 1963. From January, 1963 to January, 1969 the statistics have been assembled by the present writer from the *Congressional Record*.

During the time of the New Legality a significant number of Amendments actually have been adopted. The partial reform of the "lame-duck" tenures of Congress (and the Executive) was effected by the ratification of the Twentieth Amendment just as Franklin D. Roosevelt began his first term. On the heels of this came the Twenty-First Amendment, repealing the Eighteenth. The New Deal itself was the target of the Twenty-Second, which limited the people's right to elect a President to two terms. It was adopted in 1951. The Twenty-Third, granting at last to the voters of the District of Columbia a modicum of electoral freedom, was adopted in 1961. The abolition of the poll tax as a voting prerequisite in national elections, a byproduct of the civil rights movement of the sixties, was adopted three years later, while the Twenty-Fifth Amendment, on Presidential disability and succession, was adopted in 1967 as a sensible reaction to the assassination of President Kennedy and his succession by a man with a known history of heart attack.

The long struggle to do something about the Electoral College, an anti-democratic mechanism which had never worked, seemed closer to success after the confused Presidential election of 1968. Numerous Congressional proposals on the subject were revived, and President Nixon gave a general if somewhat ambivalent endorsement to the idea of a change. The American

Bar Association went on record as supporting a complete abolition of the Electoral College and the election of a President and Vice-President by direct popular vote, a position supported by the majority of legal scholars in the nation. In the age of the doctrine of "one man, one vote," this position seemed to be the most logical one.

As suggested in the corresponding Appendix in the earlier volume, these statistics are revealing rather than significant; they indicate the subjects which were uppermost in the public mind at the particular time, and where the number of bills on a given subject waxes and wanes, one may discern a sort of politics of numbers. For years, for example, proposals for an "equal rights" amendment for men and women have been showered upon Congress; yet none has ever been reported out onto the floor of either House. The Supreme Court cases on prayer in the public schools provoked an enormous number of bills seeking to override the holdings. The apportionment cases resulted in a comparable outburst of proposals, spearheaded by the so-called Dirksen amendment, but to date none of the proposals has cleared both Houses of Congress.

Perhaps most symptomatic of constitutional development in this period has been the number of proposals for amendment to legalize certain activities of the Federal government which, after the constitutional crisis of 1937, were legalized by judicial decision instead. Federal surveillance over wages and hours, collective bargaining, child labor, social security and related subjects have all been found in this category. Reference to Appendices D and E will confirm the judicial shift of position which obviated the need to seek amendments. Whether the judicial shift was a tacit form of amendment is a subject of continuing dispute between conservatives and progressives.

By the end of the sixties, approximately six thousand proposals for constitutional change had been offered in Congress since 1789. The twenty-five amendments which actually have been adopted in this period demonstrate the built-in restraints upon popular impulse represented in Article V of the Constitution itself. Yet the expedition with which certain amendments have been adopted, when the good sense of the people was enlisted, suggests that the methodology of Article V is essentially sound. Between this continuing capacity to respond to persuasively presented proposals, and the ultimate change in judicial interpretation wrought by the cataclysms of the mid-century, the Constitution of the United States seems reasonably assured of continuing viability.

TABLE I. Proposed Amendments, 1933-1940

Subjects of Proposed Amendments	Congresses and Sessions							
	73rd/1st	73rd/2nd	74th/1st	74th/2nd	75th/1st	75th/2nd	76th/1st	76th/2nd
Agricultural assistance				6	4		2	
Alcoholic bev.: state prohib.			1		2	1	2	
Aliens, Indians: employment	1		1					
Indian rights							1	
suffrage	2		2		3		2	
Appropriations: item veto	1	1		4	7	1	2	
Armed forces					1			
Business-govt. competition							1	
Congress: powers generally	2	1	6	7	5	1	2	
Constitution: amending proc.	3	2	3	1	5			
due process redefined							1	
XIV Amend.: repeal				2	1		1	
XVI Amend.: repeal								
XVII Amend.: repeal						1		
XXI Amend.: repeal							1	
D.C. suffrage	2	1	2	1	2		6	
Domestic relations			1	1	3	3	1	1
Electoral College: reform		1	1		1		1	
Equal rights	2		3		3		4	
House of Repr.: general	1							
equal powers with Senate			1		1			
four-year terms			4		8	1	2	1

TABLE I. Proposed Amendments, 1933-1940 (Cont'd.)

Subjects of Proposed Amendments	Congresses and Sessions							
	73rd/1st	73rd/2nd	74th/1st	74th/2nd	75th/1st	75th/2nd	76th/1st	76th/2nd
Judiciary: appointments	1							
election	1		1	1				
numbers							3	
qualifications							3	
salaries	2				4		2	
tenure	2	1	2		5		1	
Supreme Court: advisory opinions					1			
composition of			3		9		2	
judicial review			3	3	16		1	
jurisdiction			1					
Justices generally	1				1			
retirement, tenure					10		1	
Labor: child labor	2		1	1	8		2	1
wages, hours			5	2	6	5	1	
right to work		1	1	1	1		1	
Old age assistance			1				11	
President: appts. reconfirmed					1			
tenure, term	1		1	1	7		7	
elections (and see Elect. Coll.)	3	1	1	1	10		2	4
Religion: pub. funds prohib.						1		
States: powers generally		1	1	2				

TABLE I. Proposed Amendments, 1933-1940 (Cont'd.)

Subjects of Proposed Amendments	Congresses and Sessions							
	73rd/1st	73rd/2nd	74th/1st	74th/2nd	75th/1st	75th/2nd	76th/1st	76th/2nd
Taxes: income, estate, etc.	2				2	1	5	
limitations on power						1		
securities	11	14	15	4	27	5	10	
Treaties: ratification generally			1					
War: conscription	4	4	4		6	3	7	
declaration			5		11	5	4	
prohibition of	1		1	1	1		1	
Total amendments proposed	43	27	71	39	174	30	95	7
Total reported out of committee	10	0	3	0	14	2	6	1
debated on floor	5	0	1	0	1	0	2	0
Total passed by one House	1	0	0	0	0	0	0	0

TABLE II. Proposed Amendments, 1941-1950

Subjects of Proposed Amendments	Congresses and Sessions									
	77th/1st	77th/2nd	78th/1st	78th/2nd	79th/1st	79th/2nd	80th/1st	80th/2nd	81st/1st	81st/2nd
Alcoholic bev.; state prohib.	2		1				1		1	
Aliens, Indians; Indian rights										
suffrage	3		4		2		2		1	1
Appropriations: item veto	1		1		1	1	2		1	
limitations										2
Armed forces								2		
Budget: balancing			2		1	1	1		1	
Business-govt. competition	1									
Capital punishment abolished						1	1		1	
Citizenship limitations		2			1		1			
Congress: disaster, emergency								1		2
limit to terms			4		2	2	4			
member qualifications									2	
power generally				1						
succession, disability						1				
Constitution: XIV Amend.: repeal										
XXII Amend.: repeal							7	1	1	1
D.C. suffrage	2		2		3		3		2	2
Domestic relations	1		1	1	2		1			
Education: Federal interference			1							
non-sectarian support for								1		
Elections generally									1	

TABLE II. Proposed Amendments, 1941-1950 (Cont'd.)

Subjects of Proposed Amendments	Congresses and Sessions									
	77th/1st	77th/2nd	78th/1st	78th/2nd	79th/1st	79th/2nd	80th/1st	80th/2nd	81st/1st	81st/2nd
Electoral College—abolish	5			4	1	1	9	1	11	
Equal rights		1	6		11	1	9	1	15	
Foreign aid limitations									1	
House of Rep.: equal powers	1						4			
four-year terms				1	1		3			
Judiciary: numbers							1	1		
qualifications							1			
removal	1		1		1		1			
tenure		1	2	1			1			
Supreme Court: composition of	2		1	1	1	2	1			
Justices generally		1				1				
retirement							1			
Jury trials						1				
Labor: child labor	1		1							
collective bargaining						1				
right to work	1		1		1		1			
Legislation: procedure generally	1		1							
Old age assistance	1									
President: appointments reconfirmed					1					
Ex-President in Senate					1				1	
powers generally						1	1			
qualifications							1			
succession, disability					1		2			

TABLE II. Proposed Amendments, 1941-1950 (Cont'd.)

Subjects of Proposed Amendments	Congresses and Sessions									
	77th/1st	77th/2nd	78th/1st	78th/2nd	79th/1st	79th/2nd	80th/1st	80th/2nd	81st/1st	81st/2nd
President (cont.)										
tenure, term	7		7	8	12	1	18		3	1
veto generally			1	1	2					
elections (see Elect. Coll.)	1			4	5		9	1	4	1
Religion: recognition of God, Christ							2		1	
public funds prohibited	1						1			
Segregation								1		
Taxes: income, estate, etc.		1	1	1	1		2			
limitations on power				1						
securities	4		1							
Treason redefined								1	2	
Senate: general					1		1		1	
news states' number									1	
Treaties: general									2	
ratification	1	1	8	4	9					
Vice-President: abolish					1		1			
add second, third					1		1			
Congress to fill vacancy							1			
Voting: anti-poll tax	1	1	2	2	2		2	1	2	1
18-year minimum age	4	4	7		4	1	4		3	

TABLE II. Proposed Amendments, 1941-1950 (Cont'd.)

Subjects of Proposed Amendments	Congresses and Sessions									
	77th/1st	77th/2nd	78th/1st	78th/2nd	79th/1st	79th/2nd	80th/1st	80th/2nd	81st/1st	81st/2nd
War: declaration	5									
Total amendments proposed	43	12	57	29	68	15	102	10	64	12
Total reported out of committee	2	0	5	3	20	1	16	1	13	0
debated on floor	0	0	0	0	2	0	1	0	2	0
Total passed by one House	0	0	0	0	2	0	1	0	2	0
Total passed by both Houses	0	0	0	0	0	0	1*	0	1†	0

*Became XXII Amendment.
†Became XXIII Amendment.

TABLE III. Proposed Amendments, 1951-1960

Subjects of Proposed Amendments	Congresses and Sessions									
	82nd/1st	82nd/2nd	83rd/1st	83rd/2nd	84th/1st	84th/2nd	85th/1st	85th/2nd	86th/1st	86th/2nd
Aliens, Indians: Indian rights	1		1							
suffrage	1									
Apportionment: Congress		1	3							1
state					1					3
Appropriations: item veto	1	4		2	6		10	2	14	3
limitations	5	4	10	2	6	3	10			
revenue requirements									1	
Armed forces			2		1					
Budget: balancing			2	1	1	1	4		5	3
Business-govt. competition		1	2		2		2			1
Capital punishment abolished										1
Citizenship limitations							1			
Civil rights, treaties on	4	6	14		11					
Congress: disaster, emergency	2		2	2	3					
limit to terms				2	2					
member qualifications	1		2						1	
succession, disability	1		1			1			1	
Constitution: amending proc.				10	2	3	1			
XVI Amend.: repeal	1						1		4	
XXII Amend.: repeal						2	3			
D.C. suffrage	5		3	1	6	2	5		7	1
Education: Federal interference				1					6	1

TABLE III. Proposed Amendments, 1951-1960 (Cont'd.)

Subjects of Proposed Amendments	Congresses and Sessions									
	82nd/1st	82nd/2nd	83rd/1st	83rd/2nd	84th/1st	84th/2nd	85th/1st	85th/2nd	86th/1st	86th/2nd
Elections: general		3					1		1	
Electoral College: abolish	8	1	16	1	16	1	6	1		3
amend, reform			1		1		1			
Equal rights	10		12	2	13	1	12	1	61	1
Executive agreements	2	10	3		1		2		1	1
Foreign aid limitations			1		1		1		1	
House of Repr.: equal powers	5		2		1	2	1		2	
four-year terms			5	4	5		5	1	2	1
recall of members										
Judiciary: appointments	1						2			
election							1			
removal	1		1							
restrictions on		1								
tenure	2	1	1				3		2	1
Supreme Court: composition	1		3		3				1	
judicial review								1	2	
jurisdiction		1	2		2			1	1	
Justices generally			2			2	2	1		
retirement, terms							6		4	
Obscenity									1	
Postmasters' appointments									1	

TABLE III. Proposed Amendments, 1951-1960 (Cont'd.)

Subjects of Proposed Amendments	Congresses and Sessions									
	82nd/1st	82nd/2nd	83rd/1st	83rd/2nd	84th/1st	84th/2nd	85th/1st	85th/2nd	86th/1st	86th/2nd
President: appointments reconfirmed									1	
Ex-President in Senate						1				1
powers generally		4								
qualifications						1	1	1	3	1
succession, disability						1		2	2	2
tenure, term	4		2							
elections (see Elect. Coll.)	4	7	10		9	6	7	13	13	3
Religion: recognition of God, Christ	2		2		4	2	17			
Segregation				1					1	
Senate: new states' numbers	1		2		2					
States: powers generally			1			2				
admission			1	5	7	2	10	13	2	3
Federal relations				1	1	1	4		1	
Taxes: income, estates, etc.	3		3	2	3	1	1	1		
limitations on power		1	1		1			2	16	2
Treason redefined	1			2	1	2	2		1	
Treaties: general	4	2	12	4	1	1	5		7	2
ratification generally					1					
supremacy of Constitution	1	2	17	2	11	1	5		6	2
Vice-President: additional			1				1			
Voting: anti-poll tax	3	1	7				1			
18-year minimum age			1	3	6		4		3	2
War: conscription	1	1	1							1

TABLE III. Proposed Amendments, 1951-1960 (Cont'd.)

Subjects of Proposed Amendments	Congresses and Sessions									
	82nd/1st	82nd/2nd	83rd/1st	83rd/2nd	84th/1st	84th/2nd	85th/1st	85th/2nd	36th/1st	86th/2nd
Total proposed amendments	77	49	151	46	129	36	138	28	175	33
Total reported out of committee	12	6	24	2	10	0	15	5	24	1
debated on floor	0	1	3	0	2	0	0	0	2	1
Total passed one House	0	1	5*	0	1	0	0	0	1	0

*i.e., two passed without formal floor debate.

TABLE IV. Proposed Amendments, 1961-1968

Subjects of Proposed Amendments	Congresses and Sessions							
	87th/1st	87th/2nd	88th/1st	88th/2nd	89th/1st	89th/2nd	90th/1st	90th/2nd
Aliens, Indians: Indian rights							1	
Apportionment: Congress				1				
state	11	9	10	66	106	1	14	
Appropriations: item veto	3	1	1		3			
limitations	1	1	1	1	3			
revenue requirement			1					
Armed forces								1
Budget: balancing			5	7	7		4	
Business-govt. competition			1		1			
Capital punishment abolished	1							
Citizenship limitations	2				1		4	1
Congress: disaster, emergency	3	1	4		3		1	
limit to terms	2		1	6				
members' qualifications	1			1		2	2	
Civil rights							10	
Constitution: amending proc.	1		1	1	1		4	
due process redefined			29		3	1		
XIV Amend.: amend			1					
XXII Amend.: repeal	4		1					
Court of the Union			7		1		1	
Criminal law, crimes					3	2	4	3
D.C. suffrage	2		2	2	1	1	29	
Domestic relations			1					

TABLE IV. Proposed Amendments, 1961-1968 (Cont'd.)

Subjects of Proposed Amendments	Congresses and Sessions							
	87th/1st	87th/2nd	88th/1st	88th/2nd	89th/1st	89th/2nd	90th/1st	90th/2nd
Education: Federal interference	5	2					1	
Elections generally	1		5		5		2	1
Electoral College: abolish			22		22		20	20
amend, reform	18	3	6					
Equal rights	134	12	105	2	88	39	130	22
House of Rep.: equal powers		1	1				6	
four-year terms	2				14	6	4	
number of members			7		8			
Judiciary: appointments	1						3	6
election		1					1	12
removal, retirement					1		1	
restrictions on			1		1	3	1	
tenure				2				5
Supreme Court: composition of	1	1	1	1	1	4	4	6
judicial review	1				1	2	10	
jurisdiction			1	1				
Justices generally			5	1	5	1	3	7
retirement			1	1			1	
Obscenity				1				
Postmasters' appointments					1		2	2
Public prayer	57		135	20	31		45	5
President: appointments reconfirmed						1		
Ex-President in Senate	2	2						

TABLE IV. Proposed Amendments, 1961-1968 (Cont'd.)

Subjects of Proposed Amendments	Congresses and Sessions							
	87th/1st	87th/2nd	88th/1st	88th/2nd	89th/1st	89th/2nd	90th/1st	90th/2nd
powers generally	39	1					1	
qualifications	1		1	5	1		1	
succession, disability	8		12	10	32		2	
tenure, term			1		1			
elections (see Elect. Coll.)					1	7	16	5
Religion, recognition of God, Christ establishment of	5		12	3	5	21	2	
Segregation		1		2	3	1	3	
States: admission	1			1			4	
Federal relations	1							
Senate: general	1	1	1	1	6		1	
Taxes: income, estate, etc.	10		1		1			
limitations on power		2	1		4	3	2	
Treason redefined	2					1		
Treaties: general	5		1		2			
ratification generally			1					
Voting: voting rights					4		4	1
anti-poll tax	6	6					1	
18-year-old minimum age	7	6	2	1	19	8	54	8
Total proposed amendments	283	101	393	135	390	105	400	109
Total reported out of committee	34	6	0	2	2	1	4	0
debated	1	0	0	1	2	1	0	0
Total passed one House	1	0	0	1	1	0	0	0
Total passed both Houses	1*	0	0	0	1†	0	0	0

*Became XXIV Amendment.
†Became XXV Amendment.

Appendix C

Statutes on the Federal Judiciary, 1932-1968

The furore over constitutional decisions of the Supreme Court in the mid-thirties and mid-fifties dramatized the political impact of the Court's decision-making role in the process of national government, but it paled in significance in comparison with the periodic enactments of Congress, over the period from 1932 to the end of the sixties, which quietly laid the foundation for a modern and highly efficient system of judicial administration. The last years of the Hoover administration saw the first concrete steps toward the completion of the program of modernization of the Federal judiciary for which Chief Justice Taft had labored so long. Attorney General William D. Mitchell devoted much of his time in the Justice Department to a final draft of a bill which Congress passed on the eve of the New Deal, authorizing the Supreme Court to draft uniform rules of procedure in appeals in criminal cases. Attorney General Cummings, Roosevelt's first successor to Mitchell, followed this accomplishment with a draft bill, which Congress enacted in 1934, extending the authorization to include uniform rules of civil procedure.

Even the statutes enacted in the passionate context of the great Court fight of 1937 were important legislative steps toward a more efficient administration of justice, while a 1939 law created an Administrative Office of the United States Courts, and in 1940 the authority over uniform rules was extended to its logical full dimension by applying it to criminal trial procedure as well. The Administrative Procedure Act of 1946, while it was criticized by many contemporary observers as an involved and sometimes retrogressive statutory effort, at least sought to codify the informal processes of judicial review of the work of regulatory agencies which had developed since 1912. In 1948 came a comprehensive modernization of the Judicial Code of 1911, with another general overhaul taking place ten years later. The Criminal Justice Act of 1964, while a complement to the Civil Rights Act of the same year, significantly documented Congress' disposition to accommodate the new constitutional propositions set out by the Court in the civil liberties and defendants' rights decisions of the late fifties and early sixties.

A systematic, scholarly process of research and drafting of procedural modernization, rules of evidence, redefinition of the jurisdiction of state and Federal courts with respect to each other's business was progressively encouraged during this period. Permanent committees on rules of procedure were attached to the Judicial Conference of the United States; the Chief Justice annually used his "state of the judiciary" address to the American Law Institute to suggest new areas of study for this professional academy of the bar; and the establishment of the Federal Judicial Center in 1968, to administer continuing projects of research into the improvement of judicial administration, all indicated a forward-looking attitude of the judiciary itself.

The representative statutes which follow provide a chronology of this process of modernization. They should be fitted into the list of general Congressional enactments in Appendix D, so as to discern their relationship to such complementary legislation as the executive reorganization acts of the forties and the procedural safeguards written into some of the civil liberties statutes of the sixties. Taken with the corresponding list of statutes in the preceding volume of the present study, they document a continuing effort at strengthening the whole judicial process which virtually parallels the constitutional events occurring in this period.

February 24, 1933. Criminal Appeals Rules Act, Ch. 119, 47 Stat. 904.

The power to draft uniform rules of procedure had been the third and climactic step in Chief Justice Taft's plan for a modern judiciary, following the statutes of 1922 and 1925 which created the Judicial Conference, facilitated the transfer of judges to sit in areas of crowded dockets, and broadened the discretionary jurisdiction of the Supreme Court. This statute authorized the drafting of uniform rules of appellate procedure in criminal cases in the Federal courts.

June 19, 1934. Rules of Civil Procedure Act, Ch. 651, 48 Stat. 1064.

Complementing and substantially broadening the rule-making power of the preceding statute, this act vested in the Supreme Court authority to promulgate uniform rules in civil cases, and to merge actions at law and in equity. Chief Justice Hughes, in January, 1935, appointed a committee of lawyers, jurists and legal scholars to undertake the drafting of the new rules, which were adopted in due course. Following the final extension of the rule-making power in criminal trials, in 1940, the Court came to rely on permanent committees of experts to keep up to date the rules in both civil and criminal procedure, admiralty and general appellate processes.

March 1, 1937. Supreme Court Retirement Act, Ch. 21, 50 Stat. 24.

This was the first Congressional response to Franklin Roosevelt's controversial Judiciary Reform Bill. It separated the bill's proposal for retirement of Supreme Court Justices on a guaranteed income on the same basis as other Federal judges, thus removing an economic inhibition against voluntary retirement.

August 24, 1937. Judicial Procedure Reform Act, Ch. 754, 50 Stat. 751.

The remainder of Roosevelt's bill which survived the bitter political fight from February through August covered certain long-overdue reforms in procedure without reaching the New Deal objectives to modernize the ideology of the Supreme Court. The statute provided for government intervention in any suits involving constitutional questions, the expediting of appeals in such suits, the clarification of the authority of three-judge courts in such suits, and the facilitating of assignments of judges within a circuit to relieve judges temporarily incapacitated.

June 7, 1939. Administrative Office of the Courts Act, Ch. 501, 53 Stat. 1223.

This statute created the Administrative Office of the United States Courts, thus providing a managerial service for the Federal judiciary, a clearing-house for information on the degree of congestion of court dockets, and better fact-finding procedures for preparation of judicial budget requests. It established an executive officer for the Judicial Conference of senior circuit judges, and provided for the organizing of a judicial council within each of the circuits.

June 29, 1940. Criminal Pleading and Trial Rules Act, Ch. 445, 54 Stat. 688.

Completing the legislative steps toward full power to draft uniform rules, this statute rounded out the 1933 statute on appellate procedure by extending the uniform rules to the trial level in criminal cases.

June 9, 1944. Amended Expediting Act, Ch. 239, 58 Stat. 272.

Following the case of *United States v. Aluminum Co. of America* (see Appendix E), Congress adopted this statute providing that where the Supreme Court cannot muster a quorum (because of Justices disqualifying themselves on a particular case) the appeal shall be referred to the intermediate appellate court of the circuit in which it originated.

June 11, 1946. Administrative Procedure Act, Ch. 324, 60 Stat. 237.

After legislative efforts dating from 1929, and a detailed two-year study by the Department of Justice, this statute codified the procedure for hearings, making of rules and judicial review of actions by regulatory agencies. The statute emphasized full publicity of administrative proceedings, timely notice to all affected parties, fixed times for public hearings and limitations on types of evidence to be admissible. Cf. *Morgan v. United States* (two cases, 1936 and 1938) in Appendix E.

August 2, 1946. Federal Tort Claims Act, Tit. IV, 60 Stat. 812, 842.

An autonomous section of the Legislative Reorganization Act of 1946, this statute waived government immunity in certain types of personal injury claims against the United States or government contractors. Agency heads were authorized to settle monetary claims below a certain figure, and provision was made for satisfying these and any adjudicated claims without the necessity for individual private bills passed by Congress.

June 25, 1948. Judicial Code (Revision) Act, Ch. 646, 62 Stat. 869.

This was a comprehensive modernization of the Judicial Code of 1911, redefining the relationships and organization of courts within the Federal judiciary system, providing for their jurisdiction, etc. It preserved the essential features of the 1911 code brought up to date by the dozens of amendments which had been adopted over the ensuing thirty-seven years.

June 29, 1950. Administrative Orders Review Act, Ch. 1189, 64 Stat. 1129.

Complementing the Administrative Procedure Act of 1946, this statute systematized the process of judicial review for several specific groups of agencies: the Federal Communications Commission, certain offices of the Department of Agriculture, and the several maritime boards.

June 23, 1953. Court of Claims Amendment Act, Ch. 253, 67 Stat. 226.

In this and companion statutes (Act of July 14, 1956, Ch. 585, 70 Stat. 432, Act of August 25, 1958, P.L. 85-755, 72 Stat. 848), Congress undertook to clarify the status of the Court of Claims and the Court of Customs and Patent Appeals as "constitutional" rather than "legislative" courts, primarily to determine their jurisdiction over cases under the Federal Tort Claims Act of 1946. Several decisions of the Supreme Court—cf. *O'Donoghue v. United States* and *Williams v. United States* in 1933 and *National Mutual Ins. Co. v.*

Tidewater Transfer Co. in 1949, in Appendix E—had cast substantial doubt on the permissible extent of the jurisdiction of these courts; but see also *Glidden Co. v. Zdanok* (1962), discussing the effect of these statutory efforts at clarification.

July 11, 1958. Judicial Conference Amendment Act, P. L. 85-513, 72 Stat. 356.

Directing the Conference to inaugurate a continuing study of the operation and effect of rules of practice and procedure in all Federal courts, this represented the ultimate culmination of the long struggle for systematic updating of court rules throughout the Federal system.

August 20, 1964. Criminal Justice Act, P. L. 88-455, 78 Stat. 552.

Accepting the general principle of recent judicial decisions on the right to counsel for indigent defendants, the statute provided for reimbursement for legal services out of the public funds, provided for representation in appeals, and directed all Federal trial courts to provide for the effective operation of the process of appointing counsel in such cases.

Appendix D

Selected Acts of Congress, 1932-1968

The statistical tables which precede the selected statutes for this period, like the tables in the corresponding Appendix in the first volume of this study, summarize the Federal, state and local laws which have been invalidated and the judicial precedents which have been overruled. As a statistical documentation of the New Legality, these tables are of fundamental significance. At first comparison with the corresponding tables in the first volume, little difference appears between the judicial record of the Fuller, White and Taft Courts and that of the Courts after 1932; if anything, the figures show a decline from the totals of both the White and Taft Courts in the statutes and ordinances held void.

There are, however, certain facts of considerable significance latent in the statistics on the invalidation of Federal and state legislation in the period since 1932. The first has to do with the Congressional acts held invalid in 1935—not only is it the highest number in the twentieth century, and indeed in any year in American history, but all of the acts were foundation stones for the first New Deal. The second has to do with the long hiatus in judicial hostility toward Federal legislation—after 1936 and until 1960 (a twenty-four-year period) only six Congressional acts were invalidated, even in part, and not more than one in any single term of the Court.

The third fact emerging from a scrutiny of these statistics is the substantial decline in judicial hostility toward state statutes and municipal ordinances for the period from 1937 to 1954. The sudden jump in statistics for state laws held invalid thereafter reflects the determination of the Warren Court to assert a preemptive Federal authority in areas of segregation, apportionment and rights of criminal defendants—areas in which local rather than Federal law had been the rule.

But more important than any of these is the fact to be discerned in the final column in these tables—the precedents overruled by later judicial opinions. The story begins with the last four years of the Hughes Court, reaches its climax in the first term of the Stone Court, and has continued at a fairly consistent plateau to the present. The ultimate confirmation of the New Legality lies in these figures, documenting the extent to which the Court committed itself to terminating the ruling effect of earlier judicial decisions enunciated in a prior frame of national reference. Between 1889 and 1932, eighteen earlier cases had been overruled; between 1932 and the end of the 1968 term in June, 1969, more than a hundred earlier cases had been overruled.

The period of the New Legality's birth may be described as the years 1937 to 1942, for there is a fundamental correlation between the absence of judicial decisions invalidating Federal statutes and the sudden climax in the number of precedents overturned. The one logically required the other: for if the Court had discovered a new basis for the validity of Congressional (and Presidential) exercise of power under the Constitution, it necessarily had to distinguish or deny the rules of scores of earlier cases which had been held diametrically the opposite. For the conservative, this was the ultimate evidence of judicial betrayal; for the progressive and certainly for the activist, it was a *sine qua non*.

The list of Federal, state and local laws which have been set aside, and the number of prior decisions overruled, for the period of the present study through 1964 has been compiled from *The Constitution of the United States of America* (Washington, rev. ed., 1965), at pp. 1397-1401 and 1473-1537. The present writer has added the statistics for the period 1965-68.

Because, following the estrangement between President Roosevelt and Congress bred in the great Court fight of 1937, the readiness of Congress to enact New Deal legislative programs was significantly reduced, the White House came to rely on the Executive Order to a degree greater than in previous administrations, to implement certain of its legislative grants of authority. The expanding role of the Executive Order in this context is described in a special note supplementing this Appendix.

The Hughes Court, 1932-1941*

October Terms	Statutes and Ordinances Invalidated				Overruled Opinions
	U.S. Laws	State Laws	Ordinances	Total	
1930†		13		13	2
1931	1	16		17	1
1932	1	7		8	3
1933		6		6	4
1934	2	7		9	
1935	7	13		20	
1936	3	10		13	
1937		9		9	2
1938		8	1	9	4
1939		4	2	6	6
1940†		4	2	6	4
Totals	14	97	5	116	26

*First two years of Hughes Court overlap last two years of corresponding table in first volume.
†Hughes took office Feb. 14, 1930, and retired July 1, 1941.

The Stone and Vinson Courts, 1941-46, 1946-53

October Terms	Statutes and Ordinances Invalidated				Overruled Opinions
	U.S. Laws	State Laws	Ordinances	Total	
1941		4		4	13
1942		4		4	2
1943	1	3	5	9	4
1944		3	1	4	6
1945*		4		4	
1946	1	6	1	8	4
1947		4	1	5	4
1948		7	1	8	1
1949		6	1	7	11
1950		9		9	2
1951		4	2	6	
1952†	1	7	1	9	1
Totals	3	61	13	77	48

*Stone died April 22, 1946; Vinson took office Oct. 7, 1946.
†Vinson died Sept. 8, 1953

The Warren Court, 1953-1969

October Terms	Statutes and Ordinances Invalidated				Overruled Opinions
	U.S. Laws	State Laws	Ordinances	Total	
1953		4	1	5	
1954		8		8	3
1955	1	1	1	3	
1956		6	1	7	2
1957	1	4	2	7	3
1958	1	5	2	8	2
1959		6	1	7	1
1960	3	8	2	13	5
1961		14		14	2
1962		11	1	12	3
1963	1	20		21	10
1964	2			2	7
1965		11	1	12	
1966		7		7	4
1967	2	4		6	3
1968*		6	2	8	2
Totals	11	105	14	130	52

*Warren's retirement was announced to be effective at end of 1968 term in June, 1969.

March 9, 1933. Emergency Banking Relief Act, Ch. 1, 48 Stat. 1.

Validating Franklin D. Roosevelt's drastic action in closing all banks under authority of the 1917 Trading with the Enemy Act, this statute, passed in a single day by the special session of Congress, gave the Chief Executive broad discretionary powers over all national banks and Federal Reserve banks in their transactions in currency, credit, gold, silver and foreign exchange. Sound banks in the Federal Reserve System were reopened under special license of the Treasury Department. The act also authorized the Treasury to call in all gold and gold certificates in the country. The emergency legislation effectively halted the money panic of 1933.

March 20, 1933. Economy Act of 1933, Ch. 3, 48 Stat. 11.

A clause in Section 11 of this act, repealing "all laws granting or pertaining to yearly renewable war risk insurance," was held to violate the contracts clause of the Constitution in *Lynch v. United States*. This was accordingly the first of the New Deal statutes to be invalidated (in part) in the courts.

March 22, 1933. Beer-Wine Revenue Act, Ch. 4, 48 Stat. 16.

Anticipating the repeal of prohibition, this statute amended the Volstead Act to legalize the sale of light wines and beer and thus stimulate the economy.

March 31, 1933. Civilian Conservation Corps Act, Ch. 17, 48 Stat. 22.

The first of the major unemployment relief acts, this statute created 250,000 jobs for men in reforestation and conservation, road construction and flood control projects.

May 12, 1933. Agricultural Adjustment Act, Ch. 25, 48 Stat. 31.

The first statutory program for agricultural relief, this law and the National Industrial Recovery Act of June 16 marked the climax to the Hundred Days of emergency New Deal legislation. This statute sought to encourage crop reduction by guaranteeing parity prices to farmers who voluntarily curtailed production, provided for the refunding of farm mortgages and established a special levy on processors of the agricultural products to finance the crop-reduction subsidies. The processing tax and crop control features of this first Agricultural Adjustment Act were held unconstitutional in *United States v. Butler* (1936).

May 12, 1933. Federal Emergency Relief Act, Ch. 30, 48 Stat. 55.

The second major unemployment relief statute, this act provided for outright grants to local governments—as distinguished from the Hoover loan program—for state-administered work programs complementing the Federal CCC program.

May 18, 1933. Tennessee Valley Authority Act, Ch. 32, 48 Stat. 58.

The multiple purposes of this statute included flood control, power generation, reforestation and the development of the general economic and social well-being of an entire region. Although widely criticized as an attempt to introduce state planning of the social economy, the act was upheld in 1936 in *Ashwander v. Tennessee Valley Authority.*

May 27, 1933. Federal Securities Act, Ch. 38, 48 Stat. 74.

Aimed at reforming stock market practices in selling securities, the statute compelled full disclosure of pertinent financial data to prospective investors, through registration of new issues with the Federal Trade Commission. The following year a special commission was created to administer security market surveillance.

June 5, 1933. Gold Repeal Joint Resolution, Ch. 48, 48 Stat. 112.

By this enactment Congress cancelled gold clauses in all Federal and private obligations and made all debts payable in legal tender. Although the Supreme Court held this action invalid as to clear government promises to pay in gold, it also ruled that the private holder of such promises was not entitled to unjust enrichment when the nation was not on the gold standard; *Perry v. United States* (1935).

June 6, 1933. National Employment System Act, Ch. 49, 48 Stat. 113.

Creating the United States Employment Service in cooperation with established state agencies, and financed by matching state and Federal funds, this statute dealt with a long-standing problem of exploitation of job-seekers by private employment agencies.

June 13, 1933. Home Owners Refinancing Act, Ch. 64, 48 Stat. 128.

This act created the Home Owners Loan Corporation to refinance home mortgages for nonfarm families, exchanging HOLC bonds for other claims against residential property, the bonds then being converted into a single first mortgage.

June 16, 1933. Banking (Glass-Steagall) Act, Ch. 89, 48 Stat. 162.

This statute created the Federal Deposit Insurance Corporation to guarantee individual bank deposits up to $5,000 (later $10,000). It also separated deposits from investment affiliates of banks, broadened Federal Reserve Board control over speculation on credit, and authorized the establishment of branch banking.

June 16, 1933. National Industrial Recovery Act, Ch. 90, 48 Stat. 195.

The climax of the Hundred Days of legislation, this statute undertook to promote industrial recovery through a series of fair competition codes, establishing the right of collective bargaining among employees and creating two major supervisory agencies, the National Recovery Administration (NRA) and the National Labor Board. Title II of the statute created a Public Works Administration (PWA) to stimulate the economy by "pump priming" projects such as road construction and public buildings.

In 1935 the major portions of Title I were invalidated by the Supreme Court. *Panama Refining Co. v. Ryan* held invalid Section 9 (c), the "hot oil" provision subjecting petroleum production to quotas established under state law, as an unlawful delegation of Congressional authority. *Schechter Poultry Corp. v. United States* shortly thereafter held that the code authority of the statute was an unconstitutional delegation of public power to private groups through the executive.

June 16, 1933. Emergency Railroad Transportation Act, Ch. 91, 48 Stat. 211.

Seeking to deal with the growing problems of railroad bankruptcies, Congressional action in this statute revised the Transportation Act of 1920 to bring railroad holding companies under the jurisdiction of the Interstate Commerce Commission and to place rate-making procedures under the surveillance of a Coordinator of Transportation.

June 16, 1933. Farm Credit Act, Ch. 97, 48 Stat. 257.

A Farm Credit Administration had been created by Executive Order in March. This statute empowered the FCA to offer short-term and medium-term credits for agricultural production at low interest rates, thus making long-term mortgages on farm properties (rather than on properties plus production) obtainable at more advantageous rates.

June 16, 1933. Deficiency Act, Ch. 101, 48 Stat. 307.

Section 13 of this law, reducing salaries of Federal judges by 15 percent, where the judges were retired but available for assignment, was held invalid under Article III, Section 1 of the Constitution prohibiting reduction of judges' salaries while in office. *Booth v. United States* (1934).

January 30, 1934. Gold Reserve Act, Ch. 6, 48 Stat. 337.

With this session of Congress, the New Deal alternated between further emergency legislation and the beginning of long-term legislative programs to consolidate its reforms. This statute empowered the President to limit the devaluation of the dollar, transfer into the Treasury any gold stocks remaining in the Federal Reserve System, and apply any profits from government sales of gold to an Exchange Stabilization Fund.

January 31, 1934. Farm Mortgage Refinancing Act, Ch. 7, 48 Stat. 344.

This statute created the Federal Farm Mortgage Corporation to issue bonds in exchange for consolidated farm loan bonds and invest them directly in mortgage loans. By this means the New Deal sought further to reduce the interest burden on farm debtors by making possible the refinancing of their principal debts at lower FFMC rates.

February 15, 1934. Civil Works Emergency Relief Act, Ch. 13, 48 Stat. 351.

This statute was the transition between the FERA of the previous year and the expanded Works Progress Administration (WPA) of the following year.

February 23, 1934. Crop Loan Act, Ch. 23, 48 Stat. 354.

Complementing the mortgage refinancing act of January 31, this statute broadened the authority of the FCA to extend loans on the planting, cultivating and harvesting of agricultural produce.

April 7, 1934. Farm Relief (Jones-Connally) Act, Ch. 103, 48 Stat. 528.

Encouraged by the experience under the first AAA—and under pressure from producers not covered by the original act—this was the first of several extensions of coverage by the act under the parity support program. This extension included cattle, peanuts, flax and sorghum.

April 21, 1934. Cotton Control (Bankhead) Act, Ch. 157, 48 Stat. 598.

This statute departed from the voluntary principles of the first AAA by providing for compulsory reduction of excess cotton production, with benefit payments to offset the reductions.

April 27, 1934. Home Owners Loan Act, Ch. 168, 48 Stat. 643.

This law broadened the 1933 statute to cover costs of repairs as well as mortgages. Section 6 of this statute, providing for converting state savings and loan associations into Federal associations upon approval of 51 percent of the stockholders, was held invalid under the Tenth Amendment in *Hopkins Savings Association v. Cleary* (1935).

May 9, 1934. Sugar (Jones-Costigan) Act, Ch. 263, 48 Stat. 670.

Another amendment to the original Agricultural Adjustment Act, extending the benefits to sugar producers and financing the benefits by a tax on processors, this was part of the original AAA invalidated by *United States v. Butler* in 1936.

May 18, 1934. Criminal Code Amendments, Ch. 299, 48 Stat. 780.

This law, fixing penalties for killing or assaulting Federal officers, was one of a series of statutes broadening the scope of Federal criminal law. Others related to extortion messages sent in interstate commerce (Ch. 300, 48 Stat. 781); strengthening the Federal Kidnapping (Lindbergh) Act of 1932 (Ch. 301, 48 Stat. 781); making a specific crime out of interstate flight to avoid arrest (Ch. 302, 48 Stat. 782); concerning prison insurrections (Ch. 303, 48 Stat. 782); and providing for offenses against banks (Ch. 304, 48 Stat. 783).

May 24, 1934. Municipal Bankruptcy Act, Ch. 345, 48 Stat. 798.

This statute permitted municipal corporations the same privileges in bankruptcy open to private corporations, and provided for a grace period of two years to consolidate and adjust municipalities' debt burdens when 51 percent of the creditors consented. Held unconstitutional under the Tenth Amendment in *Ashton v. Cameron County District* (1936).

June 6, 1934. Securities Exchange Commission Act, Ch. 404, 48 Stat. 881.

This statute created the SEC as a specialized agency to take over the program of surveillance of securities and their markets begun by the act of the previous year. The new commission was given authority to regulate trading in stocks and bonds, and to license stock exchanges.

June 7, 1934. Corporation Bankruptcy Act, Ch. 424, 48 Stat. 911.

This law provided for reorganization of corporations not legally bankrupt but unable to liquidate assets to meet current obligations, in cases where two-thirds of the creditors consented.

June 12, 1934. Farm Mortgage Foreclosure Act, Ch. 446, 48 Stat. 929.

Authorized the Land Bank Commissioner to make loans to farmers for the purpose of recovering farm lands owned by them prior to foreclosure.

June 19, 1934. Communications Act, Ch. 652, 48 Stat. 1064.

Replacing the former Federal Radio Commission with a new agency, the Federal Communications Commission, and transferring to it certain activities (i.e., relating to telephone and telegraph) of the Interstate Commerce Commission, this statute typified the New Deal tendency to devise specialized administrative regulatory agencies to handle the complex subject-matter of a technological society.

June 19, 1934. Silver Purchase Act, Ch. 674, 48 Stat. 1178.

A revival of the old silver bloc program of the Western states, this law authorized increased government purchases of silver to an amount equal to one-third of the Treasury's stocks of gold, at the same time nationalizing the existing silver stocks and purchases of foreign and domestic silver.

June 19, 1934. Labor Disputes Joint Resolution, Ch. 677, 48 Stat. 1183.

As collective bargaining disputes developed under Section 7 (a) of the NIRA, impeding the progress of the industrial recovery program envisioned in the statute, the National Labor Board authorized under Title I of the 1933 act was found to lack the administrative authority to negotiate settlements. An Executive Order in December, 1933 reorganized the existing board in an effort to broaden its effectiveness. With collective bargaining efforts still stalemated, a new agency known as the National Labor Relations Board was created by this Joint Resolution, which authorized the President to create regional boards with broader powers to compel arbitration of labor disputes. The resolution was intended to run to the terminal date of the NIRA in June, 1935. Although the *Schechter* case cut short the operation of the NIRA, Congress had already begun work on a labor law (the Wagner Act) which converted the NLRB of the Joint Resolution into the new NLRB of July 5, 1935.

June 27, 1934. Railroad Retirement Act, Ch. 868, 48 Stat. 1283.

This statute undertook to create a social security system on an industry-wide basis, requiring all interstate railroads to participate in funding a program of unemployment compensation and retirement benefits. The law was held unconstitutional in *Railroad Retirement Board v. Alton Railroad Co.* (1935).

June 28, 1934. Federal Farm Bankruptcy (Frazier-Lemke) Act, Ch. 369, 48 Stat. 1289.

This act authorized suspension of bankruptcy proceedings when a majority of creditors agreed to permit farmers to retain possession of their properties at reasonable interest for five years, in lieu of outright repurchase of their foreclosed farms at a 1 percent interest rate. The statute was found unconstitutional in *Louisville Joint Stock Bank v. Radford* (1935).

June 28, 1934. National Housing Act, Ch. 847, 48 Stat. 1246.

Creating the Federal Housing Administration, this law sought to stimulate housing construction while improving standards of such construction and stabilizing home financing.

June 28, 1934. Tobacco Control Act, Ch. 866, 48 Stat. 1275.

Modeled after the Bankhead Cotton Control Act, this law authorized a compulsory production quota system for tobacco planters and subjected planters to an ad valorem tax in cases where they refused to participate in the system.

April 8, 1935. Emergency Relief Appropriation Act, Ch. 48, 49 Stat. 115.

The so-called Second New Deal program began with this statute, creating the Works Progress Administration (WPA) which had a twofold objective of developing a continuing program of public works for unemployed and establishing a yardstick for wages and hours. The statute also vested in the Chief Executive authority to create new administrative agencies as deemed necessary to implement other parts of the Federal relief program. Acting on this authority, Roosevelt by Executive Order on May 1 created the Resettlement Administration to rehabilitate families on submarginal lands and to develop subsistence programs and homesteads for low-income urban residents—the so-called "greenbelt towns" near Washington, Cincinnati and Milwaukee. Roosevelt by two other Executive Orders on May 11 created the Rural Electrification Administration and on June 7 the National Youth Administration.

April 25, 1935. Soil Conservation Act, Ch. 85, 49 Stat. 163.

Established the Soil Conservation Service as a permanent agency of the Department of Agriculture; this act represented the government's commitment to a continuing program of control and promotion of soil conservation in the national interest.

July 5, 1935. National Labor Relations (Wagner-Connery) Act, Ch. 372, 49 Stat. 449.

With this, and the Social Security Act the next month, the major legislative projects of the Second New Deal were completed. Other New Deal statutes either took the form of complementary legislation, like the succeeding amendments to the Agricultural Adjustment Act, or revived in somewhat different form some of the features of the earlier New Deal laws struck down by the Supreme Court (see Note in Appendix E).

The Wagner Act created a new National Labor Relations Board with broader powers to define appropriate bargaining units within industrial plants, supervise elections upon request of workers and certify the duly chosen representative. The Board also had the power to hear complaints of unfair employer practices and to issue cease and desist orders. The Wagner Act was upheld, in a case indicating a turning point in constitutional jurisprudence, in *NLRB v. Jones and Laughlin Steel Corp.* (1937).

August 14, 1935. Social Security Act, Ch. 531, 49 Stat. 620.

The final piece of major legislation in the New Deal program, this statute (1) created a cooperative Federal-state system of unemployment compensation which tended to make substantially more uniform the numerous unemployment insurance plans of various states, financed by a payroll tax; (2) levied a tax in equal amounts upon employers and employees to fund a program of old-age and survivors' insurance; and (3) authorized grants of Federal funds to states to finance local programs of aid to disabled and dependent persons and to develop certain social services.

In two cases in 1937—*Stewart Machine Co. v. Davis* and *Helvering v. Davis*—the key tax features of the statute were held constitutional.

August 23, 1935. Banking Act, Ch. 614, 49 Stat. 684.

A major revision of the original Federal Reserve Act of 1913, this statute vested control over regulation of credit in an Open Market Committee of the Federal Reserve System, confined the System's purchases of government securities to the open market, authorized the Board of Governors to increase reserve requirements of member banks when deemed necessary, and authorized national banks to make real estate loans.

August 24, 1935. AAA Amendments, Ch. 641, 49 Stat. 750.

Following the Jones-Connally, Bankhead and Tobacco Control Acts of the previous year, these amendments to the first AAA codified the intervening amendatory statutes and generalized the compulsory features of the Cotton and Tobacco Control Acts. The amendments were held to be an unconstitutional use of the taxing power in *Rickert Rice Mills v. Fontenot* (1936).

August 26, 1935. Public Utility Holding Company Act, Ch. 687, 49 Stat. 803.

The statute empowered the Federal Power Commission to regulate interstate transmission of electric power by such holding companies, vested similar authority over gas in the Federal Trade Commission, and broadened the powers of the SEC over financial practices. The most drastic provision was a "death sentence" clause providing that any public utility holding companies which were unable, at the end of a five-year period, to demonstrate a local useful and efficient function were to be dissolved. By 1952 it was reported that the administration of this act had resulted in the dissolving of more than 750 holding company affiliations.

August 28, 1935. Farm Mortgage Moratorium (Frazier-Lemke) Act, Ch. 792, 49 Stat. 942.

This was one of a number of legislative attempts to overcome the adverse constitutional decisions of the Supreme Court. After the original Frazier-Lemke Act of 1934 was held unconstitutional in *Louisville Joint Stock Bank v. Radford,* this statute in substantially similar terms offered farmers extended credit, provided for repurchase of foreclosed farms at contemporary appraisals, and authorized suspension of foreclosures with creditors' consent for a period of five years. This statute was upheld in 1937 in *Wright v. Vinton Branch*; see also the note accompanying Appendix E.

August 30, 1935. Bituminous Coal Conservation Act, Ch. 824, 49 Stat. 991.

This first Guffey (Guffey-Snyder) Act created a "little NRA" to preserve the acknowledged beneficial effects of the production, price and labor codes under the NIRA. A 15 percent tax was levied on coal producers, with 90 percent of the tax being remitted upon compliance with the provisions of the statute. Although this statute sought to meet the constitutional objections of the *Schechter* decision, by making the code-like regulations a part of the Congressional enactment instead of delegating a code authority to private parties, the Court held the Guffey Act to be an unconstitutional use of the tax power in *Carter v. Carter Coal Co.* (1936). A direct challenge to this decision was represented in the second Guffey (Guffey-Vinson) Act of 1937.

June 19, 1936. Anti-Price Discrimination (Robinson-Patman) Act, Ch. 592, 49 Stat. 1526.

Amending the Clayton Act to prohibit price discrimination between different purchasers, with increased penalties for such practices aimed at destroying competition.

June 26, 1936. Merchant Marine Act, Ch. 858, 49 Stat. 1985.

Congress in this statute responded to years of advocacy in favor of greater governmental support of transoceanic domestic ship construction. The act replaced the Federal Shipping Board of the First World War with a Federal Maritime Commission, provided funds for loans to shipbuilders with proviso for converting such ships to naval auxiliaries in wartime.

June 30, 1936. Government Contracts (Walsh-Healey) Act, Ch. 881, 49 Stat. 2036.

The primary objective of this statute was to establish a national standard for wages, hours, prohibition of child labor and acceptable working conditions by requiring the meeting of these standards by private contractors working with the government.

April 26, 1937. Bituminous Coal (Guffey-Vinson) Act, Ch. 127, 50 Stat. 72.

In another challenge to Supreme Court nullification, this statute reenacted the basic provisions of the first Guffey bill invalidated in the *Carter Coal Co.* case. The new law omitted the wage-hour restrictions which the Court had originally found objectionable, but in 1938 the general wage-hour law reintroduced these features of labor policy, and they were upheld in *United States v. Darby* (1941).

June 3, 1937. Agricultural Adjustment Act of 1937, Ch. 296, 50 Stat. 246.

Encouraged by the reversal of judicial position on constitutional questions after the winter of 1937, Congress reenacted the basic provisions of the AAA, which was subsequently upheld in *Mulford v. Smith*. See also the note in Appendix E.

July 22, 1937. Farm Tenant (Bankhead-Jones) Act, Ch. 517, 50 Stat. 522.

This statute created the Farm Security Administration and authorized low-interest 40-year loans to tenant farmers whose applications for money to purchase farm properties were approved by the FSA. Other objectives of the statute were the retirement of sub-marginal lands from use, and improvement of wages, hours and living conditions for migratory workers.

August 16, 1937. Municipal Bankruptcy Act, Ch. 657, 50 Stat. 653.

The 1934 statute on this subject was held unconstitutional in *Ashton v. Cameron County District*. Taking its cue from the New Legality taking shape in the Supreme Court, Congress reenacted the substance of the law and the following year, in *Bekins v. United States,* saw the Court uphold the constitutionality of the fundamental principles it had invalidated two years before. See note to Appendix E.

September 1, 1937. United States Housing (Wagner-Steagall) Act, Ch. 896, 50 Stat. 888.

The first significant Federal effort in slum clearance, through the creation of a Federal Housing Authority vested with power to undertake a systematic program of low cost public housing.

June 23, 1938. Civil Aeronautics Act, Ch. 601, 52 Stat. 973.

Rounding out the New Deal administrative program on transportation generally, this statute created the Civil Aeronautics Authority to promote domestic development of air transport, regulate rates and enforce standards of air safety.

June 25, 1938. Food, Drug and Cosmetic (Wheeler-Lea) Act, Ch. 675, 52 Stat. 1040.

A major revision and updating of the original 1906 statute, codifying a great number of amendments which had been enacted by Congress in the intervening years. Section 301 (f) making it an offense to refuse entry or inspection to Federal officers was held a denial of due process in *United States v. Cardiff* (1952). The statute as a whole, however, with substantially increased powers over misbranding vested in the Food and Drug Administration and over false advertising vested in the Federal Trade Commission, represented a major victory for consumer interests in securing protective legislation.

June 25, 1938. Fair Labor Standards (Wage-Hour) Act, Ch. 676, 52 Stat. 1060.

The three major objectives of this law, complementing the Wagner Labor Act, were the establishment of a minimum wage (originally set at 40 cents an hour), fixing of a forty-hour limit to the work week, and prohibiting child labor. The law was held constitutional in 1941 in *United States v. Darby.*

June 30, 1938. Federal Firearms Act, Ch. 850, 52 Stat. 1250.

As part of the growing Federal legislation with reference to interstate crime, this statute sought to proscribe traffic in certain types of firearms commonly used by gangsters. Section 2 (f) establishing a presumption of guilt based upon prior conviction and present possession of a proscribed weapon was held invalid under the Fifth Amendment in *Tot v. United States* (1943).

February 10, 1939. Internal Revenue Code, Ch. 2, 53 Stat. 1.

The first codification of the tax laws of the United States, Subtitle A grouped income, estate and gift tax measures, Subtitle B covered levies on documents of transaction and production, Subtitle C related to manufacturing and processing, and Subtitles D and E defined organization and procedures.

April 13, 1939. Administrative Reorganization Act, Ch. 36, 53 Stat. 561.

Over objections of entrenched agency interests and Congressional suspicion that it would be used to consolidate the President's political control over the

Executive Department, Congress passed this enabling legislation in an effort to control spiraling costs of government. The statute enabled the President to consolidate and regroup various administrative agencies under reorganization plans subject to Congressional review; where Congress expressed no objection by nullifying resolutions, the reorganization plans were implemented by Executive Order. Five major plans for reorganization and consolidation were enacted within the next eighteen months.

August 2, 1939. Political Activities (Hatch) Act, Ch. 410, 53 Stat. 1147.

In response to complaints that large numbers of WPA votes in certain states had been improperly solicited or coerced during the 1938 elections, Congress provided by this law for the prohibition of political activity by any Federal officers below the policy level. The act was amended the next year to apply to state and local employees whose salaries came in whole or part from Federal funds.

November 4, 1939. Neutrality Act, Ch. 2, 54 Stat. 4.

A stringent embargo on arms exports had been adopted by Congress in 1937 at the height of isolationist sentiment stimulated by the ideological aspects of the Spanish Civil War. With the outbreak of World War II, the 1939 statute amended the prior act and permitted the "cash and carry" export of arms to belligerent powers.

June 28, 1940. Alien Registration (Smith) Act, Ch. 439, 54 Stat. 670.

A stringent law aimed at the surveillance of resident aliens by fingerprints and periodic registrations, the anti-subversive provisions of the statute were criticized as conflicting with the guarantees of the First Amendment. The Vinson Court upheld the basic provisions of the Smith Act, including its challenge to freedom of association and expression, in *Dennis v. United States* (1951), but it was critically reexamined in 1957 in *Yates v. United States* and in 1961 in *Communist Party v. Subversive Activities Control Board*.

September 16, 1940. Selective Training and Service Act, Ch. 720, 54 Stat. 885.

This was the first peacetime draft law in national history, providing for a one-year program of registration and selection of 2,000,000 men between the ages of twenty-one and thirty-five.

October 14, 1940. Immigration and Nationality Act, Ch. 876, 54 Stat. 1169.

A stringent tightening of the immigration and naturalization laws, Section 401 (g) as subsequently amended provided for loss of citizenship in the case of desertion in time of war. This section was held unconstitutional under the Eighth Amendment in *Trop v. Dulles* (1958).

March 11, 1941. Lend-Lease Act, Ch. 11, 55 Stat. 31.

The appalling reverses to Anglo-French arms in 1940 had been aggravated by the near-exhaustion of British credits for purchasing war supplies from the United States. At President Roosevelt's urging, this statute was enacted to permit any nation whose defense was deemed by the President to be vital to the defense of the United States to receive such supplies by sale, transfer, exchange or lease. More than $50,000,000,000 worth of such aid was extended during World War II.

December 18, 1941. First War Powers Act, Ch. 593, 55 Stat. 838.

Following American entry into the war, Congress passed an omnibus bill vesting in the President a further authority to reorganize Executive Department agencies in the national interest, expedite the awarding of contracts for war supplies, seize enemy properties and impose censorship.

January 30, 1942. Emergency Price Control Act, Ch. 26, 56 Stat. 23.

The Office of Price Administration (OPA) was created to supervise and fix price and rent ceilings, combat profiteering and speculation, expedite defense purchases without excessive waste, and place limits on wages and other income from production.

March 27, 1942. Second War Powers Act, Ch. 199, 56 Stat. 176.

Complementing the earlier statute, this law broadened the controls over interstate transportation, created a system of priorities, expedited naturalization proceedings for foreign-born members of the armed services, redefined the censorship power, and permitted a new ratio of metallic content in five-cent coins.

November 15, 1943. Urgency Deficiency Appropriation Act, Ch. 218, 57 Stat. 450.

In an effort to oust certain controversial government officeholders, Section 304 of this appropriation act specifically named Goodwin B. Watson, foreign affairs specialist with the Federal Communications Commission; William E. Dodd, Jr., a witness before the House Un-American Activities Committee, and Robert Morss Lovett, governmental secretary to the Virgin Islands. These men were barred from the governmental payroll, a provision held by the Court to be a bill of attainder in *United States v. Lovett* (1946).

June 22, 1944. Servicemen's Readjustment Act (GI Bill), Ch. 268, 58 Stat. 284.

Title I of this law expanded authority of the Veterans Administration to expedite construction of veterans' hospitals; Title II provided for veterans education, Title III for loans to purchase homes, farms or businesses, and Title IV for employment assistance.

September 27, 1944. Amendments to Immigration and Nationality Act of 1940, Ch. 418, 58 Stat. 746.

Sections 401 (j) of the 1944 amendments and 349 (a) (10) of the 1952 amendments (P.L. 414, 66 Stat. 163) sought to deprive draft evaders of citizenship. Both sections were held to violate the Fifth and Sixth Amendments in *Kennedy v. Mendoza-Martinez* (1963).

July 31, 1945. Bretton Woods Agreement Act, Ch. 339, 59 Stat. 512.

Authorizing the United States to participate in the Final Act of the United Nations Monetary and Financial Conference (Bretton Woods) of July 23, 1944, this act provided for American financial support for the International Bank for Reconstruction and Development (World Bank) and the International Monetary Fund. Bretton Woods and Dumbarton Oaks were the two major international conferences which led to the United Nations Conference in San Francisco in the spring of 1945.

December 20, 1945. United Nations Participation Act, Ch. 583, 59 Stat. 619.

Authorizing United States participation in the international organization drafted at San Francisco, thus committing the nation to full partnership in the successor to the old League of Nations and officially terminating the isolationist tradition.

April 16, 1946. Broadcasting Coercive Practices Act, Ch. 138, 60 Stat. 89.

Known as the Anti-Petrillo Law, this statute aimed at specific demands of the musicians' union leader, James Petrillo, which allegedly compelled broadcasters to employ a minimum number of union members for any performances, and pay penalties for the use of recordings rather than "live" performances. The statute reflected the growing Congressional dissatisfaction with labor practices which anticipated the Taft-Hartley Act. Criticized but upheld in *United States v. Petrillo* (1947).

August 1, 1946. Atomic Energy Act, Ch. 724, 60 Stat. 755.

The complexities of the nuclear age were recognized by this law; the preamble declared that with the demonstrated military consequences of the release of atomic energy, the "effect of the use of atomic energy for civil purposes upon the social, economic and political structures of today cannot now be determined." Complete government control of fissionable material was decreed for the present, along with severe penalties for divulging information on reactor processes—although the government itself had already approved release of the so-called Smyth Report giving the essential details.

August 6, 1946. Legislative Reorganization Act, Ch. 753, 60 Stat. 812.

A sweeping restatement, if not a complete modernization, of the Federal legislative process, complementing the administrative reorganization programs carried out just before World War II. Title IV of this statute was denominated the Federal Tort Claims Act (see Appendix C).

June 27, 1947. Labor-Management Relations (Taft-Hartley) Act, Ch. 120, 61 Stat. 136.

Passed over President Truman's veto, this statute reflected the shift from the heavily pro-labor position of the New Deal years to the postwar concern for a limiting of union power. The act banned the closed shop, permitted suits against unions for strike-incurred damages, imposed a sixty-day "cooling-off" period, required public disclosure of union finances and required a non-Communist oath of union officers. The oath was held constitutional in *American Communications Association v. Douds* (1950).

December 30, 1947. Stabilization Act, Ch. 526, 61 Stat. 945.

Concerned with continuing postwar inflation, at the same time that it sought to respond to constituents' restlessness under the extended price control programs of the war period, Congress modified the authority of the original OPA and stipulated limits to the powers of the Office of Economic Stabilization created the previous year by Executive Order. This was one of several legislative attempts—always compromised by desires to accommodate opposing constituent interests—by which Congress undertook to deal with inflation over the next five years.

January 27, 1948. Information and Educational Exchange Act, Ch. 36, 62 Stat. 6.

In another of a series of enactments which signalled the commitment of the United States to a broad participation in international affairs, Congress in this statute created the United States Information Service with powers to engage in dissemination of publications for all types of foreign media on American affairs, to inaugurate a continuing program of research in both communications and content, and to cooperate with private programs (e. g., Radio Free Europe) in a variegated plan of international information.

April 3, 1948. Foreign Assistance Act (Marshall Plan), Ch. 169, 62 Stat. 137.

Further reflecting the nation's commitment to postwar internationalism, this statute provided (Title I) for "economic cooperation" in rebuilding war-devastated economies, (Title II) for emergency children's relief, and for specific aid (Title III) to Greece and Turkey and (Title IV) China.

June 25, 1948. Displaced Persons Act, Ch. 647, 62 Stat. 1009.

Recognizing another novel problem—that of stateless persons—Congress authorized the relaxation for a limited period of the immigration quotas to permit entry of refugees from Communist or former Axis countries.

May 5, 1950. Uniform Code of Military Justice, Ch. 169, 64 Stat. 107.

Article 3 (a) subjecting ex-servicemen to court martial after discharge, for crimes committed while in service, was held to violate the Fifth and Sixth Amendments. *Toth v. Quarles* (1955); *Reid v. Covert* (1957), and three 1960 cases—*McElroy v. United States, Kinsella v. United States* and *Grisham v. Hagan.*

June 5, 1950. Act for International Development, Ch. 220, 64 Stat. 204.

This was one of a series of statutes in which Congress reviewed and modified the foreign aid programs begun by the Marshall Plan.

September 23, 1950. Subversive Activities Control Act, Ch. 1024, 64 Stat. 987.

Another postwar problem, of militant international Communism and domestic infiltration, reached critical proportions in the eyes of the Congresses of the early fifties. This statute was passed amid the public excitement over the atomic espionage cases and the conviction of Communist Party leaders under the Smith Act, affirmed in *Dennis v. United States* (1951). But in 1964 Section 6 of this statute, forbidding a member of a registered Communist organization to seek or obtain a passport, was held unconstitutional in *Aptheker v. Secretary of State.*

June 27, 1952. Amendments to Immigration and Nationality Acts, P.L. 414, 66 Stat. 163.

The amendments were another phase of the Congressional program seeking to control subversive activities. Section 352 (a) (1) depriving naturalized persons of citizenship after residing for three years in the state of prior origin was held unconstitutional in *Schneider v. Rusk* (1964).

April 1, 1953. Reorganization Plan I, 67 Stat. 18.

The new Department of Health, Education and Welfare was established in this plan, merging the former Federal Security Agency and other government activities concerned with education and related social subjects.

August 24, 1954. Communist Control Act, Ch. 886, 68 Stat. 775.

Climaxing the virulent Congressional hostility toward subversives, this statute undertook to outlaw the Communist Party in the United States. It complemented the Internal Security (McCarran) Act of 1951 limiting Communist entry and departure from the country for subversive purposes, by penalizing membership in the Party as illegal thereafter.

August 16, 1954. Internal Revenue Code, Ch. 736, 68A Stat. 3.

A comprehensive legislative effort to modernize the basic tax structure of the nation, codifying the various amendments to the 1938 code and purporting to simplify individual tax return procedures, encouraging small business by more liberal definitions of depreciation and retained earnings, etc.

September 9, 1957. Civil Rights Act, P.L. 85-315, 71 Stat. 634.

The first Congressional enactment on the subject in the twentieth century, this law created a Commission on Civil Rights as a fact-finding agency on which subsequent legislation could be based, and sought to strengthen the Federal power to enforce voting rights.

July 29, 1958. National Aeronautics and Space Act, P.L. 85-568, 72 Stat. 426.

Recognizing that space activities required both governmental control and government subsidy, this statute created a coordinating agency (NASA) to develop national capabilities in space, to subsidize experimental research in space science and technology, and to serve as a central clearing house for information on space developments.

August 12, 1958. Departmental Information (Anti-Secrecy) Act, P.L. 85-619, 72 Stat. 547.

The "people's right to know" had been advocated by news media for a number of years, resulting in this Congressional enactment seeking to classify categories of information and ensure the greatest degree of accessibility to public records by reporters.

September 14, 1959. Labor-Management Reporting and Disclosure Act, P.L. 86-257, 73 Stat. 519.

In an effort to combat allegedly widespread racketeering practices among union leaders, this so-called Landrum-Griffin Act was passed to require strict accounting of all union funds, limit their use in union elections, and provide for judicial surveillance of alleged mishandling.

May 6, 1960. Civil Rights Act, P.L. 86-449, 74 Stat. 86.

A revision and strengthening of the general provisions of the 1957 statute, this act reflected one of the growing problems of civil rights in a listing of criminal provisions for interstate flight to avoid prosecution for destroying schools, churches and other public buildings.

September 22, 1961. Peace Corps Act, P.L. 87-293, 75 Stat. 612.

Implementing President Kennedy's proposal for citizen involvement in the problems of underdeveloped countries, the statute undertook to make available to interested nations the technological knowledge of individual Americans living with the individual nationals to whom they would offer training.

December 16, 1963. Higher Education Facilities Act, P.L. 88-204, 77 Stat. 363.

Federal aid to education, already introduced in earlier laws on agricultural and technological training (cf. Morrill Act), was extended to physical facilities of higher education by this act. It provided for a variety of grants to public and private colleges and universities to cover part of the construction costs of libraries, laboratories and other instructional facilities.

July 4, 1964. Civil Rights Act, P.L. 88-352, 78 Stat. 241.

This statute substantially broadened the strengthened Federal powers in the whole area of racial equality. The Civil Rights Commission created by the 1957 statute was given greater authority in its fact-finding function and was complemented by a new Community Relations Service. In addition to further proscribing interference with voting rights, the accelerated desegregation of schools and other public facilities was provided for, and the Federal courts given greater authority to review remanded civil rights cases to ensure conformity with the holding.

July 9, 1964. Urban Mass Transportation Act, P.L. 88-365, 78 Stat. 302.

Implementing President Johnson's finding that transportation was a major complication of contemporary urban life, this statute authorized Federal aid in planning and construction of new transportation facilities, and research and development on both transportation and the related problems of air pollution from propulsion fuels.

August 20, 1964. Economic Opportunity (War on Poverty) Act, P.L. 88-452, 78 Stat. 508.

Another objective of President Johnson's "Great Society" was implemented in this statute creating a domestic Job Corps with complementary work-training, work-study and work-experience programs, assistance for disadvantaged children of school age, and provision for urban and rural community action programs to eliminate local poverty conditions.

April 11, 1965. Elementary and Secondary Education Act, P.L. 89-10, 79 Stat. 27.

Broadening earlier Congressional aid to public education, this law provided for Federal funds for areas where government military establishments placed a disproportionate burden on local school facilities ("Federal impact" areas), and made available various economic aids for children of low-income families.

June 30, 1965. Social Security Act Amendments (Medicare), P.L. 89-97, 79 Stat. 286.

After years of advocacy, Congress finally acceded to the argument that the United States should follow the lead of all other advanced countries in providing government-subsidized hospitalization and health benefits to aged citizens.

August 6, 1965. Voting Rights Act, P.L. 89-110, 79 Stat. 437.

Finding that the voting rights provisions in the 1957, 1960 and 1964 acts were a piecemeal approach to a problem which virtually created alternatives as loopholes for evasion, a group of Senators led by Mike Mansfield and Everett M. Dirksen advanced a bold new legislative concept which placed virtually all suffrage issues under the surveillance of the Department of Justice. The statute was a wholesale implementation of the Fifteenth Amendment, Section 1. Federal courts were directed to appoint special examiners whenever any voting rights questions were raised, and to suspend any tests required of electors where it was suspected that their purpose was to frustrate the exercise of the right. State autonomy in the administration of electoral and voting processes was to be suspended by the courts upon finding of such frustration, to be restored only upon satisfactory evidence offered to the courts of a permanent and effective correction of the objectionable practices.

September 9, 1965. Department of Housing and Urban Development, P.L. 89-174, 79 Stat. 667.

The steady growth of Federal legislation in the general subject-area, augmented by the problems of systematic control of urban blight and equal

housing opportunities, resulted in raising the subject to the level of a
Cabinet department in this statute.

November 8, 1965. Higher Education Act, P.L. 89-329, 79 Stat. 1219.

Completing the Federal aid to education aspect of the "Great Society,"
this law provided for the development of community and continuing education
services, financial aid to college libraries, general assistance to developing
institutions, and broader grants in aid to students.

October 15, 1966. Department of Transportation Act, P.L. 89-670, 80 Stat. 931.

The third new Cabinet office to be added in little more than a decade, the
recognition of this problem of urbanized society committed the Executive
Department to a permanent policy of administration of public and private
activities in this subject-area.

November 3, 1966. Demonstration Cities and Metropolitan Development Act, P.L. 89-754, 80 Stat. 1255.

Another facet of the "Great Society" concerned the establishment of pilot
or model projects, government-subsidized, demonstrating efficacious programs
of reclamation of slums and blighted areas, improved living conditions for
urban areas, and the like. Although Congress enacted the principle in this
statute, sparse appropriations for the projects limited its early effectiveness.

April 11, 1968. Civil Rights Act Amendments, P.L. 90-284, 82 Stat. 73.

The continuing cultural clash between racial groups which had led to
periodic demonstrations and quasi-insurrections in various parts of the
country prompted Congress to enact this legislation to impose greater penalties
on interference with Federally protected rights of voting and education, to
promote stricter fair housing rules, to regulate the practice of civil disobedience and to enlarge the criminal sanctions with reference to interstate
travel for purposes of fomenting riots.

June 19, 1968. Omnibus Crime Control and Safe Streets Act, P.L. 90-351, 82 Stat. 197.

Complementing the foregoing act, and representing a closing commentary
on the issues besetting American society at the end of the present study, this
statute provided for cooperative programs of recruiting and training of law
enforcement officers between the Department of Justice and state and local
governments, sought to offset certain Supreme Court opinions concerning
confessions in criminal prosecutions, prohibited wiretapping and slightly
strengthened the control of firearms.

Executive Actions and the New Legality

The critical commentary of the Supreme Court in the "Hot Oil" case in the winter of 1935 pointed up the fact that there was at that time no official publication for the thousands of Presidential Proclamations, Executive Orders, rules and regulations of administrative agencies, and other legal instruments which had the force of law and fundamentally affected the status of parties liable thereunder. By the Act of July 25, 1935 (Ch. 417, 49 Stat. 500) the *Federal Register* was established as the official daily gazette in which these documents were to appear. In 1937 the statute was amended to provide for the regular compiling of documents of continuing and general effect, in the *Code of Federal Regulations.* The first edition of the *C. F. R.* appeared in 1938 and the second in 1949; the latter is kept up to date with periodic revisions for individual titles, the most important ones being revised annually.

The table which follows summarizes statistics from one or the other of these editions to illustrate the growth of this function of the Executive Department, particularly during the New Deal. The number of Presidential Proclamations and Executive Orders from 1889 to the present, as complete as rather incomplete government records reveal them, has been included.

Presidential Proclamations and Executive Orders (there is no clear-cut distinction between them) embrace trivial, routine and ephemeral issues as well as major governmental initiatives. They are usually issued in pursuance of specific Congressional enactments, except as they may relate to subjects constitutionally within the jurisdiction of the Executive Department (e. g., Proclamations of neutrality in instances of hostility between two or more foreign powers).

The significance of the New Deal use of the Presidential Proclamation and Executive Order lay in the fact that these instruments became a fortuitous medium for implementation of Rooseveltian programs after the political *entente* between the White House and Congress broke down in the course of the great judiciary fight of 1937. The legislation of the second New Deal, like that of the first, had contained broad and general delegations of implementing authority to the Chief Executive; when the statutes of the second New Deal were affirmed by the revolutionized Court, Roosevelt was able to continue his administrative programs through Proclamation and Executive Order.

Prior to the twentieth century, fewer than two hundred Executive Orders had been issued and Proclamations were confined largely to ceremonial announcements. Although the table shows a steady increase in the number of these instruments after 1889—attesting to the growing variety of governmental programs requiring administrative decisions—no President before or since Franklin Roosevelt undertook to employ them for such wide-ranging executive purposes. Theodore Roosevelt used them to expedite his conservation policies, and Wilson, to implement preparedness and wartime programs; under the New Deal, they became an important auxiliary device in bringing the New Legality into being.

In the Steel Seizure Case of 1952 the Court interposed its only significant limitation upon the process, insisting that the Executive Department was free to act only within guidelines which made clear what Congress' intention had been in delegating the authority which the President was thereafter free to implement. Whether or not this was a gratuitous limitation placed upon an inherent executive function when the general welfare was in question, as suggested by critics of the majority opinion, the Court has not been disposed to dilate further upon the subject since that case.

Proclamations and Executive Orders, 1889-198

Administration	Dates	Proclamations	Exec. Orders
Harrison	Mr. '89-Mr. '92	67	
Cleveland	Mr. '93-Mr. '97	50	[38]
McKinley	Mr. '97-Sept. '01	54	[67]
T. Roosevelt	Sept. '01-Mr. '09	338	[873]
Taft	Mr. '09-Mr. '13	365	[683]
Wilson	Mr. '13-Mr. '21	409	[1,380]
Harding	Mr. '21-Aug. '23	79	[470]
Coolidge	Aug. '23-Mr. '29	203	[1,382]
Hoover	Mr. '29-Mr. '32	166	[985]
F. D. Roosevelt	Mr. '33-Apr. '45	610	3,517
Truman	Apr. '45-Jan. '53	355	891
Eisenhower	Jan. '53-Jan. '61	387	483
Kennedy	Jan. '61-Nov. '63	168	203
Johnson	Nov. '63-Jan. '69	324	319

Information on Proclamations from annual volumes of *United States Statutes at Large;* information on Executive Orders after 1935 from annual summaries in *Federal Register;* bracketed statistics for period before New Deal represents data, probably incomplete, reconstructed from first edition of *Code of Federal Regulations.*

Appendix E

Principal Constitutional Cases, 1932-1968

As with the counterpart to this Appendix in *The Old Legality*, the chronological arrangement of cases, with details as to the composition of the Court, the administration in the White House and the Department of Justice, and the division of Justices on specific cases, is intended to serve as a documentary description of the development of constitutional thought throughout the period. All of the important cases cited in the text itself are included here, and to these are added a number of other cases which have invalidated or significantly interpreted Federal and state statutes, or municipal ordinances, or have corroborated, distinguished or overturned prior decisions. Taken together, these data document the definition of *The New Legality*.

The chronological table of cases in the first volume carried the history from the opening year of the second century of the Constitution, through the end of the Taft Court and the first two years of the Hughes Court to the beginning of the New Deal. The present chronology overlaps the antecedent table by reiterating—although it also adds to—the data on the Hughes Court from February, 1930 to the October term of 1932. This has been done to present in one whole the significant decisions of Hughes' Chief Justiceship, during which the cataclysmic reversing of ideological poles took place. For the same reason, the data on the Warren Court are carried to the end of the October, 1968 term—to June, 1969.

To discern the features of the great ideological change in the last part of the 1930's, the key cases of the first and second New Deal legislative programs are described in somewhat more detail than others in this Appendix. In addition, the table of cases is followed with a special note comparing the statutory details, the points by which the reversing cases were distinguished from the earlier cases invalidating New Deal laws, and the contrasting jurisprudential rationale in the decisions.

1930

February 24. THE HUGHES COURT (February, 1930-June, 1941). Hughes, C. J.; Brandeis, Butler, Holmes, McReynolds, Sanford, Stone, Sutherland, Van Devanter.

March 23. Thomas D. Thacher becomes Solicitor General.

May 26. Texas & N. O. R. Co. v. Brotherhood of Railway & Steamship Clerks. 281 U. S. 548.

Argued May 1, 2, 1930. Hughes, C. J., for the Court.

Sustaining the right of employees under the Railway Labor Act to a free choice of their representatives for collective bargaining. The Court in 1935 refused to analogize from this, in invalidating industry-wide social security (*Railroad Retirement Board v. Alton Railroad Co.*).

June 2. Justice Roberts succeeds Sanford.

1931

February 24. United States v. Sprague. 282 U. S. 716.

Argued January 21, 1931. Roberts, J., for the Court; Hughes, C. J., not participating.

Dismissing a novel holding of the intermediate courts, that the Prohibition Amendment had never been in effect because relating to personal liberties of individuals and thus in conflict with the reserved powers of the people.

April 20. Aldridge v. United States, 283 U. S. 308.

Argued March 16, 1931. Hughes, C. J., for the Court; McReynolds, J., dissenting.

Holding that a Negro defendant charged with murder of a white man was entitled to raise the question of racial prejudice in examination of prospective jurors.

May 18. Stromberg v. California. 283 U. S. 359.

Argued April 15, 1931. Hughes, C. J., for the Court; McReynolds and Butler, JJ., dissenting.

Invalidating a California "red flag" statute as unconstitutionally denying to American citizens the right to freedom of expression, including unpopular radical opinions and symbols.

May 18. Tax Commission v. Jackson. 283 U. S. 527.

Argued March 5, 1931. Roberts, J., for the Court; Butler, McReynolds and Van Devanter, JJ., concurring; Sutherland, J., dissenting.

Holding that Indiana, in classifying businesses for tax purposes, could use a basis other than value of goods, i. e., the number of stores in a chain, and applying a tax which increased progressively with the number of retail outlets owned by a business. But see Roberts' opinion in the Florida "chain store tax" case of *Liggett v. Lee* in 1933.

May 25. Indian Motorcycle Co. v. United States. 283 U. S. 570.

Argued April 25, 1929; reargued October 24, 27, 1930. Van Devanter, J., for the Court; Stone, J., dissenting.

Federal tax on the sale of motorcycles to a municipal police department held invalid as a burden on a local governmental function.

May 25. Federal Trade Commission v. Raladam Co. 283 U. S. 643.

Argued April 24, 1931. Sutherland, J., for the Court.

One of a series of cases throughout the years since this Commission was formed, narrowly construing the Commission's power to prosecute suspected deceptive business practices in favor of private freedom of enterprise. Here the Court declined to uphold a Commision order against claims of an "obesity remedy" manufacturer.

June 1. Near v. Minnesota. 283 U. S. 697.

Argued January 30, 1931. Hughes, C. J., for the Court; Butler, Van Devanter, McReynolds and Sutherland, JJ., dissenting.

Invalidating a Minnesota law authorizing the closing of publications alleged to be guilty of false charges against public officials.

November 23. Bandini Petr. Co. v. Superior Court, 284 U. S. 1.

Argued October 13, 14, 1931. Hughes, C. J., for the Court.

Sustaining a California law which prohibited unreasonable waste of natural resources by oil producers.

November 23. Santovicenzo v. Egan. 284 U. S. 30.

Argued October 22, 1931. Hughes, C. J., for the Court.

Holding a treaty between the United States and a foreign nation to control the disposition of alien property within a state, any state law to the contrary notwithstanding.

November 30. Hoeper v. Tax Commission. 284 U. S. 206.

Argued October 15, 1931. Roberts, J., for the Court; Holmes, Brandeis and Stone, JJ., dissenting.

The majority held unconstitutional a Wisconsin statute taxing the combined income of a husband and wife where each has independent income. Holmes' dissent argued that where the state had a reasonable objective of discouraging tax evasion, no Federal question was involved.

1932

January 4. First National Bank v. Maine. 284 U. S. 312.

Argued December 10, 1931. Sutherland, J., for the Court; Stone, Brandeis and Holmes, JJ., dissenting.

Holding that where a stockholder dies in Massachusetts owning shares in corporate property in Maine, an estate tax in Massachusetts bars a similar tax in Maine. The dissent challenged the assumption that such double taxation was necessarily unconstitutional.

March 14. Justice Cardozo succeeds Holmes.

March 21. New State Ice Co. v. Liebmann. 285 U. S. 262.

Argued February 19, 1932. Sutherland, J., for the Court; Brandeis and Stone, JJ., dissenting; Cardozo, J., not participating.

The majority held that an Oklahoma ordinance withholding licenses to distribute and sell ice in competition with companies already licensed was unconstitutional because it regulated businesses not "affected with a public interest." This *laissez-faire* formula by which the Court determined the validity or invalidity of government regulation was soon to be abandoned by the Hughes Court in 1934 *(Nebbia v. New York)*.

March 21. Heiner v. Donnan. 285 U. S. 312.

Argued February 21, 1932. Sutherland, J., for the Court; Stone and Brandeis, JJ., dissenting; Cardozo, J., not participating.

Holding that a tax law creating a presumption that gifts made within two years of death were in anticipation of death, and therefore subject to estate tax, was contrary to due process under the Fifth Amendment. Stone's dissent pointed out that the purpose of the law—to reach taxable wealth which was distributed in evasion of the tax—was a policy decision for Congress to make.

April 11. Smiley v. Holm, 285 U. S. 355.

Argued March 16, 17, 1932. Hughes, C. J., for the Court; Cardozo, J., not participating.

In this early reapportionment case, the Court held that where a state failed to redistrict after census returns established a reduction in its Congressional representation, candidates for the House of Representatives were to be elected at large.

April 11. Burnet v. Coronado Oil Co. 285 U. S. 393.

Argued January 15, 1932; reargued March 16, 1932. McReynolds, J., for the Court; Stone, Roberts and Brandeis, JJ., dissenting.

Holding exempt from Federal taxation public school lands leased to private companies, where a portion of the revenue from the extracted oil from the lands went to public schools. Overruled in *Helvering v. Mt. Producers Corp.* (1938).

April 11. Coombes v. Getz. 285 U. S. 434.

Argued March 21, 1932. Sutherland, J., for the Court; Cardozo, Brandeis and Stone, JJ., dissenting.

Holding that where a suit was brought between parties to a contract, prior to repeal of a state law creating the cause of action under the contract, the repeal could not operate to impair the right created under the contract. Cardozo dissented with the observation that such a contract right was always liable to state action withdrawing it.

May 2. Nixon v. Condon. 286 U. S. 73.

Argued January 7, 1932; reargued March 15, 1932. Cardozo, J., for the Court; McReynolds, Butler, Sutherland and Van Devanter, JJ., dissenting.

Invalidating under the Fourteenth Amendment a Texas statute giving political parties the right to limit the qualifications of voters in primaries, where this resulted in all-white primaries. The majority held that this was "state action" even though implemented by political parties.

May 16. Champlin Refin. Co. v. Commission, 286 U. S. 210.

Argued March 23, 1932. Butler, J., for the Court.

Upholding an Oklahoma statute compelling oil refineries to refrain from wasting by-products—e. g., natural gas—of drilling for oil.

October 18. Wood v. Broom, 287 U. S. 1.

Argued October 13, 1932. Hughes, C. J., for the Court; Brandeis, Stone, Roberts and Cardozo, JJ., dissenting.

Reversing judgment of a three-judge court and holding that Federal courts could not enjoin state officials persisting in malapportionment.

November 7. Powell v. Alabama. 287 U. S. 45.

Argued October 10, 1932. Sutherland, J., for the Court; Butler and Mc-Reynolds, JJ., dissenting.

One of the "Scottsboro cases," affirming that the right to counsel in felony cases was guaranteed to defendants under the Fourteenth Amendment.

November 7. United States v. Shreveport Grain & El. Co. 287 U. S. 77.

Argued October 19, 1932. Sutherland, J., for the Court; Brandeis, Stone and Cardozo, concurring.

Holding that the Pure Food and Drug Act in defining administrative powers to implement the regulations in the statute did not unconstitutionally delegate legislative powers to a non-legislative branch.

1933

January 23. Twentieth Amendment ratified.

February 6. Anglo-Chilean Nitrate Sales Corp. v. Alabama. 288 U. S. 218.

Argued January 19, 1933. Butler, J., for the Court; Cardozo, Brandeis and Stone, JJ., dissenting.

The majority held that where a state has licensed a foreign corporation to do business within its borders, it cannot thereafter burden interstate commerce with a tax on doing business. The dissent argued that the corporation solicited and obtained a privilege which was offered in the knowledge that the state had a right to tax the privilege.

March 4. Franklin D. Roosevelt inaugurated President.

Homer S. Cummings becomes Attorney General.

March 13. Appalachian Coals, Inc. v. United States. 288 U. S. 344.

Argued January 9, 10, 1933. Hughes, C. J., for the Court; McReynolds, J., dissenting.

In a revival of the "rule of reason" of the turn-of-the century trust cases, the Court held that the creating of a selling agent, with power to fix prices, by competing coal dealers was not a violation of the Sherman Act. In contrast to the philosophy of the *Schechter* case in 1935 invalidating the NIRA, Hughes here held that cooperative regulation of the market, to cope with a universally recognized evil, was not an attempt to restrain trade in the interest of monopoly.

March 13. Liggett Co. v. Lee. 288 U. S. 517.

Argued January 12, 13, 1933. Roberts, J., for the Court; Brandeis, Cardozo and Stone, JJ., dissenting.

A Florida chain store tax setting rates higher for national chains than for local chains was held to be unconstitutionally discriminatory. Brandeis' lengthy dissent marshalled economic arguments in support of a state's power to control bigness of an industry when it threatened the survival of local outlets.

May 5. J. Crawford Biggs becomes Solicitor General.

May 29. Williams v. United States. 289 U. S. 553.

Argued April 12, 1933. Sutherland, J., for the Court.

Holding that Court of Claims was "legislative" rather than "constitutional" court like district and intermediate courts (cf. *O'Donoghue v. United States,* 289 U. S. 516), on assumption that its limited jurisdiction also limited its dignity. Cf. Appendix C.

December 4. Southern R. Co. v. Virginia. 290 U. S. 190.

Argued October 17, 18, 1933. McReynolds, J., for the Court; Hughes, C. J., Cardozo and Stone, JJ., dissenting.

Denying a state commission power to order railroads to eliminate grade crossings in interest of public safety where there was no provision for review of the order.

December 5. Twenty-First Amendment ratified.

1934

January 8. Home Building & Loan Assn. v. Blaisdell. 290 U. S. 398.

Argued November 8, 9, 1932. Hughes, C. J., for the Court; Sutherland, Butler, McReynolds and Van Devanter, JJ., dissenting.

Sustaining a Minnesota mortgage moratorium law on ground that economic welfare of the state and legislation to protect it were within reserved powers of state, particularly where the mortgagee's rights were not extinguished but merely postponed.

December 5. Booth v. United States. 291 U. S. 339.

Argued January 17, 1934. Roberts, J., for the Court.

In the light of the retirement question during the 1937 Court fight (see also Appendix C), this case and a companion case *(Amidon v. United States)* are interesting for their holding that judges in the lower Federal courts continued in office after retirement and thus were protected from diminution of salaries.

March 5. Nebbia v. New York. 291 U. S. 502.

Argued December 4, 5, 1933. Roberts, J., for the Court; McReynolds, Butler, Sutherland and Van Devanter, JJ., dissenting.

The long-standing doctrine that government regulation could apply only to business "affected with a public interest" was discarded with the majority holding that any business was subject to reasonable regulation. The opinion also held that the legislature had the primary power to determine the occasion of regulation, and barred judicial intervention unless the legislature exceeded its constitutional power. Here a New York law setting prices for milk producers was held to be reasonable.

May 28. Worthen Co. v. Thomas. 292 U. S. 426.

Certified Question Submitted May 2, 1934. Hughes, C. J., for the Court; Sutherland, Butler, McReynolds and Van Devanter, JJ., concurring.

Distinguished the Minnesota mortgage moratorium law from an Arkansas law exempting proceeds of life insurance policies from garnishment, where the latter statute was not limited to or justified by economic emergency.

June 4. Lynch v. United States. 292 U. S. 571.

Argued May 7, 1934. Brandeis, J., for the Court.

Holding that Congress could not reduce government expenditures by repudiating contractual obligations of the United States, this case involving Federal war risk insurance foreshadowed the *Gold Clause* cases.

December 3. Borden's Farm Products v. Baldwin. 293 U. S. 194.

Argued November 6, 7, 1934. Hughes, C. J., for the Court; Stone and Cardozo, JJ., concurring.

This case sought to establish further guidelines for application of New York Milk Control Law, the constitutionality of which had been generally upheld in *Nebbia v. New York.* So far as intrastate regulation was concerned, the Court found plenary power in the state legislature.

1935

January 7. Panama Refin. Co. v. Ryan. 293 U. S. 388.

Argued December 10, 11, 1934. Hughes, C. J., for the Court; Cardozo, J., dissenting.

The first major New Deal case invalidating a section of the NIRA, relating to petroleum production controls. This "hot oil" decision strongly criticized the draftsmanship of the statute as not specifying the limits to the delegation of legislative power or providing notice to affected parties concerning their liability.

February 18. Norman v. Baltimore & Ohio R. Co. 294 U. S. 240.

Argued January 8-10, 1935. Hughes, C. J., for the Court; McReynolds, Butler, Sutherland and Van Devanter, JJ., dissenting.

First of the *Gold Clause* cases, the opinion in this and a companion case (*United States v. Bankers Trust Co.*) sustained the power of Congress to suspend specie payments in the national interest and thus sustained the suspension of gold clauses in private contracts.

February 18. Nortz v. United States. 294 U. S. 317.

Argued January 10, 1935. Hughes, C. J., for the Court; McReynolds, Butler, Sutherland and Van Devanter, JJ., dissenting.

The second of the *Gold Clause* cases held constitutional the suspension of specie payments on Treasury notes since the holder of the note sustained no loss by the suspension, being required by law to turn in gold even if he could receive it in payment.

February 18. Perry v. United States. 294 U. S. 330.

Argued January 10, 11, 1935. Hughes, C. J., for the Court; Stone, J., concurring; McReynolds, Butler, Sutherland and Van Devanter, JJ., dissenting.

In the final *Gold Clause* case, the majority (as well as the dissenters) first held that the government could not repudiate gold clauses in Liberty Bonds, representing a borrowing on the credit of the United States to pay in specie. Hughes, however, then held that since the claimant would be unjustly enriched by the government's payment of his bond in gold, and could not prove any damage resulting from his being paid in paper money, he was not entitled to insist upon his contract right.

March 4. Baldwin v. G. A. F. Seelig. 294 U. S. 511.

Argued February 11, 12, 1935. Cardozo, J., for the Court.

In another case growing out of the New York Milk Control Law, the Court in this unanimous opinion held that local price fixing authority did not extend to milk imported from outside the state.

March 11. Stewart Dry Goods v. Lewis. 294 U. S. 550.

Argued February 8, 1935. Roberts, J., for the Court; Cardozo, Brandeis and Stone, JJ., dissenting.

Graduated taxes on retail sales were held to violate the equal protection clause of the Fourteenth Amendment.

March 23. Stanley F. Reed becomes Solicitor General.

April 1. Norris v. Alabama. 294 U. S. 587.

Argued February 15, 18, 1935. Hughes, C. J., for the Court; McReynolds, J., not participating.

Conviction of Negro defendant set aside where both grand jury and trial jury were shown consistently to bar Negroes as jurors.

April 1. Grovey v. Townsend. 295 U. S. 45.

Argued March 11, 1935. Roberts J., for the Court.

Reflecting its ambivalence toward the matter of Federal rights and Negro disfranchisement, the Court in this case reversed a trend begun in 1927 *(Nixon v. Herndon)* and continued in 1932 *(Nixon v. Condon)* and now held that denying a Negro voter the right to vote in a party primary was not "state action." Reversed in *Smith v. Allwright* (1944).

April 29. Aero Mayflower Transp. Co. v. Commission. 295 U. S. 285.

Argued April 4, 1935. Cardozo, J., for the Court.

Affirming a Georgia tax on private vehicles using state highways, the revenue going to the upkeep of the highways, as not burdening interstate commerce or violating the equal protection clause by exempting farm and dairy trucks.

May 6. Railroad Retirement Board v. Alton R. Co. 295 U. S. 330.

Argued March 13, 14, 1935. Roberts, J., for the Court; Hughes, C. J., Brandeis, Cardozo and Stone, JJ., dissenting.

Overturning a major New Deal statute seeking to establish a social security system within an industry, the majority held the law to be an invalid use of the commerce power. The decision was rendered moot by the later *Social Security* cases. See Note at end of this Appendix.

May 20. Herndon v. Georgia. 295 U. S. 441.

Argued April 12, 1935. Sutherland, J., for the Court; Cardozo, Brandeis and Stone, JJ., dissenting.

Dismissing a convicted defendant's appeal from a state court on the ground that a general allegation that the trial violated the Federal Constitution was too vague to raise a Federal question. The dissent anticipated the defendants' rights cases of the 1960's by arguing that a Federal question arose at any stage in a trial where an individual's Federal rights were jeopardized.

May 27. Schechter Poultry Corp. v. United States. 295 U. S. 495.

Argued May 2, 3, 1935. Hughes, C. J., for the Court; Cardozo and Stone, JJ., concurring.

Invalidating Title I of the NIRA, the Court declared that there was an excessive delegation of legislative power to the executive, that the guidelines for drafting codes of unfair competition between private groups were inadequate, and that much of the subject-matter of the law was local rather than interstate in nature. See Note following this Appendix.

May 27. Louisville Joint Stock Land Bank v. Radford. 295 U.S. 555.

Argued April 1, 2, 1935. Brandeis, J., for the Court.

By a unanimous opinion the Court held unconstitutional the first Frazier-Lemke Federal Farm Bankruptcy Act. Refusing to analogize from the Minnesota state mortgage moratorium, the Court insisted that this first Frazier-Lemke Act denied creditors their security under the due process clause. Congress enacted a new Frazier-Lemke Act, meeting the constitutional objections of the *Radford* opinion, and this was upheld in *Wright v. Vinton Branch* (1937). See Note to Appendix.

May 27. Humphrey's Executor v. United States. 295 U. S. 602.

Argued May 1, 1935. Sutherland, J., for the Court; McReynolds, J., concurring.

In a final blow at the White House on this "Black Monday," the Court denied the President a power to remove an administrative appointee without the consent of Congress.

December 9. Hopkins Federal Savings & Loan Assn. v. Cleary. 296 U. S. 315.

Argued November 18, 19, 1935. Cardozo, J., for the Court.

Invalidating so much of the Home Owners' Loan Act as permitted the conversion of state savings and loan associations into Federal associations in contravention of the law of the state creating the original association, as an infringement of the Tenth Amendment.

December 16. Colgate v. Harvey. 296 U. S. 404.

Argued October 14, 15, 1935. Sutherland, J., for the Court; Stone, Brandeis and Cardozo, JJ., dissenting.

Invalidating a Vermont income tax law on the ground that an exemption of unsecured loans within the state, which did not include those made outside the state, infringed upon "privileges and immunities of citizens of the United States" under the Fourteenth Amendment. The dissent pointed out that the effect of the majority holding was to hamstring local tax powers. Reversed in *Madden v. Kentucky* (1940).

1936

January 6. United States v. Butler. 297 U. S. 1.

Argued December 9, 10, 1935. Roberts, J., for the Court; Stone, Brandeis and Cardozo, JJ., dissenting.

Invalidating the first AAA, this decision holding agriculture to be a purely "local" subject with which the Federal government should not be concerned made a virtual shambles of the first New Deal recovery program. The majority opinion condemned the processing tax as a non-revenue measure intended to regulate agricultural production, but left unanswered the question of government liability to refund such taxes. Congress enacted several statutes, including a new AAA, seeking to deal with these problems, and these were ultimately upheld by a new Court. Cf. *Anniston Mfg. Co. v. Davis* (1937), *Mulford v. Smith* (1939), Appendix D and Note to this Appendix.

January 13. Rickert Rice Mills v. Fontenot. 297 U. S. 110.
Argued December 16, 17, 1935. Roberts, J., for the Court.

This was one of eight cases challenging the AAA processing taxes, held invalid under the *Butler* decision.

February 17. Grosjean v. American Press Co. 297 U. S. 233.
Argued January 14, 1936. Sutherland, J., for the Court.

Holding an advertising tax on major newspapers in Louisiana—allegedly levied by Huey Long against press critics—to be an unconstitutional infringement on press freedom.

February 17. Brown v. Mississippi. 297 U. S. 278.
Argued January 10, 1936. Hughes, C. J., for the Court.

Invalidating convictions based on coerced confessions.

February 17. Ashwander v. TVA. 297 U. S. 288.
Argued December 19, 20, 1935. Hughes, C. J., for the Court; Brandeis, Cardozo, Roberts and Stone, JJ., concurring; McReynolds, J., dissenting.

Upholding the TVA, the majority ruled that the government had explicit constitutional power to construct dams to provide power for wartime munitions, as well as to improve navigability of waterways. A by-product of these activities such as electricity was a disposable property of the government.

March 30. Fisher's Blend Station v. State Tax Commission. 297 U. S. 650.
Argued March 9, 1936. Stone, J., for the Court.

A radio broadcasting station licensed by a Federal agency was held not subject to any state tax which burdened interstate commerce.

April 6. Jones v. SEC. 298 U. S. 1.
Argued March 10, 11, 1936. Sutherland, J., for the Court; Cardozo, Brandeis and Stone, JJ., dissenting.

The conservative majority in this decision castigated the Commission for seeking to compel an applicant for a license to testify as to his stock plan even after he had withdrawn his application. The dissent argued that the effect of his holding was to encourage questionable promoters to frustrate an inquiry by withdrawing applications if threatened.

April 26. St. Joseph Stockyards Co. v. United States. 298 U. S. 38.

Argued March 2, 1936. Hughes, C. J., for the Court; Roberts, Brandeis, Cardozo and Stone, JJ., concurring.

Affirming the general right of administrative regulatory agencies, when provided with adequate Congressional guidelines, to fix and enforce rates to be charged by the regulated businesses.

May 18. Carter v. Carter Coal Co. 298 U. S. 238.

Argued March 11, 12, 1936. Sutherland, J., for the Court; Hughes, C. J., Cardozo, Brandeis and Stone, JJ., concurring.

Invalidating the first Bituminous Coal Conservation (Guffey) Act as an invasion of states' rights—in the face of seven *amicus* briefs of states advocating the upholding of the act. The majority insisted that national power did not coincide with national problems unless there was explicit authority for such power in the letter of the Constitution. Substantially modified in *Sunshine Coal Co. v. Adkins* (1940).

May 25. Ashton v. Cameron County District. 298 U. S. 513.

Argued April 29, 1936. McReynolds, J., for the Court; Cardozo, Brandeis, Stone, JJ., and Hughes, C. J., dissenting.

The first Municipal Bankruptcy Act of 1934 was struck down by a five-to-four majority holding that the law invaded the rights of the state. The dissent refuted this premise by pointing out that no municipality could invoke the law unless its state's laws permitted. Overruled, in effect, in *United States v. Bekins* (1938).

June 1. Morehead v. New York ex rel. Tipaldo. 298 U. S. 587.

Argued April 28, 29, 1936. Butler, J. for the Court; Hughes, C. J., Stone, Brandeis and Cardozo, JJ., dissenting.

The same narrow majority of conservatives, including Roberts, struck down the New York minimum wage law for women as infringing upon the constitutional rule against impairment of contract rights. Stone, among the dissenters, answered that a freedom to contract to work for less than a living wage was a freedom which could be limited in the public interest. Reversed in *West Coast Hotel Co. v. Parrish.*

1937

January 4. Kentucky Whip & Collar Co. v. Illinois Central R. Co. 299 U. S. 334.

Argued November 20, 1936. Hughes, C. J., for the Court; Stone, J., not participating.

Upholding the use of the commerce clause to implement a statute prohibiting transport of convict-made goods into states prohibiting the goods.

January 4. DeJonge v. Oregon. 299 U. S. 353.

Argued December 9, 1936. Hughes, C. J., for the Court.

Invalidating the Oregon criminal syndicalism law as infringing upon the free speech guarantee of the First Amendment, and limiting "clear and present danger" to overt acts.

January 11. United States v. Hudson. 299 U. S. 498.

Argued November 17, 18, 1936. Van Devanter, J., for the Court; Stone, J., not participating.

Sustaining the Silver Purchase Act of 1934.

January 20. President Roosevelt inaugurated for second term.

March 29. West Coast Hotel Co. v. Parrish. 300 U. S. 379.

Argued December 16, 17, 1936. Hughes, C. J., for the Court; Sutherland, Butler, McReynolds and Van Devanter, JJ., dissenting.

Upholding the Washington state law fixing minimum wages for women, specifically overruling *Adkins v. Children's Hospital* (1923) and in effect reversing the *Morehead* decision of the previous June. This decision, timed to have a maximum effect on the Roosevelt judicial reform bill in the Senate, marked the beginning of the constitutional revolution of the Hughes Court. See Note to this Appendix.

March 29. Wright v. Vinton Branch. 300 U. S. 440.

Argued March 3, 4, 1937. Brandeis, J., for the Court.

In a second case on this important decision day, the Court unanimously upheld the second Frazier-Lemke Federal Farm Bankruptcy Act, passed by Congress in virtually the same language as the original but considered by the Court to have met the constitutional objections in the *Radford* case. See Note to this Appendix.

March 29. Sonzinsky v. United States. 300 U. S. 506.

Argued March 12, 1937. Stone, J., for the Court.

The regulatory tax feature of the National Firearms Act was upheld as a use of the tax power within the discretion of Congress.

March 29. Virginia R. Co. v. System Federation. 300 U.S. 515.

Argued February 8, 9, 1937. Stone, J., for the Court.

Upholding an amendment to the Railway Labor Act promoting collective bargaining in interstate transportation, this decision on the heels of the *West Coast Hotel* and *Wright* decisions broke the back of the New Deal effort to push Roosevelt's Court bill through Congress.

March 29. Highland Farms Dairy v. Agnew. 300 U. S. 608.

Argued March 8, 1937. Cardozo, J., for the Court; Van Devanter, Sutherland, McReynolds and Butler, JJ., dissenting.

Sustaining a Virginia price-fixing law on the basis of the rule in *Nebbia v. New York*.

April 12. NLRB v. Jones & Laughlin Steel Corp. 301 U. S. 1.

Argued February 10, 11, 1937. Hughes, C. J., for the Court; McReynolds, Butler, Sutherland and Van Devanter, JJ., dissenting.

In a succession of Labor Board cases, of which this was the prototype and all of which were five-to-four decisions, the majority upheld all essential features of the National Labor Relations Act. The right to organize for bargaining purposes, said Hughes, was "a fundamental right" whose recognition is "an essential condition of industrial peace." Congress could properly utilize the commerce power and general welfare clause to ensure industrial peace in the public interest, the opinion concluded. The holding and its reasoning were totally new in American constitutional law, and made clear the commitment of the Court to a new jurisprudence.

April 26. Herndon v. Lowry. 301 U. S. 242.

Argued February 8, 1937. Roberts, J., for the Court; Van Devanter, Butler, McReynolds and Sutherland, JJ., dissenting.

Invalidating a Georgia criminal syndicalism statute which proscribed speech advocating violence at an indefinite future date, as failing to establish a clear and present danger.

May 17. Anniston Mfg. Co. v. Davis. 301 U.S. 337.

Argued April 2, 1937. Hughes, C. J., for the Court; Cardozo and Stone, JJ., concurring; McReynolds, J., dissenting.

This case denied recovery of processing taxes paid under the first AAA, even though they had been declared unconstitutional, where the cost of the tax had been passed on to others not party to the suit.

May 24. Carmichael v. So. Coal & Coke Co. 301 U. S. 495.

Argued April 7, 8, 1937. Stone, J., for the Court; McReynolds, Sutherland, Butler and Van Devanter, JJ., dissenting.

One of several cases on this date sustaining the principle of social security. This decision upheld an Alabama unemployment compensation law enacted in coordination with the Social Security Act.

May 24. Stewart Machine Co. v. Davis. 301 U. S. 548.

Argued April 8, 9, 1937. Cardozo, J., for the Court; McReynolds, Sutherland, Butler and Van Devanter, JJ., dissenting.

Upholding the unemployment compensation feature of the Social Security Act, as a valid use of the tax power by Congress to deal with a national problem of insurance against hardships from joblessness.

May 24. Helvering v. Davis. 301 U. S. 619.

Argued May 5, 1937. Cardozo, J., for the Court; McReynolds and Butler, JJ., dissenting.

In this Social Security case, the old-age benefits of the statute were upheld. More importantly, the majority opinion repudiated the dictum in the *Butler* case, that the general welfare clause was limited to the subjects of the specifically enumerated powers of government and held instead that it was a separate and general source of authority in the Federal government. See Note at end of this Appendix.

October 4. Justice Black succeeds Van Devanter.

November 8. Dodge v. Board of Education. 302 U. S. 74.

Argued April 28, reargued October 14, 1937. Roberts, J., for the Court.

Sustaining a state law reducing teachers' annuities as not in violation of the contract clause of the Constitution.

November 8. Hale v. Board of Assessment. 302 U. S. 95.

Argued October 18, 19, 1937. Cardozo, J., for the Court; Sutherland, Mc-Reynolds and Butler, JJ., dissenting.

Sustaining an Iowa income tax laid on the interest from tax-exempt state bonds.

December 6. Palko v. Connecticut. 302 U. S. 319.

Argued November 12, 1937. Cardozo, J., for the Court; Butler, J., dissenting.

Upholding a state law providing for a second trial in a criminal case, where the second conviction resulted in a more severe sentence, as not double jeopardy under state law where it might be under the Bill of Rights. By its gratuitous statement that the Bill of Rights was not incorporated by general reference into the Fourteenth Amendment, the Court prepared the way for a judicial wrangle over this matter for the next three decades. Reversed in *Benton v. Maryland* (1969).

December 13. Smyth v. United States. 302 U. S. 329.

Argued November 18, 19, 1937. Cardozo, J., for the Court; Stone, J., concurring; McReynolds, Sutherland and Butler, JJ., dissenting.

The Court sustained the Secretary of the Treasury in calling in gold-clause bonds in advance of their maturity date, where right of such action had been reserved, even though the effect of such action was to enable the United States to pay off the bonds in depreciated currency.

December 20. Nardone v. United States (I). 302 U. S. 379.

Argued November 15, 1937. Roberts, J., for the Court; Sutherland and Mc-Reynolds, JJ., dissenting.

Affirming a provision of the Communications Act of 1934 as making inadmissible in Federal courts any evidence obtained by wiretapping. Cf. second *Nardone* case in 1939, and subsequent cases which have failed to resolve the issue definitively.

1938

January 3. McCart v. Indianapolis Water Co. 302 U. S. 419.

Argued December 15, 1937. Per curiam; Cardozo, J., not participating; Black, J., dissenting.

On a procedural question involving a utility's attempt to enjoin state rate fixing, Black began his attack on long-established procedures of utility valuation for rate purposes, which he insisted were prejudicial to consumer interests.

January 3. Alabama Power Co. v. Ickes. 302 U. S. 464.

Argued December 6, 7, 1937. Sutherland, J., for the Court; Black, J., concurring.

Upholding the right of the Federal government, under Title II of the NIRA, to subsidize municipal power plants and dismissing private utility's complaint as showing only damage resulting from lawful competition.

January 31. Justice Reed succeeds Sutherland.

January 31. Conn. Gen. Life Ins. Co. v. Johnson. 303 U. S. 77.

Argued January 14, 1938. Stone, J., for the Court; Cardozo, J., not participating; Black, J., dissenting.

The majority opinion held invalid a California tax on a Connecticut insurance contract. Black's dissent challenged this long-established rule.

January 31. Indiana ex rel. Anderson v. Brand. 303 U. S. 95.

Argued January 10, 1938. Roberts, J., for the Court; Black, J., dissenting. Cardozo, J., not participating.

Upholding a contractual right of tenure for public school teachers of more than five years' employment with the school system, as against a repeal of the tenure statute, under the contract clause.

February 14. South Carolina Hwy. Dept. v. Barnwell Bros. 303 U. S. 177.

Argued January 4, 1938. Stone, J., for the Court; Cardozo and Reed, JJ., not participating.

This opinion was the culmination of a long series of cases in which Stone had steadfastly contended that in the absence of a preemption of the subject-matter by Congress, and where the state regulation imposed on interstate transportation was a reasonable and local concern (e. g., upkeep of state highways), the regulation was not a burden on interstate commerce.

February 28. Western Livestock v. Bureau. 303 U. S. 250.

Argued January 31, 1938. Stone, J., for the Court; McReynolds and Butler, JJ., dissenting; Cardozo, J., not participating.

Upholding a New Mexico tax on an interstate publication as a reasonable means of compelling the publication to share the local tax burden, the effect on interstate commerce being remote.

February 28. Lauf v. Skinner. 303 U. S. 323.

Argued January 12, 1938. Roberts, J., for the Court; Cardozo and Reed, JJ., not participating; Butler and McReynolds, JJ., dissenting.

Reversing action of lower Federal court granting injunction in labor dispute where state law permitted union action which management sought to enjoin by suing in Federal court.

February 28. NLRB v. Pennsylvania Greyhound Lines. 303 U. S. 261.

Argued February 4, 1938. Stone, J., for the Court; Cardozo and Reed, JJ., not participating.

Holding that an employer found in violation of the National Labor

Relations Act prohibiting company unions could be compelled to withdraw recognition of such union.

March 5. Robert H. Jackson becomes Solicitor General.

March 7. Helvering v. Mt. Prod. Co. 303 U. S. 376.

Argued February 10, 1938. Hughes, C. J., for the Court; Cardozo and Reed, JJ., not participating; Butler and McReynolds, JJ., dissenting.

Overruling *Burnet v. Coronado Oil & Gas Co.* (1932) and holding that a tax on income from lands leased from school districts is not a tax laid on an instrumentality of the state.

March 28. Electric Bond & Share Co. v. SEC. 303 U. S. 419.

Argued February 7-9, 1938. Hughes, C. J., for the Court; Cardozo and Reed, JJ., not participating; McReynolds, J., dissenting.

Upholding power of Congress to require all holding companies to register with the Commission as being within the commerce power.

March 28. Lovell v. Griffin. 303 U. S. 444.

Argued February 4, 1938. Hughes, C. J., for the Court; Cardozo, J., not participating.

This was one of the so-called "handbill cases" of the late thirties, mostly involving the Jehovah's Witnesses and their sectarian publications. This opinion held invalid, under the First Amendment, a Georgia city ordinance requiring a license for distributors of literature.

March 28. Santa Cruz Fruit Pkg. Co. v. NLRB. 303 U. S. 453.

Argued March 7, 1938. Hughes, C. J., for the Court; Reed and Cardozo, JJ., not participating; Butler and McReynolds, JJ., dissenting.

This case substantially extended the jurisdiction of the National Labor Relations Board over intrastate activity when the effect upon interstate commerce was shown to be direct and substantial.

March 28. New Negro Alliance v. Grocery Co. 303 U. S. 552.

Argued March 2, 3, 1938. Roberts, J., for the Court; Cardozo, J., not participating; McReynolds and Butler, JJ., dissenting.

Picketing of retail stores allegedly guilty of racial bias was held not to be a conspiracy in restraint of trade.

April 25. Morgan v. United States. 304 U. S. 1.

Argued March 10, 11, 1938. Hughes, C. J., for the Court; Black, J., dissenting; Cardozo and Reed, JJ., not participating.

Holding, in this and a prior appeal of the same case (298 U. S. 268), that administrative agencies were required to afford full and fair hearings to parties before fixing rates for their marketing activities.

April 25. United States v. Bekins. 304 U. S. 27.

Argued April 7, 1938. Hughes, C. J., for the Court; Cardozo, J., not participating; McReynolds and Butler, JJ., dissenting.

Affirming the revised Municipal Bankruptcy Act and substantially nullifying ("distinguishing") the rule in *Ashton v. Cameron County District.*

April 25. Erie R. Co. v. Tompkins. 304 U. S. 64.

Argued January 31, 1938. Brandeis, J., for the Court; Butler, McReynolds and Reed, JJ., concurring; Cardozo, J., not participating.

Overturning a long-standing rule *(Swift v. Tyson)* dating from 1842, the Court denied the existence of a Federal common law and directed that in the absence of Federal or state statutes Federal courts were to apply the common law of the state in which the Federal court was sitting.

April 25. United States v. Carolene Products Co. 304 U. S. 144.

Argued April 6, 1938. Stone, J., for the Court; Black and Butler, JJ., concurring; McReynolds, J., dissenting; Cardozo and Reed, JJ., not participating.

The opinion rejected an argument that a statutory definition of "adulterated" food, being arbitrary, was a denial of due process. Stone then discussed the presumption of validity of Congressional enactments and speculated whether the presumption should be scrutinized more exactingly when individual rather than economic rights were involved.

May 16. NLRB v. Mackay Radio. 304 U. S. 333.

Argued April 5, 6, 1938. Roberts, J., for the Court; Cardozo and Reed, JJ., not participating.

Sustaining the broad authority of the NLRB to modify its fact-finding procedure where the contentions of all parties are adequately reviewed.

May 23. Helvering v. Gerhardt. 304 U. S. 405.

Argued April 7, 8, 1938. Stone, J., for the Court; Black, J., concurring; Butler and McReynolds, JJ., dissenting; Cardozo and Reed, JJ., not participating.

Breaking with the long-established tradition of immunity of state employees from Federal taxation, this case held employees of the New York Port Authority subject to Federal income tax. The next year, in *Graves v. New York ex rel. O'Keefe,* the liquidation of the old rule was completed.

May 23. Johnson v. Zerbst. 304 U. S. 458.

Argued April 4, 1938. Black, J., for the Court; Reed, J., concurring; Cardozo, J., not participating; McReynolds and Butler, JJ., dissenting.

One of the early right-to-counsel cases, holding that the Sixth Amendment requires protection of the defendant's right to counsel in Federal courts.

December 5. Consolidated Edison v. NLRB. 305 U. S. 197.

Argued October 14, 17, 1938. Hughes, C. J., for the Court; Butler, McReynolds, Reed and Black, JJ., dissenting in part.

Continuing the trend toward broad Federal jurisdiction in labor law, the majority here upheld NLRB jurisdiction over in-state employees of a utility whose employment was substantially affected by utility's interstate activities.

December 12. Missouri ex rel. Gaines v. Canada. 305 U. S. 337.

Argued November 9, 1938. Hughes, C. J., for the Court; McReynolds and Butler, JJ., dissenting.

One of the opening chinks in the "separate but equal" doctrine, this opinion held that a state offering higher education to white students was compelled to offer substantially similar education to students of other races who were residents of the state.

1939

January 20. Frank Murphy becomes Attorney General.

January 30. Justice Frankfurter succeeds Cardozo.

January 30. Currin v. Wallace. 306 U. S. 1.

Argued January 4, 1939. Hughes, C. J., for the Court; McReynolds and Butler, JJ., dissenting.

Upholding provisions of the Tobacco Control Act, the Court foreshadowed its progressive validation of the general program of aid to agriculture which Congress established in connection with the second Agricultural Adjustment Act.

January 30. Tennessee Electric Power Co. v. TVA. 306 U. S. 118.

Argued November 14, 15, 1938. Roberts, J., for the Court; Butler and Mc-Reynolds, JJ., dissenting; Reed, J., not participating.

The Court rejected a challenge to the TVA in which private utilities complained that PWA funds were unfairly used to construct public power plants which bought TVA power under the private utilities' rates.

February 27. NLRB v. Fansteel Metallur. Corp. 306 U. S. 240.

Argued January 12, 13, 1939. Hughes, C. J., for the Court; Frankfurter, J., not participating; Stone, Reed and Black, JJ., dissenting in part.

Plagued by the legal issues arising with the sit-down strikes, the Court in this case upheld the right of employers to discharge employees engaged in illegal acts.

February 27. NLRB v. Columbia E. & S. Co. 306 U. S. 292.

Argued January 11, 12, 1939. Stone, J., for the Court; Frankfurter, J., not participating; Black and Reed, JJ., dissenting.

This case expanded upon the *Fansteel* rule. The dissent argued that sit-down strikes were symptoms of prior unfair labor tactics by management which ought to be the real subject of judicial consideration.

February 27. NLRB v. Sands Mfg. Co. 306 U. S. 332.

Argued January 12, 1938. Roberts, J., for the Court; Frankfurter, J., not participating; Black and Reed, JJ., dissenting.

The majority held that where employees repudiate a *bona fide* collective bargaining agreement made by their representatives, discharge for failure to follow the contract is not an unfair employer practice.

March 27. Graves v. New York ex rel. O'Keefe. 306 U. S. 466.

Argued March 6, 1939. Stone, J., for the Court; Frankfurter, J., and Hughes, C. J., concurring; Butler and McReynolds, JJ., dissenting.

Complementing the *New York Port Authority* case of the previous year, this decision affirmed the right of states to tax income of Federal employees. Overruling *Collector v. Day* (1870) and succeeding cases.

April 17. Justice Douglas succeeds Brandeis.

April 17. Mulford v. Smith. 307 U. S. 38.

Argued March 8, 1939. Roberts, J., for the Court; Butler and McReynolds, JJ., dissenting.

Refuting virtually all of the rationale of the *Butler* decision invalidating the first AAA, the majority here found broad constitutional authority for the AAA of 1938.

April 17. Rochester Tel. Corp. v. United States. 307 U. S. 125.

Argued March 7, 1939. Frankfurter, J., for the Court; Butler and McReynolds, JJ., concurring.

In another step toward greater latitude in the exercise of constitutional powers, the Court in this case relaxed the policy of strict judicial surveillance of regulatory agencies and restated the standards for review of agency orders.

May 15. United States v. Morgan. 307 U. S. 183.

Argued October 20, 21, 1938; reargued April 20, 1939. Stone, J. for the Court; Reed, J., not participating; Butler and McReynolds, JJ., dissenting.

This opinion continued the trend begun in the *Rochester Telephone* case, broadening the discretionary powers of regulatory agencies.

May 22. Guaranty Trust Co. v. Henwood. 307 U. S. 247.

Argued February 8, 9, 1939. Black, J., for the Court; Hughes, C. J., Stone, McReynolds and Butler, JJ., dissenting.

Majority refused to permit payment of railroad bonds in foreign currency greater in dollar value than face of bonds, as circumvention of Congressional gold standard resolution of 1933.

May 22. Lane v. Wilson. 307 U. S. 268.

Argued March 3, 1939. Frankfurter, J., for the Court; McReynolds and Butler, JJ., dissenting; Douglas, J., not participating.

In 1915 the Court had outlawed an Oklahoma "grandfather clause" which preserved rights of white voters while denying those of Negroes. The current case invalidated all state laws since 1915 which did not ensure equal opportunity to voters of all races under the Fifteenth Amendment.

May 22. O'Malley v. Woodrough. 307 U. S. 277.

Argued April 28, 1939. Frankfurter, J., for the Court; McReynolds, J., not participating; Butler, J., dissenting.

The Revenue Act of 1932 subjected to a Federal income tax the salaries of Federal judges appointed after the enactment of the law. This opinion sustained the tax liability of the statute against a claim that it violated the constitutional rule against reduction of income of judges during tenure.

June 5. Coleman v. Miller. 307 U. S. 433.

Argued October 10, 1938; reargued April 17, 18, 1939. Hughes, C. J., for the Court; Frankfurter, Black, Douglas and Roberts, JJ., concurring; Butler and McReynolds, JJ., dissenting.

In a rare opinion discussing the process of constitutional amendment, the Court rejected an attack upon a Kansas legislative vote ratifying the Child Labor amendment after having rejected it in 1925. The Court held that the question of whether a proposed amendment was still subject to ratification was a political one for Congress to answer, but where Congress had not set a reasonable terminal date for ratification the amendment presumably still lay before the states.

June 5. Hague v. CIO. 307 U. S. 496.

Argued February 27, 28, 1939. Roberts and Black, JJ.; Stone and Reed, JJ.; Hughes, C. J., in separate opinions in lieu of a Court opinion; McReynolds and Butler, JJ., dissenting; Frankfurter and Douglas, JJ., not participating.

The three divergent opinions of the majority invalidated a Jersey City ordinance which sought to prevent union organizers from distributing literature or holding meetings on labor subjects. The case introduced the concept of freedom of expression as a vehicle for enforcing labor's organizational rights.

June 5. United States v. Rock Royal Cooperative. 307 U. S. 533.

Argued April 24, 25, 1939. Reed, J., for the Court; Black and Douglas, JJ., concurring; Butler and McReynolds, JJ., dissenting.

Affirming the constitutionality of the Agricultural Marketing Agreement Act of 1937, under which cooperatives could be formed to fix prices of foodstuffs in interstate commerce. See Note to Appendix.

December 4. United States v. Lowden. 308 U. S. 225.

Argued November 6, 1939. Stone, J., for the Court.

Holding that the Interstate Commerce Commission may lawfully require merging carriers to use part of the resulting savings to compensate employees whose interests or status are affected by the merger.

December 11. Weiss v. United States. 308 U. S. 321.

Argued November 13, 14, 1939. Roberts, J., for the Court.

Applying the earlier *Nardone* rule to intercepted telephone messages and holding them inadmissible as evidence in Federal courts.

December 11. Nardone v. United States (II). 308 U. S. 338.

Argued November 14, 1939. Frankfurter, J., for the Court; Reed, J., not participating; McReynolds, J., dissenting.

Qualifying the earlier *Nardone* rule with proviso that the defendant has the burden of proving the fact of wiretapping and the materiality of this fact to the case against him.

1940

January 2. Chicot County Drainage Dist. v. Baxter State Bank. 308 U. S. 371.

Argued December 7, 1939. Hughes, C. J., for the Court.

Affirming the constitutionality of the second Municipal Bankruptcy Act and largely nullifying if not overruling the holding in *Ashton v. Cameron County District*. See Note to Appendix.

January 2. AF of L v. NLRB 308 U. S. 401.

Argued December 7, 1939. Stone, J., for the Court.

The Court denied the right of one union, losing a collective bargaining election, to demand court review of the Board's order certifying the other union as winner.

January 2. Avery v. Alabama. 308 U. S. 444.

Argued December 7, 1939. Black, J., for the Court.

Although the case affirmed a conviction in a state criminal proceeding, the Court in reviewing the conviction observed that the right to counsel in felony cases was not satisfied merely by appointment of counsel but had to include opportunity for consultation and preparation of defense.

January 2. NLRB v. Falk Corp. 308 U. S. 353.

Argued December 8, 11, 1939. Black, J., for the Court; McReynolds, J., not participating.

Denying lower courts power to review or modify Board orders for an election to select a bargaining unit.

January 29. Robert H. Jackson becomes Attorney General. Francis Biddle becomes Solicitor General.

January 29. Madden v. Kentucky. 309 U. S. 83.

Argued December 14, 1939. Reed, J., for the Court; Hughes, C. J., concurring; Roberts and McReynolds, JJ., dissenting.

Overruling in part *Colgate v. Harvey* and asserting a reasonable latitude in states to levy taxes at different rates where the purpose was to equalize the tax burden.

February 5. Justice Murphy succeeds Butler.

March 4. Nat. Liquorice Co. v. NLRB. 309 U. S. 350.

Argued February 7, 1940. Stone, J., for the Court; Douglas and Black, JJ., dissenting; Murphy, J., not participating.

Affirming the Board's authority to set aside a contract with company union where majority of employees had voted for representation by outside union.

April 22. Thornhill v. Alabama. 310 U. S. 88.

Argued February 29, 1940. Murphy, J., for the Court; McReynolds, J., dissenting.

A state anti-picketing statute was held unconstitutional under the First Amendment, extending the doctrine enunciated in the *Hague* case.

May 6. Tigner v. Texas. 310 U. S. 141.

Argued March 29, 1940. Frankfurter, J., for the Court; McReynolds, J., dissenting.

Sustaining constitutionality of a Texas law which exempted agricultural groups from definitions of combinations in restraint of trade.

May 20. Cantwell v. Connecticut. 310 U. S. 296.

Argued March 29, 1940. Roberts, J., for the Court.

Another "handbill case" in which a statute forbidding sale of religious literature without license was held unconstitutional, as was a conviction for common law breach of the peace in playing a provocative recording as part of the religious statement.

May 20. Sunshine Coal Co. v. Adkins. 310 U. S. 381.

Argued April 29, 1940. Douglas, J., for the Court; McReynolds, J., dissenting.

Affirming the constitutionality of the second Bituminous Coal Conservation (Guffey) Act and substantially nullifying the argument set out in the *Carter Coal Co.* case. In neither case did the Court explain how the commerce clause might support a fair price for coal but not a correlative fair wage for labor. See Note to this Appendix.

May 27. Apex Hosiery Co. v. Leader. 310 U. S. 469.

Argued April 1, 2, 1940. Stone, J., for the Court; Hughes, C. J., McReynolds and Roberts, JJ., dissenting.

Sit-down strikers had been fined treble damages under the Sherman Act in the original trial of this case. Sustaining a Court of Appeals reversal of the trial court, Stone argued that the Sherman Act did not apply to union activity where, as here, the activity was manifestly aimed at improving working conditions and not at effecting a monopoly in trade.

June 3. Minersville School District v. Gobitis. 310 U. S. 586.

Argued April 25, 1940. Frankfurter, J., for the Court; McReynolds, J., concurring; Stone, J., dissenting.

This first "flag salute" case held that the state could lawfully compel public school students to recite the Pledge of Allegiance. Religious objectors were denied relief on the ground that the law did not itself seek to promote or restrict religious beliefs. The Court reversed the present decision three years later in *West Virginia State Board of Education v. Barnette.*

November 25. Smith v. Texas. 311 U. S. 128.

Argued November 14, 1940. Black, J., for the Court.

Invalidating an indictment of a Negro by a grand jury from which Negroes were excluded. The case marked the accelerating of a trend toward more affirmative assertion of individual rights protected by the Federal Constitution.

November 25. American Ins. Co. v. Avon Park. 311 U. S. 138.

Argued November 12, 1940. Douglas, J., for the Court.

While the Court conceded the constitutionality of the second Municipal Bankruptcy Act, it set aside in this case a proceeding under the act where the necessary consent of two-thirds of the creditors was only obtained by including claims held by the municipality's own fiscal agent.

December 9. Wright v. Union Central Life Ins. Co. 311 U. S. 273.

Argued November 20, 22, 1940. Douglas, J., for the Court.

Following the general principle set out in *Wright v. Vinton Branch*, the Court here sustained the right of farmer debtors to have foreclosed property reappraised or its value fixed by a court, after which a reasonable time for redemption would be allowed.

1941

January 20. Franklin D. Roosevelt inaugurated for third term.

January 20. Hines v. Davidowitz. 312 U. S. 52.

Argued December 10, 11, 1940. Black, J., for the Court; Stone and Mc-Reynolds, JJ., Hughes, C. J., dissenting.

This was one of a series of cases in which the Hughes Court supplemented the commerce clause as a source of authority for the Federal government with the concept of preemption of a field of activity. Here the Pennsylvania alien registration law was held invalid because the Federal Smith Act had preempted the field of immigration and naturalization and its related subject-areas. See Appendix D.

February 3. United States v. Darby. 312 U. S. 100.

Argued December 19, 20, 1940. Stone, J., for the Court.

Upholding the Fair Labor Standards Act of 1938 and overruling *Hammer v. Dagenhart* (1918) in declaring child labor to be a proper subject for regulation under the commerce clause. The decision substantially qualified the rule in the *Carter Coal Co.* case and rendered moot the question of the validity of the Child Labor Amendment. See Note to this Appendix.

February 3. Opp Cotton Mills v. Administrator. 312 U. S. 126.

Argued December 20, 1940. Stone, J., for the Court.

A companion case, specifically affirming the wage and hour provisions of the FLSA as within the scope of the commerce power.

February 3. United States v. Hutcheson. 312 U. S. 219.

Argued December 10, 1940. Frankfurter, J., for the Court; Murphy, J., not participating; Stone, J., concurring; Roberts, J., and Hughes, C. J., dissenting.

Overruling, in effect, *Duplex Prtg. Press Co. v. Deering* (1921) and reviving Clayton Act's exemption of labor unions from the definition of conspiracies in restraint of trade.

February 10. Milk Drivers Union v. Meadowmoor Dairies. 312 U. S. 287.

Argued December 13, 16, 1940. Frankfurter, J., for the Court; Black, Douglas and Reed, JJ., dissenting.

Although criticized as inconsistent with the *Hutcheson* rationale, this case sustained the right of a state to enjoin union picketing where the picketing tends to provoke violence. The Court shortly thereafter *(Bakery Drivers v. Wohl*, 315 U. S. 769; *Carpenters' Union v. Ritter's Cafe*, 315 U. S. 722) retreated somewhat from the broad permissiveness in these picketing cases. Cf. *Giboney v. Empire Storage & Ice Co.* (1949).

April 28. Olsen v. Nebraska. 313 U. S. 236.

Argued April 8, 9, 1941. Douglas, J., for the Court.

Overruling *Ribnik v. McBride* (1928) and upholding a state law fixing fees charged by private employment agencies.

May 26. United States v. Classic. 313 U. S. 299.

Argued April 7, 1941. Stone, J., for the Court; Douglas, Black and Murphy, JJ., dissenting; Hughes, C. J., not participating.

A Louisiana voter alleged that his ballot had been falsified. In a prosecution under the Federal Criminal Code, the majority opinion held that Congressional elections involved Federally protected rights and that these rights could be secured against individual as well as against state action. The case inclined the Court toward a more affirmative concept of individual rights deriving from national citizenship.

September 5. Francis Biddle becomes Attorney General.

October 6. THE STONE COURT (October, 1941-June, 1946).
Stone, C. J.; Roberts, Black, Reed, Frankfurter, Douglas, Murphy.
Justice Byrnes succeeds McReynolds.
Justice Jackson succeeds Stone, J.

October 21. Edwards v. California. 314 U. S. 160.

Argued April 28, 29, 1941; reargued October 21, 1941. Byrnes, J., for the Court; Douglas, Jackson, Black, Murphy, JJ., concurring.

Invalidating a state law forbidding the transporting of indigent persons into the state. The concurring opinion suggested that the law should be invalidated on the basis of national citizenship and the right to travel freely in all states.

November 17. Charles Fahy becomes Solicitor General.

December 8. Bridges v. California. 314 U. S. 252.

Argued October 18, 21, 1940; reargued October 13, 1941. Black, J., for the Court; Frankfurter J., dissenting.

In this and a companion case *(Times-Mirror v. Superior Court)* the majority opinion asserted the concept of an absolute freedom of expression in the First Amendment, limiting the contempt power with reference to criticism of pending cases to instances of actual interference with the administration of justice.

1942

January 12. Georgia v. Taylor. 315 U. S. 25.

Argued December 15, 16, 1941. Byrnes, J., for the Court; Roberts, J., not participating.

Striking down Georgia's "peonage law," whereby debts owed or money advanced were to be "worked out" on the creditor's land, as contrary to the Thirteenth Amendment.

January 19. Glasser v. United States. 315 U. S. 60.

Argued November 13, 14, 1941. Murphy, J., for the Court; Frankfurter, J., Stone, C. J., dissenting in part; Jackson, J., not participating.

Holding that the Sixth Amendment protected a criminal defendant from having the court, over his objection, appoint a counsel to represent him and another defendant jointly, where the original defendant alleges that this jeopardized his own case.

February 2. Cloverleaf Butter Co. v. Patterson. 315 U. S. 148.

Argued December 9, 10, 1941. Reed, J., for the Court; Stone, C. J., Frankfurter, Murphy and Byrnes, JJ., dissenting.

Holding that state regulations affecting interstate commerce may be nullified at any time Congress elects to preempt the field. One of the cases emphasizing the preemption doctrine which agitated Congress in the fifties.

March 9. Chaplinsky v. New Hampshire. 315 U. S. 568.

Argued February 5, 1942. Murphy, J., for the Court.

Upholding a state "actionable words" statute, prohibiting the use of insulting or provocative language in public, as not infringing upon the guarantees of the First Amendment.

March 16. FPC v. Natural Gas Pipeline Co. 315 U. S. 578.

Argued February 10, 11, 1942. Stone, C. J., for the Court; Black, Frankfurter, Douglas and Murphy, JJ., concurring.

This decision extended the general rule of the post-1937 Court, asserting the general Federal power over control of prices in interstate commerce, to natural gas as it had been extended to other commodities. It also anticipated the decision in the *Hope Natural Gas* case of 1944 which repudiated the restrictive formulae for rate fixing which had been laid down by the *laissez-faire* Court of the nineties.

March 30. Allen-Bradley v. Wisconsin Employment Board. 315 U. S. 740.

Argued March 2, 1942. Douglas, J., for the Court.

Upholding a state law regulating picketing and other union tactics as not inconsistent with the policy of the NLRA, Congress not having clearly asserted its preemption of the field.

June 1. Betts v. Brady. 316 U. S. 455.

Argued April 13, 14, 1942. Roberts, J., for the Court; Black, Douglas and Murphy, JJ., dissenting.

In the continuing issue of incorporation of the Bill of Rights into the Fourteenth Amendment as applied to the states, the narrow view prevailed in this case, denying that the Sixth Amendment was generally incorporated. The majority held that appointment of counsel for indigent defendants is not a general constitutional right but merely a policy matter resting upon legislative initiative. Overturned in *Gideon v. Wainwright* (1963).

June 1. Faitoute v. Asbury Park. 316 U. S. 502.

Argued April 28, 1942. Frankfurter, J., for the Court; Reed, J., concurring.

Sustaining a New Jersey municipal bankruptcy law against a claim that the Federal bankruptcy law had preempted the field.

June 8. Jones v. Opelika. 361 U. S. 584.

Argued February 15, 1942. Reed, J., for the Court; Stone, C. J., Murphy, Black and Douglas, JJ., dissenting.

Distinguishing the rule in *Lovell v. Griffin*, the majority sustained an Alabama municipal ordinance licensing street vendors as not infringing upon freedom of expresson or religion. One of the themes of the dissent was the incorrectness of the holding in the first "flag salute" *(Gobitis)* case involving the same religious sect; within a year, *Gobitis* was to be reversed.

July 31. Ex Parte Quirin. 317 U. S. 1.

Argued July 29, 30, 1942. Per curiam opinion July 31; full opinion October 29 by Stone, C. J., for the Court; Murphy, J., not participating.

In a special term of the Court, petitions for habeas corpus were sought by German saboteurs landed by Nazi submarine and captured in civilian clothing. The Court found the petitioners subject to the Articles of War and not entitled to release to civil courts.

November 4. Wickard v. Filburn. 317 U. S. 111.

Argued May 4, 1942; reargued October 13, 1942. Jackson, J., for the Court.

Holding that where Congress had constitutionally fixed quotas for production of wheat, it could compel compliance with quotas in the case of wheat grown for home consumption rather than the grain market, if it reasonably believed this was necessary to stabilize the market.

December 14. Davis v. Department of Labor. 317 U. S. 249.

Argued November 18, 1942. Black, J., for the Court; Frankfurter, J., concurring; Stone, C. J., dissenting.

As distinguished from the narrow construction of compensable injuries, in the 1920s, the Court here held that where there is any doubt whether maritime injuries are covered by state or Federal law, the doubt may be resolved in favor of state law rather than denying workmen any right of compensation.

1943

January 4. Parker v. Brown. 317 U. S. 341.

Argued May 5, 1942; reargued October 12, 13, 1942. Stone, C. J., for the Court.

Accepting the principle in *Davis,* the Court now unanimously held that where preemption is not manifest, a state law will be sustained in order to preserve remedies for parties seeking relief thereunder.

February 1. Tileston v. Ullman. 318 U. S. 44.

Argued January 13, 14, 1943. Per curiam.

The Court dismissed a suit brought by a physician alleging that Connecticut's law preventing him from giving patients information on contraceptives endangered the patients' lives. The opinion found no standing to sue where the physician rather than the patients brought the action. This was one of a series of cases which finally resulted in a decision that the Connecticut law was unconstitutional *(Griswold v. Connecticut).*

February 1. SEC v. Chenery Corp. 318 U. S. 80.

Argued December 17, 18, 1942. Frankfurter, J., for the Court; Black, Reed and Murphy, JJ., dissenting; Douglas, J., not participating.

Majority ruled that Commission orders were reversible where they could not be sustained on grounds found by the Commission itself.

February 15. Justice Rutledge succeeds Byrnes.

March 1. McNabb v. United States. 318 U. S. 332.

Argued October 22, 1942. Frankfurter, J., for the Court; Reed, J., dissenting; Rutledge, J., not participating.

This case established the rule that an accused person must be taken before a judicial officer without delay following his arrest. Cf. *Mallory v. United States* (1957).

May 3. Murdock v. Pennsylvania. 319 U. S. 105.

Argued March 10, 11, 1943. Douglas, J., for the Court; Reed, Frankfurter, Roberts and Jackson, JJ., dissenting.

One of a series of cases in which the majority moved to revise its position on license fees and other requirements of ordinances which might be burdens on religious practices. The majority returned to the rule in *Lovell v. Griffin* in holding such ordinances invalid under the First Amendment.

May 10. Lockerty v. Phillips. 319 U. S. 182.

Argued May 3, 1943. Stone, C. J., for the Court.

Sustaining the validity of the wartime price control law and the OPA regulations issued under it.

June 1. Mayo v. United States. 319 U. S. 441.

Argued April 16, 1943. Reed, J., for the Court; Black, J., concurring.

Holding that property of the United States brought into a state for distribution there under Federal law is exempt from state inspection fee.

June 7. Tot v. United States. 319 U. S. 463.

Argued April 5, 1943. Roberts, J., for the Court; Black, J., concurring; Murphy, J., not participating.

Invalidating a section of the National Firearms Act which created a statutory presumption of violation where the accused had a prior conviction of illegal use of firearms.

June 14. Taylor v. Mississippi. 319 U. S. 583.

Argued April 15, 16, 1943. Roberts, J., for the Court.

Anticipating the reversal of the rule in the early "flag salute" litigation, this case dismissed a conviction of one counseling children to refuse the salute on religious grounds.

June 14. West Virginia Board of Education v. Barnette. 319 U. S. 624.

Argued March 11, 1943. Jackson, J., for the Court; Black, Douglas and Murphy, JJ., concurring; Reed and Frankfurter, JJ., dissenting.

The main "flag salute" case, overruling the 1940 *Gobitis* case and holding flag salute statutes to infringe upon the free exercise of religion guaranteed as an absolute in the First Amendment.

June 21. Hirabayashi v. United States. 320 U. S. 81.

Argued May 10, 11, 1943. Stone, C. J., for the Court. Douglas, Murphy, Rutledge, JJ., concurring.

Sustaining the constitutionality of a wartime curfew order applied to Japanese-Americans, the Court arguing that a military emergency represented in racial identification with a belligerent power justified the enforcement of the curfew on a racial basis.

June 21. Schneidermann v. United States. 320 U. S. 118.

Argued November 9, 1942; reargued March 12, 1943. Murphy, J., for the Court; Douglas, Rutledge, JJ., concurring; Stone, C. J., Roberts and Frankfurter, JJ., dissenting.

Reversing a denaturalization verdict in Federal trial court on ground that the government had failed to establish the contemporary subversiveness of the defendant.

December 20. Magnolia Petr. Co. v. Hunt. 320 U. S. 430.

Argued October 20, 1943. Stone, C. J., for the Court; Jackson, J., concurring; Douglas, Murphy, Black and Rutledge, JJ., dissenting.

In a controversial ruling, Stone contended that the full faith and credit clause requires that the final judgment of a court in one state bar an action on the same case in another state.

December 20. Dobson v. Commissioner of Internal Revenue. 320 U.S. 489.

Argued November 8, 1943. Jackson, J., for the Court.

Holding that a judgment of the Federal Tax Court is not appealable if no error of law is alleged.

1944

January 3. FPC v. Hope Natural Gas Co. 320 U. S. 591.

Argued October 20, 21, 1943. Douglas, J., for the Court; Black and Murphy, JJ., concurring and specifically dissenting from the dissent of Frankfurter, J.; Reed, Frankfurter and Jackson, JJ., dissenting; Roberts, J., not participating.

Another case loosening the ties of the Court to the doctrines of "fair value" and "just and reasonable" rates which had served to limit government regulation of utilities since the nineties. Frankfurter's dissent, to which Black and Murphy objected, suggested that Congress had adopted as its own policy the judicial doctrines as to due process and thus bound the subsequent courts to abide by the doctrines.

January 3. Mercoid Corp. v. Mid-Cont. Inv. Co., 320 U. S. 661.

Argued December 9, 1943. Douglas, J., for the Court; Black and Murphy, JJ., concurring and dissenting from dissent by Frankfurter; Roberts, Reed, Frankfurter and Jackson, JJ., dissenting.

Holding that the Court in its equity jurisdiction had discretion to deny relief to a patent holder who had used his patent to restrain use of unpatented material. Frankfurter had observed that "contributory infringement" of patent rights was "an expression both of law and morals." Black objected that "a socially undesirable practice may seek acceptance under the guise of conventional moral symbols." Case illustrated one facet of the Black-Frankfurter disputation of these years.

January 31. Mahnich v. Southern SS. Co. 321 U. S. 76.

Argued January 5, 1944. Stone, C. J., for the Court; Roberts and Frankfurter, JJ., dissenting.

An admiralty case, this is chiefly notable for Roberts' lengthy protest against the succession of overruled decisions in the Stone Chief Justiceship.

January 31. Warehouse Co. v. Bowles. 321 U. S. 144.

Argued November 18, 1943. Jackson, J., for the Court; Douglas, Black and Murphy, JJ., dissenting.

Exempting a public warehouse in California from the Emergency Price Control Act which specifically provided for such exemptions, the minority opinion protested that even if the provision did not violate the equal protection clause it frustrated price control policy.

March 6. Anderson v. Abbott. 321 U. S. 349.

Argued February 8, 1943; reargued January 12, 13, 1944. Douglas, J., for the Court; Jackson, Roberts, Reed and Frankfurter, JJ., dissenting.

Majority opinion held that where legislative policy was to reach all stockholders of national banks in assessment for liquidation, transfer of shares to a holding company would not be allowed to defeat legislative purpose. Dissent criticized the opinion for assuming to declare what legislative policy was intended.

March 27. Yakus v. United States. 321 U. S. 414.

Argued January 7, 1944. Stone, C. J., for the Court; Roberts, Murphy and Rutledge, JJ., dissenting.

The majority upheld the general authority of the OPA, where Congress had provided sufficient guidelines, even when the authority included criminal sanctions if these sanctions or the question of criminality had been submitted to a jury. The opinion also emphasized the rule that litigants must raise the constitutional issue "in due time" or lose the right to have the issue reviewed on appeal.

March 27. Bowles v. Willingham. 321 U. S. 503.

Argued January 7, 10, 1944. Douglas, J., for the Court; Rutledge, J., concurring; Roberts, J., dissenting.

Upholding rent control powers of the OPA, against the complaint that the control had to go into effect before it could be reviewable.

March 27. Tennessee Coal & Iron Co. v. Muscada Local. 321 U. S. 590.

Argued January 13, 14, 1944. Murphy, J., for the Court; Frankfurter and Jackson, JJ., concurring; Stone, C. J., and Roberts, J., dissenting.

This case upheld the general principle of "portal-to-portal" pay, and in the process raised the question of liability of management for retroactive adjustments in pay potentially representing millions of dollars.

April 3. Smith v. Allwright. 321 U. S. 649.

Argued November 10, 12, 1943; reargued January 12, 1944. Reed, J., for the Court; Frankfurter, J., concurring; Rutledge, J., dissenting.

In an attempt to evade the "state action" holding in *Nixon v. Condon* (1932), Texas repealed all statutory primary election laws and left the question of voter qualification to the political parties. The Court held that where the primary is an integral part of the electoral process, any political party action is part of the state action and where it denies Negroes the right to vote in the primary is in violation of the Fifteenth Amendment.

May 1. Ashcraft v. Tennessee. 322 U. S. 143.

Argued February 28, 1944. Black, J., for the Court; Jackson and Roberts, JJ., dissenting.

One of the early cases in which criminal conviction was set aside upon the demonstration of coerced confession. Dissent warned that reasonable safeguards of suspects should not be synonymous with immunity from all questioning.

June 5. United States v. S. E. Underwriters Assn. 322 U. S. 533.

Argued January 11, 1944. Black, J., for the Court; Stone, C. J., and Frankfurter, J., dissenting; Jackson, J., dissenting in part; Roberts and Reed, JJ., not participating.

Overturning a long line of decisions to the contrary, the majority held fire insurance to be interstate commerce subject to the Sherman Act. The dissenters argued that such a reversal of constitutional doctrine threatened havoc among state insurance laws. The majority replied that its holding did not necessarily preempt the field occupied by state law. Two questions were raised, but not answered, by the case: the nature of preemption, and the interpretation of the Sherman Act as it was understood in 1890 as against its understanding in 1944. Cf. *United States v. Yellow Cab Co.*, 332 U. S. 218 (1947), where Court extended commerce power although conceding defendants were not subect to anti-trust action. Congress criticized this opinion, and specifically disclaimed presumption of preemption in this area; cf. Ch. 20, §1, 59 Stat. 331.

June 12. Baumgartner v. United States. 322 U. S. 665.

Argued April 26, 1944. Frankfurter, J., for the Court; Murphy, Black, Douglas and Rutledge, JJ., concurring.

Rejecting an argument for denaturalization, brought ten years after citizenship had been granted, that defendant at that time had not renounced all foreign allegiance, where evidence was not beyond dispute.

June 12. Hartzell v. United States. 322 U. S. 680.

Argued April 25, 1944. Murphy, J., for the Court; Roberts, J., concurring; Reed, Frankfurter, Douglas and Jackson, JJ., dissenting.

Holding that convictions under 1917 Espionage Act required persuasive evidence of clear and present danger.

December 18. Korematsu v. United States. 323 U. S. 214.

Argued October 11, 12, 1944. Black, J., for the Court; Frankfurter, J., concurring; Roberts, Murphy and Jackson, JJ., dissenting.

The majority upheld a wartime Civilian Exclusion Order, barring Japanese-Americans from certain West Coast areas, as being "constitutional at the time it was made."

1945

January 8. Thomas v. Collins. 323 U. S. 516.

Argued May 1; reargued October 11, 1944. Rutledge, J., for the Court; Douglas, Black, Murphy, Jackson, JJ., concurring; Stone, C. J., and Roberts, Reed and Frankfurter, JJ., dissenting.

The majority (two justices and three concurring Justices) held unconstitutional a Texas statute enjoining labor organizers from engaging in their activities until an organizers' license had been issued.

January 20. President Roosevelt inaugurated for fourth term.

March 26. Georgia v. Pennsylvania R. Co. 324 U. S. 439.

Original action. Argued January 3, 1945. Douglas, J., for the Court; Stone, C. J., Roberts, Frankfurter and Jackson, JJ., dissenting.

The majority opinion granted the motion of a state to bring an anti-trust action against a group of railroads. The dissent argued that adequate relief could have been obtained in a Federal trial court, and that equitable relief for a sovereign state was impractical.

April 12. Harry Truman succeeds Roosevelt as President.

May 7. Screws v. United States. 325 U. S. 91.

Argued October 20, 1944. Douglas, J., for the Court; Rutledge, J., concurring; Black and Douglas, JJ., dissenting.

A tenuous majority of four Justices plus one reversed conviction of state law enforcement officer charged with killing Negro suspect. The majority, however, did accept the argument that violation of Federally protected rights was subject to Federal prosecution even though defendant might act under color of state law.

May 7. Jewell Ridge Coal Corp. v. Local No. 6167. 325 U. S. 161.

Argued March 9, 1945. Murphy, J., for the Court; Stone, C. J., and Jackson, Roberts and Frankfurter, JJ., dissenting.

This opinion followed the *Muscada* case in applying the "portal-to-portal" pay scale to mining unions. Jackson's dissent contended that the parties to the contract could exclude such a pay scale if they operated within the statutory framework, but the case is principally remembered as the occasion for the famous "feud" between Jackson and Black.

June 18. Southern Pacific R. Co. v. Arizona. 325 U. S. 761.

Argued March 26, 27, 1945. Stone, C. J., for the Court; Rutledge, J., concurring; Black and Douglas, JJ., dissenting.

Invalidating a state law limiting the length of trains passing through the state, as interfering with interstate commerce and having no direct relation to public safety or welfare.

June 18. Associated Press v. United States. 326 U. S. 1.

Argued December 5, 6, 1944. Black, J., for the Court; Douglas and Frankfurter, JJ., concurring; Roberts and Murphy, JJ., dissenting; Jackson, J., not participating.

Holding exclusive membership provisions of a wire news association to be a conspiracy to restrain trade in news communications, against the purpose of the First Amendment.

June 18. Bridges v. Wixon. 326 U. S. 135.

Argued April 2, 3, 1945. Douglas, J., for the Court; Stone, C. J., Roberts and Frankfurter, JJ., dissenting.

One of a long series of cases in which the militant labor leader challenged the validity of deportation proceedings allegedly based on his unpopular utterances. The majority here sustained his petition for habeas corpus from a detention order held to be invalid.

July 1. Tom Clark becomes Attorney General.

October 1. Justice Burton succeeds Roberts.

October 8. J. Howard McGrath becomes Solicitor General.

1946

January 14. New York v. United States. 326 U. S. 572.

Argued December 7, 8, 1944; reargued December 4, 1945. Frankfurter, J., for the Court; Stone, C. J., and Reed, Murphy and Burton, JJ., concurring; Douglas and Black, JJ., dissenting.

Holding New York State liable to a Federal tax on the commercial sale of mineral waters from state properties.

February 25. Duncan v. Kahanamoku. 327 U. S. 304.

Argued December 7, 1945. Black, J., for the Court; Murphy and Stone, JJ., concurring; Burton and Frankfurter, JJ., dissenting; Jackson, J., not participating.

One of the first cases holding that martial law could not supplant civil law and procedure with reference to civilians where the wartime conditions did not make civilian processes unenforceable.

April 22. Girouard v. United States. 328 U. S. 61.

Argued March 6, 1946. Douglas, J., for the Court; Stone, C. J., Reed and Frankfurter, JJ., dissenting; Jackson, J., not participating.

The majority opinion rejected the argument that conscientious objectors were ineligible for naturalization; overruling *United States v. Schwimmer* (1929), *United States v. McIntosh* (1931) and *United States v. Bland* (1931).

April 29. First Iowa Cooperative v. FPC. 328 U. S. 152.

Argued March 8, 1946. Burton, J., for the Court; Frankfurter, J., dissenting; Jackson, J., not participating.

The opinion distinguished between the exclusive power of the FPC to issue water power licenses relating to navigable streams, and state laws relating to the applicants' title to riparian rights or to local power franchises.

June 3. United States v. Lovett. 328 U. S. 303.

Argued May 3, 6, 1946. Black, J., for the Court; Frankfurter and Reed, JJ., concurring; Jackson, J., not participating.

Invalidating, as a bill of attainder, part of a Congressional appropriation act specifically barring certain named persons from the Federal payroll unless their Presidential appointments were renewed and reconfirmed.

June 3. Morgan v. Virginia. 328 U. S. 373.

Argued March 27, 1946. Reed, J., for the Court; Rutledge, Black and Frankfurter, JJ., concurring; Burton, J., dissenting; Jackson, J., not participating.

Invalidating state "Jim Crow laws" as they affected interstate transportation.

June 10. Colgrove v. Green. 328 U. S. 549.

Argued March 7, 8, 1946. Frankfurter, J., for the Court; Rutledge, J., con-

curring; Black, Douglas and Murphy, JJ., dissenting; Jackson, J., not participating.

In this four-to-three decision (Stone, C. J., having died) on one of the early reapportionment cases, Frankfurter contended that the Court had no jurisdiction to review a "political" and local question of the failure of Illinois to reapportion its Congressional districts.

June 10. Anderson v. Mt. Clemens Pottery Co. 328 U. S. 680.

Argued January 29, 1946. Murphy, J., for the Court; Burton and Frankfurter, JJ., dissenting; Jackson, J., not participating.

Another "portal-to-portal" case in which the majority held employees entitled to pay for time spent in preparing for work. Congress specifically criticized the judicial interpretations in the "Portal-to-Portal Act" of 1947; Ch. 52, 61 Stat. 84.

June 24. THE VINSON COURT (June, 1946-September, 1953).

Vinson, C. J.; Black, Frankfurter, Douglas, Reed, Murphy, Jackson, Rutledge, Burton.

1947

February 10. Everson v. Board of Education. 330 U. S. 1.

Argued November 20, 1946. Black, J., for the Court; Jackson, Frankfurter, Rutledge and Burton, JJ., dissenting.

Majority upheld New Jersey law permitting reimbursement to parents of parochial school children for cost of transportation. The case affirmed the extension of First Amendment provisions on religious freedom to the states through the Fourteenth Amendment.

February 10. United Public Workers v. Mitchell. 330 U. S. 75.

Argued December 3, 1945; reargued October 17, 1946. Reed, J., for the Court; Frankfurter, J., concurring; Douglas and Rutledge, JJ., dissenting in part; Black, J., dissenting; Jackson and Murphy, JJ., not participating.

Rejecting government employees' testing of the Hatch Act as improperly brought, where parties were seeking relief from an abstract or hypothetical threat to political freedom.

March 6. United States v. United Mine Workers. 330 U. S. 258.

Argued January 14, 1947. Vinson, C. J., for the Court; Jackson and Frankfurter, JJ., concurring; Black and Douglas, JJ., concurring in part; Murphy and Rutledge, JJ., dissenting.

Upholding fine levied against John L. Lewis and union for ignoring an injunction and precipitating a strike contrary to their contract.

May 5. Harris v. United States. 331 U. S. 145.

Argued December 12, 13, 1946. Vinson, C. J., for the Court; Frankfurter, Murphy, Jackson and Rutledge, JJ., dissenting.

Sustaining the right of government agents to seize illegal matter in possession of suspect, where search itself was duly authorized.

June 23. United States v. California. 332 U. S. 19.

Argued March 13, 14, 1947. Black, J., for the Court; Frankfurter, J., dissenting.

One of series of unsuccessful suits by states to claim paramount property right in tidelands oil reserves.

1948

January 12. Sipuel v. Board of Regents. 332 U. S. 631.

Argued January 7, 8, 1948. Per curiam.

Affirming the "equal, though separate" rule of segregated higher education set out in the *Gaines* case.

January 19. Oyama v. California. 332 U. S. 633.

Argued October 22, 1947. Vinson, C. J., for the Court; Black, Douglas, Murphy and Rutledge, JJ., concurring; Reed, Burton and Jackson, JJ., dissenting.

Invalidating state law escheating lands indirectly held by alien through son who was citizen.

February 16. Woods v. Miller Co. 333 U. S. 138.

Argued February 6, 1948. Douglas, J., for the Court; Frankfurter and Jackson, JJ., concurring.

Upholding postwar rent control act, where state of war constructively continued and purpose of act was to control inflation bred by housing shortages as direct consequence of wartime conditions.

March 8. Illinois ex rel. McCollum v. Board of Education. 333 U. S. 203.

Argued December 8, 1947. Black, J., for the Court; Frankfurter, Jackson, Rutledge and Burton, JJ., concurring; Reed, J., dissenting.

Invalidating state "released time" policy where public facilities were used for voluntarily requested religious instruction for public school children.

March 29. Winters v. New York. 333 U. S. 507.

Argued March 27, 1946; reargued November 19, 1946; reargued November 10, 1947. Reed, J., for the Court; Frankfurter, Jackson and Burton, JJ., dissenting.

Invalidating, as too vague to define the crime, a New York statute prohibiting distribution of publications devoted to bloodshed and lust.

May 3. Shelley v. Kraemer. 334 U. S. 1.

Argued January 15, 16, 1948. Vinson, C. J., for the Court; Reed, Jackson and Rutledge, JJ., not participating.

Holding that while racially restrictive covenants as to real estate may be valid as between parties to the agreement, judicial enforcement constitutes impermissible "state action."

June 7. Takahashi v. Fish & Game Commission. 334 U. S. 410.

Argued April 21, 22, 1948. Black, J., for the Court; Murphy and Rutledge, JJ., concurring; Reed and Jackson, JJ., dissenting.

Outlawing a state statute prohibiting alien residents from commercial fishing in coastal waters, as discriminatory under Fourteenth Amendment.

June 14. Trupiano v. United States. 334 U. S. 699.

Argued March 9, 1948. Murphy, J., for the Court; Vinson, C. J., and Black, Reed and Burton, JJ., dissenting.

Holding valid the arrest of party seen by law enforcement officer in process of illegal act, in course of raid without warrant, but denying admissibility of evidence seized in same raid without warrant. Overruled in *United States v. Rabinowitz* (1950).

June 14. Lichter v. United States. 334 U. S. 742.

Argued November 20, 21, 1947. Burton, J., for the Court; Murphy, J., concurring; Jackson and Douglas, JJ., dissenting.

Upholding constitutionality of Renegotiation Act under which Congress asserted right to renegotiate wartime contracts to control profiteering.

1949

January 3. Lincoln Federal Union v. Northwestern I. & M. Co. 335 U. S. 52.

Argued November 8-10, 1948. Black, J., for the Court; Murphy, J., dissenting in part; Frankfurter, J., concurring.

Upholding state "right to work" laws on the ground that no specific Federal right is infringed.

January 3. AF of L v. American Sash Co. 335 U. S. 538.

Argued November 8-10, 1948. Black, J., for the Court; Murphy, J., dissenting in part; Frankfurter, J., concurring.

In a companion case, Court held that provisions of these laws were not open to challenge by union members as discriminatory.

January 20. Harry Truman inaugurated for full term.

April 4. Giboney v. Empire Storage and Ice Co. 336 U. S. 490.

Argued January 4, 5, 1949. Black, J., for the Court.

Qualifying the rule of *Thornhill v. Alabama,* the Court here upheld a Wisconsin statute prohibiting picketing viewed as coercing employees to violate a valid contract.

April 25. California v. Zook. 336 U. S. 725.

Argued February 8, 1949. Murphy, J., for the Court.

Sustaining a state law regulating passenger lines, even where the business was largely interstate, against claim that Congress had in fact preempted the field.

May 16. Terminiello v. Chicago. 337 U. S. 1.

Argued February 1, 1949. Douglas, J., for the Court; Vinson, C. J., Frankfurter, Jackson and Burton, JJ., dissenting.

Invalidating an ordinance prohibiting breaches of peace by provocative speech as infringement upon First Amendment.

June 20. Nat. Mut. Ins. Co. v. Tidewater Transf. Co. 337 U. S. 582.

Argued November 8, 1948. Jackson, J., for the Court; Rutledge, J., concurring; Vinson, C. J., Douglas, Frankfurter and Reed, JJ., dissenting.

Majority upheld Congressional enactment giving Federal courts jurisdiction over suits between District of Columbia parties and citizens of other states even though no Federal question was involved.

June 27. Wolf v. Colorado. 338 U. S. 25.

Argued October 18, 1948. Frankfurter, J., for the Court; Black, J., concurring; Douglas, Murphy and Rutledge, JJ., dissenting.

The majority ruled that in a state trial involving state criminal charge, the exclusionary rule in *Weeks v. United States* (1914) did not apply to evidence which would be inadmissible in Federal courts. Overruled in *Mapp v. Ohio* (1961).

August 24. J. Howard McGrath becomes Attorney General.

October 3. Justice Clark succeeds Murphy.

October 12. Justice Minton succeeds Rutledge.

1950

April 24. Cassell v. Texas. 339 U. S. 282.

Argued November 10, 1949. Reed, J., for the Court; Frankfurter, Burton, Clark and Minton, JJ., concurring; Jackson, J., dissenting; Douglas, J., not participating.

Reversing criminal conviction based on indictment by grand jury from which Negroes were excluded.

May 8. American Communications Assn. v. Douds. 339 U. S. 382.

Argued October 10, 11, 1949. Vinson, C. J., for the Court; Frankfurter and Jackson, JJ., concurring in part; Black, J., dissenting; Douglas, Clark and Minton, JJ., not participating.

Upholding non-Communist affidavit in Taft-Hartley Act, on ground that Congress has power to protect public interest from politically motivated strikes fomented by subversive officers of unions. But cf. *United States v. Brown* (1965).

June 5. Sweatt v. Painter. 339 U. S. 629.

Argued April 4, 1950. Vinson, C. J., for the Court.

The beginning of the end of the "equal but separate" doctrine, where the Court held that a state university must admit qualified Negroes when facilities in segregated state university were unequal.

June 5. McLaurin v. Oklahoma Regents. 339 U. S. 637.

Argued April 3, 4, 1950. Vinson, C. J., for the Court.

Segregation of Negro students within all-white university held unconstitutional.

June 5. United States v. Louisiana. 339 U. S. 699.

Argued March 27, 1950. Douglas, J., for the Court; Jackson and Clark, JJ., not participating.

Another of a series of suits in which the Court asserted paramount Federal rights in tidelands oil reserves, unless Congress (as it subsequently did) waived these rights.

June 5. United States v. Texas. 339 U. S. 707.

Argued March 28, 1950. Douglas, J., for the Court; Frankfurter, J., in "separate opinion"; Reed and Minton, JJ., dissenting; Jackson and Clark, JJ., not participating.

A companion suit, rejecting the argument that Texas had a claim over submerged oil lands by virtue of its prior status as a republic.

December 11. Blau v. United States. 340 U. S. 159, 332.

Argued November 7, 1950. Black, J., for the Court; Clark, J., not participating; Minton and Jackson, JJ., dissenting.

Two cases, in the first of which the Court reversed a contempt citation where defendant had relied on constitutional provision against self-incrimination. In the second, the husband of the defendant was absolved of contempt in declining to give testimony which was protected by the rule on marital confidences.

1951

January 15. Niemotko v. Maryland. 340 U. S. 268.

Argued October 17, 1950. Vinson, C. J., for the Court; Black and Frankfurter, JJ., concurring.

Overturning city ordinance which required license from local officials for use of public park for peaceable discussion.

January 15. Feiner v. New York. 340 U. S. 315.

Argued October 17, 1950. Vinson, C. J., for the Court; Frankfurter, J., concurring; Black, Douglas and Minton, JJ., dissenting.

Sustaining conviction of one who refused to desist from inflammatory utterance when authorities, reasonably believing that speech would provoke violence, requested him to desist.

January 15. Dean Milk Co. v. Madison. 340 U. S. 349.

Argued December 7, 1950. Clark, J., for the Court; Black, Douglas and Minton, JJ., dissenting.

Invalidating a city ordinance limiting milk sales to approved plants within five miles of city limits, as unreasonable burden upon interstate commerce.

February 26. Rogers v. United States. 340 U. S. 367.

Argued November 7, 1950. Vinson, C. J., for the Court; Black, Frankfurter and Douglas, JJ., dissenting; Clark, J., not participating.

Sustaining contempt conviction where refusal to testify on ground of self-incrimination is for benefit of another.

February 27. Twenty-Second Amendment ratified.

April 12. Gerende v. Board of Supervisors. 341 U. S. 56.

Argued April 9, 1951. Per curiam; Reed, J., concurring.

Maryland loyalty oath as prerequisite to listing of candidacy on electoral ballot upheld.

April 30. Joint Anti-Fascist Committee v. McGrath. 341 U. S. 123.

Argued October 11, 1950. Burton, J., for the Court; Black, Douglas and Frankfurter, JJ., concurring; Vinson, C. J., and Reed and Minton, JJ., dissenting; Clark, J., not participating.

Sustaining power of Attorney General to prepare list of subversive groups under Executive Order to aid work of Loyalty Review Board.

June 4. Dennis v. United States. 341 U. S. 494.

Argued December 4, 1950. Vinson, C. J., for the Court; Frankfurter and Jackson, JJ., concurring; Black and Douglas, JJ., dissenting.

Upholding Smith Act against challenge by Communist defendants, after lengthy trial in lower court. Majority rejected argument that a theoretical "right of revolution" exists in Constitution and declared that "clear and present danger" arises when groups advocating overthrow of government are in readiness to make their attempt. But cf. *Yates v. United States* (1957), and the cases of *Scales v. United States* and *Noto v. United States* (1961), as narrowing the *Dennis* doctrine.

June 4. Garner v. Board of Public Works. 341 U. S. 716.

Argued April 25, 1951. Clark, J., for the Court; Burton, Frankfurter, Black and Douglas, JJ., dissenting.

Scienter (guilty knowledge) held essential to proving that one taking loyalty oath was guilty of false swearing.

1952

January 2. Rochin v. California. 342 U. S. 165.

Argued October 15, 1951. Frankfurter, J., for the Court; Black and Douglas, JJ., concurring; Minton, J., not participating.

Reversing a conviction on a narcotics charge, where law enforcement officers upon forcibly entering defendant's bedroom compelled him to eject morphine capsules he had swallowed.

March 3. Day-Brite Ltg. Co. v. Missouri. 342 U. S. 421.

Argued January 10, 1952. Douglas, J., for the Court; Frankfurter, J., concurring; Jackson, J., dissenting.

Statute requiring employers to grant four hours from work without penalty on election day held to be reasonable under due process clause.

March 3. Doremus v. Board of Education. 342 U. S. 429.

Argued January 31, 1952. Jackson, J., for the Court; Douglas, Reed and Burton, JJ., dissenting.

Dismissing, for want of jurisdiction, appeal from New Jersey supreme court ruling upholding state law requiring Bible reading in public schools. Cf. *Engel v. Vitale.*

March 3. Adler v. Board of Education. 342 U. S. 485.

Argued January 3, 1952. Minton, J., for the Court; Black, Frankfurter and Douglas, JJ., dissenting.

One of a series of loyalty oath cases sustaining state laws upon condition that parties knew the nature of the subversive organization in taking oath as to membership. These cases were steadfastly narrowed in the late 1960s: cf. especially *Elfbrandt v. Russell* (1966).

April 28. Beauharnais v. Illinois. 343 U. S. 250.

Argued November 21, 1951. Frankfurter, J., for the Court; Black, Douglas, Reed and Jackson, JJ., dissenting.

Upholding a state "group libel" law as within the police power of the state and not infringing upon the First Amendment.

April 28. Zorach v. Clauson. 343 U. S. 306.

Argued January 31, February 1, 1952. Douglas, J., for the Court; Black, Frankfurter and Jackson, JJ., dissenting.

Upholding a New York "released time" law under which school children could leave public school premises to attend requested religious instruction on private premises.

May 27. James McGranery becomes Attorney General.

June 2. Youngstown Sheet & Tube Co. v. Sawyer. 343 U. S. 579.

Argued May 12, 13, 1952. Black, J., for the Court; Frankfurter, J., concurring; Douglas, Jackson, Burton and Clark, JJ., separately concurring; Vinson, C. J., Reed and Minton, JJ., dissenting.

President Truman's seizure of the major steel companies, to avert a prospective nationwide strike, was based on general executive authority alleged to be implied in Article II of the Constitution. In six separate opinions the Court sustained the companies' injunction against the Secretary of Commerce, denying the implied executive authority in the absence of a Congressional enactment under the "necessary and proper" clause of Article I.

December 2. Walter J. Cummings, Jr., named Solicitor General (but not confirmed).

December 15. Wieman v. Updegraff. 344 U. S. 183.

Argued April 16, 1952. Clark, J., for the Court; Burton, Black, Douglas and Frankfurter, JJ., concurring; Jackson, J., not participating.

Invalidating an Oklahoma loyalty oath where persons were barred from public payrolls solely because they belonged to organizations on the Attorney General's subversive agencies list and without proof of their knowledge of the nature of the organizations.

1953

January 20. Dwight D. Eisenhower inaugurated as President.

January 21. Herbert Brownell becomes Attorney General.

February 9. Brown v. Allen. 344 U. S. 443.

Argued April 29, 1952; reargued October 13, 1953. Reed, J., for the Court; Jackson, Burton and Clark, JJ., "noting position in concurrence"; Frankfurter, Black and Douglas, JJ., "noting position" and dissenting.

One of the early tests of post-conviction review of criminal convictions in state courts, in which defendants sought habeas corpus in Federal courts alleging denial of constitutional rights. The general effect of the majority holding was to deny Federal habeas corpus where the writ or a similar remedy was still available in the state courts.

March 9. United States v. Kahriger. 345 U. S. 22.

Argued December 16, 17, 1952. Reed, J., for the Court; Douglas, J., concurring in part.

Upholding a requirement of the revenue law, requiring reporting of income from gambling devices, against a claim that this amounted to potential self-incrimination when the information could be used to support a gambling charge. Overruled in *Marchetti v. United States* (1968).

May 25. Avery v. Georgia. 345 U. S. 559.

Argued April 30, 1953. Vinson, C. J., for the Court; Black, Reed and Frankfurter, JJ., concurring; Jackson, J., not participating.

Invalidating a process of impaneling juries where names were on cards of different colors, where result was exclusion of Negroes from jury call.

June 15. Burns v. Wilson. 346 U. S. 137.

Argued February 5, 1953. Vinson, C. J., for the Court; Minton and Jackson, JJ., concurring; Douglas and Black, JJ., dissenting; Frankfurter, J., filing "separate opinion."

Affirming the right of the military court to try a serviceman for crimes allegedly committed in service. The dissent urged that if there was reasonable doubt as to jurisdiction, habeas corpus should issue. See *Reid v. Covert* (1957) and *Kinsella v. United States* (1960).

June 15. Barrows v. Jackson. 346 U. S. 249.

Argued April 28, 29, 1953. Minton, J., for the Court; Vinson, C. J., dissenting; Reed and Jackson, JJ., not participating.

Extending the rule in *Shelley v. Kraemer* to bar enforcement of a racial covenant against a co-covenantor. Over objections that defendant relied on constitutional rights of non-Caucasians when none was party to this suit, Court accepted standing of defendant where state court might deny non-Caucasians opportunity to test their rights themselves.

June 19. Rosenberg v. United States. 346 U. S. 273.

Argued June 18, 1953 (special term); per curiam *opinion filed this date; subsequent opinion of Court by Vinson, C. J.; Jackson and Clark, JJ., concurring; Black and Douglas, JJ., dissenting.*

Meeting to consider a stay of execution for spies convicted under Espionage Act of 1917, the Court rejected the argument that this statute had been impliedly repealed by the Atomic Energy Act of 1946.

October 5. THE WARREN COURT (October, 1953-June, 1969).

Warren, C. J.; Black, Reed, Frankfurter, Douglas, Jackson, Burton, Clark, Minton.

1954

February 8. Irvine v. California. 347 U. S. 128.

Argued November 30, 1953. Jackson, J., for the Court; Clark, J., concurring; Black, Frankfurter, Douglas and Burton, JJ., dissenting.

In a remarkably negative tone, the majority sustained a conviction based on police "trespass" since the offense was against property instead of against the person of the defendant, as it had been in *Rochin*. This case marked the beginning of a judicial campaign to overrule *Wolf v. Colorado*.

February 25. Simon E. Sobeloff becomes Solicitor General.

March 15. Alabama v. Texas. 347 U. S. 272.

Argued February 3, 4, 1954. Per curiam; Reed, J., concurring.

Original action brought to test constitutionality of Submerged Lands Act (1953) by which Congress waived title to tidelands oil reserves. Denied.

May 17. Brown v. Board of Education. 347 U. S. 483.

Argued December 8-11, 1952; reargued December 7-9, 1953. Warren, C. J., for the Court.

One of four cases in which the "separate but equal" doctrine was held unconstitutional, reversing *Plessy v. Ferguson* (1896) as it had been extended to segregated schools. The unanimous opinion held that the subject (public education) had to be considered in the light of contemporary conditions rather than historical conditions.

November 22. Berman v. Parker. 348 U. S. 26.

Argued October 19, 1954. Douglas, J., for the Court.

The case involved the power of the Federal government to undertake a redevelopment program for the District of Columbia. In the process of affirming the power, the Court asserted that there was a police power in the Federal government analogous to that in the states.

1955

March 28. Justice Harlan succeeds Jackson.

March 28. Williamson v. Lee Optical Co. 348 U. S. 483.

Argued March 2, 1955. Douglas, J., for the Court; Harlan, J., not participating.

Rejecting argument that Oklahoma statute forbidding opticians' advertising was unconstitutionally discriminatory, Court declared that for such discrimination to be improper it had to be invidious, not merely legislative distinction between evils of varying magnitudes.

May 31. Brown v. Board of Education (II). 349 U. S. 294.

Argued April 11-14, 1955. Warren, C. J., for the Court.

In its original ruling of desegregation, the Court had invited reargument on the feasibility of implementing the opinion. In this opinion the Court announced that it would be governed by equitable principles but would require the states to proceed with "all deliberate speed."

November 7. Toth v. Quarles. 350 U. S. 11.

Argued February 8, 9, 1955; reargued October 13, 1955. Black, J., for the Court; Reed, Minton and Burton, JJ., dissenting.

The Court here began its retreat from the rule in *Burns v. Wilson,* holding that ex-servicemen like other civilians were entitled to trial in civil courts even though alleged crime was committed during service.

1956

March 26. Ullman v. United States. 350 U. S. 422.

Argued December 6, 1955. Frankfurter, J., for the Court; Reed, J., concurring; Douglas and Black, JJ., dissenting.

Sustaining Immunity Act of 1950, encouraging witnesses to testify with proviso that their testimony would not be used against them, as satisfying the essential requirements of the Fifth Amendment. But cf. *Miranda v. Arizona* (1966).

April 2. Pennsylvania v. Nelson. 350 U. S. 497.

Argued November 15, 16, 1955. Warren, C. J., for the Court; Reed, Burton and Minton, JJ., dissenting.

Affirming the holding of the Pennsylvania supreme court, which found the state sedition law inoperative because Congress had preempted the field. The case began the general Congressional outcry against the "preemption doctrine."

April 9. Slochower v. Board of Education. 350 U. S. 551.

Argued October 19, 1955. Clark, J., for the Court; Reed, Burton, Minton and Harlan, JJ., dissenting.

Invalidating a provision of the New York City charter providing for summary dismissal of employees who invoked the privilege against self-incrimination as denial of due process.

April 23. Griffin v. Illinois. 351 U. S. 12.

Argued December 7, 1955. Black, J., for the Court; Frankfurter, J., concurring; Burton, Minton, Reed and Harlan, JJ., dissenting.

Invalidating an Illinois statute which denied indigent defendant right to copy of his transcript for appeal purposes without cost. The opinion held that where post-conviction review is available, all defendants must have equal opportunity to have their record submitted.

May 21. Ry. Employees v. Hanson. 351 U. S. 225.

Argued May 2, 1956. Douglas, J., for the Court; Frankfurter, J., concurring.

The Court ruled that the union shop provision of the Railway Labor Act, rather than the open shop provision of the Taft-Hartley Act, applied to interstate railroad unions.

June 11. Reid v. Covert. 351 U. S. 497.

Argued May 3, 1956. Clark, J., for the Court; Warren, C. J., Black and Douglas, JJ., dissenting; Frankfurter, J., "reserving opinion."

In this and a companion case *(Kinsella v. Krueger)* the majority held that wives of servicemen stationed abroad could be tried by military courts for criminal activity. The following year (354 U. S. 1) this holding was reversed, the Court then averring that civilians were entitled to civil trial when not themselves under military law.

October 16. Justice Brennan succeeds Minton.

1957

January 20. President Eisenhower inaugurated for second term.

February 25. Breithaupt v. Abram. 352 U. S. 432.

Argued December 12, 13, 1956. Clark, J., for the Court; Warren, C. J., Black and Douglas, JJ., dissenting.

Sustaining against a plea of self-incrimination a blood test obtained from accused while he was unconscious.

March 27, Justice Whittaker succeeds Reed.

April 29. Pennsylvania v. Board of Trusts. 353 U. S. 230.

Without argument. Per curiam.

The "first Girard College case," holding that where a government unit is represented on the governing board of a privately endowed school, there is colorable state participation in the school's segregation. See also *Brown v. Pennsylvania*, 392 F. 2d 120 (1968), cert. den. 391 U. S. 921 (1968).

May 6. Konigsberg v. State Bar of California. 353 U. S. 252.

Argued January 14, 1957. Black, J., for the Court; Frankfurter, Harlan, Clark, JJ., dissenting. Whittaker, J., not participating.

One of a number of bar admissions cases in which applicants were challenged for refusing to testify as to political affiliations or beliefs. The majority in this case rejected the argument that as future officers of the court applicants waived rights of privacy in matters of personal beliefs. See same case on review in 1961.

May 29. J. Lee Rankin becomes Solicitor General.

June 3. Jencks v. United States. 353 U. S. 657.

Argued October 17, 1956. Brennan, J., for the Court; Burton, Clark and Harlan, JJ., dissenting; Whittaker, J., not participating.

Holding unconstitutional a conviction based on undisclosed FBI reports, where trial court had denied access to records on ground that defense had failed to demonstrate inconsistency between testimony and report. The case precipitated a violent Congressional reaction.

June 17. Watkins v. United States. 354 U. S. 178.

Argued March 7, 1957. Warren, C. J., for the Court; Frankfurter, J., concurring; Clark, J., dissenting; Burton and Whittaker, JJ., not participating.

Reversing a contempt citation for refusal to answer questions of House Un-American Activities Committee where questions related to other witnesses.

June 17. Sweezy v. New Hampshire. 354 U. S. 234.

Argued March 7, 1957. Warren, C. J., for the Court; Frankfurter and Harlan, JJ., concurring; Clark and Burton, JJ., dissenting; Whittaker, J., not participating.

Reversing a conviction of a witness for refusing to answer question put by the state attorney general as one-man investigating committee of state legislature, as inadequately safeguarding inividual's rights.

June 17. Yates v. United States. 354 U. S. 298.

Argued October 8, 9, 1956. Harlan, J., for the Court; Clark, Black and Douglas, JJ., dissenting in part; Brennan and Whittaker, JJ., not participating.

In an opinion greatly narrowing the effectiveness of the Smith Act, the majority ruled that the advocacy of overthrow of the government as proscribed by the statute meant overt action rather than abstract argument. In effect, the decision overturned the *Dennis* case and provided for a new trial for the original defendants.

June 17. Service v. Dulles. 354 U. S. 363.

Argued April 2, 3, 1957. Harlan, J., for the Court; Clark, J., not participating.

Holding that where a foreign service officer had repeatedly been cleared by prescribed loyalty review procedures, the Secretary of State could not dismiss him by independent action.

June 24. Mallory v. United States. 354 U. S. 449.

Argued April 1, 1957. Frankfurter, J., for the Court.

Setting aside a conviction of one who had been subjected to prolonged interrogation without being apprised of his constitutional rights, and particularly where the interrogating officers had failed to comply with procedural requirement that suspect be arraigned without delay.

June 24. Roth v. United States. 354 U. S. 476.

Argued April 22, 1957. Brennan, J., for the Court; Warren, C. J., and Harlan, J., concurring; Douglas and Black, JJ., dissenting.

Sustaining both Federal and state obscenity statutes as not infringing upon First Amendment, and suggesting a test of obscenity as reference to sex in manner appealing to "prurient interests." Although vigorously criticized thereafter, the *Roth* test has not yet been replaced by a more definite standard.

July 11. Wilson v. Girouard. 354 U. S. 524.

Argued July 8, 1957 (special session) Per curiam; Douglas, J., not participating.

Upholding against constitutional claims of defendant a decision by the United States to waive its own jurisdiction over member of armed forces charged with crime against foreign national, under treaty providing for such waiver. This decision, added to the "Fifth Amendment" decisions of *Jencks, Yates, Service* and *Mallory*, precipitated the Congressional attack upon the Court the following session.

November 8. William P. Rogers becomes Attorney General.

1958

March 31. Perez v. Brownell. 356 U. S. 44.

Argued May 1, 1957; reargued October 28, 1957. Frankfurter, J., for the Court; Warren, C. J., Whittaker, Black and Douglas, JJ., dissenting.

Sustaining Nationality Act of 1940 wherein Congress provided for expatriation of native born citizen who participated in foreign elections. Overruled in *Afroyim v. Rusk* (1967).

March 31. Trop v. Dulles. 356 U. S. 86.

Argued May 2, 1957; reargued October 28, 29, 1957. Warren, C. J., for the Court; Brennan, J., concurring; Frankfurter, Burton, Clark and Harlan, JJ., dissenting.

Holding under Eighth Amendment that use of expatriation or denaturalization as punishment for conviction for military crimes under Nationality Act is unconstitutional.

June 30. Beilan v. Board of Education. 357 U. S. 399.

Argued March 4, 1958. Burton, J., for the Court; Frankfurter, J., concurring; Warren, C. J., Douglas, Brennan and Black, JJ., dissenting.

Majority sustained Pennsylvania statute which provided, with due notice to parties liable, for discharge of employees of school boards who failed to satisfy superiors as to knowledge of subversive nature of organizations in which they held membership. Cf. *Keyishian v. Board of Regents* (1967).

June 30. NAACP v. Alabama ex rel. Patterson. 357 U. S. 449.

Argued January 15, 16, 1958. Harlan, J., for the Court.

Alabama had first demanded right to examine association's membership list as condition for licensing it as foreign corporation doing business within the state. When NAACP refused condition and undertook to organize local office, it was cited for contempt. In setting aside contempt citation, the Court ruled that the state action interfered with freedom of association.

June 30. Lerner v. Casey. 357 U. S. 468.

Argued March 4, 1958. Harlan, J., for the Court.

Qualifying the *Slochower* doctrine, and relieving some of the anti-Court pressure in Congress, the opinion upheld a dismissal of an alleged security risk where state inquiry under pertinent state law provided adequate constitutional safeguards.

June 30. Speiser v. Randall. 357 U. S. 513.

Argued April 8, 9, 1958. Brennan, J., for the Court; Black, Douglas and Burton, JJ., concurring; Clark, J., dissenting; Warren, C. J., not participating.

Invalidating California statute withholding tax exempt status from otherwise qualified parties who refused to subscribe to state loyalty oath.

September 12. Cooper v. Aaron. 358 U. S. 1.

Argued September 11, 1958 (special session). Warren, C. J., and all Justices by name, for the Court.

The Court unequivocally rejected attempt by Little Rock authorities to prevent desegregation of schools until court order had been further tested. The Court in the process rejected the theory that the states had a reserved power to interpret the Federal Constitution on their own authority, since all state and local officers were bound by oath to support the Constitution and laws of the United States.

October 14. Justice Stewart succeeds Burton.

1959

March 30. Bartkus v. Illinois. 359 U. S. 121.

Argued November 15, 1957; reargued October 21, 22, 1958. Frankfurter, J., for the Court; Warren, C. J., Black, Brennan and Douglas, JJ., dissenting.

Another of the cases in which the dimensions of the Bill of Rights as extended to the states was discussed. Here defendant, acquitted in Federal court of a criminal charge, was tried in the state court on an identical indictment and convicted. The majority held that there was no double jeopardy since this guarantee of the Fifth Amendment did not extend in terms to the states.

June 8. Lassiter v. Northampton Elementary Board. 360 U. S. 45.

Argued May 18, 19, 1959. Douglas, J., for the Court.

Upholding a non-discriminatory literacy test for voters in North Carolina where they were required to read the state constitution in English.

June 8. Uphaus v. Wyman. 360 U. S. 72.

Argued November 17, 18, 1958. Clark, J., for the Court; Warren C. J., Brennan, Black and Douglas, JJ., dissenting.

Upholding New Hampshire subversive control statute, where it related to subversive activity against the state, as not in conflict with Smith Act which had preempted field with reference to activity against nation. But cf. *DeGregory v. Attorney General of New Hampshire* (1966).

June 8. Barenblatt v. United States. 360 U. S. 109.

Argued November 18, 1958. Harlan, J., for the Court; Warren, C. J., Black, Brennan and Douglas, JJ., dissenting.

Sustaining contempt of Congress citation where witness refused to answer questions as to his own Communist affiliation. Dissent argued that the effect of majority opinion was to deny rights under First and Fifth Amendments. Cf. *Russell v. United States* (1962).

June 29. Kingsley Pictures v. Regents. 360 U. S. 684.

Argued April 23, 1959. Stewart, J., for the Court; Black, Douglas, Frankfurter, Clark and Harlan, JJ., concurring separately.

Holding unconstitutional a New York motion picture censorship statute under First and Fifth Amendments. This was one of a series of decisions, dating from the early 1950's, which formed the basis for a broadly liberal concept of permissive publication and portrayal in drama.

November 23. Henry v. United States. 361 U. S. 98.

Argued October 20, 21, 1959. Douglas, J., for the Court; Black, J., concurring; Warren, C. J., and Clark, J., dissenting.

The majority held invalid a conviction for possession of stolen goods, where government agents had stopped defendant's car to search for illicit liquor and unexpectedly found stolen goods.

December 14. Smith v. California. 361 U. S. 147.

Argued October 20, 1959. Brennan, J., for the Court; Black, Douglas and Frankfurter, JJ., concurring; Harlan, J., concurring in part and dissenting in part.

Los Angeles ordinance fixed absolute criminal liability in booksellers possessing obscene publications for sale. The ordinance was held unconstitutional where it failed to require evidence of *scienter*.

1960

January 18. Kinsella v. United States. 361 U. S. 234.

Argued October 22, 1959. Clark, J., for the Court; Whittaker and Stewart, JJ., concurring; Harlan and Frankfurter, JJ., dissenting.

One of several cases in which Court held that servicemen's dependents, charged with crimes overseas, could not be subjected to court martial but were entitled to civil trial.

February 23. Bates v. Little Rock. 361 U. S. 516.

Argued November 18, 1959. Stewart, J., for the Court; Black and Douglas, JJ., concurring.

Court set aside convictions and fines of NAACP officials who had refused to divulge names of local members, as infringing upon freedom of association.

February 29. United States v. Raines. 362 U. S. 17.

Argued January 12, 1960. Brennan, J., for the Court; Frankfurter and Harlan, JJ., concurring.

Government officials had brought suit under Civil Rights Act of 1957 against state officials discriminating against Negro voters. District Court had held the suit to be beyond the scope of the Fifteenth Amendment, but Supreme Court reversed, asserting that the subject was within the scope of the Amendment and the 1957 statute a proper implementation of it.

March 28. Abel v. United States. 362 U. S. 217.

Argued February 24, 25, 1959; reargued November 9, 1959. Frankfurter, J., for the Court; Warren, C. J., and Douglas, Black and Brennan, JJ., dissenting.

Sustaining search and seizure under an administrative warrant issued by Immigration and Naturalization Service, in notorious spy case.

June 20. Flemming v. Nestor. 363 U. S. 603.

Argued February 24, 1960. Harlan, J., for the Court; Black, Douglas and Brennan, JJ., dissenting.

Majority upheld amendment to Social Security Act cancelling old age benefits in cases of deported aliens. Dissents condemned amendment as tantamount to bill of attainder in confiscating an accrued property right.

November 14. Gomillion v. Lightfoot. 364 U. S. 339.

Argued October 18, 19, 1960. Frankfurter, J., for the Court; Whittaker and Douglas, JJ., concurring.

Invalidating state gerrymandering statute intended to minimize Negro vote, as contrary to Fifteenth Amendment.

December 12. Bush v. Orleans Parish School Board. 364 U. S. 500.

Without oral argument. Per curiam.

Dismissing motions to stay injunctions against segregation, and also dismissing doctrine of "interposition" of state authority against enforcement of Federal authority.

1961

January 20. John F. Kennedy inaugurated as President.

January 21. Robert F. Kennedy becomes Attorney General.

January 23. Archibald Cox becomes Solicitor General.

February 27. Braden v. United States. 365 U. S. 431.

Argued November 17, 1960. Stewart, J., for the Court; Black, Douglas, Brennan, JJ., and Warren, C. J., dissenting.

Upholding contempt conviction of witness before Un-American Activities Committee for refusing to answer questions of Communist activities where questions were held to be pertinent to subject of inquiry.

March 6. Silverman v. United States. 365 U. S. 505.

Argued December 5, 1960. Stewart, J., for the Court; Douglas, Clark, and Whittaker, JJ., concurring.

Setting aside convictions based on "bugging" devices for eavesdropping on suspects.

March 20. Rogers v. Richmond. 365 U. S. 534.

Argued November 8, 9, 1960. Frankfurter, J., for the Court; Stewart and Clark, JJ., dissenting.

Reversing conviction based on allegedly coerced confessions, where Court found original trial over question of admissibility of confessions lacked elemental safeguards of due process.

March 29. Twenty-Third Amendment ratified.

April 17. Burton v. Wilmington Pkg. Authority. 365 U. S. 715.

Argued February 21, 23, 1961. Clark, J., for the Court; Harlan, Frankfurter and Whittaker, JJ., dissenting.

Holding invalid under Fourteenth Amendment a policy of refusing to serve Negroes by a restaurant licensed by public agency. This case represented progressive broadening of "state action" doctrine begun in *Shelley v. Kraemer.*

April 24. Konigsberg v. State Bar. 366 U. S. 36.

Argued December 14, 1960. Harlan, J., for the Court; Warren, C. J., and Black, Douglas and Brennan, JJ., dissenting.

This second "bar association" case, by 5-4, held opposite of 1957 case, also 5-4. Present majority held that state could properly demand of candidate for admission to bar information concerning associations which might affect his qualifications for admission.

June 5. Communist Party v. Control Board. 367 U. S. 1.

Argued October 11, 12, 1960. Frankfurter, J., for the Court; Warren, C. J., and Black, Douglas and Brennan, JJ., dissenting.

The lengthy majority opinion sustained in principle the constitutionality of the Subversive Activities Control Act of 1950. Two years later, however, in *Communist Party v. United States,* 331 F. 2d 807, the Court of Appeals ruled that only party officials, rather than the party itself, could be subject to the act. The Supreme Court denied certiorari, leaving open the question of whether such individual officials were entitled to the constitutional defense against self-incrimination. On this, cf. *Albertson v. Subversive Activities Control Board* (1965).

June 5. Scales v. United States. 367 U. S. 203.

Argued April 29, 1959; reargued October 10, 1960. Harlan, J., for the Court; Warren, C. J., Black, Douglas and Brennan, JJ., dissenting.

Sustaining, although narrowly defining, the evidentiary provisions of the "Jencks Act," the Court held that where a trial court properly followed these provisions a conviction for advocating violent overthrow of authority would be sustained.

June 5. Noto v. United States. 367 U. S. 290.

Argued October 10, 11, 1960. Harlan, J., for the Court; Warren, C. J., Black, Douglas and Brennan, JJ., dissenting.

In a companion to *Scales*, the Court here reversed a conviction where it found only advocacy of overthrow as an abstract proposition. Cf. *Brandenburg v. Ohio* (1969).

June 19. Torcaso v. Watkins. 367 U. S. 488.

Argued April 24, 1961. Black, J., for the Court; Frankfurter and Harlan, JJ., concurring.

Outlawing an old Maryland law, requiring officeholders to take oath to belief in God, as contrary to freedom of religion clause in First Amendment.

June 19. Poe v. Ullman. 367 U. S. 497.

Argued March 1, 2, 1961. Frankfurter, J., for the Court; Brennan, J., concurring; Black, Douglas, Harlan and Stewart, JJ. dissenting.

Another attack on the Connecticut anti-birth control law, dismissed by narrow majority as presenting no justiciable Federal issue. Cf. *Griswold v. Connecticut* (1965).

June 19. Culombe v. Connecticut. 367 U. S. 568.

Argued January 16, 1961. Frankfurter, J., for the Court; Warren, C. J., Brennan, Douglas and Black, JJ., concurring; Harlan, Clark and Whittaker, JJ., dissenting.

Setting aside conviction based on confession where accused was denied counsel and not properly arraigned.

June 19. Mapp v. Ohio. 367 U. S. 643.

Argued March 29, 1961. Clark, J., for the Court; Black and Douglas, JJ., concurring; Stewart, Harlan, Frankfurter and Whittaker, JJ., dissenting.

Overruling *Wolf v. Colorado* and holding the constitutional guarantees against illegal search and seizure extended to the state through the Fourteenth Amendment.

December 11. Garner v. Louisiana. 368 U. S. 157.

Argued October 18, 19, 1961. Warren, C. J., for the Court; Douglas and Harlan, JJ., concurring.

One of a series of "sit-in" cases in which the Court invalidated convictions of Negroes under "breach of peace" laws as denial of due process.

December 11. Cramp v. Board of Public Instruction. 368 U. S. 278.

Argued October 16, 1961. Stewart, J., for the Court; Black and Douglas, JJ., concurring.

Invalidating Florida teacher loyalty statute where oath vaguely related to membership in "Communist Party."

1962

February 19. Chewning v. Cunningham. 368 U. S. 443.

Argued December 4, 5, 1961. Douglas, J., for the Court; Harlan, J., concurring.

Invalidating conviction based on trial without counsel, one of a series of cases in which the Court began to develop the right-to-counsel rule.

March 26. Baker v. Carr. 369 U. S. 186.

Argued April 19, 20, 1961; reargued October 9, 1961. Brennan, J., for the Court; Douglas and Clark, JJ., concurring; Harlan and Frankfurter, JJ., dissenting; Whittaker, J., not participating.

First of the reapportionment cases, in which the majority held the Federal District Court had jurisdiction under Fourteenth Amendment to require state legislature to redistrict lower house of legislature on equitable basis.

April 16. Justice White succeeds Whittaker.

April 30. Carnley v. Cochran. 369 U. S. 506.

Argued February 20, 21, 1962. Brennan, J., for the Court; Warren, C. J., Harlan, Black and Douglas, JJ., concurring; White, J., not participating.

Setting aside conviction of an illiterate defendant where evidence failed to show that assistance of counsel had been "intelligently and understandingly waived."

June 25. Engel v. Vitale. 370 U. S. 421.

Argued April 3, 1962. Black, J., for the Court; Douglas, J., concurring; Stewart, J., dissenting; Frankfurter and White, JJ., not participating.

The New York Regents' prayer case, in which the majority held that the anti-establishment clause of the First Amendment prohibits the state from composing any prayer or other expression of religious attitude for use in public schools.

June 25. Manual Enterprises v. Day. 370 U. S. 478.

Argued February 26, 27, 1962. Harlan, J., for the Court; Warren, C. J., Brennan, Douglas and Black, JJ., concurring; Clark J., dissenting; Frankfurter and White, JJ., not participating.

Another of the obscenity cases in which the majority found no liability under the First Amendment where, "taken as a whole," publications do not flout "contemporary notions of rudimentary decency."

June 25. Glidden Co. v. Zdanok. 370 U. S. 530.

Argued February 21, 22, 1962. Harlan, J., for the Court; Clark, J., and Warren, C. J., concurring; Douglas and Black, JJ., dissenting; Frankfurter and White, JJ., not participating.

Defining the Court of Claims and Court of Customs and Patent Appeals as "constitutional courts" under Article III of the Constitution.

June 25. Robinson v. California. 370 U. S. 660.

Argued April 17, 1962. Stewart, J., for the Court; Douglas and Harlan, JJ. concurring; Clark and White, JJ., dissenting; Frankfurter, J., not participating.

Extending Eighth Amendment prohibition of "Cruel and unusual punishment" to states via Fourteenth Amendment, with reference to a state law committing narcotics addicts to prison on mere finding of addiction.

October 1. Justice Goldberg succeeds Frankfurter.

1963

January 14. NAACP v. Button. 371 U. S. 415.

Argued November 8, 1961; reargued October 9, 1962. Brennan, J., for the Court; Douglas and White, JJ., concurring; Harlan, Clark and Stewart, JJ., dissenting.

Virginia statutes prohibiting attorneys' acting as intermediaries or soliciting cases held inapplicable to associations whose primary aim is to apprise members of their constitutional rights.

February 18. Bantam Books, Inc. v. Sullivan. 372 U. S. 58.

Argued December 3, 4, 1962. Brennan, J., for the Court; Black, Douglas and Clark, JJ., concurring; Harlan, J., dissenting.

Invalidating Rhode Island law which created a censorship commission which, if convinced of obscenity of a publication, was empowered to discourage dealers from selling the publication or to initiate criminal proceedings. The majority held that the definition of obscenity was unconstitutionally vague.

February 18. Kennedy v. Mendoza-Martinez. 372 U. S. 144.

Argued October 10, 11, 1961; reargued December 4, 1962. Goldberg, J., for the Court; Douglas, Black and Brennan, JJ., concurring; Harlan, Clark, Stewart and White, JJ., dissenting.

Invalidating sections of Nationality Act of 1940 and Immigration and Nationality Act of 1952 depriving alleged draft evaders of citizenship without providing for normal safeguards of due process.

February 25. Edwards v. South Carolina. 372 U. S. 229.

Argued December 13, 1962. Stewart, J., for the Court; Clark, J., dissenting.

Setting aside breach of peace convictions of Negroes who peaceably assembled to petition legislature for relief from discriminatory laws.

March 18. Townsend v. Sain. 372 U. S. 293.

Argued February 19, 1962; reargued October 8, 9, 1962. Warren, C. J., for the Court; Goldberg, J., concurring; Stewart, Clark, Harlan and White, JJ., dissenting.

The first of a "trilogy" of cases (*Fay v. Noia*, 372 U.S. 391; *Sanders v. United States*, 373 U. S. 1) in which the Court declared that Federal District

Court review of state criminal convictions would lie where state record failed to show adequate review of prisoner's constitutional rights.

March 18. Gideon v. Wainwright. 372 U. S. 335.

Argued January 15, 1963. Black, J., for the Court; Douglas, Clark and Harlan, JJ., concurring.

Overruling *Betts v. Brady*, and holding that equal protection under Fourteenth Amendment requires counsel to be appointed for indigent defendants in all criminal proceedings.

March 18. Douglas v. California. 372 U. S. 353.

Argued April 17, 1962; reargued January 16, 1963. Douglas, J., for the Court; Clark, Harlan and Stewart, JJ., dissenting.

A companion to *Gideon*, extending the right of counsel to indigents in carrying criminal convictions to appellate courts.

March 18. Gray v. Sanders. 372 U. S. 368.

Argued January 17, 1963. Douglas, J., for the Court; Stewart and Clark, JJ., concurring; Harlan, J., dissenting.

Overthrowing Georgia's county-unit voting system in primaries where this system resulted in disproportionate weight to votes in counties of widely varying population.

March 25. Gibson v. Florida Legislative Invest. Committee. 372 U. S. 539.

Argued December 5, 1962; reargued October 10, 11, 1962. Goldberg, J., for the Court; Black and Douglas, JJ., concurring; Harlan, Clark, Stewart and White, JJ., dissenting.

In another NAACP case where a state agency sought to compel divulgence of membership lists, majority held that the state failed to establish a reasonable relationship between the information sought and the state interest involved.

May 20. Lombard v. Louisiana. 373 U. S. 267.

Argued November 5-7, 1962. Warren, C. J., for the Court; Douglas, J., concurring; Harlan, J., dissenting.

One of the "lunch counter sit-in" cases in which Negroes seeking to break down segregated service policy were convicted under state "criminal mischief statute." The majority held the statute unconstitutional.

May 20. Wright v. Georgia. 373 U. S. 284.

Argued November 7, 1962. Warren, C. J., for the Court.

Where Negroes had been ordered by police officer to leave public park customarily used by white persons, their convictions were set aside on ground that the order amounted to an order to give up exercise of constitutional rights.

May 27. Lopez v. United States. 373 U. S. 427.

Argued January 14, 1963. Harlan, J., for the Court; Warren, C. J., concurring; Brennan, Douglas and Goldberg, JJ., dissenting.

Sustaining a conviction on a bribery charge, where part of evidence admitted into trial was obtained by a concealed tape recorder.

May 27. Watson v. Memphis. 373 U. S. 526.
Argued April 17, 18, 1963. Goldberg, J., for the Court.

Ordering desegregation of a public park, this case together with *Wright v. Georgia* marked the beginning of a systematic broadening of the desegregation doctrine.

June 3. Goss v. Board of Education. 373 U. S. 683.
Argued March 20, 21, 1963. Clark, J., for the Court.

Rejecting a school transfer plan which offered an option of perpetuating segregated public schools.

June 10. Ker v. California. 374 U. S. 23.
Argued December 11, 1962. Clark, J., for the Court; Harlan, J., concurring; Warren, C. J., Brennan, Douglas and Goldberg, JJ., dissenting in part.

In a divided opinion, eight of the Justices agreed that Fourth Amendment standards as to search and seizure extended to state criminal proceedings, but disagreed on whether the instant search (without warrant) and seizure of marijuana which was object of search was reasonable.

June 17. Abingdon School Dist. v. Schempp. 374 U. S. 203.
Argued February 27, 28, 1963. Clark, J., for the Court; Douglas, Brennan, Goldberg and Harlan, JJ., concurring; Stewart, J., dissenting.

In another "school prayer" case, the majority held contrary to the First Amendment a state law requiring religious exercises in schools.

June 17. Sherbert v. Verner. 374 U. S. 398.
Argued April 24, 1963. Brennan, J., for the Court; Douglas and Stewart, JJ., concurring; Harlan and White, JJ., dissenting.

Reversing a South Carolina court which had denied unemployment compensation to Seventh Day Adventist who was unable to accept Saturday employment because of her faith.

November 22. Lyndon B. Johnson succeeds to Presidency.

1964

January 23. Twenty-Fourth Amendment ratified.

February 17. Wesberry v. Sanders. 376 U. S. 1.
Argued November 18, 19, 1963. Black, J., for the Court; Clark, J., dissenting in part; Harlan and Stewart, JJ., dissenting.

Another of the basic reapportionment cases, extending the one man-one vote principle to House of Representative elections.

March 9. New York Times v. Sullivan. 376 U. S. 254.
Argued January 6, 1964. Brennan, J., for the Court; Black, Douglas and Goldberg, JJ., concurring.

Enunciating a new "public official" rule in which defamatory statements relating to public officers were held nonactionable under First Amendment without proof of actual malice.

March 23. Preston v. United States. 376 U. S. 374.

Argued February 25, 1964. Black, J., for the Court.

Denying admissibility of evidence obtained in search of suspect's car, where evidence was not related to charge of arrest, made without warrant and at a place remote from place and time of arrest.

March 23. Stoner v. California. 376 U. S. 483.

Argued February 25, 1964. Stewart, J., for the Court; Harlan, J., concurring in part and dissenting in part.

Denying admissibility of evidence obtained by search without warrant where hotel room clerk let officers into defendant's room.

April 20. Brotherhood of R. Trainmen v. Virginia. 377 U. S. 1.

Argued January 31, 1964. Black, J., for the Court; Clark, J., dissenting; Stewart, J., not participating.

The majority held that unions could not be enjoined, under First Amendment freedoms, from counseling their members as to how and when to seek legal service in settling claims and recommending specific attorneys for this service.

May 18. Schneider v. Rusk. 377 U. S. 163.

Argued April 2, 1964. Douglas, J., for the Court; Clark, Harlan and White, JJ., dissenting; Brennan, J., not participating.

Holding discriminatory under the Fifth Amendment a provision of the Immigration and Nationality Act of 1952 expatriating naturalized citizens who reside abroad in their country of origin for a fixed period of years.

May 18. Massiah v. United States. 377 U. S. 201.

Argued March 3, 1964. Stewart, J., for the Court; White, Clark and Harlan, JJ., dissenting.

Denying admissibility of incriminating evidence elicited from suspect in absence of his attorney.

May 25. Griffin v. School Board. 377 U. S. 218.

Argued March 30, 1964. Black, J., for the Court; Clark and Harlan, JJ., dissenting in part.

Outlawing Virginia tuition grant system as it was used to aid white children to attend segregated private schools and closing public schools to frustrate integration.

June 1. United States v. Aluminum Co. of America. 377 U. S. 271.

Argued April 23, 1964. Douglas, J., for the Court; Harlan, Stewart and Goldberg, JJ., dissenting.

Sustaining government's anti-trust suit against "oligopolistic" combination dominating if not restraining trade.

June 1. Baggett v. Bullitt. 377 U. S. 360.

Argued March 24, 1964. White, J., for the Court; Clark and Harlan, JJ., dissenting.

Outlawing 1931 Washington state loyalty oath as unconstitutionally vague.

June 15. Reynolds v. Sims. 377 U. S. 533.

Argued November 13, 1963. Warren, C. J., for the Court; Clark and Stewart, JJ., concurring; Harlan, J., dissenting.

In this and five companion cases following, the Court rounded out its basic rationale on reapportionment as applied to state and national government. In this case from Alabama, majority held that equal protection clause required that one man-one vote principle apply to both houses of a state legislature.

June 15. WMCA, Inc. v. Lomenzo. 377 U. S. 633.

Argued November 12, 13, 1963. Warren, C. J., for the Court; Harlan and Stewart, JJ., dissenting.

Complementing the *Sims* case, this opinion held that Federal courts could review formulae for apportionment to detect any "built-in bias."

June 15. Md. Committee for Fair Representation v. Tawes. 377 U. S. 656.

Argued November 13, 14, 1963. Warren, C. J., for the Court; Clark, J., concurring; Harlan and Stewart, JJ., dissenting.

Rejecting apportionment plans which vary with one legislative house or the other with resultant malapportionment in one or the other.

June 15. Davis v. Mann. 377 U. S. 678.

Argued November 14, 18, 1963. Warren, C. J., for the Court; Clark, J., concurring; Stewart and Harlan, JJ., dissenting.

Where apportionment seeks to balance urban and rural economic strength in a state legislature, it is held to violate the one man-one vote rule.

June 15. Roman v. Sincock. 377 U. S. 695.

Argued December 9, 1963. Warren, C. J., for the Court; Clark, J., concurring; Stewart and Harlan, JJ., dissenting.

Rejecting another argument excusing malapportionment, that Congress in admitting a state to the Union had accepted the fact of malapportionment.

June 15. Lucas v. Colorado General Assembly. 377 U. S. 713.

Argued March 31, April 1, 1964. Warren, C. J., for the Court; Clark, Stewart and Harlan, JJ., dissenting.

Invalidating a state constitutional referendum where the electoral majority acceptance of apportionment imbalance conflicts with the equal protection clause.

June 15. Malloy v. Hogan. 378 U. S. 1.

Argued March 5, 1964. Brennan, J., for the Court; Douglas, J., concurring; Harlan, Clark, White and Stewart, JJ., dissenting.

Qualifying, if not overruling, *Twining v. New Jersey* (1908) and holding Fifth Amendment rule against self-incrimination extended to states through Fourteenth Amendment.

June 15. Aguilar v. Texas. 378 U. S. 108.

Argued March 25, 26, 1964. Goldberg, J., for the Court; Harlan, J., concurring; Clark, Black and Stewart, JJ., dissenting.

Confirming partial incorporation of Fourth Amendment into Fourteenth, majority held that search warrants issued on hearsay must be reviewed by issuing magistrate as to reasonableness of the circumstances.

June 22. Jacobellis v. Ohio. 378 U. S. 184.

Argued March 26, 1963; reargued April 1, 1964. Brennan, J., for the Court; Black, Douglas, Stewart and Goldberg, JJ., concurring; Warren, C. J., and Harlan, J., dissenting.

Wrestling further with the problem of obscenity and free speech, majority here asserted protection of a work unless it is "utterly devoid of redeeming social importance."

June 22. Bell v. Maryland. 378 U. S. 226.

Argued October 14, 15, 1963. Brennan, J., for the Court; Douglas and Goldberg, JJ., concurring; Black, Harlan and White, JJ., dissenting.

One of a series of "sit-in" cases (cf. *Garner v. Louisiana*, 368 U. S. 157; *Peterson v. South Carolina*, 373 U. S. 244), Brennan holding convictions subject to vacating in light of later legislative enactments affecting defendants' rights. Dissent urged restraint in indefinite expansion of Fourteenth Amendment restraints on state sovereignty.

June 22. Escobedo v. Illinois. 378 U. S. 478.

Argued April 29, 1964. Goldberg, J., for the Court; Harlan, Stewart, White and Clark, JJ., dissenting.

Expanding upon the *Gideon* doctrine of a constitutional right to counsel, the majority ruled that the right matures when a police investigation comes to focus on a specific suspect.

June 22. Aptheker v. Secretary of State. 378 U. S. 500.

Argued April 21, 1964. Goldberg, J., for the Court; Black and Douglas, JJ., concurring; Clark and White, JJ., dissenting.

Outlawing Section 6 of the Subversive Activities Control Act of 1950 which denied passports (i. e., right to travel) to native-born citizens because of their alleged radical affiliations.

December 14. Heart of Atlanta Motel v. United States. 379 U. S. 241.

Argued October 5, 1964. Clark, J., for the Court; Black, Douglas and Goldberg, JJ., concurring.

Upholding the "public accommodations" section of the Civil Rights Act of 1964, as within the commerce power and not in derogation of due process.

December 14. Katzenbach v. McClung. 379 U. S. 294.

Argued October 5, 1964. Clark, J., for the Court; Black, Douglas and Goldberg, JJ., concurring.

In a companion to the *Heart of Atlanta Motel* case, the Court extended the "public accommodations" rule to public eating facilities.

1965

January 18. Fortson v. Dorsey. 379 U. S. 433.

Argued December 10, 1964. Brennan, J., for the Court; Harlan, J., concurring; Douglas, J., dissenting.

One of numerous cases filling in details in the basic reapportionment decisions, in this instance holding that equality in population ratios need only be "reasonable."

January 18. Henry v. Mississippi. 379 U. S. 443.

Argued October 13, 1964. Brennan, J., for the Court; Black, Harlan, Clark and Stewart, JJ., dissenting.

Qualifying the rule in the 1963 "trilogy," the Court here ruled that where a state defendant knowingly and intelligently waives his Federal claims in the state court, Federal habeas corpus will not issue.

January 18. Cox v. Louisiana. 379 U. S. 536, 559.

Argued October 21, 1964. Goldberg, J., for the Court; Black, Clark, White and Harlan, JJ., concurring in part and dissenting in part.

Two cases, in the first of which the Court invalidated a Louisiana breach of peace statute which left to the discretion of local officials the permission to use streets for peaceful demonstrations. In the s cond, a statute prohibiting demonstration "near" public buildings was held void for vagueness.

January 20. President Johnson inaugurated for full term.

February 13. Nicholas DeB. Katzenbach becomes Attorney General.

April 5. Pointer v. Texas. 380 U. S. 400.

Argued March 15, 1965. Black, J., for the Court; Harlan, Stewart and Goldberg, JJ., concurring.

Where *Gideon* had extended to the states the Sixth Amendment guarantee of the right to counsel in criminal cases, this opinion now added the guarantee of the right to confront and cross-examine witnesses against him, another element of the Sixth Amendment.

April 28. Griffin v. California. 380 U. S. 609.

Argued March 9, 1965. Douglas, J., for the Court; Harlan, J., concurring; Stewart, J., dissenting; Warren, C. J., not participating.

Comment on defendant's failure to testify in his defense was now held to be unconstitutional self-incrimination extended from the Fifth Amendment to the states through the Fourteenth.

May 3. Zemel v. Rusk. 381 U. S. 1.

Argued March 1, 1965. Warren, C. J., for the Court; Black, Douglas and Goldberg, JJ., dissenting.

Distinguishing *Kent v. Dulles*, the majority here upheld a statutory ban on travel to Cuba where it applied uniformly to all citizens.

June 7. United States v. Brown. 381 U. S. 437.

Argued March 29, 1965. Warren, C. J., for the Court; White, Clark, Harlan and Stewart, JJ., dissenting.

Holding Section 504 of the Taft-Hartley law, making it a crime for Communists or ex-Communists to hold labor union office, invalid as a bill of attainder.

June 7. Griswold v. Connecticut. 381 U. S. 479.

Argued March 29, 1965. Douglas, J., for the Court; Warren, C. J., Goldberg and Brennan, JJ., and Harlan and White, JJ., concurring separately; Black and Stewart JJ., dissenting.

After years of unsuccessful attacks on the state anti-birth control statute, the Court in this case supported the attack on the ground that "specific guarantees in the Bill of Rights have penumbras" which include the personal right to knowledge which may not be frustrated by government edict.

June 7. Linkletter v. Walker. 381 U. S. 618.

Argued March 11, 1965. Clark, J., for the Court; Black and Douglas, JJ., dissenting.

Limiting the exclusionary rule on evidence in state courts, asserted in *Mapp v. Ohio*, to convictions appealed since the date of that case.

August 24. Thurgood Marshall becomes Solicitor General.

October 4. Justice Fortas succeeds Goldberg.

November 15. Albertson v. Subversive Activities Control Board. 382 U. S. 70.

Argued October 18, 1965. Brennan, J., for the Court; Clark, J., concurring.

Completing the process of circumscribing the statute, after sustaining its general constitutionality in 1961 *(Communist Party v. SACB)* but leaving undisturbed an appellate court holding in 1964 that the party as an organization could not be registered under the act. The Court here held that individuals could not be compelled to register as agents for the party without violating the Fifth Amendment right of freedom from self-incrimination.

December 6. Rogers v. Paul. 382 U. S. 198.

Without argument. Per curiam. White, Harlan, Clark and Fortas, JJ., dissenting in favor of oral argument.

Ordering prompt transfer of Negro students where the Court was satisfied that inaction by state was for purpose of perpetuating school segregation.

1966

January 17. Evans v. Newton. 382 U. S. 296.

Argued November 9, 10, 1965. Douglas, J., for the Court; White, Black, Stewart and Harlan, JJ., dissenting.

Holding that where private trustees maintain segregated private park at general public expense, their function is essentially public in nature and therefore subject to the standards demanded by the Fourteenth Amendment.

February 21. Rosenblatt v. Baer. 383 U. S. 75.

Argued October 20, 1965. Brennan, J., for the Court; Clark, Douglas and Stewart, JJ., concurring; Black, Douglas and Harlan, JJ., concurring in part and dissenting in part.

Extending the *Sullivan* "public official" doctrine to cover critical commentary on persons in any supervisory capacity in a public facility.

February 23. Brown v. Louisiana. 383 U. S. 131.

Argued December 6, 1965. Fortas, J., for the Court; Brennan and White, JJ., concurring; Black, Clark, Harlan and Stewart, JJ., dissenting.

Reversing breach of peace convictions of Negroes engaged in "stand-in" to protest segregation of public library. Black's dissent, denying the right of demonstrators to disrupt lawful public activity, was basis of majority holding in *Adderley v. Florida* (1966).

March 7. South Carolina v. Katzenbach. 383 U. S. 301.

Argued January 17, 18, 1966. Warren, C. J., for the Court; Black, J., concurring in part and dissenting in part.

In an original bill of complaint, South Carolina challenged the Voting Rights Act of 1965, particularly as to the provisions for bringing certain state electoral practices under Federal surveillance. The Court held the statute within the constitutional powers of Congress under the Fifteenth Amendment.

March 21. Memoirs v. Attorney General. 383 U. S. 413.

Argued December 7, 8, 1965. Brennan, J., for the Court; Black, Stewart and Douglas, JJ., concurring; Clark and Harlan, JJ., dissenting.

Extending the *Roth* obscenity doctrine and reiterating the test that to incur liability a publication must be "utterly without redeeming social value."

March 21. Ginzburg v. United States. 383 U. S. 463.

Argued December 7, 1965. Brennan, J., for the Court; Black, Douglas, Harlan and Stewart, JJ., dissenting.

In this case the majority applied the *Roth* test and found the defendant properly convicted of "prurient appeal."

March 21. Mishkin v. New York. 383 U. S. 502.

Argued December 7, 1965. Brennan, J., for the Court; Harlan, J., concurring; Douglas, Black and Stewart, JJ., dissenting.

In another obscenity case on this date, the majority found that publication aimed at deviant sexual groups and element of *scienter* present was properly held liable under existing statutes.

March 24. Harper v. Board of Education. 383 U. S. 663.

Argued January 25, 26, 1966. Douglas, J., for the Court; Black and Harlan, JJ., dissenting.

Invalidating state poll tax as denial of equal protection under Fourteenth Amendment.

March 28. United States v. Guest. 383 U. S. 745.

Argued November 9, 1965. Stewart, J., for the Court; Clark, Black and Fortas, JJ., concurring; Warren, C. J., Harlan, Brennan and Douglas, JJ., concurring in part and dissenting in part.

Remanding a case to trial court with instructions to prosecute case under Civil Rights Act of 1964 upon rule that a right of interstate travel exists and warrants judicial inquiry into conspiracies to deprive citizens of this right.

March 28. United States v. Price. 383 U. S. 787.

Argued November 5, 1965. Fortas, J., for the Court; Black, J., concurring.

Reversing a trial court which dismissed charges against defendants under Civil Rights Act of 1964 where statute provided for prosecution of any persons acting under "color of law" to deprive others of their constitutional rights. Cf. *United States v. Williams*, 341 U.S. 70 (1951). The principles enunciated in the *Price* and *Guest* cases were eventually incorporated in provisions of the Civil Rights Act of 1968. See Appendix D.

April 4. DeGregory v. Attorney General of New Hampshire. 383 U. S. 825.

Argued February 24, 1966. Douglas, J., for the Court; Harlan, Stewart and White, JJ., dissenting.

Upholding defendant in refusal to answer questions about prior rather than current affiliation with subversive groups, as lacking a nexus between defendant and activities under study.

April 18. Elfbrandt v. Russell. 384 U. S. 11.

Argued February 24, 1966. Douglas, J., for the Court; White, Clark, Harlan and Stewart, JJ., dissenting.

Holding Arizona loyalty oath unconstitutional under First Amendment protection of right of association, where statute failed to require proof of specific intent to further unlawful aims of an association, through defendant's affiliation.

April 19. Seagram & Sons v. Hostetter. 384 U. S. 35.

Argued February 23, 1966. Stewart, J., for the Court.

Sustaining New York price-fixing law on liquor, as within the powers reserved to the state under the Twenty-First Amendment.

June 6. Shepard v. Maxwell. 384 U. S. 333.

Argued February 28, 1966. Clark, J., for the Court; Black, J., dissenting.

Reversing a conviction in a sensational murder trial because blatant publicity attendant upon the proceedings had prejudiced defendant's right to a fair and impartial trial.

June 13. Miranda v. Arizona. 384 U. S. 436.

Argued February 28, March 1, 1966. Warren, C. J., for the Court; Clark, J., dissenting in part; Harlan, Stewart and White, JJ., dissenting.

In this and three companion cases, the right-to-counsel doctrine was further extended to require presence of counsel during interrogation of suspects and responsibility of interrogators to inform suspects of their right to remain silent.

June 13. Katzenbach v. Morgan. 384 U. S. 641.

Argued April 18, 1966. Brennan, J., for the Court; Douglas, J., concurring in part; Harlan and Stewart, JJ., dissenting.

Holding invalid a New York statute which required literacy in English, as this was enforced against Spanish-reading Puerto Ricans, as conflicting with the Voting Rights Act of 1965.

June 20. Johnson v. New Jersey. 384 U. S. 719.

Argued February 28, March 1, 2, 1966. Warren, C. J., for the Court; Harlan, Stewart and White, JJ., concurring; Black and Douglas, JJ., dissenting.

Limiting the retroactive effect of the right-to-counsel rule in *Escobedo*.

June 20. Schmerber v. California. 384 U. S. 757.

Argued April 25, 1966. Brennan, J., for the Court, Harlan and Stewart, JJ., concurring; Warren, C. J., Black and Douglas, JJ., dissenting.

Sustaining law enforcement officers in administering blood test for alcoholic content, as not amounting to self-incrimination.

June 20. Georgia v. Rachel. 384 U. S. 780.

Argued April 25, 26, 1966. Stewart, J., for the Court; Warren, C. J., Douglas, Brennan and Fortas, JJ., dissenting.

Majority denied that new civil rights enactments by Congress automatically compelled removal of such cases from state to Federal courts without explicit showing of doubt that litigants' rights could be protected in state courts. Dissent protested that purpose of removal was to facilitate rather than to limit removal wherever reasonable doubt as to impartial state trial existed.

November 14. Adderley v. Florida. 385 U. S. 39.

Argued October 18, 1966. Black, J., for the Court; Douglas, Fortas, Brennan, JJ., and Warren, C. J., dissenting.

Limiting the freedom of assembly for purposes of protesting against alleged discriminations, the majority held that conviction for trespass when ordered to leave non-public premises did not deny freedom of expression which could be exercised elsewhere.

December 5. Bond v. Floyd. 385 U. S. 116.
Argued November 10, 1966. Warren, C. J., for the Court.

State action in denying legislative seat to duly elected and qualified member, because of his militant criticism of national policy, held unconstitutional.

December 12. Lewis v. United States. 385 U. S. 206.
Argued October 17, 1966. Warren, C. J., for the Court; Brennan and Fortas, JJ., concurring; Douglas, J., dissenting.

Sustaining conviction, against Fourth Amendment complaint, where undercover investigator was invited by defendant to his home for purpose of transacting illegal business.

December 12. Fortson v. Morris. 385 U. S. 231.
Argued December 5, 1966. Black, J., for the Court; Warren, C. J., Douglas, Brennan and Fortas, JJ., dissenting.

Overturning a District Court ruling, based on *Gray v. Sanders,* which had held invalid state constitutional provision for election of a governor by a legislature in event of a failure of any candidate to receive a majority of the popular vote. The majority found nothing in the one man-one vote doctrine to prohibit such procedure as practical device.

December 12. Hoffa v. United States. 385 U. S. 293.
Argued October 23, 1966. Stewart, J., for the Court; Warren, C. J., Clark and Douglas, JJ., dissenting; White and Fortas, JJ., not participating.

Sustaining conviction of labor leader based on testimony of undercover agent where defendant's conversations with agent were voluntary even though unwitting. Cf. companion case *(Osborn v. United States)* where an accused person's voluntary conversation, tape-recorded, was ruled admissible.

1967

January 9. Time, Inc. v. Hill. 385 U. S. 374.
Argued April 27, 1966; reargued October 18, 19, 1966. Brennan, J., for the Court; Harlan, Black and Douglas, JJ., concurring; Warren, C. J., Fortas and Clark, JJ., dissenting.

In a divided opinion, the official opinion set aside a judgment obtained under New York's privacy statute because it was unclear that the statute required proof of reckless disregard for truth. The concurring judges argued that the case should be retried to settle this issue, but warned that they would, if the case were then appealed, review on the basis of the broad freedom of press concepts under the *Sullivan* rule.

January 9. Swann v. Adams. 385 U. S. 440.
Argued December 6, 1966. White, J., for the Court; Harlan and Stewart, JJ., dissenting.

On a previous hearing *(Swann v. Adams,* 378 U. S. 553) the Court had found Florida reapportionment plan inadequate. In now rejecting a revised

plan, the Court made clear that substantial deviation from equal representation in electoral districts would not be approved without persuasive reasons
for justifying the deviation.

January 16. Garrity v. New Jersey. 385 U. S. 493.

*Argued November 10, 1966. Douglas, J., for the Court; White, Harlan,
Clark and Stewart, JJ., dissenting.*

Invalidating a statute threatening forfeiture of public office where office
holder refused to waive privilege against self-incrimination.

January 16. Spevak v. Klein. 385 U. S. 511.

*Argued November 7, 1966. Douglas, J., for the Court; Fortas, J., concurring;
Harlan, Clark and Stewart, JJ., dissenting.*

Expanding *Garrity* doctrine and overruling earlier case of *Cohen v. Hurley*
(366 U. S. 117), majority held that threat of disbarment as penalty for
availing oneself of constitutional immunity was invalid.

January 23. Keyishian v. Board of Regents. 385 U. S. 589.

*Argued November 17, 1966. Brennan, J., for the Court; Clark, Harlan, Stewart
and White, JJ., dissenting.*

Substantially limiting the rule in *Adler v. Board of Education* (1952)
and New York's "Feinberg law," as being "overbroad" in penalizing association by public employees in allegedly subversive groups, in the light of
Elfbrandt v. Russell.

February 10. Twenty-Fifth Amendment ratified.

February 20. Chapman v. California. 386 U. S. 18.

*Argued December 7, 8, 1966. Black, J., for the Court; Stewart, J., concurring;
Harlan, J., dissenting.*

Overturning conviction in case where trial judge commented to jury on
defendant's failure to testify, against state constitutional provision barring
reversals in state appeals court for "harmless error."

February 20. Cooper v. California. 386 U. S. 58.

*Argued December 8, 1966. Black, J., for the Court; Warren, C. J., Douglas,
Brennan and Fortas, JJ., dissenting.*

Applying California's "harmless error" provision, majority upheld conviction where search and seizure of suspect's car was under valid forfeiture
statute and for purpose closely related to arrest.

March 10. Ramsey Clark becomes Attorney General.

March 13. Klopfer v. North Carolina. 386 U. S. 213.

*Argued December 6. 1966. Warren, C.J., for the Court; Stewart and Harlan,
JJ., concurring.*

Holding that indefinite postponement of prosecution after indictment,
and over defendant's protest, deprived him of right to speedy trial under
Sixth Amendment.

March 20. McCray v. Illinois. 386 U. S. 300.

Argued January 10, 11, 1967. Stewart, J., for the Court; Warren, C. J., Douglas, Brennan and Fortas, JJ., dissenting.

Sustaining, against Sixth Amendment claims, arrest made by narcotics squad officers without warrant but upon reliable information from undercover source.

May 15. In re Gault. 387 U. S. 1.

Argued December 6, 1966. Fortas, J., for the Court; Black and White, JJ., concurring; Harlan, J., concurring in part and dissenting in part; Stewart, J., dissenting.

Extending the privilege against self-incrimination and right to counsel to juvenile court proceedings.

May 29. Afroyim v. Rusk. 387 U. S. 203.

Argued February 20, 1967. Black, J., for the Court; Harlan, Clark, Stewart and White, JJ., dissenting.

Overruling *Perez v. Brownell* and denying Congress power to strip individuals of citizenship under implied sovereign power over foreign relations.

May 29. Reitman v. Mulkey. 387 U. S. 369.

Argued March 20, 21, 1967. White, J., for the Court; Douglas, J., concurring; Harlan, Clark, Black and Stewart, JJ., dissenting.

Sustaining the California supreme court, which had held a restrictive housing amendment ("Proposition 14") to its state constitution to conflict with the equal protection clause of the Fourteenth Amendment. Harlan's dissent continued his argument warning that the indefinite expansion of Fourteenth Amendment limits upon state action would fatally undermine the Federal system.

June 5. Camara v. Municipal Court. 387 U. S. 523.

Argued February 15, 1967. White, J., for the Court; Clark, J., dissenting.

In earlier cases (*Frank v. Maryland*, 359 U. S. 360; *Eaton v. Price*, 364 U. S. 263) a 5-4 majority had sustained convictions where householders had refused inspection of premises without warrant. These cases were now overruled in favor of Fourth Amendment interpretations in *Mapp v. Ohio* and *Ker v. California* as extended to the states. *See v. Seattle* was a companion case.

June 12. Loving v. Virginia. 388 U. S. 1.

Argued April 10, 1967. Warren, C. J., for the Court; Stewart, J., concurring.

Outlawing a state miscegenation statute.

June 12. Berger v. New York. 388 U. S. 41.

Argued April 13, 1967. Clark, J., for the Court; Douglas, J., concurring; Black, Harlan and White, JJ., dissenting.

Majority held invalid a New York statute defining permissible eavesdropping for inadequacy of judicial supervision and protective procedures. See *Katz v. United States* in next term.

June 12. Curtis Pub. Co. v. Butts. 388 U. S. 130.

Argued February 23, 1967. Harlan, J., for the Court; Warren, C. J., Black, Douglas, Brennan and White, JJ., concurring.

In this and a companion case (*Associated Press v. Walker*) the Court by a wide division but no dissents sought to restate the libel rule in *Sullivan*. In the first case the Court held that a publication relating to a well-known sports figure could be found liable for defamatory statements recklessly made. In the second case the Court held that reasonable efforts to report accurately on rapidly moving public events would reduce liability to proof of malicious intent.

June 12. United States v. Wade. 388 U. S. 218.

Argued February 16, 1967. Brennan, J., for the Court; Clark, J., concurring; Warren, C. J., Fortas, Douglas, Black, White, Harlan and Stewart, JJ., concurring in part and dissenting in part.

In a remarkable demonstration of non-unanimity, with eight Justices qualifying their concurrences, the Court ruled that police "line-ups" in absence of counsel made inadmissible identifications based solely on the "line-ups." Congressional criticism of the ruling was reflected partly in the provision in the Omnibus Crime Control and Safe Streets Act of 1968 for admissibility of certain types of eyewitness identification. Cf. also *Gilbert v. California*, 388 U. S. 263.

June 12. Stovall v. Denno. 388 U. S. 293.

Argued February 16, 1967. Brennan, J., for the Court; White, Harlan and Stewart, JJ., concurring in the result; Douglas, Fortas and Black, JJ., dissenting.

Limiting the retroactive effect of the *Wade* doctrine, the Court sought to establish the validity of criminal process under "old standards" (i. e., before Wade) on a parity with different process under the "new standards" established in *Wade*.

June 12. Jacobs v. New York. 388 U. S. 431.

Without oral argument. Per curiam; Brennan and Fortas, JJ., dissenting on procedure; Warren, C. J., dissenting.

Obscenity convictions dismissed as moot since time of suspended sentences had run. Dissents warned that unless reviewed, states might "insulate their law" from constitutional appeal by regular use of suspended sentences, which would expire before appeal could be heard.

October 2. Justice Marshall succeeds Clark.

November 6. Mora v. McNamara. 389 U. S. 934.

Certiorari denied. Stewart and Douglas, JJ., dissenting; Marshall, J., not participating.

In an unusual dissent from a routine order of the Court, denying review of an attempt by three noncommissioned officers to block orders for their shipment to Viet Nam, Stewart and Douglas urged that the Court might have considered the fundamental constitutional issues springing from the Congressional "Gulf of Tonkin resolution" of 1964.

December 5. Zwickler v. Koota. 389 U. S. 241.

Argued October 12, 1967. Brennan, J., for the Court; Harlan, J., concurring in the judgment.

In setting aside a New York law against distribution of anonymous handbills, the Court stressed the difference between an allegation of "vagueness," which might be left for lower court determination, and "overbreadth," which was a proper constitutional issue because it raised questions of infringement.

December 11. United States v. Robel. 389 U. S. 258.

Argued November 14, 1966; reargued October 9, 1967. Warren, C. J., for the Court; Brennan, J., concurring in result; White and Harlan, JJ., dissenting; Marshall, J., not participating.

Invalidating a section of Subversive Activities Control Act of 1950 which made criminal the acceptance of employment in defense industry by member of group known to be on subversive list, the majority held that this abridged constitutional right of association.

December 18. Katz v. United States. 389 U. S. 347.

Argued October 17, 1967. Stewart, J., for the Court; Douglas, Brennan, Harlan and White, JJ., concurring; Black, J., dissenting; Marshall, J., not participating.

Overruling *Olmstead v. United States* (1928) and *Goldman v. United States* (1942), under the general prohibitions of the Fourth Amendment. "Bugging" by electronic eavesdropping, authorized by proper judicial order, and not involving physical trespass, was suggested by the majority as permissible.

1968

January 16. Schneider v. Smith. 390 U. S. 17.

Argued December 12, 13, 1967. Douglas, J., for the Court; Black and Fortas, JJ., concurring; Stewart, White and Harlan, JJ., concurring in result; Marshall, J., not participating.

Applying the standard in *Robel* to hold invalid a statutory procedure for screening of merchant seamen for security purposes.

April 1. Avery v. Midland County. 390 U. S. 474.

Argued November 14, 1967. White, J., for the Court; Harlan, Fortas and Stewart, JJ., dissenting; Marshall, J., not participating.

Applying the principles of the reapportionment cases to local government units and declaring that there is no constitutional ground for substantial departures from equal population as a basis for representation.

April 8. United States v. Jackson. 390 U. S. 570.

Argued December 7, 1967. Stewart, J., for the Court; White and Black, JJ., dissenting; Marshall, J., not participating.

Discerned by some observers as a beginning of a judicial attack on the death penalty, the majority invalidated a provision of the Federal Kidnapping Act which authorized capital punishment "only if the jury should so recommend." Cf. *Boykin v. Alabama* (1969).

April 22. Ginsberg v. New York. 390 U. S. 629.

Argued January 16, 1968. Brennan, J., for the Court; Stewart, J., concurring in result; Harlan, J., concurring; Fortas, Douglas and Black, JJ., dissenting.

Affirming a New York state conviction of distributor of "girlie" publications to minors, as properly within the police power of the state to limit the type of material tending to flow into the hands of minors. Fortas protested that the decision amounted to arrogating to the state a parental responsibility for surveillance of minors' reading matter.

May 20. Levy v. Louisiana. 391 U. S. 68.

Argued March 27, 1968. Douglas, J., for the Court; Harlan, Black and Setwart, JJ., dissenting.

Invalidating a statute which limited recovery for parent's wrongful death to legitimate children; majority opinion rejected proposition that illegitimates are "nonpersons," and if persons constitutionally protected against invidious discrimination. Cf. companion case of *Glona v. American G. & L. Co.*, 391 U. S. 73.

May 20. Duncan v. Louisiana. 391 U. S. 145.

Argued January 17, 1968. White, J., for the Court; Black, Fortas and Douglas, JJ., concurring; Harlan, J., dissenting.

Extending to the states the jury trial guarantee of the Sixth Amendment.

May 20. Amalg. Food Employees v. Logan Valley Plaza. 391 U. S. 308.

Argued March 14, 1968. Marshall, J., for the Court; Douglas, J., concurring; Black, Harlan and White, JJ., dissenting.

Affirming the right of peaceful picketing of a privately owned shopping center. Majority opinion found that such a center had all the attributes of a public place; Black, who had written the original opinion in *Marsh v. Alabama* relied upon by the majority, protested that *Marsh* doctrine had applied only to private developments with all the attributes of a community.

June 10. Terry v. Ohio. 392 U. S. 1.

Argued December 12, 1967. Warren, C. J., for the Court; Black, Harlan and White, JJ., concurring; Douglas, J., dissenting.

With some limitations, the majority found a "stop and frisk" law constitutionally permissible against the argument that such police power was void under the search and seizure prohibition.

June 10. Flast v. Cohen. 392 U. S. 83.

Argued March 12, 1968. Warren, C. J., for the Court; Douglas, Stewart and Fortas, JJ., concurring; Harlan, J., dissenting.

Qualifying the rule in *Frothingham v. Mellon* (1923) as to the circumstances creating standing to bring a constitutional suit, and affirming such standing where the party can establish his interest in the Federal spending power as a taxpayer and also can point to a specific constitutional limitation which allegedly has been breached.

June 10. Maryland v. Wirtz. 392 U. S. 183.

Argued April 23, 1968. Harlan, J., for the Court; Douglas and Stewart, JJ., dissenting; Marshall, J., not participating.

Supporting the government action in extending the jurisdiction of the National Labor Relations Board to state hospitals and schools.

June 10. Board of Education v. Allen. 392 U. S. 236.

Argued April 22, 1968. White, J., for the Court; Harlan, J., concurring; Black, Douglas and Fortas, JJ., dissenting.

Supporting a New York law lending textbooks to children in primary and secondary schools, as applied to parochial school students.

June 17. Jones v. Alf. Mayer Co. 392 U. S. 409.

Argued April 1, 2, 1968. Stewart, J., for the Court; Douglas, J., concurring; Harlan and White, JJ., dissenting.

Sustaining Congressional enactment prohibiting racial discrimination in the purchase or sale of real estate.

June 17. Powell v. Texas. 392 U. S. 514.

Argued March 7, 1968. Marshall, J., for the Court; Black and Harlan, JJ., concurring; White, J., concurring in the result; Fortas, Douglas, Brennan and Stewart, JJ., dissenting.

Qualifying the rule in *Robinson v. California* (1962) which had limited incarceration of drug addicts, a narrow majority (four Justices plus one) declined to apply the rule to set aside the conviction of a chronic alcoholic. Dissent and division of majority cast doubt on the general power of the state to convict and incarcerate such persons under all circumstances.

October 12. Erwin N. Griswold becomes Solicitor General.

October 15. Williams v. Rhodes. 393 U. S. 93.

Argued October 7, 1968. Black, J., for the Court; Warren, C. J., White and Stewart, JJ., dissenting.

In test of state voting laws with reference to ability of third parties to get on ballots, majority held that right to vote was of such fundamental importance that state had to demonstrate beyond doubt its compelling interest in setting higher standards for small political followings to obtain a place on ballot.

November 18. Firemen v. Chi., R. I. & P. R. Co. 393 U. S. 191.
Argued October 22, 1968. Black, J., for the Court; Douglas, J., dissenting; Fortas, J., not participating.

"Full train crew" laws challenged by carriers were sustained by majority opinion on ground that it was exclusively within legislative competence to determine whether burden placed on carriers was outweighed by safety of employees in limiting hours and conditions of work.

1969

January 20. Richard M. Nixon inaugurated as President.

January 20. Hunter v. Erickson. 393 U. S. 385.
Argued November 13, 1968. White, J., for the Court; Black, J., dissenting.

Invalidating Akron city charter amendment which, like California's "Proposition 14," would have barred city council from enacting open housing ordinance, as violation of equal protection clause.

January 21. John Mitchell becomes Attorney General.

March 10. Shuttlesworth v. Birmingham. 394 U. S. 147.
Argued November 18, 1968. Stewart, J., for the Court; Harlan, J., concurring; Black, J., concurring in result; Marshall, J., not participating.

Latest in a long series of tests of local police power *versus* freedom of peaceful demonstration, this case held that where right to parade in demonstration was limited by undefined power to issue parade permit, the permit ordinance was unconstitutional.

April 7. Stanley v. Georgia. 394 U. S. 557.
Argued January 14, 15, 1969. Marshall, J., for the Court; Black, J., concurring.

Holding unconstitutional a statute which made mere personal possession of allegedly obscene material a crime.

April 21. Street v. New York. 394 U. S. 557.
Argued October 21, 1968. Harlan, J., for the Court; Warren, C. J., Black, White and Fortas, JJ., dissenting.

Dismissing, by 5-4 majority, conviction for burning American flag as symbolic expression of protest; Harlan's opinion suggested that facts of case indicated prosecution might have been for unpopularity of defendant's argument and thus infringement on his First Amendment rights.

May 5. Moore v. Ogilvie. 394 U. S. 814.
Argued March 27, 1969. Douglas, J., for the Court; Stewart and Harlan, JJ., dissenting.

Overruling *MacDougall v. Green* (1948) and invalidating Illinois electoral statute which required signatures of voters from fifty counties to accompany petition for independent candidates to be placed on ballot. Majority contended that statute failed to ensure equitable standard of electoral representation. But cf. *Williams v. Rhodes.*

April 21. Shapiro v. Thompson. 394 U. S. 618.

Argued June 17, 1968; reargued October 23, 24, 1968. Brennan, J., for the Court; Stewart, J., concurring; Warren, C. J., Black and Harlan, JJ., dissenting.

Affirming judgment of three-judge court that statutory requirements of prior local residency to qualify for public welfare was unconstitutionally discriminatory.

May 15. Justice Fortas resigned after series of allegations generated by Justice Department as to conflicts of interest.

June 2. O'Callahan v. Parker. 395 U. S. 258.

Argued January 23, 1969. Douglas, J., for the Court; Harlan, Stewart and White, JJ., dissenting.

Extending the *Kinsella* rule on servicemen and non-military offenses, majority held such defendants were entitled to civil trial even while in service, where crime was not "service-connected."

June 2. Gaston County v. United States. 395 U. S. 285.

Argued April 23, 24, 1969. Harlan, J., for the Court; Black, J., dissenting.

In this and a related case in this term *(Allen v. Board of Elections,* 393 U. S. 544) Court majority gave broad construction to provision of Voting Rights Act of 1965 as to illicit voting qualifications found in state laws.

June 2. Daniel v. Paul. 395 U. S. 298.

Argued March 24, 25, 1969. Brennan, J., for the Court; Black, J., dissenting.

Extending the "public accommodation" standard of the Civil Rights Act of 1964 to private recreational facility.

June 9. Brandenburg v. Ohio. 395 U. S. 444.

Argued February 27, 1969. Per curiam; Black and Douglas, JJ., concurring.

Invalidating a state criminal syndicalism law.

June 16. Powell v. McCormack. 395 U. S. 486.

Argued April 21, 1969. Warren, C. J., for the Court; Douglas, J., concurring; Stewart, J., dissenting.

Reversing lower courts and finding House of Representatives improperly barred Congressman Adam Clayton Powell from his seat when he met the specific qualifications set out in Article I of Constitution.

June 23. Benton v. Maryland. 395 U. S. 784.

Argued December 16, 1968; reargued March 24, 1969. Marshall, J., for the Court; White, J., concurring; Harlan and Stewart, JJ., dissenting.

Overruling *Palko v. Connecticut* (1937) and holding double jeopardy standards of Fifth Amendment extend to states through Fourteenth. Marshall's opinion declared that once it is decided that a particular Bill of Rights guarantee is "fundamental to the American scheme of justice" it applies to both Federal and state law.

June 23. Warren E. Burger becomes Chief Justice.

The Supreme Court and the
First and Second New Deals

The cases recapitulated in outline form below will suffice to document the shift in constitutional ideology of the Supreme Court in the critical years in which the statutory implementation of the first New Deal, so called, was systematically invalidated, and the immediately following period in which comparable statutes of the second New Deal were sustained. While it is literally true that Congress in its second enactment undertook to correct specific flaws as the Court might have pointed them out, and while it is also true that on review of the second enactment the Court found a means of distinguishing between the former invalid law and the present valid one, the procedure did not disguise the fact that an intellectual shift of one hundred and eighty degrees had taken place. It was volubly attested in the dissents of the conservative minority, and was equally well illustrated in the rationale of the new majority.

This shift—representing the end of half a century of *laissez-faire* jurisprudence with which the Constitution's second century was ushered in—has already been described in Chapters 3-5 of the text. Because it is one of the major turning points in American constitutional history, however, it warrants this further documentation. The outline which follows cites the case which invalidated the original proposition of law, with a representative quotation from the prevailing majority view, followed by a comparable example from the case which reversed the constitutional posture of the Court on this subject and set it on the course it has continued to the present.

1. The issue of agricultural relief.

May 12, 1933. Agricultural Adjustment Act undertook to establish program of crop controls and price subsidies under processing taxes, acting under general welfare clause.

January 1, 1936. Roberts, for the Court in *United States v. Butler:*

> Congress has no power to enforce its commands on the farmer to the ends sought by the . . . Act. It must follow that it may not indirectly accomplish those ends by taxing and spending to purchase compliance. The Constitution and the entire plan of our government negative any such use of the power to tax and to spend as the act undertakes to authorize. It does not help to declare that local conditions throughout the nation have created a situation of national concern; for this is but to say that whenever there is a widespread similarity of local conditions, Congress may ignore constitutional limitations upon its own powers and usurp those reserved to the states. If, in lieu of compulsory regulation of subjects within the states' reserved jurisdiction, which is prohibited, the Congress could invoke the taxing and spending power as a means to

accomplish the same end, [this] would become the instrument for total subversion of the governmental powers reserved to the individual states.

June 6, 1937. Reenactment of Agricultural Adjustment Act under commerce clause, with nominal modifications in original machinery.

April 17, 1939. Chief Justice Hughes, in an opinion upholding the Tobacco Control Act on January 4 *(Currin v. Wallace)*, sought to distinguish it from the *Butler* attack on the parent statute by quoting older cases to the effect that "Congress is amply authorized to pass measures to protect interstate commerce." Roberts, in *Mulford v. Smith*, relied on the *Currin* holding to uphold the second AAA; but Butler in dissent pointed out that the basic objective in both statutes had been to regulate agricultural production, a power explicitly denied to the Federal government in *Butler*.

*　　*　　*

June 28, 1934. The first Frazier-Lemke farm mortgage moratorium law sought to relieve bankrupt farmers by permitting them to readjust their debts in terms of current prices, or to operate their farms under court order under certain terms.

May 27, 1935. Brandeis, for a unanimous Court in *Louisville Bank v. Radford*, acknowledged that bankruptcy laws had gradually progressed from a basic concern to ensure equitable distribution of assets to creditors to a concern that the debtor be finally discharged of his obligations. But here the Court held that the law operated to discharge the debtor without any assurance of ultimate distribution of assets to creditors, and thereby deprived the latter of property without due process.

August 28, 1935. The second Frazier-Lemke Act was passed by Congress, with a proviso for the staying of claims.

March 29, 1937. Brandeis, again for a unanimous Court in *Wright v. Vinton Branch*, upheld this statute as satisfying the due process clause where Congress made clear its intent to provide debtors with relief without extinguishing creditors' right to future settlement.

2. The issue of industrial relief.

June 16, 1933. The first New Deal climaxed in the passage of the National Industrial Recovery Act, Title I of which undertook to delegate to the executive broad authority to negotiate with industry on matters of price-fixing, production controls and the like.

May 27, 1935. Chief Justice Hughes, in *Schechter Poultry Corp. v. United States*, after pointing out the numerous admitted flaws in the hastily drafted legislation, then added:

> It is not the province of the Court to consider the economic advantages or disadvantages of such a centralized system. It is sufficient to say that the Federal Constitution does not provide for it. Our growth

and development have called for wide use of the commerce power. .....
But the authority of the Federal government may not be pushed to such
an extreme as to destroy the distinction, which the commerce clause itself
establishes, between commerce "among the several states" and the internal
concerns of a state.

July 5, 1935. Approximately six weeks after this decision, Congress
enacted the National Labor Relations Act, a statute enlarging upon the
Labor Disputes Joint Resolution of 1934 (see Appendix D) and Title II of
the NIRA. While the judicial review of the NLRA was not technically a
counterpoint to the *Schechter* decision, its rationale was diametrically opposed to the dictum in *Schechter*.

April 12, 1937. Hughes delivered the opinion of the Court in *National
Labor Relations Board v. Jones & Laughlin Steel Corp.:*

> The grant of authority to the Board does not purport to extend to
> the relationship between all industrial employees and employers. . . . It
> purports to reach only what may be deemed to burden or obstruct
> [interstate] commerce and, thus qualified, it must be construed as con-
> templating the exercise of control within constitutional bounds. It is a
> familiar principle that acts which directly burden or obstruct interstate or
> foreign commerce, or its free flow, are within the reach of the Congres-
> sional power.

*   *   *

August 30, 1935. The principal effort to salvage some of the benefits
from Title I of the NIRA was the first Guffey Bituminous Coal Act, creating
a "little NRA" for the coal mining industry.

May 18, 1936. In finding this statute unconstitutional, Sutherland for
the majority voiced the firm conviction of the Old Legality:

> The proposition, often advanced and as often discredited, that the
> power of the Federal government inherently extends to purposes affecting
> the nation as a whole with which the states severally cannot deal or
> cannot adequately deal, and the related notion that Congress, entirely
> apart from those powers delegated by the Constitution, may enact laws
> to promote the general welfare, have never been accepted but always
> definitely rejected by this Court.

April 26, 1937. With slight modifications, a second Guffey Act was
passed, with its prospects for being upheld depending upon a changing
constitutional rationale.

May 20, 1940. Douglas, speaking for the Court in *Sunshine Coal Co. v.
Adkins,* explicitly refuted the Sutherland dogma:

> It was the judgment of Congress that price-fixing and the elimination
> of unfair competitive practices were appropriate methods for prevention
> of the financial ruin, low wages, poor working conditions, strikes, and
> disruption of the channels of trade which followed in the wake of the
> demoralized price structures in this industry. If the strategic character of

this industry in our economy and the chaotic conditions which have prevailed in it do not justify legislation, it is difficult to imagine what would. To invalidate this act we would have to deny the existence of power on the part of Congress under the commerce clause to deal directly and specifically with those forces which in its judgment should not be permitted to dislocate an important segment of our economy and to disrupt and burden interstate channels of trade. That step could not be taken without plain disregard of the Constitution.

3. The issue of personal economic security.

With the enactment of unemployment compensation and old age retirement benefits in the Social Security Act, the New Deal completed the basic steps in developing a welfare-oriented, nationally planned surveillance of the economic system. Where, in the *Alton Railroad* case in the spring of 1935 and the *Morehead* case in the spring of 1936, the majority had made sweeping recitals of the evils of paternalistic capitalism or government, the rationale of the New Legality was on the verge of its own breakthrough. In the late summer of 1935, with the Social Security Act, and the early summer of 1938, with the Fair Labor Standards (Wage-Hour) Act, Congress stated the ultimate legislative propositions for the New Legality. When, in the Social Security cases in 1937 and in *United States v. Darby* in 1941, the Court unequivocally upheld the propositions as principles of constitutional law, the New Legality was an accomplished fact.

May 24, 1937. Ninety days before enactment of Social Security by Congress, the Court in invalidating a pension plan under the Railroad Retirement Act had confidently declared: "The meaning of the commerce and due process clauses of the Constitution is not so easily enlarged" by Congressional authorization to management and labor to reach voluntary agreements on old age pensions. "It is an attempt for social ends to impose by sheer fiat" an industry-wide social security system. Now, in rebuttal, Cardozo speaking for the majority said of the nationwide system:

> The problem is plainly national in area and dimensions. Moreover, laws of the separate states cannot deal with it effectively. Congress, at least, had a basis for that belief. . . . Apart from the failure of resources, states and local government are at times reluctant to increase so heavily the burden of taxation to be borne by their residents for fear of placing themselves in a position of economic disadvantage as compared with neighbors or competitors. . . .
> Whether wisdom or unwisdom resides in the scheme of benefits set forth. . . , it is not for us to say. The answer to such inquiries must come from Congress, not the courts. Our concern here, as often, is with power, not with wisdom.

February 3, 1941. Stone, who within six months would become Chief Justice, in speaking for the Court on the child labor prohibition in the Wage-Hour Act, pronounced the peroration on the Old Legality, which had closed the doors to Federal regulation of the subject for more than a generation. Now, declaring the rule in *Hammer v. Dagenhart* to be totally defunct, Stone said:

> The power of Congress over interstate commerce "is complete in itself, may be exercised to its utmost extent, and acknowledges no limitations other than are prescribed by the Constitution." [Marshall, C. J., in] *Gibbons v. Ogden.* . . . That power can neither be enlarged nor diminished by the exercise or non-exercise of state power. . . . Congress, following its own conception of public policy concerning the restrictions which may appropriately be imposed on interstate commerce, is free to exclude from the commerce articles whose use in the states for which they are destined it may conceive to be injurious to the public health, morals or welfare, even though the state has not sought to regulate their use. . . .
>
> Such regulation is not a forbidden invasion of state power merely because either its motive or its consequence is to restrict the use of articles of commerce within the states of destination; and is not prohibited unless by other Constitutional provisions. It is no objection to the assertion of the power to regulate interstate commerce that its exercise is attended by the same incidents which attend the exercise of the police power of the states.

In the final analysis, the breakthrough in constitutional law which came in the period following the 1937 crisis was simply a recognition by the Court of a maximum (rather than, as under *laissez-faire,* a minimum) latitude in the lawmaking bodies, Congressional and state, to determine for themselves the subject matter to which their constitutional powers could be applied. Once that had been determined upon, the restrictive interpretation of the commerce power, the tax power, the general welfare and "necessary and proper" clauses which had been the hallmark of the Old Legality for the period from the eighties to the Great Depression had to give way. This was the theme of the period of Stone's Chief Justiceship, which inevitably took on the appearance of chaos; but it was the chaos of dismantling the obsolete which was necessary to make way for the new structure.

If the freedom of government to act was the basic principle evolving from the Hughes-Stone decade, from 1937 through 1946, the next logical question—to be disposed of by the Warren Court—was the obligation created by the Constitution itself, to compel action in the face of inaction. This led in turn to the epochal decisions in *Brown v. Board of Education, Baker v. Carr,* and *Gideon v. Wainwright.* With these propositions placed at its apex, the New Legality which came into being in the New Deal was virtually completed.

Bibliography

The following paragraphs complement the Bibliography in *The Old Legality,* focussing upon materials relating to the Court and the Constitution for the period since 1932. There have been a substantial number of new titles in the interval since the first volume of this study went to press, and these are included in the present note, attesting to the undiminishing output of commentary on constitutionalism in our day.

It is obvious that the closer one comes to the present, the fewer are the primary source materials which can be available. There have been, as noted below, a few published collections of public papers of individual Justices, of variable quality as reference books, but none of the Court members of recent decades has deposited significant amounts of documents in collections available for scholarly study. What individual Justices will actually permit to be preserved and examined, also, varies with their sense of the balance between judicial proprieties and the responsibility to history.

For the period of the present study, a relatively small but highly informative body of documents has become available in the judiciary files in the various Presidential libraries. Beginning with Franklin D. Roosevelt's plan to construct a library for his private and public papers at Hyde Park, New York, Congress has vested in the National Archives the responsibility for accepting and maintaining such depositories. These now include, in addition to the Roosevelt Library, those of Herbert Hoover at West Branch, Iowa, Harry S Truman at Independence, Missouri, Dwight D. Eisenhower at Abilene, Kansas, John Fitzgerald Kennedy at Cambridge, Massachusetts and Lyndon B. Johnson at Austin, Texas. The Roosevelt, Truman and Eisenhower Libraries were of particular value to the author of the present work, and the vast treasury of materials on the New Deal to be found at Hyde Park has already provided much of the material for Arthur M. Schlesinger's volumes on *The Age of Franklin D. Roosevelt,* Leonard Baker's interesting recapitulation of the judiciary fight of 1937, *Back to Back: The Duel Between F. D. R. and the Supreme Court,* and—probably the most fascinating work of all for students of the Court and Constitution—*Roosevelt and Frankfurter: Their Correspondence, 1928-1945,* edited and annotated by Max Freedman.

While the staffs of the Presidential Libraries and the National Archives, as well as those of the Supreme Court Library and, of course, the Library of Congress, are consistently cooperative, there is often more difficulty in using recent documents still within the jurisdiction of the Department of Justice. It is understandable that some contemporary records must be classified in the public interest, for a reasonable period of time; it is also conceded that the Department, unlike the foregoing agencies, is not organized primarily to serve the needs of researchers. The most annoying problem, however, is the shifting policy on accessibility of materials—one administration making certain documents available to some scholars, the following administration withdrawing the same documents from other scholars who by accident of time happen to come along later.

Despite the lack of primary source material in the form of papers of individual members of the Court, the secondary works, in both book and periodical form, relating to the Justices are of primary importance in understanding the personalities and careers of the men themselves. And despite the fact that nine of these men were in active service on the Court as the study reached its stopping point, a surprising amount of printed literature exists for most of them. A number of the Justices for this period—Cardozo, Douglas, Frankfurter, Jackson, Rutledge—were highly productive writers, whose own works bear study in any effort to understand their interests and viewpoints. Representative titles for these men have been cited within their biographical sketches in Appendix A, and should be referred to in connection with the bibliographies which follow.

BLACK, HUGO LAFAYETTE. Not surprisingly, Justice Black has been the subject of a number of studies from his first years on the Court. His first decade is treated in John P. Frank's *Mr. Justice Black: The Man and His Opinions* (New York, 1949). This was followed the next year by Charlotte Williams' competent biography, *Hugo L. Black: A Study in the Judicial Process* (Baltimore, 1950). Wallace Mendelson's brief monograph, *Justices Black and Frankfurter: Conflict in the Court* (Chicago, 1961) was one of the early scholarly analyses of the nature of activism and restraint as practiced by these two protagonists. An illuminating collection of Black's opinions was edited by Irving Dilliard under the title, *One Man's Stand for Freedom: Mr. Justice Black and the Bill of Rights* (New York, 1963). Most recent is Stephen P. Strickland's *Hugo Black and the Supreme Court: A Symposium* (Indianapolis and New York, 1967).

Black's career has been studied in periodical literature from his earliest judicial activity to the present. W. M. Barnett in "Mr. Justice Black and the Supreme Court" in 8 *Univ. of Chicago L. Rev.* 20 (December, 1940) gives a contemporary assessment of the subject, while Daniel M. Berman's "Mr. Justice Black: The Early Years," 8 *Catholic Univ. L. Rev.* 103 (May, 1959), provides a retrospective view. Berman also has written, "Freedom and Mr. Justice Black: Record After Twenty Years," 25 *Missouri L. Rev.* 155

(April, 1960). Another early assessment was written by Fred Rodell, "Justice Hugo Black," 59 *American Mercury,* 153 (August, 1944), 762 (December, 1944), 60 *id.* 508 (April, 1945).

The famous interview between the Justice and Professor Edmond Cahn, under the title, "Justice Black and First Amendment Absolutes," appears in 37 *N.Y.U. L. Rev.* EDT (June, 1962). In much the same vein is C. A. Reid's article, "Mr. Justice Black and the Living Constitution," 76 *Harvard L. Rev.* 673 (February, 1963). Of numerous symposia, two of the most useful are in 65 *Yale Law J.* 449 *et seq.* (February, 1956) and in 14 *U.C.L.A. L. Rev.* 397 *et seq.* (January, 1967). To the question of whether the Justice has turned conservative in recent years, the most effective answer is provided by a onetime law clerk of the jurist, A. E. Dick Howard, in "Mr. Justice Black: The Negro Protest Movement and the Rule of Law," 53 *Va. L. Rev.* 1030 (June, 1967).

BRENNAN, WILLIAM JOSEPH. The Justice delivered a series of papers before the Center for the Study of Democratic Institutions which was then published under the title, *The Bill of Rights and the States* (Santa Barbara, Calif., 1961). A collection of his opinions has been edited by Stephen J. Friedman under the title, *An Affair with Freedom* (New York, 1967).

An informative background article to Friedman's book is his "Mr. Justice Brennan: The First Decade," in 80 *Harvard L. Rev.* 7 (November, 1966). Two early studies are the article by F. P. McQuade and A. T. Kardos, "Mr. Justice Brennan and His Legal Philosophy," 33 *Notre Dame Lawyer,* 321 (May, 1958) and the article by Daniel M. Berman, "Mr. Justice Brennan: A Preliminary Appraisal," 7 *Catholic Univ. L. Rev.* 1 (January, 1958).

BYRNES, JAMES FRANCIS. The brief Court tenure of this Justice has not invited any detailed studies in book or periodical literature. He is best understood in his own two books, *Speaking Frankly!* (New York, 1947), a vindication of his own policies in the late New Deal period, and *All in a Lifetime* (New York, 1958), an autobiography.

CARDOZO, BENJAMIN NATHAN. The considerable professional writing of this jurist is suggested in some of the titles appearing under his name in Appendix A. A book list about Cardozo approaches equally respectable proportions, beginning with Bernard L. Shientag's *Opinions and Writings of Benjamin N. Cardozo* (New York, 1930). James P. Pollard studied the first years on the Supreme Court in *Mr. Justice Cardozo: A Liberal Mind in Action* (New York, 1935), and Beryl H. Levy traced some of the seminal doctrines of the jurist in *Cardozo and Frontiers of Legal Thinking* (New York, 1938). Moses J. Aronson wrote an article, "Cardozo's Doctrine of Social Justice," in 4 *J. Social Philos.* 5 (October, 1938) and also edited a volume of *Essays Dedicated to Benjamin N. Cardozo,* published jointly by Columbia, Harvard and Yale Universities in 1939. A doctoral dissertation on *The Judicial Philosophy of Justice Cardozo: A Study in*

Mediation (Seattle, 1958) reflects the continuing interest in the intellectual heritage left by this member of the Court.

Margaret E. Hall has assembled a representative group of works in *Selected Writings of Benjamin Nathan Cardozo* (New York, 1947, 1967). Among professional journals there is a short but insightful piece by Justice Douglas, "Mr. Justice Cardozo," in 58 *Michigan L. Rev.* 549 (February, 1960), a symposium under the general title, "Judicial Process Revisited," 71 *Yale L. J.* 195 *et seq.* (December, 1961), and a good review of his later career in "Mr. Justice Cardozo and the New Deal Court," 12 *J. Public L.* 383 (1963).

CLARK, TOM C. Two useful articles on this Justice are C. B. Dutton's "Mr. Justice Tom C. Clark," 26 *Indiana L. J.* 169 (Winter, 1951), and John P. Frank's "Justice Tom Clark and Judicial Administration," 46 *Texas L. Rev.* 1 (November, 1967).

DOUGLAS, WILLIAM ORVILLE. The prodigious output of this jurist is suggested by the selected titles in Appendix A, which are only representative of his writing. Vern Countryman has written a general study of his work on the Court in *Douglas of the Supreme Court* (New York, 1959), and Gilbert L. Oddo has written on *Mr. Justice Douglas and the Roosevelt Court* (Washington, 1952).

Amid a long list of periodical literature, the following may be mentioned: two symposia respectively appearing in 39 *Washington L. Rev.* 1 *et seq.* (Spring, 1964) and in 73 *Yale L. J.* 915 *et seq.* (May, 1964); two articles by Leon Epstein, "Economic Predilections of Justice Douglas," 1949 *Wisconsin L. Rev.* 531 (May, 1949) and "Justice Douglas and Civil Liberties," 1951 *id.* 125 (January, 1951); two Washington correspondents wrote on the subect in "Mr. Justice Douglas," by Richard L. Neuberger, 185 *Harper's,* 312 (August, 1942), and "Washington's Angry Scotsman," by Jack Alexander in 215 *Saturday Evening Post,* 9 (October 17, 1942), and Fred Rodell did an article on "Bill Douglas, American," in 61 *American Mercury,* 656 (December, 1945), 62 *id.* 251 (February, 1946).

FORTAS, ABE. In the brief and controversial career of this member of the Court, one particularly timely and thoughtful essay was produced under his name—*Concerning Dissent and Civil Disobedience* (New York, 1968)—which remains an ironic commentary on the constitutional issues which contributed to the Senate hostility to the man himself.

FRANKFURTER, FELIX. Another of the scholars on the bench—the title of the single biography on the man which has been written to date—Justice Frankfurter produced a series of books which illuminated some of the major constitutional issues in national history. *The Case of Sacco and Vanzetti* (Boston, 1927) precipitated a furore in its day, but his work on *The Business of the Supreme Court* (New York, 1928) in collaboration with James M. Landis, and on *The Labor Injunction* (New York, 1930) in collaboration with Nathan Greene are considered by scholars to be the definitive treatment of these subjects. *The Commerce Clause Under Marshall, Taney and Waite* (Chapel Hill, 1937), originally delivered as the Weil Lectures on American Citizenship at the University of North Carolina, is one of the best succinct statements on constitutional history in its formative period, only equalled in quality by his *Mr. Justice Holmes and the Supreme Court* (Cambridge, 1961), a reprint of both his biographical note on Holmes in the *Dictionary of American Biography* and three lectures on American civilization delivered at Harvard University in 1938.

Frankfurter has been the subject of three highly useful and complementary books: Helen Shirley Thomas wrote *Felix Frankfurter: Scholar on the Bench* (Baltimore, 1960); Harlan B. Phillips transcribed some of the interviews from Columbia University's project in Oral History as *Felix Frankfurter Reminisces* (New York, 1960); and Max Freedman edited the letters sent by the jurist to the New Deal leader in *Roosevelt and Frankfurter: Their Correspondence, 1928-1945* (Boston, 1967). Mendelson's study of *Conflict on the Court,* already mentioned, is also highly pertinent for an understanding of the Justice and his work. Mendelson has also edited two collections: *Felix Frankfurter: A Tribute* (New York, 1964) and *Felix Frankfurter: The Judge* (New York, 1964).

Among many articles on Frankfurter, two symposia—in 67 *Yale L. J.* 179 *et seq.* (December, 1957) and in 76 *Harvard L. Rev.* 1 *et seq.* (November, 1962)—and a series of papers in tribute and appraisal in 26 *Univ. of Chicago L. Rev.* 1 *et seq.,* 205 *et seq.* (Autumn, 1958 and Winter, 1959) are particularly valuable. Archibald MacLeish's "Felix Frankfurter: A Lesson in Faith," in 1966 *Supreme Court Review,* 1 (Chicago, 967), and Emmerich Handler's "The Fourth Amendment, Federalism and Mr. Justice Frankfurter," 8 *Syracuse L. Rev.* 1 66 (Spring, 1957), are also recommended.

GOLDBERG, ARTHUR. Although the tenure of this Justice was relatively brief, it was the subject of a book by Daniel P. Moynihan, *Defenses of Freedom: Public Papers of Arthur J. Goldberg* (New York, 1966), and one article, "Constitutional Prejudice for Liberty and Equality: Mr. Justice Goldberg," by J. F. Marvin in 34 *Univ. of Missouri/Kansas City L. Rev.* 289 (June, 1966).

HUGHES, CHARLES EVANS. A wealth of original material on the two periods of Hughes' service on the Supreme Court is to be found in his papers deposited in the Library of Congress, including a detailed autobiography in manuscript form. The author is grateful for the kind permission of the Chief Justice's daughter, Mrs. William T. Gossett, to examine and quote from these papers. It is also gratifying to know that the autobiographical notes and other selected papers are now being edited for publication, for the unique role played by this jurist during one of the critical constitutional eras in modern times warrants the fullest study.

The definitive biography of the jurist is Merlo J. Pusey's *Charles Evans Hughes* (New York, 1952), a two-volume work of insightful scholarship.

Complementing this is an intensive study of Hughes as a judge in Samuel Hendel's *Charles Evans Hughes and the Supreme Court* (New York, 1951). C. Herman Pritchett includes a substantial discussion of Hughes' administrative abilities as Chief Justice in his work on *The Roosevelt Court* (New York, 1948) from the time of the confrontation of 1937 until the coming of Fred Vinson and the changing of the bench to the Truman Court. Hughes' own authoritative work, *The Supreme Court of the United States* (New York, 1929), is based upon a series of lectures he delivered at Columbia University in 1927 and provides significant perspective for the Chief Justice's own constitutional predilections as well as remaining a valuable commentary on the bench itself.

Edwin McElwain's article, "Business of the Supreme Court as Conducted by Chief Justice Hughes," 63 *Harvard L. Rev.* 5 (November, 1949), is a good supplement to Pritchett's volume, mentioned above. Alpheus Thomas Mason has a good summary of his judicial contributions in "Charles Evans Hughes: An Appeal to the Bar of History," 6 *Vanderbilt L. Rev.* 1 (December, 1952). Another summary is by M. W. Loper, "The Court of Charles Evans Hughes: Contributions to Civil Liberties," 12 *Wayne L. Rev.* 535 (Spring, 1966).

JACKSON, ROBERT HOUGHWOUT. Perhaps the most complex of the varied personalities to serve on the Court, Jackson has been the subject of a continuing series of professional studies of his jurisprudence. His own book, *The Struggle for Judicial Supremacy* (New York, 1941), was a well-documented though critical contemporary study of the constitutional crisis under the New Deal. Eugene C. Gerhardt's *America's Advocate—Robert H. Jackson* (Indianapolis, New York, 1958) is the basic biographical study. Two recent studies are Glendon Schubert's *Dispassionate Justice: A Synthesis of the Judicial Opinions of Robert H. Jackson* (Indianapolis, New York, 1969) and *Mr. Justice Jackson: Four Lectures in His Honor* (New York, 1969), delivered by Chief Judge Charles Desmond of the New York Court of Appeals, Professor Paul Freund, Associate Justice Potter Stewart and Lord Shawcross, chief prosecutor at the Nuremberg trials.

Since his death, the Justice has been the topic of a number of law review articles, including the highly informative symposium in 8 *Stanford L. Rev.* 3 *et seq.* (December, 1955). W. B. Lawless' study, "Mr. Justice Jackson: The Struggle for Federal Supremacy," 37 *Notre Dame Lawyer,* 489 (May, 1962), and D. J. Simpson's "Robert H. Jackson and the Doctrine of Judicial Restraint," 3 *U.C.L.A. L. Rev.* 325 (April, 1956), cover two key aspects of his jurisprudence. Appraisals of his work are numerous; among the more informative are Louis L. Jaffe, "Mr. Justice Jackson," 68 *Harvard L. Rev.* 940 (April, 1955), and T. Taylor, "Robert H. Jackson, 1892-1954— The Nuremberg Trials," 55 *Columbia L. Rev.* 488 (April, 1955). Another good study is Walter F. Murphy's "Mr. Justice Jackson, Free Speech and the Judicial Function," 12 *Vanderbilt L. Rev.* 1019 (October, 1959).

MURPHY, FRANK. A rather surprising amount of literature appears on this Justice, including three booklength studies which, in their varied approaches to the subject, suggest the numerous facets of Murphy's own public career. Harold Norris' *Mr. Justice Murphy and the Bill of Rights* (New York, 1965) focusses upon the Justice's principal contribution to the libertarian rationale, while both of the other books discuss the jurist as politician: Richard D. Lunt's *The High Ministry of Government: The Political Career of Frank Murphy* (Detroit, 1965) devotes most of its theme to the pre-Court career of the subject, while J. Woodward Howard's *Mr. Justice Murphy: A Political Biography* (Princeton, 1968) uses the politician as a medium for understanding the constitutionalist.

Howard's "Justice Murphy: The Freedom Years," 88 *Vanderbilt L. Rev.* 473 (March, 1965), is a sort of preview of the main theme of his book. John P. Frank's "Mr. Justice Murphy: The Goals Attempted," 59 *Yale L. J.* 1 (December, 1949), is a good complement to the Howard book and article. A. P. Man, Jr. has a good summary of Murphy's accomplishments in "Mr. Justice Murphy and the Supreme Court," 36 *Virginia L. Rev.* 889 (November, 1950), and former Solicitor General Charles Fahy has an interesting analysis of "The Judicial Philosophy of Mr. Justice Murphy" in 60 *Yale L. J.* 812 (May, 1951). The disparate views of the jurist's career are summarized in Eugene Gressman's "The Controversial Image of Mr. Justice Murphy," 47 *Georgetown L. J.* 631 (Summer, 1959).

REED, STANLEY FORMAN. In 1950 Mark J. Fitzgerald wrote a doctoral dissertation on *Justice Reed: A Study of a Center Judge* (Chicago, 1950). Other dimensions of Reed's judicial career are emphasized in F. William O'Brien's *Justice Reed and the First Amendment* (Washington, 1958) and his article, "Mr. Justice Reed and Democratic Pluralism," 45 *Georgetown L. J.* 364 (Summer, 1957).

ROBERTS, OWEN JOSEPHUS. The last member of the pre-New Deal Court has been the subject of several revisionist studies. His own Oliver Wendell Holmes Lectures, *The Court and the Constitution* (Cambridge, 1951), reflect his own view of the great changes in both the bench and the Constitution which he experienced in his own tenure. A recent doctoral dissertation of particular interest is E. Adrian Leonard's *Mr. Justice Roberts and the Constitutional Revolution of 1937* (South Bend, Ind., 1967). Another doctoral dissertation is William O. Trapp's *The Constitutional Doctrines of Owen J. Roberts* (Ithaca, N. Y., 1943). The famous eulogy and apology by Felix Frankfurter, dispelling the rumor that Roberts shifted a vote in the *West Coast Hotel Co.* case, appears in a symposium in 104 *University of Pennsylvania L. Rev.* 311 *et seq.* (December, 1955).

RUTLEDGE, WILEY BLOUNT. A series of lectures at the University of Kánsas appears under Rutledge's name in *A Declaration of Legal Faith* (Lawrence, Kansas, 1947). Fowler V. Harper has written a well-balanced biography in *Justice Rutledge and the Bright Constellation* (Indianapolis,

New York, 1965). L. E. Mosher has published two studies—"Mr. Justice Rutledge's Philosophy of Civil Rights," 24 *N.Y.U. L. Q. Rev.* 661 (October, 1949), and "Mr. Justice Rutledge's Philosophy of the Commerce Clause," 27 *N.Y.U. L. Rev.* 218 (April, 1952). Another study of "Justice Rutledge on Civil Liberty," by Landon G. Rockwell, appears in 59 *Yale L. J.* 27 (December, 1949). A symposium on the Justice appears in 35 *Iowa L. Rev.* 541 *et seq.* (Summer, 1950).

STONE, HARLAN FISKE. Alpheus Thomas Mason's *Harlan Fiske Stone: Pillar of the Law* (New York, 1956) is one of the best examples of what judicial biography should be. It draws extensively upon the Stone papers, most of which are in the Columbia University libraries, and its analysis of Stone's own jurisprudential development is superlatively carried out. Some of the evolutionary phases of this analysis are strikingly illustrated in several law review articles which Professor Mason published while his full-length work was in progress—e. g., "Harlan F. Stone: In Defense of Individual Freedom, 1918-20," 51 *Columbia L. Rev.* 147 (February, 1951); "Harlan F. Stone Assays Social Justice, 1912-1923," 99 *Univ. of Pennsylvania L. Rev.* 887 (May, 1951); "Harlan F. Stone and FDR's Court Plan," 61 *Yale L. J.* 791 (June-July, 1952); and "The Core of Free Government, 1938-40: Mr. Justice Stone and 'Preferred Freedoms,' " 65 *id.* 597 (April, 1956).

Samuel J. Konefsky's *Chief Justice Stone and the Supreme Court* (New York, 1946) is an excellent analysis of Stone's jurisprudence, based on his opinions over three decades in broad areas of the commerce and taxing power, administrative regulation and civil liberties.

A doctoral dissertation by Joseph Kise, *Constitutional Doctrines of Harlan F. Stone* (Cambridge, 1938), and Alfred Lief's *Public Control of Business: Selected Opinions of Harlan F. Stone* (New York, 1940) are of limited value when contrasted with the perspectives provided at the end of Stone's Chief Justiceship. In this connection, see John P. Frank's "Harlan Fiske Stone: An Estimate," 9 *Stanford L. Rev.* 621 (May, 1957).

VINSON, FRED M. Little has been written about this Chief Justice as yet, but C. Herman Pritchett's *Civil Liberties and the Vinson Court* (Chicago, 1954), a sequal to his definitive work on *The Roosevelt Court,* evinces both scholarship and prescience in describing the libertarian issues which were building up during this period between the New Deal and the Warren Chief Justiceship.

WARREN, EARL. A widely varying list of studies on the fourteenth Chief Justice already exists. Some are popular and general in their treatment, as Irving Stone's *Earl Warren, a Great American Story* (New York, 1948); Bill Severn's *Mr. Chief Justice: Earl Warren* (New York, 1968); John P. Frank's *The Warren Court* (with pictures by Yousuf Karsh) (New York, 1964); and Luther A. Huston's *Pathway to Judgment* (Philadelphia, 1966). Henry M. Christman collected some *Public Papers of Chief Justice Earl Warren* (New York, 1959), although it is reported that the major part of the

Chief's public papers will be deposited in the Earl Warren Center which has been developed at the University of California.

Two full-length biographies appeared almost simultaneously—Leo Katcher's *Earl Warren: A Political Biography* (New York, 1967) and John Weaver's *Warren: The Man, the Court, the Times* (Boston, 1967). The latter is particularly useful for the Chief's California background, drawn from interviews with contemporaries. Among various studies of the Warren era may be mentioned Alexander M. Bickel's *Politics and the Warren Court* (New York, 1965) and Archibald Cox's *The Warren Court* (Cambridge, 1968).

Law review commentary will doubtless proliferate since the retirement of the Chief in June, 1969. Among insightful articles which have been published to date may be mentioned Sam Kagel's and Virginia B. Smith's "Chief Justice Warren and Labor Law," 49 *California L. Rev.* 126 (March, 1961), and I. M. Heyman's "The Chief Justice, Racial Segregation, and the Friendly Critics," *id.,* 104 (March, 1961).

The Court and the Constitution in the past thirty years have been the subject of a remarkable number of studies, both general and specialized. The constitutional crisis of 1937 has produced a number of works, among which may be mentioned two doctoral dissertations—Joseph R. Saylor's *Court Crisis of 1937* (Austin, Tex., 1945) and E. K. MacColl's *Supreme Court and Public Opinion: A Study of the Court Fight of 1937* (Los Angeles, 1953). But the most substantial dissertation on the changing shape of the Federal judiciary after the New Deal is Richard K. Burke's *The Path to the Court: A Study of Federal Judicial Appointments* (Nashville, 1958).

Among literally dozens of booklength works mostly published in the past decade, a good introduction may be had in the collection of papers in tribute to Princeton's constitutional scholar, Alpheus Thomas Mason, edited by Gottfried Dietze under the title, *Essays on the American Constitution* (Englewood Cliffs, N. J., 1964). Another perspective may be gained by Beryl H. Levy's *Our Constitution: Tool or Testament?* (Port Washington, N. Y., 1941, 1965), originally written following the great constitutional shift of the late Hughes Court. Another retrospect—on the one hundred and fiftieth anniversary of *Marbury v. Madison*—is Edmond N. Cahn's *Supreme Court and Supreme Law* (Bloomington, Ind., 1954). Among other general studies is Arthur E. Sutherland's *Constitutionalism in America* (New York, 1965), written as a book for laymen but admirably elucidating for the specialist as well.

Charles L. Black, Jr. in his *The People and the Court* (New York, 1960) and Alexander M. Bickel in *The Least Dangerous Branch* (Indianapolis, New York, 1962) both stress the role of the Supreme Court in scanning the Constitution for basic safeguards to the democratic process. Both of these books are representative of the Yale Law School emphasis on "legal realism" —a type of constitutional jurisprudence considerably beyond what Chief Justice Taft viewed so critically during his New Haven years—and they are

508   Court and Constitution in the Twentieth Century

complemented by still another Yale scholar's work in Eugene V. Rostow's *The Sovereign Prerogative: The Supreme Court and the Quest for Law* (New Haven, 1962).

Edmund Morgan's *Congress and the Constitution* (Cambridge, 1966) is one of the few studies which has been made of the role of Congress in shaping our constitutional law. Two books which document the uprising on Capitol Hill in the second Eisenhower administration are C. Herman Pritchett's *Congress versus Supreme Court, 1957-1960* (Minneapolis, 1961) and Walter F. Murphy's *Congress and the Court* (Chicago, 1962), a study on which the present author relied heavily. A recent thoughtful study of the jurisdictional limitations which can be placed upon the Court is Raoul Berger's *Congress v. the Supreme Court* (Cambridge, 1969).

For a continuing assessment of the Court's constitutional business, reference again must be made to the annual reviews in the November issue of the *Harvard Law Review,* the sections on constitutional law and related subjects in New York University Law School's *Annual Survey of American Law,* and the annual collection edited by Philip M. Kurland in the *Supreme Court Review* published by the University of Chicago Law School. On the great issue of integration and its collateral issues, the best collection of primary documents is in the *Race Relations Reporter,* published for more than a decade after *Brown v. Board of Education* by the Vanderbilt University Law School.

The role of the Presidency, especially after the four terms of Franklin D. Roosevelt, has assumed new significance in the record of constitutional development. The basic study is Edward S. Corwin's *The President: Office and Powers* (New York, 1957). E. S. Redford has touched upon a significant area in *The President and the Regulatory Commissions* (Washington, 1960), and Theodore C. Sorensen gives a glimpse of the Kennedy administration at work in *Decision Making in the White House* (New York, 1963). Richard E. Neustadt has a discerning study in *Presidential Power* (New York, 1960), and Laurin L. Henry another in *Presidential Transitions* (Washington, 1960). John M. Smith's *Powers of the President During Crises* (Washington, 1960) and J. W. Anderson's *Eisenhower, Brownell and the Congress* (University, Ala., 1964), a study of the struggle for the Civil Rights Act of 1957, are both valuable. With Anderson's work should be read Daniel M. Berman's *A Bill Becomes a Law: The Civil Rights Act of 1960* (New York, 1962).

On constitutional rights generally, Edmond N. Cahn's *The Great Rights* (New York, 1963) is a good starting point. The definitive collection on the subject is Thomas I. Emerson's two-volume work, *Political and Civil Rights in the United States* (Boston, 3rd ed., 1967). Walter Gelhorn's *American Rights: The Constitution in Action* (New York, 1960) is a concise statement of the civil liberties law, while the practical application of the law is illustrated in the *Civil Rights and Liberties Handbook* of the National Lawyers Guild (Berkeley, Calif., 1963). David Fellman's *The Limits of Freedom* (New

Brunswick, N. J., 1959), Paul G. Kauper's *Civil Liberties and the Constitution* (Ann Arbor, 1962) and Donald O. Johnson's *Challenge to American Freedoms: World War I and the Rise of the American Civil Liberties Union* (Lexington, Ky., 1963) effectively round out the list.

David Fellman's *The Constitutional Right of Association* (Chicago, 1963) and Charles E. Rice's *Freedom of Association* (New York, 1962) are two good specialized works on this aspect of the Bill of Rights. On the subject of religious freedom, see Paul G. Kauper's *Religion and the Constitution* (Baton Rouge, 1964), Charles E. Rice, *The Supreme Court and Public Prayer* (New York, 1964) and A. P. Stokes, *Church and State in the United States* (New York, 1964). Two works of particularly high value are the *Papers and Proceedings* of the Conference on Prejudicial News Reporting in Criminal Cases (Chicago, 1964), a discussion jointly sponsored by the schools of law and journalism at Northwestern University and edited by Fred E. Inbau; and James C. N. Paul, *Federal Censorship: Obscenity in the Mail* (New York, 1961).

Other studies on civil rights, in the context of recent constitutional issues, include Donald B. King's collection on *Legal Aspects of the Civil Rights Movement* (Detroit, 1965); Milton R. Konvitz, *A Century of Civil Rights* (New York, 1961); Burke Marshall, *Federalism and Civil Rights* (New York, 1964); Jack W. Peltason, *58 Lonely Men: Southern Federal Judges and School Desegregation* (New York, 1961); and the wealth of information in the various *Reports* of the United States Commission on Civil Rights (Washington, 1959-61). A specialized study of value is Clement Vose's *Caucasians Only: The Supreme Court, the N.A.A.C.P. and the Restrictive Covenant Cases* (Berkeley, 1959).

David Fellman's *The Defendant's Rights* (New York, 1958); O. John Rogge's *The First and the Fifth* (New York, 1960); Erwin N. Griswold's *The Fifth Amendment Today* (Cambridge, 1955); Sidney Hook's *Common Sense and the Fifth Amendment* (New York, 1957); and Lewis Mayer's *Shall We Amend the Fifth Amendment?* (New York, 1959) are all pertinent in view of the recurrent proposals to limit the rights of individuals in criminal actions. The most authoritative handbook in this subject-area is *Constitutional Limitations on Evidence in Criminal Cases* (Ann Arbor, 1966) by B. James George, Jr.

In the area of reapportionment, see Andrew Hacker's *Congressional Redistricting* (Washington, 1964) and Robert S. McKay's *Reapportionment: the Law and Politics of Equal Representation* (New York, 1965). The most comprehensive study on this subject is Robert G. Dixon's *Democratic Representation: Reapportionment in Law and Politics* (New York, 1968).

Notes

CHAPTER 1   *Progressives in Power: Harvest Home*

[1] 284 U. S. v-vii (1932).

[2] Charles Evans Hughes, Autobiographical Notes (Library of Congress), p. 226.

[3] *New York Times,* January 17, 1932.

[4] Adolf A. Berle and Gardiner C. Means, *The Modern Corporation and Private Property* (New York, 1932), p. 44.

[5] Oliver Wendell Holmes, *Collected Legal Papers* (New York, 1920), p. 295; Felix Frankfurter, *Mr. Justice Holmes and the Supreme Court* (Cambridge, 1961), p. 21; Abrams v. United States, 250 U. S. 616 (1919); Hughes, Autobiographical Notes, p. 226.

[6] Laski to Holmes, May 29, 1932, in Mark DeW. Howe, ed., *The Holmes-Laski Letters* (Cambridge, 1953), II, p. 1389.

[7] Hughes, Autobiographical Notes, ch. xxiii, p. 17.

[8] Cf. Ch. 22, 16 Stat. 45.

[9] Hughes, Autobiographical Notes, ch. xxiii, p. 17; *New York Times,* August 14, 1932.

[10] Hughes, Autobiographical Notes, ch. xxiii, p. 17.

[11] Quoted in William E. Leuchtenburg, *Franklin D. Roosevelt and the New Deal* (New York, 1963), p. 19.

[12] Frankfurter, *op. cit.,* p. 32; *New York Times,* January 14, 1932.

[13] *New York Times,* January 15-21, 1932.

[14] 75 *Cong. Rec.,* 4488; *New York Times,* February 16, 1932.

[15] *New York Times,* July 17, 1917; February 16, 1932.

[16] Merlo Pusey, *Charles Evans Hughes* (New York, 1952), II, p. 682; Benjamin N. Cardozo, *The Nature of the Judicial Process* (New Haven, 1921), p. 66; cf. Techt v. Hughes, 229 N. Y. 222, 128 N. E. 185 (1920).

[17] IRT Co. v. Lavin, 246 N. Y. 65, 159 N. E. 863 (1928); Babington v. Yellow Cab Co., 250 N. Y. 14, 164 N. E. 726 (1928); dissent in People v. Gitlow, 234 N. Y. 132, 195 App. Div. 773 (1922).

[18] McPherson v. Buick Motor Co., 217 N. Y. 382, 111 N. E. 1050 (1916).

[19] New State Ice Co. v. Liebmann, 285 U. S. 262 (1932).

[20] Coombes v. Getz, 285 U. S. 434 (1932).

[21] Cf. Bandini Petr. Co. v. Superior Court, 284 U. S. 8 (1931); Champlin Refin. Co. v. Commission, 286 U. S. 210 (1932).

[22] Burnet v. Coronado Oil Co., 285 U. S. 393 (1932).

[23] Nixon v. Condon, 286 U. S. 73 (1932).

[24] Chafee, "The Supreme Court Rules That —" 37 *Current History* 295, 302 (December, 1932).

[25] Nelles, "Toward Legal Understanding," 34 *Columbia L. Rev.* 1041, 1069 (June, 1934).

[26] Lilienthal, "Public Utilities During the Depression," 46 *Harvard L. Rev.* 745, 774 (March, 1931).

[27] *id.*, 775.

[28] Corwin, *Twilight of the Supreme Court* (New Haven, 1934), p. 184.

[29] Cf. Herbert Hoover, *Memoirs* (New York, 1952), II, ch. 28.

[30] S. Crowther, "Everybody Ought to Be Rich" (interview with J. J. Raskob), 46 *Ladies Home J.* 9 (August, 1929).

[31] Department of Commerce, Bureau of the Census, *Historical Statistics of the United States* (Washington, 1957), p. 14.

[32] Cf. Dixon Wecter, *The Age of the Great Depression* (New York, 1948), ch. 1.

[33] 69 *Cong. Rec.* 9524.

[34] *id.*, 9527; W. A. White, *A Puritan in Babylon* (New York, 1938), p. 347.

[35] *id.*, p. 344.

[36] Cf. Wecter, *op. cit.*, ch. 1.

[37] Leuchtenburg, *op cit.*, p. 19.

[38] Mauritz A. Hallgren, "Mass Starvation in Philadelphia," 134 *Nation* 255, 277 (March 9, 1932).

[39] Charles R. Walker, "Relief and Revolution," 88 *Forum* 73, 74 (August, 1932).

[40] Cf. W. F. Swindler, *The Old Legality, 1889-1932* (New York, 1969), Appendix D.

[41] Editorial, "Mr. Hoover Stands Pat," 135 *Nation* 157 (August 24, 1932).

[42] Cf. A. M. Schlesinger, Jr., *The Crisis of the Old Order* (Boston, 1957), ch. 33.

[43] Cf. Schlesinger, *The Coming of the New Deal* (Boston, 1959), ch. 1.

[44] Raymond Moley, *After Seven Years* (New York, 1939), p. 45.

[45] Cf. James M. Burns, *Roosevelt, The Lion and the Fox* (New York, 1956), ch. 8.

[46] *New York Times,* October 6, 1932; October 10, 1932.

[47] Byrnes, *All in a Lifetime* (New York, 1958), p. 65; Raymond Clapper, MS Diary (Library of Congress), July 29, 1936.

[48] Cf. Leuchtenburg, *op. cit.*, ch. 2.

[49] 113 *Literary Digest,* 10 (May 7, 1932); Avis D. Carlson, "Deflating the Schools," 167 *Harper's,* 705, 706 (November, 1933).

[50] Johnson, "The Average American and the Depression," 35 *Current History,* 671, 673 (February, 1932).

[51] Franklin D. Roosevelt, *Public Papers and Addresses* (New York, 1933), II, p. 28.

[52] Schlesinger, *Crisis of the Old Order,* ch. 35; Burns, *op. cit.,* ch. 8.

[53] Elliott Roosevelt, ed., *F. D. R.: His Personal Letters, 1928-1945* (New York, 1950), I, pp. 332, 333.

[54] 21 *Time,* 12 (March 13, 1933).

[55] Roosevelt, *Public Papers,* II, p. 15.

[56] 115 *Literary Digest,* 5 *et seq.* (March 11, 1933); 136 *Nation,* 278 (March 15, 1933).

[57] Cf., generally, Leuchtenburg, *op. cit.,* ch. 3; Burns, *op. cit.,* ch. 9; Moley, *op. cit.,* ch. 4.

[58] Harlan D. Phillips, ed., *Felix Frankfurter Reminisces* (New York, 1960). pp. 245-48; Burns, *op. cit.,* chs. 9, 10.

[59] Cf. Schlesinger, *Coming of the New Deal,* pp. 265-66.

[60] Samuel Rosenman, *Working With Roosevelt* (New York, 1952), p. 550.

[61] *id.,* ch. 7; Schlesinger, *Coming of the New Deal,* chs. 11, 12.

[62] *id.,* ch. 12.

[63] Leuchtenburg, *op. cit.,* ch. 3.

[64] Cf. Schlesinger, *Coming of the New Deal,* ch. 20.

[65] Cf. Wecter, *op. cit.,* ch. 8; Leuchtenburg, *op. cit.,* p. 55.

[66] Cf. Appendix D.

[67] 77 *Cong. Rec.* 753.

[68] *id.,* 753-54.

[69] Moley, *op. cit.,* p. 184.

[70] 77 *Cong. Rec.* 4212 *et seq.*

[71] Roosevelt, *Public Papers,* II, p. 246.

[72] Cf. Schlesinger, *Coming of the New Deal,* ch. 6.

[73] Cf. John Corbin, "The New Deal and the Constitution," 90 *Forum,* 92 (August, 1933).

[74] Cf. E. E. Witte, "Background of the Labor Provision of NIRA," 1 *U. Chicago L. Rev.,* 572 (March, 1934).

[75] Cf. Rexford G. Tugwell, *The Industrial Discipline and Governmental Acts* (New York, 1933), ch. 8.

[76] Berle and Means, *op. cit.,* pp. 355-56.

[77] Moley, *op. cit.,* pp. 193-94.

[78] *id.,* p. 194.

[79] Pound, "Common Law and Legislation," 21 *Harvard L. Rev.* 383 (April, 1908).

[80] Beck, "The Future of the Constitution," 19 *Am. Bar Assn. J.* 493, 540 (September, 1933); Parker, "Is the Constitution Passing?" *id.,* 570, 575 (October, 1933).

[81] Cf. Leuchtenburg, *op. cit.,* pp. 81-82.

[82] Cf. G. A. King, "The Gold Clause—Can It Constitutionally Be Abrogated by Legislation?" 2 *Geo. Washington L. Rev.* 131 (January, 1934).

[83] *New York Times,* May 23, 1934.

[84] *New York Times,* June 12, 1934; July 7, 1934.

CHAPTER 2   *New Deal and Old Court*

[1] Hughes, Autobiographical Notes, ch. xxiii, p. 13.

[2] *id.,* p. 17.

[3] Max Freedman, ed., *Roosevelt and Frankfurter: Their Correspondence, 1928-1945* (Boston, 1967), p. 273.

[4] Jackson, *Struggle for Judicial Supremacy,* ch. 9.

[5] Roosevelt, *Public Papers,* II, pp. 356-57.

[6] *id.,* III, p. 421; *New York Times,* September 18, 1934.

[7] *New York Times,* September 18, 1934; October 2, 1934.

[8] *New York Times,* September 30, 1934.

[9] *New York Times,* December 23, 1934.

[10] 117 *Literary Digest,* 10 (June 20, 1934).

[11] Home B. & L. Assn. v. Blaisdell, 290 U. S. 398, 429-47 (1934).

[12] *id.,* 448, 453, 473.

[13] Nebbia v. New York, 291 U. S. 502, 523-31, 536 (1934).

[14] *id.,* 558-59.

[15] Harold Ickes, *Secret Diary* (New York, 1954), I, p. 273.

[16] *Washington Post,* December 11, 1934, quoted in Pusey, *Hughes,* II, p. 734.

[17] Panama Refining Co. v. Ryan, 293 U. S. 388, 428-33 (1934).

[18] Carl B. Swisher, ed., *Selected Papers of Homer Cummings* (New York, 1939), pp. 107-10.

[19] *id.,* p. 112; "New Deal Meets Tests in Courts," 119 *Literary Digest,* 5, 6 (January 19, 1934).

[20] Norman v. B. & O. R. Co.; United States v. Bankers Trust Co. (two cases), 294 U. S. 240; Perry v. United States, 294 U. S. 330; Nortz v. United States, 294 U. S. 317 (1935).

[21] Ickes, *op. cit.,* I, pp. 273-74; cf. Legal Tender Cases (Hepburn v. Wallace), 8 Wall. 603 (1870); (Knox v. Lee), 12 Wall. 457 (1871).

[22] Cf. John M. Blum, ed., *From the Morgenthau Diaries* (Boston, 1959), I, pp. 126-27.

[23] Undated MS in Roosevelt Papers (Hyde Park).

[24] Blum, *op. cit.,* p. 130; 25 *Time,* 11 (February 25, 1935).

[25] Norman v. B. & O. R. Co., 294 U. S. 240, 304, 307 (1935).

[26] Nortz v. United States, 294 U. S. 317 (1935).

[27] 294 U. S. 330 (1935).

[28] *id.,* 356.

[29] *id.,* 369, 378, 381; *New York Times,* February 24, 1935; "Justice McReynolds' Dissent in the Gold Clause Cases," 18 *Tenn. L. Rev.* 768 (June, 1945).

[30] Quoted in Pusey, *Hughes,* II, p. 738.

[31] Cf. Home B. & L. Assn. v. Blaisdell, 290 U. S. 398 (1934).

[32] *New York Times,* February 22, 1935; March 7, 1935; Richard L. Neuberger and Stephen B. Kahn, *Integrity: The Life of George W. Norris* (New York, 1937), p. 349.

[33] *New York Times,* March 23, 1935.

[34] Pusey, *Hughes,* II, pp. 688-90; and cf. Appendix C.

[35] Swisher, *Cummings Papers,* p. 147; Neuberger and Kahn, *op. cit.,* p. 353.

[36] Schlesinger, *The Politics of Upheaval* (Boston, 1960), p. 261.

[37] Cf. 79 L. Ed. 1471 ff.; 1571 ff.; 1613 ff.

[38] Swisher, *Cummings Papers,* p. 127.

[39] 79 L. Ed. 1574; Donald M. Richberg, *My Hero* (New York, 1954), p. 194.

[40] *id.,* pp. 195-96.

[41] Stewart Dry Goods Co. v. Lewis, 294 U. S. 550 (1935).

[42] Grovey v. Townsend, 295 U. S. 45 (1935).

[43] Retirement Board v. Alton R. Co., 295 U. S. 330, 362 (1935).

[44] *id.,* 375, 388-89, 391.

[45] Schechter Poultry Co. v. United States, 295 U. S. 495, 528 (1935).

[46] *id.,* 553.

[47] Louisville Bank v. Radford, 295 U. S. 555, 602 (1935).

[48] Humphrey's Exec. v. United States, 295 U. S. 602, 625 (1935).

[49] 119 *Literary Digest,* 10 (June 8, 1935).

[50] Richberg, *op. cit.,* p. 195.

[51] Eugene C. Gerhardt, *America's Advocate: Robert H. Jackson* (Indianapolis, New York, 1958), p. 99.

[52] Cf. Mason, *Brandeis,* chs. 36, 38, 39.

[53] Stone to Moore, May 30, 1935, quoted in Mason, *Stone,* p. 395.

[54] Roosevelt, *Papers,* IV, p. 200.

[55] *id.,* pp. 201-02.

[56] Roosevelt to Armistead Brown, July 6, 1935, in Roosevelt Papers (Hyde Park).

[57] Cf. Appendices D and E.

[58] Cf. Acts of June 11, 1934, July 5, 1935 and August 30, 1935, in Appendix D.

[59] Roosevelt to Hill, July 6, 1935. Roosevelt, *Papers,* IV, 297.

[60] Cf. 6 *Newsweek, 38* (September 21, 1935).

[61] Hart Coal Co. v. Sparks, 7 F. S. 16, 28 (1934).

[62] Penn v. Glenn, 10 F. S. 483, 487 (1935).

[63] United States v. Sutherland, 9 F. S. 204, 210 (1934); Stout v. Pratt, 12 F. S. 864, 867 (1935).

[64] Ickes, *op. cit.,* I, p. 467.

[65] George Creel, *Rebel at Large* (New York, 1935), pp. 291-92.

[66] Leuchtenburg, "The Background to Franklin D. Roosevelt's 'Court-Packing Plan," *Supreme Court Review, 1966* (Chicago, 1967), pp. 370 ff.

[67] United States v. Butler, 80 L. Ed. 480-81 (1936).
[68] 297 U. S. 1, 44 (1936).
[69] *id.*, 62.
[70] *id.*, 62, 69.
[71] *id.*, 87.
[72] *id.*, 80-84.
[73] Jackson, *op. cit.*, pp. 157-64.
[74] Ickes, *op. cit.*, I, p. 524.
[75] Cf. Appendix E.
[76] 80 *Cong. Rec.* 1882.
[77] Act of June 6, 1934, Ch. 404, 48 Stat. 881; cf. Appendix D.
[78] Jones v. Securities Exchange Commission, 298 U. S. 1, 23 (1936).
[79] *id.*, 32.
[80] James M. Landis, *The Administrative Process* (New Haven, 1938), pp. 140-41.
[81] Carter v. Carter Coal Co., 298 U. S. 238, 291 (1936).
[82] *id.*, 294.
[83] *id.*, 311-12.
[84] *id.*, 320-21, 331.
[85] Colgate v. Harvey, 296 U. S. 404, 424 (1935).
[86] *id.*, 445.
[87] Ashton v. Cameron County District, 298 U. S. 513, 531, 541 (1936).
[88] Morehead v. New York ex rel. Tipaldo, 298 U. S. 587, 610 (1936).
[89] *id.*, 635.
[90] Ickes, *op. cit.*, I, p. 614.
[91] Roosevelt, *Papers,* IV, pp. 191-92.

CHAPTER 3   *Court Reform Revisited*

[1] Schlesinger, *Politics of Upheaval,* chs. 32, 33.
[2] Henry Wallace, *Whose Constitution?* (New York, 1936), p. 91.
[3] *id.*, pp. 92, 93.
[4] Robert S. Allen and Drew Pearson, *Nine Old Men* (New York, 1936), chs. 2, 4-11.
[5] *Philadelphia Record,* December 1, 3, 4, 1936; January 4, 5, 1937.
[6] Stuart Alsop and Turner Catledge, *The 168 Days* (New York, 1938), p. 27.
[7] Rosenman, *Working With Roosevelt,* pp. 144-47; Burns, *Roosevelt, The Lion and the Fox,* ch. 15.
[8] Clapper, Diary, January 20, 1937.
[9] Roosevelt, *Public Papers* (New York, 1941), V, pp. 1, 2.
[10] *id.*, IV, p. 639.
[11] 81 *Cong. Rec.* 8.
[12] Alsop and Catledge, *op. cit.*, ch. 2.

[13] *Report of the Attorney General for 1913* (Washington, 1914), p. 5.

[14] Leuchtenburg, "Background to Court-Packing Plan," pp. 387-92.

[15] *New York Times,* January 30, 1937; Clapper, Diary, February 5, 1937.

[16] Richberg, *My Hero,* p. 222.

[17] Rosenman, *op. cit.,* pp. 153-54.

[18] *id.,* p. 155.

[19] *id.,* p. 156.

[20] Burns, *op. cit.,* pp. 293-95.

[21] Alsop and Catledge, *op. cit.,* p. 65; Ickes, *Secret Diary,* II, p. 65.

[22] *id.,* p. 66; Alsop and Catledge, *op. cit.,* p. 67.

[23] *id.,* p. 67.

[24] Roosevelt, *Papers,* V, p. 55

[25] *id.,* p. 57.

[26] *id.,* p. 58.

[27] Clapper, Diary, February 5, 1937.

[28] Leonard Baker, *Back to Back: The Duel Between FDR and the Supreme Court* (New York, 1967), ch. 1; Alsop and Catledge, *op. cit.,* p. 69.

[29] *id.,* p. 135.

[30] Clapper, Diary, February 8, 1937.

[31] McIntyre to Roosevelt, March 11 (?), 1937. Roosevelt Papers.

[32] Frankfurter to C. C. Burlingham, March 13, 1937; Freedman, *Roosevelt and Frankfurter,* pp. 390-92.

[33] Cf. F. H. Stinchfield, "The American Bar and The Supreme Court Proposal," 12 *Washington L. Rev.,* 164 (April, 1937).

[34] Cf. Pusey, *Hughes,* II, ch. 70.

[35] Cf. dates of argument in West Coast Hotel Co. v. Parrish in Appendix D; and cf. Hughes, Autobiographical Notes, ch. xxiii, p. 31.

[36] United States v. Hudson, 299 U. S. 498 (1937); Ashwander v. TVA, 297 U. S. 288 (1936).

[37] Leuchtenburg, *Franklin D. Roosevelt and the New Deal,* p. 235.

[38] Act of March 1, 1937; Ch. 21, 50 Stat. 24; cf. Appendix C.

[39] Leuchtenburg, *Franklin D. Roosevelt and the New Deal,* p. 236.

[40] Alsop and Catledge, *op. cit.,* p. 53.

[41] *id.,* pp. 164 ff.

[42] *id.,* pp. 86 ff.

[43] Clapper, Diary, February 8, 1937; Burns, *op. cit.,* pp. 305 ff.; Rosenman, *op. cit.,* p. 159.

[44] Roosevelt, *Papers,* V, pp. 116, 120-21.

[45] Burton K. Wheeler, *Yankee from the West* (New York, 1962), p. 320.

[46] *id.,* p. 320.

[47] Hughes, Autobiographical Notes, ch. xxiii, p. 20.

[48] Wheeler, *op. cit.,* p. 327.

[49] *id.,* p. 328; Pusey, *Hughes,* II, p. 754.

[50] *id.,* p. 755.

⁵¹ Wheeler, *op. cit.,* pp. 329-30.

⁵² *id.,* p. 330.

⁵³ *id.,* p. 331.

⁵⁴ U. S. Senate, Judiciary Committee. *Hearings on Reorganization of the Federal Courts (S. 1392),* March 10-16 (Washington, 1937), *passim.*

⁵⁵ Pusey, *Hughes,* II, p. 771.

⁵⁶ West Coast Hotel Co. v. Parrish, 300 U. S. 379, 389 (1937).

⁵⁷ *id.,* p. 391.

⁵⁸ *id.,* p. 409.

⁵⁹ Wright v. Vinton Branch, 300 U. S. 440, 455 (1937).

⁶⁰ Sonzinsky v. United States, 300 U. S. 506, 513 (1937).

⁶¹ Virginia R. Co. v. System Federation, 300 U. S. 515, 554-58 (1937).

⁶² NLRB v. Jones & Laughlin Steel Corp., 301 U. S. 1, 37 (1937).

⁶³ Alsop and Catledge, *op. cit.,* Part IV.

⁶⁴ Roosevelt, *Papers,* V, p. 154; Clapper, Diary, April 20, 1937.

⁶⁵ *id.,* April 28, 1937.

⁶⁶ *id.,* May 6, 1937.

⁶⁷ Alsop and Catledge, *op. cit.,* pp. 208-16.

⁶⁸ *id.,* pp. 210-12.

⁶⁹ U. S. Senate, Judiciary Committee. *Adverse Report (S. 1392)* (Washington, 1937), *passim.*

⁷⁰ Stewart Machine Co. v. Davis, 301 U. S. 548, 585-88 (1937); and cf. also Helvering v. Davis, 301 U. S. 619 (1937).

⁷¹ Quoted in Pusey, *Hughes,* II, p. 766.

⁷² Freedman, *Roosevelt and Frankfurter,* p. 399.

⁷³ *New York Times,* July 10, 1937.

⁷⁴ Clapper, Diary, May 25, 1937.

CHAPTER 4   *The Shaping of a New Court*

¹ Ashurst to Roosevelt, January 10, 1937; Roosevelt Papers (Hyde Park).

² Ickes, *Secret Diary,* II, p. 182; Cummings to Roosevelt, August 9, 1937; Roosevelt Papers (Hyde Park).

³ Ickes, *op. cit.,* p. 182; Roosevelt Papers (Hyde Park).

⁴ Ickes, *op. cit.,* p. 183.

⁵ *id.,* p. 183; Charlotte Williams, *Hugo L. Black: A Study in the Judicial Process* (Baltimore, 1950), ch. 3.

⁶ *id.,* ch. 4.

⁷ *id.,* p. 66; Freedman, *Roosevelt and Frankfurter,* p. 457.

⁸ Wheeler, *Yankee from the West,* p. 339; Williams, *op. cit.,* p. 19.

⁹ Ickes, *op. cit.,* pp. 190-91; Williams, *op. cit.,* p. 14.

¹⁰ Ickes, *op. cit.,* p. 191.

¹¹ *id.,* p. 192; cf. Ex parte Levitt, 302 U. S. 633 (1937).

¹² Williams, *Black,* pp. 14-15.

[13] *id.,* pp. 21-22.

[14] *id.,* p. 22.

[15] *id.,* ch. 2.

[16] *id.,* p. 24; *New York Times,* September 14, 1937.

[17] *New York Times,* September 27, 1937.

[18] *New York Times,* September 30, 1937.

[19] Williams, *Black,* p. 29.

[20] *id.,* pp. 31-36.

[21] Cf. Burns, *Roosevelt: The Lion and the Fox,* chs. 17, 18; Wecter, *Age of the Great Depression,* ch. 14; Leuchtenburg, *Franklin D. Roosevelt and the New Deal,* ch. 14.

[22] Hughes, Autobiographical Notes, ch. xxiii, p. 18; cf. Horace Binney to Sutherland, August 19, 1937, Sutherland Papers (Library of Congress). Sutherland wrote to Nicholas Murray Butler on January 12, 1938: "It had been my intention to retire nearly a year ago, but felt I could not do so in self-respect while the Court was under fire." Sutherland Papers.

[23] Cf. M. J. Fitzgerald, *Justice Reed: A Study of a Center Judge* (Chicago: Univ. of Chicago Doctoral Diss., 1958), *passim.*

[24] Cf. Schlesinger, *Politics of Upheaval,* p. 261.

[25] Cf. Phillips, *Frankfurter Reminisces,* ch. 27.

[26] Wallace Mendelson, ed., *Felix Frankfurter: A Tribute* (New York, 1964), pp. 59, 137, 164.

[27] Phillips, *op. cit.,* ch. 27; Ickes, *op. cit.,* II, pp. 545, 563; Mason, *Stone,* p. 482.

[28] *id.,* p. 482; Ickes, *op. cit.,* II, p. 546.

[29] *id.,* p. 540.

[30] U. S. Senate, Judiciary Committee. *Hearings . . . on the Nomination of Felix Frankfurter to Be a Justice of the Supreme Court of the United States* (Washington, 1939), pp. 107, 122-26.

[31] *id.,* p. 100.

[32] Ickes, *op. cit.,* II, p. 589.

[33] Roosevelt, *Public Papers,* VII, p. 527.

[34] Cf. Burns, *op. cit.,* chs. 16-18.

[35] Cf. Leuchtenburg, *Franklin D. Roosevelt and the New Deal,* pp. 238, 274.

[36] Roosevelt to Schwellenbach, March 21, 1939; Schwellenbach to Roosevelt, March 25, 1939. Roosevelt Papers (Hyde Park).

[37] Laski to Roosevelt, March 27, 1939, quoted in Freedman, *Roosevelt and Frankfurter,* pp. 490-91.

[38] Cf. Appendix A. Cf. chart prepared February 16, 1937 by WPA showing average age of Court from beginning to that date, in Roosevelt Papers (Hyde Park).

[39] Mason, *Stone,* chs. 6, 15, 32, 33.

[40] Cf. Sheldon Goldman. "Judicial Appointments to the United States Court of Appeals," 1967 *Wisconsin L. Rev.* 186 (Winter, 1967).

[41] Cf. Richard K. Burke, *The Path to the Court* (Nashville: Vanderbilt Univ. Doctoral Diss., 1958), pp. 215 ff., 281 ff.

[42] *id.*, pp. 314 ff.; 351 ff.

[43] Burns, *op. cit.*, ch. 18.

[44] Cf. L. W. Howard, *Mr. Justice Murphy: A Political Biography* (Princeton, 1968), pp. 219-28.

[45] Richard L. Lunt, *The High Ministry of Government: The Political Career of Frank Murphy* (Detroit, 1965), p. 215.

[46] Freedman, *Roosevelt and Frankfurter,* p. 581.

[47] Hughes, Autobiographical Notes, ch. xxiii, p. 31; Frankfurter, in 104 *Univ. of Pennsylvania L. Rev.* 313-16 (December, 1955).

[48] Roberts, Memorandum to Frankfurter, November 9, 1945, quoted in Freedman, *Roosevelt and Frankfurter,* pp. 393-95.

[49] Schechter Poultry Corp. v. United States, 295 U. S. 495, 546 (1935).

[50] United States v. Butler, 297 U. S. 1 (1936); Carter v. Carter Coal Co., 298 U. S. 238, 307, 318 (1936).

[51] NLRB v. Jones & Laughlin Steel Corp., 301 U. S. 1, 37 (1937).

[52] United States v. Bekins, 304 U. S. 27, 49-51, 54 (1938).

CHAPTER 5 *Seedtime of a Modern Constitution*

[1] Cf. Tables in Appendix E.

[2] 152 *Nation,* 273 (March 8, 1941); 55 *Current History,* 8 (July, 1939).

[3] *id.*, p. 8; and cf. "Statesmanship on the Court," 9 *American Scholar,* 139 (Spring, 1940).

[4] Jackson, *Struggle for Judicial Supremacy,* chs. 9, 10; and cf. Jackson, *The Supreme Court in the American System of Government* (Cambridge, 1955).

[5] Cf. statutes and cases in Appendices D and E.

[6] Electric Bond & Share Co. v. SEC, 303 U. S. 419, 440 (1938).

[7] Currin v. Wallace, 306 U. S. 1, 10 (1939).

[8] *id.*, p. 14.

[9] Mulford v. Smith, 307 U. S. 38, 48 (1939).

[10] United States v. Rock Royal Cooperative, 307 U. S. 533, 574 (1939).

[11] Sunshine Coal Co. v. Adkins, 310 U. S. 381 (1940).

[12] United States v. Lowden, 308 U. S. 225, 239 (1939).

[13] United States v. Darby, 312 U. S. 100, 114 (1941).

[14] Gibbons v. Ogden, 22 U. S. (Wheat.) 196 (1924).

[15] Indiana ex rel. Anderson v. Brand, 303 U. S. 95, 108-09 (1938); but cf. Dodge v. Board of Education, 302 U. S. 74 (1937).

[16] Hale v. Board of Assessment, 302 U. S. 95, 101 (1937).

[17] Smyth v. United States, 302 U. S. 329, 356 (1937).

[18] Guaranty Trust Co. v. Henwood, 307 U. S. 247, 258 (1939).

[19] Alabama Power Co. v. Ickes, 302 U. S. 464, 483 (1938); and cf. Tennessee Electric Power Co. v. TVA, 306 U. S. 152 (1939).

[20] Helvering v. Gerhardt, 304 U. S. 405, 425 (1938).

[21] Helvering v. Therrell, 303 U. S. 218 (1938).

[22] Helvering v. Mountain Producers Corp., 303 U. S. 376 (1938).

[23] Graves v. New York ex rel. O'Keefe, 306 U. S. 466, 480 (1939).

[24] O'Malley v. Woodrough, 307 U. S. 277, 281 (1939).

[25] NLRB v. Pennsylvania Greyhound Lines, 303 U. S. 261, 264-69 (1938).

[26] Santa Cruz Fruit Pkg. Co. v. NLRB, 303 U. S. 453, 466-67 (1938).

[27] Leuchtenburg, *Franklin D. Roosevelt and the New Deal,* pp. 239-40.

[28] *id.,* p. 241.

[29] *id.,* p. 242.

[30] United States v. Hutcheson, 312 U. S. 219 (1941).

[31] Virginian R. Co. v. Federation, 300 U. S. 515 (1937); Lauf v. Skinner, 303 U. S. 323 (1938); New Negro Alliance v. Grocery Co., 303 U. S. 552 (1938); and cf. Allen-Bradley Local 1111 v. Wisconsin Empl. Rel. Bd., 315 U. S. 740 (1942).

[32] NLRB v. Mackay Radio, 304 U. S. 333 (1938); NLRB v. Fansteel Metall. Corp.; 306 U. S. 240 (1939); Consol. Edison v. NLRB, 305 U. S. 197 (1938); NLRB v. Columbia E. & S. Co., 306 U. S. 292 (1939).

[33] Hague v. CIO, 307 U. S. 496 (1939); AFL v. NLRB, 308 U. S. 401 (1940); NLRB v. Fuller, 308 U. S. 453 (1940); Nat. Licorice Co. v. NLRB, 309 U. S. 350 (1940).

[34] United States v. Darby, 312 U. S. 100 (1941); Opp Cotton Mills v. Administrator, 312 U. S. 126 (1941).

[35] Swift v. Tyson, 41 U. S. (16 Pet.) 1 (1842); Erie R. Co v. Tompkins, 304 U. S. 64 (1938).

[36] *id.,* 78.

[37] Black & White Taxi & Trans. Co. v. Brown & Yellow Taxi & Trans. Co., 276 U. S. 518, 533 (1928).

[38] Cf. ICC v. Union Pac. R. Co., 222 U. S. 541 (1912).

[39] Rochester Tel. Corp. v. United States, 307 U. S. 125, 146 (1939).

[40] FCC v. Pottsville, 309 U. S. 134 (1940).

[41] NLRB v. Sands Mfg. Co., 306 U. S. 332 (1939).

[42] Tigner v. Texas, 310 U. S. 141, 147 (1940).

[43] Plessy v. Ferguson, 163 U. S. 537, 552 (1896).

[44] Missouri ex rel. Gaines v. Canada, 305 U. S. 337, 344 (1938).

[45] Cf. ch. 13 *infra.*

[46] Nardone v. United States, 302 U. S. 379 (1937); Nardone v. United States, 308 U. S. 338 (1939).

[47] Weiss v. United States, 308 U. S. 321 (1939); and cf. Benanti v. United States, 355 U. S. 96 (1957); Rathbun v. United States, 355 U. S. 107 (1957).

[48] Cf. Opp Cotton Mills v. Administrator, 312 U. S. 126 (1941).

[49] Avery v. Alabama, 308 U. S. 444 (1940).

[50] Cf. ch. 14 *infra.*

51 Thornhill v. Alabama, 310 U. S. 88 (1940).

52 Cf. Lovell v. Griffin, 303 U. S. 444 (1938); Cantwell v. Connecticut, 310 U. S. 296 (1940).

53 *id.*, 304.

54 Minersville School District v. Gobitis, 310 U. S. 586 (1940).

55 Board of Education v. Barnette, 319 U. S. 624 (1943).

56 Walton Hamilton and George Brock, "The Supreme Court Today," 103 *New Republic*, 178 (August 5, 1940). Cf. also Marquis Childs, "Minority of One," 214 *Saturday Eve. Post*, 14 (Sept. 20, 1941).

57 Willkie, "The Court Now Is His," 212 *Saturday Evening Post*, 29, 71 (March 9, 1940).

58 Cf. Rosenman, *Working With Roosevelt*, pp. 75-76.

59 Burns, *Roosevelt: The Lion and the Fox*, ch. 17; Leuchtenburg, *op. cit.* ch. 11.

60 C. O. Hardy, "An Appraisal of the Factors Which Stopped the Recovery Development in the United States," 29 *Am. Econ. Rev.* (Supp.), 170 (March, 1939).

61 Cf. Appendix D.

62 Burns, *op. cit.*, ch. 20; Rosenman, *op. cit.*, ch. 13.

63 Leuchtenburg, *Franklin D. Roosevelt and the New Deal*, pp. 312-22.

64 *id.*, chs. 12, 13.

65 Frances Perkins, *The Roosevelt I Knew* (New York, 1946), pp. 125-28, 134.

66 White, "Thoughts After the Election," 30 *Yale Rev.* (n.s.) 217 (December, 1940).

67 Lubell, "Post Mortem: Who Elected Roosevelt?" 213 *Saturday Evening Post*, 9, 10 (January 25, 1941).

68 Cf. Rosenman, *op. cit.*, ch. 16.

69 *id.*, ch. 24.

CHAPTER 6   *Aftermath of Revolution*

1 Pusey, *Hughes*, II, p. 786.

2 Cf. Swindler, *The Old Legality*, ch. 17.

3 152 *Nation*, 685 (June 14, 1941).

4 Pusey, *Hughes*, II, ch. 63. Cf. also Swindler, *The Old Legality*, ch. 17.

5 Cf. Burke, *Path to the Court*, chs. 2, 3.

6 Pusey, *Hughes*, II, p. 802; Mason, *Stone*, pp. 563-68; and cf. John H. Clarke to Roosevelt, June 4, 1941, and R. C. Leffingwell to Roosevelt, June 13, 1941. Roosevelt Papers (Hyde Park).

7 37 *Time*, 15 (June 21, 1941).

8 "That Liberal Majority," 154 *Nation*, 729 (June 27, 1942).

9 Cf. Wallace Mendelson, *Justices Black and Frankfurter: Conflict in the Court* (Chicago, 1961), *passim.*

[10] Mason, *Stone,* p. 574.

[11] United States v. Darby, 312 U. S. 100, 124 (1941).

[12] 21 *Newsweek,* 40 (June 28, 1943).

[13] 10 *U. S. News,* 18 (June 13, 1941).

[14] Mason, *Stone,* pp. 565, 592-93, 707.

[15] Cf. 23 *Newsweek,* 44 (March 13, 1944).

[16] DiSanto v. Pennsylvania, 273 U. S. 34 (1927); South Carolina Hwy. Dept. v. Barnwell Bros., 303 U. S. 177 (1938); So. Pac. R. Co. v. Arizona, 325 U. S. 761 (1945).

[17] *Am. Bar Assn. Report for 1934* (Baltimore, 1934), pp. 539 ff.

[18] McFarlane, "Administrative Agencies in Government and the Effect Thereon of Constitutional Limitations," *id.,* p. 326; Landis, *The Administrative Process,* pp. 15-16.

[19] 300 U. S. 379, 391.

[20] Williams, *Black,* ch. 5.

[21] McCart v. Indianapolis Water Co., 302 U. S. 419, 428 (1938); Conn. General Life Ins. Co. v. Johnson, 303 U. S. 77, 85 (1938); New York Life Ins. Co. v. Gamer, 303 U. S. 161, 171 (1938).

[22] Sartor v. Arkansas Natural Gas Corp., 321 U. S. 620 (1944); and cf. FPC v. Hope Natural Gas Co., 320 U. S. 591 (1944); Erie R. Co. v. Tompkins, 304 U. S. 64 (1938).

[23] Louis L. Jaffe, "The Supreme Court Today," 174 *Atlantic,* 76 (December, 1944).

[24] Rodell, "Felix Frankfurter, Conservative," 183 *Harper's,* 449, 457 (October, 1941).

[25] Milk Drivers Union v. Meadowmoor Dairies, 312 U. S. 287, 299-317 (1941).

[26] Rodell, *loc. cit.,* p. 458.

[27] 47 *Time,* 21 (June 24, 1941).

[28] Mason, *Stone,* pp. 468-70.

[29] *id.,* pp. 469-72.

[30] Schlesinger, "The Supreme Court: 1947," 35 *Fortune,* 73, 75 (January, 1947).

[31] Mason, *Stone,* chs. 34, 35.

[32] *id.,* p. 275.

[33] Pusey, "The Roosevelt Supreme Court," 58 *American Mercury,* 516, 597 (May, 1944); and cf. Marquis Childs, "Minority of One," 214 *Saturday Eve. Post,* 14 (Sept. 20, 1941).

[34] Powell, "Our High Court Analyzed," *New York Times,* June 18, 1944; Herman Pritchett, *The Roosevelt Court* (New York, 1948), p. 25; FPC v. Hope Natural Gas Co., 320 U. S. 541, 619, 624, 628-60 (1944).

[35] Mercoid Corp. v. Mid-Continent Inv. Co., 320 U. S. 661, 672, 678 (1944).

[36] *id.,* 672-74.

[37] Mason, *Stone,* pp. 608-09.

[38] Mahnich v. Southern SS. Co., 321 U. S. 76, 111-13 (1944).

[39] *id.*, 113.

[40] Cf. Yonkers v. United States, 320 U. S. 685, 692 (1944).

[41] Mason, *Stone,* p. 611.

[42] Anderson v. Abbott, 321 U. S. 349, 369 (1944).

[43] Cf. 30 *Am. Bar Assn. J.* 484 (August, 1944).

[44] Sears, "The Supreme Court and the New Deal: An Answer to Texas," 12 *Univ. of Chicago L. Rev.* 140, 141 (February, 1945).

[45] Mason, *Stone,* ch. 38.

[46] Cf. Marquis W. Childs, "Minority of One," 214 *Saturday Evening Post,* p. 14 (September 20, 1941).

[47] Mason, *Stone,* 765-69.

[48] Cf. 23 *Newsweek,* p. 42 (February 14, 1944); Powell, *loc. cit.* n. 34 *supra,* p. 17.

[49] Rosenman, *op. cit.,* 445-51; Burns, *op. cit.,* p. 466.

[50] Undated memorandum, Harry S Truman Papers (Independence, Missouri).

[51] Cf. Schlesinger, *"The Supreme Court: 1947,"* p. 78; 44 *Time,* 21 (October 9, 1944).

[52] Mason, *Stone,* p. 593.

[53] Girouard v. United States, 328 U. S. 61, 79 (1946).

[54] Cf. Mason, *Stone,* chs. 46, 47.

[55] *Washington Post,* March 2, 1945, quoted in Mason, *Stone,* pp. 799-800.

[56] Cf. Tables in Appendix D.

CHAPTER 7   *Experimental Constitutional Law*

[1] George L. DeLacy, Presidential Address, 23 *Nebraska L. Rev.* 7 (November, 1944).

[2] Cf. John E. Hewitt, "Constitutional Law," 1943 *Annual Review of American Law* (New York, 1944), p. 93.

[3] Wickard v. Filburn, 317 U. S. 111, 120, 121 (1942).

[4] Mason, *Stone,* pp. 430-31; Burnet v. Coronado Oil & Gas Co., 285 U. S. 393, 406n (1932); and cf. James W. Moore and Robert S. Oglebay, "The Supreme Court, *Stare Decisis,* and the Law of the Case," 21 *Texas L. Rev.* 514 (May, 1943). Cf. also Smith v. Allwright, 321 U. S. 649, 665 (1944).

[5] Jones v. Opelika, 316 U. S. 584, 624 (1942), citing Minersville School District v. Gobitis, 310 U. S. 586 (1940).

[6] 316 U. S. 594, 600.

[7] West Virginia State Board of Education v. Barnette, 319 U. S. 624, 638, 642 (1943).

[8] Fay v. New York, 332 U. S. 261, 294 (1947).

[9] Wolf v. Colorado, 338 U. S. 25, 26 (1949).

[10] Edwards v. California, 314 U. S. 160, 174 (1941).

[11] *id.,* 178.

[12] Mason, *Stone,* pp. 579-80.

[13] United States v. Classic, 313 U. S. 299, 320 (1941).

[14] Cf. dissent in Cloverleaf Butter Co. v. Patterson, 315 U. S. 148, 170 (1942).

[15] Faitoute v. Asbury Park, 316 U. S. 502, 511 (1942).

[16] 8 *Newsweek,* 23 (December 8, 1941); Wickard v. Fillburn, 317 U. S. 111, 124 (1942).

[17] Parker v. Brown, 317 U. S. 341, 362 (1942).

[18] United States v. S. E. Underwriters Assn., 322 U. S. 533, 540 (1944).

[19] *id.,* 578, 584.

[20] Magnolia Petroleum Co. v. Hunt, 320 U. S. 430, 436 (1944).

[21] Cf. United States v. Morgan, 307 U. S. 183 (1939); Scripps-Howard v. FCC, 316 U. S. 4 (1942).

[22] Davis v. Dept. of Labor, 317 U. S. 249 (1943).

[23] Cf. SEC v. Chenery Corp., 318 U. S. 80 (1943).

[24] Cf. Arthur T. Vanderbilt, "War Powers and Their Administration," 1942 *Annual Review of American Law* (New York, 1943), p. 106.

[25] *id.,* 110-13.

[26] Vanderbilt, "War Powers," 1943 *Annual Review of American Law* (New York, 1944), pp. 116, 139-49.

[27] United States v. Curtiss-Wright Export Corp., 299 U. S. 304 (1936).

[28] Burns, *op. cit.,* ch. 19; and cf. Appendix D.

[29] Yakus v. United States, 321 U. S. 414, 424 (1944).

[30] Bowles v. Willingham, 321 U. S. 503, 519 (1944).

[31] Hirabayashi v. United States, 320 U. S. 81, 100, 106, 109 (1943).

[32] Korematsu v. United States, 323 U. S. 214, 217, 225, 233, 242 (1944).

[33] Schneidermann v. United States, 320 U. S. 118, 135-37 (1943).

[34] Baumgartner v. United States, 322 U. S. 665 (1944).

[35] Hartzell v. United States, 322 U. S. 680 (1944).

[36] Bridges v. Wixon, 326 U. S. 135, 152 (1945).

[37] Bridges v. California, 314 U. S. 252 (1941).

[38] 326 U. S. 151, 156.

[39] Screws v. United States, 325 U. S. 91, 113, 134, 138 (1945).

[40] *id.,* 100-05.

[41] *id.,* 116-18, 131-33.

[42] *id.,* 138.

[43] *id.,* 142-45, 158-61.

[44] Robert K. Carr, "Screws v. United States," 31 *Cornell L. Q.* 48, 66 (September, 1945).

[45] Cf. ch. 15.

[46] Colgrove v. Green, 328 U. S. 549, 564 (1946).

[47] United States v. Lovett, 328 U. S. 303, 319 (1946).

[48] Colegrove v. Green, 328 U. S. at 554.

[49] *id.,* 566.

[50] *id.,* 572.

[51] Powell v. Alabama, 287 U. S. 45 (1932).

[52] Betts v. Brady, 316 U. S. 455, 473 (1942).
[53] *id.,* 473.
[54] *id.,* 477.
[55] Cf. Yale Kamisar, "Betts v. Brady 20 Years Later: The Right to Counsel and Due Process Values," 61 *Michigan L. Rev.* 219 (October, 1962).
[56] Cf. Kamisar, "Right to Counsel and the Fourteenth Amendment," 30 *Univ. of Chicago L. Rev.* 1 (Autumn, 1962).
[57] Cf. Tables in Appendix D.
[58] Edwards v. California, 314 U. S. 160 (1941).
[59] Georgia v. Taylor, 315 U. S. 25 (1942).
[60] Mayo v. United States, 319 U. S. 441 (1943).
[61] Thomas v. Collins, 323 U. S. 516 (1945).
[62] Morgan v. Virginia, 328 U. S. 373 (1946).
[63] 323 U. S. xix (1944).
[64] Hand, "Chief Justice Stone's Concept of the Judicial Function," 46 *Columbia L. Rev.* 696 (September, 1946).
[65] Cf. Mason, *Stone,* ch. 48.
[66] 323 U. S. xix (1944).
[67] 333 U. S. xx, xxiii (1947).
[68] 90 *Congressional Record,* 1680.
[69] Cf. Schlesinger, "Third Term Issue," 64 *American Mercury,* 407, 410 (April, 1947).
[70] Corwin, *The Presidency: Office and Powers* (New York, 1957), p. 276.
[71] *New York Times,* February 25, 1944.
[72] Neustadt, *Presidential Power* (New York, 1960), p. 180.
[73] Corwin, *Presidency,* p. 277.
[74] 90 *Congressional Record,* 1681.
[75] *id.,* 1771, 1773.

CHAPTER 8   *The Vinson Interlude*

[1] Pusey, *Hughes,* II, pp. 801-02; memorandum from Charles G. Ross to Merlo Pusey, July 11, 1950. Truman Papers.
[2] *New York Times,* June 7, 1946.
[3] *New York Times,* June 9, 1946.
[4] Justice Burton to Truman, June 7, 1946. Truman Papers.
[5] Jewell Ridge Coal Corp. v. Local No. 6167, 325 U. S. 161 (1945); Anderson v. Mt. Clemens Pottery Co., 328 U. S. 680 (1946); and cf. Tennessee Coal & Iron Co. v. Muscada Local, 321 U. S. 590 (1944).
[6] 18 *U. S. News,* 81 (June 21, 1946); and cf. Joe Short to Eugene C. Gerhardt, February 18, 1952. Truman Papers.
[7] 18 *U. S. News,* 82.
[8] *New York Times,* June 11, 1946.
[9] Memorandum, Truman to Joe Short, December 10, 1951. Truman Papers.

[10] Schlesinger, "The Supreme Court: 1947," p. 79.

[11] Gerhardt, *America's Advocate,* ch. 15; Williams, *Black,* pp. 177-79; cf. also *New York Times,* September 19, 1945.

[12] *New York Times,* June 13, 15, 1946.

[13] *New York Times,* June 18, 1946.

[14] 92 *Congressional Record,* 7064 ff.

[15] Anderson v. Mt. Clemens Pottery Co., 328 U. S. 680, 691 (1945).

[16] *id.,* 694.

[17] Harry A. Mills and Emily C. Brown, *From the Wagner Act to Taft-Hartley* (Chicago, 1950), ch. 10.

[18] 48 *Time,* 21 (November 18, 1946).

[19] Mills and Brown, *op. cit.,* ch. 10.

[20] 93 *Congressional Record,* 1562.

[21] *id.,* 2081, 2114, 2121, 2244, 2351, 2365; cf. P. L. 49, 61 Stat. 84.

[22] United States v. United Mine Workers, 70 F. S. 42 (1946); United Mine Workers v. United States, 330 U. S. 258 (1947).

[23] *id.,* 269, 284, 290.

[24] *id.,* 308, 328.

[25] *id.,* 306.

[26] *id.,* 312.

[27] *id.,* 339.

[28] Cf. Taft, "Toward Peace in Labor," 121 *Colliers,* 21, 38 (March 6, 1948).

[29] Cf. Louis Stark, "Labor Act: What It Leaves of New Deal Gains," 36 *Survey Graphic,* 380 (July, 1947).

[30] Cf. Hartley, *Our New National Labor Policy* (New York, 1948), chs. 5, 6.

[31] *id.,* chs. 11-14.

[32] Note, "Constitutionality of the Portal-to-Portal Act," 47 *Columbia L. Rev.* 1010 (September, 1947); Mills and Brown, *op. cit.,* ch. 11.

[33] *id.,* ch. 10.

[34] 49 *Time,* 17 (June 23, 1947); *id.,* 13 (June 30, 1947).

[35] *id.,* p. 13.

[36] *id.,* p. 15.

[37] Mills and Brown, *op. cit.,* chs. 12-15.

[38] Cf. Thomas F. Mulroy, "Taft-Hartley Act in Action," 15 *Univ. of Chicago L. Rev.* 595 (Spring, 1948).

[39] Cf. *New York Times,* September 15, 17, 1948.

[40] Cf. Eric F. Goldman, *The Crucial Decade* (New York, 1956), pp. 83-89.

[41] *id.,* pp. 81, 87.

[42] Cf. 62 *Time,* 23 (November 15, 1948).

[43] Cf. Goldman, *op. cit.,* ch. 6.

[44] C. Herman Pritchett, *Civil Liberties and the Vinson Court* (Chicago, 1954), chs. 1-4.

[45] John P. Frank, "The United States Supreme Court, 1946-47," 15 *Univ. of Chicago L. Rev.* 1, 44, 49 (Autumn, 1947); "The United States Supreme Court, 1951-52," 20 *id.,* 1, 68 (Autumn, 1952).

[46] *New York Times,* June 16, 18, 1953.

[47] Cf. McGrath to Truman, September 15, 1949. Truman Papers.

[48] Cf. Goldman, *op. cit.,* chs. 6, 7, 10.

[49] Cf. Fowler Harper, "Record of J. Howard McGrath," 173 *Nation,* 441 (November 24, 1951); J. M. Snyder, "Education of Newbold Morris," 74 *American Mercury,* 11 (June, 1952); 39 *Newsweek,* 25 (April 14, 1952); 32 *U. S. News,* 52 (April 11, 1952).

[50] United States v. California, 332 U. S. 19 (1947).

[51] United States v. Louisiana, 339 U. S. 699 (1950); United States v. Texas, 339 U. S. 707 (1950); cf. Ch. 65, 67 Stat. 29.

[52] United Public Workers v. Mitchell, 330 U. S. 75 (1947); United States v. Petrillo, 332 U. S. 1 (1947); Lichter v. United States, 334 U. S. 742 (1948); Hirota v. MacArthur, 335 U. S. 876 (1948).

[53] 330 U. S. at 105, 111; 332 U. S. at 16.

[54] 335 U. S. at 876, 881.

[55] Pritchett, *op. cit.,* ch. 9.

[56] American Communications Assn. v. Douds, 339 U. S. 391, 393, 396 (1950).

[57] *id.,* 417, 433, 445.

[58] *id.,* 449.

[59] Blau v. United States, 340 U. S. 159; 340 U. S. 332 (1950).

[60] Rogers v. United States, 340 U. S. 367, 378 (1951).

[61] Niemotko v. Maryland, 340 U. S. 268, 273; Kuntz v. New York, 340 U. S. 290, 295; Feiner v. New York, 340 U. S. 315, 321, 329 (1951).

[62] Garner v. Bd. Pub. Wks., 341 U. S. 716, 727 (1951); and cf. Gerende v. Bd. of Superv., 341 U. S. 56 (1951).

[63] Wieman v. Updegraff, 344 U. S. 183, 191 (1952).

[64] Cf. Bernard Schwartz, "Administrative Law," 1951 *Annual Review of American Law* (New York, 1952), pp. 133-35.

[65] Joint Anti-Fascist Committee v. McGrath, 341 U. S. 823, 835, 853, 855 (1951).

[66] Cf. Pritchett, *op. cit.,* ch. 12; Gerhardt, *America's Advocate,* ch. 17.

[67] Adler v. Board of Education, 342 U. S. 485 (1952).

[68] Dennis v. United States, 341 U. S. 494, 508 (1951).

[69] *id.,* 549.

[70] *id.,* 580.

[71] *id.,* 585.

[72] Pritchett, *op. cit.,* pp. 71-77.

[73] Everson v. Board of Education, 330 U. S. 1, 28 (1947).

[74] Illinois ex rel. McCullom v. Board of Education, 333 U. S. 203 (1948).

[75] Zorach v. Clauson, 343 U. S. 306 (1952).

[76] Doremus v. Board of Education, 342 U. S. 429 (1952).

[77] Harris v. United States, 331 U. S. 145, 154 (1947).

[78] *id.,* 163, 164.

[79] Johnson v. United States, 333 U. S. 10, 16 (1948).

[80] Trupiano v. United States, 334 U. S. 699 (1948).

[81] *id.,* 713.

[82] United States v. Rabinowitz, 339 U. S. 56 (1950).

[83] Adamson v. California, 332 U. S. 46, 59 (1947).

[84] Wolf v. Colorado, 338 U. S. 25 (1949).

[85] Townsend v. Burke, 334 U. S. 736 (1948).

[86] Pritchett, *op. cit.,* pp. 157-59.

[87] McNabb v. United States, 318 U. S. 332 (1943); Upshaw v. United States, 335 U. S. 410 (1948).

[88] Stein v. New York, 346 U. S. 156 (1953).

[89] Cf. Morgan v. Virginia, 328 U. S. 375 (1946).

[90] Missouri ex rel. Gaines v. Canada, 305 U. S. 337 (1937); Sipuel v. Board of Regents, 332 U. S. 631 (1948); Sweatt v. Painter, 339 U. S. 629 (1950); McLaurin v. Board of Regents, 343 U. S. 637 (1950).

[91] Youngstown Sheet & Tube Co. v. Sawyer, 343 U. S. 579 (1952).

[92] *id.,* 610.

[93] Cf. Powell, "Behind the Split in the Supreme Court," *New York Times,* October 9, 1949.

CHAPTER 9   *The Transition of Liberalism*

[1] W. Hamilton, "Preview of a Justice," *48 Yale L. J.* 819, 823 (March, 1939); cf. S. J. Konefsky, "Felix Frankfurter and the Conscience of a Constitutional Judge," 31 *Brooklyn L. Rev.* 213 (April, 1965).

[2] Frankfurter, *The Commerce Clause Under Marshall, Taney and Waite* (Chapel Hill, 1937), pp. 36, 72, 80.

[3] Hand, "Mr. Justice Frankfurter," 62 *Harvard L. Rev.* 353, 355 (January, 1949); Jaffe, "The Judicial Universe of Mr. Justice Frankfurter," *id.,* 357 (January, 1949).

[4] Hook, "Liberalism and the Law," 23 *Commentary,* 46 (January, 1957).

[5] Freund, "Mr. Justice Frankfurter," 76 *Harvard L. Rev.* 18 (November, 1962).

[6] Schenck v. United States, 249 U. S. 47 (1919); Abrams v. United States, 250 U. S. 616, 624 (1919).

[7] Minersville School District v. Gobitis, 310 U. S. 586, 594 (1940).

[8] Board of Education v. Barnette, 319 U. S. 624, 646 (1943).

[9] Niemotko v. Maryland, 340 U. S. 268, 284 (1951).

[10] Dennis v. United States, 341 U. S. 494, 540 (1951).

[11] Cf. Nathaniel L. Nathanson, "Separation of Powers: The Justice Revisits His Own Casebook," in Wallace Mendelson, ed., *Felix Frankfurter: The Judge* (New York, 1964), pp. 1-29.

[12] Cf. Frankfurter, "Reflections on the Reading of Statutes," 47 *Colum. L. Rev.* 517 (May, 1947).

[13] Mendelson, *Conflict in the Court,* ch. 3.

[14] *id.,* ch. 4.

[15] Mahnich v. Southern SS. Co., 321 U. S. 76, 105 (1944).

[16] Cf. Georgia v. Evans, 316 U. S. 160 (1942).

[17] Cf. Frankfurter, "Reading of Statutes," p. 540.

[18] Apex Hosiery Co. v. Leader, 310 U. S. 472 (1940).

[19] United States v. United Mine Workers, 330 U. S. 258, 308 (1947); United Brotherhood v. United States, 330 U. S. 395, 413 (1947); Textile Workers Union v. Lincoln Mills, 353 U. S. 448, 460 (1947).

[20] AFL v. American Sash & Door Co., 335 U. S. 538, 542 (1949); Textile Workers v. Lincoln Mills, 353 U. S. 448, 521 (1947); Gibson v. Phillips Petr. Co., 352 U. S. 874 (1956).

[21] Street Ry. Employees v. Wisconsin Board, 340 U. S. 383, 399 (1951); Pennsylvania R. Co. v. Rychlik, 352 U. S. 480 (1957).

[22] *id.*, 498.

[23] Ry. Employees v. Hanson, 351 U. S. 225 (1956).

[24] Cf. Frankfurter, *Justice Holmes and the Supreme Court*, pp. 45-73.

[25] Freedman, *Roosevelt and Frankfurter*, p. 383; Haley v. Ohio, 332 U. S. 596, 602 (1947).

[26] Cf. Griffin v. Illinois, 351 U. S. 12, 16 (1956).

[27] Cf. Frankfurter, "Reading of Statutes," p. 545.

[28] Herdman v. Pennsylvania R. Co., 352 U. S. 518, 524 (1957).

[29] Cf. Mendelson, *Felix Frankfurter: A Tribute* (New York, 1964).

[30] United States v. Lovett, 328 U. S. 303, 321 (1946).

[31] *id.*, 327-29.

[32] Cf. J. B. Grossman, "Role Making and the Analysis of Judicial Behavior: The Case of Mr. Justice Frankfurter," 11 *J. Pub. L.* 285 (1962).

[33] Gerhardt, *America's Advocate*, ch. 7.

[34] Cf. Paul A. Freund, "Individual and Commonwealth in the Thought of Mr. Justice Jackson," 8 *Stanf. L. Rev.* 9 (December, 1955).

[35] Gerhardt, *America's Advocate*, p. 306.

[36] Dobson v. Commissioner, 320 U. S. 489 (1943); Gerhardt, *op. cit.*, p. 306.

[37] Farmers Reservoir & Irrigation Co. v. McComb, 337 U. S. 755, 771 (1949).

[38] Cf. Jackson, *Supreme Court in the American System of Government, passim.*

[39] Cf. Missouri v. Holland, 252 U. S. 416 (1920); Schlesinger v. Wisconsin, 270 U. S. 230 (1926).

[40] West Virginia ex rel. Dyer v. Sims, 341 U. S. 22, 31 (1951).

[41] New York v. United States, 326 U. S. 572 (1946).

[42] Rochin v. California, 342 U. S. 165, 169-70 (1952).

[43] Wolf v. Colorado, 338 U. S. 25 (1949).

[44] Mapp v. Ohio, 367 U. S. 643, 672 (1961).

[45] 338 U. S., at 342.

[46] 367 U. S., at 659.

[47] *id.*, 680-82.

CHAPTER 10   *The Jurisprudence of Activism*

[1] Cf. Arthur S. Miller, "Toward a Concept of Constitutional Duty," *1968 Supreme Court Review* (1968), p. 199.

[2] Black, "William Orville Douglas," Symposium in 73 *Yale L. J.* 915 (May, 1954); Jack Alexander, "Washington's Angry Scotsman," 215 *Saturday Evening Post*, 9, 10 (October 17, 1942); Richard L. Neuberger, "Mr. Justice Douglas," 185 *Harper's*, 312, 317 (August, 1942).

[3] Leon Epstein, "Economic Predilections of Mr. Justice Douglas," 1949 *Wisconsin L. Rev.* 531, 536 (May, 1949).

[4] Fortas, "Mr. Justice Douglas," 73 *Yale L. J.* 918 (May, 1954).

[5] Warehouse Co. v. Bowles, 321 U. S. 144, 156 (1954).

[6] Anderson v. Abbott, 321 U. S. 349, 366 (1944).

[7] Wright v. Union Central Life Ins. Co., 311 U. S. 273, 281 (1940).

[8] Epstein, *loc. cit.*, pp. 548-52.

[9] American Ins. Co. v. Avon Park, 311 U. S. 138, 140 (1940).

[10] Helen Shirley Thomas, "Mr. Justice Douglas and the Concept of 'Fair Trial,'" 18 *Vanderbilt L. Rev.* 701 (March, 1965); and cf. John W. Hopkirk, "William O. Douglas: His Work in Preparing Budget Proceedings," *id.*, p. 698.

[11] FPC v. Hope Natural Gas Co., 320 U. S. 591 (1944).

[12] Georgia v. Pennsylvania R. Co., 324 U. S. 439 (1945).

[13] Cf. Epstein, *loc. cit.*, p. 552.

[14] Cf. Irving Dilliard, *One Man's Stand for Freedom* (New York, 1963), pp. 3-27.

[15] Berman, "Freedom and Mr. Justice Black: Record After Twenty Years," 25 *Missouri L. Rev.* 155 (April, 1960).

[16] Edmond Cahn, "Justice Black and the First Amendment Absolutes," 37 *N. Y. U. L. Rev.* 540 (June, 1962); and cf. C. A. Reid, "Mr. Justice Black and a Living Constitution," 76 *Harvard L. Rev.* 673 (February, 1963).

[17] Berman, *loc. cit.*, pp. 156-58.

[18] Galvan v. Press, 347 U. S. 522, 532 (1954).

[19] Konigsberg v. State Bar, 353 U. S. 252 (1957).

[20] Konigsberg v. State Bar, 366 U. S. 36, 67-69 (1961).

[21] Speiser v. Randall, 357 U. S. 513, 532 (1958).

[22] Watkins v. United States, 354 U. S. 178 (1957); Barenblatt v. United States, 360 U. S. 109 (1959).

[23] *id.*, 138, 143.

[24] *id.*, 148.

[25] Cf. Communist Party v. Subversive Activities Control Board, 367 U. S. 1, 137 (1961); Dennis v. United States, 341 U. S. 494, 579 (1951).

[26] Cf. ch. 8 *supra*.

[27] In re Summers, 325 U. S. 561, 573 (1945).

[28] 353 U. S. 252.

[29] 366 U. S., at 44-49.

[30] Everson v. Board of Education, 330 U. S. 1 (1947); McCullom v. Board of Education, 333 U. S. 203 (1948); Zorach v. Clauson, 343 U. S. 306, 315 (1952).

[31] Torcaso v. Watkins, 367 U. S. 488, 492, 495 (1961).

[32] Engel v. Vitale, 370 U. S. 421, 430 (1962).

[33] Bridges v. California, 314 U. S. 252, 262 (1941).

[34] United Public Workers v. Mitchell, 320 U. S. 75, 105, 109 (1941).

[35] American Communications Assn. v. Douds, 339 U. S. 332, 445 (1950).

[36] Dennis v. United States, 341 U. S. 494, 579, 580 (1951).

[37] Wieman v. Updegraff, 344 U. S. 183, 194 (1952).

[38] Yates v. United States, 354 U. S. 298, 339 (1957).

[39] Smith v. California, 361 U. S. 147, 155 (1959).

[40] Duncan v. Kahanamoku, 327 U. S. 304, 322 (1946).

[41] Johnson v. Zerbst, 304 U. S. 458, 468 (1938).

[42] Betts v. Brady, 316 U. S. 455, 476 (1941).

[43] Carnley v. Cochran, 369 U. S. 506, 518 (1962).

[44] Gideon v. Wainwright, 372 U. S. 335 (1963).

[45] Bartkus v. Illinois, 359 U. S. 121, 150, 155 (1959).

[46] Adamson v. California, 332 U. S. 46, 68, 89 (1947).

[47] *id.*, 90.

[48] Douglas, *We, The Judges* (New York, 1956), ch. 5.

[49] *id.*, p. 82.

[50] Flemming v. Nestor, 363 U. S. 603, 628 (1960).

[51] Scherbert v. Verner, 374 U. S. 398 (1963).

[52] Everson v. Board of Education, 330 U. S. 1 (1947); McCollum v. Board of Education, 333 U. S. 203 (1948).

[53] Zorach v. Clauson, 343 U. S. 306 (1952).

[54] Engel v. Vitale, 370 U. S. 421 (1962).

[55] Douglas, *We, The Judges,* p. 353.

[56] Rodell, "Justice Douglas: Anniversary Fragment for a Friend," 26 *U. Chi. L. Rev.* 2 (Autumn, 1958).

[57] Douglas, *We, The Judges,* ch. 8.

[58] Douglas, *Freedom of the Mind* (New York, 1964), p. 24.

[59] Dennis v. United States, 341 U. S. 494, 588 (1951).

[60] Cf. Feiner v. New York, 340 U. S. 315 (1951).

[61] Cf. Communist Party v. Subversive Activities Control Board, 367 U. S. 1, 169 (1961).

[62] Elfbrandt v. Russell, 384 U. S. 11, 19 (1966).

[63] Aptheker v. Secretary of State, 378 U. S. 500, 519 (1964); and cf. Kent v. Dulles, 357 U. S. 116, 125 (1958).

[64] Zemel v. Rusk, 381 U. S. 1, 23 (1965).

[65] Griswold v. Connecticut, 381 U. S. 479 (1965).

[66] *id.*, 484-85.

[67] Gideon v. Wainwright, 372 U. S. 335, 345 (1963).

[68] Cf. Griswold v. Connecticut, 381 U. S. 479 (1965); Klopfer v. North Carolina, 386 U. S. 213 (1967); Duncan v. Louisiana, 391 U. S. 145 (1968); Stanley v. Georgia, 394 U. S. 557 (1969).

[69] Douglas, *We, The Judges*, pp. 432-33.

[70] *id.*, 433.

CHAPTER 11 *Congressional Confrontation*

[1] *New York Times,* June 5, 1952; Merlo Pusey, *Eisenhower the President* (New York, 1956), pp. 17-18; Emmet John Hughes, *The Ordeal of Power* (New York, 1962), ch. 2.

[2] Sherman Adams, *First Hand Report* (New York, 1961), p. 13.

[3] Pusey, *op. cit.*, ch. 1.

[4] *New York Times,* March 12, 1952.

[5] Pusey, *op. cit.*, p. 22.

[6] *id.*, ch. 2; Hughes, *op. cit.*, ch. 3.

[7] Adams, *op. cit.*, ch. 3.

[8] *id.*, ch. 4; Hughes, *op. cit.*, ch. 3.

[9] *id.*, p. 67.

[10] *id.*, pp. 67-68.

[11] Undated fragment, Eisenhower Papers (Abilene, Kansas).

[12] Pusey, *op. cit.*, pp. 287-88.

[13] John Weaver, *Warren, The Man, the Court, the Times* (Boston, 1967), ch. 13; and cf. Knowland to Eisenhower, September 25, 1953, Eisenhower Papers.

[14] 62 *Time*, 17 (October 12, 1953); Leo Katcher, *Earl Warren, A Political Biography* (New York, 1967), pp. 295-96, 300-02.

[15] Weaver, *op. cit.*, chs. 8-10; Katcher, *op. cit.*, chs. 14-24.

[16] Weaver, *op. cit.*, pp. 192-94.

[17] *New York Times,* October 1, 1953: Katcher, *op. cit.*, pp. 306-07.

[18] *New York Times,* October 1, 1953.

[19] Minnick to Eisenhower, October 13, 1953, Eisenhower Papers; 100 *Cong. Rec.*, 2043-44, 2359-62, 2381.

[20] Cf. Gerhardt, *America's Advocate*, ch. 16.

[21] Brownell to Eisenhower, November 5, 1955. Eisenhower Papers.

[22] *New York Times,* November 20, 1954.

[23] Cf. Donald R. Richberg, "The Bricker Amendment and the Treaty Power," 39 *Va. L. Rev.* 753 (October, 1953); J. B. Whitten and J. E. Fowler, "The Bricker Amendment—Fallacies and Dangers," 48 *Am. J. of Int. Law*, 23 (January, 1954).

[24] 101 *Cong. Rec.* 2830-31.

[25] *id.*, 3012, 3022.

[26] *id.*, 3034.

[27] Eisenhower to Harlan, November 16, 1955. Eisenhower Papers.

[28] Memo to Sherman Adams, October 13, 1956; Brownell to Eisenhower, October 11, 1956; Eisenhower to Harley Dodge, October 4, 1956. Eisenhower Papers.

[29] 103 *Cong. Rec.* 3936-46.

[30] Brownell to Eisenhower, March 8, 1957. Eisenhower Papers.

[31] Rogers to Eisenhower, October 7, 1958; Lawrence E. Welsh to Robert E. Hampton, October 7, 1958; Hampton to Sherman Adams, October 8, 1958. Eisenhower Papers.

[32] Cf. 105 *Cong. Rec.* 6999, 7452, 7832.

[33] Schwartz, "Supreme Court, October 1956 Term," 32 *N. Y. U. L. Rev.* 1202 (November, 1957).

[34] *New York Times,* February 13, 1956; 102 *Cong. Rec.* 2556.

[35] 102 *Cong. Rec.* 4460.

[36] *New York Times,* June 13, 1956; Byrnes, 40 *U. S. News,* 50 (May 18, 1956).

[37] *New York Times,* February 14, 15, 22, 1957.

[38] 108 *Cong. Rec.* 3376, 6771, 7452, 8387, 9869, 11117.

[39] Cf. Walter Murphy, *Congress and the Court* (Chicago, 1962); *New York Times,* February 22, 26, March 25, 1958.

[40] *New York Times,* April 9, 10, 1958.

[41] Cooper v. Aaron, 358 U. S. 1, 4, 18-19 (1958).

[42] *New York Times,* February 22, 1959.

[43] *New York Times,* August 21, 1958.

[44] Virginia Commission on Constitutional Government, *Report of the Conference of Chief Justices* (Richmond, 1959), p. 33.

[45] *id.,* p. 36.

[46] Cf. W. F. Swindler, "The Current Challenge to Federalism: The Confederating Proposals," 52 *Geo. L. J.* 1 (Fall, 1963).

[47] 105 *Cong. Rec.* 7452.

[48] *id.,* 7452-53.

[49] *id.,* 7468, 7471.

[50] Kurland, "Equal in Origin and Equal in Title to the Legislative and Executive Branches of the Government," 78 *Harv. L. Rev.* 143 (November, 1963).

CHAPTER 12 *Storm on Capitol Hill*

[1] Hughes, *Ordeal of Power,* p. 58.

[2] 40 *Am. Bar Assn. J.* 955 (November, 1954).

[3] Adams, *First Hand Report,* p. 336; Weaver, *Warren,* ch. 14.

[4] Hughes, *Ordeal of Power,* p. 243.

[5] Katcher, *Warren,* pp. 341-43.

[6] *id.,* p. 401.

[7] Irvine v. California, 347 U. S. 128, 139 (1954).

[8] Peters v. Hobby, 349 U. S. 331 (1955).

[9] Murphy, *Congress and the Court,* ch. 5.

[10] Griffin v. Illinois, 351 U. S. 12 (1956).

[11] *id.,* 19.

[12] Pennsylvania v. Nelson, 350 U. S. 497, 504 (1956).

[13] Slochower v. Board of Education, 350 U. S. 551, 557 (1956).

[14] *id.*, 559; cf. Elfbrandt v. Russell, 384 U. S. 11 (1966).

[15] Cole v. Young, 351 U. S. 536, 556 (1956).

[16] Railway Employees v. Hanson, 351 U. S. 225, 233 (1956).

[17] 101 *Cong Rec.* 31.

[18] 102 *Cong. Rec.* 6583.

[19] *id.*, 6384.

[20] *id.*, 6385.

[21] House Rep. 2576 (84th Cong., 2d Sess.), pp. 2, 13.

[22] Murphy, *Congress and the Court*, ch. 7.

[23] *id.*, ch. 6.

[24] Mallory v. United States, 354 U. S. 449 (1957).

[25] *id.*, 453.

[26] Pennsylvania v. Board of Trusts, 353 U. S. 230 (1957).

[27] Jencks v. United States, 353 U. S. 657, 670 (1957).

[28] *id.*, 681-82.

[29] Watkins v. United States, 354 U. S. 178, 195, 202 (1957).

[30] Sweezy v. New Hampshire, 354 U. S. 234, 250, 252 (1957).

[31] *id.*, 265-67.

[32] Yates v. United States, 354 U. S. 298, 320 (1957).

[33] Murphy, *Congress and the Court*, pp. 112-13.

[34] Service v. Dulles, 354 U. S. 363, 388 (1957).

[35] Donald C. Morgan, *Congress and the Constitution* (Cambridge, 1966), ch. 1.

[36] 104 *Cong. Rec.* 10525, 10543.

[37] Murphy, *Congress and the Court*, p. 239.

[38] *id.*, p. 211.

[39] *id.*, p. 151.

[40] Palermo v. United States, 360 U. S. 343, 352-53 (1959).

[41] Murphy, *Congress and the Court*, ch. 8.

[42] Hughes, *op. cit.*, pp. 242-43; J. W. Anderson, *Eisenhower, Brownell, and the Congress* (University, Alabama, 1964), ch. 1.

[43] President's Committee on Civil Rights, *To Secure These Rights* (Washington, 1946), ch. 2.

[44] *id.*, p. 13.

[45] Screws v. United States, 325 U. S. 91 (1945); United States v. Williams, 341 U. S. 58 (1951); Pennsylvania v. Board of Trusts, 353 U. S. 230 (1957).

[46] Anderson, *op. cit.*, pp. 28-43, 60-62.

[47] *id.*, pp. 88-103.

[48] 103 *Cong. Rec.* 12806.

[49] *id.*, 12812.

[50] Murphy, *Congress and the Court*, pp. 117-20.

[51] *id.*, ch. 6.

[52] Trop v. Dulles, 356 U. S. 86, 120 (1957).

[53] *id.*, 103.

[54] Beilan v. Board of Education, 357 U. S. 399 (1958); Lerner v. Casey. 357 U. S. 468 (1959); Barenblatt v. United States, 360 U. S. 109 (1959); Uphaus v. United States, 360 U. S. 72 (1959).

[55] Greene v. McElroy, 360 U. S. 474 (1959).

[56] Cf., *inter alia,* 71 *Time* 19 (February 17, 1958); 71 *Time* 15 (March 17, 1958); 72 *Time* 21 (November 17, 1958).

[57] 104 *Cong. Rec.* 18687.

[58] *id.,* 18690.

[59] *id.,* 18690.

[60] Murphy, *op. cit.,* pp. 199-201, 208-10.

[61] 104 *Cong. Rec.* 18750.

[62] Murphy, *op. cit.,* pp. 212-17.

[63] 104 *Cong. Rec.* 18928.

[64] Murphy, *op. cit.,* pp. 218-19.

[65] 104 *Cong. Rec.* 19575-76. The legislative day was August 23.

[66] Hughes, *op. cit.,* ch. 9.

[67] Jackson, *Struggle for Judicial Supremacy,* p. 315.

[68] Katcher, *op. cit.,* pp. 381-82.

CHAPTER 13 *The Jurisprudence of Desegregation*

[1] Plessy v. Ferguson, 163 U. S. 537, 551 (1896).

[2] *id.,* 559, 560.

[3] Buchanan v. Warley, 245 U. S. 60 (1917).

[4] Gunnar Myrdal, *An American Dilemma* (New York, 1944), I, ch. 29.

[5] Missouri ex rel. Gaines v. Canada, 305 U. S. 337 (1938).

[6] Nixon v. Herndon, 273 U. S. 536 (1927); Aldridge v. United States, 283 U. S. 308 (1931); Norris v. Alabama, 294 U. S. 587 (1935); Powell v. Alabama, 287 U. S. 45 (1932).

[7] Morgan v. Virginia, 328 U. S. 375 (1946); Sipuel v. Oklahoma, 332 U. S. 631 (1948); Sweatt v. Painter, 339 U. S. 629 (1950); McLaurin v. Oklahoma State Regents, 339 U. S. 637 (1950); Shelley v. Kraemer, 334 U. S. 1 (1948).

[8] Myrdal, *op. cit.,* chs. 8, 13.

[9] "The Negro Citizen in the Supreme Court," 52 *Harv. L. Rev.* 823 (March. 1939).

[10] Myrdal, *op. cit.,* ch. 29.

[11] Cf. Kilpatrick, *The Southern Case for School Segregation* (New York, 1962), ch. 1.

[12] *id.,* p. 22.

[13] Hays, *A Southern Moderate Speaks* (Chapel Hill, 1959), pp. 3, 100.

[14] Carter, *First Person Rural* (Garden City, 1963), p. 98.

[15] Brown v. Board of Education, 345 U. S. 972-73 (1953).

16 Cf. Symposium, "American Federalism: The General Perspective," 54 *Colum. L. Rev.* 489 (April, 1954).

17 *New York Times,* December 9, 1953; Brief for Appellants, esp. pp. 40-67.

18 *New York Times,* December 9, 1953.

19 *New York Times,* December 9, 1953.

20 Weaver, *Warren,* ch. 14.

21 *New York Times,* May 18, 1954.

22 Brown v. Board of Education, 347 U. S. 490-91.

23 *id.,* 493.

24 *id.,* 494-95.

25 *New York Times,* May 18, 1954.

26 Brown v. Board of Education, 349 U. S. 294, 300-01 (1955).

27 Quoted in J. J. Kilpatrick, ed., *We, the States* (Richmond, 1964), pp. 275 ff.

28 Cf. 1 *Race Relations Reporter,* 252, 445, 462 (1956).

29 *id.,* 435, 437, 438, 440, 443, 591, 753, 948.

30 Cooper v. Aaron, 358 U. S. 1, 19 (1958).

31 United States v. Louisiana, 188 Fed. Supp. 916, 926 (1960).

32 Bush v. Orleans Parish School Board, 364 U. S. 500-01 (1960).

33 Cf. Goss v. Board of Education, 373 U. S. 683, 688-89 (1963), and cases cited therein.

34 *id.,* 689.

35 Watson v. Memphis, 373 U. S. 526, 532-33 (1963); and cf. Wright v. Georgia, 373 U. S. 284 (1963).

36 Rogers v. Paul, 382 U. S. 198 (1965).

37 Griffin v. School Board, 377 U. S. 218 (1964).

38 Cf. the extensive review of the reports of this Commission, and committee reports and debates in Congress, contained in Sen. Rep. 162 (89th Cong., 1st Sess.), April 21, 1965.

39 *id.,* pp. 6-12.

40 Cf. Schlesinger, *The Thousand Days* (Boston, 1964), 972.

41 *New York Times,* June 20, 1963.

42 Cf. "Civil Rights Act of 1964: Sources and Scope of Congressional Power," 60 *Northwestern L. Rev.* 574 (Sept.-Oct., 1965).

43 Cf. 110 *Cong. Rec.* 6528.

44 *id.,* 501, 7483, 10209.

45 Cf. P. L. 88-352, 78 Stat. 241.

46 Cf. Sen. Rep. No. 162, note 38 *supra.*

47 *id.,* pp. 13ff.

48 Civil Rights Cases, 109 U. S. 3, 24 (1883).

49 Shelley v. Kraemer, 334 U. S. 1, 14 (1948).

50 Burton v. Wilmington Pkg. Authority, 365 U. S. 715, 726 (1961).

51 Lombard v. Louisiana, 373 U. S. 267, 273 (1963).

52 110 *Cong. Rec.* 5083-93.

53 Cf. *Annual Survey of American Law,* 1964 (New York, 1965), pp. 21-27.

[54] Heart of Atlanta Motel Corp. v. United States, 379 U. S. 241, 250-52 (1964).

[55] *id.,* 259-61.

[56] Katzenbach v. McClung, 379 U. S. 294, 305 (1964).

[57] Evans v. Newton, 382 U. S. 296, 299 (1966).

[58] *id.,* 301.

[59] Cf. ch. 6 *supra.*

[60] Feiner v. New York, 340 U. S. 315, 321 (1951).

[61] *id.,* 322, 331; and cf. Beauharnais v. Illinois, 343 U. S. 250 (1952).

[62] Edwards v. South Carolina, 372 U. S. 229, 237 (1963).

[63] Cox v. Louisiana (1st), 379 U. S. 531, 551, 557 (1965); Cox v. Louisiana (2nd), 379 U. S. 559 (1965).

[64] 379 U. S. 575, 585, 591 (1965).

[65] Brown v. Louisiana, 383 U. S. 131, 133, 141, 150 (1966).

[66] *id.,* 151 *et seq.*

[67] Adderley v. Florida, 385 U. S. 39, 47 (1966).

[68] An exhaustive documentation of the administration of the several modern civil rights statutes, complemented by the 1965 Senate report cited in notes 38 and 39 *supra,* appears in H. Rep. No. 914 (88th Cong., 1st Sess.), November 20, 1963.

[69] *id.,* pp. 20ff.

[70] *id.,* pp. 30ff.

[71] Cf. P. L. 89-110, 79 Stat. 437.

[72] South Carolina v. Katzenbach, 383 U. S. 301, 325 *et seq.* (1966).

[73] Katzenbach v. Morgan, 384 U. S. 641, 648 (1966).

[74] United States v. Price, 383 U. S. 787 (1966); and cf. United States v. Guest, 383 U. S. 745 (1966).

[75] Loving v. Virginia, 388 U. S. 1 (1967).

CHAPTER 14 *Restatement of the Bill of Rights*

[1] Cf. Schlesinger, *The Thousand Days,* pp. 696-98.

[2] Cf., generally, William J. Brennan, Jr., "Federal Habeas Corpus and State Prisoners—An Exercise in Federalism," 7 *Utah L. Rev.* 423 (Fall, 1961).

[3] Cf. Ralph F. Bischoff, "Constitutional Law and Civil Rights," 1963 *Annual Survey of American Law,* 1 (1964).

[4] Schlesinger, *The Thousand Days,* p. 698.

[5] Cf. Paul Freund, "Supreme Court in Contemporary Life," 19 *Southwestern L. J.* 439 (September, 1965).

[6] Schlesinger, *The Thousand Days,* chs. 8, 24.

[7] H. Rep. No. 1698 (88th Cong., 2d sess.), pp. 1, 2 (1960).

[8] 108 *Cong. Rec.* 4171.

[9] *id.,* 4198 *et seq.;* 4243 *et seq.*

[10] *id.,* 5072-5106.

[11] Bates v. Little Rock, 361 U. S. 516, 523 (1960).

[12] Konigsberg v. State Bar, 366 U. S. 36, 44, 56 (1961).

[13] Malloy v. Hogan, 378 U. S. 1, 9-11 (1964).

[14] Spevak v. Klein, 385 U. S. 511 (1967); and cf. Garrity v. New Jersey, 385 U. S. 493 (1967).

[15] Cramp v. Bd. of Pub. Instr., 368 U. S. 278 (1961).

[16] Gibson v. Florida Legis. Inv. Comm., 372 U. S. 539, 547 (1963).

[17] Baggett v. Bullitt, 377 U. S. 360 (1964).

[18] United States v. Brown, 381 U. S. 437, 455 (1965).

[19] Dennis v. United States, 384 U. S. 855, 875 (1965).

[20] Elfbrandt v. Russell, 384 U. S. 11, 17 (1966).

[21] Bond v. Floyd, 385 U. S. 116, 135 (1966).

[22] Keyishian v. Bd. of Regents, 385 U. S. 589, 604 (1967).

[23] Scales v. United States, 367 U. S. 203 (1961); Noto v. United States, 367 U. S. 290 (1961).

[24] 367 U. S. 259, 300.

[25] Communist Party v. Subv. Act. Cont. Bd., 367 U. S. 1, 137 (1961).

[26] *id.,* 145 *et seq.*

[27] Communist Party v. United States, 331 F. 2d 807 (1963); cert. den. 377 U. S. 968 (1964); Albertson v. Subv. Act. Cont. Bd., 382 U. S. 70 (1965).

[28] Albertson v. Subv. Act. Cont. Bd., 382 U. S. at 77 (1965).

[29] Aptheker v. Secy. of State, 378 U. S. 500, 515 (1964); and cf. Kent v. Dulles, 357 U. S. 116 (1958), and Zemel v. Rusk, 381 U. S. 1 (1965).

[30] 108 *Cong. Rec.* 7599 *et seq.*

[31] *id.,* 7604.

[32] *id.,* 7639.

[33] Weaver, *Warren,* p. 285.

[34] *id.,* 289; and cf. Katcher, *Warren,* ch. 1.

[35] 108 *Cong. Rec.* 7639.

[36] *id.,* 7640.

[37] *New York Times* v. Sullivan, 376 U. S. 255 (1964).

[38] Rosenblatt v. Baer, 383 U. S. 75 (1966).

[39] Time, Inc. v. Hill, 385 U. S. 374, 388 (1967).

[40] Curtis Pub. Co. v. Butts, 385 U. S. 130; Associated Press v. Walker, 385 U. S. 130 (1967).

[41] 385 U. S., at 165.

[42] Cf. A. B. Hanson, "Developments in the Law of Libel: Impact of the *New York Times* Rule," 7 *Wm. & M. L. Rev.* 215 (1966).

[43] Roth v. United States; Alberts v. California, 354 U. S. 476, 496, 508 (1957).

[44] *id.,* 503.

[45] *id.,* 512.

[46] Manual Enterprises v. Day, 370 U. S. 478, 481 (1962).

[47] Jacobellis v. Ohio, 378 U. S. 184, 191 (1964).

[48] Memoirs v. Attorney General, 383 U. S. 413, 418, 427 (1966).

[49] Mishkin v. New York, 383 U. S. 502, 508 (1966).

[50] Ginzburg v. United States, 383 U. S. 463, 470 (1966).

[51] 383 U. S. at 455.

[52] *id.*, at 491.

[53] Jacobs v. New York, 388 U. S. 431 (1967) and cases following; but cf. Ginsberg v. New York, 390 U. S. 629 (1967).

[54] Mapp v. Ohio, 367 U. S. 643, 653, 660 (1961).

[55] Ker v. California, 374 U. S. 23, 34 (1963).

[56] Aguilar v. Texas, 378 U. S. 108, 110 (1964).

[57] Preston v. United States, 376 U. S. 364 (1964).

[58] Stoner v. California, 376 U. S. 483, 488 (1964).

[59] Schmerber v. California, 384 U. S. 757, 770 (1966).

[60] McCray v. Illinois, 386 U. S. 300 (1967); and cf. Lewis v. United States, 385 U. S. 206 (1966).

[61] Cooper v. California, 386 U. S. 58, 59-60 (1967).

[62] Benanti v. United States, 355 U. S. 96, 99 (1957); and cf. Nardone v. United States (1st), 302 U. S. 379 (1937); Nardone v. United States (2nd), 308 U. S. 338 (1939); Schwartz v. Texas, 344 U. S. 199 (1952).

[63] Rathbun v. United States, 355 U. S. 107 (1957); and cf. On Lee v. United States, 343 U. S. 747 (1952).

[64] Silverman v. United States, 365 U. S. 505 (1961); Lopez v. United States, 373 U. S. 427 (1963); Hoffa v. United States, 385 U. S. 293 (1966).

[65] Berger v. New York, 388 U. S. 41, 55 *et seq.* (1967).

[66] Stein v. New York, 346 U. S. 156 (1953); and cf. Brown v. Mississippi, 297 U. S. 278 (1936) and Ashcraft v. Tennessee, 322 U. S. 143 (1944).

[67] Spano v. New York, 360 U. S. 315 (1959); Culombe v. Connecticut, 367 U. S. 568, 635 (1961).

[68] Rogers v. Richmond, 365 U. S. 534 (1961); Mapp v. Ohio, 367 U. S. 643 (1961).

[69] Chewning v. Cunningham, 368 U. S. 443, 446 (1962).

[70] 370 U. S. 908 (1962).

[71] Cf. Transcript of Record in Gideon v. Cochran (later *sub. nom.* Gideon v. Wainwright), Docket No. 155, October Term, 1962.

[72] Cf. Briefs Amici Curiae in same case.

[73] Petitioner's Brief in same case, *passim.*

[74] Gideon v. Wainwright, 372 U. S. 335, 339 (1963).

[75] *id.*, 345, 349.

[76] Douglas v. California, 372 U. S. 353, 357 (1963).

[77] *id.*, 360.

[78] Crooker v. California, 357 U. S. 433 (1958); Cicenia v. LaGay, 357 U. S. 504 (1958); Spano v. New York, 360 U. S. 315 (1959); Massiah v. United States, 377 U. S. 201 (1964).

[79] Escobedo v. Illinois, 378 U. S. 478, 480-82 (1964).

[80] *id.*, 488, 492.

[81] *id.*, 492.

[82] *id.,* 495.

[83] P.L. 88-455, 78 Stat. 552,

[84] Miranda v. Arizona, 384 U. S. 436, 473 (1966).

[85] *id.,* 488 *et seq.*

[86] *id.,* 499.

[87] *id.,* 504, 514 *et seq.*

[88] *id.,* 526.

[89] Johnson v. New Jersey, 384 U. S. 719 (1966).

[90] Cf. the extension of the basic principle in *In re Gault* 387 U. S. 1 (1967).

CHAPTER 15 *The Ultimate Democracy*

[1] Cf. Charles L. Black, *The People and the Court* (New York, 1960), ch. 5; Alexander M. Bickel, *Politics and the Warren Court* (New York, 1965), ch. 9.

[2] Cf. W. F. Swindler, "Reapportionment: Revisionism or Revolution?" 43 *N. C. L. Rev.* 55 (December, 1964).

[3] Baker v. Carr, 369 U. S. 186 (1962).

[4] Gray v. Sanders, 372 U. S. 368 (1963); Wesberry v. Sanders, 376 U. S. 1 (1964).

[5] Reynolds v. Sims, 377 U. S. 533; WMCA, Inc. v. Lomenzo, 377 U. S. 633; Maryland Comm. for Fair Repr. v. Tawes, 377 U. S. 656; Davis v. Mann, 377 U. S. 678; Roman v. Sincock, 377 U. S. 695; Lucas v. 44th General Assy., 377 U. S. 713 (1964).

[6] 377 U. S. at 565, 580.

[7] Cf. McKay, "Political Thickets and Crazy Quilts," 61 *Mich. L. Rev.* 645, 705-06 (February, 1963).

[8] Cf. *Historical Statistics of the United States,* p. 14.

[9] Smiley v. Holm, 285 U. S. 355 (1932); Koenig v. Flynn, 285 U. S. 375 (1932); Caroll v. Becker, 285 U. S. 380 (1932); cf. also Pac. States T. & T. Co. v. Oregon, 223 U. S. 118 (1912); Mt. Timber Co. v. Washington, 243 U. S. 219 (1917); Ohio ex rel. Bryant v. Akron Metr. Phone District, 281 U. S. 74 (1930).

[10] Wood v. Broom, 287 U. S. 1 (1932).

[11] *id.,* at 7.

[12] Cf. Highland Farms Dairy Co. v. Agnew, 300 U. S. 608 (1937).

[13] Cook v. Fortson, 68 F. S. 624 (1946), app. dism., 329 U. S. 675 (1946); Turman v. Duckworth, 62 F. S. 744 (1946), app. dism. *sub. nom.* Cook v. Fortson, 329 U. S. 675 (1946).

[14] Colgrove v. Green, 328 U. S. 549 (1946).

[15] MacDougall v. Green, 335 U. S. 281, 283 (1948).

[16] *id.,* at 289-90.

[17] Luther v. Borden, 48 U. S. (7 How.) 1 (1849).

[18] 328 U. S. at 552.

[19] South v. Peters, 339 U. S. 276, 281 (1950).

[20] Cox v. Peters, 342 U. S. 936 (1952).

[21] Kidd v. McCanless, 352 U. S. 920 (1956).

[22] Cf. Arthur Goldberg, "The Statistics of Malapportionment," 72 *Yale L. J.* 90, 102-04 (November, 1962); Swindler, *loc. cit.,* n. 69.

[23] Radford v. Gary, 145 F. S. 541, 546 (1957).

[24] Baker v. Carr, 175 F. S. 649 (1959); 179 F. S. 324 (1959).

[25] 364 U. S. 898 (1960).

[26] Cf. Transcript and Briefs, Baker v. Carr, Docket No. 103, October Term, 1960.

[27] Brief for Appellant, pp. 23 *et seq.*

[28] Brief for Appellee, pp. 42 *et seq.*

[29] Brief for United States, *amicus curiae,* pp. 58 *et seq.*

[30] 369 U. S. 186, 208 (1962).

[31] *id.,* 229 *et seq.;* and cf. Gomillion v. Lightfoot, 364 U. S. 339 (1961).

[32] 369 U. S. 204, 208 *et seq.*

[33] *id.,* 241, 251, 265; and cf. N. I. M. L. O. Brief, Docket No. 103.

[34] 369 U. S. at 262 *et seq.*

[35] *id.,* 266, 267, 297 *et seq.*

[36] *id.,* 330 *et seq.*

[37] 110 *Cong. Rec.* 21372-77.

[38] Cf. E. E. Schattschneider, "Urbanization and Reapportionment," 72 *Yale L. J.* 7 (November, 1962); and cf. Swindler, *loc. cit.,* nn. 99, 102, 103.

[39] Baker v. Carr, 206 F. S. 341 (1962); 222 F. S. 684 (1963); 247 F. S. 629 (1965).

[40] Cf. Swindler, *loc. cit.,* n. 76.

[41] Gray v. Sanders, 372 U. S. 368 (1963); Wesberry v. Sanders, 376 U. S. 1 (1964).

[42] 372 U. S., at 379.

[43] *id.,* 381.

[44] Wesberry v. Sanders, 376 U. S. at 8.

[45] Reynolds v Sims, 377 U. S 533 (1964).

[46] *id.,* 560, 576; and cf. nn. 48-52 *infra.*

[47] *id.,* 568 *et seq.*

[48] 377 U. S. 656.

[49] *id.,* 678.

[50] *id.,* 695.

[51] *id.,* 633.

[52] *id.,* 713.

[53] 369 U. S. 340; 372 U. S. 368, 382.

[54] 376 U. S. 20, 22, 23.

[55] *id.,* 42-45.

[56] 377 U. S. 624-25.

[57] *id.,* 533.

[58] Fortson v. Dorsey, 379 U. S. 433 (1965).

[59] Burns v. Richardson, 384 U. S. 73 (1966).

[60] Swann v. Adams, 385 U. S. 440 (1967).

[61] Avery v. Midland County, 390 U. S. 474 (1968).

[62] Norman Redlick, "Are There 'Certain Rights . . . Retained by the People'?" 37 *N. Y. U. L. Rev.* 787, 812 (November, 1962).

[63] *New York Times,* July 14, 1963.

[64] 110 *Cong. Rec.* 20215, 20218.

[85] *id.,* 21372-77.

[66] *id.,* 21377.

[67] Cf. 84 *Time* 37 (September 18, 1964).

[68] 111 *Cong. Rec.* 17843, 17845.

[69] *id.,* 17847.

[70] *id.,* 18056 *et seq.*

[71] *id.,* 18215 *et seq.*

[72] *id.,* 18221 *et seq.*

[73] *id.,* 18850 *et seq.*

[74] *id.,* 19119 *et seq.*

[75] *id.,* 19373.

[76] 112 *Cong. Rec.* 4895 *et seq.*

[77] *id.,* 8323 *et seq.*

[78] *New York Times,* April 14, 1963.

[79] 112 *Cong. Rec.* 8579.

CHAPTER 16   *Views at the Threshold*

[1] 108 *Cong. Rec.* 6331.

[2] *id.,* 18170.

[3] 66 *Newsweek* 84 (August 16, 1965).

[4] 111 *Cong. Rec.* 18769.

[5] Cf. 66 *Newsweek,* 25 (August 9, 1965).

[6] 113 *Cong. Rec.* 15726, 23376.

[7] *id.,* 24542, 24639, 24647.

[8] *id.,* 24583 *et seq.,* 24648 *et seq.*

[9] Cf. Rowland Evans and Robert Novak, "Lyndon B. Johnson: The Exercise of Power," 239 *Saturday Eve. Post* 26 (September 24, 1966).

[10] Richard Titmuss, "Poverty vs. Inequality: A Diagnosis," 200 *Nation* 130 (February 8, 1965).

[11] Cf. "Ramsey Clark Issue" in 92 *Time,* 83 (October 18, 1968).

[12] Cf. 58 *U. S. News,* 20 (March 22, 1965).

[13] Cf. E. N. Griswold, "Absolute is in the Dark," 8 *Utah L. Rev.* 167 (Summer, 1963); Griswold, "The Long View," 51 *Am. Bar Assn. J.* 1017 (November, 1965).

[14] Cf. 54 *U. S. News,* 33 (January 4, 1963).

[15] *New York Times,* June 22, 27, 1968.

[16] Cf. 72 *Newsweek,* 30 (September 23, 1968).

[17] U. S. Senate. *Hearings . . . on Nomination of Abe Fortas, of Tennessee, to be Chief Justice of the United States* (90th Cong., 2d Sess.), pp. 5-6.

[18] *id.,* pp. 13-26.

[19] *id.,* pp. 75, 77, 283.

[20] *id.,* pp. 41 ff.

[21] *id.,* pp. 180-251.

[22] *New York Times,* September 28, 1968.

[23] 93 *Time,* 17 (May 30, 1969).

[24] Cf. Alexander M. Bickel, "Is Electoral Reform the Answer?" *46 Commentary.* 41 (December, 1968).

[25] S. Bruce Jones, "Heartbreaks for the Constitution," 50 *A. B. A. Journal,* 758, 760 (April, 1964).

[26] Brennan, "Some Aspects of Federalism," 39 *N. Y. U. L. Rev.* 945 (December, 1964).

[27] Arthur Sutherland, *Constitutionalism in America* (New York, 1968), p. 549.

[28] Cf. Bickel, *The Least Dangerous Branch* (New York, Indianapolis, 1962), esp. chs. 2, 4.

[29] McCulloch v. Maryland, 4 Wheat. 316 (1819).

[30] 111 *Cong. Rec.* 1905-06.

[31] *id.,* 1905; cf. also Appendix A for both volumes of present study.

[32] Cf. Swindler, *The Old Legality,* chs. 13, 16.

[33] Brennan, *loc. cit.,* p. 947.

[34] Cf. W. F. Swindler, "The Current Challenge to Federalism: The Confederating Proposals," 52 *Georgetown L. J.* 1 (Fall, 1963).

[35] "Amending the Constitution to Strengthen the States in the Federal System," 36 *State Government* 10 (Winter, 1963).

[36] *id.,* at 11.

[37] *id.,* at 11-12.

[38] *id.,* at 13.

[39] *id.,* at 14.

[40] 49 *Am. Bar Assn. J.,* 635 (September, 1963).

[41] *New York Times,* March 18, 1967.

[42] 113 *Cong. Rec.* 5452-53.

[43] *id.,* at 5453, 5454.

[44] *id.,* 5453.

[45] *id.,* 5463.

[46] Morgenthau, "What Ails America?" 157 *New Republic* 17 (October 28, 1967).

[47] Cf. M. Janeway, "Bill Moyers Talks . . ." 222 *Atlantic,* 29 (July, 1968).

[48] 91 *Time,* 18 (April 12, 1968).

[49] Cf. Max Ascoli, "On Robert Kennedy," 38 *Reporter,* 6 (May 30, 1968).

[50] Miller, "Toward a Concept of Constitutional Duty," p. 225.

APPENDICES

[1] Richard K. Burke, *Paths to the Court* (Ph.D. diss., Vanderbilt Univ., 1958), p. 215.

[2] *id.,* pp. 254, 440.

Index

NOTE: Pages italicized indicate that act, statute or case is summarized in the appendices, or that biography and/or bibliography for Justice, Attorney General or Solicitor General is included in the appendices.

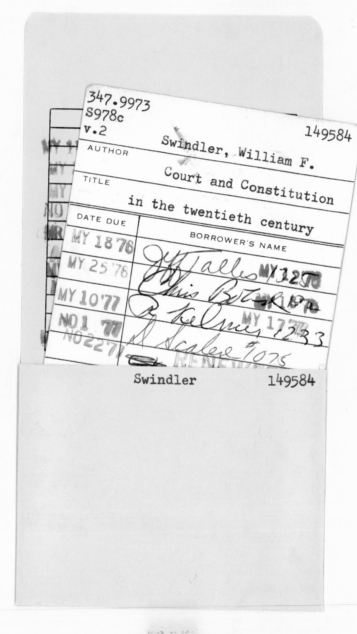